EGYPTIAN DAWN

EXPOSING THE REAL TRUTH BEHIND ANCIENT EGYPT

ROBERT TEMPLE

arrow books

Published by Arrow Books 2011

2 4 6 8 10 9 7 5 3 1

First published in Great Britain in 2010 by
Century
Random House, 20 Vauxhall Bridge Road,
London SW1V 2SA

www.randomhouse.co.uk

Addresses for companies within The Random House Group Limited can be found at:
www.randomhouse.co.uk/offices.htm

The Random House Group Limited Reg. No. 954009

A CIP catalogue record for this book
is available from the British Library

ISBN 9780099414681

The Random House Group Limited supports The Forest
Stewardship Council® (FSC®), the leading international forest
certification organisation. All our titles that are printed on
Greenpeace approved FSC® certified paper carry the FSC® logo.
Our paper procurement policy can be found at
www.randomhouse.co.uk/environment

Typeset in Ehrhardt MT by Palimpsest Book Production Limited,
Falkirk, Stirlingshire

Printed and bound in Great Britain by
CPI Bookmarque, Croydon CR0 4TD

AUTHOR'S NOTE

I dedicate this book firstly to my wife Olivia, who helped me at all stages, both at the archaeological sites in Egypt and in preparation of this book. She also took many of the photos. She was the associate director of our Project for Historical Dating, visited and assisted at all the sites, and supervised most of the logistics, travel and planning arrangements. She has been of invaluable help to me in countless ways for all of my books from the 1970s until the present, and without her editorial judgement and suggestions my books would have been greatly inferior and less clear. She has always challenged me to explain things better and has improved my expression, phraseology, and exposition for everything I have published. She has been a full-time collaborator, not always properly recognised as such, and even our closest friends have not fully realised the extent to which she was intimately involved in all of my work. Apart from all of that, she is in her spare time the most wonderful woman in the world.

I also dedicate this book to Amy Yuan, Meng Fanjing, Clara Coleridge Hebblethwaite, and Jessica Coleridge Williams.

In addition, I wish to dedicate this book to certain authors, artists, scientists, editors, and scholars who are presently or were when they were alive close friends of mine, and who I believe have exemplified the highest standards of original thinking and fearless exposition of the truth as they saw it:

Michael Baigent, David Bohm, Mark Booth, Cecil Collins, Richard Gregory, Lu Gwei-djen, John Michell, Peter Mitchell (Nobel Laureate for Chemistry, 1978), Joseph Needham, Rupert Sheldrake, Chandra Wickramasinghe, and Arthur M. Young.

Long may the struggle against ignorance, stupidity, vanity, and egotism continue. All of the above have made major contributions in the battle against the darkness.

ACKNOWLEDGEMENTS

My first thanks go to my wife Olivia, who as usual has contributed the most to this book, not least by organising the Egyptian research trips, and later by advising on the entire content of the book, as well as proof-reading it, and also translating some of the French material used in my research.

I am grateful to the Egyptian Supreme Council of Antiquities for granting permission to myself, Olivia, and Professor Ioannis Liritzis to carry out the archaeometric research at Giza, and granting us special access to the Sphinx Temple and Valley Temple which had apparently not been granted to anyone else for some decades. I am also grateful to Dr Zahi Hawass for granting permission to us to descend into and study the Osiris Shaft at Giza, which lies beneath the Chephren Causeway, and is a site specifically identified with his own personal research.

Special thanks and acknowledgement must be made to my colleague Professor Ioannis Liritzis, Head of the Department of Mediterranean Studies at the University of the Aegean at Rhodes. Ioannis is the inventor of the new dating technique known as optical thermoluminescence, which can date when two pieces of cut stone which have been pressed together were last exposed to sunlight, and hence can date stone structures directly. (A description of this technique and an account of how Ioannis discovered it may be found in the main text.) Ioannis and I decided to collaborate on archaeometric work in both Greece and Egypt, and some of our Egyptian work is reported here, hence the announcement following the list of contents, and the introductory account of 'the

Liritzis Dating Method.' The remainder of our findings will appear in a joint book at a later date. All of our Egyptian findings were submitted to Dr Zahi Hawass considerably in advance of publication here, though we are unaware of his having taken any steps towards publication of them in Egypt, which was his right under the new terms of cooperation with foreigners.

I am grateful to Professor Gunter Dreyer, Head of the German Institute at Cairo, for inviting us to date the tomb of King Khasekhemui (last king of the Second Dynasty) at Abydos during the course of his excavation of it.

I am especially grateful to Mark Booth, formerly of Century Books, for commissioning this book, and the enthusiastic and friendly support he gave to ensuring that these findings would become available to the general public.

The preparation of the Giza Plateau plans and the meticulous checking of data using advanced software would not have been possible without the graphic collaboration of Jonathan Greet, who is also designer and maintainer of this book's website www.egyptiandawn.info, on which a vast number of further illustrations relating to the book may be found.

Much of this book would have been impossible without the extensive and dedicated assistance in German translation of my friend Eleonore Reed. Together we translated the relevant works of Uvo Hölscher and Hermann Ricke, which was a task of the most extreme difficulty. I am immensely grateful to her for this. I am also grateful to Professor Horst Jaritz, former Director of the Swiss Institute in Cairo, for assisting me to translate a particularly difficult passage in Ricke's report on his excavation of the Sphinx Temple.

I also wish to express my gratitude to the following:

Michael Lee for scanning all of the illustrations and photos appearing in this book and on its website, which was a highly specialised task requiring a great deal of skill, especially when older material was used, which often required painstaking digital enhancing and cleaning up of images. My agent Bill Hamilton of A. M. Heath for his attention to this project over a considerable period of time. Mohammed Nazmy for assisting us in making travel and accommodation arrangements in Egypt. Simon Cox for making available to me the Egyptian ordnance survey maps and other books and materials, as well as for useful discussions. My friend Stefano Greco for finding and translating the work by Annibale Brandi from Italian, which is found as an Appendix. Tessa Dickinson for translating numerous Egyptological articles from French and assisting in other ways. Livia Puggini for assisting with some further German translation work. Chris Prior for making a mathematical calculation at my request which I used in this book.

Olivia and I owe a great debt to our good friend the late Michael Scott of Tangier for taking us to Mezorah many years ago and enabling us to study and photograph the rarely-visited site. Thanks are also due to the late Gordon Browne of Morocco for useful information and discussions on that subject. And I am particularly grateful to James Mavor for sending me information about his survey of Mezorah and giving me the permission to reproduce his survey drawing (which may be seen on this book's website) and quote from his article on the subject.

I am grateful to Mrs Kathleen Kottler of California for making available material by and photos of her father, the late Dr Patrick O'Mara, and for giving me permission to quote from his writings.

John Pye has been ever helpful in assisting me to acquire rare publications, as has Shirley Lancaster.

The editing of this book was made very pleasant and efficient by the remarkably cheerful and delightful Briony Nelder of Century. I am grateful also to Penny Isaac for her conscientious copy-editing.

CONTENTS

Author's Note   v

Acknowledgements   vii

The Liritzis Dating Method   1

1   Exposing the Big Lie   4

2   The Osiris Shaft at Giza and its Mysteries   43

3   The Pyramids Are Too Old   81

4   The True Locations of the Royal Tombs at Giza   151

5   A King Eight Feet Tall   194
    The Dating Results   210
    Conclusions   211

6   The 'Lost Kings' and a Pyramid of the First Dynasty   213

7   The Sphinx and Valley Temples of Giza   279
    The Valley Temple   286
    The Sphinx Temple   340
    The Dating Results   362

8   Stonehenge in Africa   370

APPENDICES: 435

One   Two Previously Unknown Nineteenth-Century
        Accounts of the Great Pyramid's Passages   437

Two   Palermo Stone 'Measurements'   444

Three   Translation of the Introduction to Uvo Hölscher's
        Excavation Report on the Valley Temple at Giza   450

Notes   468

Colour Plate Section Captions   489

Index   503

For supplementary illustrations and documents see:
www.egyptiandawn.info
The dating results reported in this book were acquired by Professor
Ioannis Liritzis and the author as a result of joint research trips by
themselves and Olivia Temple to Egypt, with official permission of the
Egyptian Supreme Council of Antiquities.

. . . let them march in silence over the pale incandescence of the plain; and kneeling at last, in the smoke of dreams, there where the peoples annihilate themselves in the dead powder of earth . . . all the salt of the earth shudders in dream. And sudden, ah sudden, what would these voices with us? Levy a wilderness of mirrors on the boneyard of streams, let them appeal in the course of ages! Erect stones to my fame, erect stones to silence; and to guard these places, cavalcades of green bronze on the great causeways!. . .

St John Perse, *Anabase* (translated by T. S. Eliot, 1930)

THE LIRITZIS DATING METHOD

The dating work referred to in this book has been based upon the development of a revolutionary new dating technique for archaeology, known as *optical thermoluminescence*. It was invented and perfected by my Greek colleague Professor Ioannis Liritzis. Another technique called simply *thermoluminescence*, for dating pottery, and with a somewhat similar name, has been known for a long time. But Ioannis's technique is new, and it dates stone, not pottery.

Until now, it has not been possible for archaeologists to date stone structures directly. All the dates for buildings and structures which you read about are based upon *indirect* methods. Pieces of pottery scattered around a site, or a bit of wood or other organic matter, can be dated. (Wood and organic matter are dated by the well known Carbon 14 method.) Then a conclusion is drawn that perhaps the building is of the same date as the bits and pieces found around or within it. At least the archaeologist hopes so! For what else can he do? He can't date the building itself. But now it can be done. And as it has become possible, everything will change drastically. Instead of the indirect process of 'dating by association', which until today has been practised for all stone buildings and structures, Ioannis can achieve direct dating of those structures themselves.

Professor Ioannis Liritzis was previously a nuclear physicist, and through his knowledge of that field he was able to work out a technique whereby he could calculate the date of the last exposure to light of two pieces of stone which have been pressed together. (I give an explanation of his technique as well as how he developed it in a moment.) If we can pinpoint the date when the stones were pressed together for the construction of the building, we have dated the building. Much that was previously guesswork can now become certainty. Although our dating results tend to be spread over several centuries, so that they cannot tell us on their own whether something was built in the reign of a particular king, we can safely classify structures into broader periods of time. In Egypt, for instance, we can say whether something is Old Kingdom, Middle Kingdom, or New Kingdom.

Before he developed his new technique, Ioannis was very familiar with the thermoluminescence method for dating pottery, which he himself used. And he also knew of the OSL (optically stimulated luminescence) dating technique, used especially to date geological sediments, such as marine and fluvial sand and muds, and loess deposits. Sometimes OSL is used in archaeology, as for instance to date a geological sediment lying over an archaeological site or a burial. It can also be used to date ceramics. OSL dates the time which has elapsed since certain minerals, such as quartz and feldspar, were last exposed to daylight. But no one had ever made use of the concepts underlying this technique to date stone structures.

Ioannis had gone off on his own to try to work out how one might possibly date the walls of a monument directly. He thought about the limestone blocks being cut, and then carved to fit into a wall. He imagined himself being a tiny crystal of limestone experiencing all of this. There he was in his imagination, a 'calcitic crystal', subject to all the environmental stresses which such crystals experience, and he tried to imagine what they were. As a crystal, he absorbed a lot of free electrons from the surrounding radiation of his environment. Some of these came from cosmic rays. Others came from radiation emitted by the radio-isotopes of uranium, thorium, potassium, and rubidium which were in his vicinity, as well as the gamma rays emitted by his environment. (This bombardment is called the 'dose rate', as if the crystal were being forced to swallow medicine.) The crystal which Ioannis had become was heavily-dosed, and had been forced to swallow lots of electrons, which had been squeezed into microscopic holes in the crystal called 'electron traps'. But then suddenly, as a crystal, Ioannis was ripped from the womb of his limestone block and exposed, naked, to the sun. The energy from the sunlight caused all of the electrons to start rushing out of their electron traps, and basically the crystal started vomiting up all of its medicine. Within only a few hours, the crystal was stripped bare of all of its electrons, and all of its electron traps were empty. Then suddenly, darkness descended, and the crystal was squeezed against another block of limestone, and it never saw the sun again. Slowly, gradually, the electrons returned and began to fill in all the holes once more. But it took a long, long time. The shock of the sunlight, like a cold shower, was never to return, and the traumatized crystal made its way back to normality with a great deal of psychological counselling.

Having experienced all of this as a crystal in his mind, Ioannis had a eureka moment. As he puts it:

'And there was light! An idea came as a striking light! I was inspired! The sunlight exposure had provided the answer.'

Suddenly he realized that the flooding of the limestone crystal with sunlight (which he calls 'bleaching'), and the emptying of its electron traps, could be considered as setting a 'stone clock' to zero. Then when the crystal was covered in darkness again and could begin swallowing its medicine once more, with the electrons creeping in as normal from the ambient radiation, the crystal's clock would be set ticking afresh. And if one removed the crystal again (not exposing it to the light) and counted the electrons which were in it, one could know how many years had elapsed since it had been 'bleached' by the sun. And this would give a date!

Of course there were many details which had to be sorted out as well, such as what kind of environment the stone was in – was it very radioactive or only slightly radioactive (a high dose rate or a low dose rate). That is why Ioannis carries round with him whenever he is collecting samples an extremely heavy machine called a gamma radiation detector, which is such a back-breaker when we go to remote sites!

CHAPTER ONE

Exposing the Big Lie

The most mysterious of all 'ancient mysteries' is: Where did the Egyptian civilisation come from, together with the question: Who built the pyramids, and why? Many Egyptologists are complacent about these issues. They feel that we know enough not to worry, that it is just a matter of filling in some gaps, tidying up our scraps of knowledge, coming across occasional bits of information from re-excavations of tombs which were originally robbed many thousands of years ago, and telling everybody they can relax.

But the truth is that things are not like that at all. In this book I will expose the Big Lie. I will show conclusively that many of the facts everyone is certain about are wrong. I will point to the exact locations of unopened Old Kingdom tombs which until now have been ignored, and give the physical evidence for this; I will present redatings of pyramids, temples and tombs based on a revolutionary new dating technique; I will expose faked evidence which has been credulously accepted by the Egyptological community, with the result that their chronologies prior to 2200 BC are wrong; I will explain that Cheops and Chephren cannot have built the two largest Giza pyramids; I will show that there were two simultaneous Egyptian civilisations in late prehistoric times rather than a single one; I will explore the most amazing tomb at Giza – the Osiris Shaft – and reveal the truth about it; and I will describe an existing 'Stonehenge in Africa', which is the largest megalithic ring in the world, connected with both the megalith builders of Europe and the builders of the Giza pyramids.

To this day, we are faced with the enigma of how such a great civilisation could suddenly arise, preceded only by Neolithic tribespeople. We are supposed to believe that the people of Egypt could graduate from reed huts to gigantic pyramids (the Great Pyramid's base covers an area of 13½ acres) in next to no time. Easy when you know how!?

Everything in this book will be backed up with plenty of footnotes, lots of photographs, and hard evidence. The redatings of key monuments are part of the results of a dating project undertaken with a professorial colleague, formerly a nuclear physicist, who has invented a revolutionary new dating technique. Permission for these redatings in Egypt was officially given by the Egyptian Supreme Council of Antiquities. Most of the dating results we have obtained, published and unpublished, have raised serious issues and have forced re-evaluations of chronologies.

If this sounds sensational, it is. Nor should we be afraid of change. If we have to change our ideas, that's good. I start from the premise that no one is ever correct. We are often mistaken about many matters. But what we should all aim to do is continually try to reduce our errors, try to get nearer and nearer to the truth. If we see that we are wrong, we must abandon the false path and try and find the true one. This book explores many paths.

In the next chapter, I describe my descent with a colleague into the Osiris Shaft, which goes 114 feet down beneath the surface of the Giza Plateau. At the bottom is a 'tomb of Osiris', a secret, subterranean, symbolic replica of the mythological tomb of the god who was king of the dead. His granite sarcophagus lies in the centre of a chamber surrounded by an artificial canal filled with water. No archaeological report of this site has ever been published. Religious fanatics have vandalised the site since 1944 and hacked away the four pillars that once stood around the tomb, apparently in a frenzied attempt to destroy this fantastic underground shrine. Few people have ever set eyes on this tomb of Osiris, and there are few photographs of it in existence. I was able to take photos of every stage of the descent, and of the tomb itself, and those that could not be published in this book are available on this book's website, www.egyptiandawn.info, which contains supplementary material – in particular, a vast number of additional photos.

My colleague and I were able to obtain two dating results for this tomb shaft, which challenge the basis of the entire chronology of the Giza Plateau. Furthermore, by X-ray diffraction analysis, we were able to discover that there is a sarcophagus in the shaft that was carved from a particular stone which was never used for any other stone object in the entire history of ancient Egypt. All the details of these startling discoveries are given in Chapter Two.

In Chapter Three, I reveal the unsettling news that the pyramids are *too old*. Using the revolutionary new dating technique called optical thermoluminescence invented by my colleague Professor Ioannis Liritzis, a sample taken of the third pyramid (supposed to have been built last of the three) has proved that it dates from *before* King Cheops. Therefore, the Great Pyramid (or Cheops Pyramid as it is sometimes called), the Pyramid of Chephren and the Pyramid of Mycerinus at Giza could not possibly have been built by Cheops, Chephren and Mycerinus. They were pre-existing. Cheops, Chephren and Mycerinus came along in the Fourth Dynasty and usurped them, built lots of tombs round them, which they filled with their relatives and retainers – hundreds of them! – and claimed them as their own. But they were built long before by somebody else.

So who built them? Our dating results, as well as those of the nearby Osiris Shaft, cover a wide range, and are not specific to a certain year, or even century. But they suggest that the pyramids were hundreds of years older, and possibly even a thousand years older than anyone thinks. In fact, there are no hieroglyphics in the Giza pyramids, no inscriptions, and not one shred of evidence was ever found inside any of the three pyramids to associate them with the Fourth Dynasty pharaohs, apart from some daubings in red paint inside some chambers above the King's Chamber of the Great Pyramid, which appear to mention the name of Cheops (Khufu in Egyptian, Cheops being the Greek form of his name). By a meticulous examination of all the documentary evidence about the strange find of these daubings in 1837, I have been able to demonstrate that these were forged by Colonel Henry Vyse in order to demonstrate to his financial investors that he had found something in an otherwise empty pyramid, since they had paid for him to investigate it, hoping for treasure. The full account of this act of forgery, even down to the details of the exact days on which it was carried out, and an admission by Vyse in his memoirs that the chambers contained no such inscriptions *after* the date at which he later claimed that he had found them (which is a complete contradiction), are given in Chapter Three. This means that there is no direct internal evidence at all to suggest who the real builders were of the Giza pyramids.

In Chapter Four, I turn to some strange physical evidence that I discovered and measured carefully inside the Sphinx Temple at Giza; this is normally closed not only to visitors but to archaeologists as well. I was able to obtain special access to this place, and as a result made some discoveries, which I photographed. These demonstrate in my opinion that there are still several sealed royal tombs at Giza dating prior to 2200 BC and possibly much earlier than that.

I identified the remains of lowering mechanisms for hauling forty- to sixty-ton sarcophagi down into secret caverns beneath several locations at Giza. I also discovered large boulders of cavern stalactites sitting in the Sphinx Temple, which were never mentioned by either of the excavators of the site. Because they were too heavy, they did not take them away but just left them there, where they have remained for at least 4,000 years. I took a tiny sample and showed it to an expert at the Natural History Museum in London for his mineralogical opinion. He confirmed that these stones had been removed from a limestone cave, and could not have come from any other possible source. This proves that, beneath this temple site at Giza, large caves have been excavated, which have not been entered since those days. (The sites having been covered in sand no later than 2000 BC, two of these were not even excavated until 1936, so no tomb robbing was ever possible, and thus no one can possibly have entered the caves or chambers for at least 4,000 years.) I have found no less than seven of these unopened royal tombs at Giza, and I show precisely where they are by photos and diagrams.

I also publish here, as an appendix, a previously unknown and lost work, a translation from Italian of a privately printed booklet, published in 1823, of which only a single copy survived anywhere, in a provincial Italian town where the author once lived. It was discovered and translated by my friend Stefano Greco. This booklet was written by a friend of Captain Giambattista Caviglia, who was the first to rediscover the

Subterranean Chamber of the Great Pyramid in 1817. The author describes a passage beneath the Great Pyramid. He says it extended horizontally from 'the grotto', a pocket in the bedrock, and this seems to have been obscured since that time by a collapse of gravel, so that this passage is today unknown and unexplored. I also publish a manuscript account from 1826 by a man who explored another 'lost' passage beneath the Great Pyramid. These strange descriptions from previously unknown sources raise further questions about what surprises remain in store for us within the Great Pyramid.

I describe crawling around in many shafts, tunnels and chambers at Giza that are not at all known to archaeologists. I was the first person for decades to gain entry to locked portions of the Valley Temple beside the Sphinx at Giza. The authorities had to smash the locks with hammers because the keys had long since been lost, and the locks were rusted solid. I was able to enter completely unknown spaces inside the walls of the temple, which do not appear on any of the plans: a mysterious 'blind room' chamber; hollow shafts thirty feet high, and strange, narrow passages at ground level. These resembled the holes where cobras crawl in and out, as they traditionally like to live inside the foundations of Egyptian temples; the original ancestors of those snakes were probably placed there as guardians by the last priests, to protect the crypts and concealed chambers, when Egyptian civilisation was overrun by the invading Persians more than two and a half millennia ago. These smaller 'cobra holes' led to larger spaces into which I crawled, choking on the dust. Photos of all of these discoveries are also placed on this book's website. I discuss the possible meaning of all these concealed interior features of a temple through which more than a million people pass every year, completely unaware of the secrets that lie only steps away from where they pass.

We obtained new datings for this temple, as well as the Sphinx Temple, and I compare these and discuss who could have built these huge structures, and whether they are contemporary with – or later than – the pyramids themselves. I present evidence of an archaeological find within the Valley Temple, a temple normally attributed to King Chephren of the Fourth Dynasty, which associates it instead with a much earlier king of the Second Dynasty, named King Send, of whom almost nothing is known. (His name is also spelled Sened, and means 'The Frightful', or 'The Feared One'. Some scholars suggest that Send was not a Second Dynasty king at all, but was a much earlier king more commonly known by the name of 'King Scorpion', who lived before the First Dynasty and is conventionally dated circa 3200 BC.)

Full photographic coverage of all of these findings is presented either here in the book or on the supplementary website, so that all the strange spaces I entered may be seen by the reader for him- or herself. No other photographs of most of these sights exist.

I then turn to the strange question of dates, and the enigma of who could have built these edifices. I consider the last king of the Second Dynasty. We were invited by the excavator to go to see his tomb at Abydos in southern ('Upper') Egypt, which was being re-excavated for the first time since the Victorian era. It was uncovered for only two weeks, and then covered over with sand again. I took a full set of colour photos during this time. We were asked to take dating samples, which we did, of stone, wood and pottery. These dates are discussed, and the strange nature of this king, said to have been eight feet tall, is considered. We studied the inferior use of stone by this king, whose sarcophagus chamber, as I show, was made of such crudely hacked limestone blocks that they look as if they were cut by a chimpanzee. This man was supposed to be the last king of the Second Dynasty, and to have been immediately succeeded by the first king of the Third Dynasty, who built the gigantic Step Pyramid at Saqqara only twenty or thirty years after the death of his 'predecessor'. This pyramid contains an estimated one million tons of carefully shaped stones. How, in only twenty years, could stone technology progress from the hacking of a few small stones for a pathetic grave to a huge pyramid like that, designed and constructed by masters of their craft? This is clearly impossible, and therefore necessitates a total rethink of everything that was going on in 'Archaic Egypt'. I show that there were clearly two separate Egyptian civilisations at that time: one technologically advanced and the other technologically backward. They lived uneasily side by side, and the entire question of the early 'dynasties' is thus confused and bizarre.

In looking into these murky questions, I came to realise that there was something drastically wrong with the evidence upon which

Egyptologists had relied since 1910 in constructing a supposed 'chronology' for this early period in Egypt. There is a famous stone bearing a carefully carved list known as a 'king list'. It is known as the Palermo Stone (it is kept in the museum at Palermo, in Sicily). It dates from the Fifth Dynasty and lists early kings. Unfortunately, it is only a modest fragment of what was once a huge stone. It is unquestionably genuine. However, in 1910, several fragments appeared for sale in the Cairo Bazaar, purportedly additional pieces of this stone. They are known collectively as the 'Cairo Stone' or 'Cairo Fragments'. One of these is in London, and the rest are in Cairo. Egyptologists were nearly hysterical with joy when these were discovered, and the inscriptions on them were immediately accepted as genuine historical records. When it later became clear that these could not be from the same actual stone as the Palermo Stone, little fuss was made, and people merely mumbled that, oh well, they may not be from the same one, but they were clearly from *another one*. The weakness of this argument was overlooked, because nobody wanted to give them up.

However, it can be shown conclusively, in my opinion, that five of the six fragments constituting the Cairo Stone are fakes. (And alas, the one that is not contains very little information and is not of much consequence.) What this means is that every book that has discussed early Egyptian history and chronology since 1910 is partially filled with false information fabricated by an antiquities forger. What is even worse is that these pseudo-fragments are often discussed as the Palermo Stone, without any differentiation made between them and the genuine stone, so that when historical pontifications are made about early Egyptian history on the basis of the Palermo Stone, it is impossible to know whether the information comes from a real source or from a fake source – unless you have a pre-existing knowledge of what each contains, which clearly most people, even many Egyptologists, could not be expected to have. So this leaves everything about early Egyptian history and chronology in a total mess.

But there are many other puzzles as well. Sometimes there are 'too many' kings of the same name. One example is King Teti. Everybody was very happy when there was only one, but then another one came along, and then another. Now we have three Tetis and we just don't know what to do with them. At other times, there are names with no kings. For instance, take 'Menes'. He was supposed to be the unifier of Egypt. But who was he? I explain what the name 'Menes' really meant. But one thing is for sure: there was never a king who was actually called that during his lifetime.

There are also many 'lost kings' of early Egypt, names with no facts, and there are also facts with no names. Some scholars think there were nine kings in the Third Dynasty, others that there were only three. I call attention to thirteen 'lost' predynastic kings, and show the evidence proving their existence and give translations of their names for the first time. But it isn't only kings who are 'lost'. There is also a 'lost' pyramid. This substantial pyramid was built by a king of the First Dynasty, I publish a photo of it, as it was excavated in 1937. But why does no one ever mention it?

Well, this is chaos on a grand scale. And now, just to make everything more difficult, we have discovered 'impossibly early' dates for key monuments such as the pyramids at Giza, using our new dating technique.

So what was really going on?

I have tried to investigate who could really have built the pyramids at Giza. As long ago as 1956, the physical anthropologist (a type of anthropologist who specialises in analysing skulls and skeletons) D. E. Derry published an article in *The Journal of Egyptian Archaeology* (Volume 42) entitled 'The Dynastic Race in Egypt'. In this article he reported the results of his studies (of the biometrics of northern and southern skeletons and skulls in predynastic and early dynastic Egyptian burials). His conclusions were absolute, based as they were upon careful bone and skull measurements that cannot be disputed. He said: '. . . the unexpected discovery was made that the pyramid builders were a different race from the people whose descendants they had hitherto been supposed to be. Naturally after making this discovery I was asked where the invaders had come from. My reply was that quite definitely they had not come from the south . . . If these people came from the north, they must have come across the sea . . .'

Who could these people be? Derry's exciting and shocking statement led me to do some lateral thinking. If they were from a date earlier than the Third Dynasty (conventionally dated 2686–2575 BC, although no one can really agree on how long it lasted), then they could clearly in any case not be the kings of the south, who were not able to hack a limestone block any better than a chimp. Who was there, then, in the north? Or who was there who could have entered the north by sea? This brought me to make some very bizarre discoveries about the northern regions of Egypt known as the Delta. I began to take more seriously the extraordinarily shadowy people lumped together under the vague term of 'Libyans'. Just what was a Libyan back then? Well, that turned out to be more complicated than I could ever have imagined.

A woman I had known slightly, Alessandra Nibbi, had spent most of her life trying to explain to her fellow Egyptologists that 'there was something wrong about the Delta', but they would not listen to her. By the time I realised the true importance of her work, she had died. But I was able to collect all of her printed articles by buying a complete set of *Discussions in Egyptology*, a journal published at Oxford which she had edited, and to which she contributed her strange observations, made from personal explorations of the geography of the Delta. This involved the discoveries that 'cedar of Lebanon' did not come from Lebanon, that papyrus only grows in certain specific conditions of which most Egyptologists appear to be unaware, that there was in very distant times a river route to Sinai, and other surprising things that challenged everything I thought was known about such matters.

(I was already aware that ancient place names were often misleading. For instance, Paul on the road to Damascus was not on the road to Damascus in Syria but to a Judean town of that name. Also, Jesus of Nazareth was not from Nazareth because Nazareth did not exist until more than three centuries after his death, and 'of Nazareth' is a textual error by later gospel scribes for 'the Nazarene', which was a Jewish sect opposed to the Sadducees and named after the Aramaic word *nazar*, meaning 'truth'. Also, there is a portion of the town now known as Cairo that was once called 'Babylon', even though it never had any connection with any Babylonians. So one has to watch out for these things!)

I found out that 'Libyans' was an imprecise term used to refer to anybody who lived west of Egypt, all the way to the Atlantic Coast. That is a pretty broad and vague category, covering as it does perhaps a thousand miles of territory and innumerable different peoples. Alessandra Nibbi thought some type of 'Libyans' also inhabited the entire north of Egypt from the point where the Nile divides and spreads out in the fan shape to make the Delta. But Giza is just below this point. So I wondered whether any 'Libyans' might be implicated in the building of the pyramids. But who really were these undefined peoples? People tend to talk about ancient Libyans rather glibly, and some scholars have tried to simplify the problem by creating 'eastern Libyans' and 'western Libyans'. Somehow that is supposed to help. But it is rather simplistic, like dividing American Indians into eastern and western groups. That still does not identify the Cheyenne, the Apaches, the Navajo, the Hurons, the Algonquins or the Sioux, nor does it convey very much except a decision to divide ignorance in two in the hope that two halves of a problem will somehow seem less intimidating than one whole problem.

And then I remembered that my wife Olivia and I did after all know some surprising things about some unknown ancient 'Libyans', but I had never made the potential connection with Egypt before. Many years earlier, we had visited an incredible site in the deepest wilds of Morocco, where there is the largest megalithic ring in the world. Not only had we photographed this site, which few people apart from local Moroccans have ever seen, but I had spent a great deal of time investigating it and had even written up many extraordinary discoveries relating to it, and the survival of a memory of it in ancient Greek legend as the site of the so-called 'Garden of the Hesperides', where golden apples grew, and where Atlas stood with the world on his shoulders. I was aware that the Atlantic Ocean had been named after the mythological figure of Atlas, and I believed I had the true explanation at last for the legend of the lost continent of Atlantis. I intended 'one day' to get around to writing a whole book about this. Suddenly, this half-forgotten project, stored away in a box somewhere in my study, 'clicked' in my mind.

I knew that these mysterious 'Libyans' had been able to construct walls with forty-ton stone blocks, as well as raise huge standing-stone menhirs nearly twenty feet high and weighing many tons. I even had photos to prove it. I knew that their megalithic ring had amazing astronomical correlations, and that these people were advanced mathematicians and geometers, as well as astronomers. Suddenly I realised I had a possible answer to the identity of the mysterious pyramid builders. Either these same people, or another people connected with them and residing in the Egyptian Delta, may have built or collaborated in the building of the Giza Complex. At that time they would have dominated Egypt at least as far south as Meidum (now a four-hour drive south of Cairo). The people we normally think of as 'Egyptians' at that time were based in Upper Egypt, which is the south of the country.

Egyptian Dawn now includes a full account of 'Stonehenge in Africa', which I suspect was built by the same people, whose descendants later built the Giza pyramids. At this prehistoric date, which agrees with our new dating findings, the world was a very different place from what has been imagined until now. The myth of 'Atlantis' was a fabricated tale of disinformation spread by these people, to baffle other Mediterranean maritime explorers who might stray out beyond the Pillars of Hercules into the Atlantic. For these people had settled the entire Atlantic coast all the way to Britain and Ireland and beyond, and southwards along the Moroccan coast. In other words, the builders of the earliest version of Stonehenge and Avebury in Britain are directly connected with the builders of the pyramids of Giza. 'Atlantis' as an island never existed. People were told that there was such a place, in order to encourage them to sail straight out into the middle of the ocean in search of something that was never there, in the hope that they would get lost and drown. The true 'Atlantis' was the Atlantic Coastal civilisation of the megalith builders. It was later inherited, from about 1550 BC, by the Phoenicians. It thrived on trade.

The irony is that in search of an answer to the mysteries of Giza in Egypt, I ended up connecting it with these megalith builders who are familiar to us right here at home in Britain. I have even been able to demonstrate that the region which we today call Libya is littered with standing columns with stones across the top, 'trilithons', just like those from a later stage of Stonehenge, suggesting that the communications between the North African coast and Britain persisted over millennia. It even justifies the strange remark preserved by the early English historian, Geoffrey of Monmouth, who claimed that the stones of

Stonehenge had been brought from Africa. It was not the stones themselves but the pattern and tradition of stone rings that had actually been brought to England from Africa. But the greatest achievement of these people, the founding of Memphis and the construction of the Giza Complex just below the Delta of Egypt, was overwhelmed by an invasion from the south, the original builders were expelled, and these sites were inherited and absorbed by the people we are more used to considering the real Egyptians. The secret stone technology lingered on in a dwindling form, as a royal secret, in the north, but was never allowed to spread to the south, in the uneasily 'unified' Egypt of the Archaic and Old Kingdom periods.

When the 'First Intermediate Period' of plague, social collapse and chaos occurred circa 2000 BC, the truth about all of these things was lost. By the time the Egyptians pulled themselves together again and re-established civilised life, perhaps 150 years later, in the period which we call the Middle Kingdom, 'the Libyans' were a distant memory, or people who were sometimes encountered both in battle and in trade, but no longer a dominant civilisation. Some of the early Egyptian kings had married 'Libyan' princesses as their queens, whose patron goddess was called Neith, and one of those queens was even named Neith-Hotep ('offering to Neith'), while another was named Mer-Neith ('beloved by Neith'). But the 'Libyans' faded more or less from the Egyptian view as a serious factor after 2000 BC. It is true that circa 950 BC a 'Libyan' dynasty, known as the Twenty-Second Dynasty, came to power in Egypt. But that was nothing to do with the earlier story.

The story presented in this book therefore embraces and unifies traditions of the origins of Egyptian civilisation, the construction of the pyramids of Giza, the builders of Stonehenge, and even gives a possible full explanation of the myth of 'Atlantis'. In a sense, 'Atlantis' really did exist. But it was as a coastal, not an island, civilisation of the Atlantic Ocean. This was the civilisation that originated the understanding of the earth as a sphere, that possessed a profound knowledge of astronomy, of mathematical and geometrical science, and an advanced stone technology. And I believe that the pinnacle of achievement for these people – one western branch of whom built our own Stonehenge – was the building of the Great Pyramid, the most supreme embodiment of

15

advanced ancient science ever constructed, and a triumph of ingenuity which appears to be beyond the usual capabilities of humans before or since. Even today we still could not build such a structure. This leaves open the possibility raised originally in my *Sirius Mystery*, that the connection with the star Sirius was not just an accident. For these early master-geometricians and stone technologists need not have been alone. Now at least we have a coherent reconstructed story. At last we can think with confidence of an *Egyptian Dawn*.

I now wish to reveal some discoveries about the Giza Plateau in Egypt which show that the design of the Plateau and its main monuments is every bit as impressive an achievement as the construction of those monuments themselves. The three main pyramids and the Sphinx were all planned as a unified design concept. This will become obvious when I reveal all of the new evidence. The brilliance of the intellectual feat of the planning and design of the Plateau is so overwhelming that I can think of no other architectural site on earth which was so intensively planned and which shows a comparable genius. In giving an account of this, I will be discussing only the *whole plan* of the Giza Plateau, and will ignore the individual pyramids as separate structures.

The 'Giza Plan' is essentially invisible, and was meant to be so. There is nothing obvious about it, and no casual eye was ever meant to perceive it. You may know the old proverb: 'If you want to conceal something successfully, hide it in plain sight.' Well, the Giza Plateau has been there for thousands of years and has kept its secrets very well, despite their being there for all to see.

In working all of this out, I have used the best materials available. Those are the Egyptian Government's own ordnance survey maps of the Giza Plateau. When blown up very large, one discovers that they do not have absolute precision, but they come close enough for practical analysis. I first worked everything out on paper with rulers and compasses, and then when I had finished, I joined forces with my graphic collaborator, Jonathan Greet, who is an expert at the intricacies of Adobe Illustrator software. We blew up the ordnance survey maps on a large computer screen to the size where one digital pixel was equivalent to one foot on the ground. All of our measurements were checked to a level of accuracy within two pixels, which is equivalent to two feet on the ground. Some of the things I had found on paper did not quite pass the 'two foot test' and I rejected them. If one were to accept a less stringent quality control, then there are many more correlations, but I wanted to be as rigorous as possible. Jonny was always ready with his voice of caution to say: 'Too short' or 'Too long' by a few feet, so we always dropped those. I need to add the further qualification that our accuracy also depends upon the accuracy of the ordnance survey maps themselves, and if they are slightly out, then the correlations given here might be off by as much as a few feet, but we have no way of knowing that.

The Giza Plateau, for those who have not had the good fortune to visit it in person, needs to be visualised for the sloping site that it is. It looks flat on a map, but it is not. The surveying phenomena I am about to reveal would be impressive enough if they had occurred on an entirely flat surface of ground. But these were carried out and implemented on slopes and varying levels of ground. The engineering feats involved in that are staggering to contemplate. But here I am only going to discuss the plan *itself*.

The area of the Giza Plateau falling within the Giza Plan is 10,834,564.73 square feet. To be able to specify the geometrical correlations which I discovered to within two feet in an area of nearly eleven million square feet is, I think, sufficient for the purpose.

So let us begin. Everything starts not with substance but with shadow, which is my little joke, as you will soon understand. Unless one knows what the Egyptians were after, and the importance of that shadow to them, one could never figure out the Giza Plan no matter how hard you tried. That is why they were so easily able to 'hide everything in plain sight'. For the Giza Plan *has to include the shadow*, so that its northern boundary commences far from the northern edge of the Great Pyramid. Without knowing that, you cannot even commence solving the problem of the total plan. In my previous book, *The Sphinx Mystery*, I published the 'Golden Giza Plan', which does not rely upon the shadow. But I was always aware that it was a mere portion of the answer. For there are really three simultaneous and superimposed Giza Plans, and it is the Giza Shadow Square, the first of them, which originally generated and dictated the shape and nature of the Plateau's design and its key monuments. So we will start with that. By explaining it, I will show how the entire Giza Plateau was conceived, why the three pyramids were placed where they are, and why they are the sizes that they are. Once one can comprehend the beginning of the total plan, everything else falls into place.

In attempting to 'reverse-engineer' the Giza Plateau design and figure out how the Egyptians actually went about constructing it, as opposed to the quite different manner in which I personally figured it out, I decided that their initial concept was the need for the longest possible shadow length which they could reasonably hope to achieve cast by a solid and lasting structure. The most stable possible structure of that height was a pyramid, and no other shape would have been so successful and satisfactory. We have to accept that, for whatever reasons, the Egyptians were obsessed with the calendar and they felt an imperative need to discover the true length of the solar year to as many fractions as possible. The Egyptians had a decimal system and broke their numbers down into tens, hundreds, thousands, ten thousands, etc., just as we do. But there is no evidence that they ever extended their decimal system to express fractions also as decimals. (My account of the invention of decimal fractions by the Chinese in the first century BC may be found in my book *The Genius of China*.[1]) We have never found an instance of an Egyptian writing 10.0972 or 22.25 or 17.62, or anything like that. Instead, fractions were always written as fractions, and even the way they did that was rather peculiar. I do not wish to go into the details of Egyptian fractions because it would be an unnecessary digression for this book. Suffice it to say that they often wrote down long series of them going on and on, often as a diminishing series of smaller and smaller ones. To us it seems bizarre, but to them it was normal.

So let us start with what the Egyptians must have thought was their fundamental requirement. They needed to produce a well-defined shadow at noon on every winter solstice (which would be the longest shadow of the year), which they calculated must be 648 feet long. (Obviously they used cubits, but I do not wish to confuse the reader with cubits, so I use English feet.) The credit for computing this shadow length, realizing its importance, and deducing that the true purpose of the Great Pyramid was to cast it for calendrical computation purposes, belongs to that self-educated nineteenth-century genius, Moses B. Cotsworth of York, of whom I gave an account previously in my book *The Crystal Sun* (2000).[2]

They had worked out somehow that unless they had a shadow that long they could not achieve the accuracy they needed to measure the length of the year with sufficient precision. Solstices are 'fuzzy' because the sun goes to its maximum north or south position and then appears to the naked eye to 'hover' there for two or three days, so that one cannot date the absolute moment of solstice properly without a shadow of extreme length, which alone makes it possible for its maximum shadow length to be precisely timed, to assist in identifying the 'solstice moment'. The reader will have to do without all the evidence and proof of this, some of which I have discussed in my earlier book *The Crystal Sun*, but the full account of which will appear in very great detail in a forthcoming book. There is no space here to explain all of this in full, with the accompanying diagrams which are necessary. My purpose now is only to enlighten people as to what was really going on in the strange minds of the creators of the Giza Plateau design when they set about organising its geometrical form. I should however add that Cotsworth was able to demonstrate that the fractional 'extra' portion of a day which gives the full length of the year of 365.24219 days was also probably computed by the Egyptians from a series of geometric ratios of shadow-rods observed in connection with the equinoctial shadow tip of the Great Pyramid, so that the 0.24219 of a day was actually visually displayed in front of their eyes over lengthy series of years, and was not just an abstract numerical calculation existing in their heads or on a piece of papyrus. I cannot describe the details of this ingenious physical shadow procedure here, as the very short equinoctial shadow is of no concern to us in considering the Giza Plan, which was based upon the *longest* shadow of the winter solstice, and was not based upon the short equinox shadow, which only extended 4.45 feet north of the pyramid, and was measured by a short meridian gauge of that length. In designing their Giza Plan, the Egyptians had in mind the furthest distance which their longest shadow would extend northwards, which enabled them to create a furthest northern boundary to the sacred precinct.

Having decided that they needed a shadow 648 feet long, they calculated the height of a pyramid necessary to cast the shadow they wanted, which was computed from the maximum winter solstice elevation of the sun in the sky at Giza of 36° 45', and then using this angle's cotangent of 1.339 for the very simple height calculation (I am not suggesting they used modern trigonometrical tables, but some more basic ancient method of discovering 1.339 expressed in fractions). The ancient Egyptian name for what we call the cotangent was *sekhed*. The result was the Great Pyramid. They worked out that 380 feet of the shadow would fall on the north face of the pyramid itself, leaving 268 feet spilling over and pointing north at noon. (Note: I am using Cotsworth's figures, but it is possible that only 378 fell on the pyramid and hence 270 feet was cast on the ground. However, in this discussion I will not deviate from the figures given by Cotsworth. The total shadow length is in any case the same.) 268 feet would be the longest flat shadow which the pyramid could cast at the winter solstice at noon (the 'longest meridian shadow'), and when that shadow reached its maximum, that was the moment they needed to measure with their water-clocks in order to measure the year's true duration to the many fractions they felt they required. After measuring with the water-clocks, they then synchronised with their shadow-clocks a few minutes later, due to the inconvenient fact that their shadow-clocks 'went dead' at noon for a few minutes every day. The priests who did this sort of thing were known as Unuti-priests. (These were based at Memphis. 'Unuti' means 'observers of the hours'. In a forthcoming book I describe at length the time-keeping methods of the ancient Egyptians and why they were so obsessed with accuracy and precision regarding time.)

So having realised that the shadow would spill 268 feet to the north onto the flat surface which they intended to create, they laid out the base of the Great Pyramid and then levelled the bedrock absolutely flat for 268 feet northwards to create a 'shadow floor' paved with fine limestone blocks to study the shadow every day during the year as it changed. The limestone blocks were ripped up and carried off to build mosques at Cairo centuries ago, at the same time that the casing stones (the pyramid's 'skin') were removed from the pyramid for the same purpose during the Middle Ages. Figure 1 shows the surface of the levelled

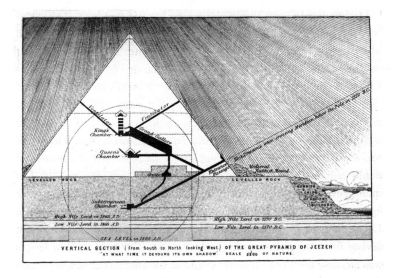

VERTICAL SECTION (from South to North looking West) OF THE GREAT PYRAMID OF JEEZEH
"AT WHAT TIME IT DEVOURS ITS OWN SHADOW" SCALE 1/500 OF NATURE.

Figure 1. This is a section view of the Great Pyramid as seen from the east, which demonstrates the carefully levelled surface to the north (which is to the right in this view) of the Great Pyramid, where the sun shadows were cast for determining the precise length of the year. In particular, there was a 'north meridian line' laid out on the surface from the base of the pyramid to measure the noon shadow at each equinox, which was less than five feet long. A stone connected with this precise spot at the base has been removed in ancient times. The rubbish mound portrayed here up against the north face of the pyramid has been long since removed. The longest shadow cast by the Great Pyramid beyond its own base extended 268 feet north at noon on the winter solstice, hence the need for a shadow floor on this levelled bedrock. (The limestone flooring of the shadow floor itself was stripped away long ago by stone robbers.) Piazzi-Smyth has drawn a line to the sky showing that in 2170 BC, the star *Alpha Draconis* would have crossed the line of sight from the Descending Passage which looked precisely at the meridian, hence allowing a perfect meridian transit or culmination to be observed every night. This is not a detail which I have chosen to discuss, as the astronomy of the Great Pyramid is too complex a subject for discussion here, and I do not necessarily go along with the *Alpha Draconis* idea. This drawing is from Charles Piazzi-Smyth, *Our Inheritance in the Great Pyramid*, London, 1880, Plate 6 at front of the book. The 'shadow floor' which lay across the levelled bedrock to the north of the Great Pyramid must be included in the Giza Precinct in order for the true plan of Giza to be revealed. If we include this northern extension beyond the base of the Great Pyramid, we get the 'Giza Shadow Square', the southwest corner of which is defined by the Pyramid of Mycerinus (see Figure 2). From the Shadow Square may be constructed (as in Figure 5) the 'Giza Perfect Square', which is slightly larger, but which shares

21

its southwest corner with the Shadow Square. The small Pyramid of Mycerinus is thus a kind of 'anchor'-object which holds both the Shadow Square and the Perfect Square in place at their common bottom southwest corner. From these two squares many geometrical correlation details may be derived for the main Giza monuments which are accurate to approximately two feet within an area of approximately 11 million square feet. The massive over-redundancy of correlations revealed within these squares cannot have a 'normal' purpose, and the fact that more than one square was used suggests an attempt at concealing the full design concept of the Plateau by means of multiple layers of design, such that if one layer were discovered, the others would remain undetected. These intellectual games played by the Egyptian priests are presumed to have a religious or 'magical' motivation, as part of a pious effort to simulate the structure of the cosmos as conceived by them, as part of their fundamental religious need to 'honour Maāt (cosmic order)'. They also clearly wished to conceal their sacred secrets from the eyes of the profane.

shadow floor extending northwards, so that the reader can visualise it clearly.

In order to find a way in which I can possibly explain what follows briefly to a general readership, it is essential to show more than one diagram of the Giza Plateau. The 'plan' of Giza is not a single plan at all, but is actually a triple-plan, and in my previous book *The Sphinx Mystery* I gave one of them, the 'Golden Plan' (Figure 7.25 in that book, which is found also on that book's website www.sphinx-mystery.info). In addition to this, there are two 'Giza squares', one slightly larger than the other, and in order to see the complete geometry, you have to superimpose one on top of the other. How the ancient Egyptians did this without either transparent tracing paper or modern computer technology is difficult to imagine. Just using different colours would not be enough on a small plan, because as we will see, it gets too complicated. The only way a drawn representation in different colours could work would be for everything to be drawn on a large plan which was at least several feet square, so that all the lines and points could be clearly seen. It would probably have been physically impossible to make a papyrus sheet which could be big enough for this, so they would have been forced to use the only other alternative available to them: a giant ox skin. Ideally, it should have been a white ox skin because otherwise they could not make out the colours properly.

In Figure 2 and Figure 5 we see the two squares separately. The

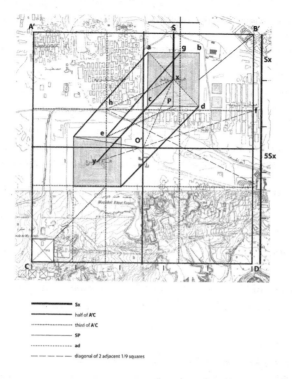

Figure 2. The Shadow Square of Giza. The northern boundary was determined by point S, which is the tip of the maximum meridian shadow cast by the Great Pyramid at noon on the day of the Winter Solstice (hence the name 'Shadow Square'). The shaded square near the top is the Great Pyramid, whose apex is x and whose corners are a, b, c, and d. The shaded square below and to the left of it is the Pyramid of Chephren, whose apex is y. At the bottom left of the Shadow Square is the small (unshaded) Pyramid of Mycerinus, whose southwest corner is point C. Solid lines may be seen dividing the Shadow Square into four equal smaller squares (with side lengths of ½ A'C), and dotted lines may be seen dividing the Shadow Square into nine equal smaller squares (with side lengths of ⅓ A'C). Since the Shadow Square was constructed by multiplying the length Sx (the total maximum meridian shadow length) times five and using that value as the side length, scales are shown at right of the design and below it, showing where those fivefold divisions occur, though they do not appear to relate to the monuments. The geometrical connections between key points on the monuments are shown by the different types of lines representing different standard lengths, as indicated by the key. For instance, the diagonal of the Great Pyramid, ad, is also equal to the distance between the apex of the Great Pyramid and the centre of the Shadow Square, as shown by the line O'x. The same distance separates x and h, and the distance occurs once again defining the distance between

the southwest corner of the Pyramid of Chephren and the southern boundary of the Shadow Square. The other monument point correlations may be seen in the plan and are described in the main text. (Design drawn by Robert Temple and graphics version by Robert Temple and Jonathan Greet)

larger one is what I have named the Perfect Square of Giza. It has a side 3,291.59 feet long (accurate to within 1 foot). The slightly smaller one is named the Shadow Square of Giza because its northern side is defined by the tip of the Great Pyramid's longest meridian shadow, which we just discussed. This square has a side 3,232.84 feet long (accurate to within 1 foot). I have labelled the four corners of the larger square A, B, C, and D, and its centre as O. I have labelled the four corners of the smaller square A', B', C, D', and its centre as O'. The reason why the letter C is the same for both is that this is the only corner they share, namely the southwest corner, which is identical with the southwest corner of the Pyramid of Mycerinus. But we start our considerations with the smaller square, since it is the shadow which generated both squares, and this bizarre process commenced with the Shadow Square itself.

In Figure 2 we see 'The Shadow Square of Giza' with certain key points of the square labelled with letters as I have already said. The tip of the maximum shadow is labelled S.

So let us follow the decision process of the Egyptians and trace the bizarre way their minds worked. They first decided they wanted a 648–foot shadow, and to get it they must build a pyramid high enough to cast it. This was to be the Great Pyramid. I have labelled its apex as point X. The total maximum meridian shadow length (at noon on the winter solstice) is thus shown by the line SX. They had, as I have already said, computed the height which their pyramid must have in order to cast this shadow. Cotsworth used the figure of 484 feet for the height of the Great Pyramid, which was the commonly accepted figure in his day. Since the top is missing today, there is no certainty of the precise height, and it tends to be estimated on the basis of the slope of the now-missing casing stones. Some estimates of the original height are as low as 481 feet.

What the Egyptians had not yet decided was the size of the base of the Great Pyramid. They decided this by multiplying the height by 2π, to obtain the length of the total perimeter of the Great Pyramid. They thus treated the pyramid as if it were the top half of a sphere, but with a square base instead of a round one, which is a form of 'squaring the circle'. I have used a height of 481.3 feet in my calculations, and taken pi as 3.1415. If we multiply 481.3 feet by 2π and divide by four, we get a median side length for the Great Pyramid of 756.00 feet, which is a generally accepted figure today for the mean side length including the casing stones. (This figure can vary slightly by some inches according to rival measurements, and if so, the projected original height of the Great Pyramid also varies slightly, but as it is only a projected height, we must rely on the base measurements for absolute accuracy, and let the projected height rise or fall accordingly.)

They now had their Great Pyramid's specifications: its height and its perimeter (which divided by four gave its base length on each side), so that the slope of the pyramid followed automatically.

John Taylor appears to have been the first person to insist that the value of pi was incorporated in the dimensions of the Great Pyramid, in a book which he published in 1859. It was his discovery that the base was equal to the height times 2π.[3]

The Egyptians then decided to create a large plan for the entire plateau, and they drew an east-west line through S, the shadow tip, which was to be the northern limit of the plan. They then multiplied the total shadow length SX by five and decided to take it as the length of each side of the total Giza Shadow Square. They had thus created the northern and southern boundaries for the first stage of their larger plan, and knew the lengths of the sides. But where should they put the eastern and western sides of the total square which they envisaged creating? They knew the lengths of those two sides but not where to place them.

They established this by dividing the base of the northern face of the Great Pyramid by the golden section at point g, with the shorter portion towards the east. (The line ab is the northern base line of the Great Pyramid. When ab is divided in golden section at g, ag is the major and gb is the minor, as seen in the diagram.) They raised a vertical line from this point g to the top of the square, which created a point which could act as a trisection point for the northern boundary of the

25

plan. They then slid this northern boundary along until this point directly above g divided the northern boundary so that one third was to the right (east) of g and two-thirds was to the left (west) of g. This anchored the entire Giza square in relation to east and west.

Having made their square stable and given it a rigidly fixed position on the plane, they divided it into nine smaller squares. We do not know why they did this, although I give some 'religious' suggestions about it in a moment, but the results of doing so created many interesting geometrical consequences. We do not know whether these appeared by accident or whether they anticipated them due to their profound knowledge of geometry.

At the same time they also divided the entire square into four smaller squares. They used the side lengths of each type of small square as standard lengths for their further geometrical constructions within the larger plan. The side length of one of the nine smaller squares is clearly ⅓ the larger square length, and the side length of one of the four smaller squares is ½ the larger square length. Surprisingly, both generate interesting correlations within the larger plan in the most astonishing way, as we will see, and both relate to one another despite being based upon different numbers.

It appears that the next thing the designers did was to take a ⅓ Shadow Square length (the side of one of the nine small squares) as a radius and swing an arc of that radius towards the southwest from the southwestern corner (point c) of the Great Pyramid. Somewhere on this arc was to be the apex of their next pyramid, which we call the Pyramid of Chephren. They then did a surprising thing: they took a ½ Shadow Square length and extended that southwestwards from the apex of the Great Pyramid. Where the ½ length line and the ⅓ length arc intersected defined the precise point which would become the apex of the Pyramid of Chephren, which I have labelled as point Y.

They then took the same ½ length line which they had used to join the apexes of the two pyramids and extended that line southwest from the northwest and southeast corners of the Great Pyramid, to designate the northwest and southeast corners of the Pyramid of Chephren. These two points thus defined the base of the Pyramid of Chephren. The plan of the Pyramid of Chephren was thus a kind of a geometrical projection of the plan of the Great Pyramid.

Despite these connections being based upon the ½ length of the side of the Shadow Square, they then reverted to the ninefold division of the Shadow Square with its ⅓ length of the Shadow Square to establish further correlations. What is especially bizarre is that some of the key points emanating from the division into nine are actually measured by the division into four. This strange finding may be seen on the diagram of the Shadow Square. I have included in the diagram the two divisions of the Shadow Square: into nine smaller squares and into four smaller squares, the sides of those squares being respectively ⅓ and ½ of the Shadow Square side length. If you look at the diagram you can see that point g (which originally established the ⅓ line length) is distant from point e by a ½ length line, despite the fact that point e is actually defined by the intersection of one of the sides of the nine smaller squares with the base of the northern face of the Pyramid of Chephren. So here we clearly see a correlation between the two pyramids of a ½ line length based upon a grid derived from a ⅓ line length. Perhaps I am very unintelligent, or seriously under-educated in geometry, but I do not understand this, even though I was the one who discovered it.

Now another strange aspect of the Giza Shadow Square manifests itself. You can establish the centre of the Shadow Square very easily, for if you draw the two diagonals of the square, the point where they cross is the centre. I have labelled it O'. If you take the length of the diagonal of the Great Pyramid (ad) and set your compass with that as its radius, with the compass point on the apex of the Great Pyramid, the arc strikes O', and you discover that the centre of the Shadow Square is the same distance from the Great Pyramid's apex as the length of the diagonal of that pyramid. How is this?

The diagonal of the Great Pyramid reappears as a measure again in that it is the same as the distance from the southwest corner of the Pyramid of Chephren to a point directly below it on the southern boundary of the Shadow Square. But why should the diagonal of the Great Pyramid appear here, in this apparently wholly unrelated context?

The same length, ad, of the diagonal of the Great Pyramid extends from the apex of the Great Pyramid to point h, which is the intersection of the four small squares at the northwest end of the Shadow Square, as seen in the diagram. The Great Pyramid apex is thus equidistant from the centre of the Shadow Square and a point defined by its ninefold division, that distance being a diagonal of the pyramid base which was independently arrived at. How is this?

Now another truly bizarre feature emerges. If we take the distance SP, which extends from the tip of the shadow (S) to the midpoint directly below it of the base of the southern face of the Great Pyramid, we find that this distance, SP, is equal to the distance from the centre of the Shadow Square, O', to the northwest corner of the Pyramid of Chephren. How is this?

Furthermore, this same distance separates the midpoint of the base of the eastern face of the Great Pyramid with point B', which is the northeastern corner of the Shadow Square. How is this?

Another strange correlation occurs if we draw a line from point P, the midpoint of the base of the southern face of the Great Pyramid, to point e, which is the point on the base of the northern face of the Pyramid of Chephren directly below point h which is intersected by one of the sides of the nine smaller squares. We find that that distance is equal to ⅓ the Shadow Square side length.

Having decided to anchor the southwest corner of the Shadow Square at C with a small pyramid, they had the problem of deciding what the size of that pyramid should be. They solved this by drawing a line southwest from a point on the base of the southern face of the Pyramid of Chephren where it is intersected by the vertical line on which h and e appear higher up, at the point of intersection between the four southwestern small squares of the Shadow Square. The length used was the ⅓ side length. The point where it terminated was designated as the northeast corner of the Pyramid of Mycerinus. As they now had specified the northeast and southwest corners of that pyramid, its plan and base dimensions were determined.

Another length used in the Shadow Square was the rectangular diagonal of two adjacent small squares. This diagonal is the distance between point h and the right paw of the Sphinx, as well as the northwest corner of the Sphinx Temple. This same length also separates the apex Y of the Pyramid of Chephren with point f on the eastern boundary of the

Shadow Square, which is the southeastern corner of the southeastern small square when the Shadow Square is divided into nine.

The Egyptians now had created for themselves a large square which covered the entire Giza Plateau. As already mentioned, as part of the internal construction of the total design, it was first divided into nine equal smaller squares. But why would they want to do this? There may have been a religious motive as well as a geometrical one for it. The Egyptians had a famous group of gods known to us by its Greek name as 'the Ennead', which means 'the Nine'. The sun god was one of them, and he presided over the group. The Egyptians may have believed they were showing reverence to the gods by having a 'geometrical ennead' portrayed at Giza in their sacred plan. In the Chester Beatty Papyrus Number One, we even find an incident recorded in a mythological tale where the sun god is described as presiding over a meeting of the Ennead precisely at noon, which the Egyptians referred to as 'the bright moment'.[4] We thus have a text which associates the sun god in his role of presiding over the Ennead, or Group of Nine, as doing so precisely at noon, and as we know, it was the noon shadow at the winter solstice which gave rise to the geometrical constructions which I have so far explained, and which I will describe in even greater detail in a moment.

In my previous books, *The Crystal Sun* (2000) and *The Sphinx Mystery* (2009), I described the dramatic winter solstice sunset shadow which the Pyramid of Chephren casts upon the south face of the Great Pyramid, and in each book I published a different photo showing this phenomenon. It is important to remember that this giant shadow *was cast on the same day as the longest noon shadow at the Great Pyramid*. The Giza Plateau is thus a Winter Solstice Shadow Centre where two gigantic shadow displays happened on the same day, one at noon and the other at sunset. The sunset shadow cast onto the Great Pyramid is at the 'golden angle', and displays on the outside surface of the Great Pyramid the same slope which appears twice on the inside, in the case of both the Ascending Passage and the Descending Passage. It was the British engineer Henry Crichton Agnew in the 1830s who first discovered the 'golden slope' inside the Great Pyramid, an angular measurement which was later confirmed by Sir Flinders Petrie. For a full explanation of all of this, the reader must consult my earlier books, because I cannot repeat it yet again here. What I did not suggest previously is that the sunset shadow on the outside of the Great Pyramid may possibly have had a calendrical purpose. It is conceivable that it may also have been precisely timed, and that timing could have been treated as a dual-timing procedure jointly with the noon shadow, in order to provide a double check on the calendrical calculations. However, I give that merely as an idea, as I have not bothered to work out any details. It does make sense, however, to have a second precisely timed event on the same day, and to compare the events year after year in order to refine one's measurements of the length of the year, as they were so obsessed with extreme accuracy. The slightly indented vertical line (called an 'apothegm') which runs down the centre of the southern face of the Great Pyramid, and which can be seen only from the air when the sunlight is at a favourable angle, may have contained when the casing stones were intact an embedded vertical gauge which would have given a precise linear measure. A photo showing this vertical indentation in the surface of the Great Pyramid may be seen in my book *The Crystal Sun*.

Now we return to further geometrical details of the Shadow Square of Giza and see how the slightly larger Perfect Square of Giza arose from it, partially in order to disguise the full plan of the Plateau from the prying eyes of the profane, and partially to render possible all the additional geometrical relationships and correlations which the Egyptians believed they needed in the Plateau's total design concept in order to be 'complete'. For if there was anything an Egyptian priest/designer hated, it was to leave out some important feature and thus be guilty of a possible oversight which could be interpreted as an act of impiety. The ancient Egyptians' behaviour thus resembled an obsessive-compulsive disorder. The Egyptians were simply dazzling in what we might be justified in considering their religio-geometrical mania.

The reader will appreciate that we are getting so many things going on here that one really needs a motion graphic as a video sequence to show it all, and I have prepared this jointly with Jonathan Greet and put it on this book's website, www.egyptiandawn.info, along with other moving sequences such as one for the set of photos which describe the descent of the Osiris Shaft (Chapter Two). But let us press on, as there

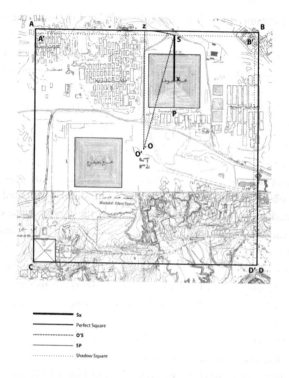

	Sx
	Perfect Square
	O'S
	SP
	Shadow Square

Figure 3. The construction of the Perfect Square of Giza (ABCD) from the Shadow Square of Giza (A'B'CD'). The Perfect Square is only slightly larger, but it has completely different properties, and many additional correlations of the key points of the monuments emerge from it. Point C, the southwest corner at bottom left, is in common between the two squares, and is the southwest corner of the Pyramid of Mycerinus. O' is the centre of the Shadow Square; the centre of the Perfect Square is slightly above and to the right of it. The 'Eye of Ra' at Giza, seen in Figure 4, cannot be constructed in the Shadow Square in such a way that it intersects any key points, but only does this in the Perfect Square. I constructed the Perfect Square by treating the line O'S as a radius and swinging it up to the vertical, thus establishing a new and slightly higher northern boundary. Point S is the tip of the maximum meridian shadow length. The length of the side of the Shadow Square is 3,232.84 feet (accurate to one foot), and the area is 10,451,254.47 square feet. The length of the side of the Perfect Square is 3,291.59 feet (accurate to one foot), and the area is 10,834,564.73 square feet. It is remarkable that two squares so close to one another in size should have such different properties in relation to the monuments, but also that *both* have deep and intimate geometrical connections with them. If the two squares are laid on top of one another, and if the Golden Giza Plan published in *The Sphinx Mystery* is laid on top of

31

them as well, then we have the total design plan for the Giza Plateau, which is a triple-plan. (The 'Eye of Ra' is an additional feature, or may be treated as part of the Perfect Square design.) No one was ever meant to discover all of these plans, as the three separate layers of mystery were supposed to be impenetrable to any investigator, so that anyone who might discover one would never discover all three. Sometimes triple-layered designs underlay major structures: this was the case with King Zoser's Step Pyramid at Saqqara and also with King Enezib's Pyramid at Saqqara, which is described in Chapter 6. (Design drawn by Robert Temple and graphics version by Robert Temple and Jonathan Greet)

is much more to say.

Now something very strange happens. We now generate the slightly larger square plan for Giza, which I have named the Perfect Giza Square, and we will find on that plan another set of bizarre geometrical relationships. The way in which this larger square was constructed again depended on the noon shadow length, but in a less direct and obvious manner. The Egyptians took the distance between O' and S, a line which we can call O'S, and erected a vertical line from O' which was equal to it. The easiest way for us to visualize this happening is that we just stick a compass point in O', use O'S as the radius, and swing an arc upwards. At the point where the arc intersects a vertical line rising from O' we specify a point on *a new northern boundary of a larger Giza square*. This is shown in Figure 3. Keeping point C at the southwestern corner fixed, we then extend the western side of the Shadow Square a short distance northwards until it reaches the new northern boundary of the new square. This is then the new northwestern corner of the larger square, and is labelled A. We measure AC and, reproducing its length, we then draw the northern boundary of the same distance, to the new northeastern corner which we label B. We then drop a vertical line to where it meets the southern boundary, and this is point D. We now have the square ABCD, which is slightly larger than the square A'B'CD' which shares its corner C with it (and which is also entirely enclosed within ABCD). Having done all this, we draw diagonals in this new square, and where they cross is the new centre, which we label O. Although O and O' are very near one another, they are not the same. Anyone attempting to analyze the Giza Plateau and discovering the Perfect Square would never normally be able to shrink the result and get the smaller Shadow Square. I say 'never normally' rather than 'never' because in fact I did it. But then I don't think in the same way that other people do, so I am able to do these things. I am 'weird' in some way which has never been defined.

This new square, the Perfect Square, then generates a number of geometrical features which relate to the three pyramids which are already there, even though they have been constructed on the basis of the *earlier* Shadow Square. In order for the Egyptians to pull this off, they must have had a great deal of truly profound geometrical knowledge, because, frankly, I don't believe there is anybody alive today who could have anticipated what would then happen. The results are so bizarre that this in a way is the most amazing aspect of all the Giza phenomena. How did the Egyptians know that a slightly larger square constructed in that manner on the basis of the same shadow tip would relate to the pyramids in such a remarkable manner? It really defies belief. And yet one presumes they must have known. This is a true mystery. As I have discovered all of these things, I keep getting the uncomfortable feeling that there are some deeper principles of geometry operating here than are apparent to us, or at least to me. The Egyptian knowledge seems to have been so profound that it embraced some kind of deeper geometrical level, almost what a physicist would call 'hidden variables', meaning dynamics at work which we do not yet understand. Just as fractals now seem obvious and yet are so recent that I actually met and talked to the man who discovered them (Benoit Mandelbrot) in my adult lifetime, I suspect there is another equally unsuspected approach to basic geometry which still awaits our discovery, but which may have been known to the pyramid builders. As I continue to describe my bizarre findings, the reader may feel inclined to agree.

The first thing one can do with the Perfect Square of Giza is to construct a giant Eye of Ra gazing upwards at the sky. It is a purely geometrical design, which is not physically represented on the ground. However, it is not just an arbitrary Eye of Ra, but is one which is constructed of two arcs and a circle, each of which intersects key points of the Giza monuments. I will now demonstrate how we create this 'Eye of Ra' within the Perfect Square, as seen in Figure 4. This giant Eye looks directly upwards at the meridian line which bisects the Perfect Square, and peers at the central point of both the day and night sky which we call the zenith.

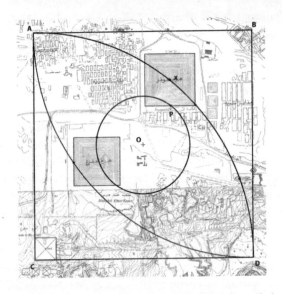

Figure 4. 'The Eye of Ra' at Giza. This can meaningfully be inscribed only in the Perfect Square (where it intersects many key points of the monuments), not in the Shadow Square (where it intersects none). If you put a compass point on B and inscribe an arc between A and D, and put a compass point on C and inscribe an opposite arc between A and D, you get the eye shape. In geometry this is known as a *vesica piscis*, and is usually derived by the intersection of two circles of equal size. It is the Egyptian hieroglyph for the letter 'r' and in Egyptian mathematics it is also the sign meaning 'fraction'. Since the Egyptians did not write vowels, it also means 'Re' or 'Ra', which is the name of the sun god. This inscribed hieroglyph intersects (1) the apex of the Great Pyramid, (2) the southeast corner of the Great Pyramid, (3) the midpoint of the waist of the Sphinx, (4) the midpoint of the base of the western face of the Pyramid of Chephren. If you take a compass point and put it on the centre of the Perfect Square, point O, and draw a circle of radius OP, it intersects both point P (the midpoint of the base of the southern face of the Great Pyramid) and the midpoint of the base of the northern face of the Pyramid of Chephren. The 'Eye of Ra' thus intersects six key points of the monuments within the Perfect Square of Giza. Because these are curves inscribed on the sloping surface of the Plateau rather than straight lines, as we find with all the other monument point correlations, the accuracy is slightly fuzzier than it is with the straight lines, and may be within a few feet of some points rather than within only one or two feet. However, as the Perfect Square contains nearly 11 million square feet, such a slightly diminished level of accuracy is still rigorous and acceptable. This 'Eye of Ra' gazes straight up at the sky, at the central point which we call the zenith. It is a fitting symbol of the solar nature of the entire Giza complex. (Design drawn by Robert Temple, graphic version by Robert Temple and Jonathan Greet)

34

First of all we put the compass point on C, which is the southwest corner of the Perfect Square. We draw an arc from A to D. We notice that this intersects the apex of the Great Pyramid, as well as the southeastern corner of the Great Pyramid and the midpoint of the waist of the Sphinx. We then put the compass point on B, which is the northeastern corner of the Perfect Square, and we swing an arc from A to D. We notice that this arc intersects the midpoint of the base of the western face of the Pyramid of Chephren. We have thus created a shape extending between A and D, two opposite corners of the Perfect Square, which is known by its Latin name as a *vesica piscis*. Normally, a vesica piscis is obtained by two intersecting circles of the same size, but in this case we have one inscribed within the Perfect Square of Giza. The vesica piscis was fundamental to Gothic architecture in the construction of the cathedrals of the Middle Ages. It was adopted by the early Christians as 'the sign of the fish' which they used as a secret sign of direction in the maze of the catacombs underneath Rome. That is because the early Christians were a collection of mystical sects known as 'Gnostics'. (Jesus himself was a 'Nazarene', which was a type of Jewish Gnostic.) Christianity was hijacked by the Emperor Constantine as a state religion and he turned it into a 'Church of Rome', which had a purely political purpose. From that time on, 'Gnostics' were persecuted or executed and their books were burned, so that the original form of Christianity only survived as an underground movement and only partially re-emerged into the open at the Reformation as Protestantism, but without most of its mystical content (other than the principle of direct individual contact with God, without the need for clerical control of this process), as it was largely just a rebellion against Roman control. The vesica piscis was used as an Egyptian hieroglyph for the letter 'r'. As such it stood for the name of the sun god Ra, also spelled by us as Re, and in Egyptian mathematics it also meant 'fraction' as a technical term, though whether this was pronounced *er* or *re* we do not know.

Within the middle of the hieroglyph 'r' inscribed in the Perfect Square of Giza we may now draw a circle with its point of origin at 0, which is also the centre of the Perfect Square. It represents the iris of the Eye. It intersects two key points of the monuments: the midpoint of the base of the southern face of the Great Pyramid and the midpoint of the base of the northern face of the Pyramid of Chephren. These two arcs and one circle which make up the Eye of Ra at Giza thus intersect no less than six key points of the Giza monuments. There is no equivalent Eye which can be drawn within the Shadow Square, and it is only the Perfect Square which generates an Eye which intersects key points of the monuments like this. This gigantic and invisible, but geometrically implied, Eye was only known to the designers and the priests, and of course, presumably to the gods. It lay there on the ground as an imagined construct in the minds of the priests, to pay invisible homage to the sun god. However, we should not dismiss it as a fantasy even though it only appears on our geometrical plans, because it really is constructed of arcs and a circle which really do intersect key points of the Giza monuments. It is thus 'real' in the sense that its design is there, and it is 'real' in the same sense that both Giza squares are there: they are there in the plans. And in paying homage to the gods, it was often considered enough to offer up these esoteric ideas and concepts, which were concealed from the eyes of the profane by the fact that there was not even anything physical to see. To the minds of the Egyptian priests, sacred geometrical designs were thus similar to silent prayers: nothing can be seen, nothing can be heard, but they exist and are powerful because they have been fully and meticulously articulated within the mental secrecy of the most elaborate acts of worship by the high priests themselves. What could be more appropriate for a solar centre like Giza than that it should secretly represent a giant solar eye staring up at the sky? This very eye reappears time and again in Egyptian paintings, and as a motif was pervasive throughout the whole of Egyptian religious culture for millennia. The actual use of the name Ra for the sun god as part of a royal name can be traced back at least to King Raneb ('Ra is my Lord'), the second king of the Second Dynasty. In some Egyptian king lists, he is said to have been succeeded by King Send, whose name has been found by excavators in the Valley Temple at Giza, as I describe in Chapter Seven (although Send's exact position in the sequence of kings is not clear, and he may have been the fifth king rather than the third king, or he may have been neither, so little do we know about such things, because of what I have referred to as the 'chronological chaos' which is discussed in Chapter Six).

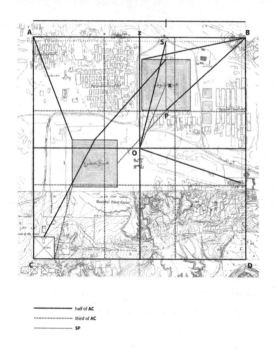

half of **AC**
third of **AC**
SP

Figure 5. The Perfect Square of Giza. This square has a side length of 3,291.59 feet (accurate to within one foot) and an area of 10,451,254.47 square feet. It was derived from the Shadow Square of Giza, by the method shown in Figure 4. The centre of this square, O, is in a slightly different location than point O', which is the centre of the Shadow Square (not shown here). If the top side of this square is divided in golden section, as shown here, with the shorter end to the right (east), and a vertical line is dropped from that point, it intersects the apex of the Great Pyramid, and also passes through the tip of the maximum meridian shadow (point S). That shadow (which originally defined the Shadow Square, from which this Perfect Square was then derived indirectly) is therefore marked by the golden section in a square of only a second order derivation, not of primary derivation, from itself. In this square, another set of correlations of key monument points emerges which is separate from those of the slightly smaller Shadow Square. The most remarkable is that the centre of this square, O, is now seen to be distant from the apex of the Great Pyramid by the distant SP, which again is derived from the shadow (Sx being the total shadow length). The distance of half of AC, which is the side of one of the four small squares into which the main square can be divided, is equal to: (1) the distance between point A, the northwest corner of the Perfect Square, and the northwest corner of the Pyramid of Chephren, (2) the distance between point B, the northeast corner of the Perfect Square, and P, which is the midpoint of the base of the southern face of the Great Pyramid, (3) the distance between point B and the northwest corner of the Great Pyramid, (4) the distance between S, which is the tip of the maximum meridian shadow, and point O, which is the centre of the Perfect Square, (5) the distance between point O and the head of the Sphinx, (6) the distance between the midpoint of the base of the northern face of the Great Pyramid and the midpoint of the base of the northern face of the Pyramid of Chephren, and (7) the distance between the midpoint of the base of the northern face of the Pyramid of Chephren and the midpoint of the northern face of the Pyramid of Mycerinus. If we take ⅓ of the distance AC, which is the side of one of the nine smaller squares into which the Perfect Square can be divided, we find that it is equal to (1) the distance between the southwest corner of the Pyramid of Chephren and the southeast corner of the Pyramid of Mycerinus, and (2) the distance between P, which is the midpoint of the base of the southern face of the Great Pyramid, and the midpoint of the base of the eastern face of the Pyramid of Chephren. All of these key monument point correlations are separate from and additional to those found in the Shadow Square. It is remarkable how each square generates its own separate but related set of monument correlations. The two squares, the Perfect Square and the Shadow Square, were meant to complement each other as well as the Golden Giza Plan reproduced as Figure 7.25 in my earlier book *The Sphinx Mystery* (see it on www.sphinxmystery.info), which actually reproduces some of these same point correlations purely on the basis of a common angle rather than as a common distance measure. The Giza Plateau was thus laid out in the most complex imaginable multiply-correlated triple design plan which was meant to be impenetrable to any investigator and to remain forever secret. It was specifically designed so that if anyone ever figured out one of the design plans they would never figure out the other two, and the decoded information would thus always be incomplete. However, they did not reckon that someone armed with modern surveys could figure out all three of them, despite the seeming impossibility of doing so. (Design drawn by Robert Temple and graphics design by Robert Temple and Jonathan Greet)

I will now briefly list the further geometrical correlations which occur between key monument points as a result of their being seen within the context of the Perfect Square. One has already been given in the description of the Eye of Ra, namely that the midpoint of the base of the northern face of the Pyramid of Chephren and the midpoint of the base of the southern face of the Great Pyramid are equidistant from O, the centre of the Perfect Square.

If we divide the Perfect Square into four small squares and take the side of one of those small squares as a measure (½ the side length of the Perfect Square), we see that it is equal to the distance between point A, which is the northwestern corner of the Perfect Square, and the northwestern corner of the Pyramid of Chephren. We can also see that it is the same as the distance between the midpoints of the bases of the northern faces of both the Pyramid of Chephren and the Pyramid of Mycerinus. The same distance also connects the midpoints of the bases of the northern faces of the Pyramid of Chephren and the Great Pyramid. This means that all three of the main Giza pyramids have these northern midpoints of theirs joined by lines of equal length to the line which connects A to the northwestern corner of the Pyramid of Chephren. But that is not all. The same length also separates the midpoints of the bases of the eastern faces of the Pyramid of Chephren and the Great Pyramid.

The same length also separates the midpoint of the base of the southern face of the Great Pyramid from the point B, which is the northeastern corner of the Perfect Square. And finally, the same length is the distance between point B and the northwestern corner of the Great Pyramid. We thus find that a unit length defined by the Perfect Square links two corners and four base midpoints of the three main pyramids with one another and with two of the corners of the Perfect Square. And this unit length occurs in other ways as well: it is the distance from the centre of the Perfect Square to any of its sides, in other words, it is half the side length of the square. But if you put a compass point on point O, which is the centre of the Perfect Square, and draw an arc of this radius eastwards from the point directly above it on the northern side of the square, it not only intersects the shadow tip S (as referred to earlier), but if you swing the compass further, it strikes the head of the Sphinx. This is the same as saying that if you inscribe a circle within the Perfect Square, it will intersect both the shadow tip to the north and the face of the Sphinx to the east. Since it was the face of the Sphinx which observed the rising sun and the shadow tip which marked the sun's longest possible noon shadow, this suggests a further correlation of solar symbolism.

If we then erase the division of the Perfect Square into four small squares and divide it instead into nine small squares, and take the side of one of those nine small squares as a measure (⅓ the side length of the Perfect Square), we find that it equals (1) the distance from the southeast corner of the Pyramid of Mycerinus to the southwest corner of the Pyramid of Chephren, and (2) the distance from the midpoint of the base of the eastern face of the Pyramid of Chephren to the midpoint of the base of the southern face of the Great Pyramid.

What is particularly bizarre about all of these correlations is that they occur with reference to the larger Perfect Square with such precision, despite the fact that the monuments were actually laid out according to the smaller Shadow Square. How can two large squares of different dimensions possibly generate so many distance correlations between the same set of key monuments? Surely if you design a set of monuments in one large square so that a large number of correlations appear, you cannot expect another equally impressive set of correlations to appear in a second large square of greater dimensions? How do the affinities of the key monuments 'carry over' from the smaller Giza square to the larger Giza square? I admit that I find this baffling, indeed astounding.

One thing I have noticed, as I have examined the measurements of the Shadow Square as compared to the Perfect Square, is that the side length of the Perfect Square is 1.0187 times the side length of the Shadow Square. This may not look familiar to anybody who has not read my earlier book *The Crystal Sun* (2000) very carefully indeed, but it is only 0.0051 different from 1.0136, the universal constant known as the Comma of Pythagoras, which I discussed at great length in that earlier book as the most important and most secret number known to the ancient Egyptians. (They expressed it as a fraction, of course, not as a decimal.) The Comma was fundamental to both musical harmony (it expresses the arithmetical difference between the mathematics of the fifth and the mathematics of the octave, as any educated musician knows very well, and which Bach tried to deal with by composing his *Well-Tempered Clavier*) and to the calendar by determining the year's precise value (establishing which was after all the main purpose of Giza), as I explained in detail in that book, and for that reason it appears to have been viewed by the Egyptians as the essential number expressing 'cosmic order'. It was also represented graphically by 'the Eye of Horus', as I have shown in the earlier book. I cannot repeat all of that information again here. But surely it cannot be an accident that the Comma of Pythagoras turns up once more, in determining the sacred design of the Giza complex. Another point to note is that the Comma, represented by the Eye of Horus, could then be said to generate another eye, namely the Eye of Ra, which we have seen appears inside the Perfect Square of Giza. It may even be that by using the Comma to enlarge the contextual dimensions of a set of geometrical relations, another set of geometrical relations deeply related to them emerges unexpectedly, and that there is a deep connection established between any two sets of geometrical relations which appear to be wholly separate if they are arithmetically related by means of the Comma. This might hint at the existence of a previously unsuspected subset of geometrical principles, a kind of 'hidden geometry' or what we might call a 'hyper-geometry'. It would be 'higher-dimensional' in a way never before imagined by us, because it would have nothing to do with what we normally call 'hyper-dimensional', but instead is more of a concealed inner dynamic which clicks into place when that specific number operates, like an invisible connective tissue activated by someone entering a numerical code. I regret that as this book goes to press tomorrow (at the time of writing), I have no opportunity to work out any laws or principles of this hidden geometrical world, if it exists. But the bizarre relationships which I have discovered between the two Giza squares strongly suggests that the Comma links them. Turning that argument on its head, it would mean that the shadow length was itself determined by the Comma, so as to make the two squares possible, and thus that the Comma was the ultimate generator of all the complex features of the Giza design plan.

Let us just stop for a moment to consider what is going on here. We started with the need for a shadow which the astronomers had calculated must be of a certain length. From that we got a pyramid high enough to cast it. Then we got the Shadow Square, in which a bewildering series of correlations between key monument points occurs. Then, again using the shadow, we extended the smaller Shadow Square to make a slightly larger Perfect Square, in which yet another, and apparently quite separate, bewildering series of correlations between key monument points occurs.

How is all this happening?

Now something even stranger occurs. If we adjust the compass so that its radius is equal to SP, and we put the compass point on O, which is the centre of the Perfect Square, we see that it touches the apex of the Great Pyramid.

How did the Egyptians ever figure all of this out?

If the reader is not baffled and exhausted by now, I am. The Egyptians were obsessive-compulsives, and did not know when to stop. They just went on and on. The trouble with ancient Egyptian mysteries is that there are just too many of them. I will skip the golden rectangles and other details of the Giza Plan which I have not described, and change subject. The reader gets the idea by now. And if you think I have revealed a lot about the Giza Plateau in this chapter, wait till you get to Chapter Four, where I describe the locations of much more than just geometrical points, but where instead I give the precise locations of seven intact royal tombs. My experience is that people always prefer a good mummy to a geometrical point any day, and if the tomb is full of lots of gold, well that's even more exciting to most readers. I hope that in Chapter Four I can be justly accused of 'putting my mummies where my mouth is'. And what is an even greater relief, you don't need any mathematics at all to open those tombs, since the illustrations to the chapter show precisely where they all are.

But first we must go beneath the surface of the Giza Plateau, precisely 114 feet down, and find something truly astounding: a replica of the Tomb of Osiris. For the full series of colour photos of the adventure described in the next chapter, please consult this book's website www.egyptiandawn.info, as the economics of book publishing make it possible to have only a limited number of photographic plates in the book itself. The book's website, maintained by the author, should always be treated as an extension of the book, and consulted by the reader when he wants to see more illustrations of anything discussed in the book.

CHAPTER TWO

The Osiris Shaft at Giza and its Mysteries

Deep below the Giza Plateau, at least 114 feet down through the solid rock, is a mysterious small island surrounded by water, in the centre of which is a huge stone sarcophagus. This is known as the Tomb of Osiris. Few people have seen it, and there are few photos of it in existence. However, I have been there, studied it and photographed it. This chapter tells the story of what it is, of how ancient it is, and explains why the shaft leading to it may be older than the pyramids themselves, before the name 'Osiris' was even in use.

Of the three pyramids at Giza, the central one is generally known by the name of the Pyramid of Chephren, Chephren being the name of a pharaoh who was the second in succession to Cheops, to whom is attributed the Great Pyramid. The Pyramid of Chephren is slightly smaller in size than the Great Pyramid, and still has a 'layer of icing' on the top, the remains of the limestone casing which once covered both it and the Great Pyramid, before those stones were stripped off by the Arabs and used to construct the city of Cairo. The Pyramid of Chephren has a very long and grand limestone causeway running down the hill in front of it towards the Sphinx, which is known as the Chephren Causeway.

The Osiris Shaft is the name now generally used to designate a deep burial shaft that is situated directly beneath the Chephren Causeway at Giza. It is sometimes also called the 'Water Shaft', or the 'Tomb of Osiris Shaft'. The reason why the name of the god Osiris has become attached to it is that at the very bottom of the shaft, in the third level, is a chamber containing a replica of the mythical 'Tomb of Osiris', mentioned a moment ago, which is traditionally described as a stone sarcophagus on an island surrounded with water, from which Osiris rose from the dead. It is meant to symbolise the site of his divine resurrection. Like Jesus, according to the Egyptian myth, Osiris died, was buried in a tomb and rose from the dead. And also like the Christian story, the open and empty tomb itself symbolised the resurrection that had taken place. Christian tradition is full of references to 'the empty tomb', and it forms the subject of some hymns. It is specifically mentioned in the four canonical gospels. The empty tomb is thus central to the entire message of Christianity. Jesus did not go to heaven direct from the cross, he did not experience resurrection immediately, he was first placed in a tomb, blocked by a heavy stone, and was only resurrected after some time spent in that tomb. Then, the fact of the empty tomb became the symbol of eternal life.

The Osiris Shaft at Giza has attracted a great deal of international curiosity. Not many people have been allowed to enter it, photos of it have been few and of poor quality, no formal archaeological report has been published – other than Selim Hassan's short note of 1944, which is quoted below – and speculation as to its true nature has run riot on the Internet. A very brief glimpse of the bottom chamber shown on American television raised more questions than it answered and, until now, no reliable direct dating was possible. Our direct dating is of some giant sarcophagi contained within this bizarre and unique place, for the shaft itself is hacked out of the solid bedrock and contains no stonework of any kind, so that the shaft itself cannot be dated. As we shall see, the huge sarcophagi are extraordinarily ancient, and one of them is made of a stone of a most puzzling type which, as far as we can determine, does not occur in any other instance in the whole of the archaeological remains of ancient Egypt.

In recent years, the Osiris Shaft has been studied by Dr Zahi Hawass, now General Secretary of the Supreme Council of Antiquities of Egypt and also Under-Secretary of State. He was responsible for pumping some of the water out of the lowest level and lifting the lid of the sarcophagus, which had been submerged there. But Dr Hawass was unable to be certain of a date for the shaft. When I suggested to him that we might be able to date the stone sarcophagi in the shaft by our new techniques, he was enthusiastic and gave us permission to descend into the shaft in order to obtain samples. We are therefore very grateful to Dr Hawass for allowing this access personally. This site was not originally part of our permission granted by the Supreme Council, and was an extension made possible on Dr Hawass's personal authority, before he became General Secretary and at the time when he was Director of the Giza Plateau. Dr Hawass takes great pride in this shaft, and people tend to consider it 'his' site. After what we found there, he should take even more pride in it, as it is far more important than he ever suspected in his most optimistic moments.

Dr Hawass called special attention to this shaft in 1999, when he appeared in a Fox Television Network (USA) programme entitled 'Opening the Lost Tombs: Live from Egypt', which was broadcast on 2 March 1999. During this programme, Hawass invited a camera crew down into the shaft, where he was interviewed discussing it. A full transcript of the portion of the film inside the shaft has been published on the Internet by an amateur enthusiast named Nigel Skinner-Simpson, a software designer with an interest in Egypt and a particular fixation on the Osiris Shaft.[1]

The quotes I take from the programme are taken from this transcript, which I presume to be accurate (except that in the inserted commentary he gets the directions of the cardinal points wrong when he attempts to give the orientations of the chambers). There was one interesting segment in this rather bad programme, and that was the Osiris Shaft portion. Hawass is seen taking a female presenter named Suzy Kolber into the shaft, where he proceeds to tell her about it, while another presenter named Maury Povich provides a voiceover. Kolber makes the inaccurate claim that Hawass had cleared the bottom of the shaft of sand, which cannot be true, since it was clear already in the 1930s. Hawass also claims that the two sarcophagi in Level Two are made of red granite, but that is not true, as we shall see, for they are not even red. But Egyptologists are seldom very clear about stones and minerals, and many Egyptian artefacts in museums throughout the world are wrongly described in terms of the materials of which they are supposedly composed.

Hawass also claims that the depth of the shaft leading from Level One to Level Two is 'fifty-five feet down', whereas in fact it is at least eighty-three feet below ground level, although the exact depth is not of particular importance. The main statement made in this part of the programme by Hawass is that pottery from Level Two was found to be of late Saitic (Twenty-Sixth Dynasty) date (ended 525 BC) or even Persian date. (Five hundred BC would be during the reign of the Persian Emperor Darius I, who had control of Egypt at that time, the last native dynasty having been conquered by the Persians twenty-five years before.) This was what one would have expected for, as we shall see, Selim Hassan had concluded that the Osiris Shaft was of Saitic date, and must have done so partly on the basis of such pottery which he had found there earlier. And the shaft was certainly reused during that period. But as we shall also see, the shaft is in fact much earlier than this, and these intruded pottery remains are therefore misleading.

The TV programme continued, with Hawass and Kolber descending to the next level, where Hawass says to her: 'Suzy, this is the "Tomb of Osiris".' Of course he did not mean it was literally the Tomb of Osiris, but rather that it was a replica of the Tomb of Osiris, although no viewer would have realised this. The camera did not really show very much at this level, and viewers would certainly have been left in a state of suspense over this astonishing revelation, of which only the briefest glimpse was offered. But the programme intended to cause this reaction, for Kolber said to Povich at the end of the segment: 'And Maury, I guess on a personal level, I am in awe of this whole thing. What a once-in-a-lifetime opportunity to be a part of this great discovery that will certainly fuel and fire the speculation that we can find the answers, perhaps details of a lost civilisation, instructions for our future – maybe . . .'

These remarks were referring to speculations about Atlantis and the visionary clairvoyance of the late Edgar Cayce, whom Kolber and Hawass discussed with each other on film during this segment. Hawass's assistant, Mark Lehner, wrote his first book on this subject, entitled *Egyptian Heritage: Based on the Edgar Cayce Readings*, in which he proposed the existence of a lost continent of Atlantis whose culture survived in Old Kingdom Egypt. Although Hawass told Kolber 'it's a legend, it's a myth', and wished to dismiss Cayce's fantasies of lost civilisations, viewers of the programme were left by Kolber with the impression that perhaps this Osiris Shaft led to a network of further tunnels, which would indeed reveal secrets of a lost civilisation. And with this kind of incitement given to millions of television viewers, it is little wonder that for many people the Osiris Shaft has come to represent a possible 'door' leading to something called the 'Hall of Records', where all the secrets of the ages are meant to be stored, awaiting rediscovery and giving modern civilisation new guidance: what Kolber refers to as 'instructions for our future'. It is obvious that the correct dating of the Osiris Shaft is a high priority, therefore, because it has become part of a wide-ranging public discourse about the mysteries of Egypt and the origins of human civilisation.

Perhaps unfortunately for Egyptologists, we have found that the Osiris Shaft is indeed extremely ancient, and it does pose a puzzle to us all. Of course, it is not old enough for the fantastic theories of an Atlantis of 10,000 BC, so far in the distant past that there is no possible connection with what is known in conventional archaeology. But possibly more disturbing, it is part of the evidence we have uncovered in Egypt that suggests that the conventional ideas about the origins of Egyptian civilisation are wrong. Drastic changes in our ideas are going to have to take place, but, alas, we are not certain what those drastic changes will be. A lot of thinking is going to have to be done, and a lot more research. This would not be quite so crucial if it were not for the fact that we are talking about possibly the earliest high civilisation in the world, and therefore the origin of high civilisation for our entire species. No 'Hall of Records' is necessary to shake us up, for these discoveries are already enough to do that on their own. In this book, I suggest a possible answer to this problem.

In modern times, the Osiris Shaft was apparently first discovered by Giambattista Caviglia in 1816 or 1817 (the period of Caviglia's initial activities at Giza), as I discovered in the Burton Manuscripts in the British Library. No account of the shaft by Caviglia himself is known to survive, but James Burton mentioned Caviglia's earlier exploration of the shaft in a document of 1826:

'In one apartment or another of all these monumental edifices was a deep shaft or well from the bottom of which a narrow passage conducted [led] to a subterranean chamber.

'One of these shafts cleared out by Mr. Caviglia was 60 feet deep and in the chamber a little to the south of the lower extremity was standing without a lid a plain but highly finished sarcophagus of the same dimensions nearly as that in the chamber of the pyramid of Cheops but of a superior polish. This discovery supplies a strong argument in favour of the pyramids being tombs.'[2]

This description appears to be of the Osiris Shaft, referring to the second level, although that is actually deeper than 60 feet. Since the third level was partially flooded until recent times, when it was pumped out by Dr Zahi Hawass, it might have been thought that no one prior to Hawass was able to explore the third level and discover the 'Osiris Tomb', and that Caviglia could not have entered it. But we are in for a surprise here, as we have documentary evidence that the lowest chamber was only a few inches deep in water in the early nineteenth century.

Caviglia's discovery of the Osiris Shaft is also recorded in a booklet published in Italian by his friend Annibale Brandi in 1823:[3]

'Caviglia descended to an underground tomb, and found a large chamber containing an impressive sarcophagus of granite with its cover, in very good condition.'

This booklet by Brandi was unknown to Egyptologists until my friend Stefano Greco, who was working with me to try to find some missing papers of Caviglia in Italy, found it in a library of a minor Italian town, Livorno. As the booklet was privately printed in the same town, it is believed that this is the only copy of the booklet surviving.[4]

Twenty years after Caviglia, the Osiris Shaft was investigated again. A local Arab named Abd el Ardi, who doubtless knew of the shaft because of his acquaintance with Caviglia (who had recently returned to Giza and worked for some time there again in 1837) pointed it out on 20 May 1837, to Colonel Richard Howard Vyse, who named it Shaft Number One at Giza, and his first note of it was as follows, recorded in Volume One of his three-volume work, *Operations Carried on at the Pyramids of Gizeh in 1837*:[5]

'The excavation of Campbell's Tomb was again resumed. Abd el Ardi pointed out a shaft near the brick peribolus, to the northward of the

Sphinx; another between that monument and Campbell's Tomb; and a third between Campbell's Tomb and the Second Pyramid, which contained water. The latter, he said, had been opened about three years before by M. Massara. I directed, therefore, Mr Hill to get a pump made, and a hose was sent for from Alexandria, in order to examine them.'

Massara therefore entered the Osiris Shaft about 1834, though no record of his doing so remains apart from this notice. Because Caviglia and Vyse, who worked together for a while in 1837 at Giza, had fallen out and were no longer on speaking terms, Abd el Ardi, who was now employed by Vyse, chose not to mention Caviglia's name in connection with the shaft, although it is evident that Massara must have learned about it from Caviglia, and Abd el Ardi must have known this very well. On 23 May, Vyse records:

'. . . a party was sent to clear out the shaft which contained the water between the Sphinx and Campbell's Tomb. [This is not the Osiris Shaft, but is the first shaft mentioned in the next diary excerpt, the second being the Osiris Shaft.]'[6]

The next day he recorded:

'The shaft westward of the Sphinx was cleared, and a party had begun that between Campbell's Tomb and the Second Pyramid. [This latter is the Osiris Shaft.] The thermometer was 115° in the shade.'[7]

Vyse's subsequent examination and clearance of the Osiris Shaft is recorded in Volume Two of his book:

The shaft between Campbell's Tomb and the Second Pyramid was examined. From the grotto at the bottom of the first shaft [Level Two] a second descended to a lower chamber [Level Three], in which square pillars had been left to support the roof; a third shaft [the canal] was full of water, which was perfectly fresh, and covered the floor to the depth of four or five inches. The level of the water was one hundred and thirteen feet seven inches below the top of the upper shaft. The Arabs said that an horizontal passage proceeded to the northward from these chambers through the side of the rock, but, owing to the drifting of the desert sand, and to the effects of repeated excavations, it is at present impossible to form an idea of the original surface of the ground.

[This was written long before the Causeway was cleared, and when much less was clear about the surface structures.] . . . (The water) may proceed from rain, but does not appear to flow from the river [the Nile]; as it does not rise and fall with it. In whatever way it [the water] may be produced, the sarcophagi could not have been intentionally immersed, and the inundations of the tombs must have accidentally arisen from the artificial channels having been stopped up, and from the water having penetrated between the strata of the rock.[8]

This is unquestionably a description of the Osiris Shaft, and in 1837 it is clear that the four square pillars in Level Three were still completely intact, and the water level was only four or five inches above the main floor (being deeper of course in the canal surrounding the island), with the large central sarcophagus already submerged in that bottom level.

This inspection of the Osiris Shaft by Howard Vyse took place on 2 June 1837, and in his table of contents he describes it as Shaft No. 1, as it is labelled on his plan of the Giza Plateau, a foldout in front of page 1 of Volume One of his work (see Figure 6 for detail of this plan showing the location of the shaft).

Three days earlier, on 30 May, Howard Vyse had recorded:

'The sand had been taken out of the shaft between Campbell's Tomb and the Second Pyramid, and a grotto was discovered at the bottom of it.'[9]

With that sentence, Howard Vyse ends Volume One of his work. From James Burton's account of Caviglia's work, already quoted, described in the unpublished manuscript I discovered in the British Museum, from the brief mention by Caviglia's Italian friend Annibale Brandi, and from Howard Vyse's account of his own men's work and his personal inspection, we can now reconstruct what occurred in the first half of the nineteenth century.

The Osiris Shaft was discovered in modern times by Giambattista Caviglia in 1816 or 1817. He used his large crew of workmen to remove a lot of sand from the shaft, so that he was able to descend easily to Level Two and view at least one of the two large stone sarcophagi there. It is very doubtful that the shaft was completely filled with sand, since it was cleverly designed to avoid this. First of all, the top level shaft

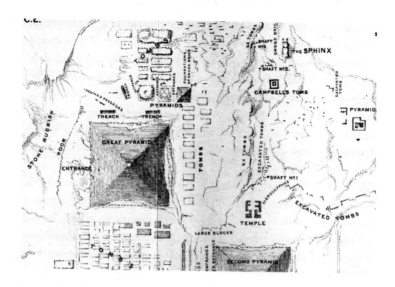

Figure 6. Detail from the folding map of the Giza Plateau drawn up by John S. Perring, appearing opposite page 1 of Volume 1 of Howard Vyse, *Operations Carried on at the Pyramids of Gizeh in 1837*, London 1840, 3 vols. The Osiris Shaft is labelled 'Shaft No. 1' on this map, near the centre of the plan shown here. The Sphinx is shown at the top, both temples in front of it being unknown at that time and still covered in sand. The Chephren Causeway, which runs over the top of the Osiris Shaft, was also covered in sand and was unknown at this time except for the point where it crosses the Osiris Shaft. The ruins marked 'temple' just above the 'Second Pyramid' (the Pyramid of Chephren) is the Funerary Temple of Chephren. This map of 1837 is not only the earliest plan showing the location of the Osiris Shaft, it is the only one.

opens beneath the Chephren Causeway, and is thus kept free of all wind-blown sand except that which blows in sideways through the narrow passage beneath the Causeway. Secondly, the main shaft is set far off to the side, beneath an overhang to the north, of Level One, so any windblown sand from the north cannot reach it, and only a small portion of that blowing into the upper passage from the south could be expected to reach it. The arrangement is such that the upper shaft could become almost full of sand before any considerable proportion would eventually spill down the main shaft to reach Level Two. But over the ages some of this did actually spill down, and it seems evident from James Burton's account that the final passage down to Level Three was clogged and that Caviglia and Burton only reached Level Two, which required a certain amount of clearing by Caviglia's men.

The next stage was in 1837 when Howard Vyse ordered his men to clear whatever sand remained in the Osiris Shaft so that he could descend into it, which he did approximately a week after they had started work. The amount of sand cleared in a week cannot have been much, and must have consisted primarily of that which blocked the way down to Level Three, and choked a considerable proportion of that level. However, even this is subject to some doubt, because there is no real evidence of sand today in Level Three, and the water is clear except for scum on top, so that it may be that it was not really sand at all which blocked the way to Level Three, but rather rubble that had been thrown down there by those who were interested in using Level Two for late burials.

But whatever it was that Howard Vyse's men took a week to clear away, Level Three was entered and was found to be intact in 1837. The square pillars, now entirely destroyed, were still there. (The destruction of these pillars is discussed later on.) And the chamber was not then flooded, by more than a few inches of excess water.

The next reference to the Osiris Shaft was an oblique comment made by Uvo Hölscher in his book of 1912, *Das Grabdenkmal des Königs Chephren* [The Funerary Monument of King Chephren],[10] which is quoted at great length later, in Chapter Seven. In his comments on the Causeway of Chephren in Chapter Three, Hölscher merely states:

'Measured on a slope, the Causeway between the Valley Temple and the Funerary Temple measures 494.6 metres in length. . . . Alongside and right next to the former ascending path [*Aufweg*], after its destruction in Persian times, shaft graves were constructed, which partly were intruded through the foundation (of the Causeway).'[11]

The only shaft grave near the Causeway which actually intrudes through the foundation of the Causeway is the Osiris Shaft, but no more is said about it, and it is doubtful that Hölscher ever entered it.

It has generally been assumed until now that the Osiris Shaft only came to light in the 1930s after Selim Hassan made some further clearance of the Chephren Causeway, removing windblown sand which had built up since Hölscher's time. His discovery was reported in the London *Daily Telegraph* for 4 March 1935, under the heading : 'Subway Found Below the Pyramids: New Discoveries in Egypt: Colonnaded Hall in Rock: 2,500 Years' Old Chambers'. In this article, Hassan was quoted as saying that he believed the chambers to be of the Saitic Period [the Twenty-Sixth Dynasty, 672 BC–525 BC], hence the headline mentioning them as being 2,500 years old. We shall see that the Osiris Shaft is much more ancient than that. Saitic shafts are 'a dime a dozen', and too late to be interesting. The Osiris Shaft, on the other hand, is as far as we know unique, and so ancient that it should force a rethink of Egyptian origins. Another notice of the find appeared in the *Illustrated London News* for 6 April 1935.

However, as I have already mentioned, it is most unlikely that the subway under the Causeway was ever wholly obscured by sand and debris, and an entrance into the subway was certainly accessible prior to Hassan's total clearance of the Causeway, from at least 1817. As for the shaft itself, protected as it is by the Causeway, which lies directly above it, it was apparently never wholly filled with sand, and has probably always been open. The shaft was certainly used in late pharaonic times, and anyone sufficiently determined, and with a long enough rope, could have descended at any time to the second level. (It is ironic that long ropes were impossible to obtain in Cairo in the mid-nineteenth century, as Vyse records with exasperation, complaining that he had to send to Alexandria for one to use in connection with the excavation of Campbell's tomb.) But, as for the third level, that was a different matter, as we have seen. So the claim made in 1935 that the Osiris Shaft was a new discovery was not true.

The first published report of the Osiris Shaft that could be called a truly archaeological account appeared in 1944, when Selim Hassan included a brief description of it in Volume Five of his famous series of excavation reports, *Excavations at Giza*.[12] In this account, Hassan records that, in his opinion, he was the discoverer of the shaft, which he assumed to be Saitic:

SHAFTS OF THE SAITIC PERIOD

During this period [the Saitic Period, or Twenty-Sixth Dynasty; 664–525 BC], it was the custom for well-to-do-persons to cut for themselves very wide and deep shafts ending in a spacious hall out of which opened a series of small chambers, each containing a sarcophagus. These sarcophagi, which are anthropoid, vary in their material according to the means of their owner, usually they are of Turah limestone, but basalt is by no means uncommon. Sometimes the shaft is cut abnormally deep and in this case it is divided into stages as it descends. The most striking example of this type of shaft is that which was cut in the causeway of the Second Pyramid [of Chephren], and discovered by me in our 6th season's work. Upon the surface of the causeway they first built a platform in the shape of a mastaba, using stones taken from the ruins of the covered corridor of the causeway. In the centre of this superstructure they sank a shaft, which passed through the roof and floor of the subway running under the causeway to a depth of about 9.00 m. At the bottom of this shaft is a rectangular chamber, in the floor of the eastern side of which is another shaft. This descends about 14 m. [this is certainly a misprint, probably for 24 m.] and terminates in a spacious hall surrounded by seven burial chambers, in each of which is a sarcophagus. Two of these sarcophagi, which are of basalt and are monolithic, are so enormous that at first we wondered if they contained the bodies of sacred bulls.

In the eastern side of this hall is yet another shaft, about 10.00 m. deep [this time the depth is correctly given], but unfortunately it is flooded. Through the clear water we can see that it ends in a colonnaded hall, also having side-chambers containing sarcophagi. We tried in vain to pump out the water, but it seems that a spring must have broken through the rock, for continual daily pumping over a period of four years was unable to reduce the water-level. I may add that I had this water analysed and finding it pure utilized it for drinking purposes. This was a great boon to the entire staff. The water came up ice-cold even in the hottest weather, and there was no occasion to stint the amount used by each person, a luxury that is perhaps unique in a desert site.

As a matter of fact, very few of the Saitic shafts have been thoroughly examined, for the reason that most of them are flooded, and unfortunately there seems little chance that we shall ever be able to get rid of this water. It would be interesting to see what result intensive pumping in the summer, following an abnormally low Nile, would give. [Note: this account was written long before the construction of the Aswan Dam, which altered all water levels.]

This account of the Osiris Shaft is very strange in several respects. The fact that the bottom chamber is at last largely dry and that pumping has finally been successful, we might owe to the effects of the Aswan Dam and the cessation of the Nile Inundations, although in many places, such as Luxor, the water table has been rising perilously, rather than falling. But the description of the Osiris Shaft given by Hassan differs significantly from what we find today. Many drastic changes have taken place at the Osiris Shaft since 1944. Hassan does not bother to describe the first level at all, but then it is essentially insignificant. It contains nothing now and probably contained nothing then (apart from wind-blown rubbish), being a mere stage of descent. The mastaba superstructure which he does describe has largely disappeared, and what remains may be seen in Plate 1. Five of the seven sarcophagi in the second level have vanished, and only the two gigantic ones remain. These are the ones that Hassan said he first imagined might have contained sacred bulls. But in the bottom chamber, the third level, the columns which Hassan could see through the water, and which Howard Vyse had seen unflooded, have now been entirely smashed, with only their tops and bottoms remaining as stumps. And if there really were additional sarcophagi, apart from the one which remains in the centre of the chamber, these too have been removed. I shall describe the shaft and its chambers more fully in a moment.

In Plate 1 and the subsequent plate on the website we may see the north and south views of the subway under the Chephren Causeway which leads to the entrance to the Osiris Shaft. A detail of Vyse's map showing the location of the subway is given in Figure 6. Within the subway, metal bars have today been placed round the actual entrance to the shaft, for the protection of the public who might fall into it, and one is tempted to add, for the protection of the shaft and its contents as well. A ladder leads down to the first level (see Plate 2), which is filled with the usual windblown rubbish that tourists continually deposit all over the Giza Plateau. Upon alighting from this ladder, a descent of about 27 feet, if you turn towards the north, and walk under an over-hang of the rock to the end of this descent stage or semi-chamber, you come to the true shaft, which plunges down into the bowels of the earth for a distance of what seems to be nearly 100 feet, though is apparently really 72 feet. Various depths for the shaft stages have been given, but as our mission was to carry out dating, we did not measure the depths ourselves, nor did we have the means to measure such a distance.

This extraordinarily deep main shaft has had a pair of parallel metal ladders tightly affixed to its south wall. These are modern ladders, for private use by the few archaeologists such as Hawass who visit the shaft, as no tourists are ever allowed in, to my knowledge. As one climbs down one of these vertiginous and sheer vertical ladders with no slope, it seems to slide in and out of the rock somewhat, inspiring little confidence as to its ultimate reliability. One has the feeling that 'its time will come', and one hopes that someone else will be climbing it when that happens. The ladder is also rather wet with moisture, so that one could actually lose one's grip on it if one did not hold very tightly indeed. A view of the main shaft and the ladders may be seen in Plate 2.

Our descent into the shaft was only made possible because Dr Hawass has had elementary lighting installed for such explorations by himself and his team. However, Dr Hawass was in Switzerland on the day we descended the shaft, and a large bullying man responsible for the electricity was unhappy about our entering it, even though we had Dr Hawass's permission and were accompanied by one of his inspectors of antiquities, who declined to descend down the dangerous ladder, and remained on the surface with my wife Olivia. Several times the electrician switched off the electric power, which had been connected by the inspector, attempting to force us to leave the shaft. Olivia protested vehemently and tried unsuccessfully to prevent him from behaving in this crazy way, as we had no torches/flashlights. I will never forget the terrifying experience of having the lights turned off suddenly while I was halfway up the main shaft ladder, leaving me with my hand on a slimy rung, hanging in space with what seemed to be fifty feet above me and fifty feet below, in absolute pitch blackness for several minutes, listening to the sound of metal bolts sliding ominously in and out of grooves in the bedrock from my weight. Ioannis was further down on the same ladder. We simply had to wait and hope, while Olivia – unknown to us – was trying to persuade the lunatic, whose English was minimal, to put the lights back on lest we fall to our deaths. She had the distinct impression that he wished we would. The inspector also tried to argue with the man in Arabic, but to no avail.

The descent of this shaft has been described by the popular Egyptological writer Robert Bauval, who was also allowed access by Dr Hawass, in his book *Secret Chamber*:

'The metal ladder was extremely moist from humidity and very slippery, making the descent a somewhat hairy experience. It was now very dark, and even with torches it was difficult to get a good perspective of this underworld environment . . . we finally reached the floor of the second level. It had seemed like forever.'[13]

Bauval believed, largely from experience of the sites and informed instinct, that the shaft and the sarcophagi must be much earlier than Saite (672 BC–525 BC), and as far as the dating of the sarcophagi is concerned, he was certainly correct in his hunch. As for the date of the shaft itself, it all comes down to whether one wants to believe that extremely ancient sarcophagi were lowered into a Saite shaft or whether the two were contemporaneous. But, as we will see, the answer to that is pretty obvious for various reasons.

Upon reaching the second level, the atmosphere is dry and you have a distinct feeling that you are very far below the surface of the earth indeed. You know that if you screamed, no one would ever hear you. The feeling of separation from the upper world is complete, and there is a curious sense of hopeless isolation, silence, and what I can only call 'deadness'.

At this second level, one is confronted with a substantial chamber containing seven niches, and in the northeast corner a further opening leading down to a third level, the level which until recent years was flooded. The descent into that third level is by a leaning ladder, about thirty more feet down. We will speak of Level Two and Level Three in our descriptions, although Level Three can certainly be considered 'the Osiris chamber', or even 'the "Tomb" of Osiris', of which it is unquestionably a replica.

Fortunately, when a madman is not at work shutting them on and off by way of intimidation, electric lights connected to the surface by long cables make it possible to inspect and study the shaft, its levels and their contents. We were thus able to take dating samples from two of the three sarcophagi; one in Level Two and one in Level Three. Several times we were left in the pitch-dark in both of these levels, as the insane electrician tried to harass us, and as Olivia each time tried to bully him into reconnecting the power, explaining to him through the translator that if he did not, how did he ever expect us to make our way back to the surface, as we had no lights at all even to find our way to the ladder. We thus managed to spend an hour and a half down the shaft, carrying out our work during the interludes when the electricity was permitted to function, and patiently waiting in the dark when it was not.

Level Two has various small bits of human bones strewn around the floor, doubtless from disturbed and plundered late burials. If one were to search carefully, one could probably find scraps of mummy wrappings. I must confess, however, that I was not tempted to do this, because mummy wrappings do not appeal to me. Hawass in the 1990s apparently gathered up most of the pottery and bones and removed them for study. But the place had been so hopelessly plundered since 1944, with all but the largest sarcophagi having been taken away (unrecorded, to unknown destinations, apparently), that there is little of any serious interest at that level other than the two gigantic sarcophagi, with their lids ajar and, of course, empty. No one could ever remove those! They must weigh forty tons apiece. They appeared to be of basalt, as they were so fine-grained, and were clearly not of Aswan granite. We were later to discover by mineralogical X-ray diffraction analysis what they really were, and this would give us a real shock.

The sarcophagi bear no inscriptions or carvings of any kind, and are thus completely plain. How these huge, weighty objects were lowered by rope and kept steady is a challenge to the imagination. What were the chances of such things swinging against the sides of the shafts, bashing the sides (there are no traces of this) or being dented or scratched themselves (there is no trace of this either)? How were they steadied and how were they lowered? We do know that the ancient Egyptians had stone pulleys for raising and lowering extremely heavy weights by the Fourth Dynasty at the latest, as Selim Hassan excavated two of them at Giza. The details of those pulleys, with photos and a discussion of their significance, are found in Chapter Four, where I discuss the sealed tombs which I believe still exist at Giza, giving their precise locations, and explaining how I located them. The importance of Hassan's discovery of the stone pulleys from the Old Kingdom will become especially obvious in my discussion of the probable locations of the intact tombs of Kings Cheops and Chephren, along with the evidence I have found which relates directly to the lowering of enormous heavy stone sarcophagi into them. All of this has obvious potential relevance to the construction of the pyramids, which I also discuss in a later chapter. In the course of my laborious researches into these matters, I unexpectedly discovered from an old commercial industrial pamphlet advertising ropes and pulleys (surprising information from which is discussed in Chapter Four) that the strongest ropes in the world up until the time synthetic fibres were invented in the twentieth century were ropes made from Egyptian cotton. Archaeologists take note: this seems to be one of the extraordinary secrets of the ancient Egyptians, which I gleaned from a dusty old industrial catalogue.

In Level Two of the Osiris Shaft, the seven niches, evidently burial niches, are arrayed along the south, west and north walls of the chamber, with none on the east. All of the niches are from floor level, and none has a raised level. As we have seen, in 1944 there were sarcophagi in all of them, but only two of those were large. The five small ones have been removed in recent decades, whereas the two large ones were obviously too heavy for any modern person to take away.

There is no doubt that the Osiris Shaft was repeatedly entered and plundered in antiquity, and we can safely assume that it was reused in the Saitic Period, as any such prominent and accessible shaft at Giza must have been. The five missing small sarcophagi were possibly of this later date. It is theoretically possible that the shaft itself is of Saitic date, but, if so, the huge sarcophagi, which are of extreme antiquity, as we shall see, would have had to have been plundered from somewhere else (presumably at Giza) and lowered down the shaft in Saitic times for reuse. Somehow this seems most unlikely, and a rather extreme measure. (We will see later that it is actually impossible.) And would the sarcophagi, if thus reused, have remained without inscriptions? There are also the considerations of the siting of the shaft, to which we will return, and, most important of all, the unitary conception of the plan of Level Three, of which its central sarcophagus is a fundamental feature, thereby tying the sarcophagus and Level Three to a common date. The likelihood of older sarcophagi being lowered into a Middle Kingdom shaft is really so small that we may effectively dismiss it.

In a niche on the south wall of Level Two is a gigantic black stone sarcophagus, which we shall call Sarcophagus One. We were unable to take a sample of this sarcophagus, so that we have done no dating or mineralogical analysis of it. Certainly it would be interesting to try again, but there were difficulties of access to a suitable point for a sample in the time available, and the constant turning off of the lights interrupted our work. With the greatest of difficulties, we did finally succeed in taking a good sample from the other giant sarcophagus in Level Two (Sarcophagus Two), which is in the end niche on the north wall, and which is grey. The location of the sample, taken from a point where the stone had already been split by ancient grave-robbers, is indicated by Ioannis in a Plate on the website. A photo of the entire sarcophagus can be seen on the website. This sarcophagus is certainly the object that is of greatest interest in the entire Osiris Shaft.

We took Geiger counter readings inside the two sarcophagi in Level Two and were astonished at the intense radioactivity given off by the stone, concentrating in the interiors of the sarcophagi. Something which seems never to have been realised by Egyptologists before is that sarcophagi made of granite, basalt and related stones are so powerfully radioactive that a corpse placed inside would be so intensely irradiated that – like the irradiated food sold in supermarkets – it would have extra 'shelf-life', and most or all of the decay bacteria in the mummy would have been killed off. Certainly this must have helped to preserve the ancient mummies as much as – or perhaps even more than – the embalming process itself. Limestone or alabaster sarcophagi would not have this property. I suggested taking these readings because of our findings in the Valley Temple, described in Chapter Seven, where the granite was so amazingly radioactive that we decided that any priests or attendants working there regularly would have contracted leukaemia or some other form of terminal cancer and probably could not have lived for more than twenty years in that environment. These radioactivity issues seem to be new findings, as neither of us has ever heard or read of such matters being mentioned before by anyone.

Our mineralogical analysis of the sample from Sarcophagus Two was our first surprise. We were convinced from visual observation that the sarcophagus was made of basalt, due to its fine-grained, glassy texture. We dismissed the idea of granite. But the laboratory report came back saying that it was a stone called dacite. This caused us both to scratch our heads in puzzlement; we tried to discover whether anything made of dacite was known in Egypt, as we had never heard of its use there. The first thing I did was check in the authoritative Lucas and Harris, *Ancient Egyptian Materials and Industries*,[14] and there was no mention of dacite at all. I then turned to Barbara Aston's *Ancient Egyptian Stone Vessels*, which contains a lengthy sixty-two-page section listing and discussing all the stones and minerals known from ancient Egyptian use.[15] Most people consider this list not only comprehensive but definitive. However, dacite is mentioned only in passing, in a survey of volcanic rocks, and the author specifically excludes it by saying it was never used for stone vessels in Egypt.[16] I then turned to the other of the three standard authorities of mineralogical knowledge regarding the ancient Egyptian civilisation, J. R. Harris, but he had nothing to say about dacite either.[17]

What is dacite and where does it occur? It is an igneous rock largely composed of feldspar and quartz, of 'aphantic' texture, meaning that its crystals are so small they can only be identified with a microscope, giving the rock a stony or dull lustre. It is 'found in lava flows and as small intrusions', and is similar to another igneous rock called rhyolite, except that rhyolite contains predominantly potassium feldspar, whereas dacite contains primarily plagioclase (soda-lime) feldspar.[18]

I consulted some books on Egyptian geology, and the only dacite deposits I could find mentioned were in the far Eastern Desert and the Sinai, which are hundreds of miles away from Giza, with no convenient route for transportation of large stones (the far Eastern Desert is beside the Red Sea and not beside the Nile, and the Sinai is on the other side of the Red Sea).[19] Jules Barthoux, who wrote about these occurrences of dacite in those out-of-the-way places, mentioned that dacite occurs mostly as veins running through other rock, for which see his drawing which I reproduce on the website. Extracting a solid block for a sarcophagus from such a vein is all the more problematical and bizarre, as most of the veins are not large enough to enable such a feat to be physically possible. These veins are sometimes vertical, making access and extraction particularly difficult. When Barthoux found a piece of dacite from a vein that was approximately 1.5 metres thick, he seemed to think it was unusually large and splendid.[20] But even that vein was not nearly large enough to produce the huge dacite sarcophagus in the Osiris Shaft. It seems that dacite is not a common Egyptian rock by any means, and it was never used for any of the tens of thousands of small stone vessels roughly contemporary with the sarcophagus (the date of which is given in a moment). In fact, there appears to be no known occurrence of its use in any ancient Egyptian artefact or construction, other than for carving this enormous Sarcophagus Two in the Osiris Shaft.

The actual locations where some dacite veins are known to exist are all hundreds of miles from the Osiris Shaft: Gebel Dukhan and Gebel Um-Sidri nearby the hills near the Wadi Mouelih, Gebel Ferani in the Sinai, and Wadi Ranga near the Red Sea. Assuming that you could locate a vein large enough to produce a huge sarcophagus at any of these locations, which is by no means an enviable task, and assuming that it is even possible at all, you would then find yourself an immensely long distance from Giza, not connected by a water route, faced with the necessity of enormous expanses of desert crossings, and all with a block or object weighing thirty or forty tons to carry. So questions certainly arise: how did they do it and, above all, why bother? Why didn't they just get some granite from Aswan (readily accessible on the Nile) or some basalt from the Fayyum (not very far south of Giza)? Why go to this incredible amount of trouble; a task bordering perilously on the impossible? And if they had found a way to do it this once, as they obviously had, why did they never do it again for the whole of Egyptian history?

Our discovery of the dacite in the Osiris Shaft has been announced by Ioannis in an article of his own in a technical journal in 2008, along with a photo of dacite.[21]

But this bizarre finding of the nature of its stone was only the first

62

surprise that this sarcophagus was to give us. For, later, when we got the dating result, we found that its date was 2800 BC, plus or minus 550 years. In other words, its possible date ranged from 3350 BC to 2250 BC. This was no late Saitic burial. At the very latest, it was Old Kingdom, but it *could* be nearly a millennium older than the time of Cheops and the Fourth Dynasty. This astounding result makes it all the more important that we make a second attempt to obtain a sample of Sarcophagus One for comparison. As for Sarcophagus Three in Level Three, our date for that provides interesting confirmation which we shall consider in a moment. Certainly, for such unexpectedly early results, it is best not to rely on a single sample, and the fact that we have two overlapping dates from the Osiris Shaft is greatly encouraging. If they had been wildly different in age, then we might have expected some error, but as that is not the case, we feel confident in these dates.

Descending into Level Three of the Osiris Shaft is an extraordinary experience. Although the chamber has been severely damaged either by treasure-seekers or by religious fanatics, it still creates an eerie and overwhelming impression. A good view may be seen in Plate 4, taken from the ladder while descending. Central to the photo is the lid of the stone sarcophagus (Sarcophagus Three), which has been raised by Dr Hawass and which now rests on two giant timbers, which appear to be railway sleepers. This was to enable him to look inside the sarcophagus, which he found to be empty and also without inscriptions. To the left in the photo may be seen a small water canal, running along the side of the central island: that is the west wall. The sarcophagus in the centre of the chamber is aligned more or less north–south, though we took no compass measurements to check magnetic directions and had no way of fixing exact geographical directions in this underground setting. (Alignments of the Giza pyramids are geographical, not magnetic, and compass readings do not indicate them. To get true north–south from a magnetic reading, you need a magnetic variation map to calculate the correction.) If we returned with a compass and a map of magnetic variation, we could doubtless compute the geographical alignments. However, as neither of us had ever entered the Osiris Shaft before, and we had little idea what we would find, we were not prepared for such contingencies. And also, as mentioned in a moment, there is iron down there, which might cause a localised distortion of any magnetic reading.

I have already published one colour photo showing part of the water canal in level Three of the Osiris Shaft in *The Sphinx Mystery*, where it is Figure 7.10 in Chapter 7.[22] (It can also be seen on the website of my previous book, www.sphinxmystery.info, in connection with a discussion of the water table level at Giza.) It is reproduced again on this book's website, www.egyptiandawn.info.

The water canal, which may be seen on the left in the photo, actually entirely encircles the central island containing the sarcophagus on all sides, except for the path from the shaft, which enters the island from the south. The four corners of the island originally had square pillars from floor to ceiling. From the account published by Hassan in 1944, which we have already seen, we know that these four pillars were intact within living memory. They have all been so viciously hacked away that only stumps remain. It is difficult to know when this could have taken place. Certainly it was not in the time of Dr Hawass, who guards the shaft so zealously and takes such a deep personal interest in it, and before that the chamber was flooded as far as we know. The only solution to this mystery seems to be to assume that the flood waters subsided or that pumping was successful in the late 1940s or the 1950s, and that the chamber was mutilated at the same time that the five sarcophagi from Level Two were removed, presumably as an act of antiquities theft. Because of the disappearance of the other sarcophagi, it seems certain that a plundering of the Osiris Shaft took place after 1944, and the damage to Level Three must have taken place then.

Afterwards, the chamber must have flooded again, until Dr Hawass was able to pump it dry, apart from the canal water, which remains. The hacking away of the four stone columns is so utterly vicious and must have required such prolonged and exhausting effort over a substantial period of time that it seems to me that it could only have had a fanatical religious motivation of some kind. Certainly, it was far beyond the capability of any casual vandals, and must have been consciously planned. I believe that the motivations must either have been those of extreme and fanatical Muslims, wishing to destroy something pre-Islamic which was so mysteriously sacred that it aroused their fears and superstitions; or, otherwise, the destruction could conceivably have been carried out for some sinister occult purpose by a secret society (in which case this would probably have happened prior to 1956, when Nasser took over Egypt). However, if a secret society had done this, it is most unlikely to have been the Egyptian Freemasons or the Rosicrucians, who would be more inclined to take a favourable interest in such a site than damage it. It would more likely be some elite esoteric society virulently opposed to them, and possibly linked to the Egyptian Muslim Brotherhood, which I have heard has some esoteric societies linked to it that are anti-Masonic. The labour involved in hacking away these columns of solid bedrock should not be underestimated. Someone or some group was absolutely determined to desecrate this sacred chamber in a drastic and permanent manner, possibly in an attempt to destroy its 'spiritual power' forever. Ordinary people may believe that such 'occult' purposes are so absurd that they find it hard to believe that people could take them seriously enough to do such a thing. But there are many people and groups in the world obsessed with occultism, and it is unwise to ignore their existence and actions entirely.

Dr Hawass has pointed out with his usual enthusiasm that this lowest chamber is a 'Tomb of Osiris', and in that he is certainly correct. It is without question a replica of that mythical island surrounded by water where the sarcophagus of Osiris is meant to lie. It is a replica of the island described in the sacred texts and is similar to, though much smaller than, the other underground Osiris Island encircled by a water canal that has been excavated at Abydos. I am referring to the famous Osireion adjoining the Temple of Seti I, both of which structures we have dated and which are discussed in my account of our work at the Temple of Seti I, which is not yet published. Hawass seems to have been the first person to recognise the true nature of this amazing chamber as an Osiris Island.

The Osiris Shaft was hacked out of the solid bedrock originally, with enormous effort, and this 'Tomb of Osiris' seems to have been created originally out of intense religious belief. In a dream I later had of the chamber I heard the Christian hymn 'Faith of Our Fathers Living Still' (familiar to me from my youth) sung as accompaniment, which is very apt; Jesus Christ died, was buried in a tomb, and rose from the dead, just as Osiris did, and the later myth owes much to the earlier one.

Originally, when the chamber of Level Three was intact, it would have presented the most amazing sight: a sarcophagus resting in the middle of an island with pillars at each corner, surrounded by an artificial river.

Level Three has a prominent vein of iron running through the rock. Such veins are not uncommon in the limestone plateau of Giza. Occasional 'crevices' in the bedrock of the Giza Plateau may be empty because they have had veins of iron taken out of them; one such crevice exists in the 'well shaft' of the Great Pyramid, for instance. The chamber of Level Three has been rather rudely hacked out of the bedrock, and the impression given by these unfinished surfaces is not a sophisticated one at all. It is all a bit too crudely done to suggest that the same people who built the perfect pyramids carved such an imperfect chamber. They simply don't match. If the pyramid builders had carved the chamber, wouldn't they have made it look smooth and beautiful? The dating result that I give in a moment may explain this.

The grey sarcophagus which is found in Level Three is not of dacite. Mineralogical analysis revealed that it was of granite. Its situation is bizarre and unique in Egypt, for it is set into a depression in the centre of the island, which in turn is in the centre of the chamber. (Although there is an Osiris Island at Abydos, it has no sarcophagus.) In Plate 4 we can see the sarcophagus lid resting on its timbers, and below it the depression, which is filled with water, just as the surrounding canal is. The actual sarcophagus itself is not only filled with water, but is underwater. Our sample thus came from the lid, as we could not reach the base of the sarcophagus.

The dating result for this sarcophagus is 1970 BC, plus or minus 400 years, thus giving a possible dating between 2370 BC and 1570 BC. Since the lowest possible date of Sarcophagus Two is 2250 BC, and the highest possible date of Sarcophagus Three is 2370 BC, there is an overlap period of 220 years for these two sarcophagi. If they are contemporary with each other, then they must date from the Fifth or Sixth Dynasties of the Old Kingdom, using conventional chronologies. In any case, we may certainly rule out a date of Sarcophagus Three during the First Intermediate Period, so that approximately 150 years of the possible dating range is impossible for social reasons, due to the total chaos of that period in history, circa 2170–2020 BC. One thing we may conclude for certain: Sarcophagus Three dates either from before the First Intermediate Period or after it; if before, then it must be from the Fifth or Sixth Dynasties.

However, it is far more likely that the sarcophagi are not contemporary with one another. Level Three is probably an afterthought, a further level created at a later period, when a 'Tomb of Osiris' was considered desirable. Although Osiris became popular during the Fifth Dynasty (conventionally dated 2498 BC–2345 BC), so that at least the concept was around, circumstantial evidence would seem to suggest that the Middle Kingdom (circa 2000 BC–circa 1750 BC by basic chronologies, which are firmly fixed astronomically) is a more likely date for Level Three and hence Sarcophagus Three. This is because we now have a dating for that larger and more grandiose underground 'Tomb of Osiris', the Osireion at Abydos, and we can demonstrate conclusively that part of it is of Middle Kingdom date. Probably the same cultural milieu that created one underground Osireion created the other. We can dismiss the possible dating between 1750 BC and 1570 BC, since it is just as unlikely that Sarcophagus Three could date from the Second Intermediate Period as it is that it could date from the First Intermediate Period. We really only have two convincing possibilities for the origin of Sarcophagus Three from its potential dating span: it is either from the Fifth or Sixth Dynasties of the Old Kingdom, or it is from the Middle Kingdom. And the chamber and the sarcophagus, so closely matched to one another and conceived of as a single entity, must be contemporaneous. Of the two possibilities, we have circumstantial evidence in favour of the latter choice, and so we tentatively presume therefore that Level Three and Sarcophagus Three are Middle Kingdom in date rather than from the end of the Old Kingdom.

The unitary nature of the planning of chamber and sarcophagus seems obvious for Level Three, as the island is surrounded by the moat and had its four corner pillars, and in the middle of the island is the depression in which rests the sarcophagus. It seems impossible to conceive of this chamber, therefore, as being anything other than a single, defined conceptual entity. Level Two is a simple burial chamber with seven niches, and it could be younger than Sarcophagus Two. But it cannot be Saite, as it has to be older than Level Three because it is higher than and leads into the lower chamber, and since Level Three is no later than Middle Kingdom, Level Two has to be at least of that date. Therefore we are forced to jettison entirely any concepts of Saite shafts and burials and are faced with the entire Osiris Shaft being Middle Kingdom at the latest, in terms of the shaft itself.

But we have already seen that Sarcophagus Two cannot be as recent as the Middle Kingdom, since its latest possible date is 2250 BC, or about the end of the Fifth Dynasty. And this takes us back to a time only a bit more than a century subsequent to the construction of the Chephren Causeway which runs across the top of the Osiris Shaft. And since it is highly unlikely that any object will be its lowest possible date from a lengthy age span, we are really left with a situation where it is hard to escape the conclusion that the Osiris Shaft was in existence *before* the construction of the giant Chephren Causeway of the Fourth Dynasty, and that the Causeway left a subway for access on purpose, although the now-vanished superstructure described by Selim Hassan in 1944 would have been a later addition, possibly Saite in date, as it is said by Hassan to have been constructed of the remains of the Causeway roof, which probably was still intact in Middle Kingdom times. For such a deep shaft to have been constructed *no later than* the Fourth Dynasty must mean that it was a highly important burial site indeed. This accords with a unique stone being used for the huge sarcophagus. And of course this also accords with the lack of inscriptions, since at that period inscriptions were not carved on sarcophagi.

The Osiris Shaft is therefore a new and fundamental element to be taken into account when considering the nature of the Giza Plateau and the Necropolis as a whole. It must now be viewed as an elementary part of the total design concept. Far from being filled in as an obstacle to the path of the Chephren Causeway, it was *accommodated* by that Causeway. That is most remarkable, if the Causeway were really built by Chephren and really built at the time we normally accept. Chephren was a highly egotistical pharaoh, to judge from his hundreds of statues of himself (see Chapter Seven). Would he under normal circumstances allow an earlier burial shaft to get in the way of his plans for what is supposed to be his own pyramid and his own Causeway? Wouldn't he be expected to fill it or at least to seal it off? Instead, he appears to have allowed his own construction to take it under its wing, as it were, by incorporating a subway for it beneath his own precious and highly personal Causeway. This is truly extraordinary. What would be his reasons for doing this?

And to return to the subject of the stone of Sarcophagus Two being dacite: who could have the power to commandeer something so rare and hard to find, and to transport such a huge block of it to Giza and lower it to the bottom of a 100-foot shaft? We may safely assume that only a king could have done this. So the burial in Sarcophagus Two may well have been a royal burial. And this might perhaps provide the justification for Chephren treating it with sufficient reverence as not to obliterate it.

But what are we to make of the fact that the possible dating range for Sarcophagus Two extends way back to predynastic times, indeed to 3350 BC? That is about 850 years earlier than the generally accepted date for the construction of the Giza pyramids. The sarcophagus, and by implication its shaft, could be of any date from that early one through to the Fifth Dynasty.

Was there in fact anything going on at Giza this early? The question of the dating of the Giza pyramids themselves is dealt with in the next chapter, in which it is made clear that the Giza pyramids are older than has been conventionally thought, and Sarcophagus Two could be a relic of the same period, and from the same culture. But what conventional results do we have to show that Giza was being used before the Fourth Dynasty? Well, we have had ample proof for a very long time indeed that Giza was used for burials during the First and Second Dynasties, and the first tomb of the First Dynasty to be discovered was found by Alessandro Barsanti (1858–1917) as long ago as 1904, and excavated by Daressy; further remains of the First and Second Dynasties at Giza were excavated by Sir Flinders Petrie, as described in his volume of excavation reports entitled *Gizeh and Rifeh* in 1907.[23] Also, a king's name inscription of the Second Dynasty was found in excavations of the Valley Temple, and I reproduce that inscription later in connection with my discussion of it in Chapter Seven. So a possible date of the main Osiris Shaft from even the First Dynasty, circa 3000 BC, cannot be ruled out, for we have long-standing evidence of burials at Giza from that time at least. It is true that that evidence presents nothing like so bold a project as the construction of this enormously deep shaft, and if the Osiris Shaft were to date from that period, it must be a major royal tomb because of the effort of construction involved.

The fact that it was originally surmounted by a mastaba (a mastaba is a rectangular, partially sunken tomb of mud brick) also provides an echo of archaic dynastic burial practices, although Hassan thought this mastaba might have been constructed later from the remains of the Causeway roof, which could have been pulled down by the Persians, or so he imagines. But there are other possible differences: if the Osiris Shaft were from that period, one would expect to find fragments of stone vases scattered on the floor of Level Two. Although I did not see any, we certainly did not make a search for such traces. We disregarded even the small bones that I noticed under our feet on the floor, as we had no time for such distractions as we struggled to get dating samples in between blackouts. A proper study of the site should be made, to see if any small fragments or traces of archaic or Old Kingdom grave goods can be found, perhaps fallen behind the giant sarcophagi in their niches, where they could not have been swept away during the theft of the other five sarcophagi and the many plundering raids that the shaft must have experienced over the millennia from grave robbers, not least in the middle of the twentieth century. The bottom of the canal in Level Three should also be searched very carefully for fragments of any remains. This would require a diver with good lights. The fact that the sarcophagi have now been demonstrated to be extraordinarily ancient justifies the closest possible scrutiny of every aspect of the shaft, canal and chambers. It is ripe for full and complete re-examination, of a forensic thoroughness, like a police murder investigation.

But now we have another problem: if the tomb was so important, why was the shaft left open? Could a royal burial possibly have taken place in such an accessible location? We cannot conclude that this must be impossible. However, the burial, whether royal or not, in such a spectacular sarcophagus must have required concealment. So we are left to conclude that there must have been a very intact sealing at the top of the shaft, and that the subway must have been carefully blocked at each end and concealed by huge stones. In other words, the shaft must have been firmly and securely sealed in Old Kingdom times when, by apparently unanimous agreement of all Egyptologists, the Giza Plateau was sacrosanct and well guarded. Therefore it could after all have been some kind of early royal burial. It would probably have been smashed open and pillaged during the First Intermediate Period, when we know that the Giza Plateau was sacked mercilessly by hordes of robbers and crowds intent on smashing the statues and relics of the preceding dynasties.

Having been left open, with its tomb despoiled, the Osiris Shaft would then have been a tempting venue for further exploitation by the Osiris-loving pharaohs of the Middle Kingdom, who could take advantage of most of the work having been done, merely dig a bit deeper and make a further chamber, and create a mystical 'Tomb of Osiris'. And who knows? Possibly the sarcophagus in Level Three was also actually used. Or it may just have been a dummy with a purely symbolic significance. For the shaft was probably never sealed after this, and the 'Tomb of Osiris' is highly likely to have been used as an esoteric initiation site for priests and possibly even pharaohs. If its purpose was primarily for religious ceremonies, there would have been no need to 'finish' the walls; it would be more effective to keep the rough-hewn look, to emphasise the cavernous and wild nature of the place. And of course it would then have been *necessary* for the shaft to remain open, for otherwise access to the 'Tomb of Osiris' would not have been possible, and rituals could not have taken place there.

What would the nature of such ceremonies have been? Osiris ceremonies are described at some length in my account of our work at Abydos (not yet published), which deals with the double structure, known as the Temple of Seti I above ground and the Osireion below ground. We have shown that these are of different dates, and that the New Kingdom Pharaoh Seti I incorporated the older structure of the Osireion into his own Temple of Osiris, but added the ritual, religious and astronomical inscriptions of the Osireion. All of the inscriptions from both structures have been studied in great detail by Rosalie David in her seminal work, *Religious Ritual at Abydos (c. 1300 BC)*.[24] Professor David has reconstructed the religious rituals, which are described in great detail on the walls, both in texts and in pictures. Unfortunately, her book is unillustrated, so that one must supplement her full account of the texts and word-pictures with illustrations published elsewhere, as I describe in the account I have written. But there are a number of observations in Rosalie David's excellent book that can be taken to relate to the Osiris Shaft, although she does not mention the shaft and indeed has never entered it.

In her book, Professor David points out that the name of Osiris is unknown before the Fifth Dynasty, and she says: 'Memphite theology places his drowning in the neighbourhood of Memphis . . .'[25] This is extremely important, because it confirms that there was a tradition at Memphis, the nearest city to Giza, that Osiris had drowned nearby. A cult centre to Osiris in the vicinity is therefore more or less a necessity. Since the 'Osiris sarcophagus' is underwater in the depression in the centre of the Osiris Island at the bottom of the Osiris Shaft, perhaps the tradition that 'Osiris drowned near Memphis' is somehow a reference to this sarcophagus being underwater, and hence also the conception of Osiris as being somehow within it must be considered as the orgin of his having been 'drowned'. This is pure speculation, but it is not an impossibility.

As I point out in Chapter Seven, there are good reasons for believing that the Valley Temple at Giza was transformed into an Osiris Temple at some point, and that Osirian rites took place there. But for the proper worship of Osiris, the God of the Dead, an underground sanctuary reproducing his tomb was preferable. As David says:

'At Abydos, the Osireion is believed to be an imitation of the burial-place of Osiris . . .'[26]

And just as that was certainly the case, we may be equally confident that the lowest level of the Osiris Shaft represented the same thing.

So what took place there? What form would the ceremonies actually have taken? Unlike the Osireion, which had inscriptions added to its walls during a later period, the Osiris Shaft is devoid of any texts or pictures depicting the ceremonies. But we may be able to glean something of what would have gone on there by analogy from the Osireion at Abydos. First of all, Osiris was the God of the Dead, and a solemn visit to a replica of his sarcophagus would have been the fundamental element of the ceremonies. But Osiris was also the God of Resurrection, so some resurrection ceremonies might well have taken place there. These might have taken the form of the empty sarcophagus being opened, and a prominent person, either a priest or a pharaoh, lying in the sarcophagus and having the lid placed over him as a sacred ordeal. This ordeal may have included the ordeal of 'drowning' within the sarcophagus, with an air tube and limited air supply. After a short time, when a ceremony beseeching Osiris to arise from the dead might have been enacted, complete with singing and praying, the lid could have been removed, and the 'resurrected' individual could arise and be 'born again'.

We are encouraged to think of some such ritual taking place because of the famous myth that Osiris was asked to lie down in a sarcophagus to test its size, and the lid was then sealed by his wicked brother Set, and he was thrown into the river and died. (Once again, in this classic tale as related by Plutarch in the first century AD, we have a motif of a 'drowned sarcophagus', since it is described as having been thrown into the river and hence submerged in water.) Later, the wife and sister of Osiris found him and raised him from the dead. If some such ceremony was enacted in the Osiris Shaft, there would have been a priestess representing Isis, and she would have presided over the resurrection. Princesses and queens of the royal house were always priestesses. For instance, as I pointed out in Chapter Five of my previous book, *The Sphinx Mystery*, Queen Mersyankh III, the wife of Chephren who was also granddaughter of Cheops, held the office of Priestess of Thoth.

Rosalie David explains that, at Abydos, a mystery play of the death and resurrection of Osiris was enacted:

From the twelfth dynasty onwards, every year at Abydos, a Mystery Play was performed in honour of Osiris, re-enacting the events of the life and death of the god. The plays are recorded on the Ikhernofret Stela [Ikhernofret was Chief Treasurer of the Middle Kingdom Pharaoh Sesostris III], and it is thought that the acts mentioned on this stela are given in the right order, since they are compatible with what is known of the Osiris myth. The play was enacted by priests and attended by pilgrims; it was celebrated partly in the temple, and the ceremony was performed for the benefit of the deceased king and for the eternal resurrection of all worshippers of Osiris. In the Temple of Denderah, the ritual reliefs show the mysteries of Osiris as they were performed in Ptolemaic times, and it can be supposed that they differed little from those at Abydos. . . . these can be reconstructed [also] in part from the reliefs and inscriptions which occur on the walls of certain temples, illustrating the ritual which attended the annual period of devotion accorded to Osiris. As well as the material which occurs in the Temple of Denderah, in the Temple of Horus at Edfu, the Crypt, the Mansion of the Prince, and the Privy Chamber of the Crypt are all connected with this cult and its Mysteries; in addition, Osirian rites occurred at Karnak in the month of Khoiak, and, in the Graeco-Roman era, the island of Philae was one of the leading centres of the cult. . . . The great festival took place in the last month of Inundation, and, at Abydos, the celebration was represented in part by a Mystery Play of eight acts. . . . Thoth was one of the chief actors in the Mysteries. . . . all the essential rites to ensure the resurrection of the god were performed prior to the festival in private chambers within the temples.[27]

We know that at Abydos, Pharaoh Seti I played the role of Osiris personally, since he is actually portrayed on the walls of the temple doing so. It is likely therefore that Sarcophagus Three of the Osiris Shaft was a secret place of initiation and ritual re-enactment of the burial and resurrection of Osiris by the pharaoh in person. Someone would have represented Isis, though we cannot tell whether this would have been a woman or a priest, and a priest dressed as Thoth would have been on hand as a leading participant in the ceremony, and advisor and assistant to the pharaoh-as-Osiris. Certainly if pharaohs really did allow themselves to be sealed inside the sarcophagus even for a few moments, it would have been a true test of nerve. In the photos, it is clear how huge and heavy the stone lid of the sarcophagus was. But possibly they did not actually carry out this physical act. After all, the sarcophagus was in a sunken pit in the central island, and as it might well always have been covered in water, it is possible that the intention was merely that it should be gazed upon through the water, and was meant to 'really contain' Osiris in a symbolic sense. If a pharaonic resurrection ritual was enacted under those circumstances, it might have been done more simply, by using a wooden coffin placed near the sarcophagus, perhaps at the foot of the small island.

The space in the chamber is limited, and the number of people partaking would have been very small. There would have been no spectators, so that the purpose was entirely private, which is why I say it would have been for magical or initiatory purposes, as there was no space for any mystery play intended for an audience. A very small procession of priests and the pharaoh would have entered the island along the pathway, and walked around the sunken sarcophagus, gazing at it mournfully and singing a dirge. A priest dressed as Set might invite the pharaoh to lie down in a wooden coffin; he would be sealed in it during a ceremony; and then Isis would open it, and Thoth would raise him up and lead him out of it into his rebirth. This might have been an annual resurrection ceremony intended to renew the life of the pharaoh. If the living pharaoh used a wooden coffin placed at the foot of the 'sarcophagus of Osiris', that might have been considered sufficient for ritual purposes.

Later, during the Saitic Period, the Osiris Shaft would have offered an excellent location for reuse by Saitic burials, and we assume that these certainly must have taken place, and that the small sarcophagi reported by Hassan in 1944 would have been Saite ones; except that one of them could have been much older and used in the rituals I have just suggested. As there seem never to have been more than two giant sarcophagi in Level Two, the remaining five niches could have held grave goods originally. But these would have disappeared during the conversion of the shaft from a true burial to an initiation centre during the Middle Kingdom.

We thus have one possible reconstruction of the complicated history of this major shaft at Giza. However, these are merely suggestions, and other researchers may have better ideas. But any alternative theories must accommodate the dates of the sarcophagi and the evident plan of Level Three as a unitary conception tied to the date of Sarcophagus Three. In fact, these are exactly the kinds of problems that can be expected to arise when, instead of speculation regarding dates, we suddenly start getting hard facts by the direct dating of stone, so that inferences by style and association are ousted from their place of primacy.

As long as the sarcophagi could not be dated directly, it was easy to dismiss the Osiris Shaft as a Saitic shaft of relatively minor importance. But now that it can no longer be dismissed in that way, we are left to grapple with the new problems outlined above.

The location of the Osiris Shaft on the Giza Plateau might have some significance. The only map in existence showing its location is the one published by Howard Vyse in 1837 (see Figure 6). We cannot assume this map to be exact in the sense of the modern geodetic survey map used for the preparation of Figure 1 in the previous chapter. However, anyone can place a ruler on Vyse's map and see clearly enough that the Osiris Shaft lies on a straight line connecting the apex of the Pyramid of Chephren with the midpoint of the Sphinx (see Figure 6). Plotting the line connecting the two end points on the modern geodetic map gives a point on the Chephren Causeway which lies on the north–south meridian line that bisects the Great Pyramid; though, in Vyse's drawing, the shaft is shown as slightly west of that point. However, the modern map makes clear that the line joining the apex of the Pyramid of Chephren with the midpoint of the Sphinx does not cross the Chephren Causeway any further west and, as we know that the shaft is beneath the Causeway, Vyse's map is slightly in error. We have to keep in mind that when Vyse made his map, the Chephren Causeway was invisible, and still buried in sand. Only the mastaba atop the Osiris Shaft protruded. The likelier error of the two possible ones to have been made by Vyse in drawing his map was to show the shaft slightly too far west. In this case, the modern point of intersection of the two lines with the Causeway is liable to be correct. Of course, someone will need to confirm this one day, but that will require a special effort with a theodolite and a small surveying team. If confirmed, the position of the Osiris Shaft will then be seen to be firmly embedded within the grand Giza design scheme, and suggests that it dates back to a time when the Giza Plans were still understood; it could even have been an integral part of them from the beginning.

As for the Osiris Shaft leading to other tunnels connecting with other locations underground in the Giza Plateau, as has been suggested by wild speculations on the Internet in recent years, where a 'cover-up' of Giza secrets is suspected as taking place in this shaft, we may dismiss such ideas. There are two 'holes' in the walls of Level Three, both on the other side of the canal from the central island and thus hard to reach, but as close an inspection as we were able to make of these left us convinced that they lead nowhere. Because of the extraordinary speculations concerning these holes, I thought it worthwhile to reproduce photos of both of them. One in the northeast corner seems to have been an attempt by an ancient tomb robber to hack through in search of something, but he must have given up, as there is nothing there after a short crawling space but a tiny hole which seems to lead to nothing. My photo of it may be seen on the website. The other, on the west wall, is another hacked opening, perhaps incorporating some natural cavity in the rock, which bends round out of sight, and appears to be large enough for a small boy to crawl into, but which almost certainly leads to nothing. According to Hawass, it goes for about six metres and then ends, but he intends to excavate it one day. Even if some extension is found, however, nothing of any size could ever be taken along it, it is so tiny. This hole may be seen on this book's website. It appears to peter out, though we could not plunge into the water and cross the canal in order to take a closer look, as we were unprepared for such a task, had insufficient time, and were suffering the continual blackouts which were making the whole undertaking perilous. Fantasies of the Osiris Shaft as a nerve-centre of Giza underground tunnels can, however, certainly be dismissed.

One other possibility exists, which should be mentioned, namely that there might be passages leading out of the chamber that can only be entered underwater (only if 'Osiris drowns'?). People who explore caves often have to dive underwater in an underground lake or river, go through an opening and come up in the next cave. If anyone wanted to disguise a connecting passage, hiding it underwater would be the perfect way to go about it. So you would dive into the moat, find the opening and go through it, come out underwater in another cave or chamber, and then rise to the surface again. Until the moat in this chamber is thoroughly explored by a diver with lights, this possibility cannot be ruled out. At the Osireion in Abydos, we do know for certain that there is a constructed conduit opening beneath water level into the canal around the island, which leads the water in. I have suggested strongly in my still-unpublished report about Abydos that the canal there should be investigated by divers. If there is an opening beneath water level leading into the canal around one Osiris Island, why should there not be one in the other?

One thing I am curious about is why there are not more fragments of rock lying around in Level Three than there are. Where are most of the remains of the four columns which were so thoroughly and viciously smashed to pieces? Although some are visible on the central island, I presume that the remainder of these must rest at the bottom of the canal. But the canal is full of water, which is covered with an opaque scum, so that one cannot see through it. The water itself is clear if the scum is pushed aside. The scum could be scraped off the canal water surface so we could look down at the bottom of the entire canal to see what it contains. If there are heaps of stone fragments from the smashed columns down there, then they would have to be cleared completely before we could see whether anything of real interest, prior to 1944 in date, is to be found at the bottom of the moat.

Another curiosity is the source of the water filling the canal: where does it come from? Obviously it must be from a spring of some sort. This in itself suggests an underwater channel or entrance of some kind, since there is no visible opening in the solid rock walls to allow water in. As the water has come from somewhere, and as there is no visible source, it can be concluded that there must be an invisible source. In other words, there must be a conduit like the one at Abydos. The chamber now seems restored to its original water level, for the water is just high enough to fill the canal around the island. This is what it must have looked like in the Middle Kingdom. In order to find the water at just the right level, the excavators of the chamber must have kept digging until they struck it, and then constructed the island and canal at the appropriate level. We must remember what Hassan said about the water: that it was drinkable. It probably comes from a spring unconnected with the polluted sources further east on the Plateau; these have been spoiled by the habitations and sewage of the neighbouring village of Nazlett. There is a serious possibility that the water comes from a constructed channel concealed underwater, because the bedrock down there is just too solid for random leaks. If such a channel exists, then its construction must have been a mammoth subterranean undertaking of the most furtive kind imaginable, since there must then be other chambers very near, in which the water was found, and a truly extraordinary plan must have been required. But where are the shafts leading down to these other chambers? There would have to be another chamber and also another access to it in order to divert the water into the canal by a conduit constructed from the other side. They say when chasing business contacts, 'follow the money trail', but here it is a case of 'follow the water trail'. Somebody urgently needs to do this. But as I am not a diver, I won't volunteer for the underwater work.

No thorough exploration of the bottom of the little canal seems ever to have been undertaken. Although there are anecdotal reports of people swimming in the chamber when the water level was higher than it is now, which must have been cool and refreshing on a hot Egyptian day, this does not seem to have been combined with diving down to find the inlet for the water, or to study the bottom of the canal. We certainly hope that these studies will take place, and that the mysteries of the 'Tomb of Osiris' may be fully revealed one day.

In conclusion, I should say that the Osiris Shaft can never now be relegated to the status of a secondary feature of the Giza Plateau on the assumption that it is a Saitic burial shaft dating from the period 664 BC–525 BC. This is now seen to be definitely not the case. The bottom level of the shaft is probably Middle Kingdom, and Level Two is probably no later than the Fourth Dynasty. And what is more, Sarcophagus Two being made of a unique stone that occurs nowhere else – to our knowledge – amongst the surviving remains of the ancient Egyptian civilisation, and being so unexpectedly ancient in date, must now be seen as one of the oldest and most precious of all carved objects to survive in the whole of Egypt. Also, the 'Tomb of Osiris' must now be viewed as being of extraordinary importance, whether as a mystical burial site, or more likely as a mystical religious site for initiations or ceremonies connected with the Osirian religion during the second millennium BC.

There is no doubt that the results we have obtained on the Plateau of Giza, including the early date for the Osiris Shaft, show that Giza as a whole must be re-evaluated. But then, so must the entire subject of the origins of the high Egyptian civilisation, which have never been clear anyway. This is not going to be an easy task. Are the existing historical chronologies of the dynasties largely accurate, so that merely the monument dates need adjusting? Or should we move the dynastic datings themselves several centuries backwards? But this would create rather large gaps in time, and how would these be filled? And since the Giza pyramids (see the next chapter, 'The Pyramids Are Too Old') and the Osiris Shaft are so old, who was it who really constructed them? Where are all the other remains of the same age that one would expect to find at Giza and elsewhere? Where are the tombs of these older kings? And were these earlier pyramid builders the mysterious 'sons of Horus', who were said in ancient Egyptian tradition to have reigned before the known kings began? If so, who were these 'sons of Horus'? And why would they construct such gigantic pyramids but leave so little else behind – except for the Osiris Shaft and the Sphinx? Or are there other tombs and structures, some of them familiar and supposedly comfortably 'dated', which need re-evaluating and redating in the light of our findings? In Chapter Four, I give the precise locations of what appear to be seven unopened royal tombs at Giza which cannot be later than the Fourth Dynasty. It seems as if our work may only just have begun.

CHAPTER THREE

The Pyramids are Too Old

The Pyramids of Giza are probably the most famous monuments from antiquity anywhere in the world. Their correct date of construction is therefore of the greatest possible significance. Everybody quite naturally wants to know who built them and when they did so. Associated with this is the question of how they were built, but that is a separate problem, except that the questions of 'who' and 'when' affect the 'how' as well.

As a result of our dating study, we have found that the pyramids of Giza are much older than they are supposed to be. This finding is the most important of all the dating results obtained by Ioannis Liritzis and myself, because it suggests that the concept of the origins of high civilisation in Egypt must be reformulated in some way. This in turn could necessitate a new conceptualisation of how civilisation evolved throughout the entire ancient world.

The pyramids of Giza are supposed to date from a very specific time in the Old Kingdom of Egypt, and to form part of a sequence of architectural development. For instance, they are meant to have followed after, and not to have preceded, the Step Pyramid at Saqqara, which is supposed to be of the preceding (Third) Dynasty, and which is made of smaller stones, is smaller than the two larger Giza pyramids, and has various features generally thought to be transitional from the earlier mastaba tombs to the true pyramid form. These ideas are repeated so often that no one really questions them and, furthermore, they seem rather obvious. The Giza pyramids are also supposed by most

Egyptologists to be the tombs of certain specific pharaohs of the Fourth Dynasty. This should all be reconsidered now, in the light of the redating we will be presenting.

The question as to how such an early construction of the Giza pyramids can possibly fit into what is already known of the chronology and history of early Egypt is now a major problem. However, in Chapter Six, the general lack of certainty within Egyptology about what really happened prior to the Fourth Dynasty will be exposed, and it is nothing new. We will see that no one has the slightest idea how many kings there were in the Third Dynasty, who they all were, or any certain knowledge of how long that dynasty lasted. Before this, in Chapter Five the strange story of the last king of the Second Dynasty is told, together with the dating results we obtained from his tomb when it was re-excavated by the German Institute in Cairo. Questions will be raised about the definitions of those early 'dynasties'. Is that what they really were? All of the king lists are incomplete or imperfect; the kings all had more than one name apiece anyway. No sooner do you find a king you can identify, such as King Teti of the Sixth Dynasty (whose small pyramid has been excavated at Saqqara), than not one but two more and earlier kings named Teti turn up; and the only thing known for certain about them is that they are both different from one another and different from the one we thought was the only one: the third one. Since we don't even really know the names of all the kings, and cannot even be certain about their so-called 'dynasties', how are we ever going to figure out whether any of these people, known or unknown, was capable of building the pyramids of Giza?

The fact that the name of the fifth king of the Second Dynasty (King Send or Sened) was excavated inside the Valley Temple of Giza is tantalising, and is discussed in Chapter Seven, but is merely suggestive. The fact that a list of names of kings supposedly preceding the First Dynasty exists on an ancient king list (the Palermo Stone), but not a single one of those names is otherwise familiar to us, and we know nothing whatever about who they were or what they did, certainly adds an interesting dimension to the puzzle. I will have more to say about these unknown early kings in the later discussions of Chapter Six. They were meant to have succeeded the gods and demigods as kings of Egypt, but who were they?

Plate 1

Plate 2

Plate 3

Plate 4

Plate 5

Plate 6

Plate 7

Plate 8

Plate 9

Plate 10

Plate 11

Plate 13

Plate 15

Plate 16

Plate 17

Plate 14

Plate 18

Plate 19

Plate 20

Plate 21

Plate 22

Plate 23

In Chapter Six, we will see that there is a case to be made for over-lapping rather than successive 'dynasties' in the early days of what is called the Archaic Period (this sort of thing happened in much later times, but has never previously been suggested for the Archaic times), of how there are many rival and competing 'king lists', with Egyptologists completely disagreeing with one another about them, about the need for additional 'phantom kings' to be inserted into existing lists of kings, of whom solid archaeological evidence exists, despite their names having vanished from official history, and other uncertainties of a highly unset-tling but stimulating kind, guaranteed both to divert and to amuse the reader who can see the humour in everything being 'a bit of a mess' as far as the origins of Egyptian civilisation are concerned.

The conventional and accepted belief is that the Great Pyramid of Giza was built by Pharaoh Cheops (Egyptian name: Khufu) of the Egyptian Fourth Dynasty, who reigned circa 2604–2581 BC according to current views of chronology. These are based on a combination of studies of fragmentary (and, as just mentioned, disputed) lists of kings, historically dateable risings of the star Sirius (where particular ones have been subjectively chosen over others, choices which may not in the light of our findings have been justified), extrapolation and guess-work. Thoroughly orthodox and conventional chronologies existed in the Victorian and Edwardian eras which would have fitted our findings better, such as that adopted by the distinguished Egyptologist James Henry Breasted (1865–1935, the founder of American Egyptology) in 1906.[1] His famous chronological scheme, known as 'Breasted's Chronology', is no longer accepted by more recent Egyptologists, who do not agree with Breasted's conclusions, which he arrived at from a variety of sources considered with the greatest care in his day. But they may find that they have to bring it back again. For Breasted's date for the Fourth Dynasty was 2900 BC–2750 BC,[2] and if we reverted to Breasted's Chronology then the Great Pyramid might still conceivably have been built by Cheops, as we shall see as we go along. But if we were to readopt Breasted's Chronology, after its having been decisively abandoned in recent times, then many living Egyptologists might feel that they would lose face, so it is to be doubted that they could ever be persuaded to agree to do this.

Breasted made a point of stressing that 'the dates in the Twelfth Dynasty are astronomically computed and correct to within three years',[3] and it is thus only the dates prior to the Middle Kingdom (i.e., dates prior to circa 2000 BC) which have been changed since Breasted's day, and where all the uncertainty still lies. This point at least is now uncontroversial. The reliability of dates for the Twelfth Dynasty and hence of the entire Middle Kingdom in Egypt, stressed by Breasted, is a matter which seems to have been confirmed and settled with finality by the leading expert in ancient Egyptian astronomy, Richard Parker, in 1977, in his paper entitled 'The Sothic Dating of the Twelfth and Eighteenth Dynasties'.[4] However, absolute chronology is not our only problem by any means for, as we shall see, the problem of superior versus inferior ancient technologies poses a far greater dilemma, and that is a problem we have to face from now on in this book.

The second-largest pyramid, the one with the limestone facing stones still in place at the top, like a coating of icing on a cake, is generally called the Pyramid of Chephren because it is conventionally believed to have been built by the Pharaoh Chephren (Egyptian name: Khafre; the correct form of his name was really Ra-kaf or Raqaf, but no one ever uses it for some bizarre reason, so we must continue to call him Khafre in order to avoid confusion). He is thought by Egyptologists to have been either the son or the brother of Cheops. We don't have much reliable information about the precise family relationships of the various leading figures of the Fourth Dynasty, because of the high degree of incest and multiple relationships between them all. Everybody in the royal family seems to have been everybody else's brother, sister, uncle, or aunt, sometimes twice over! There are also suggestions that some of the pharaohs changed their names when they rose to the throne and ceased to be princes, and that there are some cases of 'two different people' being really 'one single person'.

Also, little is known for certain about the historical events of this period. Chephren reigned circa 2572–2546 BC according to conventional schemes. In between these two pharaohs was another pharaoh called Djedefre (or actually Radjedef, which is probably the correct form of the name, though it is also not commonly used, so to avoid confusion I must once again continue to use the wrong form of the name as

EXAMPLE of the CASING-STONES of a PYRAMID, SUPER-POSED.
ON THE RECT-ANGULAR MASONRY COURSES! FROM A PHOTOGRAPH BY P.S. OF THE SUMMIT OF THE 2ᵈ PYR.

REMNANT of the ORIGINAL CASING-STONE SURFACE of the GREAT PYRAMID.
NEAR THE MIDDLE OF ITS NORTHERN FOOT. AS DISCOVERED BY THE EXCAVATIONS OF COL. HOWARD VYSE IN 1837

Figure 7. Here we see remaining casing stones of the two main Giza pyramids drawn clearly by Piazzi Smyth, to show what they were like. From Charles Piazzi Smyth, *Life and Work at the Great Pyramid*, Edinburgh, 1867, 3 vols., Volume II.

everyone else does), who for some mysterious reason did not bother to build a pyramid for himself at Giza, according to these accepted notions. He is sometimes said to have presided over the excavation or the restoration or at least the sealing of some symbolic boat pits beside the Great Pyramid at Giza, but he built no actual pyramid at Giza.[5] However, even his 'sealing the boat pit' at Giza is seriously disputed. It is not accepted by the prominent and extremely careful chronologist Anthony Spalinger in his definitive survey article, 'Dated Texts of the Old Kingdom'.[6] The evidence is in the form of a dated reference painted on a roofing block of a Cheops boat pit, but the date is to the year of a reign, without specifying whose reign. The German Egyptologist Rainer Stadelmann believed it must refer to the reign of Djedefre. However, Spalinger says:

This reference has been cited by Stadelmann in conjunction with the reign of Djedefre, Cheops's successor. However, with [Wolfgang] Helck, I feel that if this citation is valid, then Cheops has to fit. The reasons for this are simple: (1) the 11th count [which is how the date within the unspecified reign was expressed, by biennial 'cattle counts', in a method more familiar from the First and Second Dynasties] suits the evidence from the Turin Papyrus [a fragmentary king list preserved in Turin in Italy]; indeed, it actually precedes by one the figure in the next inscription, No. 8; (2) the length of Djedefre's reign is unknown but either 11 or 12 years seems quite long; (3) the quarrying was close to Cheops's death (if not before it); and (4) the pit was probably closed at the time of Cheops's interment, and a count of 11 for Djedefre does not suit that timeframe. All in all, even though one may doubt the reliability of this evidence, if the evidence is reliable then one must attribute the date to Cheops.[7]

So we see that Spalinger is even doubtful about the reliability of the evidence at all, but that, if he were to accept it, he would only do so on the basis that it was a reference to Cheops rather than to Djedefre. Another expert, Wolfgang Helck, evidently agrees with this. Hence, the often repeated story that Djedefre 'sealed a boat pit' at the Great Pyramid is not at all reliable, and probably false. Rainer Stadelmann is not as expert on matters of chronology as Anthony Spalinger. We have little choice, therefore, but to dismiss the story of Djedefre having any known association with Giza as a fairytale.

It is a bit odd, to say the least, that there was a pharaoh between Cheops and Chephren who 'skipped a beat' in pyramid building. If the pyramids were tombs of pharaohs, why was Djedefre so self-denying? And why did he shun Giza altogether? Was this a matter of personal pique? Or is something else wrong with the whole story of Giza as it has been imagined until now?

And then, finally, the smallest of the three main pyramids of Giza, which is generally called the Pyramid of Mycerinus, is believed to have been built by Pharaoh Mycerinus (Egyptian name: Menkaure; Greek name: Mykerinos), who is believed to have been the son of Chephren and to have reigned circa 2539–2511 BC according to conventional ideas.

Figure 8. This is the 'mini-king list' of a succession of pharaohs of the 4th Dynasty found carved on a cliff at Wadi Hammamat in the Eastern Desert of Egypt, between the Nile and the Red Sea. The kings' names go from right to left in historical sequence, and there are five of them, each in a royal cartouche. The first one, with the little chick, broken at the top, is the name of King Khufu, better known to us as King Cheops (the Greek version of his name). Next, to the left of him, is the name of King Radjedef, who is these days generally known as Djedefre. He was the first Fourth Dynasty pharaoh to incorporate the name of the sun god, Ra or Re, in his name. It is symbolised by the solar disc at the top, and the succeeding pharaohs to the left of him all used it as well. To the left of him is King Raqaf, these days generally known amongst Egyptologists as Khafre, and to the ordinary person as Chephren (the Greek version of his name). Egyptologists disagree amongst themselves as to whether the 'Ra' or 'Re' should really pronounced at the beginning of the name, as it is written, or whether it was only written there out of respect, and should really be pronounced at the end. The next king to the left is King Ra-Hordjedef, and the last on the left is King Ra-Biuf, or Biufre (the Greek version of his name being Bikheris). This important early list of kings was first discovered in 1949 by Fernand Debono. This list emphasises the fact that a little-known pharaoh intervened in the succession between Cheops and Chephren, and that two other pharaohs who are even less well known intervened between Chephren and Mycerinus, who is not even mentioned here. This evidence is awkward for those who advocate the theory that the three main pyramids of Giza were built by three kings in succession as their tombs, namely Cheops, Chephren, and Mycerinus. (*from Etienne Drioton, 'Une Liste de Rois de la IV Dynastie dans l'Ouadi Hammamat'*, Bulletin de la Société Français d'Égyptologie, *Number 16, October 1954, pp. 41–9.*)

Once again, the succession was not what it seems, however. Two other pharaohs actually intervened in the chronology between Chephren and Mycerinus, although many people do not realise this. The first was named Hordjedef, who built no pyramid. The second was named Bikheris (Egyptian name: Biufre), who seems to have reigned for seven years but also did not build a pyramid for himself at Giza or anywhere else. These two kings were known only as X-1 and X-2 (because there were gaps in a king list, with no names) until 1949. In that year, the Frenchman Fernand Debono discovered an inscription carved in stone in the Wadi Hammamat, a caravan corridor that leads from the Nile to the Red Sea. I reproduce this inscription here as Figure 8. The clever French Egyptologist Etienne Drioton was able to date the inscription to the Twelfth Dynasty (which commenced circa 2000 BC).[8] If you look at the bottom right corner of the figure, you can see a vertical wavy line like a series of 'v' shapes. That is the hieroglyph for the letter 'n'. Normally it is written horizontally, because it is meant to represent the rippling surface of a body of water. Only during the Twelfth Dynasty did people tilt it at right angles and write it vertically. And thus we know when this inscription was carved.

The importance of the inscription is that it preserves a partial king list of the Fourth Dynasty, commencing with Cheops, and showing his four successors. Because this inscription can be dated, and is far earlier than the New Kingdom king lists, it is historically more reliable. The list runs from the right to the left, all the names being in elliptical cartouches [the elliptical shape traditionally drawn round a king's name to set it off]. If you look at the figure, you can see the name of Khufu on the right, partially broken at the top right corner. You can readily spot his name when it appears because of the little chick, the hieroglyph for 'u'. It would take three chicks to write in hieroglyphics Marilyn Monroe's most memorable phrase: 'Boo-boopy-doo!' which in the linguistic symbols beloved of all Egyptologists would be transliterated as *bwbwpydw*. Presumably, Marilyn Monroe was unaware that she had said 'bwbwpydw', and it is merciful that she was never told, as she would have been deeply shocked, I am certain.

After the name of Cheops as Khufu we get Radjedef who, as I mentioned, is always called by scholars Djedefre. Then the next one is

Chephren as Ra-kaf, or Raqaf, who is always called today Khafre. Then we get Hordjedef, who has no Greek name. And finally we get a strange name, which Drioton prefers to transcribe as Biufre [Bioufre]. Really he says Bioufre, but one always had to 'detox' the French back into English by removing their excessive use of the letter 'o', which is one of those really embarrassing bad habits of the French, like eating blood sausages and calves' heads, which one tries to ignore in such otherwise delightful people. Biufre is not really what it says, as far as I am concerned, but who am I to disagree with Drioton, except to point out that it is really Ra-biuf, which admittedly is awkward and unconvincing as an Egyptian name, 'biuf' not being at all elegant. And since we have no other record of this name, it might even be abbreviated as Khufu's name is in this inscription, where it is only written 'Khuf'. Hence, for all we know, it could be Ra-biu-fu (if a final 'u' has been omitted as it has in Khufu's name), or Ra-biu-ef, etc. I must confess that I prefer to call him Rabiufu. In any case, this is clearly the pharaoh whose Greek name – as found in the king list written in Greek by Manetho (an Egyptian priest who wrote about Egyptian history in Greek under the Ptolemies, whose work survives only in fragments) – is Bikheris.

As for the true spellings of these kings' names, I am not the only person who refuses to assume that the prefix 'Ra-' in royal names necessarily follows rather than precedes the rest of the name. That 'Ra-' must come last is based upon a presumption of a convention of usage, of which there is no real proof. Nevertheless, the second king of the Second Dynasty was called Ra-neb,[9] and no one ever calls him Nebre, despite the fact that his name in a cartouche is written in the same manner as that of 'Khafre', and if the habit of reversing the elements of his name were followed in the same way, we would get the result Nebre instead of Ra-neb. So why is everybody so contradictory about this? Presumably it is because by Greek times the usage Chephren had become common, so that one presumes that the 're' or 'ra' part of the Egyptian name had become transposed to be the second element of the name. However, there is certainly no consistency in the way these names are expressed in transliteration by the different scholars, and it is a bit of a free-for-all, which thus adds to the confusion.

The strange anomalies of pharaohs Djedefre, Hordjedef and Bikheris intervening in this supposed sequence of events is generally glossed over. People like to speak of the sequence Cheops/Chephren/Mycerinus, as if it were continuous. Ordinary members of the educated public assume that 'one cannot slip a razor blade between them', and that their three pyramids appeared 'plonk, plonk, plonk' like three successive droppings from a giant bird in the sky. But things are never so straightforward.

People in general seem to feel very comfortable about the Fourth Dynasty. I have heard many people who know almost nothing about ancient Egypt speak of Cheops, Chephren, and Mycerinus as if they had been at school with them and, although currently out of touch, have every hope that they will reconnect with them soon through the Friends Reunited website. The reason why people 'feel at ease' with Cheops, Chephren, and Mycerinus is because they have heard the names so often that they seem somehow familiar. In other words, Cheops, Chephren and Mycerinus have had a lot of publicity. Their names are in the papers. This works on the same principle that American elections do: you buy a lot of television time, get 'name recognition', and people are relaxed enough to vote for you *because they have heard of you*. The Fourth Dynasty seems *familiar*, there is a 'comfort zone' around it. People don't like having their comfort zones interfered with, it makes them irritable and sometimes even dangerous. If you try and tell people about Djedefre, Hordjedef and Bikheris, they might get very angry with you. The existence of those three unwelcome kings makes them feel *uncomfortable*. The succession of Cheops, Chephren and Mycerinus, and their neat succession of three pyramids, makes for a nice tidy system. Don't rock the boat!

Some people hotly deny that Bikheris even existed, but they are shouting into the wind. (Those people tend never even to have heard of Hordjedef, for the obvious reason that they have not seen Drioton's article in an obscure French journal.) As for Djedefre, he is now widely acknowledged, amongst Egyptologists at least, and a wonderful bust survives showing his very impressive face. He has a very friendly expression. But he is often supposed to have tried to build a large pyramid for himself on a high hill called Abu Ruash, six miles to the northeast of Giza, within distant sight of it and sixty feet higher, rather than at Giza itself. However, as there is no pyramid actually there, it is very much a matter of dispute as to whether this 'pyramid', often called an 'unfinished pyramid', was ever really intended to be built. Certainly Djedefre was associated with – and perhaps built – a large building beside the spot, where his name has been found in the excavations, and where his magnificent bust was discovered amongst some ancient rubbish, but the structure where this was found was only of mud brick. It is often called a temple, but the evidence is very strong that it was not one, and I will come back to that.

There is a huge and deep subterranean complex there, open to the sky, which may be seen in Plate 7, but it is really just an enormous hole in the ground lined with stones. There was once something on the surface, which was unfinished, but the idea that this was ever a pyramid

RUINED PYRAMID AND CAUSEWAY OF ABOU ROASH FROM KERDASSI.

Figure 9. This drawing published by Vyse in 1840 shows the hill of Abu Ruash, which rises 60 feet above Giza to the north, and is the site of the so-called 'unfinished pyramid'. It was however much more likely to have been an excellent site for an astronomical observation shaft. The hill was approached by a long and grand causeway, which would have been necessary for access by the priests and pharaohs of those days, with their entourages. Many Egyptologists have illogically assumed that the presence of a causeway proves the necessary presence of a pyramid. However, just because the Washington Monument and Big Ben are both beside roads does not mean that one cannot be a clock tower and the other a commemorative monument. I know of no rule of logic which demands that all structures approached by causeways are required to be pyramids. (This plate faces page 7 of Volume III of Vyse.)

PYRAMID OF ABOU ROASH,
FROM THE S.W. ANGLE

Figure 10. In 1840, Howard Vyse published this drawing of the so-called 'pyramid' of Abu Ruash seen from the south-west, as it existed in 1837. (Since that time, most of this wall has been carried away stone by stone by the Arabs and used for their own purposes.) As may be seen, nowhere was there a portion of this square wall rising more than about twelve courses of stone; the scale is given by the man standing near the corner of the wall in the centre of the picture. This wall did not go across the shaft opening to the north of this structure. Many people have concluded, wrongly in my opinion, that this was the site of an 'unfinished pyramid'. However, there is no evidence whatever to support such a view. The fact that a sloping wall of approximately this height surrounded the vast excavated shaft (see Plate on the website) does not constitute evidence of a pyramid, even an 'unfinished' one. I believe this site to have been a meridianal astronomical observatory shaft, used for checking the accuracy of the calendar, and that the similar shaft (known to date at least to the Third Dynasty king named Neferka) at Zawiyet al-Aryan, many miles to the south of here, was also used for that purpose. (This plate faces page 8 of Volume III of Vyse.)

or even part of a pyramid is mere speculation. Construction engineers have suggested to me that the hole is too huge ever to have been bridge-able by *any* stone superstructure. A lot of smashed statue pieces were found in the immediately surrounding rubble, but they would suggest a structure that was *not* a pyramid rather than a pyramid, as who ever heard of a pyramid full of statues? Around the 'hole in the ground', on three sides, there was certainly a stone walled structure of some kind, rising at least twelve stone courses high (see Figures 9 and 10 showing it as it was in 1837 before most of it was carried away by the Arabs),

92

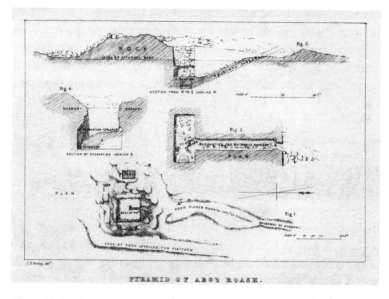

PYRAMID OF ABOU ROASH.

Figure 11. Vyse's drawings published in 1840 showing the sections and plans of the so-called 'pyramid' at Abu-Ruash, which I believe to have been an astronomical observation shaft surrounded by a stone wall. The shaft is oriented precisely to the meridian, pointing north, so that the circumpolar stars of the northern sky could be observed in their meridianal culminations every night, in order to check the accuracy of the calendar. The levelled rock platform to the east of the wall could have been used for stellar and sunrise observations. This site is conveniently situated at the top of the highest hill near Memphis, and the pyramids of Giza may be seen several miles away in the distance, down below to the south, although today they tend to be considerably obscured by mist caused by the smog of Cairo. (This plate faces page 9 of Volume III of Vyse.)

which probably had no roof, but this does not necessarily have anything whatever to do with a pyramid. Bits of granite have been found round the site, so we know granite was used there, but there is no evidence of what purpose it actually served. I have a completely different idea about what this site actually was. Diagrams of this site in section and plan may be seen in Figure 11. For the appearance of the Abu Ruash Shaft today, see Plates 5, 6 and 7.

A similar huge hole in the ground lined with stones is in the precincts of a military base on the other side of Giza known as Zawiyet el-Aryan, and is not open to archaeological inspection by anyone, for military security reasons, so that there are really two of these 'pyramids-in-reverse' which go down but not up. They both feature unroofed descending passages and chambers, open to the sky, of truly mammoth proportions, far exceeding the dimensions of any passages or chambers which have ever been found underneath or within any actual pyramids, so that they are distinguished really as a separate category of construction altogether by the sheer size of their excavation. Anyone who has ever gone down the descending passage of the Great Pyramid and developed sore legs and a stiff back, and crawled into its subterranean chamber on his hands and knees (very painful to the knees because of the stone), as one has to do, knows perfectly well that pyramids are normally cramped inside. But the great open shafts of Abu Ruash and Zawiyet el-Aryan are more like ceremonial processional ways, and a hundred people could stand down at the bottom, as perhaps they did. The notion that these are 'unfinished pyramids' is untenable in my opinion. They clearly had another purpose entirely, as they bear no resemblance to any known pyramid substructure.

The name of a Third Dynasty king called Nerferka has been found twice in excavations at the Zawiyet hole-in-the-ground. That messes up the theory that Abu Ruash was Fourth Dynasty, because its 'mate' or 'twin' clearly was earlier, and it is likely that they would have been produced in the same era. Everything is made even worse by the fact that nobody knows a thing about Neferka, who is a kind of 'ghost pharaoh'. But then, there are so many 'ghost pharaohs' that one could make a horror film about them (in which Egyptologists screaming with fear and apprehension would feature, perhaps, chased in terror by revived mummies with their wrappings coming undone; must phone my agent about this idea!).

Photos of the giant Zawiyet el-Aryan Shaft may be seen in Plates 8 and 9, and diagrams of it in Figure 13.

As far as I know, no one has ever done any studies to see whether these descending passages might have had anything to do with stellar observations. Although such observations have often been suggested as a purpose of the passages of the Great Pyramid itself before it was completed,[10] no one ever seems to have suggested this use for the

Figure 12. The two inscriptions of the name of the Third Dynasty King Neferka, inscribed in royal cartouches, which were found during the excavation of Zawiyet el-Aryan. These demonstrate that the site cannot possibly be of Fourth Dynasty date, as many Egyptologists erroneously insist, and for which there is absolutely no evidence. These are Figures 3 and 4 on page 305 of Jean-Philippe Lauer's article 'Reclassement des Rois des IIIe et IVe Dynasties Égyptiennes par l'Archéologie Monumentale' ('Rearranging of the Kings of the Third and Fourth Egyptian Dynasties on the Basis of the Archaeology of the Monuments'), *Académie des Inscriptions & Belles-Lettres, Comptes Rendus . . . 1962*, Paris, 1963, pp. 290-309, with a Response by Pierre Montet on pages 309-10.

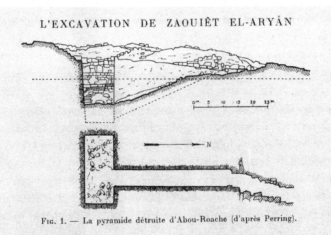

L'EXCAVATION DE ZAOUIÊT EL-ARYÂN

Fig. 1. — La pyramide détruite d'Abou-Roache (d'après Perring).

Figure 13. Jean-Philippe Lauer's section and plan of the exposed shaft and chamber at Abu Ruash, based upon the earlier section and plan drawings of John Perring in the 19th century. Note the precise north-south alignment of the shaft. This is Figure 1 from Jean-Philippe Lauer, 'L'Excavation de Zaouiet el-Aryan' ('The Excavation of Zawiyet el-Aryan').

passages of the two 'negative-pyramids', which I am certain were never actually covered up, but must have been left open in antiquity on purpose. The speculation that they were 'unfinished' comes purely from the fact that nothing was on top of them, but that is like someone insisting that because women do not have male genital organs, they are also 'unfinished'. (In fact, the lunacy of Sigmund Freud was nowhere more evident than when he insisted that all females have 'penis envy'. Egyptologists who insist that the great shafts we are discussing had to have pyramids covering them might as well say that every large hole in the ground has 'pyramid envy' . . .) It is only a modern *assumption* that because the passages and chambers were cut out of the bedrock, they must have been intended to be preliminary to the construction of pyramids which would cover them. But these shafts are so vast that no pyramid could possibly have rested on top of them without collapsing into the hole from lack of structural support. It is much more likely that these giant 'holes in the ground' were connected with astronomical observations and were meant to remain open. Why should anybody say that they were the chambers and tunnels meant to go under pyramids which were *not* built, when they do not resemble any which are known under pyramids which *were* built? Another possibility is that they were ceremonial centres, for processions down a slope to a sacred area where rituals were held. They might have had perishable roofs, or have been partially covered by canopies. Since astronomy was carried on by a special category of priests called *unuti* priests ('watchers of the hours'), the adjoining structures would have been their quarters, their 'office', and their temple. Ceremonial processions and rituals could easily have been combined with the astronomical functions of these great shafts, especially if the rituals were connected with honouring the spirits of the stars, the goddess of the night sky, and other relevant deities.

The shafts of both Zawiyet al-Aryan and Abu Ruash are known to be oriented precisely along an axis of a true north–south meridian, so they would have made excellent meridian observation shafts for purposes of calendrical accuracy and for setting of clocks by the meridianal observations of the stars and constellations as they passed overhead in succession. You merely had to stand down at the bottom of the shaft and look up along it, and watch the precise moments when stars reached the dead centre of the shaft (which is called 'culminating at the meridian'). In 1837, Vyse had already concluded that no pyramid was built at Abu Ruash, for he wrote of the site:

'. . . the edifice was not probably ever completed, or even raised to a considerable height, for scarcely any materials, and very little rubbish, are to be seen, although the situation is difficult of access.'[11]

I will return to the subject of these two 'negative pyramids' in a later chapter. But meanwhile, let us keep firmly in mind that at least one of them has already been proved to date from a period prior to the Fourth Dynasty, so that it does not fit into any cosy 'Fourth Dynasty as pyramid builders' theory in any case.

It is generally stated also that the Giza pyramids were built as personal tombs by the three pharaohs: Cheops, Chephren and Mycerinus. There is no actual convincing or incontrovertible evidence to prove that these pyramids were intended as or used as tombs, and this theory is also a matter of speculation, partially based upon the projection into the past of the clear evidence that the small pyramids of the subsequent Fifth and Sixth Dynasties were used as tombs, and also the fact that the Step Pyramid of the Third Dynasty was funerary in character. (There is, however, no evidence that King Zoser was actually buried in his Step Pyramid, and it seems to have been a funerary cenotaph with a magical and sacred purpose connected with his resurrection. In fact, I would say that, before the Fifth Dynasty, it would have been considered sacrilegious actually to inter a dead body in a pyramid, which would have been considered a form of pollution.)

But such argument-by-association is very weak, when it is closely examined on logical grounds. We have already seen in the previous chapter that the mere presence of an empty stone sarcophagus within a structure proves nothing except the presence of an empty stone sarcophagus. The idea that a sarcophagus signifies a used, as opposed to a purposely empty tomb, is a mere assumption. Just as the pyramids themselves might have been intended as giant symbolic structures, so their sarcophagi might also have been intended as symbolic. They could have been major 'statements' about resurrection, just like the tomb of Jesus, which was proudly shown in Jerusalem after the disappearance of his body from the tomb. But this idea has already been discussed, and we do not need to go over it again. In a later chapter, I will present the evidence that Cheops and Chephren are buried somewhere else, I will say precisely where and show photographs of the evidence, and I believe both of their burials are still perfectly intact and have never been opened. I also believe we could easily open these tombs and retrieve all of their contents. They would clearly vastly surpass in importance the trifling tomb of the boy pharaoh Tutankhamun, which was a desultory affair, hastily put together with odds and ends which were thrown into a chamber with little advance warning, and with no serious attempt at either magnificence or respect.

Furthermore, we are specifically told by the Greek historian Herodotus of the fifth century BC that *the pharaohs Cheops and Chephren were not buried in the pyramids that bear their names, but were rather buried elsewhere on the Giza Plateau, in their vicinity.* I cannot understand why no one has ever noticed this startling and explicit statement. Is it because people are so 'blind' to statements that contradict their assumptions that they literally *do not see them*? I have discussed this passage in Herodotus in my previous book, *The Sphinx Mystery*, and I have discussed the strange phenomenon of 'consensus blindness' in archaeology in an earlier book, *The Crystal Sun*. In *The Sphinx Mystery* I said:

'It is not often noticed either by Egyptologists or by classical scholars that Herodotus does not actually say that the underground chambers to which he refers are anything whatever to do with any of the pyramids. He says instead something quite different: that the chambers are inside the *hill*. It happens to be the same hill, or plateau, on which the pyramids also stand. In other words, he is describing underground chambers of the Giza Plateau itself, and definitely *not* underground chambers of a pyramid. The distinction seems to have eluded everyone. This overt ancient evidence *against* the 'pyramid tomb theory' is ignored by all Egyptologists, and it would not suit many of them to be forced to take note of it, since it opposes their favourite theory.'[12]

The actual passage of the text in Herodotus is found at Book II, 124.[13]

As I have already mentioned, the occurrence of empty sarcophagi inside the pyramids is not conclusive evidence at all, for empty sarcophagi of a symbolic nature were not uncommon in Egypt, as witness Sarcophagus Three in the Osiris Shaft at Giza, which we discussed in

Chapter Two, and which was probably always empty, as well as the so-called Sarcophagus Chamber of the Osireion at Abydos, which I have discussed in my account dealing with our researches at the Temple of Seti I and the subterranean Osireion at Abydos (not yet published), which appears to have been left empty on purpose, and without any access to it being possible without breaking down a stone wall. 'Empty' sarcophagi were extraordinarily common at key Old Kingdom sites in Egypt, and we should turn our attention to trying to figure out what these mean symbolically when they occur, rather than trying to fill them with bodies in our fantasies.

However, most Egyptologists accept the 'tomb theory' of the Giza pyramids unquestioningly and are not worried about the fact that it is speculation, since they consider that the speculation is sound. And since the 'tomb theory' is so widely accepted, there is a great deal of psychological resistance to any possible redating of the pyramids because, as soon as you do that, it becomes impossible for Cheops, Chephren and Mycerinus to have been buried in them, and then the 'tomb theory' in its traditional form collapses. Alternatively you have to adopt something like Breasted's Chronology, but some Egyptologists would be most hesitant to do that because it would mean going back on their earlier decision to abandon it. Many Egyptologists are more anxious to preserve the 'tomb theory' than they are to preserve the precise dates of construction per se, and so they must at all costs keep the dates of construction firmly rooted in the reigns of Cheops, Chephren and Mycerinus, for otherwise the whole edifice of their preconceptions of what pyramids were for becomes untenable.

Furthermore, as we know so much about the actual burials of earlier pharaohs, if the pyramids were really built earlier than we thought, then it becomes difficult to hold a tomb theory, since so many of those earlier pharaohs had real tombs, many of which have been found and identified quite clearly. For instance, if we start by considering King Hor-Aha of the First Dynasty: according to Walter Emery, his northern tomb at Saqqara and his southern tomb at Abydos have been located.[14] (I will be discussing this tomb in Chapter Six.) If we take the next king of the First Dynasty, Zer, his southern tomb at Abydos has been found and his northern tomb at Saqqara has been provisionally found.[15] If we take the fourth king of the First Dynasty, Uadji, his southern tomb at Abydos has been found and his northern tomb at Saqqara 'would appear to be his burial', according to Emery.[16] As for the fifth king of the First Dynasty, Udimu, his southern tomb at Abydos has been found, and a northern tomb at Saqqara, which was once thought to belong to Hemaka, has now been discovered to be Udimu's.[17] And so on. There is no need to give the complete list of such tombs because the principle is clear: these pharaohs' tombs are well known and are mastabas, not pyramids. (In Chapter Six, a remarkable exception is discussed.) If the Giza pyramids were built during the reigns of such kings, then they were not built to be tombs. These kings all had two tombs already, one for Upper Egypt and one for Lower Egypt (one being a real tomb and one being a symbolic cenotaph), and they did not need a third.

The strange phenomenon of 'double tombs' for early kings will be discussed again in Chapter Six, where other problems associated with this bizarre practice will be discussed, and once again we will find that things are not as simple as they seem.

Another thing follows from the redating: at the moment, it is conventional to say that the pyramids had to be *built* within the reign periods of Cheops, Chephren and Mycerinus respectively. This means that only a certain restricted number of years were available in order to build each pyramid. If the pyramids cease to be tied to these reigns, the periods of years collapse and there is no longer any guidance at all as to how long it might really have taken to construct the Giza pyramids. Few people other than historical chronologists would any longer care exactly how long Cheops reigned, or Chephren reigned, because it would have no further relevance to pyramid construction. Later in this book we will also briefly consider the other three large stone pyramids at Meidum and Dashur, but for the moment I am leaving them aside from the discussion to avoid too many complications at this stage. I don't want anyone to think I have forgotten them, however. One feature that I will explore in a subsequent book is that the two Dashur pyramids have a remarkable constructional relationship with each other which is not generally known, even though it is widely accepted that they were 'built by the same man'. It certainly seems that they were simultaneously planned, and I will explain why. Because of the length of this book I have had to remove a great deal of such information, which will appear in a later book.

I have already pointed out, in *The Sphinx Mystery*, what I believe to be absolutely conclusive evidence to establish that the three main Giza pyramids and the Sphinx of Giza were all constructed as a unity, a single complex, designed simultaneously. The pyramids were not constructed one by one by successive pharaohs, but were all designed at once, or at least as part of a unified plan. (Whether they were all built at the same time is not the important issue, what is important is that they were all *designed* at the same time.) I have already discussed this subject in Chapter One. The Giza Golden Plan shown in Figure 7.25 in my book *The Sphinx Mystery* makes it perfectly clear that all three pyramids and the Sphinx mutually determine one another's precise locations and sizes by radiating sighting-lines at identical angles. It is inconceivable that all four were not originated simultaneously, as a unified concept. This same construction principle will also be seen to have been at the heart of the Zoser complex at Saqqara, though it is a separate monument from a different period. In a subsequent book I will show the fantastic lengths to which the designer of the interior of the Great Pyramid went to cross-correlate every key point of the design with at least two other key points, in a spider's web of relationships of such complexity that it nearly defies belief. I should stress that all of those point-correlations are unrelated to any design theory, are purely empirical, and do not depend upon any assumptions. I have not had space here to publish these extraordinary findings, which do not relate to any previous pyramid studies whatever.

I must point out most emphatically that the obvious deep connection of Cheops, Chephren and Mycerinus with Giza, and the many activities and constructions by them at Giza (tombs, minor pyramids, boat pits, etc.) are not disproved by our redating of the pyramids, or even by my observation that the four main monuments of Giza were built as a single unified complex and not by three successive pharaohs. After all, the tombs of family members and courtiers of these kings abound on the Giza Plateau, facts which have been proved over and over again. Anyone who tried to suggest that these kings had no connection of any kind with the Giza pyramids would have to be out of touch with reality altogether. And the tomb of Hetepheres, the mother of Cheops, has been found in a shaft dug into the rock near the Great Pyramid, although the alabaster sarcophagus in this 'burial' was apparently also left empty and never contained her body. Yet another 'empty sarcophagus'. It was suggested by George Reisner that it was a reburial transferred from some other location, possibly Dashur.[18] It thus has various curious circumstances connected with it: a missing body and a possible 'reburial'; but who would 'rebury' an empty sarcophagus? Suggestions have been made that the tomb was robbed and the body stolen, but why steal a body and leave the valuable grave goods? Tomb-robbers are noted for their interest in treasure, not their necrophilia. Why would the place of burial have been altered, and where was the original one? Why was the reburial done so soon after the original burial? Why go to all the trouble of having a burial, only to dig it all up again and transfer it only a short time later? It was not customary thus to 'disturb the dead' or even to disturb empty sarcophagi. We have no idea how to explain these things, and the reburial theory is only that: a theory. These are all mysteries. But the fact that Cheops did not build the Great Pyramid does not affect this. Cheops certainly had a fixation on the Great Pyramid and wished to associate himself with it, adopt it, claim it as his own, and might have buried or reburied his mother beside it (or it is possible she outlived him and was buried there for honour's sake by a successor pharaoh). He might well have built the very small pyramids nearby, one of which might even have been for his queen, for all we know.

There are three mini-pyramids to the southeast of the Great Pyramid, known officially as the North Subsidiary Pyramid, the Middle Subsidiary Pyramid and the South Subsidiary Pyramid: they are known colloquially as the 'three queens' pyramids'. Each one has a passage and a burial chamber underneath, the chambers obviously having been robbed and stripped in distant antiquity. Traces of a fourth mini-pyramid south of the Great Pyramid have been uncovered, but not much is known of it, as it has been covered by a road. Cheops might have constructed the boat pits beside the Great Pyramid, which we have not dated. One large wooden boat has been retrieved from one of these pits and is currently on view in the museum beside the pyramid. Apparently Cheops, if not the next pharaoh, Djedefre (whose connection with the boat pit, as already discussed, probably never existed), left traces in these pits, which at the very least Cheops opened and resealed. (There was a boat pit beside the tomb of King Hor-Aha, thought to have been the 'first king of the First Dynasty', so the tradition is very old.)

A large funerary temple stood at the east side of the Great Pyramid, portions of the basalt floor of which are still to be seen (see Plate in the Chapter Four section of the website). The plan of this temple has been reconstructed, and much has been published about it, with the most extensive account of it being an entire volume by Selim Hassan.[19] (See its plan in Figure 30, in Chapter Four.) Although the analogous funerary temple to the east of the Pyramid of Mycerinus (Menkaure) was clearly later than the pyramid itself and literally jammed up against it, as Plate 12 shows so clearly, and as is discussed in connection with the Mycerinus Pyramid in a moment, no remains of this one attributed to Cheops beside the Great Pyramid survive to show us whether it was super-imposed against its pyramid or not. Cheops might, in short, have done everything *but* construct the Great Pyramid itself. And he might have held exactly the place in the chronology of Egypt and the sequences of kings of the Fourth Dynasty that is normally assigned to him. In other words, nothing need change, except that the Great Pyramid was there long before his day and he became somehow obsessed with it and built lots of things in its vicinity and possibly even renamed it 'the Horizon of Khufu' or 'the Splendour of Khufu' after himself. In other words, he could have 'recycled' the Great Pyramid in the same manner in which most pharaohs throughout Egyptian history 'recycled' monuments and put their names on them, despite the fact that they were constructed centuries earlier, and seized and moved stone blocks from earlier monuments and reused them for their own constructions. Archaeologists call this 'usurping a monument'.

But the fact remains that we have found (as the results of our sampling will show as we proceed) that the pyramids are far too old to have been built by Cheops, Chephren and Mycerinus, if one keeps them at their conventional dates, and we must then conclude that instead of *building* them, they merely *appropriated* them. (The question of the supposed workmen's graffiti of Cheops's name appearing inside the Great Pyramid will be discussed later, when we shall see that the evidence for these having been forged by Colonel Howard Vyse in the nineteenth century is essentially incontrovertible, as my analysis will show; and it is well known that he shamelessly forged a coffin of Mycerinus and inserted it into the third pyramid at Giza.)

We have established from our dating, as explained shortly, that Cheops, Chephren and Mycerinus did not build the pyramids attributed to them. So who *did* build them?

This is a gigantic and perplexing mystery. We are reduced to speaking of the 'pyramid builders', and the only identifying characteristics these people have is that they built the pyramids. Otherwise, we cannot yet identify them. But if we can't identify the 'pyramid builders', isn't there rather a large gaping hole in our ideas of how the Egyptian civilisation came to be? In fact, in Chapter Eight, I make some suggestions about the possible identity of these mysterious pyramid builders, and, at the same time, reveal a major archaeological monument elsewhere in North Africa, which I have visited and studied, but which is largely unknown at the present time, and which may provide the clue we are so earnestly looking for.

What characteristics would the 'pyramid builders' have to have?

They would have needed extraordinary mathematical and geometrical knowledge, formidable construction skills on a very large scale indeed (the Great Pyramid was the largest standing structure in the world until the nineteenth century AD; it is still the world's largest stone structure, and its base covers thirteen-and-a-half acres of ground), and a very highly advanced civilisation to sustain all this. Even though the popular image of gangs of slaves, lashed by overseers with whips, hauling stones along ramps and getting crushed in the process is a silly one (and it is time we passed beyond the fantasies of the silent film director Cecil B. DeMille, who popularised this image), certainly the pyramid builders had to be in control of the society in the area and able to marshal considerable work gangs, whether slave or free. The 'workmen's city' to the southeast of the pyramids at Giza might have housed them, though it need not have been the residence of the people who actually built the pyramids, as there was plenty of other construction to keep its teams of workers busy during the Fourth Dynasty, not least the massive number of mastabas constructed then.

The Step Pyramid at Saqqara, which is known to have been built during the reign of the first pharaoh of the Third Dynasty, King Zoser, or Djoser, or Djeser (all three spellings are correct, but I prefer the most common, Zoser), by his vizier, Imhotep, is conventionally dated circa 2670 BC. This may or may not be an accurate dating. We had no permission to take a dating sample of that pyramid in our first round of samples, despite requesting to do so, and our second round (when we were promised the permission to do this), after being repeatedly delayed by the present archaeological regime, has now been refused on the basis that no dating samples are any longer allowed to be taken out of Egypt, a general decision taken by Zahi Hawass and applying to everyone. However, as there are no laboratories capable of the technological requirements of our technique existing anywhere in Egypt, this means that our technique can no longer be used there. A dating sample for us is typically a piece of stone jointing a couple of inches long. We generally take samples from areas not visible to tourists, and there is little trace of their removal. But as I point out in Chapter Five, dealing with the confirmation of the date of the tomb of King Khasekhemui, the last pharaoh of the Second Dynasty, who is supposed to have preceded him, there is a glaring and enormous problem associated with the presumed 'succession' from King Khasekhemui to King Zoser.

The problem is not so much political or dynastic as technological, for, as we shall see as we go along, these two men, whose lifetimes overlapped, represented wholly incompatible levels of technological civilisation. The contrast was rather like that between the European colonial powers in the nineteenth century and some of the remote colonies they created in Africa, or between the technology of the white invaders of North America, who had guns, and the native Americans, who had only bows and arrows. Yes, they lived at the same time and overlapped, but the American Indians were not 'American Dynasty One' and the invading Europeans were not 'American Dynasty Two', as some remote archaeologists a thousand years from now might imagine. Something is seriously amiss in the way we view the early Egyptian dynasties. But that subject is for later chapters.

In the late 1990s, Dr Gunter Dreyer discovered through excavation some evidence that Zoser directly followed Khasekhemui. This took the form of jar seals in Khasekhemui's tomb bearing the name of Zoser, which can hardly be the case if anyone other than Zoser buried him, and which therefore seems to rule out an intervening pharaoh. But as the photos accompanying Chapter Five clearly show, Khasekhemui's limestone tomb (which was only uncovered for two weeks and then recovered, so that we were lucky ever to see it and sample it) is so crudely constructed, of roughly hewn blocks, that it resembles the kind of stonework one might expect to find amongst a tribe of savages. To go from such a barbaric and primitive construction to so highly sophisticated and astonishing a structure as the Step Pyramid with its one million tons of stone blocks in only about twenty years, as the currently accepted chronologies would have us believe, is like suggesting that you could go from a paper glider made by a schoolboy to an intercontinental ballistic missile in the same amount of time. But because most Egyptologists are so little concerned with technology and engineering, this point is rarely even considered; the fact that perhaps fewer than ten living Egyptologists have ever actually seen the tomb of King Khasekhemui with their own eyes does not help in this matter, of course. One might normally expect foreign influence to have come from somewhere, resulting in the sudden introduction of this high technology of stone, but it could hardly have come from Mesopotamia, where all construction was of mud brick. This subject is discussed further in the chapter dealing with the tomb, Chapter Five, and then considered further in subsequent chapters.

Credit must be given to a few particularly alert Egyptologists for attempting to call urgent attention to the problem that I have just mentioned. This dilemma was raised by the outstanding and uniquely respected Walter Emery, who was probably the leading expert on Archaic Egypt who has ever lived. As long ago as 1961, in his seminal work *Archaic Egypt*, Emery specifically stated the problem:

'A curious feature of Kha-sekhemui's tomb is its irregularity and faulty planning and, impressive as it is in size, it is difficult to believe that only a few years separate it from the magnificent Step Pyramid of Zoser at Sakkara.'[20]

Another distinguished Egyptologist who cited this remark by Emery and called attention to the problem again, though without solving it, was Michael Hoffman, in his 1980 book *Egypt before the Pharaohs*.[21]

Kurt Mendelssohn discussed the problem in his book, *The Riddle of the Pyramids*, in 1974:

'. . . the degree to which stone was quarried, transported and dressed for a royal tomb of the Second Dynasty bears no relation to the effort required for Zoser's funeral monument [the Step Pyramid]. In the first case it amounted to a few tons of limestone, whereas the Step Pyramid complex contains at least one million tons. It is almost impossible to conceive how this increase of production could have been achieved in just one generation.'[22]

The Egyptian archaeologist Nabil Swelim also called attention to the problem in the only book anyone has ever written devoted entirely to the Third Dynasty, *Some Problems on the History of the Third Dynasty*.[23] Because this book was published in Alexandria in Egypt (albeit in English), it is extremely rare and difficult to find, even in large libraries. I was fortunate to obtain a copy only because I purchased part of the library of Dr Kent Weeks, the Egyptologist (whom I once met in Luxor), and I thus acquired the copy that Swelim had himself given to Weeks at the time of publication, and inscribed. It has the advantage of containing the corrections made by the author throughout of the occasional misprints and typographical errors that occurred during the publication process. This book is of the most extraordinary importance, and I will be discussing it again in Chapter Six. In his book, Swelim says regarding this matter:

If . . . Netjerykhet [another name for Zoser, which Swelim prefers to use] came immediately after Khasekhemwy [the spelling of Khasekhemui preferred by Swelim], the dates of culture and tradition would coincide. But in view of the astonishing advance in stone architecture, the succession might be questioned. . . . [He then cites Emery, whose comments we have already read.] . . . Upholding the present argument is the opinion of V. Maragioglio and C. Rinaldi, about Imhotep 'Leonardo da Vinci del Nilo' [in other words, they called Imhotep the Leonardo da Vinci of the Nile]. They believe that he would not have been able to build the Step Pyramid without an ancient tradition behind him, and cannot explain how such a high standard of architectural perfection could have been reached without having been preceded by a long process of development.[24]

Swelim returns to the subject a few pages later in his book:

'Considering the incomparable differences between the burial monuments of Khasekhemwy and Netjerykhet [Zoser], mentioned above, it has been pointed out that the hitherto accepted chronology does not allow an intervening period for any form of preparation. If the mud brick layers were switched over to building with stone, it would need considerable time to master the new architectural technology . . .'[25]

But apart from these alert and questioning authors, most Egyptologists prefer to avoid the issue and simply ignore it. It is easy to ignore something when it is 'not your job', and since no Egyptologist's job is any other Egyptologist's job, that means you can ignore anything. And if you are interested in avoiding enemies who can obstruct your academic career, it is best to keep your mouth shut. That is why most of the iconoclasm that goes on within Egyptology is found either on the fringes, where there are no academic careers at stake, or amongst old or retired academics.

Thus we come to the extraordinary realisation that the confirmation of an accepted date in Egyptology can actually create more problems than it solves. The fact is that it would be far more comfortable in terms of the history of technology if we had been able to show in the following chapter that King Khasekhemui had been buried at some remote time far earlier than anyone had thought. Then the primitive state of his stone-working could be explained away. But alas, we are stuck with him more or less in his conventional time frame, meaning that he still had to be directly followed by Zoser because of Dreyer's discoveries (described in Chapter Five). And that means that, within twenty or thirty years, the impossible had to happen: the Step Pyramid at Saqqara had to be well advanced in construction, using a sophisticated stone technology that seems to be centuries in advance of what is found for the tomb of the immediately preceding king at Abydos.

It is important to stress that the advanced stone-building was taking place in a different geographical region, and that Saqqara is hundreds of miles north of Abydos. Certainly there appears to have been a geographical restriction to the advanced stone technology, and this in turn suggests a closely guarded secret northern technology, which was prohibited from spreading south or indeed getting out of royal control at Memphis. This in turn encourages us to postulate a solution for this bizarre riddle, and it might apply to our findings about the Giza pyramids as well: there must have been two parallel and overlapping ancient Egyptian civilisations, one technologically advanced and one technologically backward, one of which might have absorbed the other. But there is a massive amount of evidence from excavations, inscriptions, etc., all of which needs to be sorted through carefully, to see if such a hypothesis can hold up. This is a gigantic task which, if done fully, would require years of meticulous analysis, with the cooperation of specialists in the Archaic Period of Egypt, what we also call the First and Second Dynasties. I shall take some initial steps along this path in Chapters Five and Six, in which we shall learn some relevant facts and see just how insecure some of the most common assumptions are. Later in this book I will also demonstrate an astonishing connection between Zoser's Step Pyramid and a structure erected by a much earlier king of the First Dynasty, which has never before been noticed.

So if two different Egyptian civilisations did exist, King Zoser must represent the advanced one, and his succession so near in time to King Khasekhemui cannot be a direct succession taking place within the same technological civilisation. It is possible that such a succession took place in the sense that the Third Dynasty *absorbed* the Second Dynasty, making a temporal succession possible in the form of a takeover, like a giant corporation acquiring a smaller company (or even a larger company: what businessmen call 'a reverse takeover'). But they *cannot* have been the same civilisation. The technological discrepancy makes that absolutely impossible, unless one postulates a technological revolution more drastic and rapid even than that of the nineteenth-century Industrial Revolution of Europe. This is all fully explained in later chapters.

If we were to try to set aside this sole possibility of explaining the quantum leap in ancient Egyptian stone technology by means of a technological revolution, we would be left with an apparently insoluble dilemma: how did people with little ability to deal with limestone come within one generation to be able to construct something as grand as the huge Step Pyramid at Saqqara?

But now we have redated the Giza pyramids and found that they are far *older* than the conventional date of the Step Pyramid and also older than our date for King Khasekhemui and his primitive tomb, as we explain in a moment. So we have to jettison the theory that the Step Pyramid was a step in the evolution of stone technology, which culminated in the Giza pyramids. That may no longer be tenable. On the contrary, the Step Pyramid might now possibly be viewed as a brave and impressive attempt to emulate and copy the Giza pyramids, which were already old structures by then. In other words, Imhotep might have been trying to imitate the achievements of a bygone era. And if he did use an advanced technology, which it is obvious that he did, then he might have recreated it rather than invented it. He was apparently not able to achieve the giant size of blocks used earlier, for the blocks of the Step Pyramid are far smaller, as may be seen clearly in Plate 10. By contrast, the blocks used in the Giza pyramids range in size up to as much as 200 tons each, if one considers those used for the platform of the 'Pyramid of Chephren', which can still be seen by any tourist. A 200-ton block is equivalent in weight to approximately 350 large automobiles stacked on top of one another. No Egyptologist has ever come up with a satisfactory explanation as to how they actually got there or were produced, since the ancient Egyptians had no cranes to lift and place such monstrous stones, nor are there any conceivable rollers that could bear such weight, nor any physically imaginable means of transporting 200-ton blocks over hills and slopes, and then fitting them together with precision at the site.

If we consider the pyramids at Giza as being constructed first, the Step Pyramid of Saqqara constructed afterwards, and the small pyramids of the Fifth and Sixth Dynasties constructed last, we would then see a progressive diminishing in size of stone, so that at least there would be a coherent pattern of shrinkage of construction elements. This represents a sort of 'logic of decline'. This goes against the popular modern 'theory of universal progress'. According to this absurd theory, or I should say myth, human civilisation only ever improves, it never regresses.

Ioannis and I have done no dating work on the pyramid at Meidum or the two pyramids at Dashur. However, the Red Pyramid of Dashur contains a great deal of cedar, which can easily be dated by radiocarbon dating techniques. These three huge stone pyramids certainly pose a major further dilemma for everyone, though no one really knows for certain who built them, and there are some people who even insist that the 'collapsed' pyramid at Meidum is not collapsed at all, and others who insist that the 'bent' pyramid at Dashur was bent on purpose. Some say King Sneferu built them all. Others insist that King Huni built the pyramid at Meidum, and this suggestion is fiercely attacked as well. (In fact, no one even agrees on Huni's dynasty, much less whether he built a pyramid or not. There are even king lists that exclude his existence entirely.) As usual, no one agrees on very much. However, they are all *certain*. Despite the fact that not all of them can be correct, their *certainty* is not any less. In fact, many of these opinions are held *ferociously*.

Thus, you can get a 'ferocious Huni opinion', a 'ferocious Sneferu opinion', and so forth. The ferocity with which these views are held increases with the uncertainty of the facts. Indeed, Temple's First Anthropic Law states: *The certainty of human opinions is inversely proportional to the uncertainty of the facts.* Opinions are thus held defensively, but propagated offensively. This reminds me of religion: the more ridiculous a belief, the greater the fanaticism with which it will be held. I suppose this is like a physical requirement: the more tenuous one's hold on the log on which one is floating down the river, the more fiercely one has to try to grip it to avoid drowning. Most people feel that they are drowning in an alien cosmos, so they hold onto those logs with all their might. When viewed as a survival technique, this makes sense. Most people don't really care what they believe, as long as they don't lose their log and drown.

Ioannis's only pyramid dating sample was taken from the 'Pyramid of Mycerinus', after which the pyramid sampling permission was altered, and pyramid sampling could not continue, as will be explained in a moment. Ioannis took this sample from the red granite casing stones of the east face. Although most of the surviving casing stones of this pyramid are rough-hewn on their outer surfaces, portions of the faces are smoothed, as may be seen in Plates 12a and 12b. Ioannis took his sample from a smoothed portion because it was easier to get at the join between the blocks when the outer surfaces were smooth; for if they were rough, the join was deeper and more difficult to access, as he explained to me later. It is one of the strange features of this pyramid that so many of the casing stones were left rough in their outward-facing aspects, when they are so smooth and fit together so perfectly in other respects. They were not left rough because of any lack of ability on the part of the pyramid builders, but as a matter of choice. Either the roughness had some symbolic significance of which we are unaware today, or the pyramid builders became unaccountably lazy and could not be bothered, or there was some interruption in the work. Since the causeway of this pyramid (now recovered with sand) was never finished, it may be that the construction of this pyramid was interrupted. It has often been suggested that the outer faces of stone blocks were rough when positioned, and smoothed later, especially with granite; this enabled granite to be shipped from Aswan in the far south. Any damage caused to the blocks in transit would not be visible after the block had been smoothed in situ. In this case, the 'unfinished' theory gains further support. However, one must never be too sure about anomalies in Egyptian constructions, as they often have a purpose or an intention which is incomprehensible to us but which held importance for the builders.

One feature, which I noted when I later examined the exterior of this pyramid very closely, was that the pavement extending eastwards from the pyramid, upon which the funerary temple attributed to Mycerinus was placed, was clearly of a later construction, due to the fact that the stonework for it was jammed up against and superimposed upon the casing stones of the pyramid in a rather clumsy manner. This feature is shown clearly in the photos I took to show it, which are reproduced here as Plates 12a and 12b, and on this book's website. It almost reminds me of a car crash, the way the stones are rammed against one another by sheer brute force. The pavement and funerary temple may therefore be of a considerably later date and, as with the features mentioned in connection with the Great Pyramid that are definitely associated with Cheops, these later features may well be associated with Mycerinus because they were definitely added later. It would be interesting to take a date of this pavement to compare with the date for the casing stones. The famous statement found in a Giza tomb of the Fourth Dynasty referring to 'work being done on the pyramid (named) Mycerinus-is-divine'[26] need not refer to the building of the pyramid itself, since it does not actually speak of it; it speaks of 'work being done on the pyramid', i.e., a pyramid already in existence is having work done on it, which is quite a different thing from saying 'the construction of the pyramid'. The Fourth Dynasty of Cheops, Chephren and Mycerinus may therefore have been an 'archaising' dynasty, which became fixated on the pre-existing pyramids of Giza and built in and around them, much as their distant successors of the Saitic or Twenty-Sixth Dynasty were to do two thousand years later. But as I have pointed out previously, it was not every Fourth Dynasty pharaoh who did this, and there were more who did not than who did. Even in the immediate period from Cheops to Mycerinus, three out of six, or 50 per cent, of the pharaohs did not touch Giza, as we have seen. There must clearly have been some serious disagreement within the dynasty about all this Giza business, if more pharaohs boycotted the place than were obsessed with it. And when I say boycotted, I mean *pharaohs who were not even mentioned in one single mastaba burial.* How are we supposed to explain that? Their *complete absence* cries out for explanation, and there is none.

The dating that Ioannis obtained for the casing stones of the 'Pyramid of Mycerinus' was 3590–2640 BC. This dating absolutely rules out any connection with Mycerinus if we accept the existing chronological assumption that he reigned circa 2539–2511 BC, since those dates are more than a century after the most recent possible date for the sample.

The median date for the pyramid is 3090 BC. This takes us back to predynastic times, fifty-eight years before a conventionally accepted date for the unification of Egypt by its first pharaoh, 'King Menes', founder of the First Dynasty. However, our sample could date from as early as 3590 BC, which would be five hundred years earlier still. At a date that far back, nothing that we know of was going on at all that could possibly be described as 'high civilisation'. So we are faced with the most terrible dilemma: how could something come out of nothing? How do you get the Giza pyramids constructed when there is 'nobody there' to do it?

Probabilities over the range of possible dates cannot be established from one sample alone, and depend upon the existence of several samples, so the calculation of these awaits the further samples. However, it does not appear that these further samples will ever be allowed by the director of Egyptian Antiquities, Zahi Hawass, who has prohibited small samples of stone (and apparently even of wood) being taken to laboratories outside Egypt for analysis. Most dating work in Egypt will now inevitably grind to a screeching halt. The lack of logic in this rule defies all attempts at rational explanation. Are we to presume that a tiny fragment of wood, or a two-inch piece of stone block, is too sacred to travel beyond the borders of Egypt? One could not even take a sample to, say, Jordan. And yet Zahi Hawass is a cosmopolitan man who travels abroad a lot, not a narrow provincial, so his attitude is puzzling. Why will he not permit a few inches of wood and stone to be taken out of the country for tests for which no facilities exist in Egypt?

Our problems in dating the pyramids began in the middle of our project. Ioannis and I were granted very clear and unambiguous permission to date the pyramids by the Supreme Council of Antiquities, as seen in the reproduction of the official document on the website (both Arabic and English versions). After obtaining this document, although I knew one had to go through a further formality of multiple security clearances, I had no idea that permission, once granted by the archaeological authorities, could be 'tweaked' by other authorities, by altering the sites; it never entered my mind that security officials might take it upon themselves to override decisions already taken by Egypt's archaeological authorities and specify which monuments should or should not be examined.

With the intention of showing politeness and respect to Zahi Hawass in his role at that time as director of the Giza Plateau, I made an appointment for Olivia and myself (Ioannis was not in Egypt) to see him at his little office near the Great Pyramid on the Plateau. After some time his female secretary led us into his office, and she sat beside him throughout our meeting. I said we had come to have a few preliminary words with him about the sampling we would be doing at Giza in the future. He looked enraged rather than pleased, and would not look at me. I was deeply puzzled, as I had gone to see him with the intention of establishing friendly and cooperative relations. Thinking that perhaps he did not understand, or doubted what I was saying, I handed him the archaeological permission form signed by the authorities of the Supreme Council of Antiquities, including the then-director, G. A. Gaballah, with whom I had very amicable relations, and who is a most congenial, cultured and polite person. Gaballah is precisely the kind of person who gives Egypt a good image abroad. Another extremely polite and cultured person was Mohammed Saguir, the head of Pharaonic Archaeology, who had also signed the form, and whom I found extremely pleasant and helpful. Hawass looked at this form for a moment, screwed it up into a ball and threw it across his desk at my face, saying impatiently: 'This means *nothing*!'

I picked up the creased paper and tried to flatten it out again because I was worried about it being ruined. I asked how could it mean *nothing*? It was signed by his superiors. This only served to enrage him further, and his face turned red with fury. He said we still had to get the security clearances. I said that I realised that security clearances were necessary, and I knew that they took a long time, so we would come back in a few months when they were ready. (In fact it took nine months for these to go through, because we were 'first-timers'. Second applications are quicker and only take three months because they already have files opened for you.) I explained that I was not coming to see him with the intention of taking samples right away, I was coming to him out of courtesy to inform him well in advance that we would be turning up eventually, and to establish a preliminary liaison with him. He did not appreciate my attempts to be polite. He made it plain that he would be having a word with the security authorities about us, and the implication was clear that he might be trying to block us. There is plenty of scope for that with the security authorities, because there are six of them. In order to carry out archaeological work in Egypt, it is necessary to have permission from six separate entities: the army, the navy, the air force, the antiquities police, the ordinary police and the secret police. They all run checks on you one by one. When the army finishes with you and stamps your form as cleared, the form is carried by hand to the navy, where it sits in a tray, and when the navy finishes with you and stamps your form as cleared, the form is carried by hand to the air force, where it sits, and so on. The authorities are all in different buildings. It is estimated that each separate 'tray time' is an absolute minimum of two weeks, even for familiar faces attached to long-established foreign archaeological institutes.

When I joked to someone once in Egypt that I was delighted to know that the Egyptian Air Force did not view me as a threat to Egyptian security, as I had no jet fighter plane to call my own, this was not thought funny at all.

When our security permissions eventually came through, so that we were able to return in the next season after our original permission had been granted, we could not read it, as it was only in Arabic. We had a lot of trouble finding someone to translate it for us, as such a sensitive document cannot just be shown to a hotel concierge. Ioannis, full of enthusiasm at receiving the security clearance, went and took an initial sample from the exterior granite casing of the Pyramid of Mycerinus, as it was easy to go there on the open Plateau during normal opening hours. We would obviously have to wait to go to the Sphinx and Valley Temples, and to the Osiris Shaft, until we made elaborate arrangements for access to them. Also, we would have to consult closely with the dreaded Hawass about the interiors of the pyramids, and by arrangement with him take samples after closing hours, because of the terrible crowding of the tourists at other times. However, we then finally managed to translate the security documents, and discovered that the pyramids had been removed. We were deeply shocked, but it is impossible to argue with the army, the navy, the air force, the antiquities police, the police, and the security police, and not a good idea to try. We sought for clarification from the archaeological authorities, who ruefully said to us that, although they did not understand this, and were deeply surprised themselves, they had no power to overrule the security authorities. It seemed likely to me from his previous behaviour and remarks that Hawass might have 'had a word' with someone in one of the six bodies, and asked for this deletion to try to thwart us. We were unable to proceed with any further pyramid activity. However, our Archaeological Permission made clear that we were definitely to be granted a Phase Two, a second round of sampling, so we intended to reinstate the pyramids then, unless blocked a second time by the unknown security officials and/or Hawass. Just to show how our official documents really did 'mean *nothing*', and indeed our security permissions as well ultimately 'meant *nothing*' as well, Hawass personally granted his permission for us to date the Osiris Shaft, as described in the previous chapter. His reason for this was simple: it was *his site*. He thought we might be useful to *him*. It meant nothing that this sampling which Hawass arranged was not on any of our forms, whether archaeological ones or security ones. So he was right. They did *mean nothing*!

We were thus left with Ioannis's single sampling from the smallest pyramid, and no possibility of Ioannis getting any more from the pyramids. But as I have just pointed out, the result for this sample was dramatic.

What are we to think of a situation where the pyramids were clearly built before the commencement of the Fourth Dynasty? Our date for the 'Pyramid of Mycerinus' cannot be later than 2640 BC and, according to conventional chronologies, that is one year prior to the foundation of the Fourth Dynasty by its first pharaoh, Sneferu. Any connection between the pyramids and pharaohs Cheops, Chephren and Mycerinus is therefore impossible, unless we entirely change the chronologies.

However, it is extremely unlikely that the pyramid is as recent as its latest possible date. The dating spread is a broad one of nearly a thousand years, and in attempting to interpret such results, it is safer to deal with the median age. But even if we do that, ignoring the 500 years prior to the median age which could be correct, we would still be left with the awkward fact that the pyramids of Giza would then have been constructed before the unification of Egypt and before the reign of the first pharaoh of the First Dynasty. This leaves us in a terrible dilemma, for we no longer have the faintest idea who the pyramid builders were.

In Chapter Six I give an account of, and publish the photo of, a First Dynasty royal pyramid that was 75 feet long at the base and 43 feet high, made of mud brick. It was excavated in 1937 by Walter Emery at Saqqara. Few if any people today realise that there was such a large pyramid in the First Dynasty, which goes to show just how many unknown and unexplained factors there are at work here. It certainly does not help matters that Egyptologists decline to discuss something as crucial as a First Dynasty pyramid that was 43 feet high. Anyone would consider this an obvious subject for discussion in so-called 'histories of the pyramids', and yet it somehow manages to be overlooked.

Earlier I mentioned the only existing evidence seeming to indicate a connection between the Great Pyramid and the pharaoh Cheops (Egyptian name: Khufu). Obviously such evidence, if it exists, is extremely important, unless one assumes that there was an earlier Khufu and that the reason why the Fourth Dynasty Khufu became so fixated on the Great Pyramid was because he was named after an earlier Khufu, of whom we have lost all knowledge today but of whom the Fourth Dynasty pharaoh would have had knowledge in his time. As a matter of fact, several people have previously suggested this possibility. And I have already pointed out that when we thought we had only one King Teti, the well-known first king of the Sixth Dynasty (he is believed to have reigned 2345 BC–2333 BC), we later discovered that we had two earlier ones as well in the Archaic Period of the First and Second Dynasties,[27] giving a total of three Tetis prior to 2300 BC, so there are precedents for this kind of thing. However, I do not like postulating the existence of an earlier Khufu, because it seems an extraordinarily artificial thing to do, in the absence of any actual evidence. We have therefore to deal with the existence – within the 'relieving chambers' above the King's Chamber of the Great Pyramid (see Figure 14) – of scrawled graffiti on some stones, giving the name 'Khufu' in hieroglyphics, albeit mostly in a bizarre and atypical form. Furthermore, the particular example upon which great stress has been placed by those wishing to use this evidence to prove that the Great Pyramid was the tomb of Cheops (Khufu) has the impressive feature of appearing to continue beneath a superimposing stone, and thus to have been painted during the actual construction of the pyramid.

It must be stressed that these graffiti are the *only* known native Egyptian evidence of any kind linking the Great Pyramid with Cheops (Khufu), apart from the surrounding constructions outside the pyramid which do not constitute evidence of anything other than the pyramid surroundings, since they are demonstrably inferior to and possibly much later than the Great Pyramid. (Herodotus, born 484 BC, attributed the Great Pyramid to Cheops, but he was a Greek, and it is even thought by some scholars that he might never have really visited Egypt personally but taken his information from an earlier writer who did, named Hecataeus of Miletus (lived circa 550 BC–490 BC; not to be confused with Hecataeus of Abdera, born circa 300 BC, who was a much later Greek historian who also wrote about Egypt, and is much better known). In any case, his story cannot be treated as serious evidence of anything other than 'what people said' in Egypt in the fifth century BC.)

As is well known, there are no formal inscriptions of any kind to be found inside any of the three main pyramids at Giza. (Nor are any to be found inside the Meidum Pyramid or the two Dashur pyramids.) There is also no evidence that there were ever any paintings or indications other than empty sarcophagi (bearing no inscriptions) that these buildings were tombs, or had any particular associations with any individual pharaohs at all. Graffiti are found round the pyramids in exterior structures, but have never been found inside the Giza pyramids. The graffiti above the King's Chamber are therefore unique, and so it is hardly surprising that they have often been challenged as possible nineteenth-century forgeries.

I have not had the opportunity to inspect the graffiti myself. However, I have seen photos of some of them, and drawings of them are reproduced here in Figures 19 and 20. And in September, 2002, the National Geographic satellite TV channel broadcast a two-hour documentary on Giza and the Great Pyramid, which included footage taken in the top relieving chamber of the Great Pyramid, and showed Dr Zahi Hawass crawling around inside the chamber. It was possible in this footage to get a good look at the main graffito mentioning 'Khufu', and the impression made was not good. The painted inscription, which appears to continue under a superimposing stone, did not look at all convincing to me. Furthermore, I do not believe that it continues beneath the other stone at all. It looked as if it had been painted right up to the edge to give the impression of going underneath, but did not in fact do so. One would really have to chip away some of the other stone to see if the inscription really continues underneath or not, but I am willing to wager it does not. I have looked at the tape I made of this programme again, and am more than ever convinced that this is a fake. But, as I have already said, I am not the first person to suggest this.

In 1988, a television programme called 'The Mysteries of the

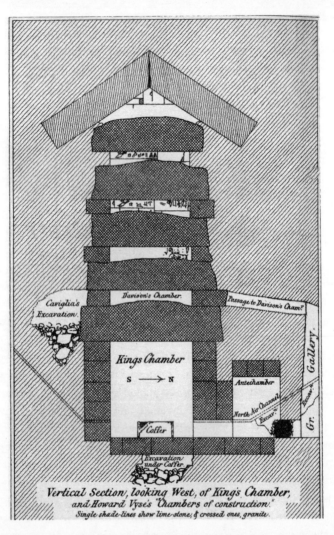

Vertical Section, looking West, of King's Chamber, and Howard Vyse's "Chambers of construction". Single shade-lines show lime-stone, & crossed ones, granite.

Figure 14. The relieving chambers over the King's Chamber, seen in a vertical section looking west, as drawn by Charles Piazzi-Smyth and reproduced by him as Plate 14, before page 97, in Volume II of Smyth's three-volume work, *Life and Work at the Great Pyramid*, Edinburgh, 1867. Smyth also shows the locations of the graffiti. It is useful also to see Smyth's drawings of the depth of the early 19th-century excavations under the coffer (these diggings are now entirely concealed, so that most people are unaware that these ever took place), and the details of Caviglia's excavations south of Davison's Chamber.

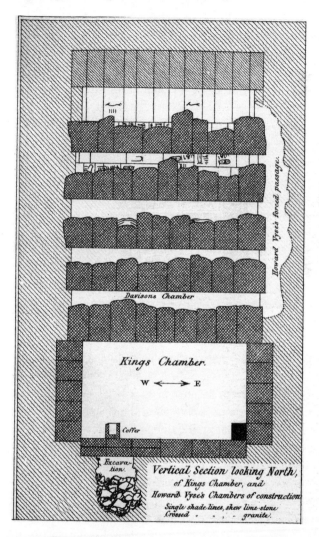

Labels within the figure:

Howard Vyse's forced passage.

Davisons Chamber

Kings Chamber.

W ⟵ ⟶ E

Coffer

Excava-
tion.

Vertical Section looking North,
of Kings Chamber, and
Howard Vyse's Chambers of construction
Single shade lines, shew lime-stone
Crossed . . „ . . granite).

Figure 15. Piazzi-Smyth's drawing of the relieving chambers above the King's Chamber seen in a vertical section looking north, being the other half of his Plate 14. The small black square in the bottom right corner of the King's Chamber is the entrance.

Pyramids . . . Live' was broadcast in America, with Omar Sharif as the presenter and William Kronick as the director. It seems to have been a slightly updated and longer version of an earlier programme made by the same director, also with Omar Sharif, eleven years earlier, in 1977, called 'Mysteries of the Great Pyramids' (which was only fifty-two minutes long), which I have never seen. As far as I know, these programmes were never transmitted in my home country of Britain. Not long before finishing this book, I was able to see a very poor second- or third-generation video cassette of an off-the-air recording of the 1988 programme. The programme showed Mark Lehner going down into the Osiris Shaft, which had a much higher water level at the bottom at that time, with the four columns already hacked away (the voiceover commentary wrongly said they had been 'worn away by the water', which is physically impossible), and picking up bits of human bones and wood from a coffin which were in the water. (The sarcophagi of Level Two were not shown.) Not much was shown of the shaft, and the emphasis was on creating an air of mystery about the place, and then moving on to another subject elsewhere. Lehner was then shown entering the 'relieving chambers' above the King's Chamber in the Great Pyramid. Once again, we saw little, but we did get a good shot of him standing upright in the top chamber, which has a pointed ceiling enabling someone to stand erect. He pointed to a large and crude cartouche containing Khufu's name on the wall of the chamber, but it looked so obviously faked to me that I could not understand anyone taking it seriously. In lower chambers, the names assigned to them were inscribed in huge letters on the walls: 'Lady Arbuthnot', 'Nelson', etc., all painted by or on the orders of Howard Vyse, who seems to have run amok with a paint pot.

The photos I have seen of others of the 'Khufu graffiti' are also extremely unconvincing and the graffiti look like the sort of thing a bored schoolboy might doodle on a bad day. Of course, they are meant to be daubs made by quarrymen or construction workers, and quarrymen and construction workers are rarely scholars. But even so, the crudity of the marks is highly unsettling. And there are various troubling anomalies. For instance, the bottom relieving chamber was discovered in 1765 by Nathaniel Davison (technically speaking, it was discovered by a Frenchman slightly before, but he is never mentioned by anyone and it is customary to say it was discovered by Davison, who I suppose we could say 'also discovered it'), and it contains no graffiti. Why are there no graffiti in this chamber, but only in the ones discovered later by the man accused by many people of forging them? If there had been any graffiti in Davison's Chamber, discovered long before Vyse came along, then there would be no controversy.

The relieving chambers above the King's Chamber were in earlier publications called by the name of the 'chambers of construction'. In 1883 Petrie published his seminal work, *The Pyramids and Temples of Gizeh*, in its first and fuller edition[28] (much larger than the heavily abridged second edition, which is the one that has been reprinted in

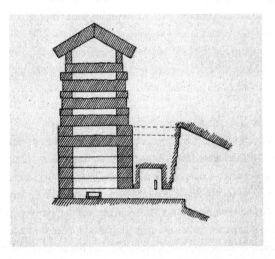

Figure 16. This drawing is from an obscure German pamphlet by Heinrich Hein, entitled *Das Geheimnis der Grossen Pyramide* (*The Secret of the Great Pyramid*), Zeitz, Germany, 1921, Figure 2, page 10. (I have prepared a full translation of this interesting pamphlet, and hope to publish it one day.) It is particularly useful in that it shows the connecting passage (represented by dotted lines) by which Nathaniel Davison in 1782 discovered what is known as 'Davison's Chamber' inside the Great Pyramid. The structure on the left shows the King's Chamber (with the coffer on the floor also shown) surmounted by a series of 'relieving chambers', the lowest of which is Davison's Chamber. At right, the termination of the Grand Gallery is shown, just below the roof of which is the entrance to the tiny passage shown by the dots.

recent years). This contains much information on these chambers. Petrie writes:

'The spaces, or "chambers of construction", as they have been called, which lie one over the other above the King's Chamber, are entered from a small passage which starts in the E. wall of the gallery [the Grand Gallery], close under the roof. This is apparently an original passage, and leads into the lower chamber; the other four spaces above that can only be entered by the forced ascent cut by Col. Howard Vyse. ... In the second chamber ... [t]here is a large cartouche of Khnumu-Khufu, nearly all broken away by Vyse's forced entrance ...'[29]

Elsewhere in his book, Petrie is wholly dismissive of the idea that 'Khnumu-Khufu' is the same person as Khufu (Cheops). Here are his comments on this crucial point:

The builder of the Great Pyramid of Gizeh is well known. Khufu (Grecianized as Kheops and Soufis, and Anglo-Grecianized as Cheops) is named both by historians and by his cartouches, which are found as quarry-marks on the building stones. But another name is found on the blocks in the Pyramid, side by side with those bearing the name of Khufu. This other name is the same as that of Khufu, with the prefix of two hieroglyphs, a jug and a ram; and it is variously rendered Khnumu-Khufu, Nh-Shufu, and Shu-Shufu. The most destructive theory about this king is that he is identical with Khufu, and that the ram is merely a symbol of the god Shu, and put as 'the determinative in this place of the first syllable of the name'. But against this hypothesis it must be observed (1) that the pronunciation was Khufu, and not Shufu, in the early times; (2) that the first hieroglyph, the jug, is thus unexplained; and (3) that there is no similar prefix of a determinative to a king's name, in any other instance out of the hundreds of names, and thousands of variants, known.[30]

In other words, Petrie believes it to be impossible that the graffito in the relieving chamber refers to Cheops. So if by chance it is authentic, it does not refer to Cheops anyway. But it is far more likely that it is a forgery, in which case Vyse certainly made a botch of it. In other words, there probably never was a 'Khnum-Khufu' in the first place, except as artificially created by someone who got his forged graffiti slightly wrong.

In 1932, Petrie wrote a scathing review of the Porter & Moss epigraphical survey volume dealing with Memphis, which had just been published. He was particularly critical about the massive failings of Porter & Moss to deal with the Giza pyramids properly (ignoring Cole's work and Borchardt's work, omitting inscriptions, etc.), and his final complaint was: 'Also Khnem-Khufu [Khnum-Khufu] does not appear in the Index.'[31] Here we see that Petrie continued to fume about the Khnum-Khufu issue, and was not a bit pleased that the separate status of 'Khnum-Khufu' had gone unrecognised in Porter & Moss, which presumably implied that they did not recognise that it was anything other than the name of King Khufu. This shows that forty-nine years after the publication of his book on the pyramids, Petrie's irritation at the glossing over of the distinctly separate nature of 'Khnum-Khufu' (whether it was a name or an epithet, as Breasted suggests, below) from the name of the pharaoh Khufu had not abated in the least.

In his pyramid book of 1883, Petrie does not mention the other painted name of Khnum-Khufu in the top, or fifth, relieving chamber, presumably because he refused to accept its validity. However, we can read of it in Mark Lehner's *Complete Pyramids*:

'Above the King's Chamber are five stress-relieving chambers, each with the same floor area as the respective chamber below. At the very top, the stones are cantilevered in the form of a pent roof to distribute the weight and stresses of the mountain of masonry above, for which there are few parallels and no precedent. [In fact, it is not certain that these chambers truly relieve any downwards stress at all, but that is another subject.] Graffiti left by the work crews on the walls add a human element. Names of the workers are combined with that of the king – here Khnum-Khufu.'[32] Just for the record, what are really mentioned are 'work gang' names, not workers' names individually.

It is more than a bit odd that the name of Khufu should be combined with that of the god Khnum, a rams'-horned divinity who is chiefly associated with the island of Elephantine at Aswan and who presided over the potters' wheel and stone masonry. James Breasted pointed out in *Ancient Records of Egypt* that the expression 'Khnum-Khufu' actually means 'Khnum protects me', and is not a name.'[33] If 'Khnum-Khufu' were to be treated as a name in a cartouche, and if it were real rather than faked, then it refers to an unknown pharaoh of unknown date, called 'Khnum Protects Me', but definitely not to Cheops. So much for the name of Cheops having been found inside 'his' pyramid.

A modern book about the pyramids, which is more illuminating in every way (other than the fact that it lacks colour illustrations) than that of Lehner's superficial survey, is J. P. Lepre's *The Egyptian Pyramids*.[34] It contains a more substantial account of the relieving chambers. He describes how Colonel Richard Howard Vyse used dynamite to blast his way into the second chamber on 14 February 1837. He mentions the graffiti painted in red ochre upon the chamber walls and the occurrences of the name of Khufu:

Hieroglyphs were in fact discovered in all four of the relieving chambers penetrated by Vyse, but they were workmen's markings, painted on at the quarries. This assertion is supported by the facts that: (1) they were of the crude, not decorative type; (2) these upper apartments were construction cavities only; and (3) some of these hieroglyphics were actually set upside down. With the markings already on them, the blocks were set into place according to how their weight and dimensions were to be oriented, and not so that the hieroglyphs would be easily readable for anyone viewing the chamber afterwards. The readings of some of these signs were actually cut off from view where the blocks were set into place behind other cross stones. Many of them had the various names of the construction gangs written on them – titles such as: 'The crew, the White Crown of Khnum-Khuf (Khufu) is powerful'; or 'The crew, Khufu excites love'.

These mentions of the Pharaoh Khufu are the only real historical testament to the builder of the Great Pyramid. His hieroglyphic name is mentioned many times on the walls of tombs and mastabas which riddle the Giza graveyard complex, those having been the burial places of his family, dignitaries and priests. But the hieroglyphics which grace the relieving chambers are the only ones bearing his name that were ever found in or on the pyramid itself. . . . The fifth or uppermost of the relieving compartments, called (Colonel) Campbell's Chamber, is in many ways the most interesting of the five. . . . There are a number of hieroglyphs painted on the ceiling, a few of which give the name of King Khufu, and one in particular which records that this stage in the construction of the monument was reached during the seventeenth year of his reign.[35]

Another account of the relieving chambers appears in *Secrets of the Great Pyramid* by Peter Tompkins, who comments:

'The most interesting discovery was not so much the chambers themselves but some red-paint cartouches daubed on the inner walls of the upper chambers. Thanks to the Rosetta Stone and Champollion's successors, one of these cartouches was recognized by Egyptologists as belonging to Khufu, believed to be the second Pharaoh of the Fourth Dynasty, called Cheops by the Greeks . . . Doubts still lingered that there might have been a far earlier king with a similar cartouche, quite unknown to Egyptologists . . . As some of the quarry marks found in the chambers are hieroglyphs signifying "year 17", Egyptologists deduced that the building had reached that stage in the seventeenth year of the king's reign. Most of the marks were roughly daubed in red paint . . .'[36]

Lepre was therefore basing his remarks upon a mere assumption when he said that the seventeenth year of Khufu's reign was referred to; what is really daubed on the stone is simply a mention of 'year seventeen'. It could be 'year seventeen' of any reign, and certainly need not be the seventeenth year of the reign of Cheops. Indeed, it is most unlikely that the year of a reign would be recorded in this way at all by a mark daubed on a stone block, because this also has been done in the wrong manner. We know from the collection 'Dated Texts of the Old Kingdom' compiled by Anthony Spalinger, referred to above, that graffiti of this kind when authentic do not simply say 'year seventeen'. It doesn't work that way. Instead, they have a jargon of their own and always say things formulaically, like: 'Year after the fourth occurrence of the [cattle] count . . .' and then they also give the month and day. Spalinger himself rejected the authenticity of this graffito, by omitting it from his list of authentic dated texts from the reign of Cheops. Since

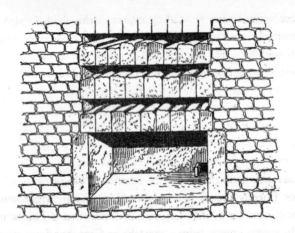

Figure 17. Longitudinal section in perspective view of the King's Chamber and three of the 'relieving chambers' above it. Figure 153 on page 228 in Georges Perrot and Charles Chipiez, *Histoire de l'Art dans l'Antiquité* (*The History of Art in Antiquity*), Paris, 1882, Vol. I, *L'Égypte*.

Figure 18. Transverse section in perspective view of the King's Chamber with the five 'relieving chambers' above it, in the Great Pyramid. At right is the top end of the Grand Gallery. Figure 152 on page 227 in Georges Perrot and Charles Chipiez, *Histoire de l'Art dans l'Antiquité* (*The History of Art in Antiquity*), Paris, 1882, Vol. I, *L'Égypte*.

Spalinger seems to be the leading expert in this field, I think we can confidently dismiss the graffito as faked on that basis alone, though, as we shall see, there are even stronger grounds for doing so.

In *Texts from the Pyramid Age*, Nigel Strudwick and Ronald Leprohon, in a section giving translations of eight 'crew name' texts from Giza, three of which mention Menkaure (Mycerinus), omit the 'dated graffito' from the Great Pyramid, but give five references presumed to be to Khufu (Cheops), although only one gives the actual name Khufu. One mentions 'Khnumkhufu', and three mention 'Horus Medjedu'.[37] Medjedu is believed to have been the alternative 'Horus name' of Cheops. However, Cheops already had another Horus name, which was Bikui-nub, meaning 'two golden falcons'. It seems that a Horus name of Medjedu is also known from a mastaba at Giza, but I am unaware of whether this is firmly established as a second Horus name for Cheops. I don't believe any other pharaoh having two Horus names has ever been known, and this is very suspicious. However, the suggestion that Cheops had an 'alternative' name of Khnum-Khufu has come to be widely accepted, despite the fact that it only rests upon the evidence of graffiti which, as we have seen, Petrie considered to be absolutely unreliable. Strudwick and Leprohon make no comment upon the reliability or otherwise of the five crew-name graffiti attributed to Khufu's time, and they seem to be unaware that the one mentioning Khnum-Khufu is unreliable, and make no comment about that.

In his book about Mycerinus, George Reisner has an appendix in which he not only lists Mycerinus's crew-name graffiti, but those of other pharaohs connected with Giza as well.[38] Strangely, these commence with two of a mysterious pharaoh named Neferka, thought to be a king of the Third Dynasty, and who was in any case certainly no later than that, of whom nothing is really known. Four are listed relating to Cheops, but only one actually mentioning Cheops specifically. There is also the one mentioning 'Khnum-Khufu', which we have already considered. And the other two mention 'Horus Medjedu', which Reisner spells Mededuw. But what is odd is that it seems to be only with Cheops that a pharaoh's 'Horus name' is used. 'Horus names' really were out of fashion by the time of the Fourth Dynasty, and this also does not ring true at all. Reisner does not consider the question of authenticity, other

129

than to reject the 'dated' graffito by not including it. However, if the 'dated' one is a fake, then the others presumably are also.

Dieter Arnold, in his book *Building in Egypt: Pharaonic Stone Masonry*, refers in passing to the graffiti from the Great Pyramid, but does not describe them or comment upon them at all, and merely gives a footnote referring the reader for information to be found in Vyse and Petrie.[39]

As I shall now make clear, there is strong reason to believe that Howard Vyse did fake all of the Khufu graffiti in these chambers. It would not have been a difficult thing to do. He apparently had plenty of motive and plenty of opportunity. He had spent £10,000 without much to show for it, and needed to come up with something fairly sensational. (I don't know exactly how much £10,000 in the 1830s would be worth in today's money, but probably half a million pounds would be a conservative estimate. Clearly, a man who had run through that amount of other people's money, without a major find, was a desperate man indeed.) He used dynamite to blast the south face of the Great Pyramid in a desperate attempt to find a way in from that side that might lead to further chambers and passages, and his total failure to find anything is recorded with gloom and finality in his book as follows:

'. . . it might be inferred that no chambers, or passages, exist in the Pyramid besides those already discovered.

'The excavation in search of a southern entrance was therefore given up, which had been carried to a considerable depth without finding the least indication of a passage, either by an inclination in the course of the stones, or by any other circumstance. The great magnitude of the building, compared with the smallness of the chambers and passages; and also the position of the entrance to the eastward in the northern front, induced a conjecture that an entrance to the westward in the southern front might conduct to passages and apartments constructed in the great space between the three chambers entered from the north. But this does not appear to be the case; and it is to be believed that the King's Chamber is the principal apartment . . .'[40]

Having discovered the higher relieving chambers above the King's Chamber by blasting with dynamite, and having forced open an 'air shaft' so that air came rushing into the chamber, but having failed to find anything further, Colonel Howard Vyse was left without enough impressive finds to justify his great expenditures. He had found nothing inside the Great Pyramid chambers and passages other than the graffiti which he so zealously had copied, published in his book, arranged for his engineer John S. Perring to publish as well, and proudly announced were 'probably the most antient [sic – this was an accepted alternative spelling of 'ancient' at that time] inscriptions in existence.'[41]

It smacks of desperation to make this exaggerated claim when he had admitted there were many such graffiti previously known to him in quarries and Giza tombs, and he described finding one himself in Campbell's Tomb near the Sphinx. Since he was familiar with several cartouches of Cheops (Khufu) from Giza, and some of these had already been published, there were numerous inscriptions from the same reign already well known to him; these were of the same reign as that claimed for the Great Pyramid graffiti. The Great Pyramid graffiti could thus not possibly be the oldest inscriptions known, when they were purporting to be of the same age as those of many others he knew. The fact that he made this strange claim, contradicting his own statements elsewhere, shows just how eager he was to be able to claim he had found something extraordinary contained within the frustratingly bare interior of the Great Pyramid, which is otherwise so notoriously lacking in any inscriptions at all. And it is odd that the only graffiti ever 'found' were in the only chambers that no one had previously entered, and to which Howard Vyse had exclusive and unlimited access by day and by night for many weeks on end. If genuine graffiti were to be found inside the Great Pyramid, one would expect to find them elsewhere, such as in the well shaft, the grotto, the Subterranean Chamber, and other out-of-the-way nooks and crannies where similar unpolished stone surfaces are found. But there is no trace of any. And the bottom relieving chamber, as already mentioned, is bare of them as well, having been discovered seventy-two years earlier by Davison.

As early as 26 April, in his book which is printed as a diary, Howard Vyse betrays his deep anxieties about not having discovered enough, by writing:

'All hopes of an important discovery were not yet given up . . .'[42]

That is a strange way to put it, considering that only the day before

131

he had discovered the third relieving chamber which he named after Nelson, and the day he wrote his despairing comments 'the best quarrymen were employed to get above the roof of Nelson's Chamber'.[43] It is obvious that Howard Vyse was deeply unsatisfied with his mere discovery of relieving chambers, and the temptation to embellish these finds was clearly strong.

Howard Vyse had unlimited time alone in the chambers with his assistants. Anyone suspecting him of having forged the graffiti should consider the evidence to be found in his own account, in which he discusses how he authorised an inscription to be painted on the wall of a relieving chamber. On 28 April, only two days after entering it for the first time, Howard Vyse records: 'Mr. Hill inscribed Nelson's great name in the chamber lately discovered.'[44] In other words, at the very same time that Howard Vyse is suspected of having, with the help of J. R. Hill, forged graffiti in the relieving chambers, he instructs the same J. R. Hill to paint a prominent modern graffito on the wall of one of those very chambers. This proves they were up there in the chambers with brushes and pots of paint. So why stop at Nelson, why not go the whole hog? Indeed, they did the same for Lady Arbuthnot's Chamber, and for Campbell's Chamber (see Plate 13, where its name painted by Hill is prominently visible). And he had already recorded that he had a keen awareness of the red paint used to daub quarrymen's marks on the ancient monuments, for on 21 April he commented about the inscription which he claims to have found in Campbell's tomb on the Plateau:

'Mr. Perring and Mr. Mash continued the survey; and in the course of it, copied the characters in the pit at the foot of the sarcophagus in Campbell's Tomb. They were inscribed with red paint between double lines, about two inches apart.'[45]

We see therefore by Howard Vyse's own testimony that, within the same month, he was conscious of the details of the size, shape and red paint of Fourth Dynasty graffiti, aware of the details of Cheops (Khufu) cartouches elsewhere [in addition, some Cheops cartouches had already been published by the Egyptologists Wilkinson and Rossellini], instructing Nelson's name to be painted on the wall of one of the relieving chambers (thereby proving that he had no compunction about writing on the walls), and very deeply frustrated that, despite finding the relieving chambers, he had not yet made an 'important discovery' after all his expenditures of time, energy and money. And this was the same month in which he had the graffiti supposedly found within the relieving chambers copied by J. R. Hill for circulation and publication. When he apparently found graffiti in Campbell's Tomb, he had them copied by John Perring, and on 12 April he hastened to send copies of them by post to William Hamilton, the prominent diplomat and anti-quary, to boost his reputation.[46] This in turn proves conclusively that he looked upon Fourth Dynasty graffiti as a key discovery, certain to secure his name in the annals of discovery, which – from his own remarks – he evidently believed his discovery of mere relieving chambers would fail to do. The day before, on 11 April, Howard Vyse records that he 'copied the quarry-marks found at the southern front of the Great Pyramid'; these are reproduced in his book and are meaningless symbols, containing no hieroglyphs or cartouches.[47]

Having made a great fuss about these uninteresting scratches found outside the Great Pyramid, having copied out and sent to Hamilton the more interesting graffiti claimed as a discovery in Campbell's Tomb, and having noted in detail the red paint and characteristics of Giza quarry marks, suddenly graffiti begin appearing in the relieving chambers themselves. Howard Vyse blasted his way by dynamite into a new chamber, then the very next day he not only copied out quarry marks but actually reported them in a letter to William Hamilton. Such was his urgency to convince others of his great accomplishments, that a mere twenty-four hours was allowed to elapse between the first discovery of a chamber and its quarry marks being boasted about to the great antiquary. This happened, for instance, with Nelson's Chamber. It was discovered on 25 April, and Howard Vyse claimed: 'Several quarry-marks were inscribed in red upon the blocks, particularly on the western side'. William Hamilton was written to the next day, and the day after, 'The quarry-marks in Nelson's Chamber were copied', and the following day, 'Mr. Hill inscribed Nelson's great name in the chamber lately discovered.'[48]

It has often been commented about the graffiti that Howard Vyse claimed to have discovered that some are upside down, and some appear to go under other blocks. But before any such features were reported of any Great Pyramid graffiti, Howard Vyse had recorded these specific features of graffiti found elsewhere on the Plateau, which he copied out in his own hand:

'I copied some hieroglyphics which Mr. Perring had observed on the ruins of the temple eastward of the Second Pyramid. These characters appeared to be upon the inner face of a stone, which must therefore have previously belonged to some other building of extraordinary antiquity; and it is to be remarked that blocks have been discovered in the tombs to the westward of the Great Pyramid inscribed with inverted hieroglyphics on their inward faces.'[49] This was entered under the date 6 May. On 9 May, Howard Vyse copied down a partial cartouche of 'Suphis', i.e. Cheops (Khufu), which he had found on a stone dug out of a mound, and which is published in his book.[50] Immediately afterwards, described under the same day, 'Lady Arbuthnot's Chamber was minutely examined, and found to contain a great many quarry-marks. Notwithstanding that the characters in these chambers were surveyed by Mr. Perring upon a reduced scale, I considered that facsimiles in their original size would be desirable, as they were of great importance from their situation, and probably the most antient inscriptions in existence. I requested therefore Mr. Hill to copy them. His drawings were compared with the originals by Sir Robert Arbuthnot, Mr. Brettel (a civil engineer), Mr. Raven and myself, and are deposited in the British Museum.'[51]

There are several things that are odd here. How can so many graffiti be so suddenly discovered? Surely, when discovering the chamber, you either see them or you do not, as they are meant to be so obvious. In the foldout engraving of them all published by Howard Vyse between pages 279 and 280 of Volume I of his book (see Figures 19 and 20), we can see that the graffiti are simply everywhere, in vast profusion, and quite impossible to miss. It seems therefore highly disingenuous to claim that a chamber which had already been discovered previously was only later, when minutely examined, found to contain graffiti. You would have to be blind not to see so many graffiti all over the walls immediately upon entering – if they had originally been there when you entered.

This sudden discovery took place on the same day that Howard Vyse was copying out a cartouche of Cheops, which he actually publishes as

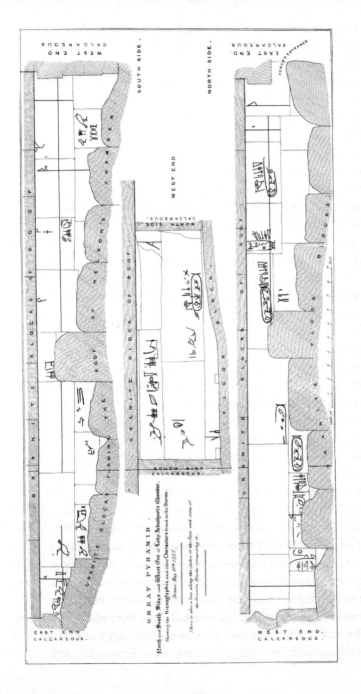

Figure 19. Folding plate opposite page 279, of Volume 1 of Howard Vyse, *Operations Carried on at the Pyramids of Gizeh in 1837*, 3 vols., London, 1840.

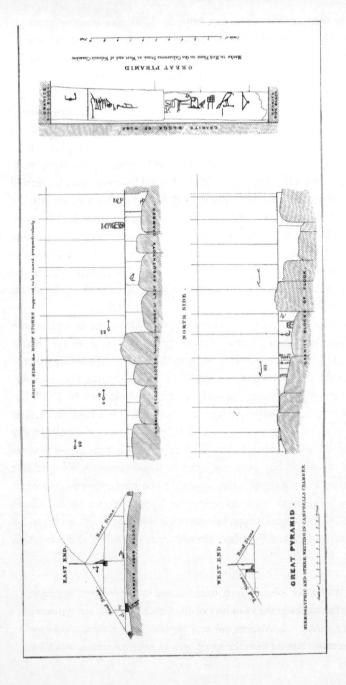

Figure 20. Folding plate opposite page 284, of Volume 1 of Howard Vyse, *Operations Carried on at the Pyramids of Gizeh in 1837*, 3 vols., London, 1840.

well. He then, on that same day, brought dignitaries into the chamber to verify the graffiti, which were supposed to have been suddenly discovered on that same day. Also, Howard Vyse contradicts himself by saying that Perring had already copied them and he thought he ought to do so again. But how could Perring already have copied them if they had not yet been 'suddenly discovered'? And furthermore, under his entry for 9 May, Howard Vyse entered the information and published the image of the partial Cheops cartouche, and then contradicts himself by claiming that it was not found until June. Why change his story in mid-sentence like that? Later, on 27 May, Howard Vyse says that he blasted his way above the chamber named Lady Arbuthnot's Chamber into the highest of the relieving chambers, which he named Campbell's Chamber. He describes all the stones and says: 'There were many quarry-marks similar to those in the other chambers, and also several red lines crossing each other at right angles [which he reproduces], with black equilateral triangles described near their intersections, in order probably to obtain a right angle.'[52]

At this point in his account, Howard Vyse inserts a lengthy text written later about the Great Pyramid graffiti by Samuel Birch of the British Museum. Birch was to go on to write an important early work on hieroglyphics entitled *Introduction to the Study of the Egyptian Hieroglyphics*, which he published twenty years later in 1857. This work by Birch has escaped notice by many scholars because, although a book of modest length in its own right, it was tucked away at the back of a book by the much more famous Sir Gardner Wilkinson, and has even evaded cataloguing by some librarians as a result.[53] However, Birch's earliest publication about hieroglyphics appears to be his treatise embodied in Howard Vyse's book. In considering the Great Pyramid graffiti, Birch records the facts that Cheops cartouches similar to those brought to his attention by Howard Vyse had already been published and were well known:

The symbols or hieroglyphics, traced in red by the sculptor, or mason, upon the stones in the chambers of the Great Pyramid, are apparently quarry-marks; . . . Although not very legible, . . . they possess points of considerable interest from the appearance of two royal names, which had already been found in the tombs of functionaries employed by monarchs of that dynasty under which these Pyramids were erected.

A cartouche, similar to that which first occurs in Wellington's Chamber, has been published by Mr. Wilkinson . . . The other name discovered . . . which he had already observed in an adjacent tomb, and conjectured to be that of Cheops, . . . is composed of elements purely phonetic, and is decidedly a name. It has also been published by Mr. Wilkinson . . . two other prenomens, in which the [solar] disc [meaning 'Ra'] is wanting, are also given by Messrs. Burton, Wilkinson, and Rossellini.[54]

This is even more suspicious. I am certainly not suggesting that Samuel Birch had anything whatever to do with any forgery. But his study of the graffiti, solicited by Howard Vyse, inadvertently reveals that the key elements of the graffiti, namely the Cheops cartouches, were already known and published by various sources, and widely familiar from elsewhere in Giza. What is more, the strange name 'Khnum-Khufu' might have originated from a Giza tomb as a non-royal name 'in which the disc is wanting', but Vyse, thinking it was a form of Cheops's name, then mistakenly inserted it into a cartouche when he forged the graffito. On this possible evidence, there might never have been a king called Khnum-Khufu.

It is often difficult for us to know at this distance in time the sequence of publications, and what was known to whom at what time. But this explicit testimony by Birch confirms that Howard Vyse had everything necessary at hand to carry out any forgeries, for all he had to do was to copy cartouches and quarry-marks, which have now been proved conclusively to have been well-known to him. So Howard Vyse had the motive, he had the means, he had the exclusive access, he had the skills, he had the time, he had the background and the materials, to commit the forgeries that I am suggesting that he committed. Furthermore, it is widely known that he was an adventurer rather than a serious scholar, and he demonstrated conclusively that he would not hesitate to damage ancient monuments by using dynamite, and would not hesitate to deface them by having the names of Nelson, Campbell and Lady Arbuthnot painted in huge letters in relieving chambers. To say that Howard Vyse is a prime candidate for mischief is an understatement.

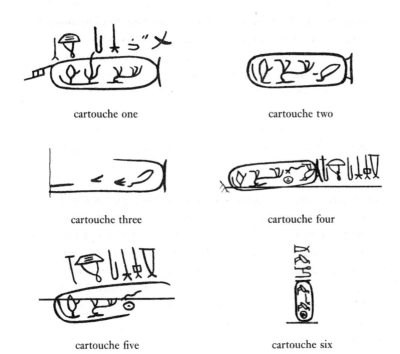

cartouche one

cartouche two

cartouche three

cartouche four

cartouche five

cartouche six

Figure 21. Here are the six whole cartouches which appear as graffiti in the 'relieving chambers' above the King's Chamber inside the Great Pyramid, and which were forged by Howard Vyse and two of his assistants. Not one of the whole cartouches represented in these Great Pyramid graffiti is correct. Not one of them gives the name 'Khufu' (the Egyptian form of Cheops). Nowhere in the graffiti does the correct Egyptian hieroglyph for 'kh' appear. That hieroglyph is a circle with thin parallel stripes drawn across it diagonally, which is generally thought to represent a round reed sieve. When writing the name 'Khufu', one always begins with that and then follows with the signs for 'u', 'f', and 'u'. The men who faked these graffiti did not understand correctly at that period in time that this was how the name of 'Khufu' was meant to be written. Instead, the circular hieroglyph is shown either with a dot in the centre (which was the sign for the sun, Ra or Re), with a dot and a line in the centre (which means nothing and is a sign which never existed), or with a splodge in the centre which is of indeterminate shape. When the solar hieroglyph is used in these graffiti, the reading is thus: '. . . -raf', and is definitely not even ' . . . khaf', much less 'khuf'. The little chicken used as a hieroglyph for 'u' by the Egyptians is so badly drawn that it looks more like an Egyptian vulture (which was a different hieroglyph entirely), or otherwise looks like a six-year-old's attempt to draw a fish. All of the whole cartouches found amongst these graffiti are erroneous and pathetic forgeries.

What I believe to be the conclusive evidence emerges from an analysis of Vyse's own record of events. A statement in his journal is entered under the date of 9 May, after the discovery of three of the four relieving chambers, on the occasion of his finding the few intact casing stones of the Great Pyramid at its excavated base, and also finding a stone outside the pyramid bearing a partial cartouche. However, these remarks actually refer to an event that took place late on 2 June, after the discovery of Campbell's Chamber, the fourth and final relieving chamber:

> A number of blocks which formed part of the casing were likewise discovered. As it was not then ascertained that the pyramid had been cased, these stones were at first supposed, from their angular shape, to have been employed in filling up, and in concealing the cavity near the entrance. They were extremely hard, and remarkably well worked; but contrary to the testimony of Abdallatif and of other Arabian authors, they did not shew the slightest trace of inscription, or of sculpture. Nor, indeed, was any to be found upon any stone belonging to the pyramid, or near it (with the exception of the quarry-marks already described, of a few lines drawn in red upon a flat stone, apparently intended for a lining), and of part of the cartouche of Suphis, engraved on a brown stone, six inches long by four broad. This fragment was dug out of the mound at the northern side on June 2d; but it did not appear to have belonged to the pyramid.[55]

We need just to stop and think for a moment what this means. In this remark made in passing, while discussing the newly discovered casing stones, Vyse actually admits that no graffiti or hieroglyphs had been discovered, as of 2 June, upon any stone belonging to the pyramid. And yet these remarks were recorded subsequent to the discovery of all four relieving chambers. This amounts to nothing less than a full confession, and the verdict can only be guilty.

Vyse discovered a total of four relieving chambers above Davison's Chamber, which he named in ascending order: Wellington's, Nelson's, Lady Arbuthnot's and Campbell's. It is necessary to list the dates and first reports of discovery of each of these as recorded in Vyse's journal,

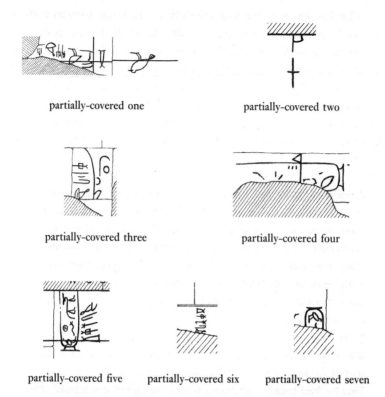

partially-covered one

partially-covered two

partially-covered three

partially-covered four

partially-covered five

partially-covered six

partially-covered seven

Figure 22. Here are the seven half-covered or partially-covered graffiti found in the 'relieving chambers' above the King's Chamber inside the Great Pyramid. Once again, as with the whole cartouches, the name of 'Khufu' does not appear anywhere. There is one pathetic attempt to simulate it, but the hieroglyph which should have read 'kh' is again erroneously shown as a disc containing a horizontal line with a dot under it, which never existed as an Egyptian hieroglyph, and the chick at the end is barely even suggested, it is so badly drawn. These sketchy markings could easily have been painted up to the edge of an adjoining stone, and there is no evidence that they continue underneath. A few of the lines shown here do not even reach the edge, but stop short of it, though without inspecting the original graffiti, it is impossible to know whether this is true of the originals or is a failure of the modern artist in his copying. There is no feature of these graffiti which is in any way convincing, and all of them appear to be fakes made by Howard Vyse and his two assistants.

141

and we will see no mention of graffiti when the chambers were actually opened. Quarry-marks are referred to, and some were drawn and reproduced by Vyse, which were written in red and largely consisted of builders' lines and what we might call doodles. But no graffiti or hieroglyphs are mentioned, until after the crushing realisation by Vyse that he had finally reached the highest chamber, and that there would be no glamorous discovery of a secret burial chamber above the King's Chamber, as he had been expecting for months. Here is the sequence of discovery of the relieving chambers, with the dates:

1. Wellington's Chamber. Discovered through a hole, 28 March, first entered by a forced passage on 30 March. Quarry-marks found [builders' symbols, not hieroglyphics], but no graffiti recorded at the time.[56]

2. Nelson's Chamber. Discovered and entered 25 April. 'Several quarry-marks [symbols, not hieroglyphic graffiti] were inscribed in red upon the blocks, particularly on the western side.'[57] Nelson's name was painted on the wall of the chamber on 28 April.[58] No hieroglyphics or graffiti were reported in the journal at the time.

3. Lady Arbuthnot's Chamber. Discovered and entered 6 May. '. . . it was quite empty.'[59] No graffiti or hieroglyphs are mentioned in the journal at the time.

4. Campbell's Chamber (the highest). Discovered and entered 27 May.[60] Vyse was dismayed to realise that there was probably no secret burial chamber above it, which he had been expecting to find, and that '. . . it was entirely empty . . . but appeared to be the last and to complete the series, as it had an inclined roof, like the Queen's and Belzoni's Chambers [Belzoni's Chamber being a chamber in the Pyramid of Chephren], composed of eleven slabs of calcareous stone, twelve feet three inches long.'[61]

In the entry in the journal for 27 May, Vyse speaks of quarry-marks in Campbell's Chamber, as follows:

'There were many quarry-marks similar to those in the other chambers, and also several red lines crossing each other at right angles, with black equilateral triangles described near the intersections, in order probably to obtain a right angle.'[62]

There is no mention of graffiti or hieroglyphs at all. On the same page as the above remarks in the printed book, Vyse reproduced drawings of two of the crossed lines with triangles. Beside these, he also reproduced a drawing of a deer lying down, though this is not mentioned in the text at all. A strange footnote appears beside the recumbent deer, which states at the foot of the page: 'This hieroglyph was not observed by Mr. Hill.'[63] Mr. Hill must have protested. (Whether this recumbent deer is today to be found in the relieving chambers, I do not know.)

Vyse then says he returned to Cairo with Mr Raven and Mr Hill, and the regular account of events in the published book is interrupted by the insertion of a text by Samuel Birch, written some time afterwards, which discusses the hieroglyphs found inside the relieving chambers. This was clearly inserted for the printer and did not appear in the original journal. It is revealing that the text by Birch is placed here, for this appears to be the moment when Vyse realised that he had failed to find a secret chamber and that he desperately needed to 'pull a rabbit out of a hat', as we say. He must have decided that he had no choice but to fake some hieroglyphs in the relieving chambers, over the access to which he had total control. The journal then resumes for 28 May, after the inserted text of Birch; there is no journal record of any graffiti or hieroglyphs on that day or the next. It is only on 30 May that Vyse's journal records:

'Mr Hill copied the hieroglyphics in Campbell's Chamber.'[64]

That is all. No hieroglyphics are mentioned in the lower chambers. We may probably safely conclude that what Vyse had actually persuaded Mr Hill to do on 30 May was not to copy hieroglyphics in Campbell's Chamber, but to fake them. The volume then ends. But we must remember that an interpolation into the journal text noted above showed Vyse admitting that on 2 June, three days later, no hieroglyphic had ever been found on any stone in the pyramid. This conclusively proves the faking of the graffiti, in my opinion. For if Hill was copying them on 30 May and Vyse admitted they didn't exist on 2 June, there is only one possible explanation as to what was really going on.

Perhaps most damning of all is the apparent forging by Howard Vyse and his colleagues of a coffin lid bearing the name of Mycerinus (Menkaure), which they claimed to have found inside the chambers of the 'Pyramid of Mycerinus'. Vyse reported this 'discovery' in his book,[65] and it was probably his most sensational find. But modern Egyptologists have proved that the find was certainly not genuine. George Reisner was restrained when he wrote:

'In 1837 Howard Vyse, during his excavation of the burial chambers of the Third Pyramid, found an anthropoid wooden coffin inscribed with the name of Mycerinus. . . . The wooden coffin itself appears to be a restoration of Dynasty XXVI, or later . . .'[66]

It appears that the 'restoration' was by Howard Vyse himself, and anyone capable of committing such a fraud was certainly capable of forging a few graffiti, as he appears to have done as well in the burial chamber of one of the three small pyramids near the Mycerinus Pyramid; why would the name of Mycerinus be daubed in red on the roof of this chamber – not a quarry-mark in this case – and be conveniently discovered by Howard Vyse,[67] unless it were part of his ongoing plan to embellish his work with sensational textual materials?

It appears that he was going round the Giza Plateau relentlessly 'spraying' the place with cartouches and graffiti, and even a fake coffin lid, to try to touch up his finds, rather like an interior decorator adding some touches here, some touches there, to bring off a good effect. He was doing this in order to try to regain some credibility and have something to show off about for all his months of effort and the huge sums of money expended. He was, after all, not an archaeologist, but an adventurer and a soldier. He had to cook up something!

There should certainly be a proper study and scholarly publication of the Great Pyramid graffiti. This has never been done in a full or satisfactory manner. (It may well be that no one has ever copied them all, as the chambers are so difficult of access: the ultimate claustrophobe's nightmare. Though I do not have claustrophobia, equally I do not have access.) As for the mention of Khufu, which appears to continue under another stone, if I hadn't seen it on film with my own eyes, I could not have imagined how utterly unconvincing it looks. And the fact that Khufu's name is given as Khnum-Khufu seems a terminal objection. Finally, it appears that one of Howard Vyse's assistants, a young Englishman of only twenty named Humphries Brewer, quarrelled with Vyse about what he insisted were the forgeries of the graffiti, and recorded this information in correspondence to his family. He said that Vyse and two assistants named Raven and [J. R.] Hill (the man who painted the name of Nelson on the wall) had entered the pyramid with brushes and red paint for the specific purpose of forging the graffiti. This amazing evidence has been discussed on the Internet, and appears to have been published first in 1985 in a book by an author who wrote: 'In 1983 a reader of [an earlier book] came forward to provide us with family records showing that his great-grandfather, a master mason named Humphries Brewer, who was engaged by Vyse to help use gunpowder to blast his way inside the pyramid, was an eyewitness to the forgery and, having objected to the deed, was expelled from the site and forced to leave Egypt altogether!'[68]

The reason why I have given so much attention to this problem of the graffiti is because our dates prove that Khufu (Cheops) could not possibly have built the Great Pyramid if he lived when Egyptologists think he did. I am trying to save the royal chronology. But if we insist that the graffiti are genuine, and that the name of Khufu genuinely refers to the pharaoh of the Fourth Dynasty, then we have no choice but to move the Fourth Dynasty very far back in time. By the principle of 'Ockham's Razor' (the principle of least complexity), we can try to find a way to alter as little as possible what we think we already know, by keeping the Fourth Dynasty and the royal chronologies in place, while shifting only the monuments backwards in time to accord with the new dating results. For, after all, it is only the monuments we have dated; we have not dated Cheops himself. And if some questionable graffiti are all that stand in the way, then we have as much right to question their authenticity as anyone else has to insist upon it.

But to go into this any further would take us much too far afield. It is sufficient here to raise the doubts about the authenticity of the graffiti, in order to put on record that we cannot by any means complacently accept them. It was essential to do this, as otherwise there would appear to be an insuperable contradiction in the dates, *unless we move Cheops further back in time*. If that happens, then the matter of the graffiti ceases to be crucial, though frankly I cannot personally accept their authenticity and, after all the evidence which has now been presented, I do not see how anybody else can continue to accept it either.

In 1980, Zecharia Sitchin, unknown to me at the time, carried out an analysis of these graffiti and also concluded that they were forged. I was unaware of this until 2009, when I saw his book for the first time. I therefore read his account after I had completed my own analysis. Anyone who wishes to know more about the subject should consult his book for additional points supporting the forgery hypothesis, the reference to which is given in the footnote.[69] Amongst other things, he points out that the hieroglyphic expert Samuel Birch wondered how some of the marks could be in semi-hieratic script many centuries before it existed in Egypt. The daubs also repeat a typographical error made by Wilkinson in a book of 1837, where the sieved disc representing 'kh' was wrongly replaced by a solar disc. Accordingly, the hieroglyph for 'kh' was not used in the graffiti, but instead the solar disc was mistakenly used, giving not 'Khufu' but 'Raufu' as the king's name. This author does a very good demolition job on Vyse as a forger in general, and gives many details about Vyse's Mycerinus forgeries which I will not go in to here.

Now we come to some previous dating work on the pyramids, which has also shown that the pyramids are hundreds of years older than is conventionally assumed. But this work, done in the 1990s using carbon-14 techniques, attempted to date the organic remains found in the mortar between the blocks of the pyramids. Many Egyptologists have refused to take the results seriously because it was so easy for them to claim that the samples were somehow 'contaminated'. Archaeologists are always claiming that organic samples are contaminated when they don't like the results. Of course, the idea that the pyramid samples were contaminated not by more recent or modern organic remains but rather were contaminated *backwards* by organic remains hundreds of years earlier than the supposed construction dates may seem rather odd, to say the least! But people who want to resist change see no difficulty in claiming such things, in their desperation to keep the status quo of a theory intact. The resounding and embarrassed silence that greeted the dating results was frankly an insult to the people who carried out the dating survey. If they had confirmed everybody's preconceptions, they would have been feted as heroes. But instead, a full report on their work has never been published, and when I asked Mark Lehner, who was one of those who carried out the survey, to give me some information about the project results, he refused.

The radiocarbon dating study was carried out by Herbert Haas, Mark Lehner, Robert J. Wenke, Willy Wölfli, James M. Devine and Georges Bonani. A preliminary report was published in 1993 at Cairo in the Egyptian journal *Annales du Service*.[70] The team announced that they had dated 17 monuments, obtaining 72 radiocarbon dates from 64 samples:

> Most samples were fragments of charred wood or other plant fibers that had been incorporated in the gypsum mortar used to level, align, and bond the stone blocks of some of the pyramids. This mortar was made by heating gypsum and small amounts of limestone in wood fires, and then mixing the anhydrous product with quartz and carbonate of sand to produce a substance that would harden when mixed with water and exposed to air. In the manufacturing process small amounts of ash, charcoal, and other organic materials were added – probably unintentionally – to the mortar. Our samples of carbonised materials from gypsum mortar ranged in amount from a few milligrams to about 3 grams.
>
> The smaller group of samples we took was not related to the mortar. These samples were from a diversity of loci and of various materials, and ranging from wood beams projecting from the core of Djoser's Step pyramid at Saqqara to unburnt reeds from mudbrick walls associated with some of the pyramid complexes.[71]

The results of most of the samples were shocking. They were centuries earlier than conventionally accepted dates. Twenty samples were removed from consideration because of doubts concerning them, and further information about them was promised in a forthcoming publication, which has still not appeared all these years later. However, the article went on to summarise the results of the remainder:

> Our calibrated age measurements differ systematically, with only a few exceptions, from the ages estimated for these monuments on the basis of written sources. . . . The remaining dates [after the removal of twenty disputed samples] average 374 years older than their estimated ages based

on ancient texts. . . . Thus our results suggest either that the historical chronology is incorrect or that there are fundamental problems with the analytical methods or the correction factors that were applied to calculate the radiocarbon dates. . . . In summary of our results, we have too little data to conclude that the historical chronology of the Old Kingdom is in error by several centuries, but this must be considered at least a possibility. . . . If some of the Egyptian pyramids are much older than previously thought, some of the explanatory 'models' of the processes that produced the first Egyptian states would have to be reconsidered. The cultural connections between Egypt and Mesopotamian civilisations would also have to be re-examined. Alternatively, if our age estimations have been in error because of biological 14C dilution or inaccuracies in correction curves, we must assume that many other dates obtained from Egyptian materials are also suspect.[72]

We are now in a position to substantiate the findings of this earlier dating survey, which has until now effectively been suppressed and ignored within Egyptology because it is 'inconvenient'. And whereas 'biological contamination' of dozens of samples – *backwards*, one must stress! – has been used as an excuse to overlook these earlier findings, no 'biological contamination' of our stone samples is possible, so people will have to think again if they wish to sweep inconvenient findings under the carpet.

No monument-by-monument account of the samples taken by this earlier survey, or of the results, has ever been published. This means that we cannot cross-correlate our results with theirs, because they have never specified what theirs were. In other words, we do not even know for certain that they took a sample from the Pyramid of Mycerinus and, if they did, what date they got from it. Whereas they informed us as long ago as 1993 that all but twenty of their results averaged 374 years 'too early', they did not identify the samples or give the dates for each. So we are left stumbling in the dark and do not know what to make of their study other than in very general terms.

Eight years later, in 2001, the results of another radiocarbon study were published. Four of the same men participated in it, joined by four new people. This report appeared in a journal of the University of

Arizona and was entitled 'Radiocarbon Dates of Old and Middle Kingdom Monuments in Egypt'.[73] For some strange reason, even though four of the authors had been authors of the 1993 report from *Annales du Service*, the existence of the earlier report is nowhere mentioned and is actually eliminated from the footnotes. This is bizarre and unexplained. In the new report, only four paragraphs of discussion precede the list of samples and dates. In these introductory paragraphs there are no general statements, as there were in the report in *Annales du Service*, calling attention to the fact that the study had yielded dates that were too early for conventional chronologies. Instead, the authors go out of their way to state that their findings are nothing to worry about:

'The results confirmed the sequence of the monuments and their ages as they were established by historians, but the match between 14C and historic dates was only approximate and left open the possibility of a difference between the two chronologies.'[74]

This is an extraordinarily coy statement! The dating results of many samples are then listed without comment, taking several pages, and it is clear that most of the dates are too early. Presumably this glaring discrepancy between theory and practice is what the opening statement means by 'leaving open the possibility of a difference'. The only possibility left open, in my opinion, is that of being deaf, dumb, blind and in denial, or of reading the results and drawing the obvious conclusions: *the monuments are earlier than they are supposed to be.*

In the list of dates from samples, the Great Pyramid is dated between 2604–2828 BC, the 'Pyramid of Chephren' is dated between 2634–2876 BC, and the 'Pyramid of Mycerinus' is dated between 2582–2858 BC. All of these dates are 'too early', though nowhere does the article actually say so. (In fact, they would be acceptable to the now jettisoned Breasted Chronology, which I mentioned earlier in this chapter.) If these dates are correct, and if the currently accepted chronologies are correct, then the three pyramids cannot have been built by Cheops, Chephren or Mycerinus. And yet the authors do not call attention to this at all. Considering it is so important, and that the entire basis of the conventional assumptions about the Old Kingdom in Egypt is at risk, one would have expected at least a murmur to have arisen. Instead, one gets the impression that the authors of the report are hoping that nobody will notice. And why should they 'forget' their previous publication and eliminate all mention of it from their footnotes? It strikes me that they were hoping nobody would ever notice that four of them had once put their names to an article in which they dared to call into question the fundamentals of Egyptological preconceptions.

From all of this it is clear that a great deal of previous evidence was amassed (although some of it has never been published) to indicate what our own study has now shown, namely that the Giza pyramids are unquestionably older than they are supposed to be. But instead of shouting this from the rooftops, or should we say, the pyramid-tops, the authors of the reports give the impression of speaking to the world through a wet towel. They appear to have just 'dumped' their results in a list. I, on the other hand, think that it is time that facts were faced, and I have no hesitation is saying at the top of my voice: *the pyramids are earlier than anyone thought, and I do not apologise for saying so!*

In my previous chapter on the Osiris Shaft I gave two other surprisingly early dates from the Giza Plateau. In particular, the earlier of the two dates gives the possibility of the production of a giant stone sarcophagus well before the Fourth Dynasty, and possibly in predynastic times. The study by Ioannis Liritzis and myself of the Osiris Shaft therefore reinforces our findings regarding the pyramids. The Osiris Shaft is 'too early', just as the pyramids are 'too early'. They both seem to be relics of some civilisation that we somehow can't identify. And just to make everything more intriguing still, the Osiris Shaft sarcophagus is made of an anomalous material otherwise unknown to Egyptology. So the mystery deepens.

What does all of this mean? The fact is, we don't know. But I have some ideas that I will be putting forward in the coming chapters which may go some way towards answering some of our questions. However, before that, we need to consider the evidence I have discovered about a series of intact and unopened royal tombs at Giza, where they are, and why we should get busy trying to open these tombs which would revolutionise ancient Egyptian history.

CHAPTER FOUR

The True Locations of the Royal Tombs at Giza

Could the tombs of the famous pharaohs Cheops and Chephren have been so carefully concealed at Giza, in the vicinity of the pyramids but not in them, that they are still intact? Herodotus, the ancient Greek historian (circa 484 BC–425 BC) specifically stated that these tombs were elsewhere on the Plateau and hence not inside the pyramids that today – as in his time – bear their names. Later in this chapter I will quote his Greek words on this specific point, which strangely has been ignored until now, and I will reveal precisely where at Giza I believe these intact tombs actually are. I will also show photographic and pictorial evidence to support this claim. I believe that these tombs have remained untouched from the Old Kingdom until today, and that they could easily be opened and all of their contents retrieved.

Before I realised any of this, I unexpectedly came across evidence of what I now believe must be other, and probably earlier, royal tombs at Giza, which are still sealed, and none of which can possibly be later than the Fourth Dynasty. In fact, I have discovered no less than five more of these sealed tomb locations and, for all we know, the entire series of Fourth Dynasty pharaohs might be down there waiting to experience their 'resurrection' at the hands of modern archaeology. Alternatively, four of the seven 'tombs' I have located might not actually be tombs, but something else, a kind of subterranean Sanctuary of Sokar (the earlier name for Osiris as god of the dead), full of awesome and mysterious things that are so often alluded to in the Egyptian religious texts. What I am referring to are 'the Secrets which are concealed in Rostau', underground mysteries mentioned in the Pyramid Texts, the Coffin Texts, and the various netherworld texts, for century after century, by the Egyptian priests. And where was Rostau? It was that portion of Giza at the Sphinx, where stand the two temples known as the Valley Temple and the Sphinx Temple, and the Sphinx precinct itself.

The key to this strange enigma was revealed to me as a result of having had special access to a site that is normally closed to all visitors at Giza, which led me to make an unusual discovery. I believe that the underground tombs or mystery sites are still intact and could be opened, and all their amazing contents retrieved. In this chapter, I give the details. Those photos which cannot fit into the book's plates section may be found on this book's website, which is www.egyptiandawn.info. I am not referring to the intruded and now empty burial chamber beneath the Sphinx which I discussed in *The Sphinx Mystery* (where I reprinted 281 years' worth of eyewitness accounts of people who entered it), or to any other previously known structures. Who knows, perhaps one of these unopened and cleverly concealed chambers or chamber complexes is the legendary 'Hall of Records'. Since I believe I have found seven separate subterranean structures at Giza containing huge and heavy sarcophagi or other objects, and because Cheops and Chephren required only one tomb each, I have been rather puzzled as to what the other five subterranean chambers or chamber complexes could actually be.

In January 2001, Ioannis Liritzis, Olivia and I were given permission by the Egyptian Supreme Council of Antiquities to do some archaeological work inside the Sphinx Temple and the Valley Temple at Giza. The Valley Temple is the huge megalithic structure near the Sphinx through which tourists used to pass when they visited the pyramids and Sphinx by entering from the village in front of the Sphinx which is called Nazlett el-Sammann, although this public entrance is to be closed. This temple contains many fascinating locked portions, which I will describe fully later, and it is a far more complex building than anyone realises. It is honeycombed with a secret internal structure. I have crawled into many small holes in the walls and roof and I have found unreported chambers, shafts and passages galore inside the thick walls of the Valley Temple. I am certain that there must be just as many surprises underground as I found above ground.

I describe what I found in the Valley Temple in Chapter Seven, and photos of many of the chambers and shafts are reproduced for this book or on the website. Most of these features have never appeared on any published plans of the temple, are unknown to contemporary Egyptologists, who have never had access to them, and have never been seen even by the Giza Plateau inspectors themselves. The female inspector who accompanied us had worked on the Giza Plateau for ten years and had never set foot in any of the closed areas of the Valley Temple or entered the Sphinx Temple at all. None of the inspectors at Giza could remember anyone in living memory having entered some of the places in the Valley Temple; the locks had rusted into place and had to be smashed with hammers. The keys to them were lost anyway.

The Sphinx Temple is next door to the Valley Temple, and the whole of it is closed to tourists. Hoopoes make their nests there, and are generally undisturbed. To enter this area one must have special archaeological permission. Few archaeologists have any reason to go there, and so it is rarely visited. It is the very ruined-looking structure that sits directly in front of the Sphinx and looks as if it has been under water for centuries. In fact, it was under the sand for at least 4,000 years and was only excavated in 1936. Before that its existence was entirely forgotten, and it is probable that no one had seen it since the end of the Old Kingdom, circa 2200 BC. It was certainly completely unknown during the New Kingdom period, when structures were built on top of its sand mound.

What I discovered, only a small distance from the Sphinx inside the Sphinx Temple, was at first interpreted by me as being the probable tomb of Cheops. But, as we will see, following this evidence further, I decided that his tomb was in another location which I will discuss later on. As for the tomb of Chephren, following up the clues gathered about the probable location of the tomb of Cheops, I believe I have found it also on the basis of similar evidence, and that it is elsewhere on the Giza Plateau, as I will explain. As for what is beneath the Sphinx Temple, I believe it must be something else. But, whatever it is, it contains extremely heavy objects which were lowered into it, so it must be important. It has also been constructed by vastly enlarging some natural subterranean spaces within the limestone bedrock, as we will see.

Let us start by turning to the evidence for this large subterranean structure beneath the Sphinx Temple. It is where the trail of evidence started. This is why it was so important that I was able to spend time in the Sphinx Temple in January 2001. After I had closely scrutinised many more obvious things clamouring for my attention, I finally saw it. But even then I did not appreciate the details of its significance. I merely knew that there was something anomalous and wrong about it, so that I made a very close study of it, measured it carefully, and took many photos. It was only after I had returned to England and studied my photos and made a careful translation of Herbert Ricke's excavation report about this feature, and given it a lot of thought, that the solution occurred to me. In order to see what this feature was, I had to be completely open to a new possibility – but first I had to rule out all the 'normal' possibilities. So you see, I had my own struggle with 'consensus blindness'.

This strange feature is called by Herbert Ricke, the German excavator, a 'waste-water conduit' or 'water drain' (*Abwasserleitung*). At casual glance, it might easily be assumed that this is what it must be. After all, what else could it be? And most people would just leave it at that. But I am one of those people who will never accept any conventional explanation for anything without examining it to see whether it can really be true or not. If people assume something to be true, I am always suspicious. Assumptions are unsafe. Temple's Second Anthropic Law states: 'With regard to assumptions or interpretations of evidence, accuracy is in inverse proportion to certainty and in direct proportion to uncertainty.' An easier way of stating this is: 'The more certain a person is of being correct, the more likely it is that he or she is wrong, and the more uncertain a person is of being correct, the more likely it is that he or she may actually be correct.'

As I looked at this strange feature in the floor of the Sphinx Temple, I became more and more puzzled. I called it to the attention of Olivia and my colleague, Ioannis. They agreed with me that it looked too small to be a drain of any kind. That is, although it superficially appeared to be a drain, how could it really function properly when it was so narrow that it could barely take away any liquid? We had a spirit level with us and we placed it on the inner end of the 'drain' and saw clearly that the 'drain' sloped *inwards*, not outwards, so that it couldn't possibly have drained anything away from the structure. If it had really been a 'drain' of any kind, it would have had to drain something *in*, not *out*. And why would anybody want to do that?

I became somewhat obsessed by this feature of the Sphinx Temple and its mystery, and no one could drag me away until I had studied it as closely as was possible with the means I had at hand.

The 'conduit' was first of all a channel, which had been very carefully cut out of the bedrock and then meticulously filled with granite, so tightly that it seemed almost physically impossible to have done it. It is one thing to fit stones together so tightly that you cannot fit a razor blade between them, but to fit a stone *into the bedrock* to the same degree of precision is so uncanny that one really is tempted to believe that only *cast stone* poured in as a slurry and then set hard could possibly be bedded down so tightly in the rock floor.

Apart from granite fitted into the bedrock like this, I have often found myself wondering how anyone could possibly cut such brittle and friable stone with such precision that massive blocks weighing several tons fitted together so neatly. For Old Kingdom granite, as I know from experience, can shatter like glass when you strike it with a chisel. Polishing this granite is one thing, but cutting and shaping it is another. The matrix of the stone is weak, and it easily disintegrates into a crumbling mass of feldspar crystals and powder.

What is even more peculiar about the 'conduit', however, is that it is first inlaid with a very long, solid granite block 5.24 metres long (to the point where it disappears under the temple wall), but this in turn has a hollow running along the top of it which is then further inlaid with a series of smaller granite blocks, and you really cannot fit a razor blade between any of them. They vary in length between 64 cm and 72 cm, but are of a constant width of 42 cm, in order to fit into the central groove; the height of these little blocks is 24 cm. The overall width of the 'conduit' is 118 cm. See Plate 16, where the succession of granite blocks running along the central groove on top of the basal granite slab may clearly be seen. (I should add that I took all of these measurements myself, and that no such measurements appear in Ricke's excavation report or anywhere else.)

A space is cut in the bedrock in front of the granite blocks, which is large enough for a person to squat in, as I did when I took the close-up photo seen in Plate 17, which shows the southern end of the granite 'inlay'. From this it may be seen that a very small channel runs along under the inlaid granite blocks and emerges to follow a drain-like groove to the very end of the basal granite block. In both photos, signs of some wear may be seen to either side of the end of this drain-like groove, as if something had worn away the granite by a lateral motion across the bottom groove and thus rounded the corners off. Whatever it was, there must have been a considerable amount of pressure on the stone to accomplish this. I believe I know how and why this was done by a pattern of wear, but before I can explain, I will continue the description of the supposed 'conduit' and what I think its true function was.

In Plate 16 we can clearly see that the channel and its double-inlaid granite runs directly under the north wall of the Sphinx Temple, where a large block, and below it a much smaller block, act as convenient 'plugs' in the wall to seal the top of the 'conduit'. The temple thus sits right on top of this inward-sloping channel.

I was curious as to whether the channel continued beyond the temple wall on the other side. So I went out of the temple, round and up the bluff, and looked down on what is called the North Trench. There is no entry to the North Trench other than by jumping in and later climbing out, since the spiked metal fence at the east end has no gate and cannot be scaled. The clambering for entry and exit must take place at the west end, since the northern and southern barriers are impassable without very high ladders. Since the last excavation by Herbert Ricke in 1970, few if any people have been down into the North Trench; there is no particular reason why anyone would want to go to the considerable trouble involved, since there appears to be nothing to see.

However, despite the pleas of my accompanying inspector that it was time to go home and there was nothing to be seen in the North Trench, and that it was nearly impossible to get in, but certainly impossible to get out again, I leapt down into the trench and took my chance. I figured that if I were trapped there, someone would have to find some way to

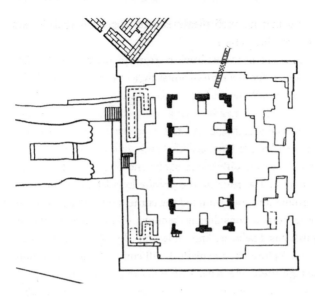

Figure 23. This is a detail from Selim Hassan's 'General Plan of the Sphinx Zone', published as Plate XVI in his excavation report of 1953. To the left are the paws of the Sphinx, and the structure in the centre is the Sphinx Temple, of which Hassan was the initial discoverer in 1936. Crossing the wall of the temple at the top (its north wall) we see clearly the path of the northern cable conduit, which Hassan believed to be a waste water drain, not realizing that it inclined inwards rather than outwards and thus could not have drained anything away, apart from the fact that it is in any case tightly blocked with small granite plugs, allowing only the narrow cable-guide channel beneath those plugs to remain open, which is too tiny for any meaningful drainage purpose anyway. Herbert Ricke, the re-excavator of the temple, stated in his report of 1970 that he had discovered this conduit for the first time, which shows that he had not bothered to read his own predecessor's excavation report of the same site, or even leaf through it, as if he had, he could not have missed the large photo of the conduit!

extricate me eventually, and I didn't mind if I spent all night there, I was going to see where the mysterious channel went. The only way I was able to justify this was to remind the inspector that Chief Inspector Mansour Radwan had told me that I should have a look at the North Trench because it would be interesting from the point of view of the wall construction. So, I overcame all protests on the grounds of this higher authority and leapt down into the trench.

Figure 23 shows a plan of the Sphinx Temple, and above the wall of the temple can be seen the North Trench (the cliff face is not depicted, so that the northern boundary of the trench is not shown). The 'conduit' may clearly be seen in the drawing passing underneath the north wall of the temple into the North Trench. It is seen at the top of the figure, as a strip at a slight angle.

The North Trench is in itself a curious feature of this strange and incompletely understood Sphinx Temple area. The southern boundary of the North Trench is the north wall of the Sphinx Temple itself, which is made of massive limestone blocks. However, when the bedrock was hacked out and levelled originally, the space was greater than that now occupied by the temple. A straight and steep cliff-face of the bedrock was cut vertically to act as what is now the northern boundary of the North Trench. The eastern end, if not for the metal fence, would be open. The western end is also cut out of the bedrock, but is not quite as high as the northern face, and is just barely accessible without ladders.

At first, when looking down into the trench from above, standing to the north, I could see a single small granite block exposed in the dust, looking like a manhole cover. Everything else was covered in a thick layer of desert dust. People often speak of sand at Giza, but desert dust is really a more accurate description of it. It is not full of quartz grains that you can feel, and has nothing in common with the kind of sand people find on a beach. It tends to flow like water and is cool in your hands. Its particles are remarkably tiny, apparently microscopic, and when stirred up it creates the most terrible choking clouds that take ages to settle back to earth again. It is always very difficult trying to crawl in this dust in a small space, because it is so hard to breathe.

When I had leapt down into the trench and investigated more carefully, I could see that the channel, its underlying granite block, and the series of small granite blocks laid into the top of this, all continued in the trench just as they had inside the temple, except that there was no evidence of a basal groove in the granite at the end of the underlying granite slab at this end. (This detail in itself is significant, as we shall see.)

I had only my hands and feet available for the clearing away of considerable quantities of tourist rubbish, and then of the thick desert dust, in order to expose the blocks, which I was therefore unable to do entirely.

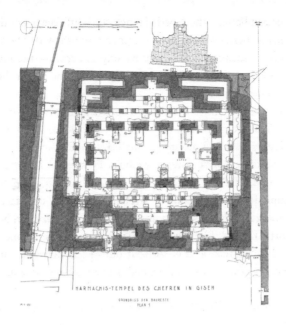

HARMACHIS-TEMPEL DES CHEFREN IN GISEH

GRUNDRISS DER BAURESTE
PLAN 1

Figure 24. This is probably the most accurate ground plan of the Sphinx Temple ever published. This remarkable labour of love was accomplished by the German archaeologist Herbert Ricke, based upon his excavations and surveys. He did not use the usual term 'Sphinx Temple' for the building, but called it the 'Harmachis Temple', after the god Harmachis (a late name for the statue of the Sphinx after it was deified). However, it is too confusing to have two names for the same temple, so we use the more usual name of Sphinx Temple, which all the English-speaking archaeologists use. This is the temple, closed to the public, which sits directly in front of the Sphinx, whose front paws and the pavement in front of them can be seen at the top of this drawing. The 'North Trench' is shown to the right of the temple. It was required to give space for the workers to construct the temple, as the north wall of this passage is a solid rock cliff, shown here in dark grey shading. The northern 'conduit', with its cable guide groove, may be clearly seen, near the middle right of the drawing, passing underneath the north wall (at right) of the temple into the North Trench and entering the bottom of the cliff face. The southern 'conduit' is not as easy to see here, but if you follow the left entrance at bottom, turn left and then right, you can see it lying across the passage and going underneath the wall either side, just before you emerge from the doorway into the passage surrounding the central court. A photo of it may be seen in Plate X. (*The illustration is Plan 1, the folding plan at the back, of Herbert Ricke* , Der Harmachistempel des Chefren in Giseh (The Harmachis Temple of Chephren at Giza), *in the series* Beiträge zur Ägyptischen Bauforschung und Altertumskunde, *Vol. 10; see notes to main text.*) This illustration is seen better in colour, as reproduced on the website.

I did have two chisels available and attached to my belt, a normal one and a spike one, which I was able to use to scrape sufficient dust from the stone surfaces to ascertain that they were indeed granite and not some other stone. Since I had no means of properly clearing these stones, I made do with cleared streaks with a flat chisel edge dragged along the stones to expose the surfaces for the purposes of the photograph in Plate 20b.

Presumably, in 1970, Ricke must have cleared these stones sufficiently to see their surfaces, but they have obviously been obscured since his time. Ricke calls attention to the fact that the channel is cut slightly into the northern cliff-face. However, he does not mention that the granite blocks stop short and do not go all the way up to the cliff-face, which is a crucial point, and bears on the possible purpose of this whole strange construction. I measured the total length of the granite from the point where it emerges from beneath the north wall of the temple to the very end of the granite just before it reaches the cliff and stops, and the length was 66.5 cm. But beyond that there is a modest space where the channel continues although the granite plugs do not. I doubt that Ricke ever cleared this portion of the channel, or he would have mentioned this feature. Since he had clearly made up his mind that he was dealing only with an insignificant, if somewhat peculiar, 'waste-water conduit', there would have appeared to be little point in being too fussy about such a detail. In his excavation plan of the temple (see Figure 24) the detail of the 'channel' reveals that it was cut a short distance into the North trench cliff-face, and the ending of the granite is also indicated. But what Ricke evidently did not do was to dig at the end of that granite.

I was disturbed by this anomaly, and suspected something odd. Using the pointed spike chisel, I thrust repeatedly down into the desert dust as far as my spike and hand could reach and was able to determine that there was no stone of any kind there. I had no means of clearing the desert dust from this substantial hole, on to which in any case I had piled a great deal of rubbish (in order to clear the 'conduit' so that it would be visible), which may be seen in the photo. But the impression I derived was that there was a low entry into the northern cliff-face here, possibly leading to a tunnel of some kind in the bedrock.

In Plate 20a, the location of this channel and its entrance into the north cliff may be seen. The potential importance of a cut entry into the cliff-face seems obvious. With a little elementary logic, the following conclusions can be reached:

1. The 'drain' inclines inwards, rather than outwards, as I demonstrated with a spirit level. Therefore, if it had 'drained' anything, it would have drained it on to the floor of the temple from outside, and not from inside the temple to the outside.

2. The mysterious channel disappears into a specially cut hole in a cliff, so that it cannot be a drain for that reason either. This is because there would have to be somewhere to drain to, or from, and something would have to have been constructed for such a purpose inside or beneath the cliff, which for drainage purposes is ridiculous, when there was a whole ground-level trench accessible and available for drainage purposes.

3. The bedrock is cut away to an unknown depth prior to reaching the cliff, after the granite terminates, and this is choked with desert dust and rubbish and has no discernible stone or rock beneath it. It therefore leads somewhere, but where?

4. The channel is meticulously and fully plugged. It should be clear to anyone that a plugged channel cannot act as a drain because it is no longer open.

5. The channel is cut out of the levelled bedrock floor, which Ricke calls the 'lower terrace' of the temple. It runs obliquely, from northeast to southwest, and thus bears no relation to the layout of the temple that lies on top of it, and which is oriented to the cardinal points squarely. It was there before the temple was, and therefore must have another purpose entirely, which did not require it to be aligned with the axis of the temple. Furthermore, this 'conduit' was once covered and concealed by the Sphinx Temple's floor, so that it could not even be seen, and its existence would have remained unknown. (Ricke did not explain how waste water could be usefully drained beneath a floor, even if the 'drain' had been inclined outwards, as he assumed, which it is not.)

6. The previous attempts to explain the channel were hopelessly wrong, so an attempt must be made to find a new explanation.

What is the previous history of discussions of this conduit? Herbert Ricke, who published (in German) the last report of the excavation of the Sphinx Temple in 1970,[1] believed that he was the first to notice or discuss the conduit. Speaking of the conduit and also of a smaller, less prominent, and more obscured conduit in the southern end of the temple, Ricke says (translated):

'They are described here for the first time, since the manner of their inclusion into the temple remains a matter of surmise.'[2]

I don't know how or why Ricke thought he was the first to discuss the conduit, for it was certainly discussed by the previous excavator of the Sphinx Temple, Selim Hassan. In his book *The Great Sphinx and Its Secrets* of 1953,[3] which contains the reports of his excavations, the cutting into the bedrock cliff-face in the North Trench is clearly visible on the right in Figure 95 on page 150, though Hassan says nothing about it in that place. And, as we shall see, he paid no particular attention to it. However, he gives very prominent attention to the conduit itself. He was the first to uncover it since Old Kingdom times, more than 4,000 years earlier. It appears very clearly drawn, crossing obliquely beneath the north wall of the temple, in his foldout plan, Plate 16, 'Sphinx Zone', following page 28, although the North Trench is not shown at all in this plan. But Figure 15 on page 27 is a large photo filling half a page, which shows the conduit very clearly, and is entitled 'A channel in the floor of the Northern passage'. Here is what Hassan says about the conduit, introducing it by first mentioning the passage which is now called the North Trench:

At the northern side of the temple is a passage measuring 31.50 x 3.0 metres, and running east–west [the North Trench]. The southern wall of the passage is formed by the northern wall of the great court [of the Sphinx Temple], while its northern wall is cut in the natural rock. At a distance of about 18.50 metres from its entrance, a channel, one metre wide, crosses the passage obliquely from east to west, passing under the southern wall to the court, and ending in a cutting in the northern wall of the passage. This channel, which has a total length of 10 metres, starts as a mere depression in the floor of the northern side of the court, and slopes to a depth of 1.25 metres at its end. It is paved with granite (Fig.

15). The tunnel by which it passes under the wall of the court is plugged with blocks of limestone.

A similar channel exists in the floor of the passage of the southern entrance; and it appears to have its source at the southern side of the eastern recess. Perhaps these were drains to carry off rainwater or libations.[4]

That is all Hassan has to say about the channels. It is very odd that Herbert Ricke was unaware of the photos and text dealing with these features in his predecessor's excavation report, especially as he comes to the same conclusion about their purpose. Of course, we have seen with the main channel that it slopes inwards – something which neither Hassan nor Ricke had noticed – and therefore could have drained away neither rainwater nor libations.

The southern channel is not plugged with granite at all, and is a rather rough piece of work, and hence not nearly so interesting. It may be seen in Plate 22. It too goes under a wall of the temple, and clearly predates the structure. I shall discuss it further later on.

Before I explain what I believe the northern channel in the Sphinx Temple actually was, and why I believe it indicates the location of a still-unopened tomb, we had better read what Herbert Ricke said about it in his 1970 excavation report. Ricke, unlike English-speaking Egyptologists, who all call the building the Sphinx Temple, chooses to call the building by the name of the Harmachis Temple, using one of the names of the Sphinx, Harmachis, which was common in the New Kingdom period. I have translated this section of his report from the German, but for the sake of accuracy in such a highly technical description, I was greatly assisted by Dr Horst Jaritz, former director of the Swiss Institute at Cairo (to whom I wish to offer my profuse thanks), who revised my translation for me, since I was so worried that I might misrepresent some detail in Ricke's account:

Water drains [*Ableitungen für Wasser*] are found at two places in the temple, both of which appear to be older than the Harmachis Temple. These probably belong to some structures of which no trace now survives [*sonst spurlos verschwundenen Einrichtung*] on the formerly clear lower terrace [this is how he refers to the levelled bedrock surface on which the temple rests]. They are described here for the first time, since the manner of their inclusion into the temple leads us to suspect their greater age. One of the drainages lies in the south-eastern part of the temple and consists of a pit in the bedrock and two channel sections (Plan I). [This drawing is reproduced here as Figure 24.] The pit lies under some remains of the north section of the enclosure wall [*Umfassungsmauer*] of the valley temple area in the core masonry of the Harmachis Temple (Plate II, *a*, under the large block in the middle of the picture, which bridges the pit). In the pit a channel chiselled in the bedrock leads in from the north, the north end of which has been built over by the core masonry of the first construction period; it is filled up with rubble, thus putting it out of action. [Ricke did not remove the rubble to examine what might be underneath.] This channel crosses the passage which connects the southern anteroom with the courtyard gallery. While constructing the door leading here into the courtyard gallery, the slot through which the lower pivot of the door-leaf would have been inset, was arranged perpendicular to the direction of the entranceway – everywhere else in the temple parallel to the direction of the entranceway, – in order not to cross the waste water conduit; in consequence, this must already have existed prior to the construction of the door. In the same pit a second channel discharges inwards from the south, which apparently was intended for the diverting of rainwater away from the Valley Temple area. This channel section seems to have been kept operational; it was also not entirely covered by the rebuilding of the Harmachis Temple.

The second waste water conduit is found on the north side of the temple (Plan I); it consists of a pit and a very carefully cut channel. The pit, which is deeply cut in the rock, lies partially under the solid rock which bounds the lower terrace on the northern side. [This refers to what is now called the North Trench, the northern edge of which consists of a substantial artificial cliff hacked out of the solid bedrock. Although the pit extends into this cliff-face slightly, the granite plugs stop well short of it, as I have pointed out earlier in my own text.] The channel leads in from the courtyard gallery under the north wall of the temple in the pit. It is comprised of two trough-like worked granite blocks tightly fitting together with a narrow semi-circular channel in them, which has been covered with finely worked square granite stones (Plate 16, *a*). The cutting in the bedrock, into which the channel has been imbedded, has been covered by a very large block during both building periods of the Harmachis Temple; the one of the second period of construction is still in situ (Plate 16, *a*). The one from the 1st period of construction has left traces in the bedrock (Figure 7 and Plate 10, *b*); it must have been of granite, for it lay in the row of granite facing of the 1st construction period. What leads one to believe that these waste water conduits as well are older than the temple, is that they have been preserved at the opening into the gallery of the court in this position which is so difficult to understand [*schwer verständliche*] and in their oblique direction within the original gentle easterly downwards slope of the lower terrace. Whether this waste water conduit was made use of after the erection of the temple or had been covered completely by a pavement is no longer discernible. One could however imagine that the court pavement might have been laid with a slope beginning from the entry of the channel, in order to carry away either rainwater or water for purification. If it were for rainwater the entry should rather have lain in the middle of the court, as was the case in the funerary temple of Chephren; water for purification could have come from an altar, which might have been erected in the court.

One might find it odd that drainage water ran in pits which would have been cut out of the very rock and which must have quickly overflowed. We have been told that 'an American woman searching for chambers under the Sphinx' bored a vertical hole in the rock in one of the pillar pits on the west side of the temple and in this hole ground water was encountered at a depth of about one metre. The rock must therefore have a porous layer, in which a sheet of groundwater can form. Such layers are visible on the stone gradation [*an der Felsstufe*] on which the Causeway of the Chephren Funerary Monument [he means the Chephren Causeway leading from the Pyramid of Chephren with the Funerary Temple which lies in front of it on the east] stands (Plate 6, *b*); they are inclined to the southeast, and could readily drain off any quantities of water towards the valley. Such softer and therefore strongly-weathered layers can be seen everywhere in the blocks of the core masonry, which have been broken in the vicinity (Plate 13).[5]

It is essential to realise that the channels were hacked out of the bedrock and the 100 tons of granite carefully and methodically laid down into the north channel *before the construction of the temple*. This is because the temple was then built on top of them, and thick limestone walls constructed across them. Ricke correctly observes that the channels must have predated the completed structure of the temple. This means that *they cannot be later than* the Fourth Dynasty and the reign of Chephren, which ended 2533 BC, according to conventional chronologies. (In any case the date cannot be later than that, as if the chronology were to be revised, it would be pushed backwards in time, not forwards.) The open question thus consists not of any later *date*, but of the *purpose* of the channels. As for the southern channel, which contains no granite plugs, I suspect it might also lead to some subterranean tomb or tunnel. But what I suggest about the northern channel does not rest only upon speculation. For the northern channel has features which provide some *evidence of an intent*.

The evidence lies in the granite blocks that fill this channel, and in some other features, primarily the mysterious tiny groove beneath the small granite blocks that are so tightly wedged into the long granite basal slab. I am convinced that the channel had nothing to do with drainage of any kind. We have already seen that it slopes inwards so could only drain inwards, and since obviously no one would intentionally flood a temple with waste water, we can happily jettison Ricke's description of this channel as a waste-water conduit. But we have also seen that enormous trouble was taken to pack this channel very tightly indeed with a gigantic slab of granite which, unless it was some form of 'cast stone', must have been brought all the way from Aswan, and must weigh about 100 tons; this was clearly an incredible feat indicating a serious purpose. Having done this, the Egyptians carved a long rectangular incision out of the entire top of the granite slab, and then excavated a further tiny groove only 9 cm deep along the centre of this rectangular incision. Then the Egyptians meticulously produced a succession of granite blocks, also presumably brought from Aswan, which were all precisely 42 cm wide and fitted so tightly into the incision in the top of the basal granite slab that it is impossible to fit a razor blade between either them and the slab or between the blocks themselves. All of these granite blocks were packed absolutely tightly over the thin groove, as if to hold something down firmly inside it.

This enormous amount of labour, expense and trouble almost defies belief. Why would such pains be taken over a 'waste-water conduit'? Whatever the purpose of this strange channel and the meticulously constructed granite plugs that fill it, and their curious configuration, it was something immensely important to the Egyptians. So, since drainage is out of the question, we are left with the baffling enigma: *what is the groove for, if not for a liquid?*

If it is not liquid, it could be solid. But solid what? Something that moves back and forth, presumably. And what is solid and moves back and forth within a long thin groove? Answer: *a cable*.

I believe that the groove was constructed as a cable-guide for lowering something incredibly heavy such as a basalt sarcophagus into a subterranean tomb. The entire channel seemed to me to be a meticulously manufactured inlet to an underground tunnel. It would have been used to moor a cable in order to lower extremely heavy objects, centrally suspended in a net, into an underground chamber. The groove would thus be for running the cable along, and the perfectly fitted granite blocks above and below would prevent the cable from moving in any direction other than backwards and forwards. We may therefore have here in this so-called 'channel' a rare surviving example of a lowering-mechanism such as we know that the Egyptians must have used in countless instances, but of which they have left no other trace that I know of (apart from the other Giza 'conduits', which I will be discussing here).

But if the 'channel' is really a lowering device, the question arises: is the possible chamber (presumably for a burial) still intact, and is whatever was lowered into it still there? The first thing to do would clearly be to investigate and find whether there is really any tunnel or chamber, but this would require a minor excavation. It seems obvious that any burial which may exist or have existed at this spot could not have been later than the Fourth Dynasty, since the Sphinx Temple was definitely built on top of this 'channel', and there is no one who believes that the Sphinx Temple could possibly be later than that. (In Chapter Seven I give the actual dates we obtained for the Sphinx Temple.)

Those who carry the cord

Figure 25. Figure 43 (Vol. I, p. 166) from Alexandre Piankoff and N. Rambova's *The Tomb of Ramesses VI*, Bollingen Series Vol. XL. 1, Pantheon Books, New York, 1954, 2 vols. The illustration is described by the text in the tomb as portraying 'those who carry the cord in the west, who divide the fields for the spirits. Take hold of the cord, seize the measuring rope of the Westerners [*the dead*]. Their spirits go to your seats, you gods. To your places, you spirits! The Divine One is in peace! The field of the spirits has been reckoned by the rope. You are correct (in measuring) for those who exist [*the blessed dead*], you are correct for those who are not [*the evil and annihilated dead*]. Re [the Sun] says to them: Correct is the rope in the West. Re is satisfied with the measuring rope. Your portion is yours, you gods. Your allotments are yours, you spirits. Behold, Re has made your field, he has distributed for you your land portions among you. Hail, the One of the Horizon [Horus]! . . . Glory to you, measurers of the fields, who preside over the rope in the West. O establish the fields to be given to the gods and to the spirits!' (translation by Piankoff, pp. 166-7). Although this giant rope represents measurements of the surface of the ground in order to mark off enclosures or 'fields' of the gods or the blessed dead, referring to their precincts and their tombs, such ropes would also have been used, threefold or fourfold, to lower heavy sarcophagi into tombs at the bottoms of deep shafts. In the early twentieth century, an international survey was undertaken by a rope manufacturer to find the strongest material in the world for ropes, and he found that the strongest was Egyptian cotton. We should thus never underestimate the strength of the ropes used in ancient Egypt, as they were made of this material.

However, there are some anomalies in the north wall of the Sphinx Temple at the precise point under which the 'channel' runs which must signify something. It seems to my eye that the giant limestone block of the temple wall, which was laid directly over the 'channel', not only juts out northwards far too much, but seems somehow to have been 'rammed in', after the construction of the main wall. The impression this gives me is that the 'channel' was there before the temple wall was built, but a large hole was left in the wall over it, and later that hole was plugged with a limestone block. In fact, Ricke seems to believe that there was originally a huge granite block in this space, during what he calls the 'first construction period', and that later, during the 'second construction period', it was replaced by this limestone block. (Ricke's two periods of construction are hypothetical, not certain. The time that might have elapsed between them, assuming there were two phases of construction at all, is not known.) This does not affect our argument, though it is a matter which might hold more clues about what was really going on. But the fact that the channel was under either one or both blocks is undisputed.

If the 'channel' was really a lowering device, then it would mean that it was cut into the bedrock and constructed first, with the Sphinx Temple then being built on top of it, with its north wall laid right across it. A gap (now filled with a huge limestone block) was left in the wall at that point; later the lowering device was actually used to lower a sarcophagus, and then finally the huge stone block plugged the hole in the temple wall when the tomb was sealed and access was no longer required: all of this must have been done with the approval of a pharaoh himself. In other words, a pharaoh would lie in the tomb indicated by the 'channel', and for all we know might still be there.

We must recall that the Sphinx Temple is known to have been entirely covered in sand during the New Kingdom, and was only cleared in 1936, for the first time since perhaps 2000 BC or even earlier. If a tomb exists in the spot I have suggested, it cannot in my opinion have been robbed, since it was physically inaccessible from the time of the First Intermediate Period. The dissolution of Egyptian civilisation towards the end of the Sixth Dynasty, circa 2200 BC, and the commencement of the First Intermediate Period, probably coincided with the covering of the Sphinx Temple with sufficient sand that tomb robbing would have been rendered impossible because the sand could simply not be shifted. Prior to that, this holy spot at Giza would have been well protected by royal guards, and tomb robbing prior to the collapse of the Sixth Dynasty can be safely ruled out. We know that the north wall of the Sphinx Temple has stood since the time the final limestone block was rammed into place above the channel. That means that the channel has never had its granite plug removed, so it remains a seal over whatever it conceals, which is therefore most definitely intact.

The opening in the north cliff-face is too small for any substantial tomb robbing to have taken place, for the opening is not big enough for anything of any size to be removed. Indeed, when the granite plugs were put into place, there was just enough space for a coffin and individual people and small objects to be let down into the tomb, if it is a tomb. And perhaps the final use for the cable would have been to lower a heavy portcullis. If so, excavators will find it is still there, and will find their way blocked.

A close inspection of the granite basal slab–ends to either side of the groove as it opens into the Sphinx Temple shows pretty clear signs of a pattern of lateral wear, as I mentioned earlier. I believe that this may be evidence of a cable bearing some heavy load swinging from one side to the other as it emerged from the groove, wearing away the granite.

Could it be that I might have located the legendary tomb of King Cheops?

A tomb of Cheops in the precinct of the Sphinx! Intact!

This could be the ultimate origin of all the traditions, through the ages, of the Sphinx guarding the tomb of an Egyptian king. And if there is any chance at all that there is an intact tomb from the Fourth Dynasty (circa 2500 BC), shouldn't we be making an attempt to open it? The minor tomb of a young king named Tutankhamun yielded hordes of priceless treasure, but that would be nothing compared to what we would certainly find within the tomb of a potentate as powerful as King Cheops. Furthermore, we could expect texts to be included, which would be the first reliable or extended texts from that period of history, predating the 'Pyramid Texts' carved on the walls of the small Fifth and Sixth Dynasty pyramids. The Tomb of Cheops would give us a direct insight into the very origins of civilisation.

However, I will explain – with evidence – why I believe the tombs of Cheops and Chephren are actually higher up the hill. So whose tomb would this be, underneath the Sphinx Temple? As explained later, in Chapter Seven, some archaeological evidence exists which associates King Send (or Sened) of the Second Dynasty with the Valley Temple next door to the Sphinx Temple. And, as explained in Chapter Seven, there is also evidence associating kings Hotepsekhemui and Nebra (or Raneb), the first and second kings of the Second Dynasty respectively, with the Valley Temple of Mycerinus (which is mentioned again later on, as site of another tomb), along with the name of King Sneferu, the first king of the Fourth Dynasty. But apart from Cheops, Chephren and King Send of the Second Dynasty, we have no archaeological evidence associating any specific early king with either the Valley Temple or the Sphinx Temple. So this presumed tomb could be the tomb of any king prior to Cheops. It might, for instance, be the tomb of King Sneferu, the founder of the Fourth Dynasty, and father of Cheops. If not a real tomb, it might be a symbolic tomb, or it might be a 'Hall of Records', or anything you like. But we must keep in mind that, whatever it is, it certainly contains at least one vastly heavy object, probably of a minimum of forty tons in weight.

However, let us not make the mistake of imagining that the tiny passage in the north cliff-face is the only way in. If we find that it does indeed lead down, we will undoubtedly discover that a vast cavern complex exists beneath the Sphinx Temple and the cliff north of it, and that this complex probably extends under the whole of the Valley Temple as well. And in this connection, I believe that we should make a closer study of the channel lying beneath the southern end of the Sphinx Temple, which we may see in Plate 22. This was probably another cable-lowering channel, but as it is not inlaid with the same careful granite blocks, it was probably a more workaday cable facility, rather than one used for a heavy sarcophagus or portcullis, and thus not requiring the same degree of strength in the sealing over of the cable hole. If so, then this lowering area might have been for much of the actual tomb treasure itself, which would have been far lighter in weight, or even for carrying workmen up and down as a more convenient access route. We should keep in mind that Ricke describes it as having two channels, which suggests a double-cable arrangement, perhaps for continual raising and lowering. Alternatively, there could have been a counterweight on the end of one cable, which was connected with the other. We will see that sophisticated and extremely robust pulleys made of basalt existed at Giza in the Old Kingdom times, as Hassan excavated two of them. (See Plates 24a and 24b.)

There is actually further striking evidence – sitting in plain sight within the Sphinx Temple – for the existence of a huge subterranean cavern and chamber complex beneath the structure. But this evidence has not been noticed by previous investigators. The prolonged inaccessibility of the Sphinx Temple to visitors is one possible reason for this, of course. Sitting very obviously on the floor of the Sphinx Temple, towards its western end, is a large mass of what appears to be alabaster. It is not part of the structure, but as it was too heavy to move, it was just left there by the various excavators. Presumably any archaeologists who gave it a glance would have imagined it was left over from construction, if they gave it much thought at all.

It struck me that it must have been sitting in the temple because it had been preserved there on purpose in antiquity, but that its significance had been overlooked during the two excavations of the temple, and it had merely been allowed to stay sitting there because it was too troublesome to remove it. I was attracted to it because it was so beautiful and white and gleaming. I did not at first appreciate its significance, but because I had been authorised by the Supreme Council of Antiquities to remove small samples of stone, I brought a small piece back with me. I thought at first that this would be useful because it appeared to be an unhewn specimen from which so many of the alabaster blocks had apparently been carved, that perhaps it had been left as a source of replacement or repair, and that an analysis of it might prove interesting in connection with construction materials. It was only later, some time after I had worked out the significance of the conduit and its cable groove, that it occurred to me suddenly what this stone might really be.

Egyptian alabaster, also known as travertine, is not the same as European alabaster (calcium sulfate), and is really a variant form of limestone, being pure calcium carbonate in regards to its chemical composition. I have been to one ancient alabaster mine in the desert east of Hawara, and the ancient Egyptians were very keen to get good supplies of this beautiful material for both construction and for works of art such as vases and statues. Being familiar as I already was with the fragments of alabaster from the Hawara Quarry, which I had been able to inspect, I recognised that the Sphinx Temple material was purer, whiter, bulkier and more beautiful. But still it took a while to grasp the true significance of it.

At the Hawara Quarry I had seen where the now-exhausted alabaster seams had run through the cliffs, and I understood that very big pieces of alabaster, which are thick as well as high, were unusual because not all alabaster seams are thick enough to yield truly large chunks. But the 'alabaster' sitting in the Sphinx Temple is very large indeed. And it is truly beautiful, a photo of the piece I brought away with me can be seen on the website. I suspected that this alabaster was not ordinary alabaster, but a special kind that is only found in caves, and not in alabaster mines. I have now come to a conclusion as to what this magnificent alabaster really is: I believe that it was extracted from an enlarged limestone cavern lying underground beneath the Sphinx and Valley Temples.

In order to test this hypothesis in a truly neutral way, I took my piece of Sphinx Temple 'alabaster' along to the British Museum of Natural History, where I often take mineral samples. I handed my piece of Sphinx Temple 'alabaster' to the geologist as one of a succession of mineral specimens for his opinion. I did not tell him anything at all about it. He didn't know it was from Egypt, and at first presumed it was from China, as so many of my other specimens are. He marvelled at its appearance and said simply: 'It's a stalactite.' I was thrilled at this confirmation of my hypothesis by an expert, as it was precisely what I had suspected myself.

In order to test the hypothesis a little further, I pretended to complain to the geologist that he could not possibly be right, saying that I had found the piece of 'alabaster', which he correctly identified as calcium carbonate, outside lying on the ground, and that it could not come from a cave. He said that it definitely came from a cave, and if I had found it outside on the ground, somebody must have left it there, because it could only occur inside a cave. He said it was a pure calcium carbonate exudation from limestone rock, which had accumulated inside a cave over the ages; this was why it had crystals on its surface. (See Plate on the website, where these may clearly be seen.) He said the water seeps through the limestone, and this pure carbonate crystal forms as a stalactite inside the cavern, which is within the limestone. Well, I then told him the truth and he agreed with me that the 'alabaster' sitting on the floor of the Sphinx Temple could only be a stalactite from a cavern in limestone, and evidently from the limestone that forms the Giza Plateau beneath or near where the stalactite mass was sitting.

If such a huge mass of stalactite had been removed from a cavern in the limestone beneath the Sphinx Temple, this could only mean that the Egyptians were busy down there enlarging natural caverns and shaping them into chambers. Furthermore, to bring such a huge piece up to the surface in itself proves the existence of raising and lowering mechanisms capable of doing that, because it must weigh two or three tons. In other words, we have here separate evidence for the necessary existence of the very cable mechanisms that I believe I have discovered in the form of the two conduits.

But there is more to this story. For a large proportion of the Valley Temple, especially the sealed portions that the public never sees, but also including the floor of the Ascending Passage, up which everyone walks when they leave the temple to go on to the Chephren Causeway and make their way towards the pyramids, is composed of gigantic masses of this very same beautiful alabaster. Often the alabaster is interspersed with red granite, providing a stunning effect. Within the Valley Temple, there is a surviving enclosed stairway leading to the roof, which is of course locked and almost never entered by anyone. At first when I went up and down this stairway I assumed that its walls were of limestone. But then I became suspicious. I pressed my torch against the wall and, sure enough, the stone round that point glowed with golden light. This translucence is a sure sign of 'alabaster' or stalactite, rather than of limestone proper, and proved that the walls only appeared to be of limestone because they were dirty and covered in the grime of desert dust, making them appear grey to the eye. But originally this enclosed stairway was a beautiful sparkling white, and if flaming torches were carried up it, a golden effulgence would have followed the bearer on all sides as he ascended. Once the roof is reached, the stone of the roof itself reverts to ordinary limestone. Limestone is opaque, but this 'Valley Temple alabaster' is translucent. The translucent quality of the 'alabaster', and also its extraordinary sparkling beauty and pure whiteness, would have seemed wonderful to the ancient Egyptians, as indeed they do to me.

It may well be that the reason the nearby capital of Memphis was known as 'White Walls' is that it had walls made of this material. If so, the caverns left after its extraction must be truly vast, like a small underground city.

The quantity of beautiful white 'alabaster' contained within the Valley Temple is overwhelming. It certainly amounts to many thousands of tons. If it all came from the caverns beneath the two temples, as seems likely, then a huge underground complex must have been created there, from which so much stalactite material could have been extracted. There must be many chambers, and if we consider the vast extent of what King Chephren, to whom the Valley Temple is attributed, is credited with having built above ground, then he – or whoever before him might really have done it – must have created something comparable beneath the surface. This underground burial complex could just possibly be a subterranean rival to the Giza pyramids themselves. Whatever it is, it will be large enough to hold a great deal of treasure, perhaps even all the temple treasures and libraries, which could have been hidden at the collapse of the Sixth Dynasty when social order was breaking down and the priests could see that the mobs would be coming to steal and destroy everything. And even more tantalisingly, it might all be perfectly intact.

We do have one famous example of evidence that this kind of concealment took place at the Valley Temple: the huge and magnificent statue of Chephren, one of the triumphs of ancient Egyptian art, which is now in the Cairo Museum. But it was found shoved down the well in the floor of the temple, an obvious act of concealment by the priests. Just imagine what could be concealed below the floors of the temples!

So what are we waiting for?

I suggested in a previous book, *The Crystal Sun*, why there were strong reasons to suspect that there would be a subterranean chamber, tunnel, or space beneath the western end of the 'Ascending Passage' which rises at a slope of 26 ½ degrees out of the Valley Temple on to the Chephren Causeway.[6] That book was published before I had access to the Sphinx Temple or made any of these discoveries, and I made the suggestion for other reasons entirely. I am now more than ever convinced of its validity. Furthermore, I have found two more granite cable grooves in the Valley Temple itself, both opening to the west of the structure through its western wall, which could have been used for raising and lowering any number of heavy objects into the subterranean depths immediately to the west of the temple. One of these practically adjoins the Ascending Passage, and could have serviced a chamber beneath it. One of these granite cable

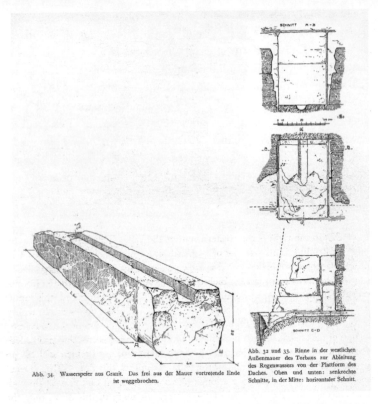

Abb. 34. Wasserspeier aus Granit. Das frei aus der Mauer vortretende Ende ist weggebrochen.

Abb. 32 und 33. Rinne in der westlichen Außenmauer des Torbaus zur Ableitung des Regenwassers von der Plattform des Daches. Oben und unten: senkrechte Schnitte, in der Mitte: horizontaler Schnitt.

Figure 26. At left we see the 'water spout of granite' which Hölscher excavated. It has broken off the other portion of it in the outer west wall of the roof of the Valley Temple. This closely resembles the great northern cable groove in the floor of the Sphinx Temple. At right, we see different views of the portion of the cable groove remaining in the wall. At top, the section view shows the same semicircular opening of the groove at the bottom of a strong and heavy stone as we saw in the Sphinx Temple, for keeping the cable from flying up or sliding to the side, and for guiding it precisely with these strong stone materials, for the lifting of huge weights. The middle drawing at right shows the plan view of an exposed portion of the groove in the wall, looking down upon it. The bottom drawing shows an east-west section looking north, the groove being obscured from sight here but travelling underneath the lowest of the three large stone blocks from right (the roof) to left. (Hölscher's own captions to these drawings, translated, read: 'Figures 32 and 33. Channel in the western exterior wall of the Valley Temple for draining of rainwater from the platform of the roof. Above and below: vertical sections, in the middle: horizontal section. Figure 34. Rainspout of granite. The end which protruded from the wall has broken away.')

176

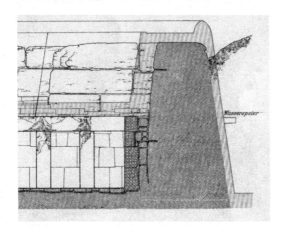

Figure 27. To the right is the western wall of the Valley Temple, with the 'water spout' protruding. This was one of two such grooves sticking out of the back of the temple which would have acted as cable guides for the lowering of heavy objects in to the subterranean spaces, which must have been accessible at the foot of the western face of the temple. Because the 'water spout' is drawn in red, this means that it is the excavator's reconstruction of how it would have appeared. In reality, he found it broken off (see Figure 28), and this is the extension of the remaining portion of the channel as that broken portion would have appeared and protruded. Above the spout the artist has sketched the mound of sand which still lay up against most of the western wall of the Valley Temple at this time (1910). (Detail from Hölscher's book, showing a longitudinal section from east to west through the Forecourt and Pillared Hall of the temple, although in this detail only the western end of the Pillared Hall is shown, at left.)

grooves may be seen in Figure 26, where four views of it are shown. It clearly resembles the 'conduits' of the Sphinx Temple, but instead of being dug into the floor, these cable grooves open on to the ceiling of the Valley Temple, where there was plenty of room for teams of men to haul the cables up and down without having to stand inside the temple itself. In Figure 28, a plan of the Valley Temple, we may see (indicated as *Entwässerung*) where both of these cable grooves emerge from the wall. Naturally, they are both assumed to be water drains by the excavator. In Hölscher's excavation report of the Valley Temple, he calls attention to a 'water spout' cut out of red granite (*Wasserspeier aus Granit*).[7] See Figures 27–29 for his drawing of this 'water spout', and note how it resembles the others we have considered. This 'spout' runs from east to

177

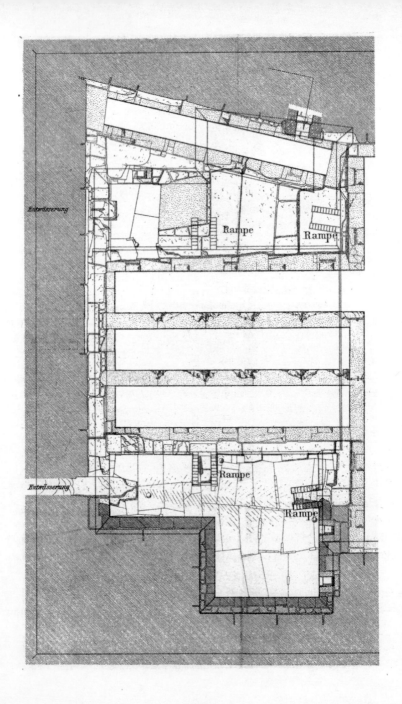

Entwässerung

Rampe   Rampe

Entwässerung

Rampe

Rampe

178

Figure 28. A detailed drawing by the excavator Uvo Hölscher of the west end of the Valley Temple at Giza, as seen in plan from above. The lines laid over this drawing in red, marking *Rampe*, are suggestions by the excavator of what he considered signs of ramps or steps. From my own close examination of the roof of this structure, I was unable to find evidence of any of these, despite the fact that I walked around inspecting the locations with the original of this and other Hölscher diagrams actually in my hand and held them side by side at each point. I am therefore inclined to doubt Hölscher's surmises about these ramps and steps, and his other suggested structures as well. The existence or non-existence of the ramps or steps is not in itself important, what is worrying is that Hölscher insisted upon the existence of features of which I could detect not one tiny shred of evidence of any kind, and even drew them (in red) on his plan of the structure as if there were certainty about them. His text contains no justification for this, so it causes concern that he wished to 'add features' to the temple, while as we shall see in Chapter 7, he omitted a vast number of far more important features from his plans and his report altogether. This erratic behaviour raises questions about his judgement. At the top of the drawing may be seen the slanting 'Ascending Passage' which rises up from the floor level of the temple at 'the golden slope' and opens onto the Chephren Causeway. I believe that a large sealed chamber exists beneath the western, elevated end of this passage, and that it has not been opened since the Old Kingdom. I first suggested this in *The Crystal Sun* (2000). At the left of this drawing, we twice see the German word *Entwässerung* ('drainage'). Hölscher believed the two 'water drains' at these points led rain water off the roof of the temple into the sand west of the temple. In Figure 26 may be seen one of these extraordinary 'waste water drains', laboriously cut out of a large piece of Aswan granite. I maintain that these 'drains' were nothing of the kind, but were cable-guide channels, or cable grooves, for the lowering of sarcophagi or other heavy stones and objects into subterranean or concealed chambers. The northern 'drain', which is the higher one in the view, would have been used for lowering objects from ground level into the concealed chamber beneath the Ascending Passage and what I believe to be the adjoining chamber south of it, which is directly below this 'drain'. The southern 'drain', seen lower in this view, would have been used to lower objects from ground level into the subterranean chamber which I believe to lie beneath the south-west corner of the temple (bottom left in this view). These 'drains', i.e. cable grooves, were made of precious granite brought from Aswan because of the strength of the stone needed to bear the enormous weights placed on the cables by stone sarcophagi weighing up to forty tons. Basalt pulleys such as those seen in Plates 24a and 24b, known to be of Old Kingdom date, would have been used for these cables. Having the operators of the cables on the temple roof would have given much greater ease and control, for attaching objects at ground level to the west of the temple and operating the cables from a position at least thirty feet (ten metres) higher than ground level helped with the stability and the steadying of the loads as they descended. But for this, a strong granite cable groove was essential. Anything made of wood would have snapped, and a weak stone would have crumbled. Today we would use steel for such a purpose.

(This is a detail from folding Plate XII of Hölscher's book.)

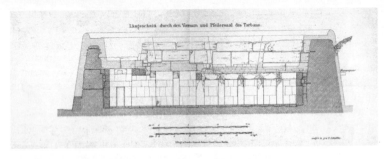

Figure 29. East-west longitudinal section of the Valley Temple, through the Forecourt (left) and Pillared Hall (centre). At right, projecting from the west wall, is a *Wasserspeier*, 'water-spout', which I believe to have been a cable channel and groove. This is from Hölscher.

west and emerges from the west wall, though its end is today broken off. They share the feature of being small and narrow, and would have been hopeless as water drains. If any of these is a cable groove, all of them are cable grooves, for they are all of the same nature, and made with infinite care and patience, and at great expense.

I have discovered so many concealed shafts, passages and chambers within the Valley Temple, which I was actually able to enter, that I can well imagine a vast number of further ones that are sealed and inaccessible. I have photographed as much as I could, despite the difficult conditions. But I consider my discoveries a mere prelude to what will eventually be found if, that is, permission can be obtained. The details of what I found are described in Chapter 7, and the photos that could not fit in this book are on the book's website.

Certainly the huge vertical shafts, which I found and photographed, concealed in the walls of the temple and not appearing on any existing plan of the structure, could have been important for access to subterranean spaces. It seems to me incredible that no one has studied the Valley Temple properly since the publication of the only excavation report of it appeared in 1912.

Earlier, I mentioned that I believe that I have found the locations of the intact tombs of Cheops and Chephren, but that they are not near the Sphinx. Once again, I have 'followed the conduits'. It became clear to me that two other mysterious conduits elsewhere at Giza bore an

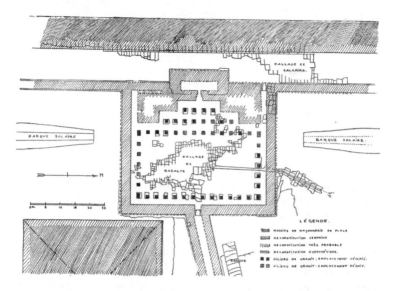

Figure 30. This is a plan of the now vanished Funerary Temple of Cheops, which sat at the foot of the eastern face of the Great Pyramid. This version of the plan is based upon an earlier one by Jean-Phillipe Lauer, re-drawn by Selim Hassan, who says: 'the reader may judge for himself if the existing remains justify [the] imaginary reconstruction'. Today, only a portion of the beautiful and magnificent basalt floor in the centre survives, so this is an attempt to reconstruct the plan from very scanty evidence. At the bottom is the Cheops Causeway, now also vanished except for foundation traces and a few odd blocks, shooting off at an angle to the right. To left and right are two oblong funerary boat pits, for 'solar barques'. The main importance of this image for our purposes is to see the prominent 'waste water drain' in the form of a limestone channel leading from the centre of the court towards the right (northwards), which passed under the north wall of the temple, and continued onto the Plateau in front of the pyramid. I believe this to be the cable-guide channel for lowering a mammoth stone sarcophagus, and other grave goods, into the tomb of Cheops, which I believe to be situated either beneath the floor of the temple at the left end of the channel, or just north of the temple at the right end of the channel. I do not believe the tomb has been robbed or opened since Old Kingdom times. (From Selim Hassan, *The Great Pyramid of Khufu and Its Mortuary Chapel*, Cairo, 1960, Figure 11, a folding plate which follows page 38, and strangely precedes the next folding plate which is called Figure 10.)

181

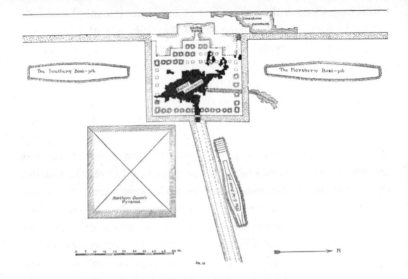

The Southern Boat-pit.   The Northern Boat-pit

Northern Queen's Pyramid

N

Figure 31. Here is another, and probably more reliable, view of the plan of the Funerary Temple of Cheops, drawn by Selim Hassan himself, of which he says that it 'shows in solid lines all the features of the temple that can be vouched for by the aid of the evidence of the rock foundations, and these can be seen by anyone who cares to examine the site.' This view shows the surviving basalt in black, and much more of the Causeway, plus an additional boat pit beside it. The cable-guide channel is more clearly shown in this view. (This is Figure 10 from Selim Hassan, *The Great Pyramid of Khufu and Its Mortuary Chapel*, Cairo, 1960. It is bound as a folding plate after Figure 11, and both are found between pages 38 and 39.)

uncanny resemblance to the ones I had been investigating at the Sphinx and Valley Temples. Both of these had also been dismissed by all archaeologists as 'water drains', and with the same lack of justification. Both were originally covered by huge temple structures, and resembled in most important features the northern channel beneath the Sphinx Temple. It is now time to consider them.

As for the tombs of Cheops and Chephren, I do not believe they are at the location of Rostau, which is the area round the Sphinx, but at more appropriate locations for those two particular kings. For these tombs, we have to move higher up the Plateau, where the evidence is to be found, as we may see in Figure 30 and Figure 31, which both come from Selim Hassan's study of the Funerary Temple of Cheops which once stood at the eastern foot of the Great Pyramid.[8] And I do believe I have located the *precise sites* of the tombs of both Cheops and Chephren at Giza, neither of which is actually inside a pyramid, and thus they are both located – as the fifth century BC Greek historian Herodotus specifically stated of the tomb of Cheops – *elsewhere beneath the Plateau.* By that is meant elsewhere than in a pyramid, contrary to all popular beliefs of today, and the assumptions of most living Egyptologists. Herodotus's testimony is specific and emphatic on this point, but has never been 'seen' by investigators for the past 2,500 years because of their consensus blindness, so that when they read Herodotus, the clear statements he made about this, while registering on the retinas of people reading him, have not impressed themselves also upon their brains. So I now give the precise words of Herodotus describing the location of the tomb of Cheops from Book II, Chapter 124: *epi tou lophou.* This means 'on the hill'.[9] Herodotus says the tomb is in underground chambers which are 'on the hill on which the pyramids stand'. It is not in the pyramid.

Henry Cary translates:

'. . . on this road [causeway] then ten years were expended, and in forming the subterraneous apartments on the hill, on which the pyramids stand, which he had made as a burial vault for himself . . .'[10]

A. D. Godley translates:

'The ten years aforesaid went to the making of this road [causeway] and of the underground chambers on the hill whereon the pyramids stand; these the king meant to be burial places for himself . . .'[11]

'The hill on which the pyramids stand' is the Giza Plateau. The tomb of Cheops was in underground chambers within that hill, not within the pyramid.

The statement is absolutely clear but has always been overlooked because it does not suit everyone's preconceptions.

Also of interest is that the subterranean tomb of Cheops within the Plateau is spoken of in connection with the Cheops Causeway, a now-vanished construction, the path of which is still known to us, and which rose from the flood plain up the hillside and culminated at the Cheops Funerary Temple (entirely vanished now also except for a portion of its magnificent basalt floor), which stood at the eastern foot of the Great

Pyramid. (See Plate on the website.) It will be seen a little later on that this detail of Herodotus's account is also important.

Whether Cheops and Chephren lived earlier in time than is conventionally thought, and thus actually built the main Giza pyramids, or whether they 'usurped' those pyramids and built death-cult edifices for themselves around them does not ultimately matter as far as their tombs are concerned. For I am convinced that their tombs were never inside any pyramids, but that they are instead very near to them. In fact, when I explain where I believe them to be, and give the evidence for their being there, it will all seem blindingly obvious, and many people will be tempted to say: 'I always thought so.'

So my suggestion as to the precise location of the intact tomb of King Cheops is that it is directly beneath the surviving portions of the great basalt pavement east of the Great Pyramid, which was once the floor of the now vanished Funerary Temple of Cheops. Here too, at this temple, we see once again the familiar pattern of a mysterious 'water drain' leading from the court of the temple out under the north wall. In this case, it is a limestone channel. Whether it once contained a long granite insert, as at the Sphinx Temple, we no longer know, as this area has been so despoiled. In this case, we have traces rather than the complete conduit and groove.

All that survives of this temple is a portion of the magnificent basalt floor, as seen in the drawings, and in the photo of this wonderful pavement on the website. The important point for us is that the conduit extends below the remaining portions of this basalt floor. The basalt blocks should be lifted to see where this channel goes. Once again, we have the proof that the conduit predates the construction of the temple itself. We also have a conclusive demonstration that it could not have drained the floor of the temple because it was under the floor. This is the same story all over again. I believe there is an intact tomb here, and that it is the tomb of Cheops. The tomb is at one or the other end of the conduit, either north of the temple where the conduit ends, or in the centre of the statue court, beneath what remains of the basalt pavement.

When you think about it, it makes sense for a pharaoh to put his tomb directly under his own funerary temple, because what could be safer than

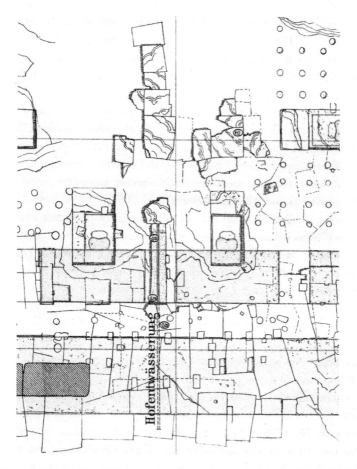

The word "Hofentwässerung" appears running vertically in the image.

Figure 32. Detail of Uvo Hölscher's excavation plan of 1909/1910 of the Funerary Temple of Chephren, from folding Plate XVIII of Uvo Hölscher, *Das Grabdenkmal des Königs Chephren* (*The Funerary Monument of King Chephren*), Erster Band (Vol. 1) of the *Veröffentlichungen der Ernst von Sieglin-Expedition* (*Publications of the Ernst von Sieglin Expedition in Egypt*), edited by Georg Steindorff, containing also contributions by Ludwig Borchardt and Georg Steindorff, J. C. Hinrich's Booksellers, Leipzig, 1912. The '*Hofentwässerung*' seen running vertically from south (bottom of the drawing) to north is the cable conduit which is presumed to have been used for lowering the sarcophagus into the Tomb of Chephren. It passed under the southern wall of the temple and ran underneath the temple floor towards the centre of the temple court. A colour image of this detail and also of a larger section of the image, giving more of the context, may be seen on this book's website, www.egyptiandawn.info. (*Collection of Robert Temple*)

to place an entire temple on top of the entrance to your tomb? That beats portcullises. In order to get at your tomb, robbers would first have to demolish the entire temple. And in this case, although the temple has now actually been demolished, the point in the centre of the statue court remains undisturbed, because that part of the pavement has survived. Think what a giant distraction to everyone's attention there is behind this temple: the Great Pyramid. Who would think of knocking down the temple to find a tomb entrance when there is a tantalising pyramid behind it, which itself looks a much more suggestive location for a tomb? And, what is more, the burial ceremony itself would have been concealed from prying eyes, because the funeral service would probably have taken place within the walls of the funerary temple, which would thus provide the 'cover' for taking the coffin there, without arousing suspicions. And then, the coffin is merely lowered down to where the sarcophagus is already waiting to receive it. The preparation of the tomb would have been far advanced by the time of the death of the pharaoh, with the empty sarcophagus waiting for the actual coffin to be lowered into it.

A similar situation exists with regard to the tomb of Chephren, which I believe is below his funerary temple, at the eastern foot of the second pyramid, which is known as the Pyramid of Chephren. Here, once again, we have a conduit running from the centre of the court under a temple wall, the southern wall in this case, which can be seen in Plates 24c and 24d. These photos, published in 1912, were taken by Uvo Hölscher,[12] the excavator of the Funerary Temple of Chephren, the remains of which sit at the eastern foot of the Pyramid of Chephren, and at which the Grand Chephren Causeway culminates. (See Plate on the website.) Here is what Hölscher had to say about it in an article published in 1909 (translated):

'Also very interesting is the discovery of an admittedly rather simple drainage system in the courtyard (Figure 4). It consists of a semicircular channel of granite. It lies open for an extent of roughly 3 metres, and then it disappears under a covering stone of granite, which itself is then again covered by a thin limestone slab. Then it continues under the pavement and reappears again south of the southern exterior walls at a great depth. Undoubtedly it served for the purpose of leading the rain water out of the alabaster pavement of the courtyard.'[13]

Let us just examine these remarks closely. What is said here is that a semicircular channel of granite (which is just what I found in the north of the Sphinx Temple) has been found which was covered by (1) 'a covering stone of granite', (2) 'a thin limestone slab', (3) an 'alabaster pavement', and (4) a wall underneath which it passes. We are expected to believe that this could be a drainage channel for waste water, despite the fact that it has three layers of stone over it and passes beneath a wall of gigantic stone blocks. What could it drain? How would the 'rain' to be drained by it ever reach it? Furthermore, it then 'reappears . . . at a great depth'. This is just what we would hope that it would do, as that must therefore lead down to the tomb. The feeble thinking that led Hölscher to imagine that 'rain water' would somehow land on the alabaster floor, pass through the alabaster floor, pass through the lime-stone slab, and pass through the granite covering, and then enter the thin groove and be drained away, shows a distinct failure of conceptual power on his part.

If you look back at what I quoted from Ricke (in translation) above, you will find that he also mentions in passing a waste-water drain at this site, leading from the central court of that temple underneath the southern wall of the temple. Presumably he obtained his information from Hölscher's 1909 article just quoted.

The photos make clear that this 'Chephren channel', which is care-fully cut out of solid granite, resembles the channel leading under the north wall of the Sphinx Temple. We can be justified in looking upon this 'channel' as yet another possible 'cable guide channel', and assume that it suggests another royal burial, either just to the south of the wall of the Funerary Temple of Chephren, or otherwise at the opposite end of the conduit, beneath the floor of the temple itself. This tomb is likely to be Chephren's. Due to the fact that no one ever took these 'water drains' seriously until now, no one since the Old Kingdom has ever realised that they were signs pointing to concealed royal tombs just below. After all, these drains were all covered by plaster and stone floors and sometimes by additional stones laid either underneath or on top of that. And then they were covered by windblown sand. Anyone catching a glimpse of them at any time would have assumed them to be drains. But even catching a glimpse of them was impossible, as we have seen,

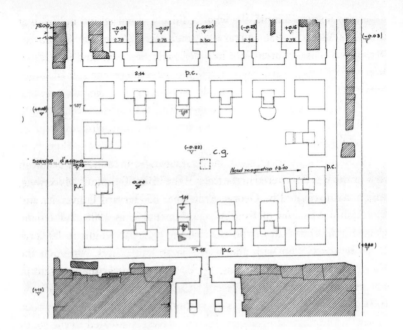

Figure 33. The plan of the central court of the Chephren Funerary Temple drawn by Vito Maragioglio and Celeste A. Rinaldi, as part of folding Plate 11 from Part Five – Plates, *L'Architettura delle Piramidi Menfite* (*The Architecture of the Pyramids of Memphis*), Rapallo, Italy, 1966. The top of the drawing is West, and the centre of the plan shows the Temple Court. The precise location of the Chephren cable guide where it runs under the foundation of the south wall of the temple is shown at middle left, where it is labelled *scarico d'aqua*, which means 'discharge of water'. It is drawn as a long thin groove leading under the south wall of the temple and extending southwards. (The Pyramid of Chephren is above this drawing; magnetic north is shown pointing right, but varies slightly from true geographical north.) The layout here resembles that of the Sphinx Temple, where the cable guide also commences inside the central court near an exterior temple wall and passes under it. Whether there is a shaft at the southern end of the channel as shown here, or whether the channel originally extended further south than this, must be established by excavation. However, the entry to the tomb of Chephren is likely to be beneath that point, and the tomb itself probably extends under the temple itself. Alternatively, the tomb is at the northern end of the conduit directly entered beneath the former temple floor.

for at the Sphinx Temple, the whole edifice was buried in sand from at least 2000 BC until 1936 and, as for the Funerary Temple of Chephren, it was also mostly buried in sand until Hölscher excavated it in 1909. It is true that some earlier writers mentioned seeing some ruined stones there, so some people did realise there was something there, but no one could be bothered to investigate properly. In any case, the 'drains' would have been covered rapidly by rubble from the dismantling of some of the large stones.

The seventh and final cable conduit suggesting an intact subterranean royal tomb was discovered in the floor of the Valley Temple of Mycerinus, which was excavated by George A. Reisner of Harvard University and the Boston Museum of Fine Arts, commencing in 1906, assisted by Cecil Firth, Oric Bates (who is discussed at some length in Chapter Eight in connection with another subject), and others. Although the Funerary Temple of Mycerinus, which sits in front of the Pyramid of Mycerinus, and which was described in Chapter Three, contains no trace of any cable conduit in its floor, there is a conspicuous occurrence of one in the floor of his Valley Temple, which is situated to the south of the Valley Temple attributed to Chephren, which sits beside the Sphinx Temple at the end of the Chephren Causeway, and which is generally referred to simply as the 'Valley Temple of Giza', as if there were no other. (I have continued this usage, and the Valley Temple of Mycerinus will thus always be referred to in full to avoid confusion.)

In the floor of the Great Open Court of the Valley Temple of Mycerinus, another one of the cable conduits occurs, placed at a similar slanting angle to the axis orientation of the temple as the one that first drew my attention in the bedrock floor of the Sphinx Temple. Naturally, it was assumed to be a drain of some kind, although Reisner, being far more observant than Hassan and Ricke had been, noted that it was *inward sloping.* Reisner really should be awarded the Order of the Gold Star for noticing that and recording it. Here is what he says of the 'drain':

'The great open court was much like that at the pyramid temple ('the Funerary Temple' of Mycerinus, as it is usually called today), except that it was not paved with stone. It measured 19.40 m. long (east–west) and 41 m. wide (north–south), and was crossed by a stone-paved pathway

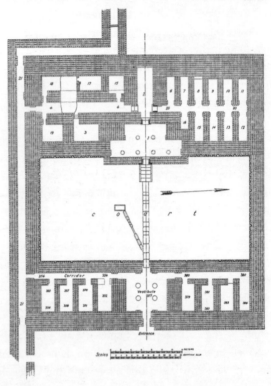

Figure 34. This is folding Plan IX (in a pocket at the back of the book) showing the Valley Temple of Mycerinus, from George Andrew Reisner's *Mycerinus*. Harvard University Press, USA, 1931. (The top of the plan is West.) The cable conduit for the tomb of Mycerinus is seen just to the left of the central stone pathway in the middle of the temple, slanting diagonally upwards into the Great Open Court. It culminates at top left in a rectangular pit carved out of a block of limestone, which has been embedded in the gravel floor, as this temple is not built on bedrock and thus it was not possible to hack a pit at the end of the conduit for the men manoeuvring the ropes, in the way that we saw at the Sphinx Temple. The stone pathway which runs up the middle of the Great Open Court passes over the cable conduit, which was thus constructed earlier. The conduit appears to terminate under the northern portion (at right) of the eastern wall of the Great Open Court, and King Shepseskaf, who succeeded Mycerinus, probably built the wall and pathway over the top of the conduit on purpose, to conceal and seal it, and then finished the temple after burying his predecessor here. The tomb of Mycerinus is therefore to be found beneath the eastern end of this conduit.

Figure 35. This is folding Plan VIII (in a pocket at the back of the book) showing the Valley Temple of Mycerinus, from George Andrew Reisner's *Mycerinus*. Harvard University Press, USA, 1931. (The top of the plan is West.) The cable conduit for the tomb of Mycerinus is seen just to the left of the central stone pathway in the middle of the temple, slanting diagonally upwards into the Great Open Court. (The jumble of structures nearly filling that Court are later in date, and not original to the temple. Figure 34 shows the Court empty, as it was originally.) At bottom, the conduit passes under a wall, just as was the case with the north conduit at the Sphinx Temple. The top left termination of the conduit is in a sunken pit carved out of limestone and sunk down into the gravel floor. This temple, unlike the Sphinx Temple, did not rest on bedrock, and so the crouching-pit had to be carved out of a limestone block which was transported to the site and embedded in the floor. This conduit is a long channel carved out of stone, with small stones hammered in on top, leaving a groove, just as at the Sphinx Temple. Reisner omitted to mention whether the stones are limestone or granite, as he did not think the 'drain' important. He did note, however, that it 'drained inwards' (i.e., could not have been a drain at all), which is more than Hassan or Ricke noticed at the Sphinx Temple when they were excavating. At the top of the plan, a real drain may be seen crossing underneath a corridor, and had the capacity to take rainwater runoff from the north to the south, as Reisner observes.

110 cm. wide, which began in the middle of the western doorway of the antechamber and ended in a stone ramp leading up to the sanctuary. . . . South of the middle of the pathway, a tank, hollowed out of a single rectangular block of limestone, was sunk in the gravel filling of the court. From its northeastern corner, an inflowing drain, slanting to the east–northeast, reached to the western door of the vestibule anteroom. This drain was a trench hollowed in blocks of stone laid end to end and covered with slabs of stone. The joints between the stones were caulked only with the plaster which lined the trench.'[14]

This 'drain' resembles the north cable conduit in the floor of the Sphinx Temple by being, once again, a narrow conduit hollowed out of 'stones' (Reisner does not tell us whether of limestone or granite) laid end to end, with stones laid on top. The design is therefore essentially the same. And, as in the case of the north cable conduit of the Sphinx Temple, the 'drain' slopes inwards, so could not possibly 'drain' the temple but only flood it. The same problem of sloping inward thus recurs.

The 'drain' of the Valley Temple of Mycerinus can be seen in two diagrams and two photos, which are Figures 34 and 35. There is no close-up photo, but the view we have of the 'drain' in Plate 25 and the successive photo on the website shows clearly how closely it resembles the north cable conduit of the Sphinx Temple.

Because the Valley Temple of Mycerinus was not built upon bedrock but upon earth, there was no possibility of digging out of the bedrock a hole for people to squat in to manipulate the cables, as at the Sphinx Temple. What seems to have happened instead is that a hollowed rectangular limestone block was sunk into the earth at the end of the conduit, to serve the same function. Figures 34 and 35 make clear that the 'drain' does not actually 'connect' with the hollowed limestone block, but merely 'touches' it slightly. There is therefore no structural connection between the two, and to interpret the hollowed block as a 'tank' makes no sense, because the 'drain' did not lead into the 'tank'. And in any case, just as was the case with the Sphinx Temple, the other end of the conduit passes underneath and disappears beneath a wall and the central stone pathway of the great open court of the temple. It was clearly constructed before the temple, just as was the case at the Sphinx Temple, for its temple was also built on top of it.

Once again, we ask the question: why would anyone go to all this trouble to lay a narrow stone conduit capped by restraining stones, which slopes inwards and could not 'drain' anything outwards, nor could it 'drain' anything inwards either, because it does not connect to anything, and then build a royal temple on top of it? This is clearly another cable conduit used to lower a heavy sarcophagus and other heavy objects into a royal tomb. It is highly likely that the tomb is that of Mycerinus. So we now have evidence of seven intact royal tombs at Giza, none of which can date from later than the Fourth Dynasty.

Another point to consider about all these 'conduits' or cable channels is that they only occur at precisely the places where it would make sense to have a royal subterranean tomb. It is not as if they are found hither and thither. Just where they would be useful for lowering heavy stone sarcophagi is where they appear. Where they are not wanted, we do not find any.

So that is it, then. Let's get digging!

CHAPTER FIVE

A King Eight Feet Tall

King Khasekhemui (pronounced as 'casa-come-ooey' with the accent on the 'oo') was the last king of the Second Dynasty of Egypt. Ioannis and I were invited by Professor Gunter Dreyer, director of the German Institute in Cairo, to attempt a dating of this king's tomb at Abydos. This was in 2001, during Dreyer's re-excavation of the tomb, which had originally been excavated a century earlier by Sir Flinders Petrie. According to the generally accepted chronologies, the burial of King Khasekhemui took place circa 2700 BC. Gunter Dreyer favours a slightly later date, and told me: 'According to our chronology, he ruled in the first part of the twenty-seventh century BC.'[1]

Ioannis, Olivia and I were taken in a four-wheel drive vehicle along the bumpy desert trail to the German Institute's site camp at Abydos. Gunter Dreyer had been excavating tombs in the great cemeteries there for more than twenty years. As we approached, a small white dog lay in a hollow in the sand, too exhausted by the heat even to raise its head and look at us. Dreyer received us cordially, and we were offered cold Coca-Colas. Then we went out into the desert, where the heat was searing and remorseless: at least 45°C. Olivia was very sensibly dressed in a light white cotton gallabiya, which she usually wears at Egyptian archaeological sites, as it protects so well against the sun. Ioannis was sweating terribly as he carried his immensely heavy gamma radiation detector, with which he takes readings at each sample's location. I busied myself with taking photos, knowing what a unique opportunity this was to see something only a handful of people in the world would ever glimpse. The Egyptian labourers, in colourful clothing, carried away bags of sand on their shoulders along the wooden gangway above the great pit where the giant tomb had been exposed. Our attempts to find even a scrap of shade during this day were fruitless, as the sun seemed to be everywhere, and there was no escaping it. Although I have been in hotter and far more desolate situations in Egypt, far out in the desert where mirages beguile the eye and one can easily become confused and dehydrated, we were at the tomb for so long that the prolonged exposure in one place was new to us. So this is what the real diggers go through day after day. Compared to them, we are birds of passage, flitting from site to site, while they grind away at one location week after week.

The first excavation of this tomb was reported by Petrie in his book *The Royal Tombs of the Earliest Dynasties*, 1901.[2] Professor Dreyer's re-excavation exposed the site once more, only very briefly; after it was completed, the entire site was recovered in sand. It will certainly not be uncovered again in the lifetime of anyone living, and possibly never. We were there to date the limestone burial chamber, which has often been described as the earliest stone structure in Egypt. Because this chamber was only uncovered for a period of two weeks, the arrangement of our visit was subject to considerable time pressures, as we were coming from two separate countries and had to coordinate our schedules. As things turned out, we were able to inspect the chamber, but on the day of our visit only two courses of stonework were visible of the six courses that exist: the lower four courses were still buried in sand. Our photos thus only show the top third of the chamber (see Plate 26). However, the exposed portion was sufficient for our dating purposes. A close-up of the limestone blocks from these two courses may be seen in Plate 27. From this photo, it can be seen that the stonework was very rough and unimpressive.

When I saw the limestone blocks, I was frankly amazed. There was no evidence of sophistication in the carving and placing of the stone blocks at all. The walls of the tomb looked like something that could have been erected by clumsy schoolboys. It seemed incredible to me – indeed, wholly unbelievable – that this was the quality of masonry in existence only a few years before construction commenced on the magnificent Step Pyramid of Zoser (sometimes spelled Djoser) at Saqqara, which is said to have been built at the beginning of the very next dynasty. I cannot understand why this issue has not been raised more loudly within the community of Egyptologists. I did not discuss the matter with Gunter Dreyer, but I did raise it with one of his colleagues, who admitted in an embarrassed manner that it was certainly a bit of a problem, and that he personally did not see any solution to it. I got the impression that there was a tacit agreement that the matter was not one that the team would be considering or even discussing amongst themselves. It is very common for excavators to confine themselves to their work, and to eschew general interpretations, no matter how drastic the issue might be. And in this case, any discussion of the issue was certain to be controversial.

I certainly have no hesitation whatever in raising this issue. To my mind, it poses one of the greatest dilemmas in the whole of Egyptology. Apparently we have two succeeding dynasties, one producing stonework so clumsy that it might as well have been laid by chimpanzees; the next, only twenty or thirty years later, producing a gigantic pyramid which is still standing proudly today and which is estimated to contain one million tons of expertly shaped stones. (Plate 10.) How can the pathetic stone structure seen in Plates 26 and 27 be separated by only twenty or thirty years from the massive and sophisticated structure seen in Plate 10?

As a historian of science I have to pose the question: *what happened??*

There seem to be only two logical possibilities. The first is that some incredible technological revolution occurred within only a few years, perhaps initiated by the brilliant Vizier Imhotep, who is known to have designed and constructed the Step Pyramid at Saqqara. We certainly have clear evidence that Imhotep's innovations in the use of stone and building techniques were revolutionary. No one questions that. But this technological revolution must have been more rapid and overwhelming than any that occurred until the most recent times, with the invention of personal computers, mobile phones, and the Internet, where society has similarly been transformed beyond all recognition within only a few years. Is it possible that something as rapid and overwhelming as this could take place four and a half thousand years ago?

However, if we hesitate to postulate such a tidal wave of change sweeping over Egypt within a fraction of a human lifetime, we would then be forced to consider the second alternative: something is wrong with our chronology, or our concept of Egyptian historical development, or both. In other words, in our struggle to conceptualise what was going on at this period in terms of political events and dynasties, we have somehow got it all wrong.

But *how* could we have got it all wrong?

The attempts to make sense of this puzzling period have been Herculean, and many excellent scholars and researchers have expended their energies to such an extent that few aspects of Egyptology have received such dogged and exhaustive attention. However, they have all been haunted by the fear that somehow the evidence was too slim. A jar sealing might turn up at any moment that could overturn their theories. (The sealings on food and wine jars in royal tombs bore royal names pressed into them and serve to identify the kings and the dynasties. They show who was around at the time the tomb was constructed.)

And it was primarily jar sealings that Gunter Dreyer was after when he re-excavated the Tomb of Khasekhemui. And he found them, in vast quantity, left behind by Petrie, who in his day did not fully appreciate their significance and did not gather them all up or sift the sand fine enough to find them. And the jar sealings found by Dreyer appear to prove conclusively three things: (1) Khasekhemui was the last king of the Second Dynasty, (2) Zoser was the first king of the Third Dynasty, and (3) Zoser (under an alternative name he had, Netjerykhet) buried Khasekhemui, since Zoser's jar sealings with his name stamped on them were found in Khasekhemui's tomb. The only alternative to the last conclusion would seem to be the possibility that Zoser reburied Khasekhemui or resealed his tomb at a later date, if it had been tampered with or robbed.

If we draw the first conclusion, that Zoser actually buried Khasekhemui, then we must also conclude that a man capable of building a gigantic stone pyramid at Saqqara was living at the time of death of a king whose tomb contained a small amount of very rough limestone masonry. Such a physical continuity must have accompanied a discontinuity of technology so wide that the word 'chasm' is inadequate.

Khasekhemui and Zoser might as well have come from different corners of the universe, to judge from their respective stone technologies, and yet one of them seems to have been present at the burial of the other.

Until this mystery can be explained in a convincing and logical manner, we can never rest easy in our minds about what was really going on in Archaic and Old Kingdom Egypt. It will not do to ignore it, and close our eyes, as most Egyptologists have been doing, by saying it is not their problem. The fact is that it is *every* Egyptologist's problem, whether he or she likes it or not. There is a collective responsibility to try and make sense of this apparently insoluble dilemma. Nobody ever made progress in understanding anything by pretending that there was no problem, or being in denial. This particular problem positively requires energetic and ingenious attempts at some kind of a solution!

Considering the crucial importance of this issue, a dating of the Tomb of Khasekhemui is extremely important. We took samples for three different kinds of dating: wood for carbon-14 dating, pottery sherds for thermoluminescence, and limestone from the tomb chamber for optical thermoluminescence.

The results for four ceramic sherds bore no relation to the tomb itself. Two of the sherds were large ones, and the results showed that they were from either the New Kingdom period or the Third Intermediate Period. They indicate merely grave-robbing, squatting, or intruded superficial burials. They can have nothing to do with Khasekhemui. The specifics of the results were: 1200 BC plus or minus 200 years, and 1100 BC plus or minus 200 years. Two other smaller sherds gave dates that were earlier than this. The first of the two small sherds from the vicinity of the burial chamber gave dates of 2210 BC, plus or minus 260 years, in other words, ranging between 2470 BC and 1950 BC. The other gave dates of 2490 BC plus or minus 260 years, thus ranging between 2750 BC and 2230 BC. Assuming that both sherds are of the same age, this would indicate a span between 2470 BC and 2230 BC, which is definitely much later than the burial, and would indicate either a disturbance of the tomb or an intruded burial during the Old Kingdom period, at which time the tomb was probably not yet entirely covered in sand, as it would have been by the time of the New Kingdom. The site was thus repeatedly interfered with in subsequent periods, as all such sites were in Egypt.

There has always been confusion over the identities of the kings of the Second Dynasty. One of the main reasons for this is that they each had three different names. Their chief names, which we like to use for them, were called their 'Horus names'. Khasekhemui is a 'Horus name', for instance. But each king also had a *nebti* (also spelled *nebty*) name and also a *nesu-bit* (or *bik-nebu*) name. Later Egyptian lists of the early kings did not call them by their Horus names, but used their alternative names instead. This is true of the New Kingdom lists, and also of the list preserved by the late historian Manetho, where the names are additionally disguised by having been turned into Greek forms. Therefore, these later lists refer to kings as if they were in code: a king referred to by his *nebti* name might be a king we know very well from his Horus name, but we just don't happen to be certain what his *nebti* name actually was, hence the information is almost useless. It is like trying to guess who played which part in a play when you have the names of the characters on one list and the names of the actors on a separate cast list, but no joint list specifying who played which role. In many cases you can piece together a partial joint list, but there are many instances where you are reduced to simple guesswork.

King Khasekhemui has always been plagued with a special problem, however. There is evidence of the existence of another king of the same dynasty whose name was almost the same: King Khasekhem. Many Egyptologists have thought that this was taking coincidence too far, and that the two men are the same. But others insist that they were different men.

Walter Emery, in his seminal book *Archaic Egypt*, says categorically: 'Kha-sekhem was succeeded by Kha-sekhemui, who was perhaps the most outstanding monarch of the dynasty . . .'[3]

Emery says that the name Khasekhem means 'The Appearance of the Power', whereas the name Khasekhemui means 'The Appearance of the Two Powers'.[4] Some people think that, after Khasekhem united the north and the south, he changed his name accordingly to Khasekhemui to celebrate the fact. But Emery thinks that 'on balance it would appear that Kha-sekhem and Kha-sekhemui were two persons, probably the eighth and ninth kings of the dynasty.'[5]

This is the position taken by Verbrugghe and Wickersham, the most recent translators of the historian Manetho (flourished circa 285–245 BC). Manetho was an Egyptian priest who wrote a history of his country in Egyptian, which only survives in fragments of a Greek translation quoted by other writers. The main importance of Manetho is that he preserved a crucial king list. In trying to make sense of the king listed by Manetho as being the king who ruled at the end of the Second Dynasty, named Kheneres, said by Manetho to have reigned for thirty years, they give a modern reconstruction of two successive kings for this period: Khasekhem, reigning twenty-one years, and Khasekhemui reigning seventeen years. They do not explain how thirty-eight years total is meant to equal the thirty years specified by Manetho.[6] They also record that, according to the Turin papyrus of late New Kingdom date, which gives an alternative king list, Khasekhem is called Hudjefa and is said to have reigned for eleven years, and Khasekhemui is called Bebti and is said to have reigned for twenty-seven years (total: thirty-eight years).[7] Of course, there is nothing to prevent Hudjefa and Bebti being the same man with two successive names; Hudjefa/Khasekhem could have changed both names and become Bebti/Khasekhemui. Verbrugge and Wickersham do not discuss the issue at all.

Erik Hornung does not recognise the separate existence of a King Khasekhem, and thus believes he and Khasekhemui were the same person. He also believes there were only five kings in the second dynasty.[8]

Michael Hoffman, author of *Egypt before the Pharaohs*, also believed that Khasekhem and Khasekhemui are the same person:

'Walter Emery, who, as we have already seen, was fond of offering alternative explanations not espoused by the majority of his colleagues, long maintained that the two spellings of Khasekhemui and Khasekhem represented two separate monarchs. While this may be true, the linguistic evidence is heavily against it as the Egyptologist Werner Kaiser has pointed out.'[9]

Michael Rice, author of *Egypt's Making*, is another author who believes that Khasekhem and Khasekhemui were the same man:

'. . . Khasekhem returned to the frontiers of Egypt to find [the god] Set, in the person of Peribsen [the name of another king], in possession of what he, the Horus [the king identified himself with the god Horus], saw as his patrimony. A series of fierce engagements took place, up and down the Valley; the outcome was victory for Khasekhem and defeat for the Set-King. Khasekhem, it is then suggested, assumed a modified throne-name, "the Horus Khasekhemwy [a more technical spelling of Khasekhemui]". This meant "In him the Two Powers are reconciled", a significant and majestic assertion indeed, in all the circumstances.'[10]

A much earlier Egyptologist, Wallis Budge, had assumed the identity of Khasekhem and Khasekhemui, but had done so erroneously in the context of believing both to be alternative names of the first king of the Second Dynasty, who he says was also called Besh, Neter-Baiu and Betchau. He speaks of Betchau's 'Horus name KHĀ-SEKHEM, which becomes KHĀ-SEKHEMUI when figures of Horus and Set appear [jointly] above the standard.'[11]

Petrie counted nine kings in the Second Dynasty, and believed Khasekhem and Khasekhemui to be two separate men, the last kings of the Second Dynasty. He spelled their names Khosekhem and Khosekhemui. However, he was careful to say that some believed the two men were the same person:

'(Khosekhem) is only known from his monuments at Hierakonpolis, and his place in the list [of kings] is uncertain. He doubtless preceded Khosekhemui, though some suppose that it is an earlier name of the same king.'[12]

However, Petrie was uncertain about Khasekhemui in other ways, saying that 'Khosekhemui may well be, therefore, the last king of the IInd dynasty, or possibly the first king of the IIIrd.'[13]

Although so much is still uncertain, enough progress seems to have been made for us to be convinced today that Khasekhemui was indeed the last king of the Second Dynasty, whereas it was Zoser (Djoser) who was the first king of the Third Dynasty. However, no one really knows what the difference is or was between the Second Dynasty and the Third Dynasty, why they were differentiated, and what relations actually existed between them. This is made even less clear now that it seems that Zoser 'buried' Khasekhemui. If there was enough continuity for that to happen, why were the dynasties considered separate? Perhaps we should be looking for a different type of answer altogether. It is at least worth considering the possibility that the Third Dynasty did not 'succeed' the Second Dynasty in real political terms, although it might have done so in terms of raw chronology. Perhaps the two entities were of a different order. It may be overly simplistic to assume that one dynasty ends and another commences. Perhaps something far more complicated was going on at that remote period, of which our real knowledge is, after all, so piecemeal and fragmentary that it amounts to little more than hints. As a historian of science rather than an Egyptologist, I would like to remind my Egyptologist friends that there are other forms of evidence than the ones they are routinely used to considering. If there is a vast technological gap between two supposedly successive entities, perhaps those entities were not really successive, even though they might have been sequential in time. Time to put our thinking caps on . . .

Some Egyptologists have reacted with surprise to Dreyer's discovery of jar sealings of Zoser in the tomb of Khasekhemui, as if this were a revolutionary finding. However, Dreyer's discoveries could be taken as a dramatic confirmation of the conclusions already reached by the remarkable researches of the Egyptologist Patrick F. O'Mara in the 1970s. O'Mara made an intensive study of the Fifth Dynasty stone that I mentioned in Chapter One called the Palermo Stone. This is, unfortunately, only a small fragment of what had originally been a much larger stone containing a complete king list of the first five dynasties. Egyptologists for generations have been driven to the utmost exasperation by the incompleteness of this crucial stone, and more than a dozen very serious and laborious attempts were made by various Egyptologists, both famous ones (Petrie, Breasted, Borchardt, etc.) and obscure ones, to try to reconstruct its lost portions.

O'Mara commenced his task by analysing all of these attempts and showing clearly what was wrong with them all. (One example: none of them had taken into account the measurement of the height of the stone, but only its width.) O'Mara then took the sensible step of applying the traditional Egyptian canon of measurement and proportion to the stone, and showed how this had routinely been done for papyri. O'Mara's approach is extraordinarily convincing, and he seems to have progressed where so many others had failed. His lengthy first book, in which he described his technique at length, is truly something for specialists. (He published many articles and four more short books, all of which are discussed in Chapter Six.) But his conclusions are in many cases remarkable. However, one will come as no surprise: he insists that Khasekhem and Khasekhemui must be the same person, and that this king was succeeded by Zoser, who had some of Khasekhemui's pottery inside his own Step Pyramid, by the way.[14] O'Mara's courage in saying the unthinkable is highly praised in the next chapter. For it was O'Mara who insisted that certain fragments of ancient king lists known collectively as the 'Cairo Stone' are fakes, against enormous opposition from Egyptologists, who hate the very idea of having to rewrite their history books. I suspect that O'Mara was correct, as we shall see later on.

We can see a portrait of King Khasekhem in Plate 30. This small statue of the seated king was excavated at Hierakonpolis, and has been pieced together from fragments. It is on display today in the Ashmolean Museum in Oxford. In this statue, the king wears the crown of Upper Egypt. Since the majority of scholars believe that Khasekhem and Khasekhemui were the same person, as we have seen, it is likely that this is the actual image of the man buried in the tomb we have dated. The fragments of this statue, before it was joined together, were published as separate photos by James Breasted in his *A History of Egypt*, who accepted Khasekhem and Khasekhemui as separate kings.[15] He reproduced these photos from their original source, James Quibell's *Hierakonpolis*, of 1900–02.[16]

Breasted also published a photo of the limestone burial chamber of Khasekhemui, reproduced from Petrie,[17] which he captioned 'Earliest stone structure in the world', and of which he enthusiastically stated in his text: '. . . and toward the end of the Second Dynasty the surrounding brick chambers of king Khasekhemui's tomb enclose a chamber built of hewn limestone, the earliest stone masonry structure known in the history of man . . .'[18]

There are certain reports preserved about both Khasekhem and Khasekhemui, or I should say about 'him'. He appears to have been something of a physical giant. As Petrie tells us: 'Sesokhris [whom Petrie equates with Khasekhem] is stated by Manetho to have been 5 cubits and 3 palms high, which would be about 8 English feet, if the short cubit of 17.4 inches were used.'[19] In the most recent translation of

Manetho, we find the statement: 'Sesokhris ruled 48 years. It is said that he was five cubits and three palms (eight and one-half feet) tall.'[20] Certainly the burial chamber was large enough to hold such a huge man, but as all trace of the body and the sarcophagus have vanished centuries – or probably millennia – ago, this strange tale can never be verified. Of course, if it were really true that the king was such a giant, it would possibly have made it that much easier for him to unite north and south by military conquest.

Emery says:

The Second Dynasty ends with two kings: Kha-sekhem and Kha-sekhemui . . . Khasekhem would thus be identical with Huzefa (Neferka-sokar?) of the Sakkara and Turin lists and with Manetho's Sesochris, who he states reigned for forty-eight years. Although this king's name is omitted on the Abydos list, there is little doubt that his control extended over the whole of Egypt, for monuments of his have been found at Hieraconpolis. But his reign appears to have been stormy and the only relics of the period, two statues, a stela and three stone vessels, record war and conquest; and although some of these events may have occurred beyond Egypt's frontier, they indicate a period of national disturbance. The two statues, one of schist and one of lime-stone, are of exceptional artistic merit and they represent Kha-sekhem seated on a throne, wearing the crown of Upper Egypt and the robe usually associated with the Sed festival [a festival of renewal of the kingship]. Around the bases of both statues is a row of contorted human figures representing slain enemies and on the front is inscribed 'Northern enemies 47,209'. It has been suggested that the 'northern enemies' were Libyans who had invaded the Delta, but we must not overlook the possibility of internal insurrection in Lower Egypt, or perhaps most likely of all, a conquest of the North by the Southerners under Khasekhem, who on that basis re-named himself Khasekhemui. As for 'Northerners' and 'Libyans', who they were and what their relationship to one another may have been, we shall have much more to say of them in a later chapter.

Further evidence of rebellion in the north comes from the three stone vessels which are identically inscribed 'The year of fighting the northern enemy within the city of Nekheb'. The goddess Nekhbet in vulture form holds a 'signet circle' within which is the word *besh* (rebels), while with the other claw she supports the emblem of the unity of Egypt before the name of Kha-sekhem.

The fragment of the stela shows part of a kneeling captive, on a platform which ends in the head of a foreigner on which rests a bow. Below is the name of Kha-sekhem and the text 'humbling the foreign lands'. It is important to note that on his statues the king is shown wearing only the White Crown of Upper Egypt [i.e., since he did not wear the joint crown, he clearly had no jurisdiction over Lower Egypt in the Delta and the North] and on the stone vases the hawk above his name also wears the White Crown. The impression gained from this admittedly limited evidence is that Khasekhem was a ruler of the Thinite family of Upper Egypt who united the Nile valley after the religious wars between the followers of Horus and Set which had probably divided the country since the reign of Perabsen [Peribsen]. His very name 'Appearance of Power' is significant, and the absence of any contemporary monument of his at Sakkara strongly suggests that his rule was centred in the far south, . . . Kha-sekhem was succeeded by Kha-sekhemui, who was perhaps the most outstanding monarch of the dynasty, for under him the final unity of the country was established and the foundation laid for the astonishing expansion and development of Pharaonic power in the Third Dynasty. . . . The struggle between the followers of Horus and Set had come to an end and his name Kha-sekhemui, 'The appearance of the Two Powers', is added to by his fuller name, 'The Gods in him are at peace'. On the numerous jar-sealings, the King's Ka name is always surmounted by the hawk and the Set animal, a further indication that some form of unity on equal terms had been achieved.[21]

In 1968, the French Egyptologist Godron made an important point about this stela that had not been noticed before. In the course of studying the inscription more closely, reconstructing a couple of incomplete hieroglyphs, and adding some details about its meaning, he also remarks that Petrie's translation of the inscription as 'humbling the foreign lands', which Emery quoted in what we have just read above, is not really accurate. He cites Weigall for originally pointing this out in the 1930s, when he said: 'this monument tells of the defeat of the "damned", a phrase which was usually applied to a usurper or to a vanquished rebel whose name had been effaced from the annals'.[22] This is a crucial historical detail which has not received proper attention. There is a world of difference between humbling foreign enemies and humbling rebels. The first interpretation implies an international status, the latter does not necessarily imply anything of the kind. Rebels can be just down the street or around the corner, whereas foreigners are abroad. The entire scale of the problem is altered by the change in the translation. Was Khasekhemui really important on the world stage (the world as defined by the Egyptians of those days, that is), or was he merely a trumped-up local potentate restricted to the southern part of Upper Egypt, who suffered from delusions of grandeur? Who is correct about the translation? Petrie? Or Weigall and Godron?

Emery continues his account of Khasekhemui as follows:

The southern tomb of Kha-sekhemui at Abydos is a fantastic construction bearing no resemblance to other monuments on that site, or indeed to any other contemporary building at Sakkara. Unfortunately, as with the other Abydos monuments, no superstructure remains, and we have only the substructure to judge of the immense size of the building. It measures 68.97 metres in length, with a varying width of between 17.6 and 10.4 metres. It consists of three parts; at the north is a door leading to three rows of thirty-three magazines for offerings and funerary equipment; then comes a stone-built burial chamber flanked by four rooms on either side, and then a further ten magazines, five on each side of a corridor leading to the south door, which is flanked by four more rooms on either side, and then a further ten magazines, five on each side of a corridor leading to the south door, which is flanked by four more rooms.

The burial chamber was at one time believed to be the oldest example of stone masonry in existence, but excavation at Sakkara and Helwan has shown that building in stone was known in the First Dynasty. A curious feature of Kha-sekhemui's tomb is its irregularity and faulty planning and, impressive as it is in size, it is difficult to believe that only a few years separate it from the magnificent Step Pyramid of Zoser at Sakkara.[23]

For the sake of completeness, I should just mention some of the ways in which stone was used before the time of Khasekhemui. First of all, upright limestone slabs were regularly used as stelae, which stood at the entrances to royal tombs, identifying the tomb with the name of the king inside. This applied to cenotaphs as well. But there is only one royal tomb so far discovered that used stone inside, prior to the time of Khasekhemui. It occurs in the tomb of King Den ('King Mutilator'), in the middle of the First Dynasty. Sir Flinders Petrie published this finding in 1901, and he commented:

'The tomb of King Den-Setui was partially cleared least year . . . The length of the passage is 78 feet over all. . . . The great brick chamber is about 50 feet by 28 feet, and 20 feet deep. . . . The astonishing feature of this chamber is its granite pavement, such considerable use of granite being quite unknown until the step pyramid of Saqqara, early in the IIIrd Dynasty. . . . Some of the slabs are of grey gneissic granite, which splits into thin masses, the western slab being 111 x 64 inches, and only 5 inches thick; other slabs are of hammer-dressed pink granite. . . . The eastern recess of the chamber was, however, all paved with brick, like the bordering of the pavement on the other sides.'[24]

Other early uses of stone all involved limestone. They were excavated between 1942 and 1954 at the archaic cemetery of Helwan by Zaki Saad. Helwan is a suburb southeast of Cairo, on the eastern bank of the Nile, opposite Saqqara. It was not a site for royal burials, but officials and nobles were buried there. Saad excavated a total of 10,258 tombs at Helwan (that's a lot of digging) and discovered that eight of them contained some limestone in their construction (a ninth was partially dug out of limestone bedrock, whereas all the rest were dug in gravel). That means that less than 0.0008 per cent of the tombs used some stone, so it was hardly common. These have all been re-examined by Wendy Wood in a survey article that was published in the *Journal of Egyptian Archaeology* in 1987.[25] She says of one: 'The stairway walls are mud brick with a lining of stone, and the steps are stone. Two limestone portcullises were found *in situ* along the north–south stretch of the stairway.' She says that although Saad dated this to the first half of the First Dynasty, it really dates to the time of the last king of that dynasty.

Wood says of another tomb: 'The substructure consists of a tapered stone stairway with two stone portcullises *in situ* and a rectangular burial chamber cut in gravel. . . . The chamber is paved and "walled up with big white limestone blocks in the same manner as [the previous tomb described] . . . and the largest limestone block (was) approximately 3 x 2 m x 50 cm.' This tomb is dated to approximately the reign of King Den of the First Dynasty.

Another of the tombs has been dated by Wood to the end of the second dynasty, in other words contemporaneous with Khasekhemui's Tomb. This is described as follows: 'The single limestone slabs laid horizontally on the north and south walls of the rectangular burial chamber measure 4 x 2m x 40.0 cm to span the long sides of the rectangle.' With these, Wood says there 'was greater care taken in dressing the stone'.

These uses of stone are minimal and unimpressive. As Wood comments: 'Even allowing for lost monuments – and an astonishing number have survived – nothing in Archaic tomb architecture is adequate preparation for the technical mastery that suddenly appears in the heart of the Third Dynasty Step Pyramid complex at Saqqara. The complex contains two granite burial chambers and a granite plug weighing approximately 3 tons that was used to seal the principal chamber under the Step Pyramid.'

In other words, the other slight evidence that survives of the uses of a few bits of stone in rare circumstances during the First and Second Dynasties is no more impressive than what we saw in the Tomb of Khasekhemui, and indeed is even less so.

Khasekhemui was certainly ambitious about the size of his structures, even if there was some lack of finesse about their design and construction. He is believed to have built the large structure at Hierakonpolis known as 'the Fort'. (See Plates 31, 32 and further photos on the website.) This building was definitely not a fort, but was probably either a palace or a large religious enclosure of some kind. The name 'Fort' became attached to it long ago and has been kept because it is familiar. Another massive Khasekhemui structure, called Shunet el Zebib in Arabic, is found at Abydos. David O'Connor has said: 'It has long been clear that none of the enclosures are fortresses, but otherwise debate continues about their functions. . . . [Shunet el Zebib's] double enclosure walls define an area of about 1 hectare or just under 2½ acres . . . The massive brick walls of this structure, today called the Shunet el Zebib, still rise as high as 10 to 11 meters, about 36 feet . . . Since 1904 this structure has been dated to pharaoh Khasekhemwy [Khasekhemui] of the late Second Dynasty, and is therefore about 4,700 years old. It is probably the oldest standing example of large-scale, monumental brick architecture in the world, in the sense that most of it has always remained free of engulfing sand or debris.'[26]

When Olivia and I visited Hierakonpolis, we were jovially received by the late Barbara Adams, whose early death is deeply regretted by all who knew her. She had devoted many years of her life to the site and knew every inch of the vast expanse of cemeteries, where she made many startling discoveries, including the remains of an elephant. (See photo of her beside an ancient bakery at Hierakonpolis on the *Egyptian Dawn* website.) She showed us the Fort, which was made entirely of mud brick. A single piece of stone stood in the centre of the vast court-yard, and there was once a pink granite gate-jamb inscribed with the name of King Khasekhemui at the entrance, which was removed to the Egyptian Museum in Cairo in 1899. This gate-jamb was discovered by Quibell in 1897.[27]

In 1932, Engelbach was able to elucidate the fact that it had once borne elaborate foundation scenes of the pharaoh establishing a sacred structure and pounding foundation stakes into the ground with the goddess Sheshet, who is always shown beside the pharaoh in such scenes, of which this is the earliest known. He managed to make these scenes partially visible by rubbing them with chalk powder and lighting them at a severe angle, and published the result. He said that these scenes were 'almost wholly erased'. He later discovered that Gaston Maspero had noticed these scenes in 1906 and commented that they had been 'chiselled out at the time when the block was re-used'.[28] Engelbach does not elaborate on this extraordinary idea suggested by Maspero.

Frankly, it is difficult to imagine that the block was reused in any way, since it was found *in situ*, and we know that this 'Fort' was not in use during the Fourth through to the Sixth Dynasties.[29] What 'reuse' can Maspero possibly have been imagining? It seems to me that an important detail has been overlooked here: we must presume that these scenes were effaced not because of any reuse of the block but on purpose while it remained *in situ*, in an attempt to erase Khasekhemui from the annals of history, as was commonly attempted for political enemies by their victorious foes and successors. As we have seen above, Khasekhem was very keen to do this himself. But who could have done this to poor Khasekhemui? It cannot have been too long after his death, for passions would have cooled and political motivations would have dwindled if very much time had passed, and his memory would have been largely forgotten anyway. I cannot imagine an attack on Khasekhemui's memory taking place later than the Fourth Dynasty, and it is more likely to have occurred at some point during the Third Dynasty. But why? This is purely speculation, with its only support being the fact reported by O'Connor that pottery ceases to be left there at some time during the Third Dynasty, indicating perhaps a ceasing of sanctity or respect for the place, which might just possibly coincide with the effacing of the carvings. But I do urge those scholars who are concerned about the political history of the period to take note of this curious anomaly, and try to figure out what it means. We have few enough clues about such things, and to overlook one is not a good idea.

Although this large edifice of 'the Fort' is extremely impressive even today, 4,500 years later, its lack of stone forms yet another striking contrast to the stone masonry of the Zoser complex at Saqqara which followed it so soon afterwards.

Khasekhemui was obviously a powerful, dynamic and probably egotistical man. He might well have killed 47,000 enemies, as he claimed. He might also have been a giant who overawed everyone he met. He wanted his name on things; he wanted large structures. But he was unable to do more with stone than stack some roughly hacked blocks on top of one another in a mere six rows, and did not even know how to finish them off properly. There is something wrong somewhere in all of this.

The dating results

Our carbon-14 dates were taken from pieces of wood which were embedded in the mud brick of the main structure of the tomb, in the vicinity of the burial chamber. There is a great deal of such wood, and taking samples was an extremely simple matter. The results we obtained were from two different laboratories. The Greek lab, Demokritos, gave results for two samples as 2834–2579 BC (68.3 per cent probability) and 2857–2502 BC (95.4 per cent probability). The other results came from Geochron Laboratories in Cambridge, Massachusetts, USA, and they were 2860–2470 BC (68.3 per cent) and 2880–2350 BC (95.4 per cent).

If we take the lowest of the upper limit dates above, it is 2834 BC. And if we take the highest of the lower limit dates above, it is 2579 BC. We are probably safe therefore in assuming that the wood dates from between 2834 BC and 2579 BC, a span of 255 years. To take the widest possible range, we would say that the dates fall between 2880 BC and 2350 BC, a span of 530 years.

Ioannis took two limestone samples from the burial chamber, one of which turned out not to be suitable for analysis. The good sample was dated by optical thermoluminescence to 3300 BC plus or minus 450 years, giving a range of 3750 BC–2850 BC.

A conventional date for the death of Khasekhemui is 2707 BC. Although our carbon-14 dates include this date within their span, neither the sherds nor the limestone are that recent. Since the earliest possible carbon-14 date is 2880 BC and the lowest possible limestone date is 2850 BC, this would suggest that the tomb of Khasekhemui dates from a period of thirty years between those two dates.

According to these findings, the tomb of Khasekhemui is between 143 and 173 years older than some conventional chronologies state, and older still than the date currently accepted by the German Institute at Cairo (early 2600s BC), by perhaps as much as 200 to 220 years.

Conclusions

It is wholly absurd to accept the standard interpretation of events in ancient Egypt at this time. It is very clear that there were technological discrepancies so glaring and extreme that we can only conclude that there must have been *two separate and contemporaneous Egyptian civilisations*. The technologically advanced civilisation was in the north (Lower Egypt). There, it was possible to build gigantic pyramids. But the technologically backward civilisation, represented by King Khasekhemui, was in the south (Upper Egypt). *These civilisations were not the same civilisation.* Yes, King Zoser must have buried King Khasekhemui. Yes, they must have been alive at the same time. But no, they were not successive kings of the same civilisation. Despite his egotistical pretensions, Khasekhemui was not the pharaoh of all Egypt, he was merely the king of the technologically backward south, who had fought some battles in the north (whether against marauding Libyans from the western desert or against native Egyptians is not known for certain), some of which he seems to have won. But he was not the king of the north; he was an intruder in that region. Now we see the real reason – never hitherto understood – why the ancient Egyptian historians clearly demarcated the 'Second Dynasty' from the 'Third Dynasty'. They were separate not only in name but in nature. The reason why the 'Third Dynasty' was not simply a continuation of the 'Second Dynasty' was that they were entirely different kingdoms; although they knew each other and had friendly enough contact for one king to bury the other, they ruled different parts of Egypt at the same time. The northern civilisation was advanced, the southern one was backward. The one was not the successor of the other. They were running in parallel for part of the time, though for how long is unclear.

This clearly gives an entirely different picture of the origins of Egyptian civilisation from any that has hitherto been suggested. In the light of this, no preconception is safe. Its implications are so staggering that every aspect of the history of that time needs to be looked at afresh. As on a train that has come to the end of the line, we must shout: *All change!*

CHAPTER SIX

The 'Lost Kings' and a Pyramid of the First Dynasty

A pyramid of the First Dynasty in Egypt? Who ever heard of such a thing? Well, that is just the trouble, most people haven't. But nevertheless, this pyramid was excavated by Walter B. Emery in 1937 at Saqqara and its remains may be seen in Plate 33 and in Figure 36. Like it or not, there it is.

This is what I call a *story*. But it is a story that nobody has wanted to tell. Why is that? Is it too embarrassing because no expert knows what to say about it or what it means?

This pyramid was the tomb of a renegade First Dynasty king named King Enezib, whose name is sometimes spelled Anedjib (both are 'correct', since 'dj' and 'z' are interchangeable in our modern spellings of Egyptian names). He was the fifth king of the First Dynasty.

How could a king as early as that have built a pyramid and yet nobody know about it?

The Pyramid of Enezib was 75 feet long at the base and would have had an original height of 43 feet, and so it was not particularly small. Its height has been calculated from its slope, which Emery says was 49 degrees, a slope which is three degrees less than that of the Great Pyramid of Giza. But Enezib's pyramid was not made of stone, it was made of mud bricks.

King Enezib seems to have been overthrown, but even if he died naturally, his successor, King Semerkhet, made every effort to efface his memory, scratching his name off precious objects and so forth. Enezib's pyramid then had its top cut off. It was thus a *decapitated*

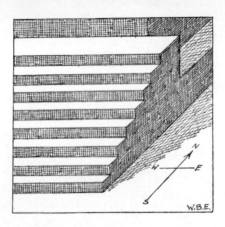

Figure 36. This cutaway diagram shows the steps of the excavated Step Pyramid tomb of King Enezib (or Anedjib), fifth king of the First Dynasty, which was discovered at Saqqara in 1937 by Emery and at first attributed to Nebetka, a royal official who lived under Enezib's reign. We see also in this drawing that the structure is oriented precisely to the cardinal points, as are the Giza pyramids. (Figure 64 from Walter B. Emery, 'A Preliminary report on the Architecture of the Tomb of Nebetka', *Annales du Service*, Cairo, Vol. 38). A fuller report on this tomb was published eleven years later in Walter B. Emery, *Great Tombs of the First Dynasty*, Volume I, Cairo, 1949, where this drawing is Figure 38–A on page 84, and the tomb has been numbered Tomb 3038. After some years of further debate and consideration, Emery decided that there might be 'some more startling possibilities' about this tomb than just belonging to a royal official. It was originally constructed as a stepped pyramid! The top was then cut off, and the pyramid form entirely concealed by a new super-structure in the conventional tomb form with a frontage of what is known as 'the palace façade' design. In 1961, Emery finally said what he thought this tomb really was; in his book *Archaic Egypt*, he said: 'The building is dated to Enezib, and, although the name of an official called Nebitka occurs on jar-sealings, etc., it would appear probable that it is the burial place of the king.' (page 82) See discussion in main text.

pyramid. That was certainly a pretty drastic thing to do, and suggests a violent hatred of pyramids by the southern kings who had established the First Dynasty. This must also have been done on the orders of Semerkhet, because Emery has established that it was done within a time span that would have included the architect's lifetime, hence must have happened right after King Enezib's death.

The strong possibility that this was a dispute between the north and the south over what exactly constituted a 'unified Egypt' is explicitly suggested by Walter Emery,[1] and is indicated by the drastic differences

Figure 37. This is the famous 'Tablet of the Kings,' carved on a wall of a corridor in the Temple of Seti I at Abydos in Upper Egypt. Since it is impossible to photograph the carving face on, due to its width and the narrowness of the corridor, this engraving of it is invaluable. (It actually extends further to the right.) Seti I, second king of the 19th Dynasty, is seen making offerings (he holds an incense pipe in his left hand) to the spirits of the royal ancestors. He is preceded by a priest. This engraving was published in Sir Norman Lockyer's *The Dawn of Astronomy*, London, 1894, p. 21. This king list is now generally known by the name of The Abydos King List. Each cartouche contains the name of an ancient king, whose spirit is being honoured. Heretical kings such as Akhenaten and his son Tutankhamun are omitted from this List, which was for ceremonial purposes, as their spirits must not be honoured. Seti I's temple at Abydos was really a 'Temple of the Royal Ancestors' culminating in himself. One of its purposes was to strengthen his claims to legitimacy by portraying him as the direct successor of all the dead kings from earliest times. It is believed that he carried out elaborate ceremonies to honour the dead kings at least once a year in person. At that time, all of their names would have been recited aloud.

between two ancient king lists, one northern one known as the Saqqara King List, and a southern one known as the Abydos King List (see Figures 37 and 38), both of which I will describe a little later on. The northern list omits Semerkhet and the four kings of the First Dynasty who preceded Enezib, and cites Enezib as the true founder of a united Egypt. As far as that list is concerned, official Egyptian history begins with him. It can be no coincidence that this list is from Saqqara, which is where Enezib built his pyramid. But the southern list, on the other hand, includes all these omitted kings. So these are the first of our 'lost

215

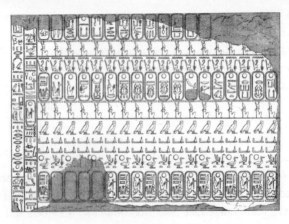

Figure 38. An illustration of part of the Abydos King List, carved on a wall of the Temple of the Ancestors of King Seti I, which is known today simply as 'The Temple of Seti I' at Abydos, north of Denderah in Upper Egypt. (From *L'Égypte: Atlas Historique et Pittoresque*, Plate I, date unknown, but late 19th century, a loose plate in the Collection of Robert Temple.)

kings' in this chapter. But, as we shall see, there were many other and probably more important 'lost kings', who form part of the ongoing mysteries of predynastic and Archaic Egypt, and what was really going on then, as well as some enigmas about the Third Dynasty of the early Old Kingdom.

The instability of First Dynasty rule is shown in a most dramatic way by Emery's discovery, which was one of the most unexpected discoveries made in Egyptology before the Second World War, although the implications of this discovery were not immediately obvious – even to Emery. It all began with his finding a puzzling tomb at Saqqara known as Tomb 3038. He discovered it in 1937, and at first he thought it was the tomb of a royal official named Nebetka or Nebitka, whose name was found on some jar sealings in the tomb. So his report described the tomb as 'the tomb of Nebetka'.[2] By the time Emery published his more extensive account of this tomb in Volume I of his *Great Tombs of the First Dynasty* in 1949, after the distressing interruption of the war was over, he had concluded that the tomb might not really be Nebetka's, but that there might be 'some more startling possibilities'.[3] And finally, by the time he published his book *Archaic*

216

Egypt in 1961, Emery was at last specific about what he meant by that: 'The building is dated to [King] Enezib, and, although the name of an official named Nebitka [which he had previously spelled Nebetka] occurs on jar-sealings, etc., it would appear probable that it is the burial place of the king.'[4]

I do not recite this evolution of Emery's thoughts on a tomb without a reason. For the *reason* is what is so astonishing about all of this. This tomb is unique for a king's tomb in the entire Archaic Period, a period constituted by what we call the First and Second Dynasties. And the strange structure of this tomb discovered by Emery appears to be connected with a political conflict of major proportions. For what amazed Emery was the strange fact that this tomb was designed and built at first *as a pyramid*. And a royal tomb in the shape of a pyramid in the First Dynasty is unique.

There are more strange things about the tomb than its original pyramid shape. There is a mystery about what happened to it, and also to its king. The tomb seems to have been a victim of a major political power struggle, and the entire appearance of the tomb was changed, for after the top of the pyramid was cut off, the structure was remodelled to look 'normal', like the tombs of the king's predecessors and successors. In other words, King Enezib seems to have been 'a heretic', who was disowned and his legacy altered by his own dynasty, but who was rehabilitated much later.

I mentioned earlier in this chapter the existence of the Saqqara King List. King Enezib was the very first king to be mentioned on the list, as if he were looked upon as the first legitimate 'king of Egypt' in the eyes of the northerners. All of the First Dynasty kings before him were ignored. His immediate successor, King Semerkhet, who opposed him, was then omitted from the Saqqara List as well, so that the northerners of later times refused to recognise him. The 'omitted' kings of the northern Saqqara List were however reinstated on the southern Abydos King List. So it seems pretty clear that there was a major north–south power struggle going on, and that King Enezib favoured the north, whereas his predecessors and his immediate successor Semerkhet favoured the south. The 'tit-for-tat' omissions and inclusions in the rival king lists would appear to make this obvious.

King Semerkhet tried to erase Enezib's name from monuments, and some stone bowls preserved beneath the Step Pyramid at Saqqara, which once bore Enezib's name, have had the name scratched out. There was certainly a campaign immediately after his reign to make him a 'non-person'. It must have been Semerkhet who altered Enezib's tomb. After all, a king's tomb could only be mutilated by order of another king. Enezib's determination to have a tomb shaped like a pyramid must have been an assertion of northern sentiment that his successor could not tolerate. Here is what Emery says in his 1961 book:

'Enezib was the first king mentioned in the Sakkara king list, and from this we may conclude that he was the first Thinite ['This' was the name of the capital of the First Dynasty] monarch to be recognised as legitimate by Lower Egypt. It is significant that his name, inscribed on stone vessels, has frequently been erased by his successor Semerkhet, who has in his turn been omitted in the Sakkara list; all of which suggests a dynastic struggle between rival claimants who received support, one from Upper and one from Lower Egypt. . . . When first excavated, the superstructure of the tomb appeared to follow the familiar design of a rectangular platform, with its exterior decorated with recessed panelling. But further digging revealed a stepped pyramid structure hidden within it. Only the lower part of the stepped structure was preserved . . .'[5]

More information about the anomalous structure is given in the full 1949 excavation report:

From an architectural point of view, this tomb is by far the most inter-esting building of the First Dynasty yet discovered, for it has undergone three distinct and radical changes in design, all apparently done by the same builder. Because of the uniform size, texture and colour of the bricks employed in all three buildings, we can be, more or less, certain that no great interval passed between these alterations. But we can gain no clue to the reason for the changes or to the architectural conception behind the first two constructions. . . . The first construction consisted of a rectangular pit . . . The superstructure consisted of a rectangular block of brickwork with vertical sides which just covered the burial pit and the subsidiary rooms, and on the north, south and west sides banks of sand and rubble were placed against them to form a foundation and

core for a series of steps arranged in pyramidal form. . . . The steps . . .
rise at an angle of 49 degrees . . .[6]

Truly this is extraordinary. The Great Pyramid's slope is just under 52 degrees, and here we have a First Dynasty royal tomb which was originally built with a slope of 49 degrees, very close indeed. As for size, King Enezib's pyramid was 22.8 metres (exactly 25 yards, or 75 feet) long from north to south, but only 10.55 metres across from east to west because the eastern face of the pyramid appears to have been truncated and is missing. Whether this was intended originally or was part of the mutilation is not known, but this is what was found by the excavators when they reached the inner structure. Plate 33 and Figure 36 therefore show this inner structure after they revealed it, having removed the outer 'normal' casing, which had entirely concealed it from view for nearly five thousand years.

Figure 39 shows what a typical royal tomb at Saqqara would have looked like when it was new, with its characteristic 'palace façade' design motif of alternating recessed and protruding panelling and the structure's flat rectangular shape known as a 'mastaba'. For a king suddenly to build a pyramid as his tomb in the midst of all of these similar mastabas must have been a great shock to everyone! To call Enezib unconventional does not do justice to the impact of his action, which would have been as upsetting to the status quo as Akhenaten was to the status quo of his day, when he also tried to change things.

The fact that alterations to it were made so soon must mean that King Semerkhet ordered the pyramid to be cut down, probably by its original architect, and the tomb to be converted to a 'normal' rectangular tomb with the standard appearance. Thus, King Enezib's 'big statement' was destroyed and covered over. It would have been tempting to think that King Enezib's First Dynasty stepped pyramid might have inspired King Zoser's Third Dynasty stepped pyramid, which was also at Saqqara. But this is impossible, because it had been decapitated and covered over, so that Zoser's architect, Imhotep, could never have seen it.

However, there is an extremely strange aspect to the Enezib story and the Zoser story, which somehow do seem to be related to one

Figure 39. Jean-Philippe Lauer's reconstruction of the tomb (or cenotaph, no one is sure which) of Queen Merneith ('Beloved of Neith', who was the goddess of the north) of the First Dynasty at Saqqara, as it would have looked when it was new, a view reconstructed by Jean-Philippe Lauer, and reproduced in several of his publications. This queen was a 'Libyan' from the Delta, probably from the capital city of Sais, who is believed to have been the wife of King Djet and the mother of King Den (the third and fourth kings of the First Dynasty).

another. The Pyramid of Enezib was decapitated and covered over by two successive stages of mastabas. (It is not clear why it was thought necessary to do this twice, so perhaps there was a 'magical' consideration due to a superstition of some kind.) But when Lauer excavated and studied the construction of Zoser's Step Pyramid at Saqqara, he discovered that Imhotep had done *precisely the reverse.* Zoser's Step Pyramid is constructed in three stages also. It starts with a mastaba, then there was a pyramid built on top of that, and then there was a further pyramid built upon that one. This may be graphically seen in two diagrams of Lauer's, reproduced as Figures 40 and 41.

So let us just consider this for a moment:

(1) Enezib's tomb consisted of a pyramid, which was cut down and covered with a mastaba, which was then covered with another mastaba.

(2) Zoser's tomb consisted of a mastaba, which was covered with a pyramid, which was then covered with another pyramid.

If Semerkhet was making a statement in converting Enezib's pyramid into a mastaba *twice,* perhaps Imhotep was making a statement by converting a mastaba into a pyramid *twice.*

Was Imhotep countering the 'bad magic' that had taken place centuries earlier with a magical construction ritual of his own, as a kind of architectural act of exorcism?

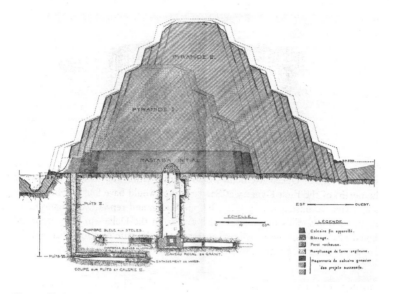

Figure 40. Jean-Philippe Lauer's diagrammatic section of the Step Pyramid at Saqqara, showing in its shaded portions its three construction phases above ground level (below ground is shown as white). Phase One is the squat rectangular mastaba at the base, labelled 'Initial Mastaba'. Phase Two is Pyramid 1. Phase Three is Pyramid 2, which is what we now see from the outside, secretly encasing the two earlier structures entirely. This was all done within the lifetime of King Zoser by his architect, Imhotep, and it was all done on purpose. The question is: why? Until now, it has been presumed, for want of any other explanation, that the pharaoh and his architect could not make up their minds, and that they first decided to build a mastaba, but were not satisfied with it, and then build a small pyramid on top of it. But then, dissatisfied still, they built yet another pyramid, much larger this time, which swallowed up both of the earlier structures (which were only discovered by Lauer's probings and excavations). However, this explanation suggests that they were rather foolish and dithering, and does not fit psychologically somehow with what we know about Imhotep as reputedly the greatest individual genius in Egyptian history. But now a surprising alternative presents itself: perhaps Imhotep was making a definite 'statement' of a political and cultural nature. For what he did was precisely the opposite of what King Semerkhet of the First Dynasty did: Semerkhet decapitated his predecessor, King Enezib's, pyramid at Saqqara and built two successive mastabas over it. Imhotep did the exact reverse, also at Saqqara, starting with a mastaba and then building two pyramids over it. This may have been intended to have, not only a political and cultural significance, but a magical significance as well: undoing the 'bad magic' of a previous age by reversing it with corrective 'good magic'. See the further discussion in the main text. This drawing is

221

folding Plate 11 in Jean Philippe Lauer, *Histoire Monumentale des Pyramides d'Égypte* (*Monumental History of the Egyptian Pyramids*), Volume 1, *Les Pyramides à Degrés* (*IIIe Dynastie*) (*The Step Pyramids of the Third Dynasty*), Cairo, 1962.

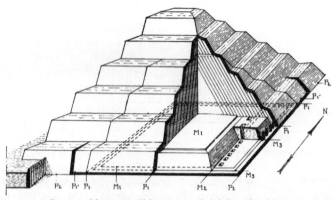

Fɪɢ. 20. — Schéma perspectif des états successifs de la Pyramide à degrés.

Figure 41. Schematic perspective view of the successive layers of the Step Pyramid of Zoser at Saqqara. Figure 20 on page 71 of Jean-Phillippe Lauer, *Histoire Monumentale des Pyramides d'Égypte* (*Monumental History of the Pyramids of Egypt*), Volume I: *Les Pyramides à Degrés* (*IIIe Dynastie*) (*The Step Pyramids* (*Third Dynasty*)), Cairo, 1962. The rectangular and flat mastaba ('M1') was the first construction (slight modifications to it are labelled M2 and M3), the step pyramid labelled 'P1' was then built on top of it, and finally the Step Pyramid as we now see it ('P2') was in turn constructed on top of that.

Or was this a purely political act? King Enezib clearly flaunted the fact that he had built himself a pyramid as a tomb, and his successor was so furious that he destroyed it and converted it into a mastaba to resemble all the others. Maybe Zoser and Imhotep were rehabilitating Enezib and making a big statement that he was right, and things were going to go their way from now on. In other words, the north was once again on top, not the south. Having buried King Khasekhemui at Abydos in the south and made their peace there, they then returned to Saqqara and began to construct a triumphalist proclamation of the

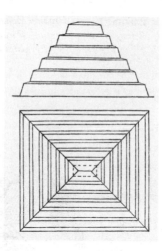

Figure 42. Elevation and plan of the Step Pyramid of Saqqara, as published by its chief excavator, Jean-Philippe Lauer. This is Figure 1 from Jean-Philippe Lauer's early article, 'Remarques sur les Monuments du Roi Zoser à Saqqarah', *Bulletin de l'Institut Français d'Archéologie Orientale*, Vol. XXX, 1930, page 334. Lauer stressed that the Step Pyramid was not square but rectangular in its plan. (The northern and southern sides are longer than the eastern and western sides, by a ratio of 6 to 5.4 at the base. This ratio changes as the structure gets higher and you move to higher levels or 'steps', so that the northern and southern sides grow longer and the eastern and western sides grow shorter the higher you go.)

supremacy of the northern viewpoint, using the secret northern stone technology to which only they had access. And just to rub everybody's noses in it and make it absolutely clear, they blatantly *reversed* the eradication process of Semerkhet, of which memories must have survived, and showed their contempt for the southern mastaba concept, which had come to symbolise the dominance of the southern kings, by putting not one but two pyramids right on top of one. It is even possible that the eastern section of Enezib's pyramid was cut away so that Imhotep could examine the internal structure and do his architectural research.

What encourages us to believe that all of this was political is the evidence that Enezib's predecessor and immediate successor were deleted from the Saqqara King List. At this point I should explain exactly what the Saqqara King List is, and answer a suggestion, made by one scholar, that these kings were omitted from it just because somebody ran out of space.

The Saqqara King List was found inscribed on the walls of the tomb of a senior priest known as a chief lector priest, whose name was Tjuloy, and who lived at the time of the New Kingdom under Pharaoh Rameses II (reigned 1279 BC–1213 BC). Tjuloy wanted to honour the 'ancestor kings', so he had fifty-eight names of kings depicted in two registers of twenty-nine each in a relief in his tomb chapel.

The name that begins his list is that of King Enezib, and then the next king, Semerkhet, who was Enezib's great enemy, is omitted, as are the four kings of the First Dynasty who preceded Enezib. The scholar Donald Redford, who has written an important book on ancient king lists and annals of the Egyptians, suggests that these omissions did not occur on purpose. He says they ran out of space on the wall. But in that case, working backwards, they should have ended with Semerkhet and not reached Enezib, But instead, Semerkhet was omitted. So why was that? How does that fit in with Redford's theory? Redford also says the list was a southern list which just happened to be inscribed in the north, because the capital of the New Kingdom was at Thebes (modern Luxor) and all lists were 'Theban lists' by that time, and that the Saqqara King List must represent 'an incursion of a Theban tradition into the Memphite region'.[7] But that isn't convincing either. Of course the more recent sections of the list came from there; where else could they have come from? But when inscribing a list at Saqqara, even if one were a southerner, one would be expected – in the matters which concerned Saqqara – to abide by Saqqaran traditions. There was no 'Saqqaran' version of any New Kingdom king list, as Saqqara never had much to do with the New Kingdom. But if you were putting up a tomb at Saqqara, you would not go against local custom. To do so would be an insult to the locals, and would also be 'bad magic'.

Redford seems keen to downplay any political significance regarding the omissions of the names of the 'lost kings'. But he contradicts this argument elsewhere in his book. He admits that with regard to king lists, 'a local tradition remained strong; and this grouped kings according to geographic clustering.'[8] Absolutely right. He also mentions, when speaking of the southern list known as the Abydos King List: '. . . the

224

strong cultic connection between the Memphite royal house of the Old Kingdom and the Abydos list is duly reflected in the orderly progression from Menes to the fifty-sixth name . . ."[9] But this is just the point about the Saqqara King List itself, that there was a strong local 'cultic tradition', which Tjuloy dare not defy, lest he offend the very hosts of his own tomb. And how much stronger could the local tradition be than at Saqqara, where the mutilated Saqqaran tomb of Enezib and the apparently pro-Enezib and anti-Semerkhet pyramid of Zoser were both to be found? But the most telling point is that Semerkhet was skipped in Tjuloy's list. If it had been a matter of wall space, he would have been the 'first king', not Enezib.

So what was going on here? Was King Enezib's stepped pyramid the first of all the pyramids of Egypt? If so, where did he get the idea? And since it was destroyed and covered over by his irate successor Semerkhet, where did Imhotep much later get the very same idea, considering that it could not have been from seeing or even knowing about Enezib's earlier structure? What was the source of these two pyramids, which were both at Saqqara, despite the fact that the second cannot have derived from direct observation of the first's remains? (I leave aside here the possibility that Imhotep may have sliced away the eastern side to investigate, as we have no evidence of this.)

This is a genuine mystery. But, like all mysteries, it must have a solution. Apart from the fact that a tradition must have survived of the mutilation of Enezib's pyramid, and was known to Zoser and Imhotep, the two Saqqara pyramids both had a common source of inspiration: some other pyramid or pyramids that inspired them both. *Can this have been the three main pyramids of Giza?*

We have seen from dating results that the Giza pyramids could go back to predynastic times. It does not mean that they did, it means that they could. But if they did not, who between predynastic times and the Fourth Dynasty could have built them without our knowing about it?

In Chapter Eight, I offer some unexpected suggestions as to the source of the knowledge and technology which could have led to the construction of the Giza pyramids by pharaohs earlier than the Fourth Dynasty, as our dating results suggest. It is absolutely clear that no pharaoh of the First Dynasty could possibly have built them, because Enezib tried to build a pyramid at Saqqara and could only do so with mud bricks, though he made a good try. Discussions of these matters have not been helped by the failure of Egyptologists to discuss or call attention to the Pyramid of Enezib. By leaving that out of the discourse, they have skewed discussions by eliminating the earliest previously dateable evidence of serious pyramid building. I should not be having to introduce Enezib's Pyramid here as a novel subject, when it has been known about since Emery's time. But the matter has been disregarded by those whose duty it was to face it.

And this brings me to the other major and mysterious 'lost kings' of this chapter. For they date from predynastic times, were kings of Lower Egypt who are clearly named on the Palermo Stone (an annals record that I mentioned in Chapter One and that I describe more fully below), but of whom all other knowledge is lost, as if a campaign of eradication of all trace of their existence had been carried out on the ground by their successors, the conquering southern kings of Upper Egypt who 'unified' Egypt and founded what we have come to call the First Dynasty. Could these 'lost kings' of the north be the true builders of the Giza pyramids? Could King Enezib have been in sympathy with them, attempted to emulate them in his small way with mud bricks and tried to build his own pyramid? After all, it wasn't that small – it was 75 feet long at the base – and he seems to have been really serious about it. Could this have been looked upon as a shocking apostasy by the passionately anti–Lower Egypt southern kings, especially by Enezib's successor (who may well have overthrown him), Semerkhet? The strange eliminations of the initial southern kings from the Saqqara King List, including Semerkhet's own omission, and Enezib's inclusion and position as '*first king of unified Egypt*' suggests a ferocious political disagreement between people who were pro–north and people who were pro–south. I believe everyone has underestimated the passions involved in all of this in ancient times. Civil wars are always the nastiest.

Thinking along these lines is encouraged by what we have already seen, namely the unavailability of advanced stone technology to the southern kings – as we saw with Khasekhemui's tomb, described in the previous chapter – but its availability at Saqqara as seen in the reign of the very next king, Zoser. There was unquestionably a technological

Plate 24a

Plate 24b

Plate 24c

Plate 24d

Plate 25

Plate 26

Plate 27

Plate 28

Plate 29

Plate 30

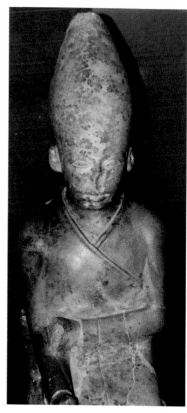

Plate 31

Plate 32

Plate 34

Plate 33

Plate 35

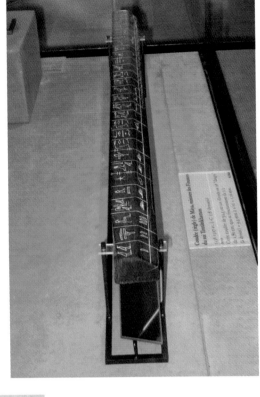

Plate 36

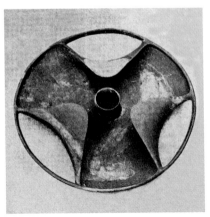

Plate 37a

Plate 37b

Plate 38

Plate 39

Plate 40

Plate 41

Plate 42

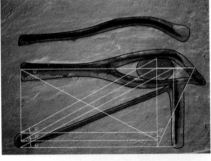

Plate 43

Plate 44

Plate 45

divide, with the northerners being able to build pyramids and the southerners not being able to build them. Only one First Dynasty king, Enezib, built a pyramid, and he was described in a northern king list as the first real king of unified Egypt, his predecessors and immediate successor expunged from the record. Perhaps there had been just as rigorous and determined an attempt to rewrite history on the part of the first kings of the First Dynasty, who wished no trace or memory of the 'lost kings' to remain. However, due to the conservatism of the Egyptian priests and the archival researches of Imhotep in the Third Dynasty (who collected the 40,000 ancient stone bowls with the names of early kings inscribed on many of them), the names were preserved on lists, and resurfaced at the end of the Fifth Dynasty on the Palermo Stone as bare names, with no other details available.

We are faced here with another chronological enigma.

The chronology of ancient Egyptian history is, as I have already pointed out, firmly established back as far as 2000 BC. Prior to that, there was something called The First Intermediate Period, which was a period of total social and political collapse. It is thought that this period was marked by floods, droughts, plagues and lawlessness. No one knows exactly how long this period lasted, but few people imagine that it was less than fifty or a hundred years, and many think it was about 150 years. I am inclined to think 150 years is a pretty reliable estimate.

Before this, there were the Fifth and Sixth Dynasties of the Old Kingdom. They were a kind of tepid afterglow of the glory of the true Old Kingdom, which consisted of the Third and Fourth Dynasties. It used to be thought that the First and Second Dynasties should be considered part of the Old Kingdom, but it has now become fashionable to speak of those as the 'Archaic Period'. One reason for that is we know so little about them. (However, it must be said that we know even less about the Third Dynasty, but people often overlook that fact.)

The unsettling thing is that prior to – let us say – 2200 BC, the chronology of Egyptian history essentially falls apart. Everything before that date is more or less lost in a kind of chronological chaos. There are many Egyptologists who do not think this. But that is because they comfort themselves with chronological assertions. They simply *decide* certain dates.

The dating results that Ioannis Liritzis and I have found for the Osiris Shaft at Giza and the Mycerinus Pyramid undermine any cosy acceptance of a 'standard chronology' prior to 2200 BC. We are by no means the first people to suggest in recent decades that all of the conventionally accepted Old Kingdom datings are 'a bit too recent', and that adjustments of one, two, three, or more centuries backwards are required. In Chapter Three, we saw that other pyramid dating results have also suggested the same thing. In Chapter Five, we have seen that an adjustment backwards of 173 years is advisable for the true date of the burial of King Khasekhemui, last king of the Second Dynasty. And I have no doubt that such modest adjustments backwards are the very least of the problem.

The chronology of these early periods rests upon the shakiest of foundations. In order to be able to discuss this subject properly, I need briefly to describe the texts and evidence that exist, upon which Egyptologists base their arguments. One of these sources is probably a fake, upon which no reliance at all should be placed, although it has been a mainstay of most of the scholarly work done on these problems since 1910.

The fake I am referring to is called the 'Cairo Stone', which I discussed briefly in Chapter One. It is not a single stone, but is rather a set of stone fragments, hence it is often referred to as the 'Cairo Fragments'. All but one of these fragments are in the Egyptian Museum at Cairo, previously called the Cairo Museum, hence the name given to the 'stone'. The largest of the fragments is also sometimes called the Cairo Stone, but the way these things are spoken of is not really consistent. The other fragment is in the Petrie Museum in London and is sometimes called the Petrie Fragment, sometimes called the London Fragment, and at other times is just called a Cairo Fragment, even though it is not in Cairo. I will discuss the details of the Cairo Stone as we go along. But first I will describe the Palermo Stone, also mentioned in Chapter One, which is, as you might expect, presently in Palermo, Sicily, hence its name. The Cairo Stone is looked upon as another portion of the Palermo Stone. It is surprising that some people still think this, despite the fact that those familiar with the physical details of the two 'stones' have long agreed that they are not pieces of the same stone at all. The Cairo Stone and the Palermo Stone have different thicknesses, for instance, and cannot possibly be part of the same physical object.

The Cairo Fragments are also of differing thicknesses from each other, suggesting that they come from separate stones. The difference in thicknesses was pointed out by Petrie in 1916, when he wrote his first article about them, entitled 'New Portions of the Annals', with which he published a very fine photo of his own Cairo Fragment which he had bought himself in the Cairo bazaar, and took back to London. It is now in London's Petrie Museum. I reproduce it in Plate 34.

Petrie says:

'Are all the pieces from the same monument, or were there two or more copies of the Annals? The internal evidence suggests that the Palermo and Cairo pieces are by different hands. On the Cairo piece the lines of the top row of kings are irregular and tilted; the main lines of the registers beneath are less regularly cut; the signs on both fragments 1 and 2 of Cairo, suggest that when fresh they were much less beautifully regular than those of Palermo. . . . Another consideration is the thickness of the slabs. The large piece at Cairo is 2.36 to 2.44 inches thick; and this is stated to be the same as the two small pieces and that at Palermo. On the other hand the piece said to be from Memphis is 3.18 inches thick, and the piece at University College [in London] is 2.09 inches thick.'

He is inclined to be charitable and to assume variations of thickness in the original slabs themselves might have been at work here, but he warns: 'Before anything can be concluded we need an accurate gauging of all sides of the larger pieces, to see how much they taper in any direction.'[10]

In 1917, the year after Petrie's article, the German Egyptologist Ludwig Borchardt published his book *Die Annalen* (*The Annals*)[11], in which he dealt with the Palermo Stone and the Cairo Fragments in rather a pompous manner, which deeply irritated Petrie and many others. However, because this book came out in the middle of the First World War, it was not seen outside of Germany for a few years. It wasn't until 1920 that Petrie was able to express an opinion on it in a review in the journal he edited, *Ancient Egypt*. Petrie was very harsh towards Borchardt and accused him of the extremely serious offence of tampering with the evidence. After criticising Borchardt regarding the stones themselves, Petrie then went on to make this astonishing accusation of scholarly dishonesty:

'A matter which casts a serious shadow on this work is the "doctoring" of two ivory tablets on p. 53. A second version of one tablet has the gratuitous insertion of [a certain numeral] put in for the sake of argument, of which there is no trace on the original. A second version of another tablet has a break smoothed out, and a perfectly clear incised line obliterated along with it, in order to make out a similar hypothetical group. Neither of these proposed readings has the least ground, and to propose fictitious readings only throws a shadow on all the rest of the material.'[12]

This is one of the most ferocious attacks on a famous Egyptologist by another and equally famous Egyptologist in the entire twentieth century. I don't believe any contemporary person has ever noticed it or is aware of it. But it must have made tsunami waves at the time. It is interesting that it took place within the context of discussions of what I have chosen to call the 'chronological chaos' of Egyptian history prior to 2200 BC. What Petrie accused Borchardt of doing was falsifying evidence from some of the ivory jar labels excavated from First Dynasty tombs (and Petrie had excavated more of these than anyone, so he knew what he was talking about, and he may very well have excavated these very ones, hence his fury) in order to support an interpretation of the Cairo Fragments. So it is evident that things were getting nasty even as early as 1917.

Another awkward aspect of the Cairo Fragments was pointed out by Petrie in 1931. It seems never to have occurred to him that the fragments might be forgeries (after all, he had bought one, so he must subconsciously have wanted it to be real). But he often referred to difficulties about them, and on this occasion he said:

'It would be impossible to have one slab nine feet long and only 2½ inches thick: There must have been several divisions. As it would be difficult to have a joint in the middle of a year space, so a whole number of spaces in each row must have been fitted in. This almost compels the width of the slabs to be uniform, in order to get on each slab a whole number of spaces in each row. Hence there is need to have slabs of equal width. According to the existing pieces it would be impossible to have four, five, seven, eight, or nine slabs, so six is the probable number.' [13]

But this is already getting a bit artificial and desperate. In order for the Cairo Fragments to be real, what Petrie is really saying is that the slabs of the annals had to be six in number, of equal width: no more, no less.

The next year, in 1932, in reviewing an article by James Henry Breasted, which referred to the Cairo Fragments, Petrie stated: 'The difference of thickness is not accounted for . . .' But he still held to his theory of six slabs side by side as the solution, and did not sense that this was too contrived to be convincing.[14]

It is ironical that Borchardt, in his 1917 book, despite apparently 'faking' some ivory tablet evidence, was correct in insisting that the Cairo Fragments differed so much in thickness, style and hieroglyphs, that they must come from at least four separate sources and could not possibly be part of the same stone. (It is possible that Petrie would have agreed with him about this if he had not been so incensed about the faking of the ivory labels.) What simply didn't occur to him, or to anyone else in those days, was that everyone had been duped and that the fragments not only came from different stones, but that they were fakes. One reason why people did not come to this conclusion early on was that for some years after their discovery, the Cairo Fragments, apart from Petrie's own, lingered in the Cairo Museum, where they were not really made available for inspection, much to everyone's frustration. Many of the scholars who wrote the books about them did not personally inspect them, but were forced to work only from photographs.

The Palermo Stone is absolutely not a fake. It dates from the latter part of the Fifth Dynasty, or at the very latest the first reign of the Sixth Dynasty. There is no doubt about this at all. This stone has been badly smashed, and is only a minor fragment of what used to be a gigantic stone bearing inscriptions recording the history of Egypt from the beginnings in the times of the gods up until the Fifth Dynasty. If only we had the whole thing. The situation is worse than tantalising, it is enough to drive people mad; and some, I would suggest, have succumbed!

The Palermo Stone on its obverse side only gives the names of three kings from the First Dynasty to the Fifth. They are Ninetjer and Khasekhemui of the Second Dynasty and Sneferu of the Fourth Dynasty. All the other names of the first four dynasties are broken or worn away. But the stone does reveal all kinds of wonderful and fascinating little details, is quaint to an extraordinary degree, and is wonderfully, sublimely archaic. After it was excavated and made such a hit with everyone, the mysterious fragments known as the Cairo Stone turned up in the hands of a Cairo antiquities dealer in 1910 and were sold to the Cairo Museum. Everybody was thrilled because, frustrated as they were that the Palermo Stone was just a fragment, they wished themselves into believing that by some miracle some more fragments of this tantalising stone had been found. After it was realised by many scholars that the stones could not physically be identical, the consensus was: no matter, it's just another copy of the same text from yet another stone. Who cares, *we've got some more of the missing pieces!* You can just imagine the heady euphoria with which delirious Egyptologists welcomed this sheer miracle, the appearance of more fragments! I feel like a terrible killjoy, but really, it just isn't so. I will explain why later, but the evidence for the faking really is solid. The Cairo Stone has been just as big a nuisance in leading everybody astray as you can possibly imagine.

Next in antiquity to the Palermo Stone, there are some other brief and partial king lists that have been found in odd places. The Wadi Hammamat List, carved in a cliff at that desert locale, is a brief king list showing a series of kings of the Fourth Dynasty, and has already been mentioned. It dates from the Twelfth Dynasty. It was reproduced as Figure 8 in Chapter Three.

There is a brief list of kings preserved on a limestone relief from the tomb of Mahu at Saqqara. It only mentions three kings' names which can still be read, one of whom (Userkaf, first king of the Fifth Dynasty) is well known, one of whom, Teti, is a puzzle, as there were three Tetis and no one really agrees about them, and the other, apparently called Djeser-nub, may or may not be a correctly deciphered name, but in any case no one knows who he is. So here is more chronological chaos.

There is a king list preserved on an intriguing object known as the Giza Drawing Board, a fragmentary wooden writing palette found in a Fifth Dynasty tomb at Giza in 1904. The object is dated to the Fifth Dynasty, so the kings listed are all early. Once again, there is a Teti: no one knows which one. Chephren and Djedefre are mentioned, but no Cheops. There is a King Bedjau, but no one really knows who he is either. As can be seen, things are a bit of a mess. Kings are mentioned in the early lists who should not exist, and kings who should exist or definitely did exist are not mentioned.

An extensive list and summary of most (but not all) of the king lists that exist is to be found in *Pharaonic King-Lists, Annals and Day-Books*, by Donald B. Redford (1986).[15] As is clear from Redford's generally thorough survey, many of the lists that exist are of no particular interest, being scrappy or corrupt, and I will not bother to mention them.

The next king list in importance is called the Turin Papyrus. As you might expect, it is in Turin and it is a papyrus. Sometimes it is called the Turin Canon (and abbreviated TC), or the Turin King List. It was intact when it was found, but then some idiots put it in a box and sent it by sea from Egypt to Italy, and by the time it arrived, it was in countless pieces. No one has ever been able to put them all back together again. Nevertheless, many chunks have been reconstituted, and a great deal of information can still be gleaned from this tattered document. The Turin Papyrus is really important; what a shame it was largely ruined.

Then there is the Abydos King List. Engravings of it may be seen in Figure 37 and in Figure 38. This amazingly long king list is carved in relief on a large wall of the Temple of Seti I at Abydos, which is an edifice that is still standing. Seti I was the second king of the Nineteenth Dynasty. The heretical pharaohs Akhenaten and Tutankhamun are omitted from this list (both of them erased from history as 'non-persons' to whose spirits incense offerings could not be made), as is the female pharaoh, Queen Hatshepsut, who could not be offered incense either because she was a woman, and, what is more, a woman who sometimes dressed as a man (literally a queen who dressed as a king). Also omitted is a heretic pharaoh of the second Dynasty named Peribsen. But great care is taken to enumerate countless early pharaohs from the dawn of

Egyptian history and, even though the names given for them tend to be garbled and confusing to us, the earnestness with which this was done at the orders of King Seti is most impressive. As I have explained in my lengthy survey, with dating results, of this temple (not yet published), the Temple of Seti I was really a temple to the Ancestors, culminating in Seti himself. Seti's son Rameses II had a similar list put into his own temple nearby, taking the list one further generation along to include his own name, but it is somewhat inferior to Seti's, and certainly adds nothing new besides Rameses himself.

Finally we come to Manetho. Manetho was an Egyptian priest whose Egyptian name is unknown, Manethon being what he called himself in Greek. He lived under the first two or three Ptolemies, the Greek pharaohs who succeeded Alexander the Great (died 323 BC) and ended with Cleopatra (died 30 BC). Manetho wrote several important works on Egyptian history and culture in Greek, which were widely circulated throughout the civilised world of his day. As is the case with so much of classical literature, only about 5 per cent of which survives, his books are all lost. However, considerable portions of king lists recorded by Manetho were copied out from his works by two other authors, and these both survive. It is somewhat confusing that these differ from one another in detail. But that is one of the hazards of working with fragments of lost texts which have not always been copied out satisfactorily. The fragments of Manetho are readily available in English translation.[16] It was Manetho who first 'created' the division of dynasties from One to Six. There was no early tradition of this numbering. Egyptologists have taken over these dynastic creations of Manetho lock, stock and barrel. Furthermore, it was Manetho who 'invented' the concept of 'dynasties' for Egypt in the first place:

'Manetho further divided the series of rulers into a series of "dynasties". *Dynasteia* was Manetho's Greek word for each grouping, and it appears that this was a new and original move. Outside of Manetho, the Greek word had the abstract sense of "governmental power" or denoted the power of a particular ruler. Only in Manetho does it acquire the sense of a sequence of potentates with a common origin or other unifying features. Manetho did not find this succession of dynasties explicitly so designated in the Egyptian or other sources he may have used.'[17]

It is important to realise, therefore, that the ancient Egyptians did not themselves necessarily distinguish between the Third and Fourth Dynasties, or between the First and Second Dynasties, or between the Fifth and Sixth. This was all invented by someone writing in Greek in the third century BC, whose works are not properly preserved anyway. It is rather annoying that we are stuck with his categories, when we can't even be certain that we have the proper description of them, gleaned as they are as mere quotes from other authors, who differ between themselves. These 'dynasties' may well be largely artificial. We need to keep that in mind as we proceed. In later times, due to the drastic defining differences between them, it is perfectly justified for us to refer to the Ptolemies as a dynasty, to refer to the Ethiopian Twenty-Fifth Dynasty as a dynasty, to refer to the rule of foreign invaders called the Hyksos as a 'Hyksos Dynasty' (although 'Hyksos Period' might be more accurate). But when we go as far back as the origins of Egyptian civilisation, to be guided by invented 'dynasties' is a recipe for just what I have suggested exists: chronological chaos.

Now, before we get down to more of the chaos itself, let us return to the matter of the faked Cairo Stone. How do we know it was faked? And if we can be certain of this, how much of what has been written about ancient Egyptian history, since the discovery of the Cairo Stone fragments in a dealer's shop in 1910, is reliable? The situation is rather dire, because so many scholars, assuming the Cairo Fragments to be genuine, have used the bogus information supposedly 'recorded' on them without distinguishing it from the genuine Palermo Stone information, and they merely refer to it all as coming from the Palermo Stone. That is pretty sloppy of them, and has caused the most appalling mess.

It is most unfortunate that Donald Redford, author of the best modern survey of the king lists, does not recognise the dubious status of the Cairo Fragments. Few scholars do. So let us turn to the source from which this revelation comes.

The discovery and demonstration that the Cairo Fragments were fakes is perhaps the greatest achievement of a remarkable scholar of chronology, Dr Patrick F. O'Mara (1914–2001). He was a professor at Los Angeles City College who, apart from writing a book to assist learners to become familiar with hieroglyphics, published a series of five books on Egyptian chronology. These were: *The Palermo Stone and the Archaic Kings of Egypt* (1979)[18], *The Chronology of the Palermo and Turin Canons* (1980)[19], *Some Indirect Sothic and Lunar Dates from the Middle Kingdom in Egypt* (1984)[20], *Some Lunar Dates from the Old Kingdom in Egypt* (1984)[21], and *Additional Unlabeled Lunar Dates from the Old Kingdom in Egypt* (1985)[22]. The fifth booklet is one, alas, which I have never seen. I tried to trace O'Mara, and contacted his old college, but was informed that he had died, that he had left a widow and daughter, but no one knew how to contact them. I persisted over a long period, and finally – by tireless detective work – managed to find his daughter, Mrs Kathleen Kottler of California, who sent me copies of all those published articles by her father that I did not already have (which are in addition to the four books mentioned above, although apparently she does not have a copy of the fifth book either), as well as the photo of him which I have reproduced as Plate 35. An obituary of O'Mara appeared in the German Egyptological journal *Göttinger Miszellen* in 2001.[23] O'Mara had contributed five articles to this journal in the last eight years of his life, between 1993 and 2001. In order to facilitate a wider familiarity with the valuable work accomplished by O'Mara in the field of ancient Egyptian chronology between 1979 and 2001, a period of twenty-two years, I have compiled what I believe to be a complete chronological list of all of his published articles on Egyptology, which may be found in the endnotes.[24]

Patrick O'Mara decided to tackle the Palermo Stone in the best possible way: from the point of view of an ancient Egyptian scribe. The Egyptians were fanatical about correct measurements, and everything had to be based on the unit of measurement called the cubit, and its subdivisions. Scribes all used 'cubit rules' (see Plate 36), which could be carried round with them as part of their standard kit. No scribe could afford to be caught without one. Cubits had subdivisions, just as feet have inches and metres have centimetres: cubits were divided into 'palms' (or 'hands') and 'fingers'. (These measurements were, as their names suggest, roughly based on an ideal 'palm' breadth and an ideal 'finger' breadth, but they were extremely precise and could not be varied.) A scribe's cubit rule would generally be fifteen fingers long, which was equivalent to three hands long. Cubit rules tended to read from right to left, and along the bottom there were fractions displayed in descending sequence as well: one third, one fourth, one fifth, one sixth, etc. There were strict canons of proportion in Egyptian art and architecture (a subject which I have discussed at considerable length in my earlier book, *The Crystal Sun*). To put it very simply, what O'Mara discovered, and what every other Egyptologist had overlooked, was that the draughtsmanship of the Palermo Stone was based rigorously on the Egyptian cubit, whereas that of the Cairo Stone fragments was not. Whoever carved the Cairo Fragments appeared to be wholly ignorant of Egyptian measurements and proportions, and could not therefore have been an ancient Egyptian scribe. *No cubit rule was used for the drafting of the Cairo Fragments*, hence those fragments *must* be fakes.

Most Egyptologists have never professionally considered art, draughtsmanship, architecture or even the underlying design principles of ancient Egypt. An Egyptologist who spends all his time on texts, or all his time on digging, might never have had a thought of this kind enter his head. Such are the dangers of overspecialisation.

Patrick O'Mara also discovered many other phoney aspects to the Cairo Fragments, however, which should have been obvious to scholars, but which they overlooked in their enthusiasm. One example is that a cartouche containing a royal name is carved vertically instead of horizontally, which is not supposed to happen. There are numerous other faults: the heights of the Nile are given in an impossible manner, suggesting that the Inundation of the Nile reached exactly the same height for some years in succession (which cannot be true); one section is directly copied from a section of the Palermo Stone (thus indicating that the Palermo Stone was used as a model by the antiquities forgers for faking the 'new fragments'); hieroglyphs are wrongly depicted; and parts of the text are incomprehensible, including even misspellings such as no real scribe would have made.

Because the forgery of the Cairo Fragments is so crucial, I am going to quote directly from O'Mara's conclusions rather than summarise them, in order to give a vivid impression of how utterly overwhelming the evidence is for these stones being fakes. By discounting the 'evidence' of these fakes, the chronology of Egypt prior to the Sixth Dynasty has thereby to be reconstructed entirely. This is surely the most extreme form of chronological chaos, but it is necessary, because so much of what is in print in many of the expert books on the subject is complete nonsense. The experts have been taken in by a cruel commercial hoax and made to look like fools.

O'Mara writes:

In 1910, not long after the pioneering efforts of Kurt Sethe and Eduard Meyer to resolve the Palermo Stone, there appeared in the Cairo antiquities market a new fragment of an ancient annals stone, a bit smaller than Palermo but of an identical or similar structure. Several much smaller fragments of like appearance were found at the same time; they too were immediately ascribed to the Fifth Dynasty. Most of the new materials were acquired by the Cairo Museum; one passed into the hands of Flinders Petrie and hence into the collection of University College, London [which houses the Petrie Museum]. A final small fragment surfaced a few years ago. The largest of these new discoveries has been known ever since as the Cairo Stone.

Study of the new companion to the Palermo Stone began immediately upon the publication of the several fragments by Gauthier in 1915. Georges Daressy, Maspero's assistant at the Museum, judged the large stone to be a fragment from the left side of the very same original block as the Palermo Stone. His essay linked the two stones together . . . Both Petrie and Ricci likewise believed the two stones to be parts of a single original and relied heavily upon data from the new stone to sustain their resolution of the old.

Ludwig Borchardt made extensive use of the Cairo Stone in his classic mathematical study of the Palermo Stone. He recognised that the two stones could not be part of the same original but held that they were to all intents identical in structure and content, except for Row I. Indeed, his final reconstruction of Palermo was based more upon the characteristics of the new companion than upon the older and more established stone itself. The two stones have been linked together inseparably in all approaches to the Palermo problem ever since, even to the extent that Palermo has been subordinated to its rival.

It is often not realized how much of our view of the chronology of the First Dynasty is drawn from the Cairo Stone. Palermo lacks any royal names in its first two historical rows whereby the reigns might be identified. . . . The structure of the Cairo Stone is totally unlike that of the Palermo Stone. Indeed, it is unlike any other annals stone or papyrus that I have measured. . . . Any interpretation must conclude that Rows I–III were not drawn in terms of conventional palm distances. [Here he is using the word 'palm' to describe the Egyptian measurement of that name, mentioned earlier, which derives from the palm of an ideal hand.] . . . Indeed, the obvious lack of a coherent and rational palm structure, together with many inconsistencies and contradictions that have been detected, point unmistakably to the conclusion that the Egyptian cubit stick was not employed in the construction of the Cairo Stone.

The Cairo Stone was not drawn with the Egyptian cubit rule and does not follow the structural principles of ancient Egyptian draughts-manship. It was not, therefore, drawn by any ancient craftsman. It is a modern fake, produced in the Winter of 1909–1910 for the antiquities market of the Cairo bazaars. It is worthless for the purposes of histor-ical research. Any and all conclusions hitherto based upon this spurious stone are invalid. . . . There is yet another statistical absurdity in the very nature of the breakage and the wearing. Why does the breaking of the stone correspond almost exactly to the surviving portion of the genuine stone? When the monument crashed down, why did not this particular piece break at the second or third register, or higher up in the upper design? It is true that the Cairo fragment extends considerably below the last row preserved in Palermo, but this part is entirely obliterated . . . The plain fact is that the surviving and legible portions of the Cairo Stone correspond exactly to the legible and calculable portions of the Palermo Stone, in defiance of statistical probability, only because the former is an imitation of the latter. The modern draftsman simply did not know what lay above and below the surviving Palermo materials and could not risk exposing himself to possible error. . . . Daressy was prob-ably right in deducing that the Cairo Stone had served for many years as a threshold in some private dwelling. The back side is thoroughly worn and scratched. The face had lain in the ground and, far more seri-ously than the Palermo Stone, is badly oxidized. But it is not worn nor scratched. The essential point is that the inscriptions were placed upon an already broken and weathered fragment, yet fresh in the sense that it was unmarked by human hand.

Many of the lines do not reach the edges of the surface. If one is to make a forgery upon an already broken stone, care must be exercised in carving lines at the edges. Heavy pressure upon stone is being exerted. If the stylus actually reaches the edge, crystals can be broken off to expose the unweathered interior. Done repeatedly, the forgery becomes self-evident. There is hence a tendency to ease the pressure in approaching the edge, and lines stop short of the mark. . . . In the large Fragment I of the Cairo group, most of the horizontal lines do not reach the edge of the surface nor do some of the vertical lines along the top edge. . . . The small Petrie fragment at University College, although superlatively drawn, has a principal line that fails to meet the edge. All these are forgeries upon blank stones, already broken and weathered.[25]

For a photo of the Petrie fragment, see Plate 34.

I have myself studied the Petrie Fragment and can confirm that not one but several of the principle lines conspicuously stop short of the surface edges of the fragment. This is so obvious that, once it is brought to someone's attention and the significance of it pointed out, it is inconceivable that the person could continue to think of it as being genuine. These characteristics cannot be ascertained from the photo (Plate 34) but only by an actual inspection of the object.

As if this analysis were not devastating enough, O'Mara then goes on to enumerate many faults with the inscriptions on the fragments as well: misspellings, wrong drawings, a Greek ending inadvertently used instead of an Egyptian one for the name of a queen [a Greek ending thousands of years before the Greeks existed takes some doing], the Nile levels already referred to being the same for some years running, as if chance had taken a holiday, and so on. How all of these blatant errors can have escaped detection by supposedly serious scholars since 1910 defies belief. Perhaps it all goes to show that when people want to believe something, you can't stop them, and they can't help themselves. It is not only called wishful thinking, it is called herd-stampede thinking.

Many experts now talk about early times in Egypt as indicated by

Figure 43. Image of a 'unifier' in his two guises, King Djer (also called Zer), second king of the First Dynasty, shown twice on a jar sealing in his tomb, seated on his throne and holding his flail as a symbol of royal authority. At left, he wears the white crown of the South, and at right he wears the red crown of the North. In front of him, his name is contained beneath the feet of a falcon surmounting a design known as a *serekh*, which was the standard presentation for a king's name at that period (later superceded by the cartouche). Standing in front of each image of Djer is a standard with a rampant jackal/wild dog at the top, representing either Upwawet ('Opener of the Ways'), Khenti-Amentiu (Chief of the Westerners, the earliest name and jackal form of Osiris), or a form of Anubis (or some conception, no longer entirely clear to us, embodying all of the above ideas of deity). This illustration is from Figure 108 of Plate XV in Sir Flinders Petrie's *Royal Tombs of the Earliest Dynasties, 1901, Part II*, Egypt Exploration Fund, London, 1901.

the Palermo Stone, when they really mean the Cairo Stone. They have accepted so unquestioningly that the latter is part of and an extension of the former that they often no longer bother to distinguish one from the other when they cite 'it': *both* are the Palermo Stone. Here are O'Mara's conclusions about the implications of all of this:

This stone and the other fragments associated with it were not found in the course of professional excavations. They simply appeared in the Cairo market and were offered for sale. They have never been authenticated by means of any published analysis. All the items must now be considered as valueless . . . Their exposure is no great loss, and we shall recoup infinitely more than we momentarily seem to have lost. The Cairo Stone has been the curse of archaic chronology. It has led us into a quagmire. Rid of the preconceptions imposed on us by Cairo, we are now free to let the Palermo Stone alone guide us in our search for the original and authentic king list.

Historians are perhaps not fully conscious of how many important details and unquestioned assumptions about early Egyptian history rest upon no other archaeological authority than the Cairo Stone. It has been utilized far more than the authentic Palermo Stone to bind together much of the structure of the Archaic Period. The attribution of Meresankh as the mother of Snefru and probably the wife of Huni rests solely upon a reading by Cerny upon the Cairo Stone. It is the sole evidence for the description of a war conducted by King Djer against the Asiatics. [The name of King Djer is not even mentioned on the Palermo Stone.]

Archaeological support for the existence of several of the early kings of the First Dynasty mentioned in later New Kingdom canons has consisted of direct and indirect evidence culled from the Cairo Stone . . . There is no ancient evidence of any kind for the existence of a First Dynasty ruler named Athothis apart from the Cairo stone. Nor of Ity and Ita. The same may be said of Menes [The true explanation of 'Menes' is reported later in this chapter; it was not a proper name but instead was an epithet which later was misunderstood as a name.] . . . the question of the *order* of the pharaohs is reopened. . . . We are now free to consider the possibility that Egyptians of later days did *not* know the correct order of their most ancient rulers. Modern archaeology may be far too humble. We know far more about many aspects of the First Dynasty than did Egyptians of the 3rd–5th Dynasties, the era of the oldest annals tradition.[26]

Few Egyptologists have taken any notice whatever of the publications of Patrick O'Mara. One reason for that might be lack of distribution, as they are so difficult to find. I only have an original copy of one of them, and the rest are photocopies from assorted libraries, as no library seems to have them all. The small publisher that brought out his books went out of business many years ago, and was far away in California, where little Egyptology takes place. O'Mara, as a professor at distant

Los Angeles City College, was not personally known to many Egyptologists. It was all too easy to ignore him. There was no Internet in his day to faciliatate communication.

In his book mentioned earlier, Donald Redford refers to one of O'Mara's books in passing in a single footnote, but otherwise says nothing about him. This is most disappointing, as it means that Redford has declined to deal with the Cairo Fragments forgery issue, which frankly I think is a major failure, considering his desire to write a definitive book about king lists. At the very least, Redford should have acknowledged that O'Mara had made his points and, if he did not accept them for some reason, say what the reason was. In fact, way back in 1982, Redford reviewed two of O'Mara's books in a scholarly journal, where he made these rather brief, and to my view wholly unsatisfactory, remarks about the Cairo Fragments:

'The Palermo Stone, being but a small fraction of the original document, has consistently defied reconstruction; all estimates as to its pristine size turn out to be rough approximations. O'Mara too meets an impasse. Having taken sixty pages to discover that precision measurement leads to a dead end, and having enunciated the chastening thought that any future attempts must proceed upon the basis of the Egyptian cubit, he nevertheless refuses to surrender and launches into other avenues that seem to promise solutions. This is a pity; he should have surrendered. . . . The Cairo fragments, of course, do not support him, and so he is at pains to dismiss them as fakes. (A rebuttal here would take too long; but I can assure him that, had he studied the fragments at first hand, he never would have reached this conclusion.)'[27] When I studied the Petrie Fragment at first hand, I realised it was a fake in less than a minute.

What could be more important to king lists than the possibility, not to mention the probability, or some would say the certainty, that one of the fundamental king lists is a forgery? But despite the fact that Redford had read and reviewed two of O'Mara's earlier publications, neither then (because it would 'take too long') nor subsequently did Redford ever give any convincing reasons why O'Mara was wrong about this point. It was offensive and unscholarly of Redford in 1982 to dismiss O'Mara's point about the Cairo Fragments being fakes on the basis that

O'Mara needed them to be fakes because they got in the way of his theories! Insults do not constitute reasoned argument. O'Mara did not want to get rid of the Cairo Fragments because he thought they were inconvenient to his theories, he pointed out numerous convincing reasons why they must be fakes and were leading everyone astray. Redford has never responded to these points in twenty-eight years, presumably because he cannot.

Stephen Quirke, who is now Professor of Egyptology at University College London and Curator of the Petrie Museum, in 1986 had some supportive things to say about O'Mara's doubts about the Cairo Fragments:

'Despite a certain isolation from current research . . . the studies of O'Mara have the merit of focusing on problems which have tended to pass without comment among Egyptologists. . . . It is also worth noting the distinct ways in which the Palermo Stone and the Cairo fragments have come down to us; even if the fragments are authentic, as usually assumed rather than affirmed, it is methodologically unsound to take them in hand with the Palermo Stone, at least at the first stages of research. Finally, the studies presented by O'Mara draw attention to the contribution of astronomy to Egyptology; this aspect of studies of chronology has received far less discussion than such an important sphere warrants.'[28]

These were extremely bold things for a young Egyptologist to dare to say, and it proves that Quirke has never been a groveller.

A much more impressive attitude than Redford's has been shown by Toby Wilkinson, in his book entitled *Royal Annals of Ancient Egypt: The Palermo Stone and Its Associated Fragments* (2000).[29] Wilkinson mentions O'Mara several times and takes his ideas into consideration, unlike other scholars who studiously ignore him. (He lists two of his books and four of his articles in his Bibliography.) Wilkinson makes a good impression as an open, rather than as a closed, scholar. Being young, he is not afraid to deal with heterodox opinions, does not run from the unusual like a scared rabbit. He also considers the problem of the Cairo Fragments being of different thicknesses, and other disturbing anomalies, rather than pretending these problems do not exist. He translates the Palermo Stone and the Cairo Fragments and clearly identifies each section with either 'PS' for Palermo Stone or 'CF1', 'CF2', etc., for the Cairo

Fragments. He renames the Petrie Fragment the 'London Fragment' and labels it LF. In this way, we can see clearly where each text comes from. So they are not all thrown together like ingredients in a pudding. This book is highly recommended for anyone interested in these early annals, but it is expensive. When I wanted to buy my own copy I had a lot of trouble because it had not yet been reprinted since the original had sold out. There was a copy for sale on the Internet for more than two thousand pounds! I declined on that occasion and waited. I got one for much less, but I still don't like to remember the price.

It is a real pity that Wilkinson does not acknowledge that the Cairo Fragments are fakes. Strictly speaking, one should probably exempt Cairo Fragment Four from this general statement, as it seems actually to have been excavated at Memphis rather than bought in a bazaar. It is, as Wilkinson admits, 'the only fragment not purchased from a dealer.'[30] It is unfortunate that it has very little text surviving on one side and nothing on the reverse, and the only king's name that can be made out on the fragment is that of Sneferu, the first king of the Fourth Dynasty. We do not learn much from the text, other than that 1,100 live captives and 23,000 'small cattle' (which may be a quaint way of describing sheep and goats, according to Wilkinson) were brought from Libya. (The Egyptian name translated as 'Libya' is *Ta Tehenu*, the literal meaning of which is 'Olive Land', and which is discussed at length in Chapter Eight, where the olives of Libya are also explained.) I suppose I should really beat my chest and say '*Mea culpa*', for maligning this fragment by speaking of the Cairo Fragments as fakes, when this tiny one is probably genuine. It might be the only surviving fragment of an annals stela that was once set up in the great Temple of Ptah at Memphis, presumably not the New Kingdom temple but an older one at the site. However, so little survives of the once-great capital city of Memphis, and we know so little of any real importance about it, despite decades of intense efforts, that it is difficult to draw conclusions about the place. Both Memphis and Heliopolis, on the other side of the Nile, are not much more than names to us: great names, but lost ones. Their stones were carried away so long ago for reuse in construction that it is painful to think of it. As Ptah is my favourite Egyptian god, I take the destruction of his temple at Memphis very hard indeed.

I have studied the cubit rule in the Louvre very closely, and it may be seen in the Plate section, as it is the kind of rule used by the scribes in carving the Palermo Stone, and people need to see one in order to understand what I am talking about. The book's website should be consulted for the complete set of photos of it.

As for the Redford book, it also lacks completely an important dimension to the king list issue, which is actually dealt with at length by O'Mara, and which I would have mentioned anyway, even if O'Mara had not brought it up. I am referring to the extensive attempts made by Imhotep, the vizier of King Zoser (first king of the Third Dynasty) to construct some kind of 'history' of the First and Second Dynasty kings. Imhotep was one of the most famous intellectuals in the history of Egypt. We know that he wrote books on medicine and architecture, as well as designing and building the Step Pyramid of Saqqara. He was also Vizier of Egypt, High Priest of Heliopolis, and High Priest of Ptah at Memphis. There seemed to be nothing that he could not or did not do. Among other things he appeared to do, which are less frequently discussed, were to reform the calendar by creating what is called the 'Civil Year', and commence the traditions of creating annals and king lists (called in Egyptian by the name of *genut*). The really interesting part of the latter project was his collection of vast quantities – more than 40,000 – of stone bowls and vases, many of which bore the names of early kings incised upon them, and all of which probably came from royal tombs. Two of these actually bear a succession of the names of four kings who followed one another and, strangely, this king list is not noticed by Redford in his book on king lists, though O'Mara makes much of it.[31] He calls it the 'Royal Block of Four', and it is indeed priceless archaeological evidence of the accurate succession of four early kings. This evidence was initially published by Jean-Philippe Lauer and Pierre Lacau in 1959, in Volume Four of the mammoth series of volumes about the Step Pyramid of Saqqara, *La Pyramide à Degrés: Inscriptions Gravées sur les Vases* [The Step Pyramid: Inscriptions Engraved on the Vases]. The relevant inscriptions are shown in Plate 4 of that volume.[32] I reproduce that photo on this book's website. Lauer is the man who reconstructed a section of the Step Pyramid complex at Saqqara, which is admired by all tourists today for the breathtaking beauty of its design. Lauer was a heroic figure, inspired by a vision and determined to realise it.

It is from his vast collection of stone bowls and vases that Imhotep clearly gathered much of his information and tried to piece together a chronology of the past, due to the paucity of other suitable written records. These bowls were all meticulously gathered and stored underneath the Step Pyramid as a gigantic hoard. It is very unfortunate that most of them were smashed after a few thousand years, when some of the subterranean ceilings collapsed on to them. The majority of the pieces are in storehouses or sheds at the Saqqara site, as I was able to discover after a considerable amount of enquiry. Many of the choice and unbroken pieces are of course in museums. But the bulk of the 40,000 bowls and vases are still at Saqqara. I was told that I might, if proper reasons were given, be allowed access to these objects to study them, but of course application is a long process, and it is not at all clear that there are proper facilities available to study tens of thousands of pieces of bowls and vases in what might be very cramped storage conditions. One would need to spread numerous examples out on big surfaces, and probably there are no such surfaces, and the lighting might not be terribly good, and the storehouses would undoubtedly be very hot to work in for hours at a time. So, guess what, I never got around to it. Which is not to say that I have given up on the idea, but it might be the dream that never happens.

I have more reasons than mere chronology to want to study the bowls and vases. Apart from the alabaster ones, which are made of an extremely soft material and were easy to fashion, the objects tend to be made of very hard stones in ways that seem technologically impossible. Some of them have curled lips, as if they had been shaped from clay; many of the hardest stones have hollow spaces which extend and curve upwards on the inside in such a way that no one can imagine any drill tool that could conceivably have created them, or could do so even today. The ones made of the hardest stones would have required diamond drills in order for them to have been hollowed out. (In fact, in my earlier book, *The Crystal Sun*, I dealt with this issue and presented the evidence that the ancient Egyptians had the use of what we call industrial diamonds. They did not have diamonds as gems, and they had no idea that the hard black stones that we call industrial diamonds had any gem qualities. But they were able to use them for drill tips.)

The technology used to create those stone bowls and vases not carved from soft alabaster is a remarkable technology, the true details of which are known to very few people. The answer to the riddle is that they were probably cast, not carved or ground. The reason why lips could be curled as if they had been made of clay, despite being of solid stone, is because those lips were curled while the material was still soft. (See Plates 37a and 37b and Figure 44 for an example of one made of schist, with 'folded lips', which was excavated by Walter Emery at Saqqara.) At a very early stage, even before the so-called 'First Dynasty', there was a secret, royally controlled technology to manufacture these miraculous bowls from liquid stone, which was then cast in moulds made from clay, or otherwise was moulded on potters' wheels while wet and soft, before it went hard. This technology was under the protection of the god Khnum, which is why his image appears on some of these bowls.[33] Khnum is often portrayed operating a potter's wheel. The same technology was sometimes used for statues made of diorite and other hard stone materials. This technology has been rediscovered in modern times by the French chemist, Joseph Davidovits. He has named it 'geopolymeric' chemistry. That is because an inorganic polymeric reaction takes place while the material is wet. The Egyptians used weathered rock particles, which could be easily disaggregated, formed a very fine aggregate, then added the necessary catalyst with water, and this formed a kind of polymeric concrete which sets hard. It is impossible to tell the difference between carved stone and cast stone with any chemical analysis or by X-ray diffraction analysis, as the results are identical. Davidovits began his professional life as an organic polymer chemist (his PhD thesis was on polyurethane), but he decided he would invent an *inorganic* polymer. Everybody thought that was impossible, and was a contradiction in terms, the word 'polymer' being, they thought, partially defined by the necessity of its being organic. However, Davidovits went on to invent a series of inorganic polymers. And by doing so, he was able to recreate some of the lost technology of early Egyptian stone bowl and vase manufacture.

There are only five people in the world at the moment who really

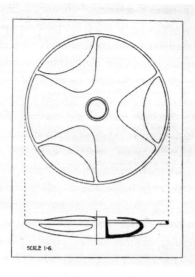

SCALE 1·6.

Figure 44. Walter Emery's drawing in section and plan of the mysterious 'schist bowl' excavated by him from the First Dynasty Tomb of Sahu at Saqqara. (Figure 58 on page 101 of Walter B. Emery, *Great Tombs of the First Dynasty*, Volume 1, Cairo, 1949.)

understand this technology: Joseph, three of his sons, and myself. I have been involved with Joseph in business for eleven years, introducing environmentally friendly geopolymeric cement technology and obtaining international patents on the technology. Joseph has also cast some giant 'pyramid bocks' of cast limestone, one weighing four tons and one weighing three tons. We believe that the three main Giza pyramids were constructed out of cast limestone, not cut limestone. And as the Egyptians had no cranes, they could not have lifted those huge blocks if they had been cut. Also, the reason why there is no space between the blocks and you can't fit a razor blade between them is that they were successively cast directly on top of one another, with only an extremely thin film of gypsum forming naturally between them each time as they cured. This subject is explained fully in Joseph's recent book (2009) on the subject, which is available in both French and English editions direct from his website www.geopolymer.org.

The stone bowls and vases were 'magical' and courtiers had to have royal permission to own one. Tens of thousands were made, but the process was a royal secret. Imhotep was especially interested in them, because he harnessed their technology on a larger scale to make the Step Pyramid out of cast limestone blocks, which he could mass-produce in sufficient quantities from limestone rubble quarried and carried in sacks. And so he had two reasons for stuffing 40,000 of the bowls and vases beneath that pyramid: technology, and as a prehistory archive. Having had an army of people gather up every bowl and vase they could find (an enormous task), which must have involved a small army of people scouring the cemeteries throughout Egypt, searching for them in looted tombs, we can be certain that Imhotep ordered the inscriptions on those bowls to be copied just as assiduously as Lacau and Lauer later copied them. I am very fortunate to own copies of the two volumes of bowl and vase inscriptions by Lauer, personally signed by him and presented to his friend Henry Fischer, much of whose library I have purchased, including all his signed Lauer offprints. (I also have signed Lauer offprints from the libraries of other Egyptologists, as I have purchased sections of the libraries of several of them.) Lauer is one of the most admirable of modern Egyptologists, and a model for the younger generations.

As we are on the subject of bowls, I will take a step backward in time to show just how topsy-turvy things can really get in terms of technology and our modern conception of 'progress', when dealing with ancient Egypt. You would think, wouldn't you, that the production of ceramic pottery would evolve and get better and better? But alas for our notion that progress only goes upwards, I will tell something about the Badarian Culture.

The Badarians take their name from a site now called Badari. We don't know who they really were. They were a prehistoric people who lived on the eastern bank of the Nile in Middle Egypt near Assiut. (This is a region where foreigners rarely go nowadays, though Olivia and I have been to that area for archaeological reasons.) In fact, they were an *early* prehistoric people. They flourished, according to conventional notions, between 4,500 and 3,250 BC. One of the things I like about the Badarians is that they were great dog lovers. They buried their dogs with reverence, which makes them just the sort of chaps I approve of. A lot of people would have us believe that these Badarians were very primitive folk, but there is one problem: their pottery. The amazing thing is that their pottery was so brilliant that it was never really equalled or surpassed in the whole of later Egyptian history. Now, what do you make of that? What happens to the idea of 'progress'?

Let's consider some of the things which have been said about the Badarian pottery. In their book *The Badarian Civilisation* (1928), the excavators Guy Brunton and Gertrude Caton-Thompson had this to say:

The most distinctive product of the Badarians was their pottery. It is hand-made, like all Predynastic pottery, and shows no trace of turning. Much of it has the surface wholly or partly covered with a fine or coarse rippling, and it was this peculiarity which led to the discovery of the culture. It had not previously been met with in the Nile Valley, and was quite new to our experience . . . The better vessels all have very thin edges; sometimes they are almost sharp. The rippling may extend over the whole outer surface of the pot, it may run half-way down, or it may remain round the rim only; but in all cases where this rippling exists it is at least at the rim. It is difficult to say exactly what instrument was used to give this effect. . . . it is quite clear that the rippled surface was considered beautiful; it was retained as a decoration, sometimes over the whole pot . . . The clay itself, of which the pots were made, is mostly very fine-grained and close . . . The excellence of its manufacture was never surpassed in later times. It is obvious that we have here the result of many ages of experiment . . . The previous stages, which must have existed, are then to be looked for elsewhere.[34]

There are many fine Badarian bowls in the Petrie museum in London, which are marvellous to behold. The Badarians had mastered the art of the production of fine linen, which they wore as their garments. The archaeological evidence shows them to have been peaceful, with no sign of any weapons in their remains. They were brilliant carvers of ivory and 'Both sexes were fond of large ivory bracelets which were worn in numbers on the forearm. Ear-studs seem to have been usual ornaments; and even a pale-green nose-stud was thought attractive, a very African touch. We may not be far wrong if we suppose the Badarians were sufficiently civilised to carry handkerchiefs. . . . The men were clean-shaven, or beardless.'

The evidence for their peaceful disposition is stated like this:

> . . . either the Badarians died out, or, as seems likely, they were dispossessed by a tribe or tribes who were practically of the same blood, but slightly more adventurous and progressive. Judging from the scanty remains that we have of the Badarians, they seem to have been a very peaceful people. There is a considerable proportion of long-lived individuals among the burials; there are no examples of broken bones or injuries; and we find no warlike weapons such as the disk-mace which is characteristic of the Early Predynastics. . . . the Badarian and the Predynastic cemeteries seem always to be on separate ground. . . . Cereals were known, but what species is uncertain. . . . It was in the manufacture of pottery that the Badarian especially excelled. Not only was it made in great quantities, but the finer qualities were never equalled in later times in the Nile Valley. The best vases are extraordinary for the thinness and excellence of the ware, and for the high finish of the delicately rippled or smooth surfaces. . . . Leather-work was carried on with considerable skill. . . . Of trade we have ample evidence. . . . the Badarians were not an isolated tribe, but were in contact with the cultures or countries on all sides of them. Nor were they nomads; their pots, some of them both large and fragile, were absolutely unsuitable for the use of wanderers. . . . [when they were buried] it was considered desirable that they should look toward the setting sun.[35]

From all of this it sounds as if the Badarians were a kind of early hippie culture, living in peace with man and beast, loving their dogs, refusing to engage in warfare, making the most beautiful pottery in Egyptian history, living often to a great age, and enjoying their life beside the beautiful River Nile in a kind of extended dream of blissful tranquillity. Eventually, more violent people came along who destroyed this idyllic existence, killed them off, and refused even to share their burial grounds. Never was the pottery of the Badarians equalled, much less surpassed. That means only one thing, that 'progress' was downwards, not upwards, as far as ceramics was concerned over the next *six and a half thousand years*. Let this be a lesson: 'progress' is not always what we think it is. Technologies can decline over time.

It is time to move on from the charming story of the lost Badarians and their idyllic existence beside a beautiful river in a day so far back in time that it preceded just about everything else that later happened in Egypt. But let us never forget the Lesson of the Badarians. For, even today, in the twenty-first century, no one can make a pot like a Badarian, and the Badarians go back to 4500 BC. In six and a half thousand years, their skills at hand-made pottery have never been equalled. Now we turn to the beginning of 'official' Egyptian history, or at least what since Manetho it has been conventional to call the 'First Dynasty'. What could be more interesting and important than the First Dynasty, for anyone who wants to understand the origins of Egyptian civilisation? As far as king lists are concerned, we know far more about the First Dynasty than we do about the Second and Third Dynasties. And plenty of First Dynasty royal tombs have been discovered, whereas hardly any have been discovered for the Second and Third Dynasties. In fact, we have *too many* First Dynasty royal tombs. As I have already mentioned earlier, in Chapter Three, each king had two tombs. One was a real tomb and one was a funerary monument, called a cenotaph. One was in the north and one was in the south. However, because no bodies of any of the kings have been found in either place, we are not certain which was the tomb and which was the cenotaph; as long as that uncertainty continues, we have to continue to call both of them 'tombs', just in case.

The reason why bodies have not been found is that all of these tombs and cenotaphs were robbed, despoiled and ransacked repeatedly over thousands of years, so it is a wonder there was anything left to find in them at all. The only bodily evidence found in any of them was found, however, in the south. In one of the tombs, a woman's arm covered in valuable gold and jewellery was found stuffed into a hole in a wall. She is presumed to have been a queen. Probably, when an ancient tomb robber was tearing apart royal mummies to strip them of their valuables, he ripped off this arm and stuffed it into a place for safe-keeping and forgot it, or was disturbed and ran away, leaving the arm behind.

This evidence strongly suggests that it was in the south where the real burials took place, and that the northern 'tombs' were the empty ones, which acted as honorary tombs, or cenotaphs.[36]

The southern location was Abydos, where all of the First Dynasty royal tombs seem to have been. (The tomb of Khasekhemui, described in Chapter Five, is very near to these tombs of the dynasty preceding his, within easy walking distance if you can stand the heat.) These extremely ancient tombs were regarded with great reverence during later ages. In the New Kingdom, they were honoured by King Seti I, for his great temple at Abydos known as the Temple of Seti I was in its intention really a Temple of the Royal Ancestors, as Caulfeild pointed out as long ago as 1903.[37] Seti's temple was oriented and placed so as to be connected on an axis with the First Dynasty tombs, which were far out in the desert but in a direct line from the temple. And Seti's temple contains the famous king list carved in stone, known as the Abydos King List, as mentioned earlier in this chapter, and illustrated as Figures 37 and 38. This is the only known Egyptian temple to feature a king list as a major feature, apart from that of Seti's son, Rameses II, who copied his father's idea and added his own name when he built a temple of his own at Abydos. The Abydos King List is carved prominently on a wall of Seti's temple, because it honours Seti's royal predecessors, and of course added legitimacy to himself, since as a pharaoh he inherited all of that tradition of more than a thousand years of pharaohship.

I have a more than usual familiarity with the Temple of Seti I and its adjoining subterranean structure, the Osireion, since I was able to have special access to them in connection with officially authorised archaeological work. I have written a lengthy account of the temple and its Osireion, which has not yet been published. This includes a thorough survey of all of the literature on the temple, including some sources that are little known. I was also able to correct major errors made by Henri Frankfort, the excavator of the Osireion, in his own extensive excavation report. And in my account, unusual dating results are reported. Unfortunately, this report does not concern the subject of this book, so its publication must be deferred until a later occasion. The matter of the ancestors is also one of the points mentioned in my account.

It is not possible to have a proper understanding of the complex structure without this awareness of the ancestral aspect, which in turn goes back to the very First Dynasty tombs that we are now considering. When my account of the Seti temple makes its appearance, there will be a slight further dimension opened on the First Dynasty tombs, for which Seti obviously had a deep superstitious reverence. One can never overestimate the religious conservatism of an ancient Egyptian of any period.

The discovery of the northern tombs of the First Dynasty at Saqqara was accomplished by the remarkable and inspired Egyptologist Walter B. Emery, a man of outstanding ability, dedication to his subject, and also intuition. As a result of being the discoverer of these tombs, which are approximately double the size of the southern tombs of the same kings at Abydos, Emery was naturally enthusiastic about promoting them as the real tombs, and considering the southern tombs at Abydos as the symbolic cenotaphs. This made sense to him because surely the larger monuments must be the real ones, and the smaller ones the dummy tombs. It is not at all unusual that Emery presumed this, despite the evidence of the bejewelled arm which I mentioned a moment ago. However, the preponderance of Egyptological opinion has been to disagree with him, and to regard the northern tombs as the cenotaphs, and the Abydos tombs as the real ones.

I am in agreement with the preponderance of opinion for once. I would suggest that a possible reason why the northern 'tombs' were larger, despite being 'dummies', whereas the southern 'tombs' were smaller despite being real, was that the northerners who had the superior technological skills were vassals to the southerners who had the military might. The 'unification of Egypt', in my opinion, was like a kind of reverse business takeover, where a subsidiary buys the parent company in a hostile bid but does not understand the patents or have the skills to run the enterprise properly, so it has to rely on its employees to survive. I suspect that the northerners, to show their obeisance to their southern rulers, made certain that the cenotaphs they built to honour the southern kings were considerably larger and more impressive than the real tombs themselves in the south. Thus they honoured their masters, but at the same time the message was not lost on those masters that the people who really knew how to get things done were their vassals in the north, and they had better not forget it. In such an atmosphere of tension and masked hostility, a situation such as that involving King Enezib was capable of igniting violent passions, and it would explain why King Semerkhet felt obliged to or simply wished to mutilate his predecessor's tomb in such a drastic manner.

Emery began his important work on royal tombs of the First Dynasty by writing his magnificent book, *Excavations at Saqqara 1937–1938: Hor-Aha*, which was published at Cairo in 1939.[38] Hor-Aha is the man whom Emery and many others choose to identify as the first king of the First Dynasty. Who could be more important than that? If we are looking for origins, here he is. There was an earlier king called Narmer, thought to be Hor-Aha's father, but scholars tend to prefer to regard him as the last predynastic king and to view his supposed son, Hor-Aha, as the first dynastic king. (It probably doesn't really make a lot of difference.) As Emery proudly states in the first sentence of his book:

With the discovery of Tomb No. 3357 at Saqqara Egyptology is presented with the third great monument which may be definitely ascribed to the reign of Hor-aha, first king of the First Dynasty. Hitherto all the available archaeological material of his reign has come from the monuments of Naqadah [Naqqada] and Abydos and conflicting evidence has been brought forward by various authorities to prove that one or other of these two tombs was his last resting place. Prior to the discovery of the Saqqara tomb the general consensus of opinion among Egyptologists appears to have been greatly in favour of Abydos as his last resting place and Naqadah as the sepulchre of his wife Neith-hotep.

The Naqadah tomb when first discovered by De Morgan was generally accepted as that of Hor-aha and it was only after its re-excavation by Garstang that the tomb was identified as that of the Queen Neith-hotep. . . . With regard to the question of the burial of Hor-aha at Abydos, as I have suggested . . . the so-called tombs of the First Dynasty at Abydos may well be cenotaphs . . . The custom of building royal cenotaphs at Abydos was certainly common in later times, for example the monuments of Senusret III and Seti I [my unpublished report on Abydos explains a direct connection between the constructions of these two pharaohs, one of the Middle Kingdom, and the other of the new Kingdom, at Abydos], and we have no reason to suppose that it was not held to in the earlier period. . . . Moreover it must be remembered that in none of the Abydos tombs were found any human remains which might be considered to be of the kings.[39]

Unfortunately, none has been found at Saqqara either. Surely they can't *both* be cenotaphs?

I have already explained why I believe that the cenotaphs were at Saqqara and the tombs were at Abydos. This all relates to the technological divide between north and south, which must have existed even at the time of this so-called 'First Dynasty'. I have already alluded to this in Chapter Five, where I pointed out the discrepancy between the northern Egyptians with their stone technology and the southern Egyptians with their lack of it.

In the fragments that survive of the history of Egypt written by the Egyptian priest with the Greek name of Manetho, who was mentioned earlier in this chapter, the first pharaoh is stated to have had the name 'Menes'. But the names given by Manetho are Grecianised, and are often difficult to match with Egyptian names, especially since the pharaohs all had more than one name anyway. So one of the great questions that has haunted Egyptology is: *Who was Menes?*

This is where there has been much disagreement. It has been suggested that Hor-Aha was Menes, it has been suggested that his father, Narmer, was Menes, and it has been suggested that neither was Menes. For decades, no one knew for certain. There were bits of evidence, tantalising, tempting, but not conclusive. The most sensible approach to this strange problem that I have ever seen (and many Egyptologists have written about it) is a small article of only three and a half pages entitled 'Menes the Memphite' by James P. Allen, published in 1992.[40] In this article, Allen points out that it is most probable that *Menes was never a name.* He believes that it comes from the Egyptian word for the ancient city of Memphis near Giza, which was supposed to have been founded by the first pharaoh of the First Dynasty. That was the tradition believed in by the time of the New Kingdom, when no one clearly remembered the name of the actual fellow who did it.

For the first 1,500 years of its existence, Memphis was not called Memphis, it was called White Walls.[41] The name Memphis, in its Egyptian form of course, only came into use in later times, during the New Kingdom. Allen believes that it was during the new Kingdom that this early king began to be referred to as 'the Memphite' (or in other words, 'He of Memphis'), which in Egyptian is written in hieroglyphs which can be Mene, Meni or Mini, from the Egyptian name for Memphis, which is Minf or Minef. So what everybody really meant when they said the name of this pharaoh was: 'You know, that king who founded Memphis, what's his name?, the Memphis guy.' And by the time the Greeks came to Egypt, when they expressed this name as Menes, everybody believed that this was the genuine name of the first king of Egypt.

This sounds very convincing to me. Allen dismisses the evidence of a couple of ivory tablets excavated in the old graves of the First Dynasty, which appeared to combine Men or Min with a pharaoh's name. Argument had raged over these for several decades. But Allen points out that it was our lack of understanding of archaic hieroglyphs that led to this confusion. It seems that with our more modern knowledge of them now, the apparent combination of Men or Min with the name of Hor-Aha on a label can now be translated as something completely different: 'The Two Ladies Shall Abide'! (That is presumed to be a reference to the cobra goddess and the vulture goddess, one representing the north of Egypt and one representing the south of Egypt, which had become united by conquest.) The apparent connection with Narmer is also dismissed as a misunderstanding. In other words, all the evidence for any royal name remotely resembling Menes in the First Dynasty or before has now been discredited.

There are precedents for this sort of thing in history. King William I of England is never referred to as King William I, but always as 'William the Conqueror'. For a considerable period, especially during the seventeenth century, he was not even called that, he was merely called 'the Conqueror'. I have read many books of that period (and this actually continued into the Victorian era) in which 'the Conqueror' is spoken of, but not identified as William. Everyone knew who was meant. At that particular time in English history, the invasion and conquest of

England by the Normans under William the Conqueror was a hot issue. People who were opposed to the tyranny of the Stuart kings invoked what seventeenth-century historians refer to as the 'Saxon Yoke Theory'. This asserted that Englishmen had been enslaved by 'the Conqueror' (which by the way was largely true), and that by rising up and fighting the English Civil War (1642–45) against King Charles I, they would be regaining their Saxon freedoms, lost since 1066, the year of the Conquest. 'The Conqueror' thus became a famous figure again, constantly invoked in political discussions of the most heated kind, upon which the fate of the realm actually hung.

I believe that Allen is correct, and that during the New Kingdom in Egypt, something similar occurred. It became relevant to speak constantly of 'the Memphite', just as Englishmen 350 years ago had once spoken of 'the Conqueror'. In England, King William I had become a semi-mythical figure called 'the Conqueror' in less than six centuries, in a country where printed books were widely circulated and extensive historical records were in the hands of a broad educated public. In contrast, the Egyptians of the New Kingdom, were living at the very least 1,500 years later (if not much more) than the first king of the First Dynasty. So imagine how foggy the notion of that king had become to a people who had no printed books, and whose priests and scribes relied upon those king lists that had chanced to survive two Intermediate Periods of chaos and destruction, with temple libraries ransacked and papyri burnt (especially during the First Intermediate Period after the collapse of the Old Kingdom) by rampaging mobs, and during periods of the collapse of government, plague, famine and natural disasters. Just as 'the Conqueror' became politically important in current discussions in seventeenth-century England, so 'the Memphite' became important in New Kingdom discussions.

At that time, the pharaohs were keen to prove their legitimacy, and Seti I built his temple to the ancestors with a grand king list carved on to a wall, with an axis oriented towards the graves of the First Dynasty kings out in the desert beyond, to the west of his temple, and with a rear door opening out upon them and their domain. Memphis had ceased to be the capital during the New Kingdom, and Thebes had taken its place; all the more reason, therefore, to invoke 'the Memphite' as an ancestor, to prove the legitimacy of succession and justify the new location of the capital by honouring the founder of the 'original capital' of a united Egypt.

At the same time, the tomb paintings and papyri of the New Kingdom constantly invoked the 'Spirits of Buto' and the 'Spirits of Nekhen', in reference to the presumed *predynastic* religious centres of Egypt: Buto in the western Delta in the north and Nekhen, known to us as Hieraconpolis, in the south. (John Wilson pointed out in 1955 that these two centres were not the actual capital cities of the north and south, and were 'never militarily or administratively significant', but had a purely symbolic and ritual importance.)[42] There was clearly a desperate need to invoke the distant past and the power of its spirits, if only to appease them by honouring them. We must remember that this was not done for 'public consumption', because there was no 'public'. It was done for 'consumption by the spirits and the gods', which was an even more urgent matter. Public opinion is as nothing compared to divine opinion, and the power of the voters of today does not rival the power of the ghosts of yesterday, much less the gods of eternity.

This clever resolution of the problem of Menes by James Allen is one of the great clarifying and cathartic acts of Egyptological thought of our time, in my opinion. Since we now know that 'Menes' was simply 'the Memphite', we can take our pick as to whether we think he was King Narmer or his son King Hor-Aha. I don't suppose it makes much difference.

Although Allen's solution to this particular aspect of 'chronological chaos' has been ignored by many Egyptologists, none of them has ever come up with a more convincing scenario; so, until someone does, we can continue to take comfort in the fact that at least someone has figured something out, even if it is only the meaning of a single word. One has to start somewhere.

In a sense, the fact that so many tombs and cenotaphs of the First Dynasty have been excavated has added to the confusion. This often happens in obscure areas of research, when investigators find that they are raising far more questions than they are answering. As soon as you have some actual physical evidence of something, you have to start interpreting and explaining it. But one must not grumble: that is just the nature of things.

In Plates 38 and 39 I show details of a famous slate palette known as the Narmer Palette. It dates from the time of King Narmer and was excavated in nearly perfect condition in the season 1897–98 at the southern site of Hieraconpolis in the predynastic Temple of Horus by the British archaeologists James Quibell and Frederick Green. In Figures 45 and 46 may be seen the entire palette designs, both back and front. This palette is one of the most important objects ever found from such an early period of Egyptian history. It is carved from a flat piece of soft green siltstone, which was extremely easy to carve. It was found near a mace head (such as that shown being wielded by King Narmer in 'smiting position' on his palette), also dating from the reign of Narmer, and another one called 'the Scorpion Mace Head', which dates from the reign of the predynastic King Scorpion, who might have been Narmer's father or grandfather.

This Narmer Palette is one of the most famous artefacts surviving from archaic times in Egypt. It has been constantly discussed for considerably more than a century now, since its initial discovery. The sacred site of Hieraconpolis ('Nekhen') was discussed in the previous chapter, Chapter Five, where some photos were reproduced showing its 'fort'. On the website I reproduce also some photos showing the vast heaps of broken pots found in the Necropolis. There are millions upon millions of pot fragments at Hieraconpolis, deposited there by pilgrims, visiting the cemetery over the course of thousands of years, who smashed pots as offerings and left the pieces in these vast heaps. It is important for the non-Egyptologist to see the vast extent of these heaps, of which my two photos give some idea, so that the sheer scale of the remains may be appreciated.

The Narmer Palette is only one of many soft stone palettes of that period which have now been excavated. Many are unadorned and might have been simple vanity items, as these palettes were either genuinely used or used 'in theory' for mineral-based pastes; these were applied to the eyes or in other ways as personal decoration. The most frequently used mineral was a copper mineral, malachite, which was ground up to make green paint. Ochre and haematite were used for red paint (the

Figure 45. (left) King Narmer, as depicted on the reverse side of the Narmer Palette, striding forth with a mace in his hand and wearing the Crown of the North (Lower Egypt), generally called 'the red crown', though in Old Kingdom times it was sometimes called 'the green crown'. The coil emitted from the centre of the turban (which resembles a Fibonacci spiral in mathematics) can clearly be seen to be made of something twisted. Petrie thought it was 'a piece of tightly twisted linen, and . . . it must have been made over a wire or other stiff foundation to keep it in position.' (*Ancient Egypt*, June, 1926, Part II, pp. 36-7). Narmer, shown on the other side of the palette in smiting position and wearing the 'white crown' of the South (Upper Egypt), as seen in Plate 38, was evidently a southern king who conquered ('smote') the North, since he did his smiting while wearing the southern crown, but progressed peacefully, evidently as a victor, wearing the northern crown, with his mace at rest. Whether Namer was 'Menes', or whether his son Hor-Aha was Menes, the Unification of Egypt by force took place from the south to the north, and resulted in the creation of what we call 'The First Dynasty'.

Figure 46. (right) King Narmer smiting an enemy, drawn from the obverse side of the Narmer Palette, and showing the details of his costume and mace.

ochre, being harder, required separate grinders). Galena, a lead mineral, was ground to make black kohl for eye-paint. One of the leading experts on early Egypt was Elise Baumgaertel. She has an entire section on palettes in her two-volume work *The Cultures of Prehistoric Egypt* (1947–

1960).[43] She points out that the palettes began with the Badarians, mentioned earlier, as purely utilitarian objects for grinding the paint used on faces and bodies. After that, the palettes took on a more sacred character.

Later palettes such as the Narmer Palette were important royal or sacred objects, recording historical events and celebrating important themes. They have also attracted the interest of historians of art. For instance, Whitney Davis has published an entire book of some length and mind-boggling complexity called *Masking the Blow*, attempting to analyse the artistic design principles and motifs of the Narmer Palette and how its 'narrative' is to be 'read'. His arguments are highly specialised, and he applies the same techniques in the book to a variety of other palettes as well.[44] He has written various other books on motifs, symbols, history of art and psychoanalysis in relation to art. So he is what many Egyptologists regard as an 'intruder' into their discipline. When I attended the International Congress of Egyptologists in Cairo in 2000, great horror was expressed in open session by a variety of Egyptologists at the thought that historians of art might wish to invade their turf and express opinions on anything, and their attitude towards historians of science was even lower still.

Because King Narmer is a candidate for 'Menes', and the other candidate is in any case his son King Hor-Aha (both of whom were undoubtedly active in conquering the north to 'unify' Egypt, which was not a process completed under a single reign), so that it really makes no difference *which* was 'Menes', the Narmer Palette has a uniquely important place in considerations of the origins of a unified Egypt. I will not attempt to discuss in detail what is represented on the palette, though some comments appear in captions to the illustrations. Suffice it to say that scenes of conquest by Narmer are, not surprisingly, portrayed, and they appear to be conquest over 'Libyans' of the Delta region of Egypt. Certainly men looking like the traditional 'Libyans' of Egyptian art over the millennia, with pointed beards, are shown receiving some very rough treatment, including decapitation. King Narmer is shown on one side of the palette wearing his indigenous crown of the south, and on the other side wearing his crown of the north, which he has gained from conquest.

A surprising number of the other slate palettes have in recent decades been identified as coming from the Delta itself, which seems to have been a major centre of their manufacture. This point is strongly made in the excellent book by Toby Wilkinson, *State Formation in Egypt* (1996), which is essentially a published version of his PhD thesis. One of the most interesting sections of that book is the last brief one, 'State Formation and the Delta'. He points out that the Delta appears to be the place of origin of the palette motif of paired animals facing each other and framing the palette.[45] (Elise Baumgaertel believes this motif was borrowed from the Sumerians, and it is not difficult to imagine the 'Libyans' being in contact with them, when one considers the discussion to come, in Chapter Eight, of their maritime capabilities.) This motif (see Plate 39) was then adopted by King Narmer on his own triumphalist Narmer Palette, possibly as an intentional use of a Delta motif to trumpet his own conquest of that very region.

Another palette now known to be of Delta origin is the one currently called the Hunter's Palette. It has a most curious history, as vividly described by Hermann Ranke in 1925, who referred to it as the 'Löwenjagd-Palette' (Lion-Hunt Palette).[46] Ranke tells the story of how it was found in three separate pieces, two in London and one at the Louvre in Paris. They were not recognised as being Egyptian at all. It was the famous Egyptologist Wallis Budge who finally recognised that these three pieces all belonged to the same object, retrieved the one in Paris, put the three together at the British Museum where he was head of Egyptian and Babylonian Antiquities, and published the result in *The Classical Review* in 1890. Eventually it was realised that the palette was definitely Egyptian, and was similar to the Narmer Palette, which was excavated later at Hieraconpolis.

Ranke points out that the bizarre hunt scene portrayed on the palette, which includes the killing of two lions, shows the hunting being done by Libyan princes wearing the customary double ostrich plumes on their heads, with some of the men carrying Libyan double axes, etc. (Amongst the Libyans, men with two plumes were higher in rank than men with one plume, and men with no plumes were real nobodies. The double plume is the ultimate origin of the double ostrich plume headdress of the god Amun at Karnak, but that is a long story that I will not tell here.) He believed the palette must be from the Western Delta, and he was probably right.

This early insight by Ranke fits in well with the insights gained only since the 1980s by excavations in the Delta, as reported by Wilkinson. Wilkinson says that it was merely the lack of excavation information about the Delta earlier on that had led to the area being unduly ignored. Wilkinson explains that the Western Delta in particular (which I discuss in Chapter Eight) was '"conquered territory", ripe for appropriation by the court without reference to pre-existing political structures.' That is, he believes, why there were so many royal estates in that area in the First Dynasty, because the conquering southern kings seized them for themselves. The Western Delta was a relatively wild and expansive place, with lots of game and grazing land, much of which was never flooded during the Inundation. These were the 'fields of the west' referred to on a First Dynasty jar sealing. And it was there that the Libyan princes with their double ostrich plumes had done their hunting before they were conquered, as portrayed on the Hunters' Palette. However, we should be wary, because conquests are rarely complete, and king after king of the First Dynasty seems to have 'conquered' the Delta. They were always doing it. The 'unification of Egypt' was not a single event, it was an ongoing process, requiring constant warfare, and resulting in repeated 'commemorative' palettes and other depictions to celebrate the 'conquests' that were never final.

King Narmer, who liked to portray himself as the ultimate conqueror, seems to have legitimised his kingship by marrying the Libyan princess Neithhotep. (Neith was the name of the goddess Neith of the north, whose temple seat was at the Western Delta capital of Sais.) There were other marriages with these Libyan princesses, and they seemed to be necessary dynastic marriages to try to 'seal the unification'.

And this brings us back to a puzzling anomaly of the Palermo Stone. I have already mentioned that only three kings' names survive on the Palermo Stone from the entire First, Second, Third and Fourth Dynasties. The obverse side of the Palermo Stone may be seen in its entirety in Figure 47. If you look at the bottom row, you can see the same pharaoh's name portrayed three times within cartouches. This name is Sneferu, the first king of the Fourth Dynasty (reading the hieroglyphs from right to left and downwards). In the last box to the left on the bottom row, side by side we see his name in a cartouche surmounted by (left) the crown of the north and (right) the crown of

Figure 47. The Palermo Stone, obverse side. This image was given to me by the officials of the museum at Palermo, and has been digitally enhanced by Michael Lee. The top row, broken at left, lists the predynastic kings of the Delta in the north of Egypt (see Figure 49 for a close-up view of this row).

Figure 48. A carving found at Dashur of King Sneferu, the first king of the Fourth Dynasty and reputed father of Cheops, seated on his throne, holding the royal flail and wearing the joint crowns of the north and the south. His name is shown above him in its cartouche. To the right are the pairs of sedge and hornet, vulture and cobra, which represent 'king of north and south'. The royal Horus falcon surmounts the inscription.

the south; both of these are apparently references to buildings named after him. Those are the only cartouches on this side of the stone. The other two kings' names that appear on this side of the stone are both from the Second Dynasty, when cartouches were not yet used, namely Ninetjer and Khasekhemui.

However, the three historical kings whose names appear on this side of the stone are greatly outnumbered by no less than seven named kings in what survives of the top row, which, as can be seen from what remains of the bottoms of inscribed compartments, originally contained at least thirteen named kings. And these seven kings are *otherwise unknown to history*. These are truly 'lost kings'. It is amusing that the 'lost kings' outnumber the 'known kings'. For those who enjoy a good joke, we could ask for nothing better.

I reproduce this top row of the Palermo Stone in an enlarged version in Figure 49, which has been specially digitally enhanced to make it absolutely clear. The larger rectangular box at the top of each section shows the name, and the seated royal figure beneath the name indicates that he is a king. The stone reads from right to left, so that these seven

Figure 49. The top row of the Palermo Stone's obverse side inscription. This shows a row of the names of a whole series of predynastic kings of Egypt, all wearing the red crown of Neith and of the North. The row is read from right to left. The seated king at the bottom of each box shows that the name written above it in hieroglyphs is that of a northern king. The first name is illegible except for the fact that it ends in '-u' (or some suggest '-pu'), the vowel 'u' being written as a chick. The next name, and the first complete one, is Seka. The next is Khaiu, the next Tiu, the next Thesh or Tjesh, the next Neheb or Niheb, the next Uazanez or Wadj-adj, the next Meka or Mekhet, and the last broken one ends in '-a'. None of the names of these kings is recorded in or on any other surviving document or monument. They are all completely 'unknown to Egyptology'. This is the only surviving evidence that they ever existed. Many scholars thus feel uncomfortable about them, and many have simply ignored this row of names and refuse to discuss them at all, I suppose lest they lose their appearance of omniscience and of being 'experts'. But when there is a single piece of evidence about something and that is it, there are no experts, and everybody is equally ignorant, so there is no shame in that. If the stone were not broken, we can see clearly by counting the bottoms of the boxes that there were at least 13 kings named, the names of seven of which are wholly visible and two partially visible. I suggest that these 'unknown kings' ruled an important northern Egyptian kingdom extending across the Delta and at least as far south as Meidum (four hours' drive by car south of Cairo today), but probably as far as Herakleopolis (somewhat further south, as discussed in Chapter 8). I believe these kings may have presided over the largely-vanished civilisation which was later conquered by the warlike southerners King Narmer and his son King Hor-Aha, creator of the 'First Dynasty' of a unified Egypt. Could this 'lost kingdom' have built the Giza pyramids, and had all trace of their existence erased by the pharaohs Cheops and Chephren when they 'usurped' them? *(This image is taken from one given to me by the museum officials at Palermo, which was then digitally enhanced by Michael Lee.)*

names in succession, preceded by ones in front and back which are partially visible, are:

(1) ... u [or some believe ... pu]
(2) Seka
(3) Khaiu or Khayu
(4) Tiu or Teyew
(5) Thesh or Tjesh or Tesh
(6) Neheb or Niheb
(7) Uasanez or Wadj-adj or Wadjenedj or Uadj-adj
(8) Meka or Mekh or Mekhet
(9) ... a

No one had ever heard of these kings before and no one has ever heard of them since. They are shown wearing the red crown of the North, so they are clearly intended to portray a series of now forgotten predynastic Kings of Lower Egypt. No tomb, monument, or trace or hint of these kings is known from any other source, and the names are unfamiliar and appear never to have been used subsequently in Egyptian history. But we cannot dismiss them just because of this, as the Palermo Stone is undoubtedly genuine, so these names must be also.

I decided to attempt to translate the strange names of these predynastic kings, as no one else ever seems to have done so. In the case of the sixth one, whereas *uadj* is well known to mean 'green', I decided to translate the second hieroglyph of the name as the creature that is actually depicted. I was surprised at what I came up with as possible meanings of these kings' names, as they seem extraordinarily primitive. Here is my list:

Seka = Man of the Ka [the ka being the spirit-double]

Khaiu = Exalted One

Tiu = Smasher

Thesh = Lake Man [very appropriate for the Delta]

Neheb = Subjugator

Uadj-adj = Green Fighting-Fish [or alternatively, Fighting-Fish of the Delta]

Mekhet = Mace Man, or Club Man

These do not sound like the sort of people one would like to meet, and my idea of fun is not to know somebody called 'Smasher', frankly.

We are faced with an entire dynasty of kings here, at least thirteen of them, with seven names surviving intact, who were active in the north of Egypt before the 'unification'. My feeling about this is that their complete disappearance from the historical record, apart from this one stone, might have been connected with a systematic campaign to eliminate all memory of them by the 'unifiers'. The earliest of the 'unifiers' from the South of whom we know the name is King Scorpion (believed to be either the father or grandfather of King Narmer), and we even have his surviving limestone mace head, showing scenes of his victory over some northerners. It was excavated at Hieraconpolis in the south in 1897 and is on display in the Ashmolean Museum at Oxford. Imagine scenarios like this:

'Scorpion versus Mace Man'

or: 'Scorpion versus Smasher'.

These may sound like really corny wrestlers on afternoon television, but there was nothing fake about the ferocity of these fellows. If they had had business cards, they would have read: *Smiting is our specialty.*

I think we were all lucky to miss predynastic Egypt, as many of us would have ended up with our heads bashed in.

We return to the problem of: *who really built the pyramids?* If we find it difficult to believe that 'Smasher', 'Subjugator', and 'Mace Man' were quite what we had in mind, we can take comfort in one thing: the demonstrable fact that a whole dynasty of thirteen kings can vanish without a trace (apart from being mentioned on one annals stone), suggests that there might be a lot of other 'lost kings' as well, including perhaps more peaceable ones whose principal aim was to construct rather than destroy.

In Chapter Eight I am much more specific about suggesting where the requisite knowledge and expertise for building the Giza pyramids might have come from, and I leave that discussion for later.

Before leaving the subject of 'lost kings', however, I just want to draw attention to a few more examples of how little is really known about the early days and the early kings. Many Egyptologists speak confidently of King Huni. They all believe he was the father of King Sneferu, first king of the Fourth Dynasty. 'Huni' is a friendly sort of name, people like saying it, and I have heard Egyptologists almost sigh as they say 'Huni'. Good old Huni! But for every cosy assumption there is a pestering sceptic. And in this case, the sceptic is Hans Goedicke. In an extremely learned article published in 1956, with an elaborate analysis of hieroglyphics of a more than usually erudite kind, Goedicke proceeded to demonstrate that the person known as Huni was not really called Huni.[47] He was able to demonstrate that the name 'Huni' was unknown until the end of the Middle Kingdom, and that 'a king with such a name is not attested by any Old Kingdom inscription'. However: 'That a king who is mentioned not only in historical lists, but also in a literary text should not have left any traces is hard to believe.'[48]

So Goedicke decided that 'Huni' must have existed, but under another name. He concluded that 'Huni' was a mistaken name, due to a scribal error. But if 'Huni' was not 'Huni', who was he? After an extremely long discourse and analysis, Goedicke concludes in a most convincing manner that his name was really *Ny-swth*, which I cannot display with the proper typography in this book, and which we can transliterate as Nishuteh. The confusion of name arose from the action of scribes hundreds of years after his time in a manner too complicated to describe here. Goedicke then goes on to reveal that he has found in the museum in Cairo a remarkable red granite cone (Object 41556) with the name of this pharaoh in a cartouche (of which he publishes a photo) and attributes its discovery at the island of Elephantine to the Egyptologist Henri Gauthier. However, I have Henry Fischer's personal copy of this original offprint, and from a note that Fischer has written at the bottom of the page, I can see that this object was really discovered in 1909 by Joseph Étienne Gauthier, not Henri Gauthier. (This explains why Henri Gauthier did not mention it in a book of his in 1907, an omission that had puzzled Goedicke. I record this fact for posterity, as there is no other record of it.) From this fact, very important historical information is gleaned by Goedicke (which would have been impossible if he had not correctly identified the misnamed 'Huni') about when Elephantine was settled as a northern outpost and how the Old Kingdom evolved; but we will not go into those details here, however interesting they might be.

I would also call attention to some cautionary remarks made by Walter Emery in his 1961 book, *Archaic Egypt*:

'The cause of the downfall of the First Dynasty is not known and the distinction between the two royal houses [of the First and Second Dynasties] is not apparent . . . [Manetho] tells us that the [Second] dynasty consisted of nine rulers who ruled for a total of 302 years. Of these kings, the order of succession of the first four is established on archaeological evidence, but after this the order and identification are very uncertain.'[49]

To be certain of only four out of nine rulers of the Second Dynasty is not very good. That leaves a lot of 'wobbly kings'. Ironically, in the next chapter, I have some evidence to present about one of them named Send, or Sendji. Of him, Emery says:

'There are no contemporary monuments of Sendji, . . . Although so little is known at present concerning Sendji, it is evident that apart from his long reign he was a monarch of importance . . .'[50]

In the next chapter I reveal some evidence relating to King Sendji which was discovered more than a century ago and then forgotten! What is more, it is evidence that was found at Giza. So in that case, one of the many 'lost kings' becomes just a little bit less lost.

Could it be King Sendji who really built the pyramids of Giza? It is not impossible. Readers should consider the remarkable find relating to him, which was made in the Valley Temple by Uvo Hölscher, as described shortly.

The situation regarding the Third Dynasty is even worse than that regarding the Second Dynasty. The disagreements about that dynasty are so great that the disputes almost remind me of 'Smasher versus Scorpion'. Some people think there were lots of kings in the Third Dynasty; others that there were barely any. And, as we have already seen in Chapter Three, one of them had his name inscribed several times at the great astronomical observation shaft at Zawiyet el-Aryan. (See Figure 50.) So there we have a site that most Egyptologists wish dearly could be assigned to the Fourth Dynasty, but which has Third Dynasty cartouches painted in it. A slight chronological problem there! There is only one book about the Third Dynasty in existence, written by an Egyptian author named Nabil Swelim, which is extremely interesting.[51] Swelim believes there were nine kings in the Third Dynasty, whereas some people think there were only three or four. It is obvious

Figure 50. The name of King Neferka, a king believed to date from the Third Dynasty (but in any case definitely not later than that), copied out by Jean-Philippe Lauer from occurrences of the name which he found when he excavated the great shaft at Zawiyet el-Aryan. The name is shown in a royal cartouche, so is obviously that of a king. It is read from right to left, the second sign being the upraised arms which are read 'ka'. No one is really certain what the sign on the right is meant to be. It has been suggested that it is an archaic hieroglyph for 'giraffe', which was called *nefer*. Others have suggested that it is a poorly drawn version of a different hieroglyph, which would mean that the name would be read Nebka, though I do not find that at all convincing. This king, who appears to have been the king who constructed the Zawiyet el-Aryan shaft, was certainly not a king of the Fourth Dynasty, the dynasty to which 'pyramid tomb theorists' would like to attribute it, whilst trying to maintain that it is an 'unfinished pyramid'. In fact, it would have been physically impossible to construct a pyramid on top of such a vast shaft, which is the case also with the smaller but similar one at Abu Ruash, but lack of engineering knowledge rarely deters an inferior Egyptologist from pushing his pet theory when it suits him. See Plates 8 and 9 and Figures 11–13 in Chapter 3, where this shaft and its twin at Abu Ruash were discussed, and where I suggested that their purpose was for rectifying the calendar by carrying out precision observations of star culminations at the meridian (north–south) line. (The shafts are oriented precisely north–south.)

that pinpointing the true number of reigns would make a big difference to the chronology of the Old Kingdom. No one has solved these problems, because there is insufficient evidence, and the Cairo Fragments mess everything up even further. There are therefore plenty of potential 'lost kings' in the Third Dynasty, just as there are in the Second.

We cannot enter further into all of these mazes of contradiction and dispute, all of these 'lost and found kings', all of these uncertainties. It is sufficient to have pointed out some of them.

I will close this chapter simply by calling attention to one last bizarre and contentious matter that affects all of these discussions. It is the subject of what came to be called the 'Dynastic Race', which was a term originated by Sir Flinders Petrie to describe a deeply puzzling finding

273

in Egypt. In 1914 a physical anthropologist [a scientist who studies ancient human bones] named Douglas Derry studied the skulls at Saqqara and compared them with predynastic skulls from the south. He discovered that they were drastically different; so different in fact that they came from a different race of people altogether. It was these people whom Petrie then called the 'Dynastic Race'. This subject has been covered up in recent times because people all over the world are now so hysterical about any discussion of race that people are afraid even to utter the word. There are several reasons for this. One understandable reason, with which all reasonable people must have full sympathy, is the abuse of the concept of 'race' by the Nazis. The words 'Semitic' and 'Aryan' are not even properly racial terms, but are linguistic terms. But that did not stop the Nazis seizing upon them and erecting fantastically evil and murderous doctrines about 'Aryans' and 'Semites' which resulted in the deaths of millions of people in the name of 'racial theories' which were merely the insane and demented ravings of lunatics. Naturally, this puts people off!

A more recent cause of hesitation to mention race is a movement of 'Afro-heritage'. I myself have written a book about 'Afro-heritage', and when I went to Harlem a few years ago I was even greeted as a hero by a black bookseller because of it. Once also in Chicago in 1978 a young black woman came up to me and said the following: 'We black people in the United States have a national secret society with a very restricted membership, of which no white person is allowed to know the name or any information at all. But we had a special meeting of the Council at which we passed a resolution that we would make one exception and only one. We would tell you of our existence without giving you our name and inform you that we all give you our deep thanks for what you did for Afro-American pride and for our people. I cannot tell you who we are, you will never hear from us again, but we voted to give you our official thanks, and I was authorised to tell you about it. Please Mr. Temple, we hope you will accept our deepest thanks for what you did. It is a pity that you are a white person and I cannot tell you any more.' She shook my hand, looked at me earnestly, turned and vanished into the crowd of a large audience at a conference where I was speaking.

In recent years, I have noticed that, unfortunately, black pride gets a bit carried away sometimes, and there have been some excesses committed in all of the enthusiasm for 'roots', which have led some people to be a bit too keen to pronounce everything to do with ancient Egypt 'African'. There are plenty of African influences in Egypt, but we must not allow modern biases to influence our study of the whole truth about any matter, especially when the tricky subject of 'race' is involved. I am one of those people who wonders whether the word 'race' even means anything at all in the scientific sense. Is there really any such thing as a 'race'? Is there anyone in the entire world whose genetic heritage is not hopelessly mixed? Why are 'white people' called 'the Caucasian race' in America? Have any of them ever been anywhere near the Caucasus? Does the 'Caucasian race' even exist? Did it *ever* exist? A recent DNA survey of the Spanish people, reported in the press, discovered that 10 per cent of them were descended from Arabs and 20 per cent of them were descended from Jews. But Arabs and Jews, as far as I can see, have never been satisfactorily defined, and I do not know what an Arab is or a Jew is, except by approximation. And I certainly know that neither of them are 'Semites', since 'Semite' is only a noun derived from the linguistic term 'Semitic', which is used to refer to language families. 'Semitic' is not and never was a justifiable 'racial' term. But if it were to be used to describe people who speak Semitic languages, then Arabs and Jews are both Semitic. So where does that leave anti-Semitism? The lack of logic of the Nazis is nowhere better shown than in their befriending of the Muslim League and the Grand Mufti during the Second World War, to try to spread 'anti-Semitism' in Egypt, which eventually led to the expulsion of the Alexandrian Jews after the War, most of whom went to America. But if the Muslim League had behaved rationally, in becoming 'anti-Semitic', it would have been anti-Arab as well as anti-Jew, and hence opposed to itself, since it was composed entirely of Arabs. Such is the mind-numbing stupidity of 'racialism', which is based upon non-existent concepts and is merely a form of the pseudo-organisation of prejudices masquerading as ideas.

So this is yet another sociological deterrent at the present time to scholarly discussions about the mysterious question of 'the Dynastic Race' in Egypt, and makes people hesitate to mention it. Consequently, we must keep in mind that the phrase 'the Dynastic Race' was coined as a means of speech to deal with differences in human skulls.

The seminal article on this subject is 'The Dynastic Race in Egypt' by D. E. Derry, published in the *Journal of Egyptian Archaeology* in 1956.[52] It had been preceded by a pamphlet by Walter Emery entitled *Saqqara and the Dynastic Race*, which was the publication of a special lecture that Emery gave at University College London in 1952.[53]

Derry's comments and findings are most extraordinary:

'The object of the present paper is to put on record a general account of the facts that led to the conclusion that another race in addition to that represented by the remains found in all reliably dated Predynastic graves occupied Egypt in Early Dynastic times.

'The earliest inhabitants of Egypt of which we have any knowledge are the so-called Predynastic people, numbers of whose cemeteries have been excavated in Upper Egypt. Where these people came from is unknown, but there is at least some evidence that they may have been the descendants of the people who inhabited what is now the Eastern Desert at a time when more frequent rain permitted sufficient vegetation to support the flocks of sheep and goats of a pastoral people. That such climatic conditions did prevail we have definite evidence. . . . The first Predynastic cemeteries were discovered by Professor Flinders Petrie in 1895 at Nakadah [Naqqada] on the west bank of the Nile, a few miles north of Luxor. At first he believed he had found a "new race", but later it was shown that these people were the autochthonous inhabitants of the Nile Valley. . . . The skeletons were sent to England and the skulls formed the subject of a special study carried out by Miss C. D. Fawcett and published in *Biometrika*, I, 408–67 (1902). In 1901 Dr George A. Reisner . . . laid bare an early Predynastic cemetery, and the human remains were packed and sent to the Medical School in Cairo, where Elliot Smith was at that time Professor of Anatomy. When Dr Reisner left Upper Egypt he settled in the vicinity of the pyramid of Cheops and began the excavation of the immense Fourth and Fifth Dynasty necropolis surrounding the pyramid . . . When I joined Elliot Smith in 1905 he had already begun a systematic examination and measurement of the human remains in this cemetery, and together we accumulated a large number of measurements to which I added many more during the following summer when, by Dr Reisner's invitation, I stayed at his camp. . . . we had at the Medical School the material, either as notes or the actual skeletons, of Predynastic and Early Dynastic cemeteries, both excavated by Dr Reisner, who at this time believed that the Egyptian culture had evolved in the Nile valley and that the people whose remains we were examining buried round the Great Pyramid were the descendants of the Predynastic Egyptians. . . . It was not until the year 1909 when, after the second season's work in Nubia, where the archaeological survey of that country brought to light an enormous amount of human material and when comparative figures of skull measurements from various series were called for, that on taking out the means of our measurements on the Fourth to Sixth Dynasty crania from the Giza necropolis, the unexpected discovery was made that the pyramid builders were a different race from the people whose descendants they had hitherto been supposed to be. . . . Even those unfamiliar with craniometry will be struck by the difference in the measurements of the skulls in the two series shown in the table on p. 83. The Predynastic people are seen to have had narrow skulls with a height measurement exceeding the breadth, a condition common also in negroes. The reverse is the case in the Dynastic Race, who not only had broader skulls but the height of these skulls, while exceeding that in the Predynastic Race, is still less than the breadth. . . . If we lump these figures [from his various tables] together and take the means of the three measurements, we obtain a result which is very striking and which is so far removed from the mean of the Predynastic people that under no circumstances could we consider them to be the same race.'

This could hardly be more explicit. Derry's article also gives various references to more technical studies containing the extended data.

Walter Emery had summed up some of the implications of these findings in his pamphlet which I mentioned a moment ago, when he said:

'Even after more than a century of scientific research in the Nile valley one, if not the principal, question facing the Egyptologist is the existence of what Petrie called the Dynastic Race. Was the Pharaonic civilization the outcome of a sudden step forward in the predynastic culture of the indigenes, or was it due to a different race whose arrival changed the whole cultural trend of the Nile valley some 5,000 years ago?'

It is clear from these statements that, in order to deal with the inflamed sensitivities of today's world, the word 'race' should stop being used, and 'people' should be substituted for it. If we talk about 'a different people', it no longer has the baggage of associations to which I have already alluded. However, in quoting from these publications, I can only use the language that they used then. Emery continues:

'On such a problem as this I should hesitate to express any views were it not for the appearance recently of additional evidence. This came to light as a result of excavations of a site in North Saqqara, which I have been directing for some years.'

He then gives a very lengthy account of various archaeological discoveries which convinced him that the leaders of society whom he calls 'the nobility and official classes' were, to judge from their tombs, wholly different from 'the lower classes'. Summing up all the relevant findings, he concludes: 'All of this plainly suggests the existence of a master race of superior culture, who gradually imposed its burial customs on the conquered indigenes.'

Finally, Emery puts the problem succinctly:

'The theory of the existence of a Dynastic Race is supported by evidence other than the archaeological. As long ago as 1914 Dr Douglas Derry, in a lecture given here at the College, drew attention to the marked difference between the Predynastic and Dynastic populations as revealed by craniometrical measurements. He considered that the theory that the Dynastic people derived from the Predynastic people was no longer tenable, that the races were distinct. Dr Derry has recently examined much of the anatomical material from Saqqara and has found no reason to modify his opinion.

'If we consider that the existence of the Dynastic Race, who brought Pharaonic civilization to the Nile valley, is proved, we must then ask: What was it and where did it come from?'

It is this question to which I propose some new answers in Chapter Eight of this book.

CHAPTER SEVEN

The Sphinx and Valley Temples of Giza

Two of the most fascinating and enigmatic structures in all of Egypt are the Sphinx Temple and the Valley Temple, which sit side by side at Giza. (See Figure 51.) One of them, the Sphinx Temple, sits directly in front of the Sphinx. It is the more ruined one, and is not open to the public. The other temple to the south of it, much more substantial as a building today, is called the Valley Temple. It is connected to the Pyramid of Chephren by a giant causeway of huge limestone blocks, known as the Chephren Causeway, which is nearly a quarter of a mile long. (See Plate 41.)

Millions of people have filed through the Valley Temple without really knowing what it was. They have entered its eastern front from the village of Nazlett el-Sammann, and then proceeded through the temple and out on to the Causeway at the rear, where they have stood and looked down on the Sphinx to their right, and then they have continued on up the gentle slope to the pyramids.

The new arrangements at Giza no longer allow entry to the Plateau at this point, so this ritual of processing through the Valley Temple as an entry point to Giza and as an approach to the pyramids is no longer the tradition that it was for so long. This was the ancient direction of approach to the Giza Plateau, and in Greek and Roman times the village called Nazlett el-Sammann was known as Busiris, a fact recorded by the Roman author, Pliny (Busiris being also the name of a city far to the north), which in Egyptian had the name of Djedu (which apparently means 'Ghost Town'). But this ancient route of approach for

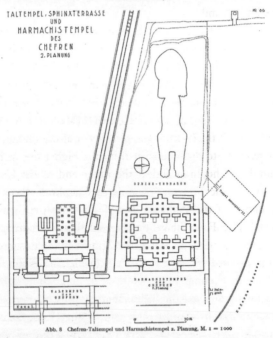

TALTEMPEL, SPHINXTERRASSE
UND
HARMACHISTEMPEL
DES
CHEFREN
2. PLANUNG

Abb. 8 Chefren-Taltempel und Harmachistempel 2. Planung, M. 1 = 1000

Figure 51. This drawing shows the Sphinx with the Sphinx Temple directly in front of it, and to the left of the Sphinx Temple is the Valley Temple. Shooting upwards from the top right hand corner of the Valley Temple and running beside the Sphinx is the Chephren Causeway, which goes up towards the Pyramid of Chephren (see Plate 41). The Sphinx Temple was first excavated in 1936 from beneath a huge mound of sand, and was unknown prior to that for about 4000 years. (This drawing is figure 8 on page 19 in Herbert Ricke's book *Der Harmachistempel des Chefren in Giseh*, Wiesbaden, 1972. Unlike other archaeologists, Ricke insists upon calling the Sphinx Temple by the name of 'the Harmachis Temple' because Harmachis was a name of the Sphinx during the New Kingdom period. He assigns both temples to King Chephren, spelled Chefren in German.)

visitors has now been abolished, so that visitors will eventually become less and less familiar with the Valley Temple, as the memory of it as part of the artery of approach by foot to Giza fades into the past. Future visitors will need to make the extra effort of descending past the Sphinx and into the building, which many will not bother to do. The temple will thus lapse back into some of its old somnolence, which it experienced for the thousands of years when nobody knew it was there and it was covered with sand.

The Valley Temple has not always been called by that name. What we now call the Sphinx Temple, for the obvious reason that it sits directly in front of the Sphinx, was only discovered in 1936. Before that, it was common to call the Valley Temple by the name of the Sphinx Temple because of its proximity to the Sphinx, although it was off to one side. But because the Valley Temple contains a great deal of granite, Flinders Petrie in 1883 called it the Granite Temple.[1] Petrie also sometimes called it 'the lower temple', to distinguish it from the higher one at the foot of the Pyramid of Chephren and at the other end of the Causeway, which we now call the Funerary Temple of Chephren. We have not attempted a dating of the Funerary Temple of Chephren, which was discussed in Chapter Four, where I suggested that it is sitting on top of the tomb of Chephren. However, we have obtained dates for both the Valley Temple and the Sphinx Temple, which I describe in this chapter.

Anyone who is interested in the history of the structures we are discussing must always remember that, prior to the 1930s, the name of the one was attached to the other. Otherwise, a great deal of confusion is possible if you read earlier writers.

As if there were not enough confusion of names already, Herbert Ricke, in his monograph about the Sphinx Temple, published in German in 1970,[2] refused to use the name the 'Sphinx Temple', but named it the Harmachis Temple. This is because the Sphinx in later times was considered to be the god Harmachis, and Ricke assumes that the temple was intended for his worship. Hence he calls the temple by the name of its presumed god. But Ricke's logic is seriously flawed. There is no evidence whatsoever that in the Old Kingdom period the Sphinx was regarded as Harmachis, a god who became identified with the Sphinx at least a thousand years later, during the New Kingdom. Ricke has merely muddied the waters by his strange insistence upon dragging yet another name upon the stage, and an unjustified one at that. What makes it even worse is that all Egyptologists are agreed that the Sphinx Temple was completely buried and its existence was unknown during the New Kingdom period, when the worship of Harmachis became attached to the Sphinx (the true significance of which no one any longer remembered). Ricke thus wishes to thrust upon this buried and unknown structure the name of a god whose worship became attached to the locality approximately a thousand years after the temple itself was covered in sand. We do not know what went on in the Sphinx Temple but, whatever it was, I think we can safely insist that the god Harmachis was never worshipped in it.

Surely the whole point of trying to discuss monuments is frustrated if we cannot adopt a common nomenclature so that we all know what we are talking about. Ricke even gives the temple a full name of 'der Harmachistempel des Chefren in Giseh' ('the Harmachis Temple of Chephren at Giza'), which attempts to force upon Chephren in the Fourth Dynasty the use of the name Harmachis for the Sphinx. If Ricke could produce any evidence for this name being used for the monument at the time of Chephren, we would feel more comfortable. But instead, this is merely Ricke's eccentric personal choice. So although in quoting Ricke we shall be forced to use his name of Harmachis Temple in the passages from his own book, we certainly reject that name in all of our own discussions and stick to the simple and obvious 'Sphinx Temple' instead.

Our dating results relate both to the Sphinx Temple and the Valley Temple. Of course, the Sphinx Temple looks older, because it is far more ruined. All Egyptologists are agreed that the Sphinx Temple was probably wholly buried from Old Kingdom times until 1936, a period of more than 4,000 years. And that is enough time underground to make anything look a bit rough.

The Valley Temple was also buried and largely forgotten until Auguste Mariette cleared most of its interior between 1853 and 1860. But an anomalous dating result that we have obtained indicates that during the New Kingdom period, the roof must have been accessible and in use, for some small limestone blocks were placed on the roof at that time. The exterior of the Valley Temple was still smothered in sand and rubble up to fifteen feet from the top until the first decade of the twentieth century, when Uvo Hölscher, as part of the Ernst von Sieglin Expedition from what was then the Kaiser's Germany, attempted to complete the excavations started by Mariette, though he did not clear the exterior of the western wall (the side near the pyramids). Hölscher published his classic volume *Das Grabdenkmal des Königs Chephren* [The Funerary Monument of King Chephren] in 1912.[3] It remains the only existing work on the Valley Temple to this day, which is an extraordinary fact, since it demonstrates the astonishing lack of interest shown in the building by generations of Egyptologists, the prime exception being Flinders Petrie, as already mentioned.

One annoying aspect of Hölscher's book is that he, like Ricke, confuses the nomenclature of the building. He insists on calling it the *Torbau*, a word meaning in German 'gatehouse' or 'gate building'. He does this in the generic sense, since there was more than one *Torbau* at Giza. Hölscher praises George Reisner for having discovered the *Torbau* of Mycerinus. Hölscher differentiates his own building (the Valley Temple) by calling it specifically the *Torbau* of Chephren. The 'Mycerinus Gatehouse' was a temple at the end of the causeway that runs down towards the river from the small Pyramid of Mycerinus, whereas the Valley Temple was at the end of the Chephren Causeway, which runs down towards the river from the Pyramid of Chephren, and hence it became to Hölscher the 'Chephren Gatehouse'. There is some logical basis for speaking of these buildings in this way, since one possible interpretation of the structures certainly is that both the 'gatehouses' were temples beside the Nile (which in those days was up next to the Giza Plateau at Inundation time), through which one proceeded by causeway to the respective pyramid of the respective pharaoh, all as part of that pharaoh's funerary cult. In fact, the 'Mycerinus Gatehouse' as well as the 'Mycerinus Causeway', are vastly inferior structures: here the builders often fell back on brick rather than stone, and none of the structures was ever properly completed.

The question as to whether we should speak of the paltry constructions attributed to Mycerinus in the same breath as the magnificent constructions attributed to Chephren is an unresolved issue of dispute. We therefore should probably not prejudge the matter by imposing terminology upon them that implies there is no difference in principle between them. In any case, the confusion caused by having yet another name for one of our structures, and calling the Valley Temple instead the 'Gatehouse of Chephren' is not worth it. Nor is the astonishingly beautiful and impressive Valley Temple dignified by being called a 'gate-house'. Even if we were to conclude for certain that it fell within such a category – and I don't believe we will ever be in a position to say that – it gives quite the wrong impression. For the Valley Temple is one of the most amazing structures in all of Egypt, and to call it a gatehouse is only one step up from calling it a doghouse.

I have retained Hölscher's quaint name of the 'porter's lodge' for one of the small chambers within the Valley Temple because I think it is so funny to use such nineteenth-century terminology for an ancient chamber, the true use or significance of which we know nothing. It appealed to my sense of humour. However, I am careful to put it in quotes, just to remind people that it is really a little joke. One might as well use a French analogy and call it the concièrge's chamber! Or perhaps we could think in military terms and call it the guard room. Since no one knows the purpose of the chamber, no one knows what to call it.

The idea that justice can be done to the Valley Temple by calling it a 'gatehouse' is contradicted by Hölscher's own ecstatic description of the building, on page one of his book:

'Nobody could be immune to the effect of this edifice, with its simplicity of forms taken to extremes, with the gigantic dimensions of its monoliths, and its precious building material. No ledge, no orna-ment, no relief, no inscription decorated the walls. Only smooth polished wall surfaces and square pillars of rose granite and a luminescent white alabaster floor!'[4]

Some gatehouse! In all passages quoted from Hölscher, I shall there-fore translate *Torbau* simply as 'Valley Temple', in order to avoid confusion.

Due to the fact that I had to write a report on the Valley Temple, and the only book about it was in German, this necessitated a most exhausting task of translation. My collaborator for German translating, Eleonore Reed (a native German speaker), joined with me in translating the relevant contents of this book dealing with the Valley Temple and the Causeway. Only someone who has tried to read Uvo Hölscher's obscure nineteenth-century German can appreciate the horror of this task. Not only did Hölscher use many academic and technical words, he even invented his own terminology from time to time. Despite Eleonore Reed being a well-educated German, and despite my own knowledge of the subject matter, and armed as we were with no less than ten separate scientific and technical dictionaries in which we could find civil engineering terms, etc., we were often reduced to imagining what on earth Hölscher was trying to say. When he invented a word, we were often reduced to despair. But I believe that in the end we achieved clarity regarding Hölscher's meaning concerning the most obscure technical details, which are often so crucial in archaeological matters. Sometimes a small detail can result in a complete alteration of the interpretation of the significance of an entire monument. One cannot be too careful, as it is the minutiae that determine everything in archaeology. It is my intention to put the lengthy translations on this book's website as free PDF downloads. The translation of the introduction is an appendix to this book.

Having translated Hölscher, our difficulties were not at an end, because one of the three reports on the Sphinx Temple is also in German: Herbert Ricke's book, which has already been mentioned. Although Ricke published his work fifty-eight years later than Hölscher, there was not fifty-eight years' worth of difference in the use of language, unfortunately. It was easier, but not a great deal easier. I had already had the excellent help of the generous Horst Jaritz, former Director of the Swiss Institute in Cairo, in translating two pages of Ricke for use in the account of the tomb locations in Chapter Four, so I knew what we were up against. Some German scholars do revel in being as obscure and technical as possible. However, we overcame these difficulties as we had overcome the others, and to Eleonore Reed I owe a great debt, for few people would have had the patience to deal with such intractable – indeed, nearly impossible material.

It is inevitable, therefore, that much of what I have to say in what follows is based upon the work reported by Hölscher and Ricke in the translations we have done of their difficult books. But fortunately, there is a brief account of the Sphinx Temple in well-written and easily comprehensible English, in *The Great Sphinx and Its Secrets*, written by the distinguished Egyptian archaeologist Selim Hassan, who discovered and excavated the Sphinx Temple in the 1930s.[5] (This lengthy and largely unknown book on the Sphinx and the Sphinx Temple is not the same as his brief book of four years earlier on the same subject, *The*

Sphinx – in both English and French editions – with which many people are familiar, but which does not contain the extensive detail to be found in the longer work.) It is unfortunate, however, that Hassan's extremely detailed and lengthy account of the Sphinx and the Sphinx Pit, as well as their history, is not matched by a lengthy account of the Sphinx Temple, of which he was the excavator. His account of the temple is remarkably brief, and he never published anything further about it, so that there is no published full excavation report of the kind we might expect of such a major monument, or of a kind to match Hölscher's report of his excavation of the Valley Temple. Probably this is why Ricke thought it worthwhile to write an account of the Sphinx Temple, to try to fill in this gap in the literature, although, as we saw in Chapter Four, Ricke clearly did not read what little Hassan did say at all carefully, and it seems that before writing his own excavation report, he did not even glance at Hassan's. Although perhaps Ricke simply had no copy of Hassan's report, as it is a very rare volume. I am fortunate to own one.

Having access to these two mysterious ancient buildings was a wonderful experience. I made many extraordinary discoveries about them, as we have already seen in Chapter Four, and as we will see further here, where I reveal some of the bizarre and unknown features of the remarkable Valley Temple. In fact, later in this chapter I shall be revealing nothing less than 'the Valley Temple that nobody knows'.

It is probably best if I first give a straightforward account of the Valley Temple, and then after that I shall reveal its mysteries, which are unsuspected by everyone. Then I shall turn to the Sphinx Temple. And finally, I shall give the dating results of both temples and discuss their implications.

The Valley Temple

The Valley Temple was unknown until the French adventurer and amateur archaeologist Auguste Mariette (see his portrait in Figure 52) decided that the evident existence of a large structure under a mound of windblown sand and rubble at the foot of Giza, very near to the Sphinx, merited some attention because it might contain a royal tomb, and he was basically a treasure-hunter. So in 1853 he commenced

Figure 52. A portrait of Auguste Mariette, drawn by Théodule Devéria in 1859, known as the Mayer Portrait of Mariette after Horace L. Mayer, who acquired it in 1930 from the heirs of Luigi Vassali. (Reproduced from William Kelly Simpson, 'A Portrait of Mariette by Théodule Devéria', in *Bulletin de l'Institut Français d'Archéologie Orientale*, Volume LXXIV, 1974, pp. 149-50, and Plate XVII.)

digging. He busied himself with this task for seven years, and largely cleared the interior, leaving the exterior untouched. It was Mariette who named the building the 'Sphinx Temple', a name it held until the true Sphinx Temple was excavated by Hassan in 1936. But, as Hölscher pointed out: 'Mariette in his time had not recognised the importance of this building. First [Charles] Piazzi Smyth [in 1865] and after him Flinders Petrie [in 1883] pointed to the connection between it and the Funerary Temple lying in ruins in front of the Chephren Pyramid. However, this connection only found an explanation when [Ludwig] Borchardt claimed the building as the "Gate in the Valley" belonging to the funerary monumental complex of Chephren.'[6]

In fact, Hölscher is not really accurate here. The Chephren Causeway was already known by Giambattista Caviglia in 1817, who partially cleared it. I have already described this in Chapter Two, in my account of the Osiris Shaft. Caviglia was the man who excavated the front of the Sphinx, and who cleared the access to – and hence rediscovered – the Subterranean Chamber of the Great Pyramid. In my previous book, *The Sphinx Mystery*,

I discussed his work at the Sphinx in great detail and published a previously unknown contemporary account of it by his friend Annibale Brandi in an appendix. In Appendix One to this book, I publish the remainder of Brandi's publication, which describes his work inside the Great Pyramid. This is an account that no Egyptologist alive today has ever seen, so I hope it will be useful. As for the Chephren Causeway, after Caviglia's work on it, the sand blew over it again, and it became effectively invisible again in a short time. It was always becoming invisible, and perhaps we should rename it the 'Vanishing Causeway'. But today it is safely on view, and it will only 'vanish' because fewer people will walk on it and see it, now that the access to the Giza Plateau has been altered.

Mariette discovered what he named the 'Well' in the anteroom of the Valley Temple (see Figure 53 and Plate on the website), a nearly rectangular pit measuring 2.2 metres by 1.5 metres on either side. Thrown down to the bottom of this deep hole dug into the pavement, upside down, he found one of the most famous statues in the world: the seated figure of the pharaoh Chephren with the wings of the hawk god Horus protectively wrapped around him from behind, which now is one of the main attractions in the Egyptian Museum at Cairo. This amazing statue, made of the most beautiful polished diorite, was intact. Many people have claimed that the statue must have been thrown into the hole by plunderers who hated the pharaoh and wanted to destroy the temple, at the time known as the First Intermediate Period, following the end of the Sixth Dynasty and the Old Kingdom, when law and order collapsed in Egypt in the aftermath of a great famine and natural disaster. And there is no doubt that much plundering, including probably of the Valley Temple, took place in those times. But I am inclined to think that the preservation intact of this magnificent work of art was intentional, and that some priests dug the pit and concealed the statue when they realised that the temple was about to be plundered. Other statues were also found in the 'Well' by Mariette, but he did not bother to record the details, as he was very sloppy and not a responsible archaeologist.

Hölscher gives an interesting account of some of the events concerning the discovery and early excavation of the Valley Temple, which we have translated from his book:

Figure 53. This is the drawing of the plan of the Valley Temple at Giza taken from the notes of Auguste Mariette, who completed his excavation of the interior of the structure in 1870. The three-pronged interior feature at bottom right shows what we call the 'magazines'. They are in fact two-stories, so that there are really six chambers there rather than three, as this plan would indicate. The tiny dark square slightly to the left of the centre of the white space at the top (which depicts the Anteroom of the temple) shows the precise location of 'the Well', in which the famous statue of Chephren was found, thrust upside down in the hole. The two front entrances of the temple (at top) are both still blocked in this diagram. The passage at bottom left is what is called the Ascending Passage, which leads up a slope and opens out onto the Chephren Causeway. Reproduced from Georges Perrot and Charles Chipiez, *Histoire de l'Art dans l'Antiquité*, Paris, 1882, Volume I: *L'Égypte.* (*Collection of Robert Temple*)

Matters entered a new phase when Mariette tried from the year 1853 onwards to find the grave of the king, Harmachis, which had been mentioned by Pliny [Natural History, XXXVI, 17, 1], within the Sphinx. [Pliny's source had confused the name of the god Harmachis with that of a king, possibly Amasis, and some Pliny scholars have corrected this.] On this occasion he accidentally hit upon the Valley Temple. He began to clear it from the top. As a result of the huge masses of sand that needed to be dealt with he found himself forced to approach his patrons the Duke of Luynes and the French Government with ever renewed demands for money. He reports this himself [he is here quoted in French, which my wife Olivia has translated]:

'The temple discovered is now up to four-fifths cleared. We still haven't found anything in this temple. But in a temple which is filled up by sand bit by bit to the ceiling there is no reason why the objects which it contains might not float and somehow find themselves trapped between two layers. All the work which has been done up to now is for the purpose of recovering the monuments on the ancient floor. Let us be courageous and go on to the bottom and since we want to reap a harvest, let's have the patience to wait until the final push!'

But these requests were in vain. The excavations were stopped even though he had reached a level only one metre above ground level. Only the announcement of the 1860 visit of the Empress Eugènie gave the Egyptian Government the incentive to resume the interrupted work at their own cost.

Mariette reports: Much later a lucky chance put into my hands the means to resume, under the order of Said Pasha, the work which four years earlier I had had to abandon. Within a few days the ground level was reached and the statue of Chephren formed the nucleus of the riches which are today collected in the Museum of Boulaq [now the Egyptian Museum in Cairo]. But for lack of a few hundred francs, the statue of Chephren would today be instead in the Museum of the Louvre. . . . This temple had been absolutely unknown until then. The plan of Wilkinson marks this spot with these words: 'pits unopened'.

Concerning the external walls uncleared by him, he says:

Seen from the outside, the temple must present itself under the aspect of an enormous cube of masonry constructed with gigantic blocks of greyish limestone. . .

. . . Regarding the access to the building, he remarks that only a single small door in the corner was visible. From this statement we can trace the many suppositions that the Valley Temple had only one door [it really has two] . . . According to Mariette's account, during his work the following were found: [He lists various finds in addition to the Chephren statue, including a statue of an 'ape', which was doubtless of the god Thoth in his symbolic form of a baboon, the animal of greatest intelligence. This statue seems to have become lost. The prescence of Thoth in this temple is however extremely significant, in suggesting that this temple was never wholly dedicated to a mere funerary cult.] . . . Specific accounts of the condition of the interior of the Valley Temple during this clearance, from which one could deduce its later usage and history, are unfortunately completely missing. Equally unclear are the circumstances of the discovery of the different statues and stelae. Mariette says only, concerning the one best-preserved statue of Chephren, that it had been found in the well. Nowadays, however, one hears everywhere the tale that all the royal statues were found lying in there, which was hardly possible, as so many statues could hardly have found space in that hole.[7]

Hölscher gives an invaluable account of the German involvement in the further clearance and excavation of the Valley Temple:

A first attempt to gain clarity about the building of the Valley Temple had already been made at times by the Leipzig Mastaba Excavations at Giza in 1905 under Georg Steindorff. But in doing so, it had soon become evident that with the relatively restricted means available, the task could not be executed. The masses of sand which needed to be shifted were too enormous. After they had created a relatively insignificant gap in front of the southern main entrance, they had to give up the task for the time being.

. . . a long time would perhaps have passed before someone might have found the courage to attempt the excavation of the funerary monument of Chephren [this is the phrase he customarily uses to describe the entire complex of the Funerary Temple of Chephren, the Chephren Causeway, and the Valley Temple], if not for the fact that the Confidential Royal Councillor [to the Kaiser] Dr Ernst von Sieglin in Stuttgart, who was already highly meritorious for his research into antiquity, became interested in this important problem and generously granted the means for an archaeological investigation of the Chephren temple complex.

An initial viewing of the excavation area undertaken by Georg Steindorff and Ludwig Borchardt in the autumn of 1908 had concluded that the work had to solve a double task, the excavation of the Funerary Temple [the one directly in front of the pyramid on the east side, which I have dicussed in Chapter Four] and the uncovering of the exterior of the Valley Temple. Furthermore, one had to investigate the pyramid as well as its surrounding walls and auxiliary complexes and to check at the same time what had been published up to then. Finally, one also had to thoroughly clear and measure up the interior of the Valley Temple, of which, even though fifty years had passed since its discovery, no sufficient account was available. . . . In addition it should only be mentioned that Borchardt had several baskets full of statue pieces and splinters collected from the surface several years ago, which are now stored in the Berlin Museum.[8]

Ludwig Borchardt meticulously described and photographed all of these finds, and published the fully illustrated account of them as an appendix to Hölscher's book.[9] Not all of the seventy-one objects described by Borchardt were actually deposited in the Berlin Museum. Some of them went to the University of Leipzig Museum. It is possible that some or all of these objects, particularly the ones in Leipzig, might have been destroyed by bombing during the Second World War, but I have not made a search for them, as this was not necessary for my work. In his account, Borchardt had to retract a suggestion, which he had made in 1898, that the statue fragments of the Valley Temple were of late origin and had nothing to do with the time of Chephren, a position rendered untenable by Hölscher's excavations. It is amusing to notice the way in which Borchardt, required to correct himself, squirms uncomfortably and huffs and puffs a bit. Borchardt also includes some further comments of great interest concerning the temple itself:

For the excavation has proved, apart from the imprints of the statues in the old pavement – which may not be decisive yet for sceptics, – that the Valley Temple had already been robbed very early on of its granite façade. And its front, destroyed in this way, had already been walled up before the New Kingdom, and that before that, high over the old level, houses had been erected. So the Valley Temple was therefore inaccessible . . . Also the back exit which led to the Causeway and the actual Funerary Temple was at the time not practicable, because it shows the same destruction as the east façade and had been even more exposed to sanding up and being covered with rubble. If this exit had at any time been the main entrance to the Valley Temple, as it was between the times of the excavations of Mariette and von Sieglin [the excavator Hölscher is not mentioned here, but rather the sponsor of his excavation, which is curious and may indicate that Borchardt and Hölscher did not like each other], then it would have been restored first. However, we could not find even the least traces of any restorative work there. We can therefore say with confidence that the Valley Temple had not been accessible from a time before the New Kingdom up to Mariette's days, and probably was not even visible. . . . Mariette's people found the remains of 9 more or less complete statues of Chephren in the Valley Temple . . . The von Sieglin Expedition established the locations for 23 statues . . . and in addition assured the places for at least a further 14 statues in the actual Funerary Temple. These 41 statues can, however, only have made up a small portion of the amount of statues which had been erected here, because the excavation has unearthed hundreds of fragments of statues in all dimensions and in the most diverse materials, from a soft alabaster to a harder metamorphic schist, up to diorite or even basalt. The temple must have been full of statues up to the point of being tasteless.[10]

All of this had been preceded by some studies by Flinders Petrie in the early 1880s (highly praised by Hölscher), not much more than twenty years after Mariette had finished his work there, who had also taken a keen interest in the Valley Temple; as already mentioned, he had called it the 'Granite Temple' because of the large amount of granite it contained. Petrie records a terrible tale about the damage wrought to the building by Mariette:

The arrangement of the Granite Temple will be seen from (my) plan . . . The causeway from the upper temple [at the foot of the pyramid] runs down the hill, in a straight line, into the passage [the 'Ascending Passage'] which slopes down into the great hall. The pillars in this hall are all monoliths of dark red granite, like that of the walls; they are 41 inches (2 cubits) square, and 174.2 high, weighing, therefore, about 13 tons each. The two larger pillars, placed at the junction of the two parts of the hall, to support three beams each, are 58 inches wide, and weigh over 18 tons each. All these pillars support beams of granite, which are likewise 41 inches square in the double colonnade, and 47.8 to 48.4 deep in the single colonnade, where their span is greater. The shorter spans are 128, and the longer 145 inches; so that the beams are not as heavy as the columns, the two sizes being 9½ and 12½ tons. Six of these beams, or a third of the whole, are now missing. The [local] Arabs say that they were found lying dislodged in the temple; and that Mariette, when clearing up the place to exhibit (at the festivities of the opening of the Suez Canal) [in 1869] had them blasted to pieces by soldiers. This seemed scarcely credible, although very similar stories are reported of that Conservator of Antiquities; but among the quantities of broken granite, which is built into a rude wall to keep back the sand, I found many pieces with polished surfaces like the beams in question, and with distinct blast-holes cut in them, quite different in character to the holes drilled anciently. This ugly story, therefore, seems confirmed.[11]

Such acts of vandalism in those days were not uncommon, alas.

Petrie made extensive measurements, some of which we have just seen, and made many extremely important comments about the Valley Temple, and published a plan of it as well on a scale of 1 to 200,[12] which, however, is incomplete, because much of the structure was still obscured by sand and rubble. For instance, the southern Entrance Hall is simply a blank, marked 'filled by sand', and showing only the beginnings of a passage heading southwards from the anteroom. The eastern half of the north wall was also invisible; and all of the exterior, including the eastern façade, was entirely uncleared at this time.

Petrie was interested in the strange chambers in the Valley Temple that we tend these days to call the 'magazines'. He called them 'loculi' (a loculus is 'a small chamber or cell in an ancient tomb for corpses or urns', according to the Oxford English Dictionary). There are six of them, and we obtained a successful granite dating sample from one of them (see Plate 42 where we are seen taking this sample). The magazines are not open to the public, and when we were granted access to them by the Egyptian Supreme Council of Antiquities, no one could remember when anyone had last been inside. None of the inspectors could recall anyone entering for more than ten years, and it might have been decades. The lock on the barred door had to be smashed because

Der Pfeilersaal
im Torbau des Chephren.
Rekonstruktion von U. Hölscher.

Figure 54. This is an imagined reconstruction of the interior of the Valley Temple of Giza. We see here the transverse hall, which runs north to south, at the eastern end of the structure. Here it is called by the name of the Pillared Hall (*Pfeilersaal* in German). A row of statues of King Chephren is envisaged here, sitting in the tranquil and eternal deathly gloom of faint light filtering in through narrow slits in the roof. The pillars are of solid granite, massive blocks weighing tens of tons each. The floor is of white Egyptian alabaster, called travertine. This is a very evocative view drawn by A. Bollacher and based upon the reconstruction by Uvo Hölscher, who excavated the structure fully for the first time. It was published as Plate 5 in Hölscher's book, *Das Grabdenkmal des Königs Chephren* (*The Funerary Monument of King Chephren*), Leipzig, 1912. Fragments of many Chephren statues have been found in the vicinity, and one large whole one is preserved in the Egyptian Museum at Cairo. It was thrown down a well beneath the temple, probably by priests who hid it there in a time of turmoil to preserve it. The Old Kingdom period of Egypt came to an end with the Sixth Dynasty, when terrible droughts and flood and plagues devastated the country for about 150 years, between approximately 2150 BC and 2000 BC. During this period, social order broke down and mobs rampaged around the Giza Plateau smashing everything, including the statues of Chephren envisaged here.

there was no knowledge of any key. Once you get inside this barred gate (see Plate on the website), there is a short passage which leads westwards into another passage at right angles to it, running north–south, with a high ceiling. From the western side of this passage extend three chambers of equal size, which are long and rectangular. A shelf of granite acts as a ceiling to them and as a floor to three corresponding chambers above them. We thus have six of these chambers in two rows of three above one another.

As Petrie writes:

Out of the great hall a doorway, in the [S.] W. corner,[13] leads to a set of six loculi; these are formed in three deep recesses, each separated in two by a shelf of granite. These recesses still have their roofs on, and are dark except for the light from the doorway, and a ventilator. The lower part of the walls of each recess is formed of granite, resting on the rock floor; this is 61.6 (inches) to 61.7 (inches) high. Above this is the granite shelf, 28 (inches) thick, which extends the whole length of the recess. In the southern recess this shelf is nearly all of one block 176 x over 72 x 28. Upon this shelf, over the lower recesses, are placed two walls of alabaster, dividing the upper three loculi; both walls are irregularly a few inches southward of the lower walls. The extraordinary length of these loculi – over 19 feet – seems strange; especially as the turn to the side loculi would prevent any coffin larger than 30 x 76 inches being taken in unless it were tipped about to get the benefit of the cubic diagonal. The doorway is only 80.45 (inches) high, so that nothing over 80 inches long could be taken in on end.[14]

Petrie was very sharp to note these facts. What on earth could have been stored in these extremely long 'magazines', considering that nothing could enter which was rigid and more than 80 inches long? That is only equivalent to a man six foot eight inches high. No sarcophagus or coffin could be brought in, because they were all bigger than that. The illumination was so faint that you could barely see anything. Only a faint hint of light comes down the intact ventilation shaft from the roof. We know from the socket hinges on the doorjamb that there was a wooden door to the passage leading to these magazines. When it was closed, the

296

magazines would have been almost dark. But when it was open, only a small amount of additional light would have entered. This area of the temple contained no light-slits such as the Pillared Hall (the court) has (see Plates on the website).

The magazines are not pleasant to enter. Thick spider webs had to be brushed aside by us for the whole length of each magazine, like pushing one's way through nineteen feet of curtains, all crawling with spiders, who got on our arms and neck and in our hair. This area of the temple is also not a healthy place to stay for long, since when we took a radiation reading, we discovered that it was so intensely radio-active from the granite that Ioannis said to me: 'Any priests working in this temple would certainly have contracted leukaemia within twenty years.' I suppose that working in there just for a few hours was equivalent to having several X-rays.

In trying to think what on earth the magazines could possibly be for, I have only been able to come up with the idea that they might have been used for the storage of corpses being 'cured' in the process of mummification. We know that a proper mummification job took seventy days, which is a long time, and you had to store the bodies somewhere in between treatments. So perhaps the mummies of the royal family, royal officials and priests were stored in these magazines, which thus acted as a kind of morgue.

It is an extraordinary fact that if the magazines were used to store corpses, the intense radioactivity in there would have acted to kill off bacteria. In fact, as we discovered in the Osiris Shaft (as mentioned in Chapter Two), when we studied the radioactivity of the sarcophagi, granite sarcophagi emit so much radiation that any mummy sealed inside one would have been intensely irradiated from the time the lid went down until the corpse was lifted out by tomb raiders, and many if not all of the bacteria present would have been exterminated. This is not the case with limestone, which is not radioactive. Someone should do some radiation tests on royal Egyptian mummies themselves!

The Egyptians might well have come to realise by trial and error that granite provided anti-bacterial protection. But they may equally well have been unaware of this, and it might have been a coincidence that granite sarcophagi were used so often.

Petrie's observations about the light-slits of the Valley Temple are interesting:

'The ventilators are a peculiar feature of the building, though somewhat like those to be seen in the tombs. They were formed by sloping slits along the top edge of the walls, a few inches wide, and usually 41 inches long. Only one remains perfect, that opening out of the chamber of loculi; this slit opens into a rectangular shaft, which rises to some way above the roof; and there opens with a square mouth of alabaster on the face of the upper court wall. [See Plate on the website for a view of this.] The mouth is on the same side of the shaft as the slit; and hence the only light entering is reflected from the side of the shaft. The slits cut for these ventilators exist all along the Western part of the great hall, and are marked on the walls in the plan. [Plate VI at the back of his book.]'[15]

Petrie also noted these things about the doors of the temple:

'All the doorways seem to have been fitted with double valve doors: the doorway to the loculi is the best to examine. There the pivot-holes cut in the granite lintel by a jewelled tube drill are plainly to be seen; with the stump of the core left by the drill, still sticking in the southern hole. On the floor beneath these is, not another hole, but a highly polished piece of black basalt, quite flat, and free from scratches. It is difficult to see what was the use of such a stone, or how the doors were worked.'[16]

Petrie's general comments on the size of the structure are also interesting:

'This Granite Temple, then, appears to have been a mass of masonry, probably cased externally with fine limestone; and measuring about 140 feet in each direction, and 40 feet high. This contained a hall about 60 feet long, 12 wide, and 30 feet or more in height, with a large recess at each end containing a statue.'[17]

The question of the date of the Valley Temple inevitably involves also the question as to whether anything earlier might have stood on the same site. Although there is no evidence of any structures, a strange find was made by Hölscher inside the temple which certainly indicates

Figure 55. This hieroglyphic inscription of the name of King Send, or Sened, 'the Frightful' or 'the Feared One', fifth king of the Second Dynasty, was found on a shard of a thin-walled diorite bowl during excavations by Uvo Hölscher at the Valley Temple at Giza in 1909, published in 1912, and its existence was never mentioned again in the archaeological literature except once in passing by George A. Reisner, who was working nearby at Giza at the time it was discovered and saw it. The royal name was not written inside a cartouche, because cartouches were not yet in use at that period. However, the sedge and the wasp at left are the indications that he is being described as 'King of Upper and Lower Egypt'. This is the only archaeological evidence of the connection of any king of Egypt with the Valley Temple, other than King Chephren of the Fourth Dynasty.

a continuity of an unexpected kind with a much earlier era than that of Chephren, as he tells us:

'Traces of older constructions were not found in our excavation site. We only encountered one shard of a thin-walled diorite bowl with the name of Send (IIIrd Dynasty). It may stem from a funerary monument in the vicinity and annexed by the priesthood of Chephren.'[18]

In fact, Send/Senda/Sened, the Senethēs of the historian Manetho's chronology, was the fifth king of the Second Dynasty, not a king of the Third Dynasty, but perhaps Hölscher only made a typographical error here. A thin-walled diorite bowl can only be one of the famous 'impossible' stone bowls of the predynastic and archaic eras, of which so many are on exhibition at Cairo, showing incredible artistry and craftsmanship. They have always aroused the awe and admiration of anyone who was interested in stone carving, as their fabrication seems beyond the skills of anyone today, except for the alabaster ones, which were in soft stone. But how such bowls were fashioned in intensely hard stones like diorite has for long defied the imagination. It is interesting indeed to learn that a diorite one was kept in the Valley Temple, and that it bore this very early pharaoh's name. The full archaeological significance of this find, however, is a matter for much speculation.

Georg Steindorff also added an appendix to Hölscher's book, in which he made his own comments about this early object, and mentioned the correct dynasty.[19] He says (I have eliminated the hieroglyphics from the quotation): 'Very important however is a small shard of a diorite bowl with the inscription (on the original running from right to left): [. . .] "the King of Upper and Lower Egypt, [. . .] [Send]." This archaic king belonged to the Second Dynasty and it is not improbable that the bowl stems from his funerary temple, unknown as to its location, and was still used as part of the cult in the sanctum of Chephren.'

This find is so little known that a book published as recently as 2006, which made attempts to be definitive at listing names of archaic kings occurring on bowls, did not mention it. The editors, Erik Hornung, Rolf Krauss and David Warburton, as well as the contributor of the relevant article dealing with the First and Second Dynasties, Jochen Kahl, clearly all had no knowledge of the fact that a bowl fragment bearing Send's name had been found in the Valley Temple at Giza.[20]

The only other archaeologist apart from Hölscher who ever mentioned this find of Send's name at the Valley Temple, as far as I have been able to discover, was George Reisner. Probably he heard about it from the excavator himself, as Reisner was excavating the Mycerinus temples from 1906 onwards, and would have overlapped in time with Hölscher's work at the Valley Temple. Reisner mentions the find in passing in his book *Mycerinus*, where he says:

'In the temples of Chephren, where few objects were found except for the statues by Mariette, eight hard stone mace heads were the only objects on which the name of the king was found. None of the stone vessels bore his name; but [there was] one fragment [which] was inscribed with the name of King Sened of Dynasty II.'[21]

This mention of Send, or Sened, is not noticed in Reisner's index, so unless you read Reisner's text through, you would never know he had mentioned him. Reisner, who published *Mycerinus* in 1931, gave a footnote reference to Hölscher's book. But no one seems either to have noticed this or to have followed it up.

Certainly the idea that a king of the Second Dynasty might have had a funerary temple at Giza, as suggested by Hölscher, is something of a shock, as they are not otherwise known there from that period. Steindorff suggests this idea too, and no one that I know of has ever followed this up either. Of course, if either of the temples existed during the Second Dynasty, then the fragment of a diorite vase might be contemporary.

Let us take a moment to consider this strange king named Send. What do some of the experts on the early period tell us about him? Walter Emery was evidently unaware of the bowl fragment found by Hölscher. Here is all he has to say about Send in his seminal book, *Archaic Egypt*:

'There are no contemporary monuments of Sendji [Send], who was apparently Sekhemib's successor and is probably to be identified with Manetho's Sethenēs whom he states reigned for forty-one years. Although so little is known at present concerning Sendji, it is evident that apart from his long reign he was a monarch of importance and we know that his cult was preserved until a late period; indeed, a bronze statue bearing his name was made in the Twenty-Sixth Dynasty [664– 525 BC], more than 2000 years after his death.'[22]

Michael Rice, in the new edition of *Egypt's Making*, has even less to say about Send, whom he calls Sened:

'Egypt did not decline in prosperity during the rule of the Second Dynasty. . . . According to some king-lists Ninetjer was succeeded by Sened, about whom virtually nothing is known. It would have been doubted that he existed at all were it not for an inscription belonging to a Fourth Dynasty priest, Sheri, who was responsible for maintaining Sened's cult at Giza, which thus had survived for at least a hundred years.'[23]

So we see that Michael Rice also had no knowledge of the find at the Valley Temple. It seems clear that few English-speaking Egyptologists have ever wanted to wade through the difficult prose of Hölscher's book, if they could even find a copy, that is. But Hornung and Krauss are German-speaking, and they have no knowledge of the find either, as mentioned a moment ago.

The king whom we have called Send is known in the Old Kingdom Annals and the Turin Papyrus as Sendi, in the Saqqara List as Sendj, and by Manetho in the Greek form as Senethēs.[24] But who was he really? Patrick O'Mara, who also did not know of Hölscher's find (as indeed no English-speaking Egyptologist seems ever to have done, or any German-speaking one since Steindorff), has an astonishing theory about him:

'. . . the name Sendi is entirely unknown from any archaeological materials directly datable to the Second Dynasty. The form of the name must conceal a well-known king from another period.

'The clue to the identity of the name is provided by the pictographic form retained in the Abydos and Turin annals – a plucked goose. . . . The plucked goose is a corruption of the scorpion. This is King Scorpion, the first warrior king of Upper Egypt.'[25]

The famous King Scorpion. Well, that is certainly an interesting theory. Many millions of people who know nothing whatever about Egypt have heard of this name, and even seen him portrayed on screen, because they have seen the Hollywood epic film *The Scorpion King*. The fact that the movie is 99 per cent fantasy is not the point, it seems. Sometimes one has to be satisfied with just getting a name registered on the public consciousness, even if it is registered wrongly. 'Having heard of' somebody is step one. Often there never is a step two.

O'Mara defends at great length his idea that King Send is an alternative name for King Scorpion, but we cannot go into those details here, except to mention that all the early kings had at least four different simultaneous names, so that such confusions are common. I did not want to pass by the subject of King Send without mentioning this extraordinary possibility, which is intriguing and challenging to conventional ways of looking at the matter. But then, with a king of whom so little is known, from an era the nature of which is so vague, anything is possible. (Anything, that is, except the Hollywood version.)

As for the priesthood of the funerary cult of Chephren, which from the time of Chephren through the remainder of the Old Kingdom was undoubtedly celebrated in this building full of his statues, Hölscher found evidence of its continuance long beyond Chephren's Fourth Dynasty, right to the very end of the Old Kingdom:

Our temple may have stood undamaged throughout several millennia. The funerary cult appears to have been cultivated regularly throughout the whole of the Old Kingdom, even if with steadily diminishing splendour. Several signs of this could be found.

The semi-circular capstones of the temple . . . are on their outsides rather badly eroded, however they are uneroded on the upright joints and the horizontal course joints. That means they must have been lying in situ for centuries, being exposed to the influences of wind and weather before they were toppled down. Since these capstones had been exposed to the assault of the destroyers, one can assume that other parts of the temple had not been destroyed any earlier either.

South of the temple, next to the brick ramp, a monument from the Sixth Dynasty was found, in which the Superintendent [*Vorsteher*] of the City beside the Pyramid of Chephren is mentioned. In the Temple court lies a limestone post which evidently had not belonged to the original temple, but must be assigned to the time of the Sixth Dynasty. On it stands a vertically inscribed king's title: in this time, therefore, the priesthood must still have had the means for such type of building activities, even if they were humble. The stone may well be a doorpost of a brick placement of a later period, of the kind found better preserved at the side entrance of the Sahu-Re Temple [at Abusir].

From all these signs, it seems to emerge that the destruction of the temple cannot have happened before the end of the Old Kingdom.[26]

Apart from the name of King Send on a bowl at the Valley Temple, the names of other early kings have also been found at Giza. In the Valley Temple of Mycerinus (as I mentioned in Chapter Three), Reisner excavated bowls bearing the names of King Hotepsekhemui, nowadays assumed to be the first king of the Second Dynasty, and King Nebra (or Raneb), nowadays assumed to be the second king of the Second Dynasty.[27] However, Reisner demonstrated from the fact that one bowl which he excavated had the name of Nebra, or Raneb, erased and replaced with that of Hotepsekhemui, that Nebra, or Raneb, was really earlier than Hotepsekhemui, so that their order of succession must be reversed, and that Nebra, or Raneb, was really the first king of the Dynasty and not the other way around,[28] but this does not matter for us in our discussion, although it is yet more evidence of the chrono-logical confusion to which I referred in Chapter Six. Since King Send, if we conservatively assume him to be the Send of the Second Dynasty, was the fourth king of the Second Dynasty, we seem to have here a pattern of Second Dynasty royal presence attested at Giza in two valley temples. Assuming that there were structures in that area of Giza asso-ciated with these Second Dynasty kings at the time, either they were demolished and all traces of them eradicated (which is a bit odd, because Reisner would have found traces in the Valley Temple of Mycerinus if such a thing had happened), or their structures were usurped and enlarged or improved in the Fourth Dynasty, thereby obliterating all structural traces of the earlier kings, whose names only survived in the archaic bowl inscriptions.

Apart from the Second Dynasty kings, Reisner also found two diorite bowls in the Valley Temple of Mycerinus bearing the name of King Sneferu, one in a cartouche and one not.[29] King Sneferu was the first king of the Fourth Dynasty, and is believed to have been the father of King Cheops. Certainly these occurrences of names of earlier kings in the valley temples at Giza are most provocative, and make one wonder. Indeed, it is even possible that at least that area of Giza was a Second Dynasty ceremonial or even burial centre, and some of the tombs there that I described in Chapter Four might actually be Second Dynasty tombs. This obviously impinges on the question of dates for the Sphinx Temple, for instance. At the very least, one is tempted to assume that the tomb of Sneferu is one of the sealed tombs in the valley temple area of Giza, as I suggested in Chapter Four for other reasons. If the Second Dynasty kings represented a tendency, whether political or otherwise, which was bitterly resented from the time of King Zoser (first king of the Third Dynasty) onwards, as suggested by the bizarre method of construction of Zoser's Step Pyramid at Saqqara and its possibly representing a 'reversing' of King Semerkhet's mutilation of King Enezib's pyramid, as described at length in Chapter Six, then perhaps the eradication of Second Dynasty traces at Giza had a deeper purpose. It may be that such a process did occur, and that it was not merely the actions of egotistical or spiteful Fourth Dynasty pharaohs, but was meant to be a serious political statement. We know almost nothing of the politics of those early days in Egypt. I merely bring this forward as a suggestion. Maybe we will make some more discoveries some day that will make all of these murky matters clearer to us.

When Hölscher commenced his work on the Valley Temple, he found the measurements of Petrie invaluable. He says:

'The next scientific material about our excavation area [after Mariette] is given by Flinders Petrie, who carried out a new measurement of the pyramids in 1881 and 1882. His acute observational abilities, and the precision of his measurements, have made his publications extraordinarily valuable for us. . . . he cleared the upper part of the Causeway and with that finally proved the connection between the Funerary Temple and the Valley Temple, which Piazzi Smyth had already previously suggested. He also gives a good description and a rather accurate ground plan of the Valley Temple. . . . His accounts are so detailed that we only need to give them a superficial verification.'[30]

Here is Hölscher's description of what he actually found when he first began his work at the Valley Temple:

Of the Valley Temple, only the interior had been excavated. The two entrance rooms were only partially cleared. Mud walls and modern walls made of broken stones, with which they tried to hold back the pressure of the sand from outside, obstructed the exits.

In the columned hall the windblown sand had already accumulated up to a height of one metre [in only half a century], so that one had to clear thoroughly here to begin with. One must doubt that this had ever been done properly before. At any rate, no one had ever paid attention to the holes in the pavement where the statues had once stood.

Of the exterior of the Valley Temple, nothing had been cleared. The lower end of the Causeway where the limestone walls are almost completely preserved must have been cleared without anyone ever recognising properly the importance of this part of the building.

The upper end of the Causeway, the foundation of which Petrie had already cleared once, was again hidden under fresh windblown sand [after only a quarter of a century].[31]

Nowadays, the Causeway is completely cleared, and our investigation and dating of a mysterious and important deep shaft directly beneath it was reported in Chapter Two on 'The Osiris Shaft'. The point where the Causeway joins the west wall of the Valley Temple may be seen in Plates on the website. As soon as one steps into the Valley Temple from the Causeway, one enters the extraordinary sloping passage known as the Ascending Passage. In my earlier book, *The Crystal Sun*, I published my discovery that this passage ascends at a slope whose angle is the same as the slope of both the Ascending Passage and the Descending Passage inside the Great Pyramid.[32] It is an angle of 26° 33' 54", known as the 'golden angle'. It is related to the 'Golden Section' or 'Golden Proportion', which was the geometrical basis of all sacred Egyptian art and architecture. To respect the 'golden angle' in a sacred ascent or descent was to honour and observe maāt, the principle of cosmic order that was thought of as regulating the universe. The same angle is observed by the Descending Passage into the Old Kingdom Mastaba of Akhet-hotep (reused and renamed the Mastaba of Neb-Kaw-Her). A very extensive discussion of the golden angle, and its religious importance to the ancient Egyptians as what I have chosen to call 'the golden angle of resurrection', due to its associations with the resurrection of Osiris as Horus, appears in my most recent book, *The Sphinx Mystery*.

When I discovered that a vast and startling winter solstice sunset shadow was cast upon the southern face of the Great Pyramid on 21 December, by the nearby Pyramid of Chephren, I measured the angle of that shadow and discovered that it too was the 'golden angle'. I published a photo of this shadow in *The Crystal Sun*,[33] and another photo of the shadow near to but not actually on the date of the solstice in *The Sphinx Mystery*, as Figure 3.10 on page 141. The placement and size of the Chephren Pyramid are perfect for casting the 'golden angle' shadow, but if they had varied, it would not have worked. I hope that people will take note of this discovery one day.

So we see that a sacred geometrical principle was embodied in one of the most prominent features of the Valley Temple, and that the angle of the Ascending Passage matched that of at least three other important Old Kingdom passages, all of which were invisible and concealed, accessible only to the priests. But it matched also the angle of the spectacularly

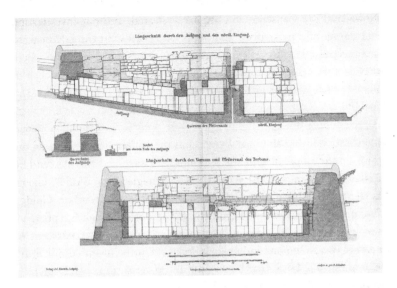

Figure 56. Above: Longitudinal section through the Ascending Passage (which ascends at the 'golden angle' of 26°33'54") and the northern main entrance of the west wall (from the Chephren Causeway) of the Valley Temple. (The small drawing below it is a section of entrance at the Chephren Causeway, showing a mount of sand at left, which covered the still unknown Sphinx Temple.) Below: Longitudinal section through the forecourt and the Pillared Hall of the Valley Temple. (Hölscher's book, a folding plate, drawn by O. Schultze.)

visible shadow cast once a year at dusk on the southern wall of the Great Pyramid. And it also matched the golden angle, which is multiply manifested in the hieroglyphic depiction of the name of the god Osiris, as illustrated on the website, and in the Uadjet Eye (also spelled Wadjet Eye or Udjet Eye). The Uadjet Eye has long been recognised as being composed of the joined hieroglyphs for mathematical fractions (see its description in Wikipedia for a quick overview of this aspect of the Eye, and see my discussion of this subject in *The Crystal Sun* for its relevance to the Comma of Pythagoras in musical harmonics and astronomy), but the Eye's rigid and canonical graphic construction on the basis of multiple golden angles has never before been noticed (see the caption to the illustration for details).

Egyptologists know that the god Ptah, who presided over Memphis near Giza, was always called by the ancient Egyptians 'he who is south of his wall'. If one considers the southern face of the Great Pyramid as representing the wall of Ptah, then what is south of it is the sacred 'golden triangle' and 'golden angle' once a year. In other words, Ptah may in that sense be identified with the sacred angle. The recurrent phrase 'Ptah who is south of his wall' was used for centuries in Egypt, without any Egyptologist having the slightest idea what it was they were talking about. But now that we have seen a gigantic cosmic display on the south wall of the Great Pyramid at the winter solstice, what more do we need?

In *The Sphinx Mystery*, I was able to reconstruct the theology of the 'golden-angled resurrection' which took place at sunrise of each equinox at Giza and was associated with the Sphinx. However, the discussion does not need to be repeated here, as it is available in my most recent previous book and can be obtained easily.

In Figure 7.25 of that book (and on its website) may be seen the Golden Giza Plan which I was able to reconstruct in *The Sphinx Mystery*. From this anyone may see that the entire Giza Plateau was one giant spider's web of interrelated and crisscrossing golden-angled lines of sight, or 'rays' as I call them for convenience. All of these sacred angles were meant to express reverence for the divine cosmic order. These matters will be discussed further, and elucidated in full, in my next book, where a great many discoveries about the geometry of the pyramids are revealed for the first time, and previous accounts of these subjects by numerous authors are also reviewed, including many forgotten accounts by engineers in foreign languages, which have been translated specially.

Just in case anyone thought the Valley Temple was just a funerary building full of statues of a pharaoh, there is another 'cosmic' aspect of it that must be mentioned. I also published this information in *The Crystal Sun*.[34] Charles Piazzi Smyth, the Victorian pyramid investigator, made an interesting observation at the Valley Temple in 1865, and recorded it on film. However, he never found occasion to publish this photo and his notes about it, and these were found among his papers after his death by Moses Cotsworth, who finally published it in a book of his own (but with attribution to Piazzi Smyth, whom he greatly revered, and whose papers he bought from his estate at auction) in

1902.[35] I then published it again in 2000, in *The Crystal Sun*. It is a very remarkable photograph indeed. It was taken precisely at noon (determined by astronomical observation) from the top of the south wall of the Valley Temple anteroom. It shows that the north wall is entirely lit and the east and west walls are entirely in shadow. The effect is most striking. Piazzi Smyth called the anteroom a 'light well', intended to show this effect of light and shadow as a precise determination of noon. Once again, we have the phenomenon of the walls being used, as with the Great Pyramid, to convey messages about important astronomical or cosmic moments, in honour of maāt, and as a celebration of cosmic order, as well as an aid to the perfect keeping of time.

Therefore, if anyone asks the purpose of the anteroom of the Valley Temple, which was open to the sky and not roofed over in antiquity, looking down into it from the roof as a 'light well' for telling the time is as good an answer as any. To say that the anteroom of the Valley Temple is a 'noon clock' would not be an exaggeration. At least for this we have photographic evidence, whereas anything else is unsubstantiated speculation. Nor were there any statue bases in this room. It seems that it was bare, as befits a 'light well' or 'sundial room'. And this would also partially explain the strange structure of the temple roof. The water clocks, which were in daily use in ancient Egypt, were probably reset once a day from the 'noon clock' of the anteroom, in order to achieve greater accuracy. I believe 'light wells' used to reset water clocks daily at noon must have existed at both the Abu Ruash and Zawiyet el-Aryan astronomical observation shafts mentioned in Chapter Three. Since the shaft at each location is interrupted midway by a modest vertical wall, before resuming its rise, and since both shafts are oriented precisely to the geographical north, these vertical walls within each shaft could have acted as the 'light wells' by becoming totally illuminated at noon, with the side walls being in total shade. It would then be no problem for the water clock to run accurately until the following dawn, and enable absolutely precise time measurements of the stellar meridian culminations observed along the shafts at night to be recorded. Thus, the calendar could be kept to the greatest possible degree of accuracy on a twenty-four-hour basis. In other words, the calendar was checked daily with the greatest of precision. Certainly the 'light well' at the Valley

Temple would have acted as a reliable clock for the whole of the Giza Plateau itself. The shadow clocks used by the ancient Egyptian Unuti priests could not tell the time at noon, at which point their readings temporarily failed, so that 'light wells' were a nesecity for determining noon.

This brings us to the subject of the roof of the Valley Temple. As may be seen from the photo reproduced as Figure 170 at the end of Hölscher's book, up until his time there were many old mudbrick buildings as well as modern ones on top of them which were crammed up against the eastern façade of the Valley Temple above the height of the temple roof. Although in ancient times, the roof only covered part of the structure, leaving other portions open to the sky, after the Old Kingdom all of these were filled with rubble and sand. Probably only portions of the roof of the Valley Temple were accessible during the New Kingdom (see our dating results), but afterwards, the entire building was clearly covered entirely, so that no one even knew it was there at all.

Many of the photos reproduced on my website are taken from the roof, which offers wonderful vantage points for looking down on the construction of most of the rooms. In Figure 57 we see Hölscher's plan of the roof, Plate XII of his book, which in the original is a two-page bi-colour foldout. In the original, he has drawn in red various proposed reconstructions of features which he believed would have been there in antiquity, including a number of steps and stairways, beside some of which on the plan you can see the German word *Rampe*. I took this foldout plan with me on to the roof of the Valley Temple and walked through it with meticulous care, attempting to find traces of these proposed reconstructed features, of which I fully expected to find some evidence. To my astonishment, I could find no evidence or trace of a single one of Hölscher's steps or stairways. I looked over and over again, barely able to accept this situation. How could he have drawn all of those things so confidently and published them on his plan without there being any evidence of them other than what came from his own imagination? And yet it seems he *did* only imagine them. So I was very sad and perplexed. It appears that we cannot accept Hölscher's reconstruction of the roof of the Valley Temple, therefore. Of course it is possible, but where is the evidence? I looked really hard. I held the plan in front of my face and peered and peered at each location, hoping for something to materialise, something that I had missed at first. But I just couldn't find any evidence at all.

Even though some steps may be seen on the roof, in the foreground of Figure 31 on page 46 of Hölscher's book, they are not there now. I believe they must have been Hölscher's own wooden steps, put there to facilitate his work, and later removed.

The roof was at different levels, and in antiquity perhaps there were wooden access ramps or steps that led from one to the other. Although the anteroom was apparently always open to the sky, we know from the many light-slits that the vast T-shaped Pillared Hall was in a kind of semi-gloom which is brilliantly evoked in the amazing lithograph (Plate V, opposite p. 20, which contains a modern photo of the ruins from the same angle) prepared for Hölscher by the artist A. Bollacher, and reproduced here as Figure 54. This drawing of what the hall might have looked like in the reign of Chephren, whether it is accurate or not, is a spectacular exercise in artistic vision based upon the reconstruction described to the artist by Hölscher himself.

Hölscher gives an account of what faced him when he commenced his work:

'At the beginning of the excavations, the Valley Temple was lying up to the height of its outer walls in the sand. In places the sand dunes consisting of windblown sand, remains of old brick buildings, and the debris of the Mariette excavations, were over fifteen meters high. In view of such enormous masses of sand, it was impossible for us to free the Valley Temple completely. We had to confine our activity in the main to the eastern side.'[36]

As he himself explains, therefore, the northern side of the temple was left uncleared, and this explains why Hölscher did not find any evidence of the Sphinx Temple, despite the fact that its remains were only a few feet away.

What is the Valley Temple like as a whole? Looking at it from the village of Nazlett, facing towards the pyramids, one sees the massive eastern façade with its two doorways, one at the south end and one at the north. You can enter through either. Once you go through one of

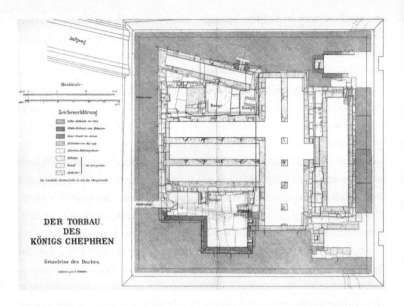

Aufgang

Maßstab

Zeichenerklärung

DER TORBAU.
DES
KÖNIGS CHEPHREN

Grundriss des Daches.

Figure 57. Plan of the entire roof of the Valley Temple, folding Plate XII from Hölscher's book. The two main entrances from the east are at right, both of which lead into the forecourt or anteroom, which then has a central door which leads into the Pillared Hall. At top, this leads into the Ascending Passage which goes at an angle towards the Chephren Causeway ('*Aufgang*') at top left. The red overlays show reconstructions envisaged by Hölscher of postulated structures, which may or may not have existed. (The colour version of this plan can be seen on the website.)

the doors, you are in one of the granite entrance halls, which are very high, though they are not large rooms otherwise. A niche made of granite very far above head height looks down on you; no one knows whether it contained a statue, or what its purpose was. (See this niche in a Plate on the website.) You turn left if you have entered by the north door, or right if you have entered by the south door. In either case, you come into the long and tall granite anteroom. This was the 'light well' or 'noon clock', and is also the room which contains the well where the statue of Chephren was found, the well being now fenced off with a railing. Then you turn towards the west and enter the vast Pillared Hall, which is in the shape of a T.

The 'top' of the T is what you enter, and the 'bottom' of the T consists of three aisles, separated by pillars, all pointing due west. If you are at the southwestern end of the building, there is a small door in the granite, locked and barred. That leads to the magazines, which have already been described. But if you go to the northwestern end, there is a door leading into a sloping corridor, which rises upwards and which we call the Ascending Passage. All of these rooms, the entrance halls, the anteroom, the Pillared Hall and the Ascending Passage, have alabaster floors and red granite walls and pillars. The red and white together make a striking colour contrast, and this must have been really impressive when they were first constructed and the colours of the stones were fresh. There are a few anomalous basalt blocks in the walls, which may be significant, and which I have discussed in *The Sphinx Mystery*, along with a photo of one. Another such photo is reproduced on the website. The anomalous occurrence of basalt blocks or other features in Egyptian structures often acts, I believe, as a sign or indicator of concealment. I discuss this symbolism in *The Sphinx Mystery*, where I also point out that no Egyptologist has ever discovered the ancient Egyptian word for basalt. In my opinion, some of the translations which say 'flint' really should say 'basalt'. I believe that the 'flint box' in the mysterious tale of the 'secret chambers of Thoth' of the Westcar Papyrus should instead be translated as 'basalt coffer', and that the mineralogical imprecision of the translation resulting from our ignorance of the word for 'basalt' has obscured the true meaning of the story. I have earlier referred to the matter of basalt in Chapter Two on 'The Osiris Shaft', where we also discovered a sarcophagus of a unique material, dacite, the Eygptian name for which is also unknown.

If you pass on up the Ascending Passage, about halfway along there are two doors on either side, opposite one another. Both are locked and barred and never open to the public. Most people go past them without a thought. The one on the left leads into the strange little chamber which Hölscher called 'the Porter's Lodge'. When you go through the door, you go down a slight ramp, and enter a rectangular chamber, which is parallel with the Ascending Passage but following the base of the temple, while the Ascending Passage rises beyond it. Its floor was once of alabaster, but has mostly been ripped away, exposing rough and lumpy limestone blocks and what seems to be bedrock at different levels, so that you can easily trip.

To see the floor properly, one would have to clear all the sand from it, which I was in no position to do. I doubt that Hölscher ever bothered to clear the floor of all of its sand either. In my opinion, it should be cleared and studied carefully. One enigma is: why was the alabaster ripped from the floor of this tiny chamber but left in the more accessible main rooms and the Ascending Passage itself? This is highly suspicious, in my opinion. The lower portions of the walls of this chamber are made of red granite, whereas the upper portions are of alabaster. No one has the slightest idea of the purpose of this tiny room. However, I believe it is the way into the subterranean chamber which I have already suggested in both *The Crystal Sun* and *The Sphinx Mystery* lies beneath the top of the Ascending Passage, and which has probably been sealed since Old Kingdom times. That is why a complete clearance and close study of this ill-lit chamber is so crucially necessary. I believe that somewhere in the floor or within the north or west walls of this chamber will be found the access to the untouched subterranean crypts of this temple. And I believe that someone suspected the same thing in antiquity, which is why the floor was ripped up. This must have happened at the very end of the Sixth Dynasty, when there was still someone left alive, perhaps a member of the temple staff or his son, who knew there was a sealed chamber there, and was struggling to find the access to a crypt which he imagined must contain gold. At the very least, I would imagine that more beautiful and intact Chephren statues must be stashed in there. The one that was thrown into the 'well' was probably too big to squeeze in. Only someone desperate to find something beneath the alabaster floor of this chamber immediately following the collapse of the Sixth Dynasty could have done this strange damage, whilst leaving the more prominent and readily accessible alabaster floors of the rest of the temple untouched. We can be certain that his motive was not to obtain alabaster.

Opposite the so-called 'Porter's Lodge' is the entrance to the stairway. If you go through that door and turn right, an ascending stairway (much of which has also been ripped away; Plate 45) takes you up to the level of the roof. You turn right again and face south, and there is a granite-framed door (Plate 46) which opens on to the roof of the temple. You have to be a mountain goat after that, because there is no way on to the main roof from that doorway unless you inch along a perilous ledge. Obviously, in ancient times, there must have been a perfectly safe means of going from the door to the roof, by simply walking over the top of the Ascending Passage, but these days, that passage is open to the sky (Plate 40, and others on the website). When I inched along the ledge, in continual danger of a nasty fall on to a stone pavement far below, I had great difficulty in persuading the male antiquities inspector or Ioannis to follow me, and it took them a considerable time to get up their courage to do so. But I had inched along so many high narrow ledges during my childhood that I took to this naturally.

If you continue up the Ascending Passage and leave the temple from its 'back door' in its western wall, you step onto the great Chephren Causeway, which extends for a quarter of a mile up the hill to the Pyramid of Chephren and his ruined Funerary Temple, which lies at the foot of the pyramid and at the end of the Causeway.

Hölscher gives a rhapsodic description of walking through the temple:

The two portals leading into the interior of the Valley Temple, which are by the way absolutely equal, are of enormous dimensions. Each half of the double door must have been about 2.80 meters wide and about 6 meters high. It was probably, as similar examples show us, constructed of hardwoods which were joined on the inside by crosspieces. From the outside one could see on the smooth surface only the nail-heads.

In the door fitting one can still see the holes for the big double bolt (Plate XI). They were artfully worked into the granite wall so that it was possible to pull out the bolt, but no further than its fitting permitted. Traces indicate that in addition to this, other locks existed, for example edge bolts.

The entrance hall which we enter has an inside height of 9.40 meters, as high as was at all possible, considering the height of the building. [This was the 'light well' or 'noon clock room'.] It was at the same time the highest of the interior halls of the entire temple precinct, and each subsequent room in the Valley Temple is lower than the preceding one.

This entrance hall is made all round, – that is, walls, ceiling, and floor, – of red granite. [My note: there are a few isolated black granite or basalt blocks, which he does not mention. I discussed these, as I said a moment ago, in my previous book *The Sphinx Mystery* because I believe they were marker stones such as those referred to in some of the ancient Netherworld texts. Some may also have been connected with shadow clock readings for this 'light well'.] On the narrow side, opposite the entrance, opens up to a great height a niche in which probably a statue may have stood as the only decoration in the room.

Now we are turning sideways, walking slightly ascending through a high two-winged door and entering the lengthy anteroom, in which the multitudes which stream through the north and south doors come together. It is about 4 meters wide, quite a size considering its granite ceiling beams must as a result be at least 5 meters long. The floor is made here, as in all other rooms of the Valley Temple from now, of polished alabaster; the walls as well as the ceiling are made of granite.

We must now briefly turn our attention to a passage which has been worked roughly into the rocky underground of this room. It is the now-famous well in which Mariette found in 1860 the beautiful Chephren statue which now belongs to the most famous pieces of the Cairo Collection. This passage does not stem from the time of the Valley Temple but, as one can see clearly, has been worked later, probably as a funerary passage, into the probably already half-ruined Valley Temple by then partially covered in sand (see Sections III and V).

But now we want to enter through the great door in the central axis into the main room of the Valley Temple, the pillared hall. It is a hall in the form of an inverted T. Sixteen monolithic granite pillars divided into one main arm with three naves and two horizontal arms with two naves each. A hall of extraordinary effect! No ornament and no profile lessens the ceremonial serenity of this architecture; only unadorned walls and undecorated square pillars, not a single line which does not necessarily belong to the construction. On the other hand, along the walls sits a large group of supernaturally sized royal statues, 23 of them, all in the same stern posture, gazing straight ahead, one hand in a fist, the other resting flat on the thigh, an image of royal dignity and strength.

Even if essentially the same, none of the figures resembles another completely. Each one is the work of an individual artist. Especially, however, they distinguish themselves from each other by the material.

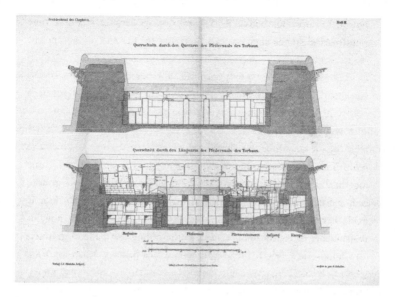

Figure 58. Hölscher's caption for this plate translated is: '(1) Transverse section through the transverse [*eastern*] portion of the Pillared Hall of the Valley Temple. (2) Transverse section through the longitudinal portion of the Pillared Hall of the Valley Temple.' The latter shows also, from left to right, the Magazine, the 'Porter's Room', the Ascending Passage, and the Stairway. The drawings are both north-south sections taken at different depths, the former being nearer the eastern end, and the latter being nearer the western end of the temple. The sloping Ascending Passage in the lower drawing is shown disappearing at an angle out of sight, above the word 'Aufgang'. The stairway to the roof is shown above the word 'Rampe'. (Plate IX of Hölscher's book, a foldout plate, drawn by O. Schultze.)

Most of them are of a white luminous alabaster, others of a blue–grey veined diorite, the tones of which play between white and black. Others are again of a metamorphic greenish slate.

It is an overwhelming impression which this hall makes upon us. The dark red granite walls and the white luminescent floor in which the statues mirror themselves in different changing hues; in addition, a light which streams at an angle in many beams through the windows which are cut partly into the wall and partly into the ceiling, shimmering as it penetrates the room, and causing the polished walls to give off numerous reflections.

The later art of the Egyptians may have produced richer and more highly developed architectural creations, but has it ever produced a more serene and ceremonial room than this one?[37]

It is impossible not to be sympathetic to Hölscher in his appreciation of the clean, unadorned simplicity of this magnificent architecture and the spectacular achievement it represents, and its strong and overwhelming beauty. This, surely, is the essence of what it means to be created in a time whose culture has not entered a stage of decadence. This is *real architecture*, and it is sublime.

As for the statues mentioned by the ecstatic Hölscher, I trust the reader will realise that he was imagining the place as it was at the time of Chephren, for the statues are all gone now, alas.

Something that has not been mentioned yet is what is found in front of the Valley Temple on the eastern side. Here there is what the archaeologists today call a 'quay'. The Nile at Inundation time came up as far as the Valley and Sphinx Temples in the Old Kingdom period, but the river has moved many miles to the east since those days, and because of the Aswan Dam, there is no Inundation at all any more. It used to last for three months, during which time the inhabited portion of the country was largely flooded, but those days are over. In fact, the structure of the 'quay' in front of the Valley Temple is rather bizarre. There is a prominent rectangular depression cut into the bedrock in the centre, and on either side there is a little stone bridge, which is directly in front of each entrance portal to the temple. (See Plates on the website.) Cut down into the bedrock under each of these two bridges are pedestrian gangways, which descend and then ascend again on the other side of the bridge. The bottoms, underneath the bridges, were evidently filled with water. These two pools are not connected with each other, and are artificially hollowed-out under the bridges, with no practical purpose that can be detected. The whole arrangement is very strange and puzzling.

I have studied the layout of these strange features and come up with a theory about what their use may possibly have been. The first point which we have to note is that the pools under the bridges were isolated, small pools, restricted to being placed under each bridge. People apparently went down into them and came up out of them on the other side.

318

Figure 59. Here the priests of Sokar, the original Lord of the Underworld (whose position was later taken by Osiris), are seen carrying the 'Sokar Barque' in procession at Giza during the annual Sokar Festival, when they made a circuit with it of the sacred areas near the Sphinx. The strange object with a bird's head sitting in the middle of the barque is a fetish which represents Sokar, in the form of a mummified hawk, with his head protruding from the mummy wrappings. The third priest from the left is wearing an animal skin (which we know from other depictions to be a leopard skin, though the spots are not visible in this picture) over his shoulder, and the medallion suspended on his chest shows that he is the chief priest of the group, while the priest following him appears to be his deputy, and carries a sacred wand or sceptre. The two main priests in the centre are not sharing in the actual bearing of the load, which is borne by the four groups of four junior priests, suggesting that as sixteen men were needed to carry it, the boat must be heavier than it appears. The exact nature of the Sokar fetish is not known, and the huge mummified portion may have contained something secret and concealed beneath the wrappings. My theory about this fetish is that a solid gold statue of Sokar was concealed inside, making the barque extremely heavy. This gold statue would have been the central cult statue of the god, normally kept in the inner sanctum of the temple. When carried outside once a year, it had to be concealed from the eyes of the profane, and also could not be exposed to the light of the sun, because Sokar was known never to emerge from his perpetual darkness. The small Sokar-head on top of the fetish merely serves to identify the fetish so that people can realize that the true Sokar is concealed inside the mummy wrappings, in keeping with his nature. This engraving of a temple carving was published in 1809 in *Description de l'Égypte*, before the decipherment of

319

hieroglyphics, but care was taken to engrave correctly the two hieroglyphs in front of the chief priest, which read SEM. This specifically identifies the chief priest in the picture as a Sem Priest, and that means that we have here a picture of the High Priest of Ptah from the Temple of Ptah at nearby Memphis, in his role as head mortuary priest, or Sem Priest, of Sokar. Ptah and Sokar were merged as a joint divinity at Giza. Later the divinity was called Ptah-Sokar-Osiris, and became a sacred trinity. The location of this temple carving is unknown, and it has possibly perished since this drawing of it was made prior to 1809. It is possible that it was carved on one of the walls of the Temple of Ptah, but was amongst the vast amount of stone carried away from Memphis and Giza for use in the construction of mosques and palaces in Cairo during the 19th century. *Collection of Robert Temple.*

The only feasable explanation for them seems to be that they were immersion pools for ritual purification as part of a ceremony. The equally strange rectangular depression, which has been cut out of the bedrock with great care in the centre of this huge forecourt, probably had a ceremonial purpose. Presumably, a large group of priests stood there, either facing the temple or, more probably, facing the rising sun in the east at dawn. In trying to figure out what possible connection the bridges and the pools might have with this, I then thought that the group of priests in the depression might split into two and file down the descending ramps, passing underneath the two little bridges and, having purified themselves in the water, emerged and come back up the ramps on the far side. Then they could have looped round and filed across the bridges, over the heads of their colleagues who were still purifying themselves beneath. Having done this, they were then heading straight for the two doors of the Valley Temple, which they would have entered. The two files would have joined one another in the anteroom, and then jointly filed through the Pillared Hall and up the Ascending Passage of the temple, and then out of the west door and onto the Causeway, where the procession would have continued all the way to the Pyramid of Chephren.

An alternative version of this scene would be to reverse it, and have the priests file out of the temple by torchlight, over the bridges in front of the two doors, pass under the bridges and purify themselves in the water, and then emerge to congregate in the rectangular area, ready to observe the rising of the sun.

Of course these are mere speculations. But we do know that major ceremonials were carried out at Giza. For instance, once a year there was the famous Feast of Sokar, with a huge and magnificent procession which went all round the area. A large sacred boat was carried in this procession, of which depictions survive. (It is reproduced in Figure 59.) What I have envisaged for the 'quays' might well have taken place as part of the extensive and elaborate Sokar ceremonies. Sokar was an underworld god who was associated with this precise area of Giza. After the god Osiris rose to prominence in the Fifth Dynasty, he was merged with the much more ancient god Sokar, who was associated with 'Rostau', or 'Rose-tau'. And it is generally thought that 'Rostau' or 'Rose-tau' was the name of the location of the Valley and Sphinx Temples. This is confirmed, for instance, by Catherine Graindorge-Héreil in her book *La Dieu Sokar* [The God Sokar], where she says specifically:

'... Sokar is master of the desert, of the kingdom of what lies below it, domains evoked by the principal sanctuaries *Rose-tau* and of *Pedju (-she)*. The first is situated in proximity to the Sphinx of Giza ... (certain) proposals tempt almost everyone to compare the toponym *Pedju (-she)* to a place possessing a flow or a body of water ...'[38]

So perhaps it is by no means unreasonable to speculate that these curious bridges and pools and the apparent assembly area in front of the temple near the Sphinx were somehow connected with the Feast of Sokar ceremonies, which also featured the carrying of a sacred barque in procession around Giza.

Hölscher wrote at great length about the details of each part of the Valley Temple, and some of his descriptions are of particular interest:

The Valley Temple is built on a rock, the surface of which has been prepared to take the wall structure or the upper pavement. Right around the foot of the building ran a drainage pavement about 75 centimetres wide – now ripped out, – perhaps of granite.

On the eastern face, of the granite cladding most of the stones of the first course of masonry are standing, 2.1 metres high throughout. The cornerstone of the southern entrance is for instance 3.9 x 1.7 x 2.15 metres in size and therefore weighs about 38,000 kilograms. One stone in the middle of the façade is 5.45 metres long and weighs about 42,000 kilograms. Towards the top, the façade consisted of granite blocks of somewhat smaller measurements. The layers and distribution of joins for the most part can still be seen on the core masonry . . . The fact that they were granite blocks can be seen by the clamp holes which served to shift them . . . The height of the façade would have not much more than what the core masonry still shows today, which is about 12.5 to 13 metres, or 24 to 25 Egyptian cubits. The slope can be measured exactly to 1:7, that is, to the height of one cubit and one palm rebound, or as about 82°.

The core masonry of the Valley Temple is visible along the whole façade. It consists of blocks of yellowish nummulitic limestone, as can be found everywhere in this area, of quite enormous measurements. Along the eastern façade lie blocks which measure 50 to 60 cubic metres, and therefore weigh around 150,000 kilograms. And such blocks have also been shifted to considerable heights.

The destroyed granite façade in the time of the New Kingdom was covered over with a mudbrick wall, and in this process the doors were covered over. After examining them closely, we have removed these brick buildings and made the doors accessible again.[39]

The only other Egyptologists to turn their attention to the Valley Temple after Hölscher were the Italians V. Maragioglio and C. Rinaldi. These two indefatigable scholars have published many volumes (exceedingly rare and difficult to find even in most specialist libraries, though fortunately I own a complete set) surveying the monuments of Egypt. In their Fifth Volume they consider the Pyramid and Complex of Chephren, which includes a section on the Valley Temple as well as a four-and-a-half page 'Excursus', or appendix, on the Sphinx Temple.[40] This volume is in two parts, the first being text, and the second being foldout plans and drawings. It is sadly obvious from the plans of both the Valley Temple and the Sphinx Temple[41] that Maragioglio and Rinaldi were not granted access to the locked portions of the Valley Temple or the North Trench of the Sphinx Temple, all of which I have personally explored most carefully, and I have detected several errors in their plans. On the plans themselves, they frequently cite Hölscher as the source, to make it clear that for the Valley Temple they are working second-hand and not directly from the monument itself, by using Hölscher's plans and measurements.

The most obvious errors in their work occur in Plate 16, where three errors also occur in the labelling.[42] In this plan they show only the eastern half of the North Trench beside the Sphinx Temple (to its north). Anyone who has been down inside the North Trench, as I have (and there are not many who have), knows it goes much further west than they show on their plan. They clearly had no access to the North Trench, which is not only sealed off but accessible only by ladder from above. When I examined the North Trench I simply leapt down into it, and had to be rescued by ladder when I had finished, as it is impossible to climb out again. I suppose it is a jump of about thirty feet. But it is important for us to keep in mind that Maragioglio and Rinaldi, who were very conscientious in their work, were prevented from achieving accuracy on all points concerning the Sphinx and Valley Temples because they were not allowed to examine and measure all parts of them properly. It was not their fault. Their work is usually first rate.

In Figure 12 of Plate 16, Maragioglio and Rinaldi show a reconstruction of some roof steps for the Valley Temple, based on Hölscher rather than on personal observation (it is obvious that they were not allowed on to the roof either). I call attention to this just in case I was wrong about my own findings on the roof, and would invite other interested people in the future to try to pursue this problem, if they can gain access, that is.

In their discussion of the Valley Temple, Maragioglio and Rinaldi are very confident, and begin by saying:

'The valley temple of Chephren stands at the southern end of the causeway and is closely connected to it; in fact, as we shall see, the covered corridor [of the Causeway] continued inside the temple. Since the building has now been completely freed from sand and rubble we can give various pieces of information that are not to be found in the book by Hölscher, who was content with clearing the east facade and cleaning up the interior.'[43]

This is a bold statement. And they express their opinion of the building as follows:

'The good preservation of the . . . temple has enabled us to ascertain that the materials used are the richest the country could offer. Their working and manner of laying are the best that have been met with.

'Beauty, richness and durability were the requisites of every Egyptian funerary edifice and here each of these features reaches the highest degree.'[44]

Maragioglio and Rinaldi do not agree with many of Hölscher's ideas of a reconstruction of the roof, but make clear that they themselves could not inspect it in person, and had to work from his photos and drawings evaluated on the basis of general principles.[45] If they had been allowed up there, they probably would have disagreed with him even more.

The account of the Valley Temple by Maragioglio and Rinaldi contains many fascinating details of construction, but it is only eight pages long (although the book is large format, and the pages are extensive). We do not need to go into the many things discussed by them which, like the many similar details given by Hölscher at much greater length in sections of his book which we have omitted, go far beyond our concerns here.

The Valley Temple That Nobody Knows

This is now the end of my general description of the Valley Temple, and at this point I want to start my account of its weirder aspects, which have never been noticed or reported before. I discovered these because of my obstinate nosiness and determination to investigate every detail of anything I am studying, which is characteristic of my compulsive nature. I never rest until I have gone as far as I can into even the most insignificant minutiae of any subject under my investigation. Any unsolved mystery is intolerable to me. I am still looking for answers to things I started looking into in my teens and twenties. No case is ever closed. However, this is not because I have any personal interest in any of these investigative projects; for me it is only the process of investigating that matters, and an attempt to achieve its completion. The ultimate aim, I suppose, is a complete information file, and since that is impossible, I am condemned to go on like this forever. I am an extreme compulsive archivist, not for my own sake, but for the sake of the Records, which must be complete. I do not wish the knowledge for myself, which is the motivation of most people. I wholly lack that 'normal' desire. I am content for information to exist without the wish to 'possess it', which is the personal failing of so many other naïve investigators. As soon as you *really wish to know something for yourself*, you will never succeed. Information must be respected, and must be allowed to exist for its own sake, just as an individual's life must be respected and allowed to exist for its own sake. This is what Albert Schweitzer called 'reverence for life', which I would extend also to 'reverence for information', information being conceived of by me as a kind of life form. Information needs to be tended as gently as seedlings in a garden. *It is alive.* The *use* of information is a separate issue. It can only be used effectively when it is not for personal benefit. Because *information is neutral*, any attempt by the user to destroy that neutrality can easily result in disaster, since the information will resist this. Information lives in Information Space, which is non-partisan. Its abuse has brought the downfall of many throughout the ages. The struggle of the world is the unending conflict between the neutrality of information and the attempts by vested human interests to misuse it. This is inevitable, because of the multiplicity of egos, all of which seek personal gain. Information can only be used productively and safely when the aim is to benefit others. Self-benefit is allowed only within this context. The real reason why our civilisation is collapsing today is because unrestrained, insane greed has become the new God to the arrogant elites who run everything. But I think most members of the powerless general public have figured that out by now, too late to do anything about it. Evil is always inconceivable except to the wicked.

When I was up on the roof of the Valley Temple, I decided I had to go higher, and climb up on to the tops of the outer temple walls, which is not easy. These walls rise much higher than the roof itself. I was not able to get up on to all of them, but the easiest to surmount was the north wall. As soon as I had done that, I discovered amazing things which no one had ever mentioned in any published work. Along the north wall of the Valley Temple there are gigantic interior vertical shafts which are hollow. See my detailed photos of these in Plates 51 and 52. They are very dramatic. I managed to persuade the male antiquities inspector to follow me, and he was greatly impressed and amazed, and could not stop gazing down the shafts. You can see him beside two of them on the website. He said no one he knew had any idea of their existence. The irony is that the electricians knew of some of these shafts, as they had run an electric cable through one of them for the purposes of the tourist *son-et-lumière* displays. But as archaeologists and electricians do not tend to converse, none of this information had become known. In my many photos of the strange features of 'the unknown Valley Temple', you may thus see various electric cables running along through shafts and passages and chambers. Until I found them, these were apparently known only to the electricians themselves who, as we have seen at the Osiris Shaft, sometimes like to keep you in the dark.

Let us start then with the north wall of the Valley Temple. As may be seen from Figure 57, which is the most sophisticated plan of the temple drawn up by its excavator, Hölscher himself, and from Figure 53, which is the earliest and simplest, drawn up by Mariette, this wall is just a big thick wall that is represented as solid: 'nothing happening there', as one might say. But all the plans of the Valley Temple are inaccurate and misleading. This fact in itself is a terrible indictment of archaeology. Is it possible that none of these distinguished and famous men ever stood on top of the north wall of the temple? Of course, in Mariette's day, it was next to a mountain of sand covering the adjoining and still unknown Sphinx Temple. Neither Petrie nor Hölscher saw the exterior base of the north wall, because at the time of their studies of this structure, that was all filled with sand and rubble. But if the vertical shafts inside the north wall were also filled with sand in their time, so that they could not be detected, who cleared them? There is no record of this ever occurring. Even if the shafts were filled with sand, it should have been obvious that they were there, if only as 'sand-filled shafts'. And yet no one ever recorded their existence, or remarked upon them – as far as I can determine, with the exception of the omnipresent electricians. I was the first to 'discover' them, though I still find this difficult to believe.

The nature of the huge voids within the Valley Temple walls may be seen clearly on the website in the series of six photos taken from the top and looking down, and in plates 51a and 51b. The first one, Plate 51a, is the one with the antiquities inspector who came up there with me. In the picture he is standing between what I have named Shaft One and Shaft Two of the north wall. Shaft Two is the gigantic open space in the foreground of the photo, which is further towards the west. Shaft

One may be seen just beyond him, and is the easternmost of the vertical shafts in the north wall. On the website I show Shaft One from the top, and here we can see how near it is to the northeast corner of the building. Below, we can see tourists milling around in front of the Sphinx Temple, and at left we can see the southeast corner of the south wall of the Sphinx Temple itself. In Plate 51a we get a better look down this shaft, and we can see clearly how the shaft was constructed. A prominent cut groove may be seen in a large stone just under the top layer, in the second course of stones, which appears to have been made for the insertion of a piece of wood. The shaft was constructed in such a way that the third course of stones from the top was built out in the form of a ledge, possibly to facilitate access to a descending wooden stairway. If so, it must have been an original feature of the temple, because it is an integral part of the interior design of the wall.

These vertical shafts within the walls of the Valley Temple are not intruded shafts made at a later date, but are original features of the edifice. They are so deep that I had to be very careful not to fall down them. At a guess, I would say they must be forty or forty-five feet deep. On the website we see another view of Shaft One from the top. No attempt was made to finish off the stonework, and the surfaces of the limestone blocks were never polished or smoothed in these interior features, although they are essentially flat.

In Plate 51b we look down into Shaft Two from the top. Although Shaft One has no electric cable, Shaft Two does have one, which may be seen clearly. Obviously, it was just thrown down from the top when the electricians were on the roof, and grabbed by someone below, to connect to the mains at ground level. A Plate on the website shows another view of Shaft Two from above, in this case indicating that two sides of the shaft are very flat and almost smooth. And once again, as with Shaft One, we see an interior ledge to facilitate descent in antiquity, which is an original part of the design. In the smoothed surfaces, we see one very clear bolt hole which has been drilled into the rock. This suggests to me the presence of a wooden 'trap door', which would originally have covered this shaft at the bottom of the first course of stonework, which could easily have been reached by someone standing at the level of the interior ledge. A further cut indentation in the stone at left, about a foot higher than the bolt hole, suggests that the end of a wooden beam rested here, but as the indentation is open at the top, the beam must have lifted upwards, and the indentation was only necessary in order to rest the end of the beam when it was lowered across the opening.

I was unable to study these shafts in greater detail from the top because I would have needed to tie a rope around myself and dangle down the holes, and there were no facilities of that kind. These shafts need to be properly explored and studied. They also offer wonderful opportunities for seeing the massive construction techniques of the temple 'from the inside'. If you descended a shaft from the top it would be like an endoscopy, but if you went up from below, it would be like a colonoscopy. This little joke is not entirely a joke, actually, because the ancient Egyptians did really believe that their temples were living entities, once they had been consecrated, 'handed over to the god', and imbued with his magical essence by the power of what theologians call 'immanence'.

Although I believe there are other vertical shafts further westwards in this north wall, I was unable to reach their tops and inspect them, as for that I would have needed assistance. The only other discovery I was able to make on the top of the north wall was another opening at the northeast corner, which may be seen on the website. I discovered a small chamber inside the wall, which was separate from, and appeared not to connect with, the vertical shafts I have just mentioned. I made attempts to enter this chamber, but was unable to do so because of a plant growing at the entrance to it, which had such sharp thorns that it was like trying to pass through a forest of razor blades. Since I had no means to remove the plant, lacking even such a simple thing as gardening gloves (not normally part of one's kit for exploring ancient ruins anyway), and not having any tool with which I could hack, I had no alternative but to retreat in disarray from this failed objective. Some of this 'razor plant' looked as if it might be cuttings placed there to block entry by someone, but as no one ever goes on to the roof of the temple, who could have done this, and what might they have concealed in the chamber that they wish to prevent anyone seeing? And so, as best I could, I peered and peered from the outside and was able to ascertain that this was indeed a small interior chamber. As it was in such a peculiar place, I believe it must have been reached normally from the inside by means of an internal passage, or possibly even yet another vertical shaft that did not open to the top. I had an uncomfortable feeling that some creature lived in this chamber who would not welcome my appearance, whether winged or creeping I did not know, but I thought I could detect signs of habitation, and what seemed most likely to me was an owl, though whether there are owls at Giza I do not know. I suppose that with the Giza Plateau being empty of people at night, an owl might make a fine living there, as there must be rodents scurrying about in all the filth left behind by the tourists. There is no doubt in my mind that there are horizontal connecting passages in this immensely thick north wall, but as I was unable to dangle down the vertical shafts on a rope, I could not see whether such access openings exist in their walls, by which one may have crossed horizontally in ancient times by means of wooden structures. This chamber guarded by the 'razor plant', however, provides indubitable evidence, to my mind, of access by an internal passage. In any case, I was soon to discover at least one horizontal internal passage linking Shaft One and Shaft Two, to which we turn next.

Olivia and I explored the base of the north wall of the Valley Temple from the passage that runs between that temple and the Sphinx Temple (see the plan in Figure 24). Although this area is closed to tourists, it is accessible to workmen, and is where the electricians entered. However, I have never found any evidence that any archaeologists have bothered to do so. In a Plate on the website we see Olivia, masked like a bandit. She is not trying to conceal her identity, but to avoid breathing in the choking 'desert dust', or what is normally called 'sand' at Giza, which rises all around you when you crawl about inside the north wall of the temple. In this particular photo, she is standing in the entrance to a chamber inside the wall. In Plate 53 we see her in silhouette as she crawls on her hands and knees along a different entry to the interior of the north wall, which is a low opening into which few have ventured. You have to crawl through the dust for a considerable way, and it does not appear to lead anywhere. I took the photo of her from inside. In fact, this narrow entry, which looks more like a cobra hole than anything intended for humans, actually leads to a horizontal passage linking Shaft One and Shaft Two at ground level. In this photo, therefore, we are looking north, and the light behind Olivia is coming from the passage between the Valley Temple and the Sphinx Temple.

In a Plate on the website we see a chamber inside the north wall of the temple at ground level which leads to a small passage running east–west at ground level between Shaft One and Shaft Two. This photo is taken facing south, and the passage commences at the back of this chamber.

In a Plate on the website we see a photo I took from within the horizontal passage looking towards Shaft Two. The electrician's cable can just be seen leading from it. This proves that the electricians were inside this passage. It may well be that it was the electricians themselves who cleared away enough sand to make entry to this passage possible, for their utilitarian purpose of laying cables. This may possibly mean that no archaeologist was ever able to enter it before that, as no one since Hölscher in 1910 really had the archaeological authority to make any clearances. If so, it is amazing how workmen can be given access to important ancient sites for promoting the tourist trade, access that has been denied to archaeologists. Perhaps the moral to be learned from this story is that if you want to discover the secrets of an ancient monument, just install a *son-et-lumière* display, and all will be revealed.

The extent of the passages and chambers at ground level inside the north wall of the Valley Temple may also be seen on the website, which shows both part of an internal passage (now partially blocked by a fallen stone) and another small opening in the wall, through which the sky may be seen.

Plate 52 is a shot that I took from the bottom of Shaft Two looking up, with the sky at the top and the electricians' cable suspended down the shaft. The massive limestone blocks which constitute the wall are here seen very clearly from the inside. I reached the bottom of this shaft by means of the internal horizontal passage leading to it from the base of Shaft One. To the right of this photo, a protruding stone ledge may be seen halfway up. The huge stone at top left has clearly been carved (or cast) in such a way that its end bends inwards, rounding its corner. Numerous holes and gaps can be seen, but it is impossible from this vantage point to evaluate them.

None of this is visible from the outside, and its existence is unknown to archaeologists. What we have to worry about is the indifference that all the archaeologists display towards this building. It is the only well-preserved temple remaining from the period of the Old Kingdom, and yet no one ever studies it. Why should it be left to me, on a dating project, to discover in my spare time in between taking dating samples with Ioannis, that the Valley Temple is riddled with a complex internal structure that is unknown to the whole of Egyptology? I believe that Egyptologists have been severely derelict in their duty and have turned a blind eye to one of the most fascinating structures in the whole of Egypt. Nothing of any note has appeared in print about the Valley Temple since the difficult German excavation report in 1912, which I took the trouble to translate at my own expense; whereas the people to whom such responsibilities should naturally fall have ignored them and defaulted on their obligations.

But the north wall of the temple is not the only place where there is concealed structure. I found much more. A Plate on the website shows a photo I took facing south inside the southern entrance hall of the Valley Temple, which is constructed of granite. At the top of the granite portions in the centre of the photo we see the bottom half of a niche, the top of which fell away long ago, and the blocks from it must have been blown up in Mariette's mad dynamiting. What do we see peeking out behind the granite? A dark hole. And, rising behind that, we have the southeastern corner of the south wall of the temple, which is limestone. I was unable to get to the top of that portion, but I feel that there is a strong likelihood that a vertical shaft exists inside the limestone which is visible here, and that it is connected with the high internal chamber, the top of which may be seen in this photo.

In a Plate on the website we see, in a photo taken by Olivia, my attempts to crawl into yet another hole in the stonework of the Valley Temple interior. But in this case, where the head goes, the body cannot follow. However, I tried. And there was yet more concealed internal structure to be seen, presumably accessible from some other interior point.

On this book's website, I show a view from the roof of the Valley Temple looking down into the granite north entrance, with a glimpse of the north niche at right, and what we see there is really remarkable. This niche is complete, unlike the southern one, which has lost its top portion. In this instance, we see that the northern niche also has a chamber behind it, just as we previously saw that the southern niche does. But the granite stone that forms the base of this north niche has been cut away at the time the temple was constructed at an odd angle, to enable access to the niche from within the wall, and we can see beyond it an intact granite entrance to an interior chamber. It is thus the case that behind each of the two granite niches were interior chambers. The only way to reach either of these chambers is by means of a very high ladder placed on the floors of the two entrances when they are not in use by tourists. I was clearly in no position to do that, so I was unable to explore the chambers, but at least I have photos proving that they exist. These chambers definitely need to be studied properly. And since they cannot have been accessed from outside in any comfortable manner, they must have been accessed by interior passages. I am convinced that the whole of the Valley Temple is positively riddled with interior features enabling communication between secret chambers, shafts and passages. But the most interesting photographic evidence is yet to come, for I will now describe the Blind Room in the south wall of the temple, and its vertical shaft and other features.

In a locked portion of the Valley Temple, as I have said earlier in this chapter, there are the six magazines, in one of which we obtained a dating result from the granite, which I will give later when I come to the dates of the two temples. The magazines are reached by going through the granite doorway, which is covered by a locked door of iron grating. The locks on this door had rusted, and the keys were lost, so the locks had to be smashed for us to get in. No one could remember when anyone was last inside. The area is totally neglected, and has not been studied since the publication of 1912. As you go in, you pass along a short passage, and a stone in the left (south) wall at chest height has been removed at some time in the past, and if you look through the opening, you can see that there is a chamber beyond. This chamber has never appeared in any published plan of the Valley Temple except for that of Petrie, which is reproduced on the website. (It is Plate VI at the back of Petrie's book, *The Pyramids and Temples of Gizeh*, first edition, 1883.) It must have been Mariette (whose excavation of the Valley Temple interior was completed in 1870) who pushed out the stone from inside and made it possible to clamber in and out of this chamber at ground level for the first time since the temple was built. However, as we see clearly in Figure 53, there is no indication whatever in Mariette's plan of the temple that the Blind Room exists, despite the fact that he had cleared the passage where the opening of the missing stone is now to be found. So perhaps this stone was removed by someone else between 1870 and 1880; in other words, an unknown person in between the time of Mariette and the time of Petrie.

In Petrie's plan of the temple (which he called 'the Granite Temple', as I mentioned previously), Petrie suggests that there was a 'forced passage, now closed' into this chamber from the east. However, I am inclined to think instead that Mariette descended into the chamber from the top of the south wall of the temple through the huge vertical shaft that leads down to it, which I will describe in a moment. This chamber was sealed on purpose in antiquity and is the type of temple chamber that modern archaeologists refer to as a 'Blind Room'. I have studied blind rooms elsewhere in Egypt, but discussion of them forms part of another account. I referred to these blind rooms in my previous book, *The Sphinx Mystery* (2009), where I pointed out that they seem to represent the sealed chamber in which the god Osiris was often represented in ancient papyri, and I reproduced some of those images from ancient papyri and quoted the related texts accompanying them.

The entrance to the Valley Temple Blind Room may be seen on the website. I took this photo facing east, with my back to the passage containing the magazines. Here, we see the locked iron grating door from the inside. To the right of the photo is what seems in the photo to be a somewhat lighter than usual stone in the higher course. This is in fact a gap, from which the stone has been removed, and if you climb up to that and wriggle through, you can gain entry to the Blind Room. In Plate 49 I show this gap from inside the Blind Room, and beyond is the passage shown in the preceding photo. In ancient times, the stone would have been in place, and the entry to the Blind Room would have been undetectable. As can be seen in this photo, the entry was very carefully made as part of the original design of the temple. The entire

Blind Room complex is situated within the massive thickness of the south wall of the temple, which in all other plans is shown as solid. No one after Petrie in 1883 ever mentioned or depicted this Blind Room. The website shows the passage from just inside the Blind Room, looking out through the gap caused by the removed stone.

In Plate 49, I show a shot of this entry to the Blind Room from further back, and we may see here that the ceiling of the Blind Room is a gigantic block of limestone, and that the entry portions of the chamber are carefully shaped and smoothed.

The description of the Blind Room given by Petrie, which he aptly calls a 'secret chamber', makes fascinating reading, and as he is the only person until now who has ever described it, I give it here. He calls the magazines the 'loculi', as I mentioned before. Here is what Petrie tells us:

On the S. side of the short passage leading to these loculi, a stone has been removed from the wall, and by climbing in, a curious irregular chamber is reached, evidently never intended to be seen. It is entirely in the rough, the N. and part of the W. side being merely the backs of the granite blocks of the hall and passage; these are irregular, in and out, but nevertheless very well dressed, flat and true in most parts. The rest of this chamber is of rough core masonry, just like the core of the upper temple [he is referring here to the Funerary Temple of Chephren, which is 'upper' because it is up the hill at the other end of the Chephren Causeway], and the floor is of rock, with a step down across it (broken line in plan) about the middle of the chamber. The base of the S.W. corner of the chamber is entirely in one block, the lower or sunken part of the rock floor being levelled up by a base plane cut in the block, and the S. and W. sides being two vertical planes in the same block, so that it forms a hollow corner all in one piece. On the S.E. the chamber is bounded by a rough wall of stone scraps built in when it was recently opened. In the chamber were found, it is said, several common mummies; perhaps of a late date, like those I found in the E.N.E. rock trench.

The history of the opening of this secret chamber seems to have been that in destroying the temple, for the sake of building stones, the pillagers began at the S.E. and S.W. corners; here they pulled stones away until they opened into this chamber, and then, finding a granite wall on one side of it, they dragged out the smallest block, and so broke through into the passage. A clearance of the outside of the temple is needed, however, to settle this as well as other questions.[46]

At the time Petrie wrote, and for long afterwards, the exterior of the south wall of the temple was completely covered in sand. Furthermore, as may be clearly seen in his plan, the southern entrance to the temple was still filled with sand and impassable, and the entire southwest corner of the temple was an unknown area. I believe Petrie was possibly in error, as a result of this, in suggesting that there was a forced entry to the chamber from the south that had later been sealed. I believe that when the ordinary mummies were lowered in what is known as 'late times' (i.e., seventh century BC or later), they came down the vertical shaft which leads to this chamber, and I believe that Mariette must have come the same way and pushed out the stone. However, as I have already pointed out, it may be seen in Figure 53 that Mariette omitted the Blind Room from his plan, so perhaps he never knew of it, and the stone was pushed out later than his time, but before Petrie's, in other words, sometime during the 1870s.

I took a photo without flash to show how dark the Blind Room is except at its southeastern end, which is illuminated by light coming down a vertical shaft in the south wall. In this shot, the careful if bizarre shaping of a huge limestone block is particularly well shown. The vast mound of windblown sand and rubbish at this point may easily be seen cascading down into the Blind Room.

On the website we see a photo taken by Olivia of myself sitting at the southern end of the Blind Room. At this point, the chamber branches to the east and forms an L-shape. A huge amount of windblown tourist rubbish, including even many large objects, litters the place, and I tried to tidy it away into a corner. I am crouching on a large amount of windblown sand that has come in through the vertical shaft in the south wall. It is clear that no one has ever bothered to clear and study the Blind Room, and this urgently needs to be done. In Plate 50a, you can see me standing at the bottom of the huge and relatively smooth vertical shaft in the south wall of the temple, which leads down into the eastern antechamber of the Blind Room. The limestone blocks here are absolutely gigantic, and must be at least 100 tons, possibly much more. On the website we see my photo of the top portion of this vertical shaft. Square holes in the limestone block can here be seen clearly, apparently used for receiving wooden beams in antiquity. There might well have been a stairway here in ancient times.

There are various anomalies to the Blind Room. For instance, in Plate 50b I show a close-up photo of a large stone plug, which seals a narrow passage leading out of the Blind Room. This needs to be investigated, as it seems that it has been in place since Old Kingdom times. A Plate on the website shows this stone plug in its context. We see here clearly that the stone plug is of granite, and that the passage and all the stones surrounding it are of limestone. This stone clearly blocks a passage leading eastwards which is about two feet high, and which must lead to the next vertical shaft further to the east, which I have not seen but merely infer; however, the fact that the passage is sealed like this with a granite plug stone must be for a very important reason. This proves that the Blind Room was not always a Blind Room, but was originally accessible from the east by this secret passage. The granite plug stone is so deeply set into the limestone passage that it is difficult to imagine how this was done, unless from the other side, and the prospect of removing it seems remote, without doing severe damage to the structure. It is interesting that no one ever attempted this in the past, and I suspect it was because it was smothered in sand for thousands of years, being so near ground level.

Opposite this eastwards passage, plugged with granite, is a westwards passage, which can be seen on the website. This must go on to link with the third vertical shaft in the south wall, which I have not inspected and merely infer. This passage has been so choked with sand and rubbish that a considerable clearance operation would be necessary before one could see anything worthwhile. Because the passage was already so filled up with sand and rubbish, I used it as my rubbish dump to push more rubbish into, in order to clear enough of the floor of the Blind Room to be able to get some idea of the chamber itself. It is not at all clear whether the horizontal limestone slab that lies atop the entrance to this passage was placed there at a date subsequent to the construction, but it appears so. The passage is blocked at the far end, but it was so inaccessible because of the sand and rubbish that I was unable to inspect this properly. Because I was desperate to find a close stone joint which might be dateable within this Blind Room, I searched intensely for a possibility, and brought Ioannis into the Blind Room to see what he thought. At top left of the photo we see the sign VT3 which marks the location of our third Valley Temple dating sample. However, this was a failure because the sample turned out to be unsuitable for dating.

So we see that the Blind Room of the Valley Temple has only ever been noticed by one archaeologist, Petrie, and has been totally ignored since his book of 1883. No one has ever made the slightest effort to clear the Blind Room, and Petrie's description of it amounts to only two paragraphs. It has never been photographed before. In fact, I think it is safe to say that no living Egyptologist is aware of its existence. Uvo Hölscher (1878–1963) must have been the last Egyptologist to enter the Blind Room, but for some reason he chose neither to mention it nor to represent it on his plan of the temple (see Figure 57) when his excavation report of the temple was published in 1912. By omitting the Blind Room from his plan, he was actually reverting to a pre-Petrie state of ignorance, since Petrie had taken care to draw the chamber in his plan, only to have all trace of it erased from Hölscher's plan. Who says that archaeology always progresses? Sometimes it takes several steps back.

There are other 'secret' aspects of the Valley Temple. In Plate 47 and others on the website I show the strange protruding limestone 'box' on the roof near the southwest corner of the temple. It seems obvious that this 'box' conceals yet another sealed chamber. Since the 'box' is placed over a space just behind the magazines, directly over the largest single 'dead area' of the temple shown in all plans, it seems equally obvious to me that there must be another sealed chamber below this one. I did not manage to climb up on top of this 'box', but in Plate 47 it may be seen that it has a perfectly flat top, which is composed of a giant flat stone slab, as if to seal it. As a matter of urgency, fibre-optic probes should be inserted into this 'box' and the space below it, where I predict substantial chambers will be found, and they may have been sealed since Old Kingdom times. After all, I can hardly be accused of wild speculation in suggesting concealed chambers within the Valley Temple when I have already found several and photographed them. This temple is positively riddled with secret passages, shafts and chambers, and it seems that no one has ever made the slightest effort to find them except for myself.

I really find it very difficult to comprehend how the only intact temple from the Old Kingdom of Egypt can be so perversely ignored like this. Even if the chambers and passages contain absolutely nothing and are all completely empty, the opportunity they offer for a close inspection of the construction techniques and architecture of the Old Kingdom is unique. Why is it that nobody can be bothered? When Maragioglio and Rinaldi made attempts to study the structure, they were not granted access and could not even gain entry to the roof. They deserve full credit for trying.

The construction of the Valley Temple is remarkable in countless ways. On the website I show a close-up photo I took of the join between two of the granite blocks in this temple. As may be seen very clearly, *there is no join*. This is one of those classic cases where 'you can't fit a razor blade between them'.

On the website I show a close-up of one of the door hinge mortise sockets drilled into the granite doorframes of the temple. These features, because they are so readily accessible, have often been discussed, by Petrie and by others since his time. But in my opinion, a proper survey of them needs to be done, and someone should produce a comprehensive monograph, however brief, of these drilled features. In my book *The Crystal Sun* (2000) I have discussed and quoted the evidence which exists for the use in antiquity of what we now call 'industrial diamonds' for drilling, and show the proof that these were commonplace no later than the first century AD throughout the Roman Empire. I point out in my lengthy discussion in that book that there is every reason to believe that 'industrial diamond' tips for drills were known and used in very early times in Egypt, and that it is by no means impossible that this was the case in Old Kingdom Egypt. I cannot repeat all of that discussion here, but the interested reader should definitely consult the evidence that I have gathered and presented in that earlier book.

On the website I show a photo of the large and anomalous black basalt block which appears in a granite wall in the anteroom of the Valley Temple. I published another view of this in *The Sphinx Mystery* (2009). When a basalt block like this appears for no good reason in an Egyptian structure, it is generally an indicator of something concealed, as I mentioned earlier. In my opinion, the granite stone just touching its upper right corner may once have been moveable, as suggested by the cutaway portion at top right of the photo, its loose join to the stone on its left, and the evident wear seen here on the right-hand edge of the adjoining block, suggesting that it was repeatedly rubbed against and damaged. On the other hand, the basalt block itself may have been moveable. The mortar to the left and upper left of the basalt block appears to be a modern cement 'touching-up' operation for the sake of the tourist industry. There is little doubt in my mind that behind these stones, within the limestone wall at their back, lie yet more cavities, passages or chambers.

On the website I show another peculiar feature, which only became clear when I examined the photo, and did not notice at the time I was in the passage leading to the magazines. This is a photo of the floor of that passage. Here we see the very strange fact that there is a rectangular hole in the granite directly beneath the opening into the Blind Room, and that it seems to have been an outlet for some strange corrosive fluid which flowed out of that hole from the Blind Room area (though the Blind Room's ostensible floor is above this level) and eroded the stone of the passage over a considerable period. For a fluid to cause this amount of erosion in the granite floor is bizarre and at present inexplicable. This too requires the most urgent investigation. It may relate to the subterranean structures, which I am convinced exist as crypts beneath this temple.

And finally, I show on the website a modern brick and cement patch in the granite masonry of the Valley Temple's interior (of a sort which must certainly predate the Second World War, and may even be Victorian). This shows a hole, probably made by treasure hunters at the end of the Old Kingdom, or otherwise by some in the 1870s when the area was once again accessible, and then tidied up. But where did this lead? Into what possible void? A fibre-optic probe could be inserted through the brick with the greatest of ease to find out.

It was as long ago as 2000, in *The Crystal Sun*, before I had the opportunity to make my close study of the Valley Temple but had only the normal tourist access that any other member of the public has, that I made the discovery that the Ascending Passage of the Valley Temple has the 'golden slope', and I became convinced that there was a sealed chamber under its western end. I have now demonstrated the existence of so many concealed internal features of this temple that this is no longer a disembodied prediction, but an inference substantiated by a great deal of incontrovertible evidence. Also, in line with the information given in Chapter Four about the possible tomb locations at Giza, this chamber, which I predicted in 2000, can now be seen to adjoin, and presumably even constitute an integral portion of the subterranean structures or crypts of the temple beneath its western wall, for which I have shown evidence with the cable guides.

Further details of my discoveries of concealed internal structure in the Valley Temple are to be found in my extended captions to many of my photos, many of which can only be consulted on the website www.egyptiandawn.info.

We have now considered the Valley Temple sufficiently, and it is time to turn our attention to the adjoining Sphinx Temple, after which I will give our dating results for these two structures and discuss their significance.

The Sphinx Temple

This temple is in a far more ruinous state than the Valley Temple and, unlike the Valley Temple, it is not familiar to people, because no one is normally allowed to enter it. When we went in, the event caused consternation to a pair of hoopoes who had evidently been nesting there for a long time in peace, and who flew off as if they had seen the ghosts of the pharaohs. Alas, they did not return as long as we were there, which I was sorry about, because hoopoes are rather fascinating to watch, and are rarely seen in Britain.

The Sphinx Temple is primarily distinguished by the fact that it is placed directly in front of the Sphinx. But there is an enigma: there is no passage between the two. Yes, believe it or not, no door existed in the Sphinx Temple to allow anyone to go out through the western wall and into the Sphinx Pit to actually look at the Sphinx. So, you might well ask, why did anyone bother to build a huge temple in front of the Sphinx, which effectively blocked the view of it and also access to it, and then forget to construct any means of communication between the two? This is positively bizarre. This means that anyone who wants to suggest that the Sphinx Temple was built for purposes of worshipping the Sphinx will have to think again, because the Sphinx was boxed in and blocked off, and there was no means of approaching it from within the building that was supposedly built for its worship.

So that is the first mystery. And then there is another: the east–west axis of the Sphinx and that of the temple are different as well. Why was symmetry not observed? If they went to so much trouble to build that huge temple, couldn't they at least have aligned it with the massive statue behind it?

Herbert Ricke called attention to this anomaly in his 1970 book on the Sphinx Temple (we have to remember that he calls it the Harmachis Temple):

'As the temple must be connected somehow with the Sphinx, it initially appears strange that its east–west axis and the axis of the Sphinx run beside each other in parallel at a distance of 14 cubits (7.35 metres). If one had wanted to have these two axes coincide, one would have had to widen considerably the lower terrace as a building site in a northerly direction, which would have meant a great expense of labour, because especially on the northern side, the bedrock stands very high. They neither undertook such an extension of the building site, nor did they consider the alternative, which would have been to plan the Harmachis Temple asymmetrically, or to set it at a right angle to the step [*Stufe*] between the two terraces, in order to direct the temple axis towards the head of the Sphinx, as was done later with the Temple of Amenophis II [see Figures 7.3 and 7.4 of *The Sphinx Mystery* for photos of this small New Kingdom temple near the Sphinx, and its visual orientation towards both the Sphinx and the Great Pyramid; full colour photos are on that book's website, www.sphinxmystery.info].'[47]

Ricke's argument that they could not align the axes because it would have meant cutting away more of the small cliff to the north of the temple does not make any sense. No civilisation that was prepared to go to the trouble of building the Great Pyramid would hesitate to cut away a small outcrop of rock because it was too much effort. To cut it away with a substantial number of men would only have taken a few days. It is more likely that the failure of the axes to coincide is intentional, as the Egyptians never made such 'mistakes' without a purpose. But to discuss these matters here would take us far beyond our concerns in this chapter. The main thing to remember always with the ancient Egyptians is that appearances can be deceptive, and are often meant to be. I have a great deal to say about this kind of thing in my lengthy study and account of the Temple of Seti I at Abydos, which is not yet published, but where I found significant construction distortions which were cleverly concealed as optical illusions. The Egyptians were expert at that sort of thing, which was one of their ways of disguising concealed locations within structures.

So we are clearly dealing with a curious structure, a temple which both blocked and did not communicate with the statue it is today presumed to have been honouring, and which deviated in an obvious fashion from that statue's axis of alignment. It is also peculiar that the two temples, the Valley Temple and the Sphinx Temple, were built side by side. What can the purpose of such an expenditure of energy possibly have been, when it could reasonably be considered a rather wasteful duplication? Surely if one is going to build two temples, one would build them in two separate places. Whatever the cult purpose of a single structure might have been, this is unlikely to have carried over to the second structure. So there must have been two purposes. And then there is the problem of competition: set side by side like that, one is continually tempted to choose a favourite, which robs one of the temples of its glory, as one will always be thought inferior to the other, and even though the choice between the two may vary with opinion, one temple will always be suffering by comparison to the other. Even the Giza pyramids were not actually next to one another, but had some breathing space between them.

No one has really come up with any answers to these questions. Nor have enough people turned their minds to them. The problems, apparently insoluble, have merely been allowed to drift.

In my previous book, *The Sphinx Mystery*, Olivia and I put forward a clear explanation of why the two temples would have been next to each other, why the Sphinx Temple did not open into the Sphinx Pit, and explained the crucial importance of the corridor between the two temples (I published many detailed photos of this in order to present the visual evidence to support my suggestions). But I did not have an answer as to the actual sacred purposes of the two temples. Of course, the Valley Temple was full of statues of Chephren, and was thus dedicated to the cult of Chephren, at least from the time of his death. Whether it was originally built for that purpose is a separate issue, and we do not need to consider that issue here. It takes us too far afield, and would necessitate a long discussion of religion and the mythology of the netherworld deity Sokar. A certain amount of this information has already appeared in *The Sphinx Mystery*, drawing upon the Netherworld texts of the Middle and New Kingdoms, and some of the strange depictions and texts of the Ptolemaic Period as well, such as the most mysterious of the crypts beneath the Temple of Denderah. Two whole chapters of *The Sphinx Mystery* deal with this religious and mythological material, and show its direct relationship with the 'golden section' and the 'golden angle'.

In *The Sphinx Mystery* I suggested that the Sphinx 'Pit' in which the Sphinx sits was in Old Kingdom times a moat filled with water brought in by sluices from the Nile, which during the period of the Inundation reached right up to the eastern edges of the Sphinx Temple and Valley Temple. Raising the water the small amount necessary to fill the Sphinx Pit, or Moat, was thus a simple matter, and I showed the water-raising equipment that would have been used for this. I also published a series of detailed photos showing the evidence of sluice-gate bolt holes and other indications of the water-flow control mechanisms that were used in the passage between the two temples, through which the water was led in. I also explained that the reason why there was no access to the Sphinx through the western wall of the Sphinx Temple is because it acted as the eastern barrier to the moat, but I gave the evidence that there was a platform on that wall (now obscured by *son-et-lumière* light fixtures) which was used as an embarking and disembarking point for using the small boats that featured in the religious and pharaonic funeral ceremonies which I believe took place on the water. I also explain the water erosion patterns in the Sphinx moat by this means, showing that they are horizontal on the body of the Sphinx because it just sat there in the middle of the water, but vertical at the sides, especially the southern side, due to the continual dredging that was necessary to clear the moat of windblown sand, with the water pouring down and scouring the sides. I also quote from the many Pyramid Texts that refer to this 'lake' and what took place on it and near it.

I believe that the pharaoh's internal organs in their four jars were washed and purified in this lake prior to his burial. However, this is all fully explained in the other book, nearly 600 pages of it with 375 illustrations; the interested reader may also wish to consult that book's extensive website, which is www.sphinxmystery.info

The discovery of the Sphinx Temple was made by Selim Hassan in 1936.

Hassan was deeply puzzled by the temple and said of it:

Judging by the style of architecture, and the absence of decoration, or inscriptions, we may safely assign this temple to a date not exceeding the middle of the Fourth Dynasty.

The fact that this temple had no direct communication with the Sphinx Court [Pit], seems to point to one of two conclusions; either it had no connection at all with the Sphinx, or, what is more probable, the Sphinx was regarded as being so holy that approach to it was forbidden to all, save only the King and the higher ranks of the priesthood. This was certainly the rule with regard to the cult images in the later Egyptian temples, but even so, the holy of holies was always provided with an easy means of access.

In the case of the Sphinx, however, we are left to assume that the royal or priestly worshipper had either to climb over the back wall of the temple by some means, or else leave the building altogether and walk round by a narrow passage, to emerge at an awkward angle in the corner of the court, either method of approach being exceedingly undignified and inconvenient.[48]

This eloquently puts the problem! Are we to imagine a hapless pharaoh creeping round through an alley between the two temples like a furtive thief, in order to gain access to the magnificent Sphinx from within the Sphinx Temple by sneaking up on him? I am convinced that my solution to this problem as presented in *The Sphinx Mystery* explains all the anomalies.

We do apparently know the name of the Sphinx Temple in antiquity, or at least Selim Hassan believes that we do. Here are some more interesting remarks by him:

> Until recent years, the name 'Temple of the Sphinx' was borne by the Valley Temple of Khafra [Chephren], and had been acquired when the true significance of that building was imperfectly understood. The real Temple of the Sphinx, which together with the cavity in which it lies was called by the Egyptians 'Setepet' the 'Elect', should be the massive construction lying in front of the Sphinx . . . Lying a few paces to the north of the Valley Temple of Khafra, it seems so far as the façade is concerned, to be designed upon the same lines . . . The two temples are both facing east, each has an entrance in the northern and southern ends of its façade, and these façades are lying in line with each other . . . Moreover, both temples are constructed of a core of local limestone masonry, and cased inside and outside with blocks of finely dressed granite. The size of some of the blocks, forming the core of the Sphinx Temple, is enormous, rivalling, and indeed, often exceeding three times the size of those used in building the Great Pyramid. Even the fact that these blocks were cut locally, does not lessen our admiration for the skill and organization that manoeuvred them into position. . . . Beyond the façades, the similarity between the two buildings ends, the interior arrangement of the Sphinx Temple being quite different from that of its neighbour, which proves that it was designed for a different use. It may be mentioned here that this building is the oldest divine temple, as distinct from a royal mortuary temple, yet discovered in Egypt.[49]

It is very disappointing that Hassan only devotes four pages of a 323-page book to a description of the Sphinx Temple. (The rest of his large book is about the Sphinx.) The situation is even worse with Maragioglio and Rinaldi, who, as I have already mentioned, devote only three and a half pages to the subject. Even Ricke only discussed the Sphinx Temple, the entire subject of his book, for about thirty pages of actual text, and some of that was merely devoted to justifying giving the name 'Harmachis Temple' to the structure. So no one has really found very much to say about the Sphinx Temple. If you were to add up all the comments made about the Sphinx Temple by every writer until now, you would probably have a lot less than fifty pages of text in total, and much of that would be repetitive. Some of the things that are said about the Sphinx Temple seem somewhat simple-minded and naive. For instance, because it is oriented to the cardinal directions, and has an eastern façade, it is claimed by some to be a solar temple. And yet those who make that suggestion do not make the same claim for the Valley Temple sitting beside it, which is also oriented to the cardinal directions and also has an eastern façade. Why would one of them be a solar temple and the other not, when they share the very same attributes upon which the solar temple hypothesis is based? Some people say, ah, the Sphinx Temple has a 'chapel' in the east and a 'chapel' in the west of its internal structure, so it must be solar. But there is absolutely no evidence of any such chapels; the narrow chambers referred to are central eastern and western recesses, which could be whatever you like, as the whim takes you – though chapels would seem to be low on the list of possibilities, as they have none of the attributes of chapels. Certainly they are too small to have been of any significance, and no group of people could have squeezed into them for any ceremony, so to 'interpret' them as solar chapels strikes me as ridiculous.

In *The Sphinx Mystery* I was able to suggest two highly specific uses to which the Sphinx Temple was put, for both of which there is hard physical evidence. Although one of these was sacred and ceremonial, while the other was purely physical, I did not address the main function and use of the temple per se. The fact that it probably sits on top of a pharaoh's tomb, as described earlier in Chapter Four, and that it was evidently used in connection with pharaonic funeral rituals, as described at length in *The Sphinx Mystery*, suggests that it was at least partly funerary, and not entirely divine, as Hassan thought.

Sometimes a sharp observer can notice something that turns out to

346

be a possible clue to something, even if we don't know to what. An example of this comes from Margioglio and Rinaldi. If you look at the Plates on the website you will see the mysterious pair of 'magazines' in the northwest corner of the Sphinx Temple. No one has the faintest idea what purpose they served. They are matched by a corresponding pair in the southwest corner of the temple. Maragioglio and Rinaldi say that they noticed traces of stone which led them to reconstruct the original appearance of these 'magazines'. According to them, the shorter ones closer to the central courtyard 'were completely faced with alabaster', whereas the longer ones along the western wall of the temple were faced with granite.[50] Assuming that they are correct about this, although we cannot resist being impressed at their ability to come to such a conclusion, it only makes the 'magazines' even more mysterious and inexplicable and, indeed, less likely actually to be magazines! However, it is always such tiny clues that one must look for. I must confess that I did not see traces of alabaster or granite in these 'magazines', but then I have not been back to the temple since finding these remarks in Margioglio and Rinaldi's text. If you look closely at the Plate on the website, which is my photo showing both the 'inner magazine' and the 'outer magazine' in the northwest corner of the temple side by side, you will see that no traces of alabaster or granite seem to be visible. They must have found extremely minute traces of some kind, and unless I went back and specially looked for these things, I can make no comment about that from personal observation. However, I must admit to being sceptical of these suggestions.

Maragioglio and Rinaldi believe that the courtyard floor of the Sphinx Temple was probably paved with 'Egyptian alabaster', like that of the Valley Temple.[51] But then again, one cannot be sure, since the floor, assuming there was one, was ripped up in antiquity and now there is only limestone bedrock. If, as I suspect, the floor of this temple was flooded during the annual Inundation every year, there may never have been a stone floor laid over the bedrock at all. During the dry period, a floor of perishable materials could have been supplied, to be removed when the flooding was due to resume some months later.

Although I have the highest possible opinion of Maragioglio and Rinaldi, who did such spectacular work over the years in studying the old monuments, their plans do occasionally contain serious errors, and this is especially the case for the Valley Temple and Sphinx Temple, unfortunately. Sometimes they merely omit their own labellings (which they actually do on their plan for the northwest magazines we have just been considering), but they also get things badly wrong on occasion, such as their wholly misleading drawing of the North Trench adjoining the Sphinx Temple, to take a single example. (As I have earlier pointed out, this is often caused by their being denied personal access to sites.) One conclusion of Maragioglio and Rinaldi with which I am forced to disagree most strongly is their notion that the small granite blocks seen in Plates on the website are the remains of the bottom course of an interior granite cladding of the eastern wall of the temple.[52] Those blocks, as I know from inspecting them closely, are entirely unconvincing for such a purpose. (See them on the website.) They are too small and derisory and look as if they were put there later on. (When viewed against the wall in front of which they sit, they remind me of some similar red blocks in a Victorian children's building blocks set.) We have demonstrated the incorrectness of Maragioglio and Rinaldi's hypothesis with our dating results, for our sample ST-3 is taken from here, and we have dated the time when the granite blocks were laid down into the bedrock. (Note that they were laid into the bedrock, not on to a pavement, which if it ever existed had already been stripped away. This crucial detail was not noted by Maragioglio and Rinaldi.) This dating result shows that this happened about two thousand years after the construction of the temple, when this interior northeast corner of the structure was accessible, possibly by way of a shaft dug down through the overlying windblown sand and rubble for the purposes of an intruded grave. At that time, the small granite blocks, which are so anomalous when seen against the gigantic limestone ones behind them, were possibly laid as part of a surrounding base for an improvised grave. The blocks are small enough that a few men could easily have carried them. The details of this result will be given with the rest of the dating results. The conclusion to be drawn is that there is no evidence whatever that the temple had an original interior granite cladding. As for the intruded shaft and grave just mentioned, I have discussed this in *The Sphinx Mystery*, as I believe that this shaft may have been known and used also in Ptolemaic and Roman times as a convenient hidden chamber for priests associated with the worship of the Sphinx as Harmachis during that era.

Although Selim Hassan thought that the Sphinx Temple must have been clad in granite on both the outside and the inside,[53] the cladding on the outside is by no means established either. Maragioglio and Rinaldi are convinced that the exterior of the eastern façade was never clad in granite except for the two doorways, which were.[54] Ricke, like Hassan, believes that the Sphinx Temple was completely clad in granite in the interior.[55] As for the exterior, he says that although the eastern wall of the temple was probably clad in granite, the western, northern and southern walls probably were not:

'The width of the east front of the Harmachis Temple was widened during the reconstruction [a second stage of construction postulated by Ricke] from 88 cubits to 100 cubits. That calculation includes the other granite cladding on the southern side which was never executed. This round number may be an indication that the northern exterior walls were not supposed to be covered with granite . . .'[56]

So now we see that none of the experts can agree on something so basic as whether the Sphinx Temple was clad in granite or not, and that Hassan, Maragioglio and Rinaldi, and Ricke, all hold completely different views on the subject. We do not have to take a position on the matter, because we did not date any granite cladding stones other than the phoney ones I just mentioned. But it was mere wishful thinking for anyone to believe that those were evidence of any interior granite cladding anyway, as the stones in question are so ridiculously small for the job that it is a relief to be rid of them as 'evidence'. It is true that various bits of granite are to be found here and there in the Sphinx Temple, but they do not appear to constitute any evidence of an interior granite cladding. We took two other granite samples from the Sphinx Temple, but neither had anything to do with interior or exterior cladding. One sample, ST-5, was from a small block tightly laid into what the archaeologists believe to have been a waste-water channel in the floor, but which I believe, as explained at length in Chapter Four, is really a cable guide for lowering a heavy sarcophagus into the crypt below. The other, ST-4, was from a granite block of unknown purpose or significance which was at the foot of a column in the Central Court. Both of these pieces of granite were apparently original to the building, but neither had any association with any wall of the temple. I am inclined to doubt that the Sphinx Temple walls had any interior cladding, and to agree with Ricke that the western, northern and southern walls were never clad in granite on the exterior. So that only leaves the eastern façade. And I am inclined to be doubtful about that also, apart from the doorways.

Ricke makes some exceedingly strange observations about this subject:

'. . . the Harmachis Temple is clearly placed in relation to the Valley Temple of Chephren . . . It adjoins it: the east fronts of both temples either are or would have been in alignment if the outer cladding of the Harmachis Temple had been completed in granite. Also, the rear [west] faces of both temples are aligned. That is, the clad west side of the Valley Temple is in alignment with the unclad west side of the Harmachis Temple. The latter evidently was not meant to be clad, for lack of space, because here the core masonry has been worked to a smooth finish.'[57]

Let's just take stock of this for a moment, and try to get a clear focus. What is he telling us? He is saying that there is a continuous western line at the back of the two temples made by the combination of a clad wall and an unclad wall, but that the continuous eastern line does not exist because it was designed for two clad walls, one of which was never clad. Something is wrong: there is clearly no continuity of conception or thinking here. One alignment is designed for differing walls but the other was designed for identical walls, but it didn't work out because they differed after all. This is one of those unsettling structural anomalies that is just as bizarre and inexplicable as the differing axes of the Sphinx Temple and the Sphinx. Surely if the idea was to match clad and unclad, then it should have been carried through consistently.

Another major difference between the two temples is by no means insignificant: it has been suggested that there was never a pavement laid in front of the Sphinx Temple as there was in front of the Valley Temple, a point which is stressed by Maragioglio and Rinaldi.[58] And according to archaeologists of today, no evidence seems to have come to light of little bridges, or pools, or any 'quay' in front of the Sphinx Temple. If so, it would seem that the processional aspect that appears to have been attached to the Valley Temple did not attach at all to the Sphinx Temple. Nor did the Sphinx Temple have any way out for people wishing to leave from the rear, whereas the Valley Temple led directly on to the Causeway and up to the pyramids. So from the point of view of ceremonial functionality, the two structures were utterly different. The Sphinx Temple was a dead end: you went in and you came out. But the Valley Temple was something you passed through.

However, in my large collection of rare photos of the Giza Plateau which I have assiduously put together over the years, I have an aerial view which shows that, in the late 1930s, quays were clearly visible in front of the Sphinx Temple. As far as I know, this photo is the only surviving visual evidence of these quays. I reproduced it as Figure 4.2 in *The Sphinx Mystery*. It seems therefore that the real reason why the Sphinx Temple 'has no quays' is because the sand blew over them and covered them up again. So, what else is new in Egypt?

The Sphinx Temple may have had a roof, or partial roof. But there was no stairway to it as in the Valley Temple. It seems that no trace of any steps or way up to the roof of any kind has been found. This is another major difference between the two adjoining temples. The roof of the Valley Temple was evidently a lively place, with everybody up there having a great time, doing whatever it was they did, some of which was certainly keeping time by observing the 'light well' every day at noon. Shadow clocks would have been up there too, but as they become imprecise exactly at noon and cannot tell the time for a period of several minutes, it was necessary to have the 'light well' to detect the exact moment of noon, which the shadow clocks could not do. This meant that the water clocks could be set, which had to happen daily, and it was the water clocks which timed the culminations of the stars at night, as obviously shadow clocks don't work at night. The Egyptians thus coordinated three separate clocks during the daytime, in order to keep perfect time. (This will all be discussed at length in a future book, which explains why they did it, and the fantastic, almost inconceivable, feats they accomplished as a result.) But the roof of the Sphinx Temple next door was apparently deserted. So the harder we look, the more we discover major differences in function between these buildings.

The main feature of the Sphinx Temple was its large Central Court, a rectangular space in the middle, with its long end north–south, surrounded by massive limestone pillars. It is thought that a covered colonnade surrounded this courtyard. It is generally thought that the Central Court was open to the sky, but no one knows for sure. However, it did not at all resemble the Pillared Hall at the centre of the Valley Temple, for that was T-shaped. It may well be that both were open to the sky, or perhaps not: who knows? And now we are beginning to realise just how much we have yet to learn.

If we imagine the appearance of the two temples side by side in antiquity, they would have made an extraordinary sight. Looking at their front facades from the east, we would have seen a dark one on the left (the Valley Temple) and a light one on the right (the Sphinx Temple). The contrast would have been startling, one being encased in dark red granite as if it had secrets to hide, and the other gleaming proudly and openly in the sun with its fresh white limestone. If one were thinking symbolically, one could say that the one on the left represented 'the concealed', and the one on the right was 'the revealed'. Since this striking contrast side by side was obviously intentional, we cannot dismiss such symbolic possibilities in the minds of the builders. Perhaps the purpose of the dark sister was to hide and that of the light sister was to proclaim. This pairing of opposites calls to mind the two sister goddesses, Isis and Nephthys, one bright and the other dark. We have evidence from a variety of sources indicating that Giza once had a Temple of Isis and a Temple of Osiris. Was the Sphinx Temple once a Temple of Isis, and the Valley Temple a Temple of Osiris (originally Sokar, who became absorbed into Osiris)?

Osiris is not meant to have come to prominence as a god until the Fifth Dynasty, so that a Fourth Dynasty temple used by Chephren might well have been commandeered in the following dynasty for the use of Osiris, perhaps even retaining a Chephren cult as an associated feature. If the Chephren statues in the Valley Temple were smashed at the end of the Fourth Dynasty in a violent attack by a mob who hated the pharaohs of that dynasty, then it might have been positively necessary to find a new use for the temple, for no one could make lots of Chephren statues again to replace those which were gone, and the sole use of the temple for a Chephren cult could have been impossible (even if it were politically advisable). We have already seen the evidence that traces of forty-one statues were identified by the excavators, but that there must have been many more. It would have been a simple matter for the Fifth Dynasty priests to dig the 'well', throw the six intact statues down it, and put the remaining fragments into the magazines, from which they were later scattered and found amongst the debris by Mariette (who did not record any locations for them). The evidence that a Chephren cult was still being serviced during the Sixth Dynasty could just as well refer to a residual or minor cult; it does not prove that the Valley Temple was in full swing exclusively as a Chephren shrine.

If one wanted to view the Valley Temple as an 'Osiris Temple' prior to the Fifth Dynasty, one would have to consider it a 'House of Sokar', since Osiris was merged with the death god Sokar of Giza during the Fifth Dynasty.

Looked at symbolically, perhaps the dark temple stood for death while the white temple stood for rebirth. And suitably to that concept, 'death' was something you went into and emerged from on the other side, as one does in the Valley Temple. But if you 'stepped into the light' of the Sphinx Temple, you could not pass through, as it was an apotheosis in itself. These remarks are meant to be merely suggestive. But certainly something was going on in the heads of the ancient Egyptians when they decided to place these two buildings in such startling contrast to one another side by side. And the ultimate explanation is likely to be sacred and symbolical, since everything the ancient Egyptians did was subservient to such principles.

If the Sphinx Temple were indeed called Setepet in antiquity, this would strengthen the idea that it was a place of rebirth where one stepped into the light and became part of the entourage of the sun god. (Those people claiming that the Sphinx Temple was a solar temple meant something different from what I am proposing; they were suggesting that it was a temple used for worshipping the sun.) It is sometimes claimed that Setepet means 'the chosen', or 'the elect', from the verb *setep*, meaning 'to choose or select'. However, if by Setepet they really meant Sethepet, the meaning would be rather different, and could be construed as the 'Place of Annihilation', which is a common name for the Netherworld, since it was there that the evil dead were annihilated while the justified dead were resurrected. (It is an interesting theological point that, in ancient Egyptian tradition, the annihilation of evil people takes place after death, and not because of death, since 'death' was entirely a state of transition by which one took leave of one's physical body, and the concept of ceasing to exist when one 'died' was inconceivable to the Egyptians, to whom ceasing to exist could only take place *after* death.) In any case, *setep* can mean 'choose or select' in the specific sense of 'choose for slaying', and the two forms of the word, though linguistically distinct in one sense because of the different consonant, are nevertheless connected, as sometimes happens in Egyptian. It may be that the priests were engaged in one of their favourite pastimes, sacred puns.

As it happens, both meanings are directly and simultaneously relevant to this place of sunrise at the equinox, where the 'Place of Annihilation' or Netherworld was literally conceived of as being at the base of the eastern horizon, while the place of being chosen for resurrection was conceived of as being directly above it. The Setepet might then have been the intermediary place between these two distinct mythological locales, so that both meanings could in a sense attach to it by pun and by affinity, though because the building was above and not below ground, the emphasis would be on the positive aspect of resurrection and eternal life. (This is all the more reason for the subterranean caverns beneath the temple to have some sacred significance beyond being only a pharaoh's tomb.) I have written so much about these matters as they relate to the area of the Sphinx in *The Sphinx Mystery* that I can only refer the reader once again to that book in order to gain a proper understanding of what all of this religious lore means in relation to this temple and its immediate surroundings.

The most mundane of all conclusions would be to think of both of the adjoining temples as funerary temples of Chephren. He already had one of those up at the top of the Causeway, at the foot of the pyramid that today bears his name. Even megalomaniacs, such as Chephren seems to have been, do not necessarily build three temples to themselves all in the same place, especially when they've also supposedly got a nice cosy pyramid to call their own.

And then there is the question of the statues. Not a single fragment of a statue was excavated in the Temple of the Sphinx – not even the tiniest little piece or chip of one. Whereas the Valley Temple contained hundreds of them! . . . Surely a case for Philip Marlowe . . .

In several Plates on the website we can see the gigantic rectangular holes in the bedrock which are found in front of each of the columns in the Central Court of the Sphinx Temple. No one knows what these were for. If they were for statue bases, then the statues must have been gigantic. If they were standing, they would have been higher than the columns, so that is not very likely. And you can see that the depressions are at an angle, which would not be the case if they were made as bases for statues, which would thus have tilted. It has been suggested that the holes were for massive rectangular plinths, upon which rested recumbent statues such as sphinxes. But it must be remembered that there are no traces of any statues, recumbent or otherwise, and also no traces of any plinths. The doors to the temple are too small for any to have been carried in (the temple would have had to have been built around them) but, more to the point, the doors are also too small for any to have been carried out. So if they were not carried out, and if they were not smashed, then what happened to them? It is tempting to conclude that they did not exist, and then their 'disappearance' can readily be explained. These holes are rather odd, and it has also been suggested that they were merely used for erecting the columns. But really, we do not know.

Selim Hassan, the excavator, assumed that statues of 'the King' rested in these holes:

'In front of each pillar is a rectangular depression cut in the rock floor, sloping somewhat towards the pillars. These were made to accommodate the bases of colossal statues of the King, purposely designed on a large scale in order that they might not be dwarfed by the immensity of the Sphinx, as would have been the case with statues that were merely life-sized. Therefore, the centre of the court was surrounded by ten huge pillars, fronted by colossal statues of the King who built the temple, and who probably sculptured the Sphinx as well.'[59]

Having made these assertions, Hassan then added a footnote as follows:

'On the other hand, the depressions in the floor may have been made to facilitate the erection of the pillars.'[60]

Hassan was not an arrogant man, and although he assumed the pillars must have been 'fronted by colossal statues of the King', he was perfectly willing to admit that on the other hand they may well not have been.

The fact is that there is not the slightest evidence that the pillars were fronted by colossal statues, of the King or of anything or anyone else. But this did not prevent Leslie Grinsell in 1947 (six years before Hassan's book appeared) from asserting with total assurance that the pillars were all fronted by sphinxes:

'Immediately east of the Sphinx and north of the granite lower temple [the Valley Temple] is the Sphinx Temple, a rectangular structure enclosing a courtyard which was lined with 10 small sphinxes, the sockets of which are still to be seen.'[61]

The certainty with which Grinsell assures us that the Sphinx Temple contained statues of sphinxes is astonishing. Where on earth did he get his sphinxes from? Hassan's book was not published until six years later, and even Hassan did not suggest sphinxes, he merely suggested royal statues. It does not build a lot of confidence in the reliability of Grinsell that he speaks of ten sphinxes in the Sphinx Temple as if he had seen them yesterday. In fact, there is no evidence whatsoever for any such sphinxes.

After Hassan, the next people to discuss the large depressions in front of the pillars were Maragioglio and Rinaldi, in 1966. Unlike the situation in the Valley Temple, where they were denied access to the locked portions and the roof, they were clearly admitted to the interior of the Sphinx Temple (although not to the North Trench, as already mentioned, which cannot be reached from inside the temple). Inside the Sphinx Temple, they made very careful and detailed measurements, which were far more informative than the information given by Hassan. They have a considerable discussion of the subject, and begin by referring to the holes in front of the pillars as follows:

In front of each of these [pillars], on the courtyard side, a hole was dug in the rock that was evidently intended to receive a structural or decorative feature.

The holes are not all of the same size. The four to the east are almost identical (1.50–1.85 x 3.10–3.30 m.) and two of them are unusual in being still filled with fine limestone masonry up to within a few centimetres of their upper rim and against the buttress of the core of the corresponding pillars. Another hole in this row is very shallow, but its bottom seems to be formed of living rock.

The two holes to north and south of the courtyard are wider than the others (2 2-.35 x 3.30 m. circa). The one to the north had the edges very much worn away and chipped, and a slightly sloping layer of limestone slabs on its bottom is perhaps the remains of a filling similar to those previously described. The hole to the south has a surface sloping towards the pier and preceded by a regular but deeper cut.

Of the four western holes, the two outer ones have dimensions similar to those on the east side (1.50–1.65 x 3 metres). Their rock bottom has steps and surfaces with carrying slopes. The two inner holes are larger (1.85 x 4.30–4.5 m.) and their rock bottom is curiously cut, reaching in both the maximum depth of one metre. It was obviously not possible to measure the vertical dimension of the holes that were full of masonry, but the others are about one metre deep, with a single possible exception, as has already been said. All the holes, but especially the two most northerly ones on the west side, have their upper edges very much worn away, perhaps as a result of the demolition that took place.

The difference in vertical section between the holes of the Temple of the Sphinx and those of the courtyard of the Upper Temple [Funerary Temple] of Chephren [at the foot of the pyramid] is so notable as to make one suppose that even the purposes for which they were dug were by no means the same and that the features for which they were prepared were also different. . . . Grinsell thinks that the courtyard of the Temple of the Sphinx 'was lined with 10 small sphinxes, the sockets of which are still to be seen'. Selim Hassan . . . on the other hand, believes that colossal statues of the King were erected in the sockets.[62]

They do not give any firm conclusion as to what they themselves thought about these holes, except to say that in them 'ornamental, rather than structural features (such as statues or triads [a statue of three figures together]) . . . found a place, at least in part'.[63] This is rather vague, to say the least, and indicates that they frankly didn't know what to think. Maybe there were some statues there, 'at least in part', i.e., in some of the holes, but possibly not in others. But they do not venture to speculate on what kind of statues, and certainly do not specify either sphinxes or kings.

By the time of Ricke's report in 1970, statues were back in force, and this time they were seated kings:

'Colossal statues had been placed around the courtyard of the Chephren Funerary Temple, just as around the courtyard of the Harmachis Temple, and also here as well as there, probably seated images of the king . . . In the Funerary Temple of Chephren there were twelve statues, in the Harmachis Temple, because of the smaller number of pillars, there were only ten places for statue bases. However, it appears as if in the bigger indentations in front of the pillars, on the narrow sides of the courtyard, . . . statues of a special type were erected . . . What these statues may have looked like remains, however, completely uncertain . . . The base holes for setting up the statues are of differing depths. The statues were therefore delivered with bases of different thicknesses. That the statues really were erected may be deduced from the fact that some base holes had then been filled up a little with stone slabs, because the bases of the statues which were erected in them had not been as high as had been predicted or expected.'[64]

That is the collected wisdom of the people who have considered this problem to date. We see that they do not really agree on details, but are inclined generally to conclude that large statues stood in the court-yard in the holes. However, none of these writers considers the fundamental problems I have already pointed out, namely that there was no way to get such plinths and statues in or out, and no trace, not even the smallest fragment, has ever been found of a single plinth or a single statue in the Sphinx Temple, whereas hundreds of fragments of royal statues have been found in the Valley Temple next door. If one assumes large statues inside the Sphinx Temple and is willing to assume that the temple was built around them, fine. But in that case, where are they now? The walls of the temple are still intact all round. The doors are too small to get them out. And not one tiny fragment of them remains.

A vanishing act without parallel. And that is why I say it is the vanishing act of something that never existed. As may be seen in a Plate on the website, we took a dating sample from a large granite block pressed against the bedrock within one of the depressions in the floor, and thereby got a date that is presumably original to the construction of the temple (sample ST-4). Clearly, if a large granite block was stuck down into the depression against the bedrock at the time of construction, it must mean something in relation to all of the depressions. But no one has previously mentioned its existence or considered it for even a moment. Is this granite block the remains of a granite plinth? It does not appear to be so. And it is certainly not the remains of part of a statue, colossal or otherwise. Did all the depressions once have such granite blocks in them? If so, why? These are questions that need considering at some future time. This temple is definitely a temple of mystery, and the mystery is largely due to our ignorance.

It is clear now that the 'holes', or 'depressions', or 'sockets' in the floor of the Sphinx Temple are entirely different from those in the adjoining Valley Temple. The Valley Temple was undoubtedly full of a bewildering number of statues of Chephren, whereas the Sphinx Temple provides no evidence that it ever contained even a single one. This is a very remarkable contrast between two temples sitting side by side, and provides further evidence – as if more were needed – that the two buildings had different functions.

I have one rather unusual suggestion as to the possible uses of the central columns of the Sphinx Temple and the strange holes in front of them, which I merely mention as a possibility. Since the Nile reached the eastern edge of the temple at the time of Inundation, and was even directed into the Sphinx Moat, as I believe, it is possible that during the period of the Inundation the floor of the Sphinx Temple may have been flooded, and was designed to be used in that condition. I therefore put forward the hypothesis that the columns were used as formal mooring posts for small ritual boats, which when the water receded rested on wooden bases fixed into those holes in the pavement. Since I believe that a small boat was used in the 'lake' of the Sphinx Moat, could it make sense that further small boats might have some ritual use within the Setepet – or Sphinx Temple – itself, as part of a complex religious enactment? The very first moment that Olivia and I walked into the Sphinx Temple, we both felt the same thing instinctively: that it had once been flooded, and that the floor had frequently been under water. It just 'felt' that way to us. Within the central court of the temple, in the midst of the columns, is a large rectangular open space. This could have constituted a small 'lake', and since lakes are so frequently mentioned in the Pyramid Texts and were of such importance to the Old Kingdom death and resurrection cults, it seems that in the dry area of Giza one could never have enough lakes.

What exactly ten small boats would do in a small lake in the middle of a temple is not easy to imagine. They would certainly fit; they could certainly be taken in and out of the temple through the narrow doors, because they could be dismantled. So all of those problems are resolved by the hypothesis. But what would their function be? We must keep in mind that sacred barques mounted on stands were of central importance in Egyptian temples, even when they were not being used for anything, but were merely carried in procession (as shown in Figure 7.22 in *The Sphinx Mystery*, which is reproduced as Figure 59 here). We know they were there even though we don't really understand why. The Temple of Seti I at Abydos had so many sacred barques inside that it even had a 'Hall of Barques'. So I do not believe that I am being in any way outrageous by suggesting that the Sphinx Temple might have contained real sacred barques that actually floated on water during the time of Inundation. There are so many precedents for barques that to invoke them as a hypothesis hardly needs any justification. However, this is just an idea, and it may be completely wrong.

In the various photos I have taken of these so-called 'pillars' in the Sphinx Temple, it can be noticed that they are rather unusual. The top half of each pillar is strangely indented, carefully and laboriously cut away. There must have been a reason for this. What could it be? If mooring ropes had been thrown round each pillar, this cutaway technique could have prevented the rope from sliding down to the base. The indentations in the pillars are particularly clear in several plates on the website. No one has commented on these features before, so consequently no one has ever suggested what their purpose might have been. These features have simply been ignored. In any case, I cannot resist the impression that somehow these pillars were utilitarian, not ornamental (which is not hard to believe, considering how unaesthetic they are in appearance!), and that each was used to secure something or, as I have said, fasten or moor something. I suppose the rectangular recesses cut away in the top portions could have been used to inset carved wooden panels. But what would be the point of that? Images of gods? But then, why the holes in front of the pillars? For the insertion of portable wooden altars upon which offerings were laid and incense was burned? Did these pillars feature somehow in processional ceremonies?

I return once again to the problem posed by our sample ST-4, which gives the date for the insertion of a small granite block very tightly packed into the inner end of one of the holes in front of the pillars. This was just as carefully done as was the insertion of the granite into the conduit, described in Chapter Four. What can the purpose of this possibly be, especially as the granite block is so very small? The fact that none of the excavators mentioned it demonstrates their lack of attention to detail. It is just such anomalies that need to be explained, and to ignore them merely leaves mystery behind like a scent trail. Alas, I cannot think of anything. I can only remark that its purpose appeared to be to raise that tiny inner portion of the hole back up to normal floor level for that short distance, possibly connected with the securing of something more firmly in the hole as a base, and strapped against the pillar. Alternatively, it may have sealed a cable hole to the subterranean chambers.

There is another difference between the Sphinx Temple and the Valley Temple that appears never to have been mentioned, and it is a detail of construction techniques. Dieter Arnold has pointed out in his book *An Encyclopaedia of Ancient Egyptian Architecture* that the Valley Temple was apparently the first building in Egypt to use cramps (sometimes called clamps) to hold the stones together. Here is what he has to say:

'They were first used in the 4th Dynasty (valley temple of Khafre [Chephren]). During the Old Kingdom their use was restricted to parts of the structure thought to be vulnerable (architrave); their usage became more extensive in the Middle Kingdom . . . Bronze cramps are less common (Khafre, copper or bronze, weighing 20–25 kg) . . .'[65]

In fact, it was the metal cramps holding the blocks of the architraves, rather than the stones themselves, that the despoilers of the Valley Temple were after when they threw the architraves down on to the floor from above at the end of the Old Kingdom (the ones that were later dynamited to smithereens by Mariette), as Uvo Hölscher originally pointed out. The metal had a considerable value, and each cramp weighed about 25 kg. It was only necessary to melt them down and sell the ingots. The robbers would have obtained hundreds of kilos of precious copper or bronze and made a small fortune for themselves.

So the temptation of the monetary value of the bronze or copper cramps of the Valley Temple was too much to resist. But what about the Sphinx Temple? What about its cramps? Well, this brings us back to the curious problem of the differences between the structures. For although the Valley Temple was full of cramps, the Sphinx Temple had none. And this is a point that no one has ever mentioned before.

Surely if the two temples had been built by the same workmen at the same time, the Sphinx Temple would have had cramps. But instead, we find only the Valley Temple described as the earliest building in Egypt to have them. Does this, therefore, mean that the Sphinx Temple is really earlier, and was built before the introduction of cramps? And while we are on that subject, let us remember that the pyramids do not have cramps either. So according to this reasoning, the Valley Temple must be a more recent structure than either the pyramids or the Sphinx Temple.

Now I give our dating results for the two structures and discuss their possible implications.

The Dating Results

We obtained one dating result from each building which was much more recent than its construction date. I have already mentioned that the roof of the Valley Temple was accessible during part of the time that the main structure was buried in the sand. Probably the reason why the roof survives so well today is that it was useful as a platform (or, in other words, as a floor!) in later times. In a Plate on the website we can see the place from which we took the limestone sample giving the more recent date. This was clearly a limestone addition of that time, as the stone even looks different. The date we obtained from this was 1050 BC, plus or minus 540 years, giving a range from 1590 BC to 510

362

BC. In other words, at some time between the reign of King Apophis of the Hyksos Period and the reign of Darius I during the Persian Occupation, somebody added a small amount of limestone to the roof of the Valley Temple. It is unlikely that the roof of the Valley Temple remained accessible after the Persian Period, as no Greek, Roman or Coptic graffiti were found on it, which would certainly have been the case if it had been possible for those inveterate scribblers to get at it. We may safely conclude therefore that the roof of the Valley Temple was buried for at least two and a half millennia before Mariette cleared it in the nineteenth century. The most likely period for the additional limestone to have been added was in fact the New Kingdom period, since the mound of the Valley Temple was chosen as a location for many mudbrick structures of New Kingdom date, as Uvo Hölscher reported and described at length. These were all cleared away in the course of excavation, but several photos and drawings of them survive. On the basis of this evidence, I am inclined to believe that the roof was really buried for at least 3,000 years before its discovery by Mariette, and that from about the end of the New Kingdom it could no longer be seen and had been forgotten.

While it may not be so surprising for the roof of a buried temple to have been accessible in later times, it is certainly surprising for the bedrock floor of a buried temple to have been accessible! And yet this is what we found in the Sphinx Temple. Our sample ST-3 was taken from the join between the small granite blocks and the bedrock which may be seen on the website, near the northeastern corner of the Sphinx Temple. The date we obtained was shockingly recent: 890 BC plus or minus 300 years, or in others words falling within the range of 1190 BC–590 BC. That is the period between the end of the Nineteenth Dynasty of the New Kingdom and the reign of the third king of the Saitic or Twenty-Sixth Dynasty (the last native Egyptian dynasty before the Persian invasion). This extraordinary dating result poses some serious problems. We know conclusively that the Sphinx Temple was buried and unknown during the New Kingdom period and during the Greek and Roman periods. In the former period, two small temples were actually built partially on top of it. In the latter period, massive steps were built over it, descending to the Sphinx Pit. (Many drawings and photographs showing all of this are to be found in my book *The Sphinx Mystery*.) It is inconceivable that the Sphinx Temple could have been cleared, or even partially cleared to any meaningful degree, during the period 1190 BC– 590 BC. How, then, does one explain the bizarre dating result which we obtained?

I believe there is only one possible answer to this question. It must have been an intruded shaft grave, dug down into what was thought to be solid earth but which turned out to be the remains of the Sphinx Temple near its eastern end. When they reached the bedrock they stopped. As it happened, they were very near the remnants of an actual limestone wall rising vertically beside the shaft. In order to form a strong and impressive surrounding for the lower level of the shaft, they used the bedrock for its base and stacked small recycled granite blocks to make a low wall as a kind of low burial-chamber lining at the bottom of the shaft. They must have encountered the gigantic base block of the limestone wall while they were doing this, because they stacked the small granite blocks up against it, misleading later archaeologists into concluding from this slim evidence that the entire temple had once been clad by granite in its interior.

We now come to the dating results of the original constructions of the two adjoining temples. Our many attempts to take samples from the 'Egyptian alabaster' of the Valley Temple met with failure, and Ioannis has concluded that he cannot get dates from that stone because it is translucent. As he puts it, this stone 'does not follow the luminescence dating criteria'. Two other samples that we took from the Valley Temple turned out upon analysis to be pure gypsum, and thus were plaster rather than stone. In the Valley Temple we were severely constrained, because we could not take any samples from areas visible to tourists.

In Plate 42 may be seen the upper magazine of the Valley Temple, from which we obtained a granite sample which gave us our only original date for that temple. The result was 2400 BC plus or minus 300 years, or the range of 2700 BC–2100 BC. Since the building cannot possibly have been built after the time of Chephren, as it was full of his statues, and the conventional date for Chephren today is slightly prior to 2550 BC, we may consider the true result as being necessarily between 2700 BC and 2550 BC, a span of only 150 years. The evidence that this building was actually constructed by and for Chephren is thus very strong, but the dating result is also compatible with the reign of Chephren having been a bit earlier than is normally assumed. (See other chapters for further discussion of the possibility that all Old Kingdom dates, at least prior to the Fifth Dynasty, should be somewhat earlier than is conventionally accepted today.)

The dating results for the Sphinx Temple are not so straightforward, however. We got three results in addition to the one later date already mentioned. Sample ST-2, which was limestone, gave a result of 2690 BC plus or minus 290 years, giving a range of 2980 BC–2400 BC. Sample ST-4 gave a result of 2300 BC plus or minus 580 years, giving a range of 2850 BC–1820 BC. And sample ST-5 gave a result of 2520 BC plus or minus 470 years, giving a range of 2990 BC–2050 BC.

If we assume all of these stones to be original with the construction of the temple, then it means that the temple was built between 2850 BC (the lowest of the high results) and 2400 BC (the highest of the low results), a span of 450 years.

Since the structure was beyond the construction capabilities of the Fifth Dynasty, we may cut this down to 350 years and consider its period of possible construction as between 2850 BC and 2500 BC.

This indicates that on the basis of the dating results, the Sphinx Temple may well have been earlier than the Valley Temple, as the range of dates all extend earlier than for the Valley Temple. On the other hand, it could also have been built by Chephren, whose conventional date of reign falls within the range as well (and so also does his reign if the chronology is revised backwards).

People will draw from these dating results the conclusions that accord with their pre-existing views. Anyone who wants to insist that both temples were built by and for Chephren is free to do so. However, I do not go along with that view myself. I believe that the Sphinx Temple is earlier than Chephren's time for several reasons. First, it appears to have been built before the use of cramps commenced in Chephren's reign, as mentioned earlier. Second, no trace of a Chephren statue was ever found there, nor of any other royal statue for that matter. Third, the evidence is strong that it had a purpose entirely different from that of a funerary memorial to a king, and was probably the temple of a god or gods (but not 'Harmachis'!). If used for pharaonic funeral rituals, it would likely have been used for those of more than one pharaoh, and hence have been a general royal funerary establishment, perhaps associated with the god Sokar (later Osiris). Fourth, the construction differences in general between the Sphinx Temple and the Valley Temple are so great that it is difficult to imagine the same architects and builders having been involved with both; if they had, the buildings would surely have a greater similarity.

Was the Sphinx Temple therefore built by the earlier pharaoh Cheops? Or by someone earlier still, such as Sneferu, the father of Cheops? Any construction date as early as 2850 BC is acceptable according to our dating results. And if one sees the large granite block resting in the pillar depression, from which we obtained sample ST-4, as not being original with the primary construction but instead a later insertion to the hole during a period of use (which is my personal view based upon direct observation), then any date as far back as 2980 BC is acceptable from our dating results. And, as may be seen from the chapter on the Osiris Shaft, and the early dates we obtained from the two stone sarcophagi that we dated there, early dates of that range are now emerging at Giza.

Perhaps the asking of questions at Giza has only just begun. My own view is that the Valley Temple was indeed built – or at the very least extensively converted by Chephren – at a time chronologically earlier than is conventionally allotted to him at present (approximately 150 years earlier), which accords with our result mentioned in Chapter Five that Khasekhemui's tomb is 173 years earlier than is conventionally thought). I also suspect that the structure might have been on the site of an earlier temple, or otherwise that much of the structure is older than the 'loculi', or magazines, where we got our one reliable 'original' date. For, after all, what we have dated are the magazines, not the whole temple. Although the temple could not have been built later than the magazines, the magazines could certainly have been inserted into an earlier temple as part of a process of conversion by Chephren, if he took an older structure and made it into a temple for himself. The fact that it became a temple to the memory of Chephren is indisputable, but it need not necessarily have been so originally. Whereas a pyramid date clearly dates a whole pyramid if it be integral to the structure, and a sarcophagus date obviously dates the whole sarcophagus, the situation is not so simple with temples, as they can be renovated, and in many cases, they can be rebuilt upon older foundations (as has happened at Edfu, for instance). Only a much better knowledge of the Valley Temple, and especially its foundations and crypts, can tell us whether the existing Valley Temple is on the site of an earlier structure.

Now that we have learned that it is impossible to date Egyptian alabaster – or travertine as it is called mineralogically – due to its translucence, we really need to go back and take some more granite samples in order to extend the dating of other parts of the structure than the magazines. However, the ban on taking dating samples out of Egypt to foreign laboratories, imposed by Zahi Hawass, renders this impossible at the present time, as there is no laboratory in Egypt able to do this highly specialised work; indeed, as the technology is so advanced, I do not see Egypt ever being able to support its own establishment. This means that unless the unwise policy of banning the taking of tiny dating samples out of the country is changed, no optical thermoluminescence dating can ever be done in Egypt again. And frankly, very little dating of any kind will be done, as the idea that Egyptian laboratories alone could date all wood and pottery samples from excavations is equally ridiculous. The banning of the taking of dating samples out of Egypt can have only one result: the end of dating. That might suit some people. And, in any case, people with special contacts can always take dating samples out, if private dating not for publication is really the aim. In that way, dating sample control amounts to a form of information control.

In conclusion, I would say that there is every reason to believe that the Sphinx Temple was built considerably before the Valley Temple (at least the Valley Temple in its 'Chephren form', if there were an earlier form), and that it probably dates to an era closer to that of the pyramids and the Osiris Shaft. And that was well before Cheops and Chephren lived. If the small piece of granite that I mentioned earlier in connection with the Sphinx Temple is not original, but was inserted some time after construction, which is highly possible, then the Sphinx Temple is probably even earlier. But perhaps most crucial of all is the evidence I gave in Chapter Four about the possible existence of a tomb or subterranean chamber complex beneath the entire structure of the Sphinx Temple. Since there is every reason to suspect that the tombs of Cheops and Chephren are further up the hill beneath the sites of their respective funerary temples, any tomb beneath the Sphinx Temple would of necessity have to be earlier than those kings. Since there is no evidence whatever connecting earlier Fourth Dynasty kings with Giza (Sneferu's associations were with Dashur), the Sphinx Temple would appear to be from an earlier epoch, and perhaps associated with the only other royal name found by excavators at the Valley Temple: King Send, whoever he was and whenever he really lived.

Thus we are led back into the mists of antiquity indeed, and become lost in what I have called in an earlier chapter the 'chronological chaos' of the Third Dynasty and of all that preceded it. So the dating results from the Sphinx Temple are thus part of the intriguing mystery of what was really going on at Giza before Cheops. Although I have written exhaustively about this in *The Sphinx Mystery* from the point of view of the Sphinx itself, we now have the evidence from Setepet, the Sphinx Temple, and thus from the entire Sphinx precinct, to brood upon as we try to unravel these strange hints about the origins of high civilisation in Egypt. The Sphinx Temple date, the pyramid date, and the second level Osiris Shaft date all seem to come together to suggest that there is more in heaven, earth, and Giza than is dreamt of in our philosophy.

Figure 60. Atlas, holding the night sky on his shoulders. From a French copper engraving of 1749 by Bernard Picart. (*Collection of Robert Temple*)

CHAPTER EIGHT

Stonehenge in Africa

When seeking a people who could possibly have provided the mathematical, astronomical and geometrical knowledge embodied in the
Great Pyramid and plateau of Giza, and who might have supplied it to
a predynastic northern Egyptian people, there is only one certain place
to turn. I am referring to that strange civilisation of the Atlantic coast,
and the people whom we call the 'megalith builders'. It is the megalithic Atlantic coastal settlements, stretching from Northern Africa to
Scandinavia, which I believe constituted the true 'Atlantis'. In other
words, I do not believe that any lost island in the Atlantic Ocean ever
existed. I believe that 'Atlantis' was a myth created on purpose by the
coastal dwellers of the eastern Atlantic Ocean for consumption by the
people of the Mediterranean, as a kind of disinformation campaign.
Later, when the megalith builders were succeeded by the Sidonians,
Tyrians, Phoenicians, etc., and later still by the Carthaginians (who originated as a Phoenician colony, Carthage having been founded about 800
BC by Phoenicians from Tyre), this myth was perpetuated and spread
amongst all other peoples who might pose a threat to the Atlantic trade.
By the time of the Phoenicians, in other words from about 1550 BC,
the Atlantic trade was to a large extent a tin trade, bringing tin into the
Mediterranean for the production of bronze, which could not be made
without it, since bronze is an alloy of copper and tin and is hence an
artificial metal, not a natural one.

One special early centre for this bronze manufacture was the island
of Cyprus, which was even mentioned as a metal-working centre by

Homer in the *Iliad* (II, 16–23). Cyprus had the copper mines, and the ships that came from the Atlantic brought the tin mined in Cornwall; these were combined, and bronze was thus produced. This was a very profitable commercial monopoly of what was, frankly, a necessary war material. At the time of the megalith builders, bronze was not yet being produced, and in the Egypt of the Old Kingdom, most metal tools were of copper, though copper alloyed with only 2 per cent of arsenic made a metal stronger than bronze, and strong arsenical copper is known from the First Dynasty. Petrie speculates that the arsenic in the First Dynasty alloy specimens probably came naturally from arsenical copper ore,[1] although the Egyptians were always very familiar with both realgar and orpiment, two minerals that yield arsenic. They also used bismuth as a hardening agent, up to 1 per cent, in the First Dynasty, which was superior for cutting purposes. Few people realise that the copper implements of the most ancient Egyptians, which are often referred to in a derogatory manner as hopelessly weak and ineffectual, were often stronger than both bronze and iron. As Petrie mentions, in reviewing a book by G. F. Zimmer: 'In reality, no metal was used to cut hard stones, but soft copper served as a bed for cutting points of emery. Actually, copper can be alloyed and hardened so as to be superior to iron, and only equalled by steel.'[2]

As for bronze itself, it makes its first appearance in the Egyptian archaeological record during the Third Dynasty, although it remained rare for many centuries thereafter. As Petrie said: 'The earliest piece of pure bronze known is the rod found in the foundations of a mastaba of the IIIrd dynasty at Meydum, which contained 9.1 per cent tin and 0.5 per cent arsenic (second analysis of unaltered core by Dr Gladstone).'[3] No one knows where the tin used in this rod came from.

From the Old Kingdom period, a small number of items made from iron began to appear. A clearly dated mass of rust from a wedge of iron was excavated at floor level in the early temple at Abydos, and dated to the Sixth Dynasty (the conventional date for which is 2345 BC–2183 BC). It was for a long time imagined that these items must have been made of beaten meteoritic iron, which was plentifully and easily discovered as dark objects lying on the light sand, collected, revered as sacred, and brought in to the court. Special ceremonial tools used for 'opening the mouth' of the deceased in funeral ceremonies were sometimes thought to be made of this iron which fell from the sky. I have written a great deal about meteoritic iron in ancient Egypt in an earlier book, *The Crystal Sun*, so I will not repeat all of that information here.

However, it now seems that much of the iron used by the Old Kingdom Egyptians was not meteoritic at all (however valued and precious meteoritic iron may have been for religious purposes, representing as it did 'pieces of the iron floor of the polar heaven' which had broken off and fallen to earth), since a metallurgist has explained and Petrie has insisted, and evidence suggests, that it could not have been turned into most of the metal objects that have survived.[4] Some iron was obtained as a by-product of the quarrying of limestone, since veins of iron occasionally run through it, as I saw for myself in the bottom level of the Osiris Shaft, described in Chapter Two, where thin veins of iron are prominently visible in the bedrock walls of the chamber. Some iron ore was obtained in antiquity up a side valley near Aswan, and smelted there, but the date of this has apparently not been ascertained and I do not believe this particular matter has received any further attention since its publication in 1917.[5]

But for the main source of iron, we now know that iron was mined in the northern Sinai, where it was extracted from the ore and turned into metal objects. Large amounts of pig iron slag are still found there in mounds in the archaeological remains. Two iron pins are known to exist in walls of the 'well shaft' of the Great Pyramid, though whether they are contemporary or were added later is unknown. The locations of these two pins are marked in the vertical section diagram of the Great Pyramid in *Great Pyramid Passages* by J. and M. Edgar. I have never had permission to go down the well shaft of the pyramid, which requires a rope and someone's skilled assistance. There cannot be many people alive today who have ever done this. So I have never seen these iron pins myself. The iron object found inside one of the Great Pyramid's 'air shafts' may be seen in a photo on this book's website. It is supposed to be preserved in storage at the British Museum, but that does not necessarily mean that anyone there really knows where it is. The only museum basement storeroom I have ever been in where everything was organised to perfection was in Stockholm, and that is because the Swedes are more orderly than God. I have been 'down under' in the British Museum, and one can say things there are 'medium' to 'medium rare', but not 'well done'. Even in Stockholm, I have to confess, I found a lost tray of objects which the curators had misplaced. (Some red faces there.) Well, I am a nuisance, I know that. That is why people do not like to let me into their cellars. As for their libraries! I was once left alone for twenty minutes in the White House Library in Washington, and during that time I did a great deal of re-arranging of the books, for instance putting Volume One and Volume Two of *Agee on Film* together instead of three shelves apart, turning books right side up which some idiot had put onto the shelves upside down, generally trying to get a bit of order in the chaos. A pity they didn't let me do the same with their foreign policy! This was during the Jimmy Carter period.

It must be kept in mind that the brief account of the Phoenician Atlantic tin trade that follows is of interest for the light it sheds on the earlier sailing routes of the megalith builders, and their Atlantic Empire. The Phoenicians were opportunists, and they rediscovered much, though not all, of their predecessors' lost world of 'Atlantis', the Empire of the Coasts. The Phoenicians turned it to profit, and their motives were commercial. However, by knowing a bit about them, we can retrace the routes and coastal civilisation of the mysterious megalith builders who preceded them. It is even possible that the Phoenicians were somehow related to or partially descended from the earlier megalith builders, and that the Phoenicians were not exclusively a 'Semitic' people, but were an admixture of Middle Eastern 'Semites' with descendants of the megalith builders, who are suspected of having been what linguists sometimes call 'Proto-Iberians', and those undefined peoples sometimes referred to by Egyptologists as 'Libyans' (whatever and whoever 'Libyans' were, for 'Libyan' is only a vague geographical term).

The myth of Atlantis created an important diversion for any Mediterraneans not in the 'club' who might somehow force their way through the naval blockades of the Straits of Gibraltar and try to discover the real trade routes. By diverting attention towards a mythical island that lay straight ahead, the true 'Atlanteans' who hugged the coasts to right and to left were getting rid of curious enquirers by steering them straight out to sea, heading fruitlessly for the middle of the ocean, where with any luck they would be lost at sea in pursuit of an illusion. Of course, some would find Madeira, some might even find the Canaries, but with any luck they would not scour the Atlantic coasts of North Africa and Europe.

It has long been recognised that tall tales were spread in ancient times to deter the curious from exploring too closely even the eastern portions of 'Libya', the name given by the Greeks to the whole of North Africa westwards of Egypt. As one example taken from many, the Rev. Watkins remarks in his book, *Gleanings from the Natural History of the Ancients*, when discussing the Libyan marvels recounted by Herodotus: 'Most probably many of these reports were industriously spread abroad by the Carthaginians to prevent troublesome neighbours from interfering with their commerce . . .'[6]

The ancient geographer Strabo (64 BC–25 AD) also wrote:

'As they [the British] have mines of tin and lead, they give these metals and the hides from their cattle to the sea-traders in exchange for pottery, salt and copper [mistranslation: should be 'bronze'] utensils. Now in former times it was the Phoenicians alone who carried on this commerce (that is, from Gades [Cadiz]), for they kept the voyage hidden from every one else. And when once the Romans were closely following a certain ship-captain in order that they too might learn the markets in question, out of jealousy the ship-captain purposely drove his ship out of its course into shoal water; and after he had lured the followers into the same ruin, he himself escaped by a piece of wreckage and received from the State the value of the cargo he had lost. Still, by trying many times, the Romans learned all about the voyage.'[7]

The translator of the above passage missed the whole point, which was that in exchange for supplying the tin to make the bronze, bronze products made with their own tin were then brought back to the British suppliers as repayment for that tin. Not having copper, they could not make their own bronze at home. An earlier translator of this same passage, realising that the Greek word *chalkos* can mean both 'copper' and 'bronze' depending on the context, got it right and said: 'Of the metals they have tin and lead; which with skins they barter with the merchants for earthenware, salt, and brazen vessels.'[8] The Britons themselves are described by Strabo as wearing tunics reaching down to their feet, covered in long belted black cloaks, and carrying canes or staffs. Many of them were nomadic and lived off their herds of livestock. The Phoenicians seemed to be scared of them, as Strabo says they resembled the goddesses of vengeance who are shown in Greek tragedies, so that they must have glowered at their visitors and looked doom-laden and ominous in their long black cloaks. (An engraving of an 'ancient Briton' done in 1676 to depict what Strabo describes may be found on the website).

In order to protect the secrets of their valuable trade routes and their livelihoods, all the successive peoples specialising in the profitable monopoly of Atlantic trade throughout ancient times spread rumours of monstrous beasts, dangerous tribes, hazardous currents, lost islands and so forth, to confuse and baffle anyone who might want to try to poke his nose into their business. I am equally convinced that they kept close guard on the Straits of Gibraltar, and attacked and burnt any ships which tried to get through, but even if a ship survived the attacks and got out into the Atlantic, it would most likely make the mistake of sailing straight out to sea, towards 'Atlantis', and never find even so much as the Phoenician town of Gades (Cadiz being its modern name, Gadir being its Punic name used by the Phoenicians), much less any other settlement of importance or trade route of value.

The centre of the Atlantic was, frankly, an excellent place to dump one's commercial rivals. This remained the case until Roman times, when the Romans broke through all obstacles and discovered many of the Atlantic routes and settlements, though not all. Such 'Atlantic' ports as Lixus on the Atlantic coast of Morocco (forty miles south of the Pillars of Hercules) and Cadiz on the Atlantic coast of Spain soon became Roman cities of great importance, and of course Britain became Roman Britain.

The megalith builders were the earliest high civilisation of the Atlantic coasts. They seem to have been more or less contemporaneous with the time when we now know that the Giza pyramids must have been built, prior to the classic period of Old Kingdom Egypt. And as they are the only civilisation of which we have any knowledge who were truly advanced in mathematics, geometry and astronomy at that time, it makes sense to postulate a contact between them and some indigenous peoples of the

Egyptian Delta, which led to the construction of the Giza pyramids. Another factor that enters here is our lack of knowledge of the 'Libyans' of that time. For, after reading what follows, it will not seem at all strange for us to realise that 'Libyans', especially the Western ones, were to some extent a branch of the megalith builders' civilisation. It seems inescapable to conclude that the megalith builders were a people whom archaeologists and linguistic historians vaguely refer to as 'Proto-Iberians', and that the Basques of the Pyrenees, the Guanches of the Canary Islands and the Berbers of North Africa are their blood relatives or descendants. The Basque language is possibly the closest-surviving language to that which must have been spoken by the megalith builders. But we will come back to these subjects. First, let us see just how close the megalithic rings really came to ancient Egypt. This in itself is a fascinating story, which is largely unknown, and which my wife Olivia and I have personally explored and researched. This story will help us understand where the 'science of the pyramids' might have come from.

One of the most important megalithic sites in the world has until now been largely unknown to archaeologists. Hidden away in an obscure corner of Morocco where no one ever goes, it has evaded their attention. When it was built thousands of years ago, it was approachable by sea, but now that approach is silted up, and the site must be visited on foot, being miles from the nearest road.

The site is called Mezorah (also spelled M'Zorah), which according to one interpretation means 'Holy Place' in Arabic, though later I will give what I believe to be the true meaning of the name. It is the largest certain megalithic ellipse in the world. It once consisted of 175 stones, of which 168 still stand. Mezorah is far larger than Stonehenge. It appears to have been constructed by the same culture as the one that built the British stone rings. For it has been laid out on a plan of a Pythagorean triangle, which is identical to the one used in laying out Britain's monuments of Woodhenge and Daviot, near Clava in Scotland, as well as some others.

In the centre of the huge ring of stones at Mezorah, a gigantic tumulus was erected, apparently by a much later culture. This tumulus was already ancient when it was excavated by the Romans in the first century BC, as described later. At that time, a skeleton was found within it.

WALL OF LIXUS.

Figure 61. This drawing showing a portion of a surviving pre-Roman wall at Lixus on the Atlantic coast of Morocco is from p. 123 of George Rawlinson, *A History of Phoenicia*, London, 1889. Rawlinson assumed this wall, which he personally inspected, to be at least Phoenician, though it could date from an earlier period, and is certainly from long before the Roman occupation of Lixus. He described it as follows: 'The blocks are squared, carefully dressed, and arranged in horizontal courses, without any cement. Some of them are as much as eleven feet long by six feet or somewhat more in height. The wall was flanked at the corner by square towers, and formed a sort of irregular hexagon, above a mile in circumference. A large building within the walls seems to have been a temple; and in it was found one of those remarkable conical stones which are known to have been employed in the Phoenician worship. The estuary of the river formed a tolerably safe harbour for the Phoenician ships, and the valley down which the river flows gave a ready access into the interior.' It is certainly possible that all or part of this wall of more than a mile in length, perhaps this very portion, dates from the pre-Phoenician occupation of Lixus. Megalithic remains of a much earlier era must have been re-cycled by the Phoenicians at Lixus subsequent to 1550 BC, if only because the utility of the stones was obvious. Until a much more careful archaeological study of the pre-Roman remains at Lixus is undertaken, it is impossible to differentiate what is wholly Phoenician from what is earlier, or what is a combination of the two, with earlier stones being recycled or built upon as foundations by Phoenician structures. Certainly these large blocks, which are presumed to be of limestone (Rawlinson does not identify the stone), are equivalent in size and shaping to many Old Kingdom Egyptian limestone blocks. Rawlinson's comments about the harbour and the inland access up river are highly relevant to what we now know about the megalithic ring at Mezorah, the existence of which was unknown to Rawlinson.

The next excavation at the tumulus occurred about 1,900 years later, in 1935–36, when a Spanish archaeologist named César Luis de Montalban cut across the mound in two huge intersecting trenches in the shape of a cross. He is said to have found three cist burials. Don César Luis de Montalbán y de Mazas was a very distinguished Spanish archaeologist, who was President of the Comisión de Monumentos (also known as the State Junta de Monumentos) of Morocco, when it was a Spanish Protectorate named Spanish Morocco. I have collected one book of his concerning his excavations of subterranean structures at the Moroccan city of Tétouan (Sp. Tetuán), which was published in 1929, a few years before he went to Mezorah.[9] He also excavated at the ancient city of Lixus on the coast near Mezorah which, although it is generally thought of as a Roman site, was founded long before that era. Montalbán excavated a remarkable ancient wall there which was constructed in the cyclopean manner, of huge blocks of stone, some of which are forty feet long and weigh many tons. The stones were laid horizontally with straight joins. He gave a photo of this wall to his friend Ellen M. Whishaw, with his permission to reproduce it, and it appears in her book *Atlantis in Andalucía* (1929),[10] which I will discuss a little later.

Before Montalbán could publish his discoveries at Mezorah, he was arrested at the site itself just as he was completing his excavations, in connection with some political matter related to the Spanish Civil War. An elderly man, he never returned, and indeed his fate is apparently unknown. I have heard it suggested that he died in jail or was executed. Nothing was ever published about his work at Mezorah, and it is possible that his notes might have been confiscated at the time of his arrest. An album of his survives in Morocco, and I once spoke to someone who had seen it, but I have not been able to locate it. During the 1980s, two preliminary reports about Mezorah, which Montalban had drafted before his arrest but had not published, were discovered in Tangier. These revealed that he had found a tomb with a skeleton to the west of the main ring itself, and he described flints which were found within the main tumulus. The whole area of Mezorah is so littered with flints that one can stuff one's pockets with them in a quarter of an hour. The site appears to have been an important Stone Age settlement.

The main ring at Mezorah was fully surveyed in the 1970s by the American surveyor and oceanographer James Watt Mavor, Junior, of the Woods Hole Oceanographic Institute in Massachusetts, USA, who found it to be a perfect ellipse of the following dimensions:

> Major axis: 59.29 metres
> Minor axis: 56.18 metres
> Focal distance: 18.95 metres
> Perimeter: 181.45 metres

The ellipse is constructed on the Pythagorean right triangle, having the ratio of 37 to 35 to 12, which Professor Alexander Thom found to be the second most commonly used at British megalithic sites. The exact figures for the ratio of the principal dimensions at Mezorah are 37 to 35.07 to 11.83.

If a 'megalithic yard' of 0.836 metres (discovered in Britain by Thom) were the unit of measure for the construction of the ring of Mezorah, then the major axis and the perimeter of the ring take on values nearly integral. According to Alexander Thom, achieving such integral measures of the perimeters of their rings was a fundamental aim of the megalithic ring-builders. He believes that these ancient people had for some reason a horror of irrational numbers such as *pi*, and that they made elaborate efforts to construct circles and ellipses that avoided them. They did this by having integral numbers of 'megalithic yards' (an ancient measure which Thom demonstrated must have been used in their construction) in both the axes of the rings, and in their perimeters. This could only be done by using a few selected Pythagorean triangles to give the ratios of the main ring dimensions. The fact that Mezorah is based on one such triangle is virtually irresistible evidence that the ring was constructed by the same people who constructed the British and French stone rings.

Professor Thom (1894–1985) was Professor of Engineering at Oxford, and after his retirement from teaching, he devoted his time for many years to surveying the megalithic remains of Britain and Britanny. He was a lean Scot with a wonderful dry sense of humour. I knew him slightly in the 1970s and 1980s. On the subject of megaliths, he wrote two books as sole author (1967 and 1971) and one jointly with his son Archie (1978), in addition to numerous articles.[11]

In line with this discussion of megalithic rings, it is worth noting that the early English historian Geoffrey of Monmouth (who lived c. 1100–c. 1155) puts the following words into the mouth of Merlin:

'They are mystical stones, and of a medicinal virtue. The giants of old brought them from the farthest coasts of Africa, and placed them in Ireland, while they inhabited that country.'[12]

He was speaking of a stone ring called 'The Dance of the Giants', at Killare, which should be transported to England 'to be set up round this plot in a circle'. Much mockery has been cast upon Geoffrey of Monmouth for his bizarre fables about the earliest British history. Transporting stones from Africa was a perfect example, it has been said, of just how silly Geoffrey of Monmouth's information was. But if we consider that the tale was garbled, then suddenly we can see that Geoffrey might have preserved some invaluable information after all. Probably the true tale was meant to be not that physical stones themselves were brought from Africa to Ireland and Britain, but *the tradition of standing stones, the techniques for erecting them, and the science of their design.*

If we interpret the tale in that way, we can see that Geoffrey might have preserved an authentic British folk memory of the existence of megalithic rings far away from Britain and Ireland to the south, even in Africa, and that the megalith builders had come from North Africa themselves. After all, Geoffrey lived about 850 years ago, and he might well have come across genuine folk memories to this effect, which are extinct today. Although such folk memories would have had to be about 3,500 years old, I have proved conclusively in my book *The Sphinx Mystery* (Chapter Three, 'An Amazing Survival', is entirely devoted to this subject) that highly specific folk memories attached to an archaeological monument survived in Egypt for 3,500 years, so we know it is possible for such things to happen.

If Mezorah represents the southerly extent of the culture responsible for the construction of the British stone rings, then we are faced with admitting the existence of a seafaring people whose culture ranged more than 2,000 miles from Sweden to the Atlantic northwest coast of Morocco. Such a prospect was no surprise to the Thom family. On one

Waterstones

128 Princes Street
EDINBURGH EH2 4AD
TEL 0843 290 8313

**

201 ISH-1   2168 0394 001

EGYPTIAN DAWN   QTY 1   7.99
  9780099414681
              TOTAL GBP   7.99
CASH   10.00
            CHANGE   2.01

A WATERSTONE'S CARD WOULD HAVE
EARNED YOU   23 POINTS TODAY
   ON ITEMS WORTH   £7.99
Apply now at thewaterstonescard.com

VAT No GB 108 2770 24

                30 05 13   16 12

occasion, Professor Alexander Thom's son, Dr Archibald Thom, told me that he and his father had been convinced for years that the builders of the rings had a 'big merchant navy which traded up and down the west coast of Europe'. Alexander Thom studied the megalithic remains of the Shetland Islands very closely. But his son carried the work even further north, and he surveyed 27 megalithic rings in Sweden, the results being published in *The Archaeological Journal*, London, Number 140 for 1984. The two Thoms, in their joint book, *Megalithic Remains in Britain and Brittany* (1978), stated that the British ring-builders must have enjoyed 'free communication in reasonably large vessels from Shetland to Scandinavia in Megalithic times'. They were certain of this because C. S. T. Calder found, associated with a Shetland megalithic monument, the remains of spruce and pine. But there has never been any pine in Shetland, and spruce was only introduced in 1548. This wood must therefore have been brought from Scandinavia.

Evidence that the ring-builders were a maritime power has thus been around for some time, in addition to which there is of course the famous 'Mycenaean dagger' design carved into stones at Stonehenge in antiquity, which has been taken by some to indicate a link with the great maritime power of the Minoans of Crete. A friend of the Thoms sought unsuccessfully to obtain permission during the Soviet era to survey a huge megalithic ring said to be in Armenia at the far end of the Black Sea. Apparently, he was thinking of the stone rings found at the site known as Zoraz Kar (*kara* in Armenian means 'stone', but it is probably a loan-word from an earlier lost language, as *kar* seems to have survived also in the name of the world's largest megalithic complex, Carnac in Britanny), 250 km southeast of the city of Yerevan and 3 km north/northeast of Sisian in the Syunik Region. Alternative spellings of the name of this site are Zorahar, Zorats Karer, Zorakarer, and Zorats Qarer, and references to it are sometimes under these spellings. Yet other names for the site are Karahunj and Angelakoth. It has come to be known as the 'Armenian Stonehenge' today, as the tourist industry has developed after the collapse of the Soviet Empire and the gaining of freedom by Armenia, which is once again an independent country.

This amazing megalithic complex consists of hundreds of basalt megaliths which are still standing. These megaliths might possibly have some connection with the civilisation that erected Mezorah, or they may be entirely unconnected. I don't believe the Armenian stones have been surveyed yet, so that would be a necessary first step to studying them properly. Armenian archaeology is hardly in the mainstream; few people outside Armenia can read the articles published in Armenian, and this subject is still wrapped in mystery as far as we in the English-speaking world are concerned.

I remain convinced intuitively that Mezorah of Morocco and Zorakar of Armenia must be linked. After all, they both include the name Zora. The Armenian one means 'Zorah-stone' or 'Zorah-of-the-stones'. *Zorah* is the Arabic word for 'dawn' or 'sunrise', presumably a loan-word from a more ancient language. Assuming that *zora* is really a proto-Iberic word meaning 'dawn' or 'sunrise' which has been borrowed in both Armenian (as *zoraz* or *zorats*) and Arabic (as *zora* or *zorah*, presumably through the medium of Berber), then its appropriateness for the megalithic rings is obvious. For, as we see later on from the survey of the site, the rings were used for observations at sunrise on the solstices and equinoxes, using stones marking those points on the horizon. The meaning of the Armenian ring would therefore literally be 'sunrise stone'. As for the Arabic Mezorah or M'zorah, I am no Arabic scholar but the M' is a prefix, which in some Semitic languages is an abbreviation of 'from', and one could construe the true meaning of M'zorah as being 'from sunrise', or more probably by extrapolation we could infer the correct meaning to be 'the place of sunrise'.

A myth about Mezorah has been preserved into modern times. It was recorded by Sir Arthur de Capell Brooke, who visited the site in 1830 under the protection of a troop of English cavalry from Tangier, and was the first modern European to 'discover' Mezorah. According to this myth, during the Great Flood, the dove from Noah's Ark landed on top of one tall menhir at Mezorah, which is still standing. This menhir is known as el Uted ('the pointer' or 'the stack'), which is five and a half metres high and is designated as Stone 130 in Mavor's survey. (It may be seen in Plates 55 and 56.) Two other menhirs (Stones 131 and 132) stood beside it but have now fallen, Stone 131 being 4.2 metres in height and Stone 132 being partly buried today.

The fact that Mezorah is known at all today is largely due to the efforts of two men whom I knew (both now dead), who were good friends of each other. Both were longstanding residents of Tangier. One was Michael Scott, a very old and intimate friend of Olivia and mine from the mid-1960s. As a boy, Michael was taken by his parents (who were British but Tangier residents) to observe Montalbán at work at Mezorah, and it made an enormous impression on him. The second, Gordon Browne, was someone I only met through Michael in Morocco, not someone I had known previously. Both men spoke fluent Arabic and had a thoroughly intimate knowledge not only of Arab culture but of the Berber tribes as well. They were also both well versed in the most obscure details of Moroccan topography, and knew the country as well as any native. In fact, Michael was a practising Sufi who actually attended a Tangier mosque in Arab dress and frequented small Sufi gatherings, and he took us to one in Tetuan to meet a Sufi master who was his close friend there. In Morocco, as in many Muslim countries, there are secret networks of Sufi mystics who keep themselves as invisible as possible to avoid trouble from the fundamentalist fanatics who like to persecute them. Michael was extremely learned in Sufi history, much of which derived from Spain. In Spain during the Middle Ages, the Muslim mystics and the Jewish mystics were very friendly with each other, and the Sufis and the Kabbalists exchanged ideas and influenced one another profoundly, a fact which is suppressed today because it is politically inconvenient to admit that it ever happened. Nowadays there are so many people who have vested interests in provoking conflicts between the Muslims and the Jews that all knowledge that Jews and Muslims ever had friendly relations with one another is considered an embarrassment. I first learned about this at the age of 18 when I studied Islamic History at university under Professor S. D. Goitein, author of *Jews and Arabs: Their Contacts through the Ages*. Dr Goitein was very outspoken on this subject, and we often discussed the issue together. Goitein was an Israeli scholar teaching in America, who was pro-Arab in his sentiments. He was convinced that the Israelis and the Arabs could and should get on together perfectly, if troublemakers would only leave them alone and stop stirring up hatreds. Alas, the real world is not made for such scholars, and the notion that troublemakers will ever cease their activities of this kind is unlikely to be realized. As we all know, this problem gets worse with every passing year, not better.

Michael Scott took Olivia and me to Mezorah in 1983. He and Gordon Browne had already introduced James Mavor to the site in 1972, which led to the survey I mentioned earlier. Mavor is an American ocean-ographer and surveyor. He returned to Mezorah several times and surveyed the main megalithic ring thoroughly. In 1976, he published his findings in English in an Austrian academic periodical, and has given me permission to reproduce his plans of the main ring. Without Mavor's laborious work, no sensible discussion of this subject would be possible. Mavor signed the offprint for me of his article, entitled 'The Riddle of Mzorah', which appeared in English in Austria, from the *Akademische Druck und Verlagsanstalt, Graz; Almogaren,* Volume VII, 1976, pp. 89–122. Mavor published the azimuths of all the stones of the ring, culminating with Stone 175 at azimuth zero. In the copy that Mavor gave me, he struck out the final sentence of paragraph three on page 97 as being erroneous. I record that detail here in case it is ever useful to someone who consults an uncorrected copy in a library.

It has always been extraordinarily difficult to find Mezorah, even if one had been there before. Maps are only of limited use. No road approaches the site nearer than several miles' distance. When we went there with Michael Scott, who had been there many times over the years, we nevertheless had to enlist the help of a local young man as a guide. However, although he lived in the immediate vicinity, he was not able to find Mezorah either. We had driven to within several miles of Mezorah in Michael's Volkswagen van and left it where the road dwin-dled away, continuing the trek on foot. We walked some miles out of the way and passed through a bog with the aid of a local horse, and enquiries of local farmers resulted in vague and unsatisfactory point-ings in general which more often than not turned out to be completely wrong, even in the opposite direction sometimes. Since rabies is endemic in Morocco, the main hazard of the journey is probably that scores of dogs assail one, snarling and barking. We were shown by Michael how they can mostly be driven away by stooping down as if to pick up a stone to hurl at them, but it is a hair-raising experience, and a stout stick is certainly advisable. (After all, rabid dogs would not be deterred by a stone anyway, and it is only the non-rabid dogs who are intimidated by the threat of having a stone thrown at them, as the locals all do every time they walk anywhere.)

The real or feigned ignorance about the whereabouts of Mezorah among the local inhabitants is utterly astonishing; it shows how rarely visited the site had been, and how little it is regarded. Within a mile of the site, one can still not find anyone to give sensible directions, even if someone local makes the enquiry himself of people he knows by name. It is difficult to believe that this ignorance is genuine. But whether real or not, it drastically contributes to the inaccessibility and continuing obscurity of Mezorah. Of course, with GPS devices, nowadays all that is necessary is to visit Mezorah once and take positional readings, and then one can find it again. Whether anyone has yet done this, I do not know. I have not been there since GPS devices became available. I have tried to find it on Google Earth, but the name is not given on the maps, and when searching the terrain visually, one gets the information that 'that zoom level' of satellite photography is not available for that area, so Mezorah (M'Zora) appears impossible to find by this means also. One would have to have access to a military satellite to find it.

If Mezorah has always been that impossible to find, how did its builders ever get there? For the answer to that question, we are indebted to Mavor's researches, aided by his experience as an oceanographer and his familiarity with estuaries and coastlines. Mavor was able to establish that Mezorah was originally approachable by boat. He says:

'Today it lies ten kilometres up a valley with but a meandering stream to connect it with the ocean.'

But this was not always so, for he continues:

'Stearns has reconstructed a sea level and climatic sequence in the Cape Ashakar region. The Neolithic period, 4000 BC to the beginning of our era, was a time of warmer climate than today and sea level two meters higher . . . all the river valleys of northern Morocco have thick alluvium including Wadi Garifa (Wad Ayacha) which leads to Mezorah. . . . In the banks of Wad Sebu in Morocco, Roman sherds have been found under nine meters deposition at Banassa. . . . Having, since ancient times, gradually filled with alluvium from the bordering hills and more distant Rif mountains, it is likely that Wad Achaya was navigable by ship almost to Mezorah at the date the monument was built and in use. The ancient settlement of Kouass, excavated by Ponisch, is at the mouth of the river. At Kouass, alongside the coast highway, is an ancient horizontal platform built up from the surrounding field with retaining walls. It is 47 meters square and one edge bears 265.8 degrees. Ponisch calls it a pre-Roman camp. Inland of the highway nearby, Ponisch excavated a Neolithic town, Fours. It is possible that the ancient settlement at Kouass had some relationship with the monuments at Mezorah. Perhaps an edifice upon the platform, which could be seen from Mezorah, signalled to sea voyagers the entrance to the estuary or river up which was to be found the holy place.'

The first recorded 'discovery' of Mezorah in historical times was by the Roman general, Quintus Sertorius, in the first century BC. During a campaign in northwestern Morocco, he and his army were marching from Lixus to Tangier, east of what is today the modern coast road (a route then impassable because of river mouths), when they came upon the site. It was described to them by the native inhabitants as the tomb of the giant Antaios (more often referred to as Antaeus, which is the Latin spelling), who had been killed at that spot by Hercules and lay buried there. The natives also said that Antaios's wife Tinge had given her name to the city Tinais, which was the Roman name for the city we now call Tangier. Sertorius was intrigued, and he excavated the great burial mound in the centre of the ring. Plutarch, in his *Life of Sertorius*, Chapter 9, tells us:

'Sertorius dug into the mound, as he did not believe what the barbarians said, so enormous was the size. But, finding the body there, sixty cubits in length, as they say, he was confounded, and, after making a sacrifice, he piled up the earth, and added to the repute and fame of the monument.'

The numerical information preserved by Plutarch is remarkably accurate, although its context has been garbled. It was not the skeleton itself, obviously, but the tumulus containing it, which had the dimensions of sixty cubits. An ancient cubit is equal to 45.72 centimetres, so that sixty cubits are equal to 27.43 metres. Mavor's measurements give the radius of the tumulus at Mezorah as 27.5 metres. Plutarch's numerical data are therefore accurate to within *seven centimetres*. This proves conclusively that Plutarch (first century AD) must have drawn from an account left by

Sertorius himself (first century BC), whose military and construction engineers obviously carried out the measurements of the tumulus for him.

This remarkable numerical evidence enables us to feel absolutely confident in regarding Mezorah as the site that was claimed in the first century BC to be the 'tomb of Antaios' discovered by Sertorius and his army.

Mavor independently concluded that Mezorah was the 'tomb of Antaios', but he did so on other grounds, as he never made the calculations that I have just given. It did not seem to have occurred to him.

There are many accounts in ancient writers of the 'tomb of Antaios' being near both Lixus and Tangier. Mezorah is between the two, and, indeed, there is nothing else which could conceivably have been the 'tomb'. Nor is there any other tumulus with these dimensions in all of Morocco. The identity of the site of Mezorah with the site encountered by Sertorius is an absolute certainty.

It is essential that we have established this fact, because by demonstrating the identity of Mezorah with the legendary tomb of Antaios, we are able to connect Mezorah with the enormous body of mythical lore related to both Antaios and Hercules. This gives us access to some textual information that we can pursue. These sources then give us the first reliable leads to genuinely ancient legends concerning this megalithic ring. We possess no such reliable legends of any real antiquity concerning any of the British or French rings, other than the passage in Diodorus Siculus, Book Two, relating to Stonehenge, which I have discussed at length in my book *The Crystal Sun*, pp. 172–185.

Mezorah is thus able to offer us wonderful clues as to the religion and culture of the megalithic people. This could revolutionise our knowledge of ancient British culture eventually, by providing us with a species of information hitherto totally lacking.

The first thing to note, then, is that the early Greek poet Pindar (518–438 BC) refers to the African site of the wrestling match between Antaios and Hercules as 'Poseidon's Shrine' (Fourth Isthmian Ode, III, 56 ff.). Poseidon (called Neptune in Latin) was the sea god, and we can receive this information about Mezorah with considerable satisfaction, for it accords with what we would expect, that a sacred centre of a maritime people would be consecrated to a god of the sea.

Atlas, who held the sky aloft in Greek mythology, was reputed to stand at the western edge of the world, and the name of the Atlantic Ocean comes from him. In myth, he is clearly envisaged as being in Morocco, near to Lixus. Indeed, Atlas was also placed originally at Mezorah, as other sources reveal, as shown in a moment. He was the father of the Hesperides maidens. Hercules, as one of his twelve labours, had to go and fetch the so-called 'golden apples of the Hesperides'. What were the golden apples, and who and where were the Hesperides maidens?

In the first century AD, Pliny (*Natural History*, Book Five, 1, 3), drawing on older authorities, tells us explicitly that the gardens of the Hesperides were near Lixus in Morocco, *at the site of the wrestling match between Antaios and Hercules*. Here was that famous garden at the western edge of the world where, Hesiod says (*Theogony*, 215) of the Hesperides that they 'tend the lovely golden apples and their trees', or, in another translation: 'the Hesperides who guard the rich, golden apples and the trees bearing fruit'.[13] Or in French: '*des belles pommes d'or et des arbres qui portent tel fruit.*'[14] The Greek word *mélon* has the basic meaning of 'apple', but it was also a general word for a round fruit, so that to the Greeks, a 'Persian apple' was what we call a peach, and a 'Kydonian apple' (used by Dioscorides) or 'golden apple' (used by Pliny) was what we call a quince.

The 'golden apples' of the Hesperides were thus not actually apples at all, but quinces. Pliny also informs us in his *Natural History* (Book Fifteen, 10) that the most golden form of quince was known in Greek as a *chrysomélon*, which literally means 'golden apple'. English translations of the Herculean myths have therefore been in error, for it was quinces rather than apples that Hercules sought in Morocco. But do quinces actually grow at Mezorah? Pliny recorded in the first century AD that 'of the famous grove in the story that bore the golden fruit nothing (remains) except some wild olives' (Book Five, 1, 3–4). But he was speaking of the immediate area of Lixus itself, being unaware of the precise location of Mezorah. However, I can resolve this problem very simply: there are indeed a number of very handsome, extremely tall quince trees growing wild in the immediate vicinity of Mezorah, and Olivia has even photographed one covered in blossom (see the website). Olivia and I have grown several types of quince over the years, and we know quince trees very well. The trees we saw were definitely quince trees, and they were taller than any we had ever seen before.

They were about thirty feet (ten metres) high. It is difficult to imagine these trees as being anything other than what botanists call 'garden escapes'. But in this case, it would appear that they are 'Garden of the Hesperides escapees'.

Due to their huge size, these trees may represent an otherwise lost variety of quince. We were there during the flowering season, so we have not seen their fruit. However, the fruit of these trees is likely to be of the large, deeply golden globular variety that one gets from 'species quince' trees. Although we have grown modern quince varieties as well, we always have a species quince growing also in our garden, and we prefer the large, magnificent fruit of the species quince to the modern quince varieties. In making quince jelly, however, they are drier and contain less juice for extraction, so you have to use more of them to make the same amount of jelly. But I must point out that we have never grown a 'species quince' tree of a height approaching those at Mezorah, nor have we ever seen a quince tree that high anywhere else in the world. The highest I have ever seen a very old quince tree grow in England has been between fifteen and twenty feet. When Olivia and I saw the magnificent grove of quince trees growing at Mezorah, I had not yet worked out the 'golden apples of the Hesperides' idea, because I had done no research prior to seeing the site. We were fascinated by the trees merely because we love and admire quince trees. If we had not been gardeners, and quince tree admirers, this information would never have been recorded, and the 'Hesperides Garden escapees' would have remained unknown.

Now we return to the astronomical issues. There is some interesting information about Atlas in the *History* of the first century BC author, Diodorus Siculus (Oldfather's translation):

'Atlas had worked out the science of astrology to a degree surpassing others and had ingeniously discovered the spherical nature of the stars, and for that reason was generally believed to be bearing the entire firmament upon his shoulders. Similarly, in the case of Hercules, when he had brought the Greeks the doctrine of the sphere, he gained great fame, as if he had taken over the burden of the firmament which Atlas had borne, since men intimated in this enigmatic way what had actually taken place.'[15]

In the earlier translation by G. Booth, published as long ago as 1700, we read of Atlas:

'They say that he was an excellent astrologer, and was the first that discovered the knowledge of the sphere; whence arose the common opinion, that he carried the world upon his shoulders; noting by this fancy, his invention and description of the sphere.'[16]

The Greek text says *ton sphairikon logon*, which means 'the principle of the sphere'. This tradition therefore assigns to 'Atlas' the knowledge of the earth as a sphere, and by implication also the study of the positions and movements of the heavenly bodies in the 'heavenly sphere', which is projected from the earth's spherical surface in astronomical science.

It is remarkable that at the end of their 1978 book mentioned earlier, the Thoms concluded that one of megalithic man's great achievements was likely to have been the discovery that 'the earth was a sphere'.[17] This was because 'from the northern Island of Unst the moon at the major standstill appeared to be circumpolar for a few days.' And the ancient historian Diodorus Siculus seems to be telling us the same thing: that the Atlantic megalith builders had discovered that the earth and the heavens-as-viewed were spherical, and passed this knowledge on to the Mediterranean peoples, represented symbolically in myth by their hero Hercules.

I have searched the literature to try and discover just what it was that Atlas really had on his shoulders. And in the older textual sources, it transpires that Atlas really bore a *pillar* (in Greek, *kion*) on his back. Aeschylus (525 BC–456 BC) has Prometheus say in his play *Prometheus Bound* (350–1): 'I am distressed by the fate of my brother Atlas, who, in the West stands bearing on his shoulders the pillar of

Figure 62. Atlas with the world upon his shoulders. (*Sevententh-century engraving, collection of Robert Temple*)

390

Heaven and Earth.'[18] An earlier translation by Buckley has: '. . . the disasters of my brother Atlas gall my heart, who is stationed in the western regions, sustaining on his shoulders the pillar of heaven and of earth . . .'[19]

And similarly, the twelfth-century author Eustathius of Thessalonica, who was a deeply learned antiquarian (1390,10), used the verb *kionophoreó*, which means 'pillar-bearing', as an epithet of Atlas.

The Greek word Aeschylus used to describe the position of Atlas, which the above translators have respectively translated as 'stands' and 'stationed', is *hestēke*, from the verb root *histēmi*, which has the specific meaning of 'making to stand still'. This is actually an astronomical term. The megalith builders were obsessed with the 'standstills' of the moon and the 'standstills' of the sun, the latter being known as the solstices ('solstice' comes from the Latin and means 'sun [*sol*] standstill'). The 'standstills' of both bodies were marked by various megalithic stones, as for instance the remarkable example of the solstice sunrise at Stonehenge, which I myself have observed from the centre of the ring (an amazing experience, well worth making any effort to have). The fact that the word for 'standstill' is thus used to describe the position of Atlas, who stands with a pillar (megalith or menhir) on his shoulder, is not likely to be coincidental. Aeschylus was, after all, a man who was one of the great dramatists of history, and a master wordsmith.

Since we know that Atlas was located in Morocco near Lixus, and we have seen that his daughters the Hesperides and their quince grove were at the 'tomb of Antaios' – namely at Mezorah, it is likely that the pillars of heaven were none other than the menhirs of Mezorah. Of the stones in the main ring, at least five (still unbroken) were very tall menhirs. There were several more tall menhirs outside the main ring, several taller than any in the ring itself. (All these are fallen now.)

Stone 30 of the main ring marks the summer solstice sunrise and stone 146 the summer solstice sunset (both indicating the summer solar 'standstill'); stones 61 and 62 mark the winter solstice sunrise and stone 118 the winter solstice sunset (all marking the winter solar 'standstill'); stones 47 and 132 mark the equinoctial sunrise and sunset respectively. The Mezorah Ring is therefore a 'ring for all seasons', since it caters for all four major solar events of the year, the two solstices, and the two equinoxes (the latter both having the same markers). The Mezorah Ring is therefore a kind of 'grand-daddy of the rings', catering for all solar tastes.

All of these sightings are from the centre of the ring and could only have taken place before the tumulus was constructed in the centre of the ring by later people, a people who clearly did not understand the astronomical purpose of the ring or know how to use it. The fact that an astronomical observer could use the Mezorah ring in this way to observe the sun standing still at the solstices also appears to be part of the Atlas myth. Bearing in mind that, as we have seen, the Greek verb Aeschylus actually uses to describe Atlas's position is *histēmi*, which literally means 'to make to stand still', the Moroccan pillar of Atlas by which one marks the solstice point *does make the sun stand still.*

Aristotle, in *The Movement of Animals* (Book III, 699a, 28–9), specifically cites a myth about Atlas which describes him as *having his feet planted upon the earth*, which in Greek is *epi tēs gēs*. As Aristotle says, in the translation by Forster which is not entirely accurate:

'Now those who in the fable represent Atlas as having his feet planted upon the earth would seem to have shown sense in the story which they tell, since they make him as it were a radius [*diametron*, for which 'radius' is a mistranslation: the word means 'diameter', not 'radius', but according to Liddell & Scott, in this specific case it means 'the axis of a sphere'], twisting [*strephonta*, really means 'making to rotate on an axis'] the heaven [*ton ouranon*] about the poles [*peri tous polous*] . . . [20] (This tallies with what we have just seen, namely the tradition of 'the sphere'.)

The translation by Farquharson says:

'And the mythologists with their fable of Atlas setting his feet upon the earth appear to have based the fable upon intelligent grounds. They make Atlas a kind of diameter twirling the heavens about the poles.'[21]

I take this to be a further description of how Atlas was really the name for the Mezorah Ring, and that the feet planted in the earth are the bases of the pillars constituting that ring, just as the 'heads' were the tips of the pillars. (The myth mentioned by Aristotle is otherwise unknown today.) Regarding the feet of the stones being planted in the earth, I should point out that some of them go several feet down below the surface, and the menhirs in particular really were 'planted'.

Clearly, we are seeing emerge here a rich tradition of mythical lore referring to the Atlantic maritime culture of the megalithic ring-builders as master astronomers. And the fact that they passed over their astronomical knowledge to 'Hercules', or the Mediterranean world, accords with what we know from the current revised chronology about the ring-builders being the more ancient culture.

If the pillar or pillars of Atlas were menhirs, could the same origin apply to the legendary 'Pillars of Hercules'? Apparently, yes. Ancient literature is full of attempts to explain that the 'pillars' only latterly came to be thought of as the two mountains astride the Straits of Gibraltar, which are called Djebel Tariq, better known as the 'Rock of Gibraltar', and Djebel Moussa on the Moroccan side. (In ancient times, these two peaks were known respectively as Kalpē and Abilyx; Abilyx is not a name of Greek origin, and may be connected with the name Lixus in some way, while Kalpē in Greek has various meanings and significations, which would lead us into too long a discussion.) The ancient geographer Strabo (first century AD) speaks of the 'pillars' at great length. He tells us (Book Three, 170–2):

> . . . some are of the opinion that the capes at the Strait are the Pillars; others, Gades [Cadiz], and others that they lie on ahead still farther outside the strait than Gades. Again, some have supposed that Kalpē and Abilyx are the Pillars . . . while others have supposed that the isles near each mountain [this is a confusion, as no such isles are known] are the Pillars . . . There are some who transfer hither . . . rocks to be the pillars which Pindar calls "the gates of Gades" when he asserts that they are the farthermost limits reached by Hercules. . . . most of the Greeks represent the Pillars as in the neighbourhood of the strait. But the Iberians [Spaniards] and Libyans [Moroccans are here meant] say that the Pillars are in Gades, for the regions in the neighbourhood of the strait in no respect, they say, resemble pillars . . . Others say that it is the bronze pillars in the temple of Hercules at Gades . . .[22]

So we see that the Moroccans and Spaniards of the first century AD did not consider the Rock of Gibraltar and its sister peak on the opposite side of the Strait to be the Pillars of Hercules, and no one could agree about what or where the pillars were! What did Strabo himself think? He says (Book Three, 170–1):

'But to deny that the isles or the mountains resemble pillars, and to search for . . . Pillars that were properly so called, is indeed a sensible thing to do . . . and that when the hand-wrought monuments had disappeared, their name was transferred to the places – whether you mean thereby the isles, or the capes that form the strait.'[23]

He was very sensible, but as he did not know of the existence of the menhirs of Mezorah, he could not identify them as the elusive Pillars.

Some further and enigmatic remarks about other pillars existing beyond Cadiz are found in Tacitus, the Roman historian of the first century AD. In his *Germania* (34) he tells us (in the translation by Mattingly and Handford):

'We [the Romans] have even ventured upon the Northern Ocean itself, and rumour has it that there are Pillars of Hercules in the far north. It may be that Hercules did go there; or perhaps it is only that we by common consent ascribe any remarkable achievement in any place to his famous name. Drusus Germanicus [brother of the Emperor Tiberius] did not lack the courage of the explorer, but Ocean forbade further research into its own secrets or those of Hercules. Since then no one has attempted it. It has been judged more pious and reverend to believe in the alleged exploits of gods than to establish the true facts.'[24]

The earlier Bohn's translation reads:

'We have even explored the ocean itself on that side [the Atlantic Ocean]; and fame reports that columns of Hercules are still remaining on that coast; whether it be that Hercules was ever there in reality, or that whatever great and magnificent is anywhere met with is, by common consent, ascribed to his renowned name. The attempt by Drusus Germanicus to make discoveries in these parts was sufficiently daring; but the ocean opposed any further inquiry into itself and Hercules. After a while no one renewed the attempt; and it was thought more pious and reverential to believe the actions of the gods, than to investigate them.'[25]

The wry humour of Tacitus is brought out better in the Bohn's translation, where we can see that he is poking fun at people who believe literally in the existence of Hercules, and attribute everything that is large in size to him.

So we see that the pillars that were 'further than Cadiz' were said to be in 'the far north'. At last we have an explicit mention by a classical author of what we can take to be the menhirs and standing stones of Britain and Brittany, which had only been hinted at by Strabo. It is more than likely that the specific reference here is to Carnac in Brittany. I have already pointed out that the word *kar* in Armenian means 'stone', is probably a loan-word from a more ancient language, and forms part of the name of the gigantic megalithic complex in Armenia known as Zoraz Kar. The name 'Zoras' applied to a huge megalithic ring must have the same origin as the 'Zorah' of Mezorah/M'zorah. So we see the three largest megalithic centres of the ancient world, all of roughly the same date, are all linked by common names. This is no coincidence.

But what of Karnak in Egypt? Could there be any conceivable connection between Carnac in Britanny and Karnak near Thebes (modern Luxor) in Egypt? At first glance, this seems impossible, since Karnak in Egypt is very many centuries later than Carnac in Britanny, with which no direct connection existed at the time. However, we must not be led astray by the appearance of impossibility. As it happens, there is a deeper connection. The Egyptian word *kar* is known to have existed in the Old Kingdom period in Egypt, and occurs in the Pyramid Texts. It means 'sanctuary'. Ahmed Eissa worked out the history and meaning of 'Karnak' in an article published in German in 1995, in which he explains that the word was generally applied to the naos [inner chamber] of a temple of the shrine of a divine statue, and: 'A *kar*-chapel can be found either in heaven or beneath the earth.' The second half of the name Karnak comes, he believes, from the word *negeg*, of Lower Egyptian origin, referring to a great egg of the primeval mound of creation, laid by a primeval bird who flew over the cosmic sea and brought the first light and the first sound to a world emerging from chaos.[26] The egg was conceived of as laid by the earth god Geb (symbolised by the sacred goose) every morning at sunrise, the egg being obviously the rising sun. (Once again, we therefore have connections with the rising sun at the horizon, so closely observed at the megalithic rings, and also at the Temple of Amun at Karnak.) And Eissa quotes a New Kingdom text as saying that 'Karnak is the horizon of the earth and the supreme mound of the First Time.'[27]

It is clear that these meanings are resonant of the cosmically sacred megalithic sites such as Carnac, which are also concerned with the horizon of the earth. What seems to have happened, therefore, is that the name lingered on throughout the ages and ended up being applied, with all its resonances of meaning, to Karnak at Thebes. In other words, Carnac and Karnak are not directly connected, but they have a deep underlying inner connection through the survival of a name charged with meaning. And sometimes the ineffable can be more important than the obvious, as any woman possessing the mysterious quality of *allure* shows so clearly.

It is well known that the earlier name of the hero Hercules was Briareōs, and that the 'Pillars of Hercules' had earlier been called 'Pillars of Briareōs' (in Greek, *Briareo stelai*). Who was Briareōs? He was a brother of Atlas and Antaios, and a sea god. According to the poet Hesiod (eighth century BC), Briareōs had fifty heads standing on his shoulders (*Theogony*, 151–2).[28] Since we have seen with Atlas that it is usually pillars that stand on shoulders, perhaps 'heads' refers also to menhirs or standing stones – fifty of them in a ring. Antaios was said in myth to have decorated Mezorah with the skulls of strangers, hinting perhaps that 'heads' really referred to the tips of the standing stones. Confirmation of this might possibly be found in the peculiar fact that in ancient Greek the word for 'head', *kephalē*, has the additional meaning of 'capital of a column'. Could this be a survival of an ancient usage going back to the Stone Age and megalithic times?

The Roman poet Lucan stated (*Pharsalia*, Book IV, ll. 593–7) that Briareōs was actually born in Morocco with Antaios. And the site of Mezorah is described by Lucan as a 'rocky tumulus' (l. 589, the Latin word used being specifically *tumulos*,[29] though none of the translators of Lucan has translated the word correctly, not realising the significance of what Lucan was reporting), which is certainly thoroughly accurate. All the classical writers quoted so far seem to have drawn on earlier accounts which are now lost.

There is an aspect of the myths relating to Mezorah that finds a curious echo, once again, in Britain. It has already been mentioned that there was a famous wrestling match at the Garden of the Hesperides between Antaios and Hercules. This match was eventually won by

Hercules, who discovered that the trick to defeat Antaois was to lift him up in the air, thereby depriving him of his contact with the Earth, which caused him to lose his strength. By this means, Antaios was overcome.

This myth reappears in Geoffrey of Monmouth's history written in the twelfth century, this time as a British legend. The combat took place in Cornwall between the native British monster Gogmagog (also called Goemagot) who was twelve cubits high, and a wanderer who had come to Britain from the Mediterranean, who in Latin was called Corineus and in Welsh was called Korineys. As Geoffrey informs us: 'And then Korineys became enraged, and took his strength to him and lifted the giant to his shoulder, and ran with him towards a sea-crag and bearing him to its highest peak, threw him over the rock into the sea, so that he went into a thousand pieces . . .'[30]

At both Mezorah and Cornwall, we thus see the tale recurring of a local giant who is only defeated by an invader who raises him aloft and holds him in the air.

What does this mean? Let us start by discovering the meaning of the name Antaios. It comes from the Greek verb *antairō*, which means 'to rise opposite to, or in the same parallel with'. This is a clear reference to the astronomical sighting uses of the Mezorah stones in connection with solar, stellar and lunar risings. Hence the name of Antaios in Greek might well embody a coded reference to the true purpose of the place. Since the name Antaios may be said, therefore, to mean 'he who rises up opposite to (someone)' or 'he who rises in the same parallel with (someone)', we clearly have here the elements of a coded astronomical myth.

No less than three Egyptologists have suggested that Antaios is actually the Egyptian god Set. As Petrie says: 'It is still uncertain what is meant by the equation of Set with the giant Antaois. Sethe has proposed *entayye* as the name of the god of Antaiopolis [the Greek name given to an Egyptian town, and derived from Antaois], and von Bissing sees in Antaois as Set the representative of earth-born strength and barbarism.'[31]

I decided to check this suggestion of the Egyptian philologist Kurt Sethe's. But as Sethe (1869–1934) lived before the current transliterations were formalised, it is difficult to know what he meant by the Egyptian word *entayye*. However, I have looked up *tayet*, and it appropriately means 'antagonist' or 'opponent', which is precisely what Antaios was in the myth, the antagonist or opponent of Hercules.[32] In trying to figure out what he may have meant by the first part of the word he suggested, I discovered that if the word were *enertayet* (and it might contract as *entayye(t)*, but I am not familiar enough with Egyptian grammar to know whether this happens in Egyptian), the meaning would be 'antagonist of stone', since the Egptian word for 'stone' is *ener*. (*Ener kem* is black granite, *ener khedj* is limestone, *ener khedj nayen* is fine Tura limestone, *ener khejen rudjet* is sandstone.)[33] On the other hand, *enertay* unexpectedly also means the two things on which Thoth stands. But as I have never heard of Thoth standing on two things, which is a mythological detail that has somehow escaped me, I am for once lost for words, transliterated or otherwise.

But what about the name of Hercules? Does it have any astronomical connotations? Yes, it does, if one realises that the Greeks had no numerals and used letters of the alphabet as numbers. This meant that every word in Greek had a numerical value. Often, the names of gods and heroes had secret meanings indicated by their numerical values. This is true for Hercules. The name Hercules (the Latin form of the name) in its Greek original is Heraklēs. The 'meaning' of this name is 'glory of Hera' (Hera being the queen of the gods). But since letters doubled as numbers in Greek, Heraklēs has the numerical value of 367 and *hē Chthōna* ('the Earth') has the numerical value of 1468. The number 367 is one quarter of 1468. Hence Hercules is 'one quarter of the Earth'. Or, to put it geometrically, Heraklēs is the side of a rhombus or square whose perimeter is *hē Chthōna*, the Earth.

We thus can see that Antaios was rising up at a certain parallel (latitude) opposite to (hence the 'opponent of') Heraklēs, who symbolized a 'quarter' of the Earth. In order for the Earth to be 'quartered', it must be divided precisely in four by the four cardinal points of north, south, east and west. This can only be done by a 'rising' at the horizon which is due east. Hence, this myth relates to sunrise at the equinox. It was only at an equinox when a body could rise at a point that was opposite to the earth quartered, and that body was the sun itself. At Mezorah, the sunrise at the equinox was marked in the stone ring. Hence, this was where the rising sun of the equinox and the quartered earth 'met'.

As soon as they 'met', Antaios was raised up aloft, and the Earth regained its power and mastery over its own affairs, because the rising had passed, at Mezorah, 'the place of sunrise'.

Although it is theoretically possible that Geoffrey of Monmouth could have known the story of the wrestling match between Heraklēs and Antaios from some classical texts, it is not particularly likely that he could have had such familiarity with the intimate details of Greek myth. He was, after all, a provincial British monk or cleric. His history is not full of classical allusions, which would lead one to see him as an expert in classical mythology. It is more likely that the myth of Corineus and Gogmagog was a genuine British myth. And it is therefore likely that it embodied a myth that went back to the culture of the megalith builders themselves. The name Gogmagog occurs in the Bible, and is clearly not the original name for the monster in British myth, but was a name borrowed from biblical lore and applied to the monster. I presume that the monster's alternative name, Goemagot, is merely a Welsh version of Gogmagog, although there are some alternative theories about that, and about the name in general.

It is obvious that the megalith builders, whose stone rings were clearly used for astronomical observation purposes, were significantly advanced in astronomy and geometry. Because they were a maritime civilisation, they must have been unrivalled navigators, and that may well be where their knowledge of astronomy and geometry received its original impetus. It will help us to understand the 'Atlantic civilisation' better, and also how it could have been in communication by sea with the Egyptian Delta, if we consider more evidence about the ships and their maritime achievements.

Clement of Alexandria (circa 150 AD–215 AD) in his *Stromata* (*Miscellanies*), Book I, Chapter 16, first paragraph, says:

'Atlas the Libyan was the first who built a ship and navigated the sea.'[34]

This is a very important titbit of an otherwise lost tradition. It shows both that Atlas was recognised as being 'Libyan' (i.e., North African, or Moroccan in this context), and that he was associated with the earliest known prehistoric maritime culture.

Countless authors, ancient and modern, have commented upon the Atlantic cultures, but these remarks have rarely been given proper attention. Perhaps the reason for this is that there is no academic discipline or academic department concerned with 'Atlantic culture'. As soon as the archaeologists of one region of the world begin to discuss it, they feel uncomfortable, because they are 'straying beyond their boundaries'. There is nothing that makes an academic more nervous than that, because it opens him up to criticism by his colleagues. The academic world is a vicious world, where no mercy is ever shown, and where the slightest slip from 'consensus behaviour' can endanger an academic's entire career. It is only people like myself, who do not depend upon the favour and approval of peers for a livelihood, who can say what they like and stray over as many boundaries as they please. With every passing year, the competition for jobs within the academic community becomes more intense, the level of fear rises and the timidity of discourse increases. One of these days, the academic world will just seize up like a sea of ice, with no movement at all, and all opinions will remain perfectly rigid. Then everybody will be safe.

The suggestion by Clement of Alexandria that the first maritime civilisation originated in 'Libya' makes a lot of sense; more sense than if we suggested that the megalith builders originated in Britain and spread to 'Libya' (i.e. Morocco). Britain was under-populated and an unlikely origin for the megalith builders' culture. 'Libya', on the other hand, is a highly likely place of origin. We know that Northern Africa was temperate many thousands of years ago, and that before the climate deteriorated and desertification ruined the land, creating the deserts, the whole northern portion of Africa was a vast savannah, teeming in game and with a large human population. All of these people had to go somewhere when their habitat became intolerable, so vast migrations took place. Some settled in the Nile Delta. Others made their way to the sea coasts, where plentiful fish could guarantee their survival, as long as they were also near fresh water for drinking purposes. It was only natural that they became increasingly familiar with boats, if only because fishing was imperative. They had every reason to want to go from point to point along the coast for trade, as some settlements had goods that other settlements did not have, and so they could exchange by barter. In this way, a coastal civilisation would have evolved, and its penetrations inland would tend to be along rivers and estuaries. If we look at the pattern of distribution of the megalithic civilisation, this is just what we find. And all along the North African coast we find this as well, for Morocco, Algeria, Tunisia and Libya are riddled with mega-lithic remains, dotted along the coasts.

Such people were vulnerable to raiding, piracy and invasion. So it was sensible for them to take refuge in remote places, such as those beyond the Straits of Gibraltar. They also tended to favour islands as trading bases, as they could only be reached by boat and could only be threatened by people possessing boats, not by land-dwellers. This was one reason for the popularity of a place like Cyprus, and the same was true of the tiny island of Ischia off the coast of Italy, at a later date; both these islands were early metallurgical centres. And later, the tin traders stockpiled their tin mini-ingots ('pieces the size of knuckle-bones') on an island called Ictis, before shipping to the Mediterranean, as the historian Diodorus Siculus records. This island was 'Almost certainly the present St.-Michael's Mount, an island in Mount's Bay of Cornwall . . .'[35] After the tin was gathered together at this small tidal island off the coast of Cornwall, it appears to have been shipped to the Isle of Wight, a larger island further east, which has been suggested as the tin traders' main shipping point. Both of these islands appear to have been 'offshore jurisdictions' where valuables could be deposited safely. If the tin which was ready for shipment had been stored onshore, it would have been susceptible to raiding parties, but by being kept on islands, it could only be 'raided' by people with boats; the traders could defend themselves more easily in sea combat.

When sailing to Britain for the tin trade, it is likely that the first sight, after the Scilly Islands, would be of Land's End, which is the furthest point west on the mainland of Britain. The true Land's End in Cornwall is marked by a single gigantic megalithic upright stone on top of a cliff, facing out to sea, which has obviously been standing there as a silent marker since the time of the megalith builders. I have been there and filmed it for television. It is some miles away from what is popularly called 'Land's End', where the tourists go. The real one is a deserted and atmospheric spot. This true 'Land's End', which is liter-ally what it is, is geographically correct, whereas the pseudo-Land's End is a town with shops where you can buy trinkets. The great megalith at Land's End is the ultimate indication that the people who erected it were a maritime culture, as it marks the furthermost extent of England to the west, and would provide the first glimpse of the mainland of Britain from the southwest by sea.

In spreading northwards from Libya, the first place for migrating peoples in antiquity to go was Spain. It is the easiest thing in the world to cross the Straits of Gibraltar by boat. You just get into your boat and you are there in no time. It is a wonderful experience taking the small ferry across the Straits from Tangier to Algeciras in Spain. Being low in the water gives you the feel of what it must have been like for the Phoenicians and their predecessors. The view is so magnificent on all sides, and it is really exciting with the spray in your face. I highly recommend this crossing to all who want to experience something of what things were like in the distant past. We crossed one late afternoon of the Spring Equinox, and it was a wonderful experience to get the 'Phoenicians' eye view' of the straits, followed by a magnificent sunset.

Spain, or 'Iberia', is often cited in old histories and chronicles as the source of the original inhabitants of Britain, so that the collected testimony on this point is vast. The Roman historian Tacitus (55 AD–120 AD) wrote in his work *Agricola*: 'The swarthy complexion and curled hair of the Silures [southern Welsh], together with their situation opposite to Spain [a reference to the ease of navigation between the two places], render it probable that a colony of the ancient Iberi [people from Iberia, i.e., Spain] possessed themselves of that territory.'[36] And in another translation: '. . . the swarthy faces of the Silures, the tendency of their hair to curl, and the fact that Spain lies opposite, all lead one to believe that Spaniards crossed in ancient times and occupied that part of the country.'[37] The Silures are reported as having inhabited in Roman times the area of South Wales north of the Severn. Modern DNA studies have shown that the Welsh are indeed related to the Basques of northern Spain.[38] And as I have pointed out before, the Basques are the remains of the 'proto-Iberians', and are probably the direct descendants of the megalith builders, as well as preserving a language similar to that spoken by the megalith builders, which linguists call 'Proto-Iberian', to distinguish it from Spanish, with which it has no connection whatever. (Spanish is an Indo-European language, which spread to Spain much later.)

The early English chronicler Nennius, who lived in the ninth century, said in his *History of the Britons*:

'. . . the Scots arrived in Ireland from Spain. The first that came was Partholomus, with a thousand men and women . . . The second was Nimech, the son of Agnomen, who according to report, after having been at sea a year and a half, and having his ships shattered, arrived at a port in Ireland, and continuing there several years, returned at length with his followers to Spain. After these came three sons of a Spanish soldier with thirty ships, each of which contained thirty wives . . . Ireland . . . was peopled to the present period, from this family [one of those just mentioned] . . . Afterwards, others came from Spain, and possessed themselves of various parts of Britain. Last of all came on Hoctor [or Damhoctor or Clamhoctor or Elamhoctor], who continued there, and whose descendants remain there to this day.'[39]

There are specific references to contacts between the British with Spain and Africa in Geoffrey of Monmouth. The mythical hero Brutus, escaping from Troy, made his way to settle in Britain. En route, he and his ships 'hoisted sail, and cleaving the waves of ocean within the ninth day they reached the Affric, and from thence . . . they sailed until they came to the land of Mauritania, and there for lack of food and drink they had to land . . . And then they came to Ackwitania [Aquitaine], and cast anchor in the port of Lingyrys [the Loire] for seven days, to see the condition of the country.'[40]

That was from the Old Welsh text. The Latin text gives some important variations:

'Without delay, therefore, they . . . set sail again, and after a course of thirty days came to Africa . . . passing the River Malua, they arrived at Mauritania, where at last, for want of provisions, they were obliged to go ashore; and, dividing themselves into several bands, they laid waste the whole country. When they had well stored their ships, they steered to the Pillars of Hercules . . . From thence they came to Aquitaine, and entering the mouth of the Loire, cast anchor. There they stayed seven days and viewed the country.'[41]

Eventually, Brutus reaches Britain and lands at Totness, seeing his new kingdom of Britain for the first time. As Geoffrey tells us: 'The island was then called Albion, and was inhabited by none but a few giants.'[42] We will recall that the megalith builders were described in Geoffrey, as quoted earlier, as 'the giants of old'. They were the ones who brought the stone rings from Africa, he said. In other words, the megalith builders were known to subsequent settlers as 'the giants'. The reason for this is obvious: they were assumed to have been giants because they were able to erect such gigantic stones, and later peoples could not imagine how they had done it unless they themselves had been giants. So this is possibly also the origin of the biblical statement: There were giants in the earth in those days. (This, by the way, was the quotation from the Bible from which Ole Rolvaag took the title of his classic novel of the early Scandinavian pioneers in America, *Giants in the Earth*.) It may well be that all the traditions of extremely ancient 'giants' preserved by later cultures refer to earlier peoples who had been able to raise giant stones, whether as megaliths or as structures, which were beyond the comprehension of their successors, leading to the assumption that they must have been giants. Geoffrey of Monmouth has many tales about the giants, not only of the famous British giant Gogmagog, but it is beyond our purpose to consider him here at any greater length. Suffice it to say that the megalith builders were considered 'giants', and there were only 'a few' of them inhabiting Britain when the next wave of settlers arrived.

The Spanish port from which all of this maritime contact with Britain and Ireland originated, at least in Phoenician times, was certainly Cadiz (anciently called Gades in Greek or Gadir in Phoenician). Whether the megalith builders had a port there, we do not know. According to Strabo, Cadiz was founded by people from Tyre.[43]

The archaeologist T. C. Lethbridge has written of the coming of the megalith builders to Britain:

The next people to appear in the islands must have been one of the most remarkable and adventurous in history. They are usually spoken of as Megalithic men because they introduced the method of building with great stones. . . . There is no doubt that they rowed or sailed the whole way up the western European seaboard and had had contact with the seafaring peoples of the Mediterranean. About two thousand years before the Birth of Christ they arrived on our western coasts where their characteristic round-bottomed 'Neolithic' pottery of Spanish types became mixed with later vessels known as 'Beakers' . . . The Beaker and Megalithic peoples seemed to have merged together . . . Characteristic Irish gold work has been found as far south as Spain and even in Palestine. It is difficult to picture the Western World at this stage; but evidently traffic by sea was considerable and the western sea-board peoples were not living in a backwater. [44]

The 'Atlanteans' must have had the ability to tack into the wind with their ships, using fore-and-aft rigging, in order to have such a vast maritime empire. They cannot technologically have relied only upon square sails, such as the peoples of the Mediterranean were limited to. It may be that those sailing vessels that are now known as Arab dhows, with their specialised sails, are descended from the ships of Atlantean design. In my book, *The Genius of China,* I describe the Chinese invention of fore-and-aft rigging, but the origins of the dhows of North Africa and the Persian Gulf have always been rather ambiguous, and we cannot prove that they drew their inspiration from China rather than from the Atlantic.

An important detail and clue is the history of Connemara in Ireland, with its fore-and-aft rigging style, which is similar to dhows, and may have Atlantean origins. Irish scholars are well aware of this, and Irish television many years ago featured an excellent and provocative documentary film on the subject by the well-known Irish filmmaker Sean O'Mordha. I was in touch with O'Mordha long ago, but never met him in person.

The fact that the megalith builders were a maritime culture was recognised early on by the Egyptologist T. Eric Peet. Peet is famous in his field as a superb scholar and one of the leading experts on Egyptian mathematics. However, he also had much wider interests. In 1912, he published a book which, though small, was nevertheless a surprisingly comprehensive general survey of megaliths around the world, entitled *Rough Stone Monuments.*[45] In it, he stated with considerable insight: '. . . megalith building is a widespread and homogeneous system, which, despite local differences, always preserves certain common features pointing to a single origin. It is thus difficult to accept the suggestion that it is merely a phase through which many races have passed. . . . There are further objections to this theory in the distribution of the megalithic buildings both in space and time. In space they occupy a very remarkable position along a vast sea-board which includes the Mediterranean coast of Africa and the Atlantic coast of Europe. In other words, they lie along a natural sea route. It is more than accident that the many places in which, according to this theory, the megalithic phase independently arose all lie in most natural sea connection with each other, while not one is in the interior of Europe.

In time the vast majority of the megalithic monuments of Europe seem to begin near the end of the neolithic period . . . it is curious that mega- lithic building, if merely an independent phase in many countries, should arise in so many at about the same time, and with no apparent reason. . . . For these reasons it is impossible to consider megalithic building as a mere phase through which many nations have passed, and it must therefore have been a system originating with one race, and spreading far and wide, owing either to trade influence or migration. . . . there (may have) extended a vast trade route or a series of trade routes, along which travelled the presence of precisely similar dolmens in Denmark, Spain, and the Caucasus. . . . (or) there is nothing a priori improbable in the idea that the megalithic monuments were built by a single invading race.

There are other considerations which support such a theory. It will be readily admitted that the commonest and most widely distributed form of the megalithic monument is the dolmen. Both this and its obvious derivatives, the Giant's Grave, the *allée couverte,* and others, are known to have been tombs, while other types of structure, such as the Maltese temple, the menhir, and the cromlech, almost certainly had a religious purpose. It is difficult to believe that these types of building, so closely connected with religion and burial, were introduced into these regions simply by the influence of trade relations. Religious customs and the burial rites connected with them are perhaps the most precious posses- sion of a primitive people, and are those in which they most oppose and resent change of any kind, even when it involves detail and not principle. Thus it is almost incredible that the people, for instance, of Spain, because they were told by traders that the people of North Africa buried in dolmens, gave up, in isolated instances, their habit of interment in trench graves in favour of burial in dolmens. It is still more impossible to believe that this unnatural event happened in one country after another. . . . An exchange of products between one country and another is not unnatural, but a traffic in burial customs is unthinkable. . . . The measurements given in the last chapter would seem to show that despite local variation there is an underlying homogeneity in the skulls of the megalithic people.

It thus seems that the most probable theory of the origin of the mega-lithic monuments is that this style of building was brought to the various countries in which we find it by a single race in an immense migration or series of migrations. It is significant that this theory has been accepted by Dr Duncan Mackenzie, who is perhaps the first authority on the megalithic structures of the Mediterranean basin. . . . One question still remains to be discussed. From what direction did megalithic architec-ture come, and what was its original home? . . . Mackenzie is . . . inclined to believe in an African origin. If he is right it may be that some climatic change, possibly the decrease of rainfall in what is now the Sahara Desert, caused a migration from Africa to Europe very similar to that which many believe to have given Europe its early Neolithic population. The megalithic people may even have been a branch of the same vast race as the neolithic: this would explain the fact that both inhumed their dead in the contracted position.[46]

The whole of North Africa is littered with megalithic remains of all sorts. In Libya, there is a vast number of 'trilithons', which resemble those of Stonehenge in England. These have been little studied, and the most extensive account of them is probably that given by H. S. Cowper in a book which was published as long ago as 1897.[47] Cowper's remarkable book contains many photos and illustrations of trilithons, with detailed descriptions of them. It needs to be said immediately that those few trilithons that have been studied in modern times have often been dismissed as 'Roman olive presses'. I would not say it is impos-sible that some of them were olive presses or, more likely, were adapted to become olive presses by having indentations bored into them to support accessory wooden structures. Much of Libya was certainly

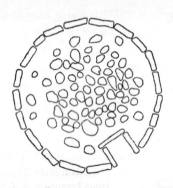

Figure 63. The plan of a megalithic stone circle in Algeria, showing how it has been filled by later people with other megalithic stones collected in the area, carried into its protective embrace, and just dumped there, presumbably for magical 'protection'. This is Figure 19 on page 94 in T. Eric Peet, *Rough Stone Monuments and Their Builders*, Harper, London and New York, 1912. This ring, the top of the drawing of it being approximately north, is one of several megalithic rings found on a hill called 'the Senam' in Msila, or M'Sila, District or Province, south-west of Algiers. The stones are limestone. In 1912, there were still three perfect rings remaining, which measured 23 ½ feet, 26 ¾ feet, and 34 ⅓ feet in diameter. Each of the rings had a break in the circumference, such as that shown here in the lower right corner, which pointed approximately southeast, obviously towards a rising point of some celestial body, but without knowing more, we cannot say what. These 'breaks' constituted open rectangular niches varying in width from two feet six inches to six feet. Algeria apparently has as many megalithic remains as Libya, but whereas the Libyan ones tend to be trilithons in square plans, the remains of Algeria appear to be rings, more like the remains of Morocco and Britain. Presumably, the differences of style indicate adjoining and related, but separate, peoples with their own sub-cultures. The largest concentration of megalithic rings and other remains in Algeria is apparently at a place called Roknia in the Guelma Region in the northeast of Algeria. At Roknia, there are more than 7,000 dolmens in a region spread over approximately one mile. This suggests that Roknia has the greatest concentration of megalithic stones anywhere in the world, far surpassing even the density of stones found at Carnac in Britanny. The story of the North African megalithic civilisation has yet to be told.

densely populated in Roman times, and the destruction of the Libyan environment seems to have taken place after the Arab conquest, which left Libya as the dry, barren and inhospitable wasteland which it largely is today. Once, Libya was flowing with water and covered in forests and crops. Alas for man's destructive powers!

Trilithon at Elkeb in Libya, from a drawing by Dr Henry Barth. This trilithon is about 45 miles south by east from Tripoli. It is 10 feet high, and the top stone is 6 foot 6 inches long. From James Fergusson, *Rude Stone Monuments in All Countries*, London, 1872, Figure 176, page 412.

A trilithon in the Khassia Hills in India. From James Fergusson, *Rude Stone Monuments in All Countries*, London, 1872, Figure 204, page 464.

One of the six trilithons standing together at Ksaea near Tripoli in North Africa, 45 miles east by south from Tripoli, from a drawing by Dr Henry Barth. From James Fergusson, *Rude Stone Monuments in All Countries*, London, 1872, Figure 175, page 411.

Trilithon at Ksaea.

Figure 64

The suggestion that the Libyan trilithons are 'Roman olive presses' does not hold up to scrutiny because of what can be seen in Plate 60. This is a photo taken in the 1890s by Herbert Weld-Blundell, an explorer who seems not to have published anything, but who gave the photo to his friend H. S. Cowper, who reproduced it in his book as Figure 49 on page 169. All of the photos in Cowper's book, including this one, are of poor quality, but in many cases they are the only ones in existence of certain of the trilithons. This is the most remarkable of them all. It shows a megalithic group of trilithons at Messa in the Cyrenaica region of Libya, which closely resembles Stonehenge. As everyone who studies Stonehenge even slightly knows, the trilithons were not original to

Stonehenge, but were added at a later stage. Originally, Stonehenge looked more like Mezorah, and had no stones lying horizontally over the tops of other stones. The widespread prevalence of over a hundred trilithons throughout Libya, some in groups, but often standing on their own, and many more torn down and destroyed, indicates a 'trilithomania' in Libya at some unknown prehistoric period, and I would suggest that these people were in contact with Britain and that their trilithons were adopted at Stonehenge under their influence. In fact, I view North Africa, from Morocco to Libya, as being the true homeland of the megalith builders, at least at that period, if not from the beginning.

The trilithon complex at Messa is so very extraordinary that there can be no doubt of its being a megalithic ruin. The name 'Messa' is also similar to the name 'Mezorah'. Cowper himself did not visit this remote site, but Weld-Blundell told him that it was 'on the Merj-Greanah road, and is at a place called Zawieh Beida, about forty miles from the latter place.'[48] Here is what Cowper tells us further about it, bearing in mind that the Libyan name for a trilithon or group of trilithons is *senam*:

In describing such a remarkable series of megalithic monuments, it is necessary to see whether we can find in any other series, points of analogy; and in doing this we have two remarkable monuments which demand attention. The first of these is the remarkable megalithic group found in Messa, in the Cyrenaica, by Mr. Weld-Blundell, and the other is the great circular Stonehenge. The parallels between these two types and the senams are indeed most striking. For, although the plans are in all three types widely diverse, we find the two main features of Stonehenge represented, one at Tarhuna and the other at Messa; for, while the Cyrenaic monument [Messa] is the outer circle of continuous trilithon of Stonehenge stretched straight, the Tarhuna senams are set up in a square. It would indeed almost be possible to construct a Stonehenge out of the Messa monument and the Tarhuna senams.

These points of similarity are so remarkable that they must not be overlooked, for it would appear that it is only on the Tripoli coast that we find any real parallels to our great ruin on Salisbury Plain.

The great difference in plan in all three groups, though very striking, is, I venture to say, more apparent than real. After examining about eighty of the senam sites the strongest impression left is that the actual and real symbol of the ritual, the idea round which all centred, was the trilithonic form itself; and this being so, the plan of the building becomes a matter of secondary importance. Ridiculous as it sounds at first[,] the tradition of Geoffrey of Monmouth, that the stones of Stonehenge were brought by the arts of the giants of old from Africa to Kildare, and afterwards by Merlin to Salisbury Plain, we may after all find a substratum of fact: we may learn some day that the worship of the trilithonic symbol did indeed make its way from Africa, or anyhow from the east, to our shores.[49]

So what is all this modern talk about 'olive presses'? An example of the casual assumption that the trilithons were mere 'olive presses' may be found in an article in *The Geographical Journal* by R. G. Goodchild in 1950.[50] Goodchild mentions the book by Cowper, for which he has much praise, but says of it that it is 'an excellent work marred only by the false conclusions as to the date and purpose of the "senam" monuments'. Goodchild reproduces one photo showing two *senams* and says in the caption: 'Roman olive-presses at Snemat, Wadi Merdun'. Goodchild is determined that the area was never significantly occupied before Roman times. He speaks of 'The archaeology of inner Tripolitania, which is, monumentally, almost exclusively Romano–Libyan . . .' Most of the *senams* are in the area of what Cowper called the Tarhuna Hills, and which Goodchild calls the Tarhuna Plateau. By somewhat tautological reasoning, Goodchild uses the *senams* to define the southern boundary of the olive-growing region, the olives of which he then wishes to use to prove that the *senams* were used for pressing the olives. He says: 'The southern limits of the main area of ancient olive cultivation can be determined with some accuracy by the distribution of Roman olive-presses, and these limits coincide almost exactly with the edge of the "high plain" climatic zone, and the beginning of the "steppe". . . . Yet the steppe and desert areas south of the Gebel were, in the Roman period, capable of supporting a considerable sedentary population . . .' So why did the olives stop?

Goodchild says of this further:

'As early as the middle of the first century BC, the inhabitants of

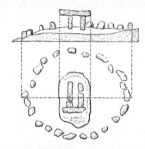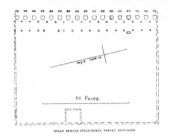

Figure 65. LEFT: Megalithic ring near Bona, Algeria, seen in section (above) and plan (below). It was discovered by M. A. Leternoux circa 1886, and this is how it looked then. Note the trilithon which is prominent in the ring. A *cippus* (stela) of late Roman workmanship bearing a Berber inscription was also found here. Bona is a prominent Mediterranean port on the northeast coast of Algeria. From James Fergusson, *Rude Stone Monuments in All Countries*, London, 1872, Figure 233, page 532 (for the relevant text, see page 405 and Figure 174).

RIGHT: Cowper's drawing of the plan of the stones at Senam Semana in Terr'gurt (see Plate X for photograph), showing the predilection in this part of Libya to arrange the large stones in rectangular enclosures rather than in round rings, which were favoured further west. Perhaps these early rectangular enclosures were the inspiration for the Predynastic, Archaic, and Old Kingdom rectangular enclosures in Egypt, if indeed they really do predate them. Too little is known to have certainty about anything relating to these Libyan megaliths. Figure 89 on page 281 from H. S. Cowper, *The Hill of Graces: A Record of Investigation among the Trilithons and Megalithic Sites of Tripoli*, London, 1897.

Lepcis Magna were able to draw on the produce of hundreds of thousands of olive-trees, and the planted areas probably increased during the Roman period. Throughout the Gebel area the traveller encounters the massive uprights of Roman olive-presses, at one time suspected of being "megalithic" monuments of prehistoric origin.'

Goodchild offers no reasons why the trilithons should be 'olive presses' or any reasons why they should not be prehistoric megaliths. But he is most insistent that the area was only lived in during Roman times, not before or after. He does, however, bizarrely contradict himself on that point because he admits that huge numbers of olive groves existed *before* the Romans, as in the last quotation just given, he speaks of how the olive groves 'probably increased during the Roman period'.

412

If something *increased* during the Roman period, it was obviously there before, but if it were there before, then it is not true that the area was uninhabited before the Romans. Clearly, logic is not Goodchild's strong point.

To the ancient Egyptians, Libya and the area extending up to and bordering the western Delta were known as 'Olive Land' from as early as predynastic times, more than three thousand years before any Romans ever set foot in North Africa. It was Percy Newberry who figured out the meaning of the name *Ta Tehenu* by which Libya was known to the Egyptians from earliest recorded times, as no one before him had ever been able to translate it. His first clue came when he was studying the ivory and wooden labels excavated in the tombs of the First Dynasty by Petrie, Griffith, Naville and others. These little labels were left from jars of offerings in the tombs, identifying their contents. One of the contents mentioned was '*tehenu* oil'. Newberry noticed that the name had a tree-branch sign beside it, a descriptive hieroglyph of the type Egyptologists call 'determinatives', because they determine the nature of the word or name. He realised that the oil must be an oil from a plant, probably a tree. In the first article in which he mentioned this, in 1912, he said of it: '. . . I suspect it may be olive oil.'[51] By 1915, Newberry was confident enough about this identification of *tehenu* with 'olive' to publish an article in Petrie's journal specifically called '*Ta Tehenu* – "Olive Land"'. [I have used the more common spelling *tehenu* rather than *djehenu* which he has given, using the linguistic symbol of the underscored 't', and have done this in the quotations which follow and the footnote, for the sake of consistency of discussion with more modern usages.] He wrote there (omitting the hieroglyphs which we cannot print here and substituting dots for them):

'No interpretation of the geographical name . . . *Ta Tehenu* has yet been given. Egyptologists usually understand the word to mean "Libya", but although this meaning is undoubtedly correct, it is not a translation of the name. Countries were often named by the Egyptians, as by other peoples, after the chief product of the land. They called Lower Egypt . . . *Ta-meh*, "Flax-land"; Middle Egypt . . . *Ta-skhemaa*, "Reed-land" . . . and Nubia . . . *Ta-pedjet*, "Bow-land", because the bow was the principal weapon of the inhabitants. *Ta Tehenu* is, of course, "*Tehenu-*land", but the question to be answered is, What is . . . *Tehenu?*'

Newberry then refers to the *tehenu* oil of the tomb offerings, points out the reasons why it must be a tree oil but cannot be oil of cedar, the name of which is known. He then describes and reproduces a photo of an archaic slate palette in the Cairo Museum, which shows pictures of olive trees, with a hieroglyphic sign beside them which for other reasons had already been read '*tehenu*'. He produces much additional evidence and concludes:

It has been remarked that *Ta Tehenu* (which we may now call "Olive-land") is usually understood to mean Libya, but Libya is a vague term. By some classical writers Libya was understood to mean the whole of Africa west of the Isthmus of Suez [i.e., reaching all the way to Morocco], by others, all the country to the west of Egypt including the Oases [also as far as Morocco]. Egyptologists generally hold to the latter definition, but there is evidence to show that in early times, at all events, Olive-land included the Mareotic lake region and all the country to the west of the Canopic branch of the Nile [see the maps in Figures 71 and 72], possibly also *much of the Delta itself.* There can be no doubt whatever that Olive-land was a very rich and prosperous country. King Sahure of the Vth dynasty [conventionally dated to circa 2487–2473 BC] captured from its people no less than 123,440 oxen, 233,400 asses, 232,413 goats and 243,688 sheep. This immense number of large and small cattle is evidence that Olive-land must have included within its boundaries very extensive grass-lands. Several centuries earlier than Sahure, [King] Narmer-Menes conquered the people of Olive-land. This conquest is recorded on a small ivory cylinder . . . found at Hierakonpolis, and it confirms the statement of Manetho [whom we discussed in Chapter Six] that the founder of the Egyptian monarchy [the first king of the First Dynasty, generally called 'Menes', as discussed in Chapter Six] undertook an expedition against the Libyans. . . . The [earliest] kings of Egypt mentioned on the Palermo Stone are figured as wearing the [red] crown of Neith [see them depicted in Figure 49, page 268], and it was by the marriage with Hetep, the chieftainess of Sais [political capital of Lower Egypt in the Delta], that Narmer-Menes united the two kingdoms of

414

Egypt under his sole authority. The kingdom which Narmer-Menes conquered was therefore the *Libyan* kingdom of Lower Egypt.[52]

Now we need to complete our consideration of the Libyan trilithons. We have seen that Libya was known as 'Olive Land' from prehistoric times, and produced olive oil, which was used as offerings in First Dynasty tombs. We thus have proof that Goodchild was talking complete nonsense when he maintained that the olive-growing areas of Libya were not inhabited before the Romans came and planted all the olive groves. (I have already pointed out that he had contradicted himself on this subject anyway.) But those olive groves had already been there for three thousand years before the Romans arrived. Furthermore, Newberry has shown the gigantic quantities of livestock possessed by the Libyans, and that as late as the Fifth Dynasty, centuries after the Libyans were 'conquered' by 'Menes', they were still a gigantic and thriving culture capable of having such vast flocks that hundreds of thousands of beasts could be captured by Pharaoh Sahure. I have added up the total number of beasts captured by Sahure, and it comes to 832,941 animals! And that is just what he managed to *capture*. It is clear then that across North Africa as a whole, even as late as 2500 BC, the 'Libyans' of all kinds must have had millions of head of livestock grazing on vast grasslands, where sand now is, and watered by rivers where dry wadis now are. It must have been something of a pastoral paradise, of enormous extent, stretching from Egypt to the Atlantic. Clearly this civilisation had the food resources and prosperity to sustain a highly advanced culture, and could produce gigantic quantities of grain, olive oil and meat for a huge population.

I am inclined to believe that the Libyan trilithons are prehistoric megaliths and were not originally 'olive presses'. Some trilithons had holes bored in their uprights, which might well have been done at some later date, whether Roman or not, in order to make them useful to farmers. And they might well have converted some to olive presses, who knows. Some of the trilithons seem to have been tampered with in other ways, with additional stones being added. No doubt a great deal of tinkering went on over the ages. But I fail to see how a site like Messa could be olive presses. There is no reason to continue laying horizontal stones over a whole row of uprights in that way if you are just pressing olives. I believe it is ridiculous even to imagine such a thing. I believe, therefore, that we can accept that the trilithons originally appeared in the area as prehistoric megaliths, but that some were adapted for utilitarian purposes during the Roman period. I do not know where the 'olive press theory' originated, but it must have been early, because it is mentioned in passing by Libyan scholar Oric Bates, who, while acknowledging that megaliths occur in the western half of North Africa, says:

'No truly megalithic monuments have been reported from Libya east of Tunisia. For over fifty years from the time of their discovery, the remains of Roman oil-presses of the *torcular* type were repeatedly asserted to be megaliths [he gives several references in addition to those we have already considered], but their real nature has now become generally recognised.'[53]

He goes on to identify the originators of the 'olive press theory' as a French author named H. Méhier de Mathuisieulx, who contributed to a French journal whose date he does not give (though this author was publishing in the early twentieth century), and two British authors, D. R. MacIver and A. Wilken, who wrote a book called *Libyan Notes* of unknown date. I have however been able to discover that this book was published in 1901 by David Randall MacIver and Anthony Wilkin (not Wilken), and contains 113 pages. In this book (page 78) the authors say that 'many supposed prehistoric monuments of Tripoli are nothing more remarkable than Roman oil-presses'. However, as these men were merely travellers and not experts on megalithic monuments by any means, I believe we can discount this theory entirely. It would not be at all unusual that trilithonic monuments might in some cases have been adapted by the local inhabitants over time for utilitarian purposes, but I do not believe that such a large number of trilithonic structures (at least a hundred) could have been erected at huge trouble and expense just for pressing olive oil. On the other hand, as there were hundreds of thousands of olive trees by Goodchild's own admission, a hundred presses made of stone would be pointless, as many thousands of presses would be needed in Libya. Clearly, perfectly adequate perishable olive presses existed in vast profusion and there was no need whatever to go to the trouble of making a few in stone. This 'olive-press theory' is thus clearly ridiculous. The *senams* must be megalithic structures, although some have been tampered with.

I believe that the strange name *senam* which is used by the locals to describe all of these structures is possibly related to the ancient Egyptian word *sensen*, which means 'joined together', being a reduplicated form of *sen*, which means 'to bind' (from the fact that *sen* is a pronoun meaning 'them'). But there may have been wordplay involved, for *senem* is a verb used to mean 'seize the heads of the vanquished by their hair'. And once again, as we saw at Mezorah, we may have an echo of the meaning of 'heads' referring to the tops of the pillars.

On this book's website, www.egyptiandawn.info I have reproduced scans of many Libyan trilithons, which the reader can study. In terms of ancient access to them, the huge map prepared by Cowper for his book makes it clear that most of them were accessible by boat from the sea from the present town of Kam by travelling westwards up the River Cinyps, which in happier times ran along the bed of the now dry and desolate Wadi Targelat. You then forked left up the Wadi Daun (which had Roman dams later on, so that it would no longer have been navigable by Roman times), and then forked left again to reach the area of Ghirah, where the *senams* began. This map may also be seen on the website, from which it may be downloaded and enlarged for closer inspection. In this respect, the concealed access by river from the sea resembles that to Mezorah, which Mavor was able to discover was used in antiquity.

There appears to have been another and more obscure route by boat to the *senams* directly southwards, along a narrow river in the present Wadi Terrgurt. *Senams* commenced at the foot of the Tarhuna Hills by this route, and then marched upwards on to the plateau itself. Presumably the river ceased to be navigable at Senam Semana, and then one had to go on by land. I also reproduce a useful map in Figure 70 showing the travels of the French traveller Méhier de Mathuisieulx, which shows clearly the location of the Plateau of Tarhuna (which the French spell Tarhouna) southeast of Tripoli.

In the mid nineteenth century, the traveller Dr Henry Barth discovered a set of six trilithons standing together 45 miles (72 km) from

Figure 66. A megalithic ring in Cyrenaica, Libya, as drawn by Giuseppe Haimann, in his book *Cirenaica*, extracted from the Bulletin of the Italian Geographical Society, 1882 (in Italian).

Tripoli at Ksaea, one of which may be seen in Figure 64. In 1886, a trilithon was found in northeast Algeria, near the coast, as part of a megalithic ring near the port of Bona. This ring and trilithon may be seen in both section and plan in Figure 65. Throughout the length and breadth of North Africa, megalithic remains, including stone rings, are extraordinarily numerous, and some of the remains are trilithons, though the trilithons seem to be rather regionally clustered. However, no one in his right mind would say that a trilithon such as the one near Bona standing in a megalithic ring was an 'olive press', unless of course the stones making up the ring are large petrified olives.

Anyone who has not been to the regions of Spain that have gigantic megalithic remains may be unaware of just how vast the megalithic culture was in that country. One can safely say that Spain was the centre of the megalithic world for the continent of Europe, at least in terms of population and sheer scale of activity and building. One of the most amazing megalithic sites there is still intact, and it made an enormous impression on me when I saw it. I found myself wondering why more

Plate 46

Plate 47

Plate 48

Plate 49

Plate 50a

Plate 50b

Plate 51a

Plate 51b

Plate 52

Plate 53

Plate 54

Plate 55

Plate 56

Plate 57

Plate 58

Plate 59a

Plate 59b

Plate 60

Plate 61

Plate 62

Plate 63

Plate 64a

Plate 64b

people in Britain seem not to be aware of it. It is called Antequera, and it is in Andalucia. Simeon Reyna has written about it.[54] The slabs of stones used to construct this dolmen are so gigantic that one of the roof stones weighs 180 tons. This exceeds the weight of any stone used in ancient Egypt, except for those forming the pavement beside the Pyramid of Chephren, which are estimated to weigh up to 200 tons each. But those are on the ground, and the ones at Antequera are *ceiling stones*. If anyone were to look for evidence of a prehistoric culture with the demonstrable ability to handle huge stones of inconceivable weight for construction purposes, and who would have the stone-handling capabilities to advise on or participate in the construction of the Giza pyramids, it is surely these very megalith builders. I reproduce some photos of the Antequera dolmens on this book's website; they are so incredible and exciting to see.

The megalithic remains of Spain have been very thoroughly studied, and published lavishly in German, commencing in 1943 at Berlin, in the middle of the Second World War. I have these huge tomes, which are almost as heavy as Antequera dolmen stones! No trouble or expense was spared, and the illustrations are amazing. The authors were George Leisner (1879–1957) and Vera Leisner (1885–1972).[55] The Leisners devoted their working lives to this immense and worthy project. Without wishing to cast any aspersions at all upon the Leisners, of whom I know nothing of a personal nature, it needs to be pointed out that the lavish expenditure of the publication of their initial volumes in the middle of the war, after the disastrous defeat of the Germans at Stalingrad, must have required the financial and political support of the Ahnenerbe (Ancestral Heritage Bureau) of the SS. As it happens, the kind of research being undertaken by the Leisners fitted perfectly with the aims and race theories of the Nazis, who in the 1930s sent archaeological and ethnographic teams to many quarters of the world (including such faraway places as Iceland and Tibet) to study 'early Aryans' (and, yes, they believed there had been 'Aryans' in Tibet, indeed that Aryans actually originated from there, but that is a long story . . .). Our knowledge of Spanish megalithic culture thus owes much to the bizarre theories and beliefs of none other than Heinrich Himmler, who must also have supplied funds for the work itself, which clearly required a substantial support staff and a significant research team. This is indeed a high irony, for it was the fascists of Spain who seem to have arrested Montalbán (who must have had republican sympathies) at Mezorah just as he finished his work there, and seized his papers, thus depriving us of his archaeological report on the megaliths of Morocco. So it all goes to show that you win some and you lose some: German fascists helped us learn about the megaliths of Spain while Spanish fascists stopped us from learning about the megaliths of North Africa.

One of the most impressive scholarly works of the early part of the twentieth century was the large folio volume *The Eastern Libyans* by Oric Bates.[56] It managed to squeak into print just before the First World War broke out. Bates was not an archaeologist; he was a geographer, a surveyor, and a very great scholar with a superb mastery of classical learning. One wonders whether there is anyone alive today who could possibly produce such a mammoth and seminal work.

Bates was in no doubt that the Libyans and peoples of northern Europe had a direct connection. He speaks about the prominence in Northern Africa of what he calls 'xanthochroids'. That weird word merely means 'people with light hair and light skin'. Sometimes he comes down to earth and just speaks of them as blonds. We could just say 'blond white people'. It has been known for a long time by Egyptologists that there were fair-haired and blue-eyed members of the royal family during the Fourth Dynasty, for instance Hetepheres, the daughter of Cheops (named after her grandmother, the mother of Cheops), who married King Djedefre, her half-brother. Some of the inlaid eyes of statues of the period show blue eyes rather than brown. These features seem to have come from the many intermarriages between Egyptian kings and Libyan princesses which took place from the First Dynasty through to the Third Dynasty. I will avoid going into detail and giving all the examples of this here because of lack of space, but these are facts which are not contested and are therefore not controversial. I should add that some amateur enthusiasts have made claims in books and articles, and on the Internet, that the world's earliest recorded queens were black Africans. To 'prove' this theory, they have claimed that the Libyan princesses who became Egyptian queens, such as the Lower Egyptian Neith Hetep and Mer Neith of the First Dynasty (especially in the 25th dynasty), who came from Sais in the Delta, were black women. Whereas it is true that black Africans did have a role in Egyptian history, and there were even some black pharaohs, the Libyan princesses/queens were pale blonde women. Black Africans came from Upper Egypt (southern Egypt), and below, not from Lower Egypt (the Delta in the north).

Here are some further comments by Bates:

> The origin, whether European, Asiatic, or African, of the Hamitic race – which, with the Arabs, now shares that part of Africa which lies north of lat. 10° N. – yet awaits solution. . . . The most important extra-African elements among the Hamites are the brachycephalic [broad-headed] Berbers and the blonds. Both, as one would *a priori* expect, are found in the north. The brachycephals are, almost certainly, invaders, since they form but a small group near the northern seaboard of the dolicho-cephalic [long-headed] African continent. The blonds are much more numerous, but are even more clearly of extra-African origin. . . . That the xanthochroids were Nordic invaders, as was long ago supposed by Broca and Faidherbe, seems . . . indubitable. . . . the African xanthropoids are found at the end of a road which was followed in historic times by another blond Nordic invasion [the Vandals; 80,000 of them crossed the Mediterranean into Africa in 428 AD and by 439 AD they had seized Carthage], (and) it is only reasonable to suppose that the xanthochroids of the Egyptian monuments and classical notices were invaders in a country primarily peopled with "autochthonous" blacks and *bruns*. One may, as did de Quatrefages, say truly that the origin of the African blonds is as yet unknown, but it is, for the reasons just given, safe to say they were immigrants.[57]

Later in the book, Bates becomes more specific about the megalith builders being blonds:

'If one attempts to divine what people these megalith builders were, the strong probability appears that they were the Nordic xanthochroids or blonds. That people seems to have come into Africa by way of Western Europe, and in the Moghreb [Maghreb is the usual spelling today; it is the region which contains Morocco, Algeria, and Tunisia], where the rude stone monuments are most numerous, the bulk of the fair Africans is found. This theory, which is fairly well sustained by other facts, and which would attribute the African megaliths to the xanthochroids whom the Berbers have partially assimilated, was first formulated and supported by General [Louis] Faidherbe [in his article 'Instructions sur l'Anthropologie de l'Algerie', published in Paris in 1873], and may still be accepted as essentially true.'[58]

Certainly Sir Flinders Petrie was of the opinion that the 'first pre-historic people' of Egypt were Libyans. He said:

> It seems now fairly clear that there were three systems of writing in Egypt, and each of these is first known with a different race. The geometrical marks of the alphabetic system appear with the first prehistoric people, who seem to have been Libyans. They belonged to the west, and were the source of all the Mediterranean alphabets. . . . the long priority of the alphabetic signs in Egypt leaves the tradition of Phoenician origin [of the alphabet] out of the case . . . Even Diodorus [Siculus] did not believe in it . . . When we see how widespread was the full alphabet, it is plain that the Phoenician had only a small part of the whole. There are 23 letters that were used in Egypt, Karia, and Spain, all unknown in Phoenicia. There were 10 other letters which the South Arabian had in common with the Mediterranean and the Runes of Northern Europe, yet all unknown in Phoenicia. It seems obvious that there was a very widespread alphabet, from which at a much later time the Phoenician selection was formed.[59]

I need hardly remind the reader that the Phoenicians, being direct inheritors of the Atlantic coastal trade routes as already explained, would naturally have been inheritors of an alphabet as well, from the same predecessors. It is notable also that Petrie recognises the existence of the alphabet in both Egypt and in megalithic Spain long before the time of the Phoenicians, and readily admits that the 'first prehistoric race' bringing culture to Egypt before the First Dynasty was Libyan, from the west. This is a direct confirmation of the hypothesis that I am advancing in this chapter. We thus have the authority of Petrie himself for what I am proposing about a Libyan (or at least joint-Libyan) origin for the first high civilisation of Egypt.

Petrie often insisted on Libyan origins. He maintained that the Egyptian city of Herakleopolis (now called Ehsnasya) had been founded by Libyans in prehistoric times:

'The site has a remarkable history. In the geologic past the Nile had found an exit to the Fayum [a large fertile area west of the Nile below Cairo] about ten miles south of the Lahun entrance. The strata collapsed into the worn channel, and lie tilted up at 45 degrees. This break in the ring of the Fayum basin gave later an easy access from the west into the Nile valley. Through this gap various waves of Libyans have come, the best known of which are the Libyan chiefs of Herakleopolis in the XXIInd dynasty. Doubtless the city was founded at first by such an invasion, which accounts for its unusual position, far from the Nile. . . . probably the canal [Bahr Yusuf] ran along the old desert edge, and the city was founded on the opposite bank. This would have been in prehistoric times, as it is a city of the earliest class . . .'[60]

Petrie is thus highly explicit in insisting that Libyans founded cities in Egypt in prehistoric times, and that one of them was south of Giza. The Egyptian name of Herakleopolis was Henen-Nesut, which is believed to mean 'palm grove of the king',[61] or sometimes Henun-Seten. The city lay west of the Nile, directly south of the Fayyum oasis region, and about the same distance south of the pyramid at Meidum (the southernmost Old Kingdom pyramid) as Meidum is south of the Old Kingdom pyramids of Dashur. So you could call Herakleopolis the effective southern boundary of what I like to describe as the 'Memphis/Giza region' (which commences at the southern base of the Delta, where the Nile divides into tributaries) before you enter what might be called 'Middle Egypt', to the south of it.

However, Petrie also believed that Libyans settled further south as well. He believed that the important prehistoric site of Naqada was founded by Libyans, who thus founded what archaeologists call the 'Naqadan civilisation':

'The first [royal] title was that of the red crown, *deshert*, which was carefully modelled in relief on a jar . . . of the first prehistoric civilisation after the Badarian . . . It is obviously a cap, like that of the Doge of Venice, with an ostrich feather stuck upright in it. We know more about it than did the historic Egyptians, who could make nothing of the traditional form which had reached them, and lengthened the feather to a line which had no meaning. This was later the crown of [the city of] Sais [in the Delta] and of the goddess Neit [Neith], thus evidently of Libyan origin, and finding this far south, at Naqada, agrees with the Libyan source of the civilisation of that period.'[62] The Egyptian name for Naqada was Nubt, and its classical name was Ombos. It is very far south, on the Nile, more than halfway from Edfu to Aswan. The fact that Libyans were there also in prehistoric times is remarkable, as it is an immense distance south of Herakleopolis. It is a strange place for the earliest known depiction of the Red Crown of the *North* to be found on a pot. It is a bit like finding a penguin at the North Pole or, more appropriately perhaps, finding a polar bear (from the Arctic Circle) at the South Pole. This all goes to show that people got around a lot more in prehistoric times than we imagine.

There are many ancient Egyptian pictures of Libyans from wall paintings and other sources, some of which I reproduce as Plate 59b, and as Figure 67. Many of these show very clearly certain recurring design patterns which appear either on the clothing of the Libyans or as tattoos on their skin. Similarities may be seen between these and the design patterns collected and reproduced by the Leisners of the Spanish/Iberian megalith builders. I reproduce those as Figure 68. The main feature in both cases is the lozenge, or the recurring lozenge as a series. These similarities further substantiate the idea that the Libyans and the Iberian megalith builders had common origins, and it should be borne in mind that the examples of the Libyan designs are mostly more than a thousand years later, so that certain cultural continuities were clearly strong over immense spans of time.

Another predynastic culture of Egypt is called the Amratian Culture, conventionally dated circa 4000 BC–3500 BC. This culture, which followed the Badarians (an early culture mentioned in Chapter Six, the ones with the best pottery) is sometimes called Naqada I. According to Sir Flinders Petrie, the Amratians were Libyans. He wrote:

'Immediately following the Badarian . . . came the Amratian civilisation . . . It is linked to the Badarian by the continuity of black-topped red pottery, the form of carinated [ridged or keel-shaped] bowls, the use of slate palettes and malachite eye-paint. Yet a great outburst of

Figure 67. A Libyan, as portrayed in New Kingdom art. From Karl Oppel, *Das Alte Wunderland der Pyramiden*, Leipzig, 1868, page 144. It was traditional for prominent Libyans to wear two feathers in their hair, and these are thought to be the origin of the double-plume appearing on the heads of various Egyptian gods, such as Amun and Sokar.

new types and new decoration shows undoubtedly a fresh people entering the land. The most obvious feature is the abundance of white line patterns on red bowls; these are all imitations of basket patterns, of which the Badarians do not show a trace. They imply an independent rise of pottery from the clay-lined basket, while the Badarian wrought clay as a pot-making material, pure and simple. The patterns are those still current in the highlands of Algeria, where also the use of haematite-faced pottery and white slip decoration is common. It is, then, to Libya that we must refer this new group of population.'[63]

Petrie also pointed out in a review of an article about ancient Malta by the French scholar, E. de Manneville: 'The carinated bowls of the Neolithic pottery [found at Malta] are most like such bowls of the early Amratian [of Egypt].'[64]

This is an important detail, because if the Amratians were 'Libyans' and pottery similar to theirs was used on Malta at about the same time, then this suggests that the 'Libyans' were a maritime people capable of sailing between the North African coast and the island of Malta, which in turn suggests that these 'Amrato-Libyo-Maltese', as we might call them, were thus a branch of the megalithic peoples. And that supports my general thesis very well indeed.

In another review, Petrie comments on the discoveries made by the German philologist E. Zyhlarx:

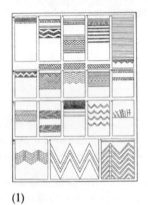

(1)

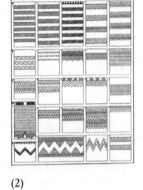

(2)

(3)

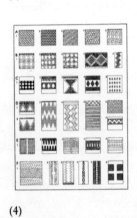

(4)

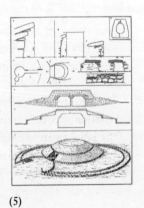

(5)

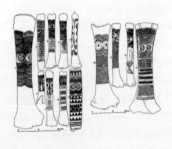

(6)

Figure 68

(1): Iberian designs found on pottery of the megalithic period in Spain. Plate 91 from Leisner, Georg, and Leisner, Vera, *Die Megalithgräber der Iberischen Halbinsel* (*The Megalithic Graves of the Iberian Peninsula*), Berlin, 1943 onwards.

(2). Iberian designs found on megalithic pottery in south-eastern Spain. Plate 90 (1) from Leisner, Georg, and Leisner, Vera, *Die Megalithgräber der Iberischen Halbinsel* (*The Megalithic Graves of the Iberian Peninsula*), Berlin, 1943 onwards.

(3). Iberian designs found on megalithic pottery in south-eastern Spain. Plate 90 (2) from Leisner, Georg, and Leisner, Vera, *Die Megalithgräber der Iberischen Halbinsel* (*The Megalithic Graves of the Iberian Peninsula*), Berlin, 1943 onwards.

(4). Iberian designs found on megalithic pottery in southern Spain. Plate 93 from Leisner, Georg, and Leisner, Vera, *Die Megalithgräber der Iberischen Halbinsel* (*The Megalithic Graves of the Iberian Peninsula*), Berlin, 1943 onwards.

(5). Reconstruction by the Leisners of the original appearance of a megalithic Iberian grave in the south of Spain. Plate 85 from Leisner, Georg, and Leisner, Vera, *Die Megalithgräber der Iberischen Halbinsel* (*The Megalithic Graves of the Iberian Peninsula*), Berlin, 1943 onwards.

(6). Ancient Iberian geometrical designs with the 'double-eye' or 'twin-sun' motif, inscribed on bones discovered in the megalithic remains. Plate 92 from Leisner, Georg, and Leisner, Vera, *Die Megalithgräber der Iberischen Halbinsel* (*The Megalithic Graves of the Iberian Peninsula*), Berlin, 1943 onwards.

'A recognition of the homogeneity between the Berber speech [of contemporary North Africa] and a Libyan component of the ancient Egyptian language carries research in Old Egyptian into a new phase of knowledge.'[65]

I do not believe much further work has been done on elucidating the Libyan linguistic elements in Old Egyptian, and their relation to Berber; or, if so, such studies have not received particular attention in our day.

Although many of the earlier Egyptologists were insistent upon a Libyan origin for the west Delta civilisation, contemporary Egyptologists have been accused of ducking the issue to an extraordinary degree. One of the most prominent contributors to the discussion was a remarkable woman whom I knew slightly, Dr Alessandra Nibbi (1923–2007). She was an Italian who was Doctor of Letters in

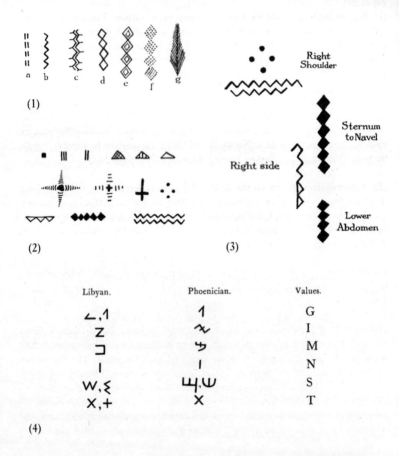

(1)

(2)

(3)

Libyan.   Phoenician.   Values.

G
I
M
N
S
T

(4)

Etruscology (study of the Etruscans), but who turned her attention to Egypt and became an Egyptologist, and settled in Oxford. From 1972 until 2007 she battled tirelessly against a sea of inertia and indifference to call the attention of Egyptologists to some anomalous matters relating especially to the Egyptian Delta, which she personally explored before it had been largely bulldozed flat, with so many archaeological sites destroyed in the pursuit of modern agriculture. She published several books and countless articles. She was one of those people with apparently limitless energy.

In 1985, she founded and edited, until shortly before her death, the

Figure 69

(1). Libyan tattoo patterns shown on figurines of 'C Group' Libyans, sometimes called 'Middle Nubians', residing in the region of Nubia between the First and Second Cataracts of the Nile. The figurines were excavated at the cemetery of Dakkah (Pselchis). Bates demonstrates that this group bears relationships to predynastic Libyans, and Bates identifies them as a branch of the Temehu Libyans of the North, who lived as a detached group for many centuries on the Nile in the far south. Bates points out that the Libyans reached these areas below Upper Egypt from Libya by travelling overland from oasis to oasis, far west of the Nile, rather than by sailing down the Nile itself. They had architectural and cultural traits wholly differing from those of the majority of black 'Nubians', and they lived partially by fishing. (Figure 98 from Oric Bates, *The Eastern Libyans*, London, 1914, page 250.)

(2). Tattoo designs shown on the skin of Libyans as depicted by the Egyptians. They are from two sources: a group of four Temehu Libyan princes portrayed on a wall of the tomb of Seti I, and three tiles preserved at Medinet Habu near Luxor; both sources are New Kingdom in date. (Figure 52 from Oric Bates, *The Eastern Libyans*, London, 1914, page 140.)

(3). Oric Bates's analysis of the various parts of the body where the different tattoo designs on the Libyans appeared. (Figure x from Oric Bates, *The Eastern Libyans*, London, 1914, page x.)

(4). Oric Bates's lists of alphabet letters as they appeared first in North Africa ('Libyan'), later in Phoenician, and as they are pronounced today, having reached us through the Greek alphabet, which derived from the Phoenician. The Phoenician letters are clearly derived from the earlier North African ones. The ultimate origin of our alphabet may thus go back to megalithic times. A closer and more comprehensive study of the monuments of North Africa, and the inscriptions which sometimes are found on them and on rocks, may yield a better understanding of these apparent origins. (Figure x from Oric Bates, *The Eastern Libyans*, London, 1914, page x.)

Egyptological journal *Discussions in Egyptology*, based in Oxford. A total of sixty-five issues appeared, of which I have managed to collect all but one now, and at any moment I have high expectations of completing my set of this truly remarkable journal. It was founded in imitation of the other small-format but much older Egyptological journal, bound also in yellow, called the *Göttinger Miszellen*, which is published in Göttingen in Germany. Between them, these two wonderful and stimulating journals have acted as necessary publishers of short articles and notices in the major Western languages, as well as frequently publishing 'unorthodox' contributions containing observations or theories which the more sober journals would be frightened to publish because they challenge conventional thinking too much.

Alessandra Nibbi's ideas are so extraordinarily interesting and relevant that at one point I considered attempting an extended survey of them here, and compiling a comprehensive bibliography for her as I have done for Patrick O'Mara (whom she frequently published in her journal). If it were not for the activities of a few polite and genteel 'trouble-makers' like Nibbi and O'Mara, Egyptology would become totally petrified and incapable of ever generating a new insight. Thus, people like Nibbi and O'Mara should be encouraged enthusiastically, because they poke the corpses of the 'walking dead', the orthodox scholars who never deviate by a hair's-breadth from consensus opinions, and make them awaken from their sleepwalking and stir slightly. However, I have had to abandon my noble idea of surveying Nibbi's ideas, however important they are in terms of what I have been discussing, because the task would be too vast, and this book would never end. I shall content myself therefore with quoting only one of her many, many articles, which appeared in her own journal in 1995, as her comments are so shocking in the light of what we have been considering:

... we are given [in a book she has just quoted] a resume from the Egyptological textbooks on the 'Libyans' without considering the fact that there is a great deal of uncertainty and assumption in piecing together the Egyptological material, and no clarity at all concerning the geographical background of these people, which cannot have been the desert. . . . We must accept the Roman use of this term which applied to all the area immediately to the west of the Nile . . . Thus the term *westerner* is more appropriate than *Libyan* for the people we are discussing . . . More recent studies of 'Libyan' people have been reluctant to separate them from the area that is Libya today and rarely attempt to identify them from any evidence. We even find references to 'ethnically Libyan pharaohs', whatever that may imply. At the seminar which formed the basis of Anthony Leahy's *Libya and Egypt c. 1300–750 B.C.* (1990), no attempt was made to define 'Libyan'. Scholars depended considerably on Leahy's earlier article on the Libyan period in Egypt which attempts to identify the foreign 'Libyan' Dynasty in Egypt as rule by men of 'Libyan extraction', even though 'the retention of their ethnic

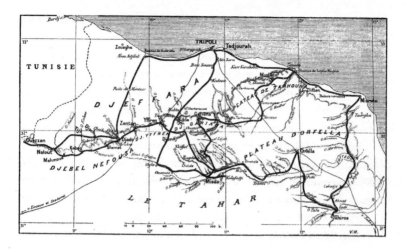

Figure 70. The late 19th-century French traveller Méhier de Mathuisieulx's map of his travels round Libya, which shows the Plateau of Tahuna (which the French spell Tahouna, as they always like to stick an extra 'o' into names, given half a chance), at upper right. This region is especially rich in trilithons, many of which were photographed by Cowper (see Plates 60–64, and many others on the website).

identity is obscured by the evidence'. In this article Leahy has to work hard to convince us that the 'Libyans' were very different from the Egyptians, which some earlier scholars [she cites two German Egyptologists, Ludwig Borchardt and Uvo Hölscher] would not have accepted. But he leaves us no wiser as to who the Libyans were.[66]

This warns us that there are no 'red-hot' scholars in this field these days!

James Henry Breasted, one of the most prominent Egyptologists at the beginning of the twentieth century (and creator of the 'Breasted Chronology' for Egyptian history which was mentioned in earlier chapters), in his book *A History of Egypt*, made it plain that he believed Libyans were crucial to the formation of Egyptian civilisation. Here are some of his comments:

[Egypt had] on the north the harbourless coastline of the Delta, and on the south the rocky barriers of successive cataracts, preventing fusion

431

with the peoples of inner Africa. It was chiefly at the two northern corners of the Delta, that outside influences and foreign elements, which were always sifting into the Nile valley, gained access to the country. Through the eastern corner it was the prehistoric Semitic population of neighbouring Asia, who forced their way in across the dangerous intervening deserts; while the Libyan races, of possibly European origin, found entrance at the western corner. . . . The Delta was, throughout the historic age, open to inroads of the Libyans who dwelt upon the west of it; and the constant influx of people from this source gave the western Delta a distinctly Libyan character which it preserved even down to the time of Herodotus [circa 484 BC–425 BC]. At the earliest moment when the monuments enable us to discern the conditions in the Delta, the Pharaoh is contending with the Libyan invaders, and the earlier kingdom of the North [the predynastic kings, some of whom are recorded on the Palermo Stone (see Figure 49)] will therefore have been strongly Libyan, if indeed it did not owe its origin to this source. The temple at Sais, in the western Delta, the chief centre of Libyan influence in Egypt, bore the name 'House of the King of Lower Egypt' (the Delta), and the emblem of Neit, its chief goddess, was tattooed by the Libyans upon their arms . . . Unfortunately, the Delta is so deeply overlaid with deposits of Nile mud, that the material remains of its earliest civilization are buried forever beyond our reach. That civilization was probably earlier and more advanced than that of the valley above.[67]

This is precisely my thesis, which frankly I arrived at before I checked to see what Breasted's views were. We have here a clear reason why we do not and possibly can never know the details of the civilisation which I believe really built the pyramids of Giza, because the home of their civilisation and the original occupation levels of their capital at Sais are mostly buried at enormous depths below thousands of years' accumulation of mud and silt of the Delta. But they must have been the highest pinnacle of achievement of these peoples of Libyan/Megalithic/'Atlantic' derivation. From the megalithic background came the mathematical, geometrical and astronomical knowledge, along with the ability to handle and build with gigantic stones equivalent to those found at Antequera in Spain (180 tons). There seems to be no other contemporary source possible

Figure 71. A map by Wilson showing Egypt northwards from Herakleopolis, the area which prior to the First Dynasty was presumably that controlled by the 'northern king' of the predynastic period. The marshy character of the Delta region of the north is well represented here. The sacred city of the Delta was Buto, seen here slightly to the left of centre just at the beginning of the marshy regions. Below it, in a drier area, was Sais, the Delta political capital.

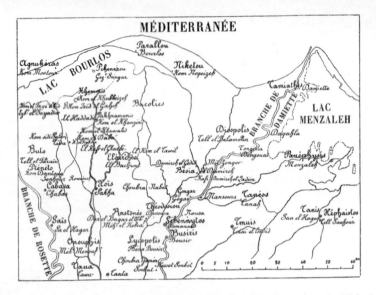

Figure 72. A map of the North Delta drawn by Georges Daressy, and published in *Annales du Service des Antiquités*, Vol. 26. Sais is near the bottom left. Busiris is in the centre, almost directly east of Sais. Tanis is at right, almost directly east of Busiris. Buto is in the middle, at far left.

for these elements of technology and culture. But how these became transformed into the fantastic achievements at Giza remains unknown. I believe I have only succeeded in showing that some of the necessary elements existed and were available to Lower Egypt at the correct time. This seems to me the only possibility for their derivation and incorporation into 'Egyptian civilisation'. By what magic this took place and resulted in the creation of such fantastic structures as the pyramids of Giza, I cannot say. The answers may, as Breasted suggests, be forever inaccessible to us. But that does not mean we should not go on trying to find these answers.

APPENDICES

APPENDIX ONE

TWO PREVIOUSLY UNKNOWN NINETEENTH-CENTURY ACCOUNTS OF THE GREAT PYRAMID PASSAGES

A Description of Giambattista Caviglia's Work inside the
Great Pyramid, Privately Published by His Friend
Annibale Brandi in 1823
Translated by Stefano Greco
(with notes by Robert Temple)

From what is believed to be the only surviving copy of:
COMPENDIOUS DESCRIPTION OF
THE PYRAMIDS OF GIZA IN EGYPT
BY
A. B.
[Annibale Brandi]
LIVORNO
BY STAMPERIA DELLA FENICE
1823

After emerging from the Great Gate of Cairo, one has to ride for at least one hour, before getting to the old city of Cairo; from there, one can go to Roda and then one crosses to Giza, land which is scarcely considered. It is located not far from the riverside of the Nile, and it has the desert at its back. One then has to travel for three hours on horses or donkeys before getting to the Great Pyramid. The distance between Giza and this Pyramid is approximately seventeen Italian miles.

The ancient historians and geographers, i.e. Herodotus, Strabo, Diodorus Siculus, Ptolemy and, most of all, Pliny, talked about the great Pyramids of Egypt, among which the most celebrated for their size and good conservation are absolutely the ones of Giza. What could I say about them, after these famous writers? Nevertheless, I will give my own feelings about them; their descriptions are well known, which is why I will not say much about them. I will only superficially say something about their construction. Whether the Great Pyramid of Giza has served as a mausoleum to an Egyptian Pharaoh, according to Herodotus, Strabo and some Arab Historians, or as the tomb of the ancient Kings of Egypt, as many authors say, is a problem for the learned. Meanwhile the opinion of a writer named Monsieur [Benoit de] Maillet seems very plausible. He says that, after putting the bodies of the King and the Queen in the Great Pyramid, they have closed it from the inside, and that the last ones to exit have gone down the well excavated in the rock, and then they have climbed up the passage; after that, by closing the entrance of it, they have left a continuously plane surface, all the way down to its base.

It is a big question if the ones who first entered it were led there by the tradition, by certain writings of the ancient writers, or only by their self-confidence, when they found the opening of the descending passage which I just mentioned.

And it is also a mystery whether before the eighth century anybody has entered the chambers of the King and the Queen through the well, because the ancient writers don't say anything about these.

From what I could see, and from what cultivated people say, certain Arab writers state that the hunger for gold brought the Caliph Mohammed to force open, around the beginning of the eighth century, an entrance into the Great Pyramid, believing he could find some treasures. They say that certain golden idols, which were found with the mummy of the King, were the small reward for many years of work and excessive expenses. Other Oriental writers say that this enterprise was the one of the Caliph Haroun el-Rashid, who lived at the time of Charles the Great

438

[Charlemagne]. Whatever they say, it is indubitable that the forced opening of the Great Pyramid was made during the dominance of the Arabs.

After a certain epoch, with great difficulty some travellers and some curious people succeeded in entering the chambers I mentioned through this forced entrance. Some intelligent men, though, thought that whatever the Pyramid had been used for, there might have been other ways to enter the interior of such a marvellous building.

Captain Giovanni Battista Caviglia from Genoa, who had been in Egypt for some time (and maybe he's still there), since he had some knowledge of science, went to the pyramids and to the Sphinx which guards the Sacred Valley [entrance to the Plateau], and he initiated the project to try to clear those passages.

He started his work in January 1817 and was able to clear the underground way, called a Passage, which led from the Pyramid to the opening of the forced entrance through which one could reach the tunnel, the chambers of the King and the Queen, and the famous well; then he made more comfortable the forced entrance, by removing the holed rock through which one had to enter [presumably the casing stones with a forced hole in them had been left around this forced entrance until this date]. Also, since he couldn't predict that in the continuation of the [descending] passage there was an entry to the well-shaft, he decided to clean the well-shaft, which was full of earth and rocks, while he was working to the horizontal opening of the passage. The well-shaft is carved out of the rock inside the Great Pyramid. Close to the middle of the well's depth, on the left side, there is a cave excavated in the rock; this is known and described by the ancient Arab writers. [This is commonly known as 'the Grotto'.]

Captain Caviglia, according to what they tell me, cleaned the cave [the Grotto] for 60 feet [if this is really true, then there has been a collapse of the gravel in the Grotto concealing this today]. Continuing to clean the descending passage, he found its connection to the well-shaft. Then, at the end of the passage, i.e. at about 380 feet from its opening, they found on its right side a chamber [the Subterranean Chamber], full of rocks and earth. [The description 'they found on its right side' refers to the fact that although you enter straight ahead, the entrance is at the extreme left corner of the chamber, so that as you enter, most of the chamber is on your right.] After he had cleared it [the Subterranean Chamber] of these [rocks and earth], he found that it did not lead to any other rooms and doesn't have any sign of opening. One should subtract 100 feet (the ones of the opening), from the length of that passage, in order to get to the entrance of the forced access. [This is an awkward way of saying that the forced entry of Mamoun leads to the Descending Passage at a point 100 feet in from its own entrance.] The fact that they [earlier people] had penetrated as far as that chamber [the Subterranean Chamber] is indicated by some letters found on its ceiling, formed by the smoke of flambeaux or candles, but when this happened is a mystery. Caviglia also cleared the chamber of the Queen very thoroughly [until then, as we know from Greaves, Sandys, and others, it had been half full of stones and rubbish and stank of a foul smell 'like a grave'], imagining he could find some way to other rooms; however, he had no results in this. He discovered that in the left corner of the tunnel [the Grand Gallery] there was a window; he climbed up to it with a ladder and he found a small room [Davison's Chamber, discovered about thirty years earlier], which was dark, of wonderful granite, and did not lead to any other place. It is true that no other writers have ever written about the continuation of this passage, nor about what happens at its end, nor about the connection to the well, nor about these other rooms.

Only Maillet guessed that the well-shaft had to be linked to the passage, but that was just a conjecture. It seems that Caviglia did nothing but clear the Great Pyramid of Giza and measure its dimensions precisely.

Also important are the discoveries made when excavating around the Andro-Sphinx [The Sphinx] and concerning the opening of various tombs located in the vicinity of the pyramids, as we will see in the continuation of these memoirs of mine. The short time that I was at the pyramids and my poor talent don't allow me to make a very exact description. However, assisted by cultivated people's advice, I continue as much as I can to describe what Mr. Caviglia accomplished.

This same Caviglia, after examining the Great Pyramid of Giza and discovering the continuation of the [*descending*] passage to the length of 280 feet further than was known, with a chamber at its end [the Subterranean Chamber], the connection between the passage and the well-shaft, and the small room of dark granite at the left corner of the tunnel [Grand Gallery], after clearing the chambers of rocks and earth, and taking note of the fact that he didn't have any other clues to find new chambers, left the Great Pyramid to look for other antiquities in the vicinity. And these initiatives of his, to say the least, were not fruitless. [I have here omitted the description of Caviglia's work at the Sphinx, and some minor tombs, which was published earlier as an appendix to my previous book, *The Sphinx Mystery*, 2009.]

... Caviglia descended to an underground tomb, and found a large chamber containing an impressive sarcophagus of granite with its cover, in very good condition. [This is apparently the so-called 'Osiris Shaft' beneath the Causeway of Chephren, described in Chapter Two. Caviglia was the first European to discover it, as James Burton also records in his manuscript record.]

... Caviglia entered and opened a small Pyramid, the one in front of the Great Pyramid, on the east side, and there he found rooms and passages that are more comfortable than the ones of the Great Pyramid. After excavating a lot in this one, and after searching in the subterranean passages, he found the space of a lodge which resembles the Antrums of Minerva; this space consists of four small caverns, excavated in the calcareous rock ...

The small pyramid [of Mycerinus] is not accessible, because so far nobody has ever succeeded in removing all the stones that surround it, and it seems, as they say, that it is not worthwhile to go to the trouble of trying to find its entrance. The other five Pyramids are very far from these, and they are in Northern Egypt, but they are not as beautiful as the ones of Giza. The perpendicular height of this Great Pyramid is 462 feet tall, i.e. 70 *tese*, and its sides are 660 feet long, i.e. 110 *tese*.

[Note: *tese* is plural for tesa, which was an Italian unit of linear measurement at this time, also sometimes used as a volumetric unit. The unit was borrowed from the French during the Later Middle Ages, the Middle French name being *toise*, from the Late Latin word *tesa*, from the earlier Latin *tensa* meaning 'outsretched arms' via Medieval Latin *tensa*, *teisa* meaning 'expanse, extent', and also from Latin *te(n)sa/tensus/tendere* 'to stretch', hence 'the stretch, reach, extent, or size of (a road).' The value of this unit varied enormously in nineteenth-century Italy between the value of 1.414 metres at Novara and the value 2.242 metres at Bardonecchia. (As a volumetric unit, it varied similarly, and was approximately two cubic metres.) Brandi is using *tese* in a loose sense, not a precise sense, to mean in the first instance 6.6 feet, and in the second instance 6 feet; however, the feet are apparently not English feet but French feet of the nineteenth century: *piedi*, or *piedi 'del Re'*. Brandi's use of this now obsolete unit of measurement, the *tesa*, and the fact that he contradicts himself in terms of its value in the two instances he gives, mean that he is only being approximate. Hence we do not really need to concern ourselves with his mention of *tese*, but just in case there are those who might worry, I have given this survey of the issue, in order to lay it to rest. R.T.]

JAMES BURTON (1826)
(UNPUBLISHED, FROM A MANUSCRIPT)
Taken from Burton's original unpublished manuscript in
the British Library:
MS. Add. 25,618:

(*Burton's description of the Grotto and 'well-shaft':*)
The well – The shaft lined with masonry above and below the grotto to support as was supposed one of those insulated beds of gravel which are frequently found in rock and which the masons call flaws.

(*Burton's description of the Subterranean Chamber:*)
The new passage. Continuing to the distance of twenty three feet beyond the door way which opened upon the bottom of the well in the same angle of inclination became narrower & took a horizontal direction for about twenty eight feet farther where it opened into a spacious chamber immediately under the central point of the pyramid. This new chamber is sixty six feet long by twenty seven feet broad with a flat roof and when first discovered was nearly filled with loose stones and rubbish which with considerable labour Mr Caviglia removed. The platform of the floor dug out of the rock is irregular nearly one half of the length from the

eastern or entrance end being level and about fifteen feet from the ceiling while in the middle it descends five feet lower in which part there is a hollow space bearing all the appearance of the commencement of a well or shaft – From hence it rises to the western end so that at this extremity there is scarcely room between the floor and the ceiling to stand upright the whole chamber having the appearance of an unfinished excavation though Mr [Henry] Salt thinks after a careful comparison of it with other subterranean chambers which have been disfigured by the combined effects of time and the rude hands of curious enquirers that it may once have been highly wrought and used perhaps for the purpose of solemn and secret mysteries. Mr Salt says he had flattered himself that this chamber would turn out to be that described by Herodotus as containing the tomb of Cheops which was insulated by a canal from the Nile but the want of an inlet and its elevation of thirty feet above the level of the Nile at its highest point put an end to this delusive idea. He thinks however from an expression of Strabo purporting that the passage from the entrance leads directly down to the chamber which contained . . . (the receptacle of the dead) that this chamber was the only one known to this author whatever might have been the intention of this deeply excavated chamber. No vestige of a sarcophagus could now be traced. On the south side of this irregularly formed or unfinished chamber is an excavated passage [*now called the Cul-de-Sac Passage*] just wide and high enough for a man to creep along on his hands and knees continuing horizontally in the rock for fifty five feet where it abruptly terminates. Another passage at the east end of the chamber commences with a kind of arch and runs about forty feet into the solid body of the pyramid. [*This suggests that there is a horizontal passage running east from the top portion of the 'subterranean well-shaft' which may have become blocked or obscured by the excavations in this shaft by Vyse and Perring eleven years later.*] Mr Salt alludes to some other passage noticed by Olivier in which the names of Paisley and Munro were now found inscribed at its extremity. [*This last paragraph appears word for word in a report sent by Henry Salt to* The Quarterly Review *in London in 1818, which suggests that Salt made use of Burton's manuscript, retaining the reference to himself in the third person.*]

APPENDIX TWO

Palermo Stone 'Measurements'

The Palermo Stone records measurements year by year of something, we don't know what. Everyone has assumed without question that these measurements must be of the differing maximum annual heights of the Nile flood every year at Inundation. This is a reasonable assumption on the face of it, because we know that nilometers (vertical gauges) were used to measure the Nile heights for thousands of years in Egypt, and that the height of the water was absolutely crucial to agriculture, and could determine whether people might starve in very bad years. All of this is well known and undisputed. But I feel very uncomfortable with the assumption that the measurements recorded on the Palermo Stone really refer to the Nile at all. One of the reasons I find this assumption unconvincing is that the measurements are too precise, down to the very tiny value of one quarter of one 'finger'. Since a 'finger' has a value of 18.71 mm or 0.7366 of an inch, the Palermo Stone measurements are thus so precise that they record variations of as little as 4.6775 mm, or 0.18415 of an inch. I cannot believe that measurements of the Nile height reached such precision, that the water surface would be stable enough to determine it, or that the gauges could possibly be so precise.

Astronomical instruments, however, would have been that precise because of the obsession with calendars and the true length of the year (a subject I intend to discuss at length in a future book). I therefore hold the opinion that what was really being measured was some astronomical quantity connected with calendrical computations. Whatever it was, it varied year by year and could be expressed as a linear measure.

In order to try to figure out what this might be, I first analysed the numerical data in the form given below. Naturally I disregarded all data coming from 'Cairo fragments' because I believe them to be fakes. So I only took the data recorded on the Palermo Stone itself.

I have produced a table in which it is possible to view the variations of the measures, many of them in substantial continuous stretches of years, expressed in both metric and English/American measures. Occasionally there is no variation. If the measurements relate to lunar motions, it should be noted that the moon's motions rise and dip five degrees above and below the ecliptic. If the Egyptians were observing these using a flat linear scale measurement and equating one angular degree with one royal cubit on their measuring instrument (ancient Egyptian knowledge of celestial degrees is something I will discuss on a future occasion, as there is no space for such a discussion here, but they did know their value and they did express them geodetically on the earth's surface as well, since they had a geographical spread of 'noon' stations used to measure shadows stretching across Egypt from east to west between Gaza and Siwa, by which they measured the size of the earth and the value of a degree), then this would make sense, because there is no recorded variation exceeding ten royal cubits, so the measurements would all be within the variations of motion of the moon as observed from the same fixed point over the year. I envisage a vertical rule marked from zero to ten standing upright and with a central slit positioned towards the dead centre of a meridian observation shaft such as those at Abu Ruash or Zawiyet el-Aryan which I discussed in Chapter Three. Then, as the moon culminated at the meridian on a certain date, a number would be obtained, which would vary with time due to the fact that the moon's motions do not coincide with the solar year. These are my early thoughts. I have not had the opportunity to think this through at all, but rather than wait until I can formulate some hypothesis, I have decided to publish the analysis of the data and the table, so that anyone who is interested might try and work it out for himself or herself.

Regarding assumptions, it is necessary to decide whether ordinary cubits or royal cubits are referred to in these measurements. An ordinary cubit contained 6 palms, and a royal cubit contained 7 palms. The data give the answer for us, because in Register Five, Box Number 4 gives a measure of 2 cubits 6 palms 2⅔ fingers. Since this exceeds 6 palms and is less than 7 palms, thus being more than an ordinary cubit and less than a royal cubit, it proves that royal cubits were being used. We are thus safe in using royal cubit conversions, and are not in danger of our numbers being out by one seventh.

Regarding the modern equivalent of a royal cubit length, Petrie found at Giza that the royal cubit was 1.71818 feet, which is 523.7 mm. We thus use 524 mm as the conversion.

Please note that the numbers in parentheses at the beginning of each line (at the far left) give the box numbers in the rows, and that they are not always consecutive (i.e., Box 4 is missing from Register Two).

Assuming royal cubit of 524 mm:

Assuming palm of 75 mm:

Assuming finger of 19 mm:

Assuming span of 262 mm:

Register One: no measurements occur. (Predynastic period.)

Register Two: (Dynastic Period)

(3)	[first year of Djer] 6 cubits	3,144 mm (10.315 feet)
(5)	4 cubits, 1 palm	2,171 mm (7.123 feet)
(6)	5 cubits, 5 palms, 1 finger	2,620 + 375 + 19 mm = 3,014 mm (9.89 feet)
(7)	5 cubits, 5 palms, 1 finger	3,014 mm (9.89 feet)
(8)	5 cubits, 1 palm	2,620 + 75 = 2,695 mm (8.84 feet)
(9)	5 cubits	2,620 mm (8.60 feet)
(10)	6 cubits, 1 palm	3,144 + 75 = 3,219 (10.56 feet)
(11)	4 cubits, 1 span	2,096 + 262 mm = 2,358 mm (7.74 feet)

(NEXT NOT CONSECUTIVE WITH ABOVE:)

Register Three:

(1)	3 cubits, 1 palm, 2 fingers	1,572 + 75 + 38 = 1,872 mm (6.14 feet)
(2)	4 cubits, 1 span	2,096 + 262 = 2,358 mm (7.74 feet)
(3)	8 cubits, 3 fingers	4,192 + 57 = 4,249 mm (13.940 feet)
(4)	3 cubits, 1 span (?)	1,572 + 262 = 1,824 mm (*uncertain*) (5.98 feet?)
(5)	5 cubits, 2 palms	2,620 + 150 = 2,770 mm (9.09 feet)
(6)	5 cubits, 1 palm, 2 fingers	2,620 + 75 + 38 = 2,733 mm (8.97 feet)

(7)   4 cubits, 2 palms (?)   2,096 + 150 = 2,246 mm (*uncertain*)
                                     (7.37 feet?)

(8)   2 cubits   1,048 mm (3.44 feet)

(9)   5 cubits   2,620 mm (8.60 feet)

(10) 4 cubits 1 span (?)   2,096 + 262 = 2,358 mm (*uncertain*)
                                       (7.74 feet?)

(11) 6 cubits, 1 palm, 2 fingers 3,144 + 75 + 38 = 3,257 mm (10.69 feet)

(12) 2 cubits, 1 span (?)   1,048 + 262 = 1,310 mm (*uncertain*)
                                       (4.30 feet?)

(13) 3 cubits, 5 palms, 2 fingers 1,572 + 375 + 38 = 1,985 mm (6.51 feet)

(NEXT NOT CONSECUTIVE WITH ABOVE:)
Register Four:

(2)   3 cubits, 4 palms, 2 fingers 1,572 + 300 + 38 = 1,910 mm (6.27 feet)
(3)   4 cubits, 2 fingers   2,096 + 38 = 2,134 mm (7.00 feet)
(4)   4 cubits, 1 palm, 2 fingers 2,096 + 75 + 38 = 2,209 mm (7.25 feet)
(5)   4 cubits, 4 palms   2,096 + 300 = 2,396 mm (7.86 feet)
(6)   3 cubits, 4 palms, 2 fingers 1,572 + 300 + 38 = 1,910 mm (6.27 feet)
(7)   4 cubits, 3 fingers   2,096 + 225 = 2,321 mm (7.62 feet)
(8)   4 cubits, 3 fingers   2,096 + 225 = 2,321 mm (7.62 feet)
(9)   1 cubit   524 mm (1.719 feet)
(10) 3 cubits, 4 palms, 3 fingers 1,572 + 300 + 225 = 2,097 mm (6.88 feet)
(11) 3 cubits, 5 palms, 2 fingers 1,572 + 375 + 38 = 1,985 mm (6.51 feet)
(12) 2 cubits, 2 fingers   1,048 + 38 = 1,086 mm (3.56 feet)
(13) 2 cubits, 2 fingers   1,048 + 38 = 1,086 mm (3.56 feet)
(14) 3 cubits   1,572 mm (5.16 feet)

(NEXT NOT CONSECUTIVE WITH ABOVE:)
Register Five:

(1)   2 cubits, 4 palms, 1½ fingers 1,048 + 300 + 28.5 = 1,376.5 mm (4.52 feet)
(2)   2 cubits, 3 palms, 1 finger 1,048 + 225 + 19 = 1,292 mm (4.24 feet)
(3)   3⅔ cubits   1,572 + 345 = 1,917 mm (6.29 feet)
(4)   2 cubits, 6 palms, 2½ fingers 1,048 + 450 + 47.5 = 1,545.5 mm (5.07 feet)
(5)   4 cubits, 2 palms, 2⅔ fingers 2,096 + 150 + 50.5 = 2,296.5 mm (7.53 feet)
(6)   4 cubits, 2 palms   2,096 + 150 = 2,246 mm (7.37 feet)
(7)   2 months, 23 days   *calendrical, not linear*

(8) 4 cubits, 2 palms, 2⅔ fingers 2,096 + 38 + 50.5 = 2,184.5 mm (7.17 feet)

(9) 4 cubits, 1⅔ palms   2,096 + 28.5 = 2,124.5 mm (6.97 feet)

(10) 2 cubits, 3 palms, 2¾ fingers 1,048 + 225 + 52.25 = 1,287.25 mm

                                  (4.22 feet)

(11) 3 cubits, 3 palms, 2 fingers 1,572 + 225 + 38 = 1,835 mm (6.02 feet)

(12) 3 cubits   1,572 mm   (5.16 feet)

(NEXT NOT CONSECUTIVE WITH ABOVE:)

Register Six:

(2) 2 cubits, 2 fingers   1,048 + 38 = 2,921 mm

                                  (9.58 feet)

(3) 5 cubits, 1 palm, 1 finger   2,620 + 75 + 19 = 2,714 mm

                                  (8.90 feet)

(4) 2 cubits, 2 palms, 2¾ fingers 1,048 + 38 + 52.25 = 1,138.25 mm

                                  (3.73 feet)

VERSO SIDE OF STONE (NOT CONSECUTIVE WITH FOREGOING:)

Register One:

(1) . . . months, 24 days   *calendrical, not linear*

(2) 4 cubits, 3 palms, 2½ fingers 2,096 + 225 + 47.5 = 2,368.5 mm (7.77 feet)

(NOT CONSECUTIVE WITH ABOVE:)

Register Two:

(2) 4 cubits, 2½ fingers   2,096 + 47.5 = 2,143.5 mm (7.03 feet)

(NOT CONSECUTIVE WITH ABOVE:)

Register Three:

(1) 2 cubits, 2¼ fingers   1,048 + 42.75 = 1,052.75 mm (3.45 feet)

(2) 3 cubits . . .   1,572 + ?? = 1,572+ mm (incomplete)

                                  (5.16 feet +)

(3) 3 + x cubits   1,572 + ?? = 1,572+ mm (incomplete)

                                  (5.16 feet +)

CUBIT = 6 palms = 24 fingers (450 mm)

ROYAL CUBIT = 7 palms = 28 fingers (524 mm)

STANDARD ROYAL CUBIT (at Giza) = 1.71818 feet (Petrie) (523.70 mm)

ROYAL CUBIT = 7 palms = 20.61–20.63 inches/ 523.5–524 mm

PALM = 4 fingers

SMALL SPAN (half an ordinary cubit) = 12 fingers (or 3 palms, ½ cubit)

LARGE SPAN (half a royal cubit) = 14 fingers (i.e., 3½ palms, ½ royal cubit)

ROYAL CUBIT assumed as 524 mm

PALM assumed as 74.86 mm, say 75 mm

FINGER assumed as 18.71 mm, say 19 mm

APPENDIX THREE

Translation of the Introduction to Uvo Hölscher's excavation report on the Valley Temple at Giza:

Hölscher, Uvo, *Das Grabdenkmal des Königs Chephren* (*The Funerary Monument of King Chephren*), Erster Band (Vol. I) of the *Veröffentlichungen der Ernst von Sieglin-Expedition* (*Publications of the Ernst von Sieglin Expedition in Egypt*), edited by Georg Steindorff, containing also contributions by Ludwig Borchardt and Georg Steindorff, J. C. Hinrich's Booksellers, Leipzig, 1912.

Translations of additional chapters and other material may be found on the website www.egyptiandawn.info

INTRODUCTION

Prehistory of the excavation

After the pyramids and funerary temples of the Fifth Dynasty at Abusir were thoroughly studied and the knowledge of them and a clear picture of the complex of the royal monuments were achieved as a result of the successful excavations of the German Institute under its Director Ludwig Borchardt, the desire became ever more urgent to obtain as well as a similarly clear picture of the older pyramid temples of the Fourth Dynasty at Giza.

However, the pyramid field at Giza is terribly damaged. Through the centuries it had been used as a quarry for old Heliopolis and Memphis, for the Roman fortress of Babylon, and for the Arab cities of Fostat and Cairo. Only the pyramids seem to have withstood time in a victorious manner. On the other hand, only barely discernible traces remained of the temples, so that one could not expect to gain a full understanding of the layout of the pyramids at Giza. However, after the publication of the pyramid complex of the Fifth Dynasty, the situation had changed completely.[1] Endowed with these historical architectural experiences one could dare to approach the terribly dilapidated cult temples of Giza.

One particular building from the pyramid times was known already. Following the example of Mariette, the lucky discoverer who excavated its interior between 1853 and 1860, it came to be called the 'Sphinx Temple'. [*Note: what we call today the Valley Temple at Giza was often called 'the Sphinx Temple' prior to 1936, because only then did Selim Hassan uncover another temple sitting beside it, and directly in front of the Sphinx, which is today correctly called the Sphinx Temple. However, just to make things unnecessarily confusing, the later expert on the Sphinx Temple, Herbert Ricke, insisted upon calling the Sphinx Temple by the name of 'the Harmachis Temple' because he thought it was for the worship of the god Harmachis, symbolized in his opinion by the Sphinx itself. However, intelligible discussion of these matters is only possible if we stick to the standard terminology!*]

Nobody could be immune to the effect of this edifice, with its simplicity of forms taken to extremes, with the gigantic dimensions of its monoliths, and its precious building material. No ledge, no ornament, no relief, no inscription decorated the walls. Only smooth polished wall surfaces and square pillars of rose granite and a luminescent white alabaster floor! Mariette in his time had not recognised the importance of this building. First Piazzi Smyth and after him Flinders Petrie pointed to the connection between it and the Funerary Temple lying in ruins in front of the Chephren Pyramid.[2] However, this connection only found an explanation when Borchardt claimed the building as the 'Gate in the Valley' belonging to the funerary monumental complex of Chephren.[3]

Was this now the type according to which we would have to reconstruct the funerary temples of the Fourth Dynasty? Who would dare to answer this question with an unequivocal yes, considering that one did

451

not even know yet if with the rooms so far revealed, the interior of the Gate building had been completely excavated, whether or not an open hall might still have been positioned before it, as with the Gate temples of Abusir, and where fantastic rumours about the building of its facade were in circulation since Mariette's time. Should the temple itself not have been decorated with richer adornment and reliefs? After all, the private graves of the Fourth Dynasty very often showed relief decorations in many places. And how should we imagine the actual complex of the funerary temples? The size of this Gate building and of the Pyramid implied immensity. Here only a thorough excavation could help. [*Note: from here on, Hölscher's name of* Torbau (*'Gate Building', or 'Gatehouse'*) *for the Valley Temple will be abandoned, and in translation we shall call the structure by its current name of the Valley Temple.*]

A first attempt to gain clarity about the building of the Valley Temple had already been made at times by the Leipzig Mastaba Excavations at Giza in 1905 under Georg Steindorff. But in doing so, it had soon become evident that with the relatively restricted means available, the task could not be executed. The masses of sand which needed to be shifted were too enormous. After they had created a relatively insignificant gap in front of the southern main entrance, they had to give up the task for the time being.

In the meantime, George Reisner had been privileged to be asked by Harvard University to tackle the Funerary Temple at the foot of the third pyramid. And shortly after that, he found the Gatehouse [*i.e., the Valley Temple of Mycerinus*] belonging to it in the valley. Precious scientific results and rich findings rewarded his careful work stretching over many years. But in relation to architecture, the results left something to be desired. For the funeral monument of Mycerinus was still completely unfinished at the early death of its constructor. Only his successor Shepseskaf finished it superficially in brick, whereby the original project was many times changed and simplified. That is, with regard to our question as to how the funerary temples of the Fourth Dynasty might have looked, the Mycerinus temple could only give us an insufficient answer.

As the ruins in front of the Cheops Pyramid [*Note: of this Funerary Temple of Cheops, only part of a pavement survives.*] also promised very little success,[4] many questioning glances[5] were directed towards the

Chephren temple, especially since, in view of the Valley Temple, one had to assume that this complex had been totally completed. On the other hand, the appearance and the exploratory excavation of Flinders Petrie revealed that this temple also was in a desolate condition of destruction. Certainly we suspect that into recent times, considerable parts of the temple had still stood upright, because Maspero[6] tells us that around 1700 [Benoit de] Maillet had still seen four big pillars of the temple erect. However, that was revealed later as an error of Maspero's, because Maillet claims[7] this not of the temple in front of the second pyramid, but of the one in front of the third pyramid, where the pillars are still standing just like that today.[8]

Nevertheless, a long time would perhaps have passed before someone might have found the courage to attempt the excavation of the funerary monument of Chephren, if not for the fact that the Confidential Royal Councillor Dr Ernst von Sieglin in Stuttgart, who was already highly meritorious for his research into antiquity, became interested in this important problem and generously granted the means for an archaeological expedition which initially should conduct a more comprehensive investigation of the Chephren temple complex.

The task

An initial viewing of the excavation area undertaken by Georg Steindorff and Ludwig Borchardt in the autumn of 1908 had concluded that the work had to solve a double task, the excavation of the Funerary Temple and the uncovering of the exterior of the Valley Temple. Furthermore, one had to investigate the pyramid as well as its surrounding walls and auxiliary complexes and to check at the same time what had been published up to then. Finally, one also had to thoroughly clear and measure up the interior of the Valley Temple, of which, even though fifty years had passed since its discovery, no sufficient account was available.

The location of the excavation area

In order to be informed about the excavation area, it is best to climb the Pyramid of Chephren[9] and have a good look around.

If we do this, we find ourselves at the edge of the Libyan Desert, the hilly landscape of which descends fairly steeply down towards the arable land to the northeast. Two sand-filled valleys which empty out like two streams from the highlands of the desert towards the arable flatlands separate from the rest of the mountain range a rock plateau which descends steeply on three sides and connects with the interior of the country behind only on the west. This plateau, which is elevated 40 to 60 metres above the plain, was as if specially created to bear the proudest necropolis of the world.

Three kings of the Fourth Dynasty have here found their resting-place: Cheops, Chephren, and Mycerinus. In addition, there is an unfinished pyramid at the southeastern slope of the plateau. It may well have been begun by Shepseskaf, possibly the son and successor of Mycerinus. [*This is no longer thought to be the case.*]

The most advantageous place had doubtless been chosen by the first king, Cheops. He put his pyramid as close as possible to the steep northeastern slope, which as seen from the arable land below appears like a plinth for the monumental structure.

By now, later on, Chephren wanted to erect a funeral monument here as well, so he had to move further towards the southwest, higher up the plateau. Whereas the pyramid of his predecessor looked more imposing from the nearby arable land because of its position, the effect of distance[10] of the new pyramid surpassed it, because it lies about 10 metres higher, and as a result of this it appears bigger.

In the same position,[11] as the second pyramid relates to the first, the third one (of Mycerinus) is to the second. However, it cannot sustain a comparison with the other two because it is considerably smaller.

The rock plateau on which the Chephren Pyramid stands declines very gradually from the northwest to the southeast. In order to be able to build the pyramid, one had first of all to construct a horizontal surface onto which one could lay out the measurements of the future edifice. For this purpose, the old builders cut away part of the high rock floor towards the north and the west and elevated towards the east the two deep areas by means of massive terrace walls. Further towards the north, west, and south, the old surrounding walls of the pyramids can be recognised. Today, however, they are severely damaged and almost submerged by windblown sand. Only stripes of weathered limestone demarcate the walls lying underneath. On the other side of the western surrounding wall lies a wide courtyard in which the remains of numerous long but narrow rooms can be discerned. Petrie has probably correctly recognised them to be the old workers' barracks.

Further towards the west, the wavelike hills of the desert, the heights and their glassy hard limestone glistening in the sun, stretch between the hills into softly undulating sandy valleys.

Towards the north and northeast one's glance wanders over the wide field of graves, stretching behind the Cheops Pyramid but also in front and on both sides of it. Nowhere does one recognise so clearly as from our high vantage point the regular street patterns in which the house-like mastabas are grouped. Closely around the Cheops Pyramid the graves of the royal family are clustered: the three small pyramids of the royal women in the southeast, and the mastabas of the princes at the south side.

Separated by a ravine from the area of the Cheops Pyramid lies our excavation field. At the exit of this ravine, in the valley, almost in the axis of the Chephren Pyramid, rises up the Great Sphinx which is now almost completely submerged in sand. It consists of a rock the form of which by its nature suggests that of a supine lion. By artificial shaping it has then been created as the symbol of the royal majesty, the resting lion with the head of the pharaoh.

To the southeast of it one recognises the so-called Sphinx Temple [*what we now call the Valley Temple, the actual Sphinx Temple of today having been still entirely covered with sand and later structures at this time and wholly unknown*] suffocated by the besieging mass of sand, the Valley Temple, part of the funerary monument of Chephren. Today we know that between this and the Funerary Temple a covered causeway existed. And now we also recognise the tongue of rock gently drawn downwards in a soft decline towards the Valley Temple, which formerly had carried this Causeway. Of this itself, hardly a stone remains. Not even its course can be clearly discerned except from a high standpoint, because the back of the rock is completely shot through with later shaft graves.

Nature then came very much to the aid of the builders in that it supplied them with a natural ascension to the temple and to the pyramid.

With this it relieved them of the effort needed to transport the material to construct difficult and costly foundations, as had been necessary for instance for the Cheops Pyramid[12] and the Abusir pyramids.

Directly in front of the pyramid lie the ruins of the Funerary Temple, where our work was meant to begin.

South of the Great Sphinx, beyond the Causeway, a place can be recognised where during the beginning of our activity, an excavation was undertaken by Count Galearza and directed by the officials of the Egyptian Antiquities Service, Ahmed Bey Kamal and G. [Georges] Daressy,[13] during which the grave of a royal mother, perhaps the mother of Chephren, came to light.

With a short glance to the sandy lowland and the Arab cemetery in the southeast, and the rock slopes rising behind, towards the unfinished pyramid of Shepseskaf, and on to the funerary complex of Mycerinus, this preliminary orientation shall be completed. There is the area where under the expert direction of George Reisner, extensive American excavations have been undertaken for the past several years.

The funerary monument of Chephren in earlier times

The information which has been transmitted to us by authors of antiquity concerning the Chephren Pyramid is very scanty, consisting of much myth and very little tangible data. After all, the Greeks and Romans were able to see little more than what there was to be seen before the commencement of our own work. The pyramid chambers were not accessible, the casing had been badly damaged on the outside, the temple had been completely destroyed, the entrance had disappeared, and the Valley Temple was probably hidden under deep sand.

Herodotus could only say[14] that the base length of the second pyramid was forty feet less than that of the first, and that its base was encased with granite. Strangely enough, he does not mention the Sphinx at all, even though it is almost certain that in those days it was lying almost completely free and that this image of the sun god Harmachis was an object of veneration at that time. Strabo said[15] that two of the pyramids were counted among the Seven Wonders of the World. Pliny reported[16] that the Sphinx had been taken for the funerary monument of the king

Harmais [*a Latin corruption of the Greek name of the Egyptian god Harmachis*]. Finally, one reads in Diodorus Siculus[17] that there exists an ascent to the peak of the second pyramid which was cut into the casing.

The Valley Temple itself is mentioned nowhere. Strabo on the other hand mentions that:[18] 'There is at Heliopolis as well as at Memphis an edifice or building of many columns of a barbaric construction, because apart from the size and quantity and number of columns, it does not contain anything graceful, nor does it contain any inscriptions.' In Lucian we read: 'In ancient times there were temples in Egypt without relief images.'[19] [*Another translation of what Lucian said is given by Herbert Strong: 'Originally the temples of the Egyptians possessed no images.'[20]*] This characterisation could refer to a building of a style similar to that of the Valley Temple, as Perrot and Chipiez have already remarked.[21] It would not have been our Valley Temple itself, because, as has been explained in Section Five, by that time it most likely was completely buried.

In the Middle Ages, and in modern times, many travellers have left us notices about the pyramids.[22] However, since in those days one was able to see even less than could be seen by the authors in Greek and Roman times, there is very little of interest to be gained from these notices.

For instance, what the Arabic writers report is mostly pure legend and fantasy. The most important of what we can find out from them is that the small pyramids of Giza – in other words, the satellite pyramids of the funerary precincts of Cheops, Chephren, and Mycerinus, were destroyed at the end of the twelfth century AD by the eunuch Karakus under the aegis of Saladin. He used the stones to build the Citadel of Cairo, the city wall and the bridges at Giza.[23] We also hear about several not unimportant communications which concur with today's findings, about the opening of the interior of the Cheops Pyramid which took place under the Caliph Mamun (813-833), the son of Harun er-Raschid, during the occasion of a visit to Egypt.

Only after the scientific rediscovery of Egypt at the beginning of the last [19th] century did investigations about our area of excavations become prevalent.

In 1818 Belzoni sought to discover the entrance of the Chephren Pyramid,[24] which at that time was not open. To begin with, he cleared a part of the lower underlying pavement between the temple and the pyramid. The damage in the pyramid yard which we found in front of the axis of the pyramid appeared to be traces left from these futile efforts. Then he turned to the north side, where he found the entry which had evidently been forced in Arabic or even earlier times. The way into the interior, however, also led through such loosely- compacted masonry, that he was afraid that his workers might become buried by the collapsing masses of stone. He was therefore forced to give up this approach and to search for the real or true old entrance passage. After he had observed that in the first pyramid the entrance does not lie exactly on the axis but was somewhat shifted towards the east, he found it there also in a similar location. The opening on the 2nd of March 1818 was immortalized by him in an inscription above the entrance. The sloping passage was filled with large stones and debris. Below, the portcullis was still in situ. After prolonged efforts they succeeded in raising it high enough so that they were able to crawl through the passage. The discoverer now entered a horizontal passage which led directly to the burial chamber. Here also the forced passage through which the grave-robbers had formerly entered also terminated. Belzoni tells us that the burial chamber once had a painted ceiling. On the walls he found a great many scribblings done with charcoal amongst which there was on the western side an Arabic inscription.[25] The sarcophagus was still in its place, the cover was broken and partly shifted to one side. Remains of cattle bones, debris, and earth were lying inside.

Then he penetrated through the descending passage, which was partly filled with rocks and rubble, down to the lower burial chamber. There he saw on the walls primitive inscriptions which he thought were Coptic. He then followed the passageway ascending northwards and noticed that there the portcullis was not in situ, and that the passage was lined with blocks. After he had convinced himself that this passage only led to the outside, he gave up the pointless attempt to open this blocked entrance.

We can actually only speak of scientific investigations of our excavation area from the time of [John] Perring and [Colonel Howard] Vyse, who worked here in the years 1837 and 1838. They undertook a new and precise examination of the second pyramid always in the thought that still further chambers might be contained within, which had not been found up to then. First of all, they reassured themselves that the lower passage which had not been opened by Belzoni really led into the open, by clearing the lower entrance in the pavement of the pyramid yard. Then Perring thought that he needed to search for the opening of the other passages in the floor of the upper burial chamber. He thus terribly destroyed the floor of the chamber and also moved the sarcophagus from its place.[26] And all in vain! Apart from this, one has to have undivided admiration for the scientific investigations and surveys of these two researchers, especially for the plans done by Perring of the entire pyramid field, as well as of the individual buildings, which have retained their value up till now, and have also been used by us extensively.

The Prussian expedition under [Karl Richard] Lepsius has, with its extensive activities in other areas, been less able to concern itself with the pyramids. The groundplan of the pyramid fields of Giza drawn by Erbkam,[27] on the other hand, shows a further improvement on Perring's, and has been unsurpassed up till today. Several valuable notices are found in the first text volume of the *Denkmäler*.[28]

The Sphinx was initially cleared in modern times by [Captain J.-B., or Giambattista] Caviglia in 1816. He found there, probably stemming from Roman times, terraced steps which led from the east towards the Sphinx, as well as the smaller temple between the paws of the colossus and the memorial stela which Thutmosis IV had erected in the 15th century BC as a memorial to the fact that he had freed the Sphinx from the suffocating desert sand.[29] Later on, Perring and Vyse in particular have continued these investigations.

Matters entered a new phase when [Auguste] Mariette tried from the year 1853 onwards to find the grave of the king, Harmachis, which had been mentioned by Pliny,[30] within the Sphinx. On this occasion he accidentally hit upon the Valley Temple. He began to clear it from the top. As a result of the huge masses of sand that needed to be dealt with he found himself forced to approach his patrons the Duke of Luynes and the French Government with ever renewed demands for money. He reports this himself [in French]:[31]

'The temple discovered is now up to four fifths cleared. We still haven't found anything in this temple. But in a temple which is filled

459

up by sand bit by bit to the ceiling there is no reason why the objects which it contains might not float and somehow find themselves trapped between two layers. All the work which has been done up to now is for the purpose of recovering the monuments on the ancient floor. Let us be courageous and go on to the bottom and since we want to reap a harvest, let's have the patience to wait until the final push!'

But these requests were in vain. The excavations were stopped even though he had reached a level only one metre above ground level. Only the announcement of the 1860 visit of the Empress Eugènie gave the Egyptian Government the incentive to resume the interrupted work at their cost.

Mariette reports: 'Much later a lucky chance put into my hands the means to resume, under the order of Said Pasha, the work which four years earlier I had had to abandon. Within a few days the ground level was reached and the statue of Chephren formed the nucleus of the riches which are today collected in the Museum of Boulaq [now the Cairo Museum]. But for the lack of a few hundred francs, the statue of Chephren would today be instead in the Museum of the Louvre. . . . This temple had been absolutely unknown until then. The plan of Wilkinson marks this spot with these words: "pits unopened".'

Concerning the external walls uncleared by him, he says:

'Seen from the outside, the temple must present itself under the aspect of an enormous cube of masonry constructed with gigantic blocks of greyish limestone. The three stelae of Thutmosis IV and of Rameses II represent the Sphinx resting upon a similar cube, which cannot be the temple that we are describing. This cube on the three stelae is ornamented with long prismatic grooves in the style of the Old Kingdom. It is not unreasonable to suppose that the temple itself had received this decoration on the outside and that seen from afar it must have reminded one in its enormous proportions of these facades of a style so original, of which the sarcophagus of Khufu-Ankh in the Museum of Boulaq [Cairo] offers a perfect example . . .'[32]

This supposition resulted in it being firmly believed in many places that the facades were ornamented as described above.

Regarding the access to the building, he remarks that only a single small door in the corner was visible. From this statement we can trace the many suppositions that the Valley Temple had only one door, lying unsymmetrical to the axis.[33]

According to Mariette's account, during his works the following were found:

1. The statue of an ape [*doubtless a baboon symbolizing the god Thoth*] on the base of which was supposed to be found the remains of an inscription.
2. Small limestone stelae venerating the Sphinx as Harmachis
3. The famous Chephren statue which had fallen head-downwards into the well.
4. Another Chephren statue of serpentine,[34] damaged, but with the head intact.
5. Fragments of eight other statues, five of them with Chephren inscriptions.
6. Chin and mouth of a fine colossal statue of alabaster, the mouth being about 15 cm. long.

Specific accounts of the condition of the interior of the Valley Temple during this clearance, from which one could deduce its later usage and history, are unfortunately completely missing [*from Mariette's account*]. Equally unclear are the circumstances of the discovery of the different statues and stelae. Mariette says only, concerning the one best-preserved statue of Chephren, that it had been found in the well. Nowadays, however, one hears everywhere the tale that all the royal statues were found lying in there,[35] which was hardly possible, as so many statues could hardly have found space in that hole.[36] Most of all, the information is missing as to where those pieces stemming from later times (the ape and the stelae) were found. Unfortunately, the necessary care in the clearing of the building has also been lacking. It can also be established[37] that those granite architraves which are now missing had crashed down at that time into the interior. As Mariette was unable to put them back into their place, in 1869 he ordered them to be destroyed by soldiers with gunpowder and then cleared away. One can still find in the vicinity today some of these granite pieces with modern holes made for explosives.

The next scientific material about our excavation area is given by

Flinders Petrie, who carried out a new measurement of the pyramids in 1881 and 1882. His acute observational abilities, and the precision of his measurements, have made his publications extraordinarily valuable for us.[38] In the upper [funerary] temple he has only scratched the surface, whereby pieces of statues and such like have been collected. But then he cleared the upper part of the Causeway and with that finally proved the connection between the funerary temple and the Valley Temple, which Piazzi Smyth had already previously suggested. He also gives a good description and a rather accurate ground plan of the Valley Temple. He dedicated careful study to the surrounding walls of the pyramid and the workers' barracks. His accounts are so detailed that we only need to give them a superficial verification.

Further works in our excavation area have not become public. In addition it should only be mentioned that [Ludwig] Borchardt had several baskets full of statue pieces and splinters collected from the surface several years ago, which are now stored in the Berlin Museum.

We have already mentioned that in 1905 during the occasion of the Leipzig mastaba excavations they did not complete the attempt to clear the southern entrance of the Valley Temple because of a lack of funds.

State prior to the excavation

We now want to summarize briefly in what condition we found the funerary monuments of Chephren at the beginning of our work.

Of the Valley Temple, only the interior had been excavated. The two entrance rooms were only partially cleared. Mud walls and modern walls made of broken stones, with which they tried to hold back the pressure of the sand from the outside, obstructed the exits.

In the columned hall the windblown sand had already accumulated up to a height of one metre, so that one had to clear thoroughly here to begin with. One must doubt that this had ever been done properly before. At any rate, no one had ever paid attention to the holes in the pavement where the statues had once stood.

Of the exterior of the Valley Temple, nothing had been cleared. The lower end of the Causeway where the limestone walls are almost completely preserved must have been cleared without anyone ever recognising properly the importance of this part of the building.[39]

The upper end of the Causeway, the foundation of which Petrie had already cleared once, was again hidden under fresh windblown sand.

The massive core blocks of masonry of the funerary temple rose high above the rubble. They had always been noticed by visitors. Also here, the traces of Petrie's excavations were recognisable. Beside it, a fragment of the granite casing of the eastern face may have been visible. The more destroyed parts of the temple, that is, the courtyard and the parts of the building towards the west, were on the other hand totally unknown. They were lying under a layer of rubble of about 1.4 metres height. Because of the protecting pyramid beside it, and also because of its high position [on the plateau], it was not so exposed to the wind, and so not much windblown sand had accumulated there. Most likely Petrie, and perhaps also commissioned or freelance antiquities thieves, have probed here, but without the slightest scientific results.

Round about the pyramid were deposited enormous rubble heaps, resulting from the breaking off of the pyramid casing. They reached in part a height of almost ten metres about the pavement of the temple yard.

Nothing was yet known about the interior surrounding wall of the pyramid. The exterior surrounding wall, on the other hand, was still clearly visible under the sand. Equally, the workers' houses were showing. The places where Petrie had been digging there were clearly indicated as gentle indentations in the sand.

Of the Queen's Pyramid, only a vague very flat rubble heap could be seen, in the middle of which some prominent great limestone blocks rose up.

We have not touched the interior of the pyramid, but we have left it in the same state in which we found it and as it has lain since Perring's investigations, which is now already over 70 years ago.

1   Borchardt, *Grabdenkmal des Königs Ne-user-re*; *Grabdenkmal des Königs Nefer-ir-ke-re* and *Grabdenkmal des Königs Sahu-re*, J. C. Hinrichs, 1907, 1909, 1910, hereinafter referred to in references in abbreviated form as Ne-user-re, Nefer-ir-ke-re, and Sahu-re.

2   Flinders Petrie, *The Pyramids and Temples of Gizeh* [London, 1883, first and fuller edition], pp. 128 and 153.

3   Compare Borchardt *Das Re-Heiligtum des Königs Ne-Woser-Re* I, p. 25; from now on referred to only in abbreviated form as 'Re-Heiligtum'.

4   In the year 1904 [Ernesto] Schiaparelli, during his mastaba excavations, had also been digging in the temple of the Cheops Pyramid and on that occasion had brought to light a basalt pavement. However, nothing is known of any further results of this excavation. [*Note: Professor Ernesto Schiaparelli of Turin University abandoned his excavations and turned over his concession to George Reisner, of the USA.*]

5   Unfortunately, nothing is known just yet about the architectural results of the French excavations at Abu Rouash.

6   *Egyptian History of Art*, German edition, p. 549.

7   [L'Abbé Jean Baptiste] Le Mascrier, *Description de l'Égypte contenant plusiers remarques curieuses sur la géographie etc. de ce pays, composée sur les Mémoires de M. [Benoit] de Maillet* (Paris, 1735).

8   Also at the time of [Richard] Pococke, the temple remnants had surely been preserved better than at the beginning of the excavations; see [The Rt. Rev. Richard] Pococke, *Description of the East*, Vol. I, p. 46, London, 1743 [*A Description of the East and Several Other Countries*, 2 vols., London, 1743-5], and the note in [Alfred] Wiedemann's *Ägyptischer Geschichte*, Supplement, p. 16, which does not correspond with it.

9   The Pyramid of Chephren lies 13.5 km southwest from the Citadel of Cairo, 20° 59' north latitude and 31° 8½' east of the Greenwich meridian.

10   The first pyramid was, according to Petrie, originally 146.59 metres high, the second was however only 143.50 metres high. The first pyramid is therefore 3.09 metres taller. The latter, however, according to Perring, lies 10.11 metres higher, so that its tip surpasses the former by 7.02 metres. Today the difference in height is considerably greater, because the tip of the first pyramid is much more damaged than that of the second.

11   Petrie gives in his *Pyramids and Temples of Gizeh* [*op. cit.*], p. 125, a triangulation of the pyramid field. According to this, the positions of the three pyramids are in a relationship to each other which has been calculated as follows:

	Distance	Direction
From the tip of the 1st pyramid to the 2nd	486.87 m	43° 22' 52"
From the tip of the 1st pyramid to the 3rd	936.17 m	37° 51' 6"
From the tip of the 2nd pyramid to the 3rd	453.95 m	34° 10' 11"

Thereby it has been selected as the starting direction of the mean north south axis [azimuth] of the first and second pyramids, which is supposed to deviate by approximately 5' east from true north.

12 Herodotus, Book II, 124, says that the erection of the ascending path to the Cheops Pyramid cost just as much labour as that of the whole pyramid; this however seems to be exaggerated.

13 G. [Georges] Daressy, in *Annales du Service des Antiquités*, Vo. X, p. 41.

14 Herodotus, Book II, 125 [*sic*]. [This is erroneous, the correct reference being 127.]

15 Strabo, Book XVII, 808. [Chapter 1, Section 33. The reference '808' is the Casaubon numbering.]

16 Pliny, *Natural History*, Book XXXVI, 17, 1: 'Harmain regem in ea [the Sphinx] conditum et volunt invectam videri; est autem saxo naturali elaborata.' [Other editions of the Latin text have said the king's name was Amasis, but Harmais tends to be accepted now, as a Latin corruption of the Greek name Harmachis.] [*Translator's note:* My old friend the late Professor D. E. Eichholz was the translator of this book of Pliny's *Natural History* for the Loeb Library (1971), and the text which he used differs from the above by adding the word *putant*: 'Harmain regem putant in ea conditum et volunt invectam videri; est autem saxe naturali elaborata.' His translation of the whole passage was: 'In front of them [the pyramids] is the Sphinx, which deserves to be described even more than they, and yet the Egyptians have passed it over in silence. The inhabitants of the region regard it as a deity. They are of the opinion that a King Harmais is buried inside it and try to make out that it was brought to the spot; it is in fact carefully fashioned from the native rock.' Eichholz very sensibly points out the similarity of this name to Harmachis. See Pliny, *Natural History*, Volume Ten, translated by D. E. Eichholz, Loeb Classical Library, Harvard University Press, USA, 1971, pp. 60-1.]

17 [Diodorus Siculus, *The Library of History*,] Book I, Chapter 63. [This statement has been edited out of modern editions of Diodorus, such as that of the Loeb Library edition. However, this statement was accepted as a genuine sentence of Diodorus by the meticulous scholars W. W. How and J. Wells in their seminal work *A Commentary on Herodotus*, 2 vols., Clarendon Press, Oxford, 1912, Vol. I, p. 230. There, when commenting on Book II, 127, of Herodotus (see Footnote 14 above), they state: 'Diodorus (I, 64) [*note that*

this is a correction to Hölscher's reference given as I, 63] tells us there was an *anabasis* ['a way up'] up one side of this pyramid.']

[18] Book XVIII, 128 [*sic*]: '. . . *oiden echei charien, oide graphikon.*' [This reference is erroneous, as there is no Book XVIII of Strabo, and Hölscher means Book XVII, Chapter 1, Section 28, the true Casaubon numbering being 804/5. The numbering '128' is incomprehensible.]

[19] [Lucian], 'On the Syrian Goddess', Section 3: '*azoanoi neoi*'.

[20] Garstang, John, ed., *The Syrian Goddess*, trans. By Herbert A. Strong, Constable, London, 1913, p. 43. Garstang, who annotated the translation extensively, makes no comment on this sentence.

[21] *Art of Antiquity*, Vol. I, Egypt, p. 311. [This reference is to the German edition of what in English was published in 2 vols. as Georges Perrot and Charles Chipiez, *A History of Art in Ancient Egypt*, Chapman and Hall, London, 1883.]

[22] Vyse, [Colonel Howard, *Operations Carried on at the Pyramids of Gizeh in 1837*, 3 vols., London,]Vol. II. This is where they have mainly been compiled. Compare also the essay 'The Wisdom of the Pyramids' ('Pyramiden-Weisheit') by A. Wiedemann in *Globus*, Vol. LXIII, Number 14, Braunschweig, 1893.

[23] A great number of testimonies about the pyramids have been compiled by the Arab historian Makrizi (1364-1442) in his great work concerning the geography and history of Egypt. A new translation of the chapter on the pyramids by Emil Gräfe in the 5th Volume of the *Leipziger Semitischen Studien* (Leipzig, 1911).

[24] From Vyse, *op. cit.*, Vol. II, pp. 294 ff.

[25] See Section Five.

[26] Vyse, *op. cit.*, vol. I, p. 196, and Vol. II, p. 99.

[27] [Karl Richard] Lepsius, *Denkmäler aus Ägypten und Äthiopien*, Abtheilung 1, p. 14.

[28] Ibid.

[29] See [James Henry] Breasted, *Ancient Records of Egypt* [5 vols., reprinted by Histories & Mysteries of Man Ltd., London, 1988], Vol. II, Section 810 ff. where the more important literature is also listed.

[30] See Note 16 above.

[31] Auguste Mariette, *Sérapeum de Memphis*, ed. by G. Maspero, pp. 91 ff.

[32] See [Auguste] Mariette, *Questions, etc.* in the *Comptes Rendus*, 1877, pp. 427-73.

[33] For example, even in [Ludwig] Borchardt's article in *Zeitschrift für Gesch. d. Architektur*, Third Year, Vol. 4, p. 68.

[34] Actually, it is a greenish metamorphic slate.

[35] For example, *Bibliothèque Égyptologique*, XVIII (*Oeuvres de Auguste Mariette*), CVIII, and Bädeker, *Ägypten*, 1906, p. 126.

[36] The provenance seems to have been stated correctly only by Petrie in *The History of Egypt*, Vol. I, p. 51.

[37] [Flinders] Petrie, *Pyramids and Temples of Gizeh, op. cit.*, p. 130.

[38] Ibid.

[39] The fact that covered causeways ascend from the valley to the funerary temple was only established at Abusir. See [Ludwig] Borchardt, *Ne-user-re*, p. 13.

NOTES TO THE CHAPTERS

Chapter One

1 Robert Temple, *The Genius of China: 3,000 Years of Science, Discovery and Invention*, Andre Deutsch, London, 2007 (new edition), p. 156.

2 John Taylor, *The Great Pyramid. Why Was It Built? And Who Built It?*, Longman Green, London, 1859, p. 22. In his calculations, Taylor used the height of 486 feet, which is too high, and his computation was thus slightly out, but his principle idea was correct. His book is more about ancient measurements than the Great Pyramid, despite its title. It contains some truly remarkable information about ancient British measurements, concerning which Taylor knew a great deal. Sir Flinders Petrie, an arch-sceptic on such matters, agreed that *pi* was incorporated in the Great Pyramid.

3 Cotsworth, Moses B., *The Rational Almanac*, York, 1905, pp. 64–7. I am fortunate to own a signed copy of this rare and enlarged second edition (the first and briefer edition appeared in 1902).

4 Gardiner, Alan H., *The Library of A. Chester Beatty: Description of a Hieratic Papyrus with a Mythological Story . . . The Chester Beatty Papyri, No. I*, Oxford, 1931, p. 25. As Gardiner remarks in his footnote 2: 'The elsewhere unknown phrase "*at the bright moment*" probably refers to a specific time of day, perhaps noon-tide.'

Chapter Two

1 http://towers-online.co.uk/pages/shaftos3.htm. Nigel Skinner-Simpson published an article about the Osiris Shaft in early 2004 in Issue Two of the magazine *Phenomena*, of which I was a contributing editor and colum-

nist, but I had nothing to do with its appearance and only saw it after it was published: 'Tunnel Talk', on pp. 25–7. There are various inaccuracies in Skinner-Simpson's article, including a ninety-degree error in his compass directions and the assertion that Zahi Hawass excavated the bottom level of the Osiris Shaft, whereas this was really done as long ago as the early nineteenth century. He maintains that the sarcophagus in that level was discovered in 1992, whereas it was already described in 1837. Skinner-Simpson says that a claim was made in 1988 on television by Mark Lehner that there were shafts going 'deeper still' beneath the water of the canal in Level Three. I know nothing of this, but as the reader will discover towards the end of this chapter, I have stressed the need to study the bottom of the canal very carefully and, if this were done, such information would soon become known.

[2] Add. Ms. 25, 618, f. 73, in the British Library. This is a document dated 1826 which is contained in the sixty-three vol. collection 'Collectanea Aegyptiaca' of James Burton, which are manuscripts dated between 1820 and 1839.

[3] 'A.B.' [Annibale Brandi], *Descrizione Compendiosa delle Piramidi di Giza in Egitto* [Compendious Description of the Pyramids of Giza in Egypt], Livorno, 1823. Translated into English by Stefano Greco, with notes by Robert Temple: the latter part dealing with the Sphinx published as Appendix Four to Temple, Robert, *Sphinx Odyssey*, Inner Traditions, USA, 2008; the initial part dealing with the pyramids published as an appendix to this book.

[4] The latter portion of the booklet (in translation by Stefano Greco) dealing with the Sphinx was published as an appendix to my previous book, *The Sphinx Mystery* (2009), and the remainder of the book, dealing with the pyramids, is published in English as an appendix to this book. A scan of the entire work in the original Italian, together with a complete English translation of the book by Stefano Greco, with my notes, is available as a free resource on the supplementary website to this book: www.egyptiandawn.info. On that website are also to be found the additional photos of the Osiris Shaft.

[5] Howard Vyse, Colonel Richard, *Operations Carried on at the Pyramids of Gizeh in 1837*, 3 vols, James Fraser, London, 1840, Vol. I, p. 266.

[6] Ibid., p. 269.

[7] Ibid., p. 272.

[8] Ibid., Vol. II, pp. 4–5.

[9] Ibid., p. 292.

[10] Hölscher, Uvo, *Das Grabdenkmal des Königs Chephren* [The Funerary

Monument of King Chephren], Vol. 1 of *Veröffentlichungen der Ernst von Sieglin Expedition in Ägypten* [Publications of the Ernst von Sieglin Expedition in Egypt], ed. Georg Steindorff, J. C. Hinrich's Booksellers, Leipzig, 1912.

11 Ibid., pp. 49–50.

12 Hassan, Selim, *Excavations at Giza*, Volume V: 1933–1934, Government Press, Cairo, 1944, p. 193.

13 Bauval, Robert, *Secret Chamber*, Century, London, 1999, p. 297.

14 Lucas, A., and Harris, J. R., *Ancient Egyptian Materials and Industries*, Dover Publications, Mineola, New York, 1999.

15 Aston, Barbara G., *Ancient Egyptian Stone Vessels: Materials and Forms*, Heidelberger Orientverlag, Heidelberg, Germany, 1994. The extraordinarily extensive survey of stones and materials used in ancient Egypt is found on pp. 11–73, but dacite is unlisted, and is mentioned only to be dismissed (see next note).

16 Ibid., p. 12.

17 Harris, J. R., *Lexicographical Studies in Ancient Egyptian Minerals*, Akademie-Verlag, Berlin, 1961.

18 Giully, James, Waters, A. C., and Woodford, A. O., *Principles of Geology*, W. H. Freeman, USA, 1959, pp. 504–6.

19 Barthoux, Jules, *Chronologie et Description des Roches Igness du Desert Arabique*, Mémoires Présentés à l'Institut d'Égypte, Tome V, Cairo, 1922, pp. 160–7.

20 Ibid., p. 167.

21 Liritzis, etc.

22 Temple, Olivia and Robert, *The Sphinx Mystery*, Inner Traditions, USA, 2009, Figure 7.10 on page 338

23 Petrie, [Sir] W. M. Flinders, *Gizeh and Rifeh*, British School of Archaeology in Egypt, London, 1907.

24 David, A. Rosalie, *Religious Ritual at Abydos (c. 1300 BC)*, Aris and Phillips, Warminster, England, 1973.

25 Ibid., p. 244.

26 Ibid.

17 Ibid., pp. 245, 244, 245, in succession.

Chapter Three

1 Breasted, James Henry, *Ancient Records of Egypt*, 5 vols, London, 1906, Vol. I, pp. 40–47. I have used the modern reprint, Histories & Mysteries of Man Ltd., London, 1988. His chronology is also presented in his book, *A History*

of Egypt from the Earliest Times to the Persian Conquest, 2nd edn, Hodder & Stoughton, London, 1948; see pp. 21 and pp. 597–601. The dates he gives for the Fourth Dynasty on p. 597 are 2900–2750 BC. He only allows 80 years to the Third Dynasty (2980–2900 BC), and he includes King Sneferu as the last king of that dynasty, although today he is generally considered to be the first king of the Fourth Dynasty. He allows 420 years for the First and Second Dynasties (3400–2980 BC).

2 Ibid., p. 40.

3 Ibid., p. 39.

4 Parker, Richard A., 'The Sothic Dating of the Twelfth and Eighteenth Dynasties', in *Studies in Honor of George R. Hughes, January 12, 1977; Studies in Ancient Oriental Civilization*, Number 39, Oriental Institute of the University of Chicago, Chicago, USA, 1977, pp. 177–189.

5 Edwards, I. E. S., *The Pyramids of Egypt*, revised edn, Viking, London, 1985, p. 121.

6 Spalinger, Anthony, 'Dated Texts of the Old Kingdom', *Studien zur Altägyptischen Kultur*, ed. Hartwig Altenmüller, Helmut Buske Verlag, Hamburg, 1994, Vol. 21, pp. 275–319.

7 Ibid., pp. 284–5.

8 Drioton, Etienne, 'Une Liste de Rois de la IV Dynastie dans l'Ouadi Hammamat', *Bulletin de la Société Français d'Égyptologie*, No. 16, October 1954, pp. 41–9.

9 Emery, Walter B., *Archaic Egypt*, Penguin Books, Harmondsworth, Middlesex, England, 1984 (orig. edn 1961), pp. 93 and 103.

10 Two books devoted to this subject are: A. Dufeu, *Découverte de l'Age et de la Véritable Destination des Quatre* [sic] *Pyramides de Gizeh Principalement de la Grande Pyramide* [Uncovering the Age and True Purpose of the Four Pyramids of Giza, Principally of the Great Pyramid], Paris, 1873; and Richard A. Proctor, *The Great Pyramid: Observatory, Tomb and Temple*, Chatto & Windus, London, 1883.

11 Vyse, Colonel Howard, *Operations Carried on at the Pyramids of Gizeh in 1837*, 3 vols, London, 1842, Vol. III, Appendix vol. written with John S. Perring, p. 8.

12 Temple, Olivia and Robert, *The Sphinx Mystery*, Inner Traditions, USA, 2009, Ch. 6.

13 Herodotus, Book II, 124; translated by A. D. Godley, Loeb Classical Library, Harvard University Press, 4 vols, 1960, Vol. I, pp. 425–7.

14 Emery, *Archaic Egypt*, op. cit., pp. 53–4. See also Emery's lengthy excavation report on this tomb: Emery, Walter B., *Excavations at Saqqara 1937–1938: Hor-Aha*, with the collaboration of Zaki Yusef Saad, Service

des Antiquités de l'Égypte, Cario, 1939, which is a model report in so many ways.

15 Emery, *Archaic Egypt,* op. cit., pp. 61–3.

16 Ibid., pp. 69–71.

17 Ibid., pp. 73–6.

18 Reisner, George Andrew, *A History of the Giza Necropolis,* Vol. II: *The Tomb of Hetep-Heres, the Mother of Cheops,* Harvard University Press, USA, 1955, photographically reprinted by John William Pye, Brockton, Massachusetts, USA, pp. 1–12.

19 Hassan, Selim, *The Great Pyramid of Khufu and Its Mortuary Chapel,* which is Vol. X, 1938–1939, of his series *Excavations at Giza,* Cairo, 1960.

20 Emery, op. cit., p. 102.

21 Hoffman, Michael A., *Egypt before the Pharaohs,* Ark Paperbacks, London, 1984 (orig. edn 1980), p. 350.

22 Mendelssohn, Kurt, *The Riddle of the Pyramids,* Thames and Hudson, London, 1974, p. 36.

23 Swelim, Nabil M. A., *Some Problems on the History of the Third Dynasty,* Archaeological & Historical Studies Vol. 7, Publications of the Archaeological Society of Alexandria, Alexandria, Egypt, 1983. These books published in Alexandria are extremely difficult to obtain, and I am fortunate to have bought the signed copy which the author gave to the Egyptologist Kent Weeks in 1983. Otherwise, I don't think I would have been able to obtain one. It is a most fascinating book, and it is a pity that I cannot here discuss its contents as it deserves.

24 *Ibid.,* pp. 14–15. These views of Maragioglio and Rinaldi are expressed in an article which I have not seen, which in his own footnote Swelim describes as: '*La Leggenda della Schiavitù del Popalo Egisiona,* last page of an undated article sent to me by the late C. Rinaldi.' Although I have a set of the extremely rare books by Maragioglio and Rinaldi on the monuments and pyramids, I do not have this article, the source and date of which were not even known to Swelim, as he makes clear.

25 Ibid., p. 21.

26 Reisner, George Andrew, *Mycerinus: The Temples of the Third Pyramid at Giza,* Harvard University Press, USA, 1931, p. 5. I have used the original edition, but there is also a photographic reprint by John William Pye, Brockton, Massachusetts, USA.

27 See their identical names and cartouches in Émile Brugsch Bey and Urbain Bouriant, *Les Livres des Rois* [The Book of Kings], Cairo, 1887, pp. 1 (First Dynasty), 3 (Third Dynasty), and 9 (Sixth Dynasty). Although cartouches were not used in the First Dynasty, Brugsch and Bouriant

have adopted the convention of the New Kingdom king lists and used them in their book. They spell Teti in the alternative and older form 'Teta'.

28 Petrie, [Sir] W. M. Flinders, *The Pyramids and Temples of Gizeh*, London, 1883.

29 Ibid., pp. 91–2.

30 Ibid., p. 152.

31 Petrie, [Sir] W. M. Flinders, review of Bertha Porter and Rosalind Moss *Topographical Bibliography* for Memphis, Vol. 3, Clarendon Press, Oxford, in *Ancient Egypt*, London, 1932, p. 55.

32 Lehner, Mark, *The Complete Pyramids*, Thames & Hudson, London, 1997, pp. 111 and 114 (foldout pages).

33 Breasted, *Ancient Records of Egypt*, op. cit., Vol. I, p. 83.

34 Lepre, J. P., *The Egyptian Pyramids: A Comprehensive Illustrated Reference*, McFarland & Company, Jefferson, North Carolina, USA, 1990. Lepre died young and was unable to follow up his excellent work.

35 Ibid., pp. 106–9.

36 Tompkins, Peter, *Secrets of the Great Pyramid,* Harper & Row, New York, 1971, pp. 64–5 (including text of a caption on p. 64).

37 Strudwick, Nigel C., and Leprohon, Ronald J. (ed.), *Texts from the Pyramid Age*, Brill, Leiden, 2005, pp. 154–5.

38 Reisner, George A., *Mycerinus,* op. cit., p. 275.

39 Arnold, Dieter, *Building in Egypt: Pharaonic Stone Masonry*, Oxford University Press, Oxford, 1991, p. 20, and footnote 80 on p. 25.

40 Howard Vyse, Colonel [Richard], *Operations Carried on at the Pyramids of Gizeh in 1837*, James Fraser, London, 1840, Vol. I, p. 287.

41 Ibid., p. 259.

42 Ibid., p. 235.

43 Ibid.

44 Ibid., p. 236.

45 Ibid., p. 232.

46 Ibid.

47 Ibid., p. 226.

48 Ibid., pp. 235–6.

49 Ibid., p. 255.

50 Ibid., p. 258.

51 Ibid., p. 259.

52 Ibid., p. 278.

53 Wilkinson, Sir J. Gardner, *The Egyptians in the Time of the Pharaohs, Being a Companion to the Crystal Palace Egyptian Collections . . . To Which Is Added*

An Introduction to the Study of the Egyptian Hieroglyphs by Samuel Birch, London, 1857.

[54] Howard Vyse, *Operations*, op. cit., pp. 279–83.

[55] Ibid., p. 258.

[56] Ibid., pp. 203–7.

[57] Ibid., p. 235.

[58] Ibid., p. 236.

[59] Ibid., pp. 255–6.

[60] Ibid., p. 277.

[61] Ibid.

[62] Ibid., p. 278.

[63] Ibid.

[64] Ibid., p. 291.

[65] Ibid., Vol. II, p. 93.

[66] Reisner, *Mycerinus*, op. cit.

[67] Ibid.

[68] Sitchin, Zecharia, *The Wars of Gods and Men*, Avon Books, 1985, following upon his earlier book *The Stairway of Heaven*, 1980, which raised the issue of Howard Vyse forging the graffiti. Sitchin has been attacked on the internet about this by a British internet writer called Martin Stower, who gives many more details about how Brewer originally went to Egypt to assist in the construction of an eye hospital, which was cancelled, so that he did some work for Howard Vyse. He protested when Raven and Hill forged the graffiti, wrote about it in letters home; these were kept in the family, etc., etc. See http://martins.castlelink.co.uk/pyramid/forging/witness1.html for discussion and other references. Although Stower is dismissive, this matter has certainly not been fully cleared up by any means. (See the following footnote for further discussion of Sitchin.)

[69] Sitchin, Zecharia, *The Stairway to Heaven*, Harper paperback, New York, 2007, Ch. 13 ('Forging the Pharaoh's Name'), pp. 337–76. This book was apparently first published in 1980, though I did not see it until 2009. I got to know Sitchin slightly at the end of July 1978, in Chicago. We attended a conference and we also appeared on a television chat show together. I am not a supporter of Sitchin's theories. I do not agree with what he says in that chapter about the Inventory Stela being an Old Kingdom stela, though I believe it does contain some copied Old Kingdom textual material (see the photo and drawing and discussion of it in my previous book, *The Sphinx Mystery*).

[70] Haas, Herbert, Lehner, Mark, Wenke, Robert J., Wölfli, Willy, Devine, James M., and Bonani, Georges, 'A Radiocarbon Chronology for the

Egyptian Pyramids', *Annales du Service des Antiquités Égyptiennes*, Publications de l'Organisation des Antiquités Égyptiennes, Tome LXXII, 1992–1993, Cairo, 1993, pp. 181–90.

71 Ibid., p. 181.

72 Ibid., pp. 182–5.

73 Haas, Herbert, Hawass, Zahi, Lehner, Mark, Nakhla, Shawki, Nolan, John, Wenke, Robert, and Wölfli, Willy, et al., 'Radiocarbon Dates of Old and Middle Kingdom Monuments in Egypt', in *Near East Chronology: Archaeology and Environment, Radiocarbon,* Vol. 43, No. 3, 2001, pp. 1,297–1,320.

74 Ibid., p. 1,297.

Chapter Four

1 Ricke, Herbert, *Der Harmachistempel des Chefren in Giseh* [The Harmachis Temple of Chephren at Giza], in *Beiträge zur Ägyptischen Bauforschung und Altertumskunde,* ed. Herbert Ricke, Vol. 10, Wiesbaden, 1970, pp. 1–43. *Note:* Ricke chooses to call the Sphinx Temple by the name of the Harmachis Temple, which is not customary among English-speaking Egyptologists.

2 Ibid., p. 15.

3 Hassan, Selim, *The Great Sphinx and Its Secrets: Historical Studies in the Light of Recent Excavations,* Government Press, Cairo, 1953.

4 Ibid., pp. 27–8.

5 Ricke, *Der Harmachistempel,* op. cit., pp. 15–16.

6 Temple, Robert, *The Crystal Sun,* Century, London, p. 375. A photo of this passage may be seen in Plate 31. I measured the slope of the passage and discovered that it was identical to the slope of both the ascending passage and the descending passage inside the Great Pyramid. This had never been noticed before.

7 Ibid., p. 47 and Figs 32, 33 and 34 on that page.

8 Hassan, Selim, *The Great Pyramid of Khufu and Its Mortuary Chapel,* Cairo, 1960. These two drawings are folding plates 10 and 11.

9 The Greek word *lophos,* meaning 'hill', sometimes survives in English as 'loaf'. My grandparents owned a farm outside Roanoke, Virginia, which had a large hill at the back named Sugar Loaf. They used to joke with their friends about their 'mountain in the back yard'.

10 Herodotus, translated by Henry Cary, Henry G. Bohn (Bohn's Classical Library), London, 1861, p. 145.

11 Herodotus, translated by A. D. Godley, Vol. I, Loeb Classical Library, Harvard University Press, USA, 1960, p. 427 (the Greek text being opposite on p. 426).

12 Hölscher, Uvo, *Das Grabdenkmal*, op. cit., Figs 47 and 48 on p. 57.

13 Hölscher, Uvo, and Steindorff, Georg, 'Die Ausgrabung des Totentempels der Chephrenpyramide durch die Sieglin-Expedition 1909' [The Excavation of the Funerary Temple of the Chephren Pyramid by the Sieglin Expedition of 1909], *Zeitschrift für Ägyptische Sprache*, Vol. 46, 1909, pp. 9–10.

14 Reisner, George A., *Mycerinus*, op. cit. p. 40.

Chapter Five

1 Email from Gunter Dreyer in Egypt to Robert Temple in London, 16 April 2001.

2 Petrie, [Sir] W. M. Flinders, *The Royal Tombs of the Earliest Dynasties* (Part II of *Royal Tombs*), Egypt Exploration Fund Memoir, Volume 21, Kegan Paul, Trench, Trübner and Co., London, 1901, pp. xx.

3 Emery, Walter B., *Archaic Egypt*, op. cit., p. 101.

4 Ibid., p. 98.

5 Ibid.

6 Verbrugghe, Gerald P., and John M. Wickersham, *Berossos and Manetho*, University of Michigan Press, Ann Arbor, Michigan, USA, 2000, p. 189.

7 Ibid.

8 Hornung, Erik, *History of Ancient Egypt*, Cornell University Press, Ithaca, New York, 1999, p. xiv.

9 Hoffman, Michael A., *Egypt before the Pharaohs*, Alfred A. Knopf, New York, 1979, p. 349.

10 Rice, Michael, *Egypt's Making*, 2nd edn, Routledge, London, 2003, p. 149.

11 Wallis Budge, [Sir] E. A., *A History of Egypt*, Volume I: *Egypt in the Neolithic and Archaic Periods*, Kegan Paul, London, 1902, pp. 208–9.

12 Petrie, [Sir] W. M. Flinders, *A History of Egypt*, Volume I, *From the Earliest Kings to the XVth Dynasty*, 10th edn, reprinted by Histories & Mysteries of Man Ltd., London, 1991, p. 34.

13 Ibid., p. 36.

14 O'Mara, Patrick F., *The Palermo Stone and the Archaic Kings of Egypt*, Paulette Publishing Company, La Canada, California, USA, 1979, p. 196.

15 Breasted, James Henry, *A History of Egypt*, op. cit. pp. 40 and 47, and Figs 20 and 21 opposite p. 38.

16 Quibell, James E., *Hierakonpolis*, 2 vols, London, 1900–02.

17 Petrie, *The Royal Tombs*, op. cit., Plate 57, 5.

18 Breasted, [Which work: *Ancient Records* or *A History of Egypt*?] op. cit., p. 42. The photo is Fig. 25 opposite p. 42.

[19] Petrie, *A History of Egypt*, op. cit., p. 36.

[20] Verbrugghe and Wickersham, *Berossos and Manetho*, op. cit., p. 133.

[21] Emery, *Archaic Egypt*, op. cit., pp. 98–102.

[22] Godron, G., 'A Propos d'une Inscription de l'Horus Kh sékhem', in *Chronique de l'Égypte*, Brussels, Tome XLIII, No. 85, 1968, pp. 34–5.

[23] Emery, *Archaic Egypt*, op. cit.

[24] Petrie, [Sir] W. M. Flinders, *The Royal Tombs of the Earliest Dynasties*. op. cit., pp. 9–10.

[25] Wood, Wendy, 'The Archaic Stone Tombs at Helwan', *Journal of Egyptian Archaeology*, Volume 73, 1987, pp. 59–70.

[26] O'Connor, David, 'The Earliest Pharaohs and the University Museum: Old and New Excavations: 1900–1987', in *Expedition*, Vol. 29, No. 1, 1987, p. 37.

[27] Quibell, *Hierakonpolis*, op. cit., Vol. I, Plate ii.

[28] Engelbach, R., 'A Foundation Scene of the Second Dynasty', in *Journal of Egyptian Archaeology*, Vol. 20, 1932, pp. 183–4, and Plate XXIV. The Maspero quotation comes from his 1906 Guide to the Cairo Museum.

[29] O'Connor, *'The Earliest Pharaohs'*, op. cit., p. 38.

Chaper Six

[1] Emery, Walter B., *Archaic Egypt*, op. cit., p. 80.

[2] Emery, Walter B., 'A Preliminary Report on the Architecture of the Tomb of Nebetka', in *Annales du Service des Antiquités de l'Égypte*, Cairo, Vol. 38, 1938, pp. 457–9 and Plates 77–85. (My copy is an original offprint.)

[3] Emery, Walter B., *Great Tombs of the First Dynasty*, Vol. I, Cairo, 1949, Plate 35-A and Figure 38-A, and page 84.

[4] Emery, Walter B., *Archaic Egypt*, op. cit., p. 82.

[5] Ibid., pp. 80–2.

[6] Emery, *Great Tombs, op. cit.*, Volume I, pp. 82–4.

[7] Redford, Donald B. *Pharaonic King-Lists, Annals and Day-Books: A Contribution to the Study of the Egyptian Sense of History*, SSEA Publication IV, Benben Publications, Mississauga, Canada, 1986, p. 27.

[8] Ibid.

[9] Ibid., p. 20.

[10] Petrie, [Sir] W. M. Flinders, 'New Portions of the Annals', in *Ancient Egypt*, 1916, Part 3, p. 115.

[11] Borchardt, Ludwig, *Die Annalen . . . des Alten Reiches* [The Annals . . . of the Old Kingdom], Berlin, 1917.

[12] Petrie, [Sir] W. M. Flinders, review in *Ancient Egypt*, 1920, pp. 123–4.

13 Petrie, [Sir] W. M. Flinders, 'A Revision of History', in *Ancient Egypt*, 1931, p. 9.

14 Petrie, [Sir] W. M. Flinders, review in *Ancient Egypt*, 1932, p. 84.

15 Redford, Donald B., *Pharaonic King-Lists*, op. cit.

16 There is a Loeb Library edition from Harvard University Press. More recent is: Verbrugghe, Gerald P., and John M. Wickersham, *Berossos and Manetho*, op. cit.

17 Ibid., p. 98.

18 Vol. 1 of *Studies in the Structural Archaeology of Ancient Egypt*, Paulette Publishing Company, La Canada, California, USA, 1979.

19 Vol. 2 of *Studies in the Structural Archaeology of Ancient Egypt*, Paulette Publishing Company, La Canada, California, USA, 1980.

20 Vol. 3, Pt 1 of *Studies in the Structural Archaeology of Ancient Egypt*, Paulette Publishing Company, La Canada, California, USA, 1984.

21 Vol. 3, Pt 2 of *Studies in the Structural Archaeology of Ancient Egypt*, Paulette Publishing Company, La Canada, California, USA, 1984.

22 Vol. 3, Pt 3 of *Studies in the Structural Archaeology of Ancient Egypt*, 1985. I have never seen this publication and only know of it from a review of it by Stephen Quirke in *Discussions in Egyptology*, Oxford, Vol. 6, 1986, pp. 101–04. O'Mara's daughter apparently has no copy of this book. I presume this book was published, like the others, by Paulette, but cannot confirm that.

23 'Obituary Notice', *Göttinger Miszellen*, Göttingen, Germany, 2001, Vol. 185, p. 4.

24 There follows a chronological list of all the articles on ancient Egyptian chronology published by Patrick O'Mara:

'Is the Cairo Stone a Fake?', *Discussions in Egyptology*, Oxford, Vol. 4, 1986, pp. 33–40.

'Historiographies (Ancient and Modern) of the Archaic Period. Pt I: Should We Examine the Foundations? A Revisionist Approach', *Discussions in Egyptology*, Oxford, Vol. 6, 1986, pp. 33–45.

'Historiographies (Ancient and Modern) of the Archaic Period. Pt II: Resolving the Palermo Stone as a Rational Structure', *Discussions in Egyptology*, Oxford, Vol. 7, 1987, pp. 37–49.

'Probing for Unlabeled Astronomical Datings in the Old and Middle Kingdoms. I. Lunar Materials in the Old Kingdom', *Discussions in Egyptology*, Oxford, Vol. 9, 1987, pp. 45–54.

'Probing for Unlabeled Astronomical Datings in the Old and Middle Kingdoms. II. Sothic and Pseudo-Sothic Materials', *Discussions in Egyptology*, Oxford, Vol., 10, 1988, pp. 41–54.

'Was the Sed Festival Periodic in Early Egyptian History?' [Pt 1], *Discussions in Egyptology*, Oxford, Vol. 11, 1988, pp. 21–30.

'Was the Sed Festival Periodic in Early Egyptian History?' [Pt 2], *Discussions in Egyptology*, Oxford, Vol. 12, 1988, pp. 55–62.

'Toward a Multi-Modeled Chronology of the Eighteenth Dynasty', *Discussions in Egyptology*, Oxford, Vol. 17, pp. 29–44.

'Dating the Sed Festival: Was There only a Single Model?', *Göttinger Miszellen*, Göttingen, Germany, Vol. 136, 1993, pp. 57–70.

'Was There an Old Kingdom Historiography? Is it Datable?', *Orientalia*, Vol 65, Fasc. 3, 1996, pp. 197–208.

'Manetho and the Turin Canon: A Comparison of Regnal Years', *Göttinger Miszellen*, Göttingen, Germany, Vol. 158, 1997, pp. 49–61.

'Can the Gizeh Pyramids Be Dated Astronomically? Logical Foundations for an Old Kingdom Astronomical Chronology. Pt I. On the Existence of Unlabeled Lunar and Sothic Dates', *Discussions in Egyptology*, Oxford, Vol. 33, 1995, pp. 73–85.

'Can the Gizeh Pyramids Be Dated Astronomically? Logical Foundations for an Old Kingdom Astronomical Chronology. Pt II: Searching for OK [Old Kingdom] Sothic and Festival Dates', *Discussions in Egyptology*, Oxford, Vol. 34, 1996, pp. 65–82.

'Can the Gizeh Pyramids Be Dated Astronomically? Logical Foundations for an Old Kingdom Astronomical Chronology. Pt III. Pepi's Jubilee: Its Promise and Its Problems', *Discussions in Egyptology*, Oxford, Vol. 35, 1996, pp. 97–112.

'Can the Gizeh Pyramids Be Dated Astronomically? Pt IV. Some Lunar Dates from the 4th and 5th Dynasties', *Discussions in Egyptology*, Vol. 38 (1997), pp. 63–82.

'The Cairo Stone [Pt I]: Questions of Workmanship and Provenance', *Göttinger Miszellen*, Göttingen, Germany, Vol. 168, 1999, pp. 73–82.

'The Cairo Stone [Pt II]: The Question of Authenticity', *Göttinger Miszellen*, Göttingen, Germany, Vol. 170, 1999, pp. 69–82.

'Palermo Stone or "Annalenstein"?', *Discussions in Egyptology*, Oxford, Vol. 45, 1999, pp. 71–86.

'The Birth of Egyptian Historiography, Fifth Dynasty Annalists at Work and the Origins of "Menes"', *Discussions in Egyptology*, Oxford, Vol. 46, 2000, pp. 49–64.

'Once Again: Who Was Menes? An Orthographical Approach', *Göttinger Miszellen*, Göttingen, Germany, Vol. 182, 2001, pp. 97–105.

'Censorinus, the Sothic Cycle, and Calendar Year One in Ancient Egypt: the Epistemological Problem', *Journal of Near Eastern Studies*, Vol. 62, 2003, pp. 17–26. [This article was accepted for publication just before O'Mara's death, and was published posthumously.]

25 O'Mara, *The Palermo Stone*, op. cit., pp. 113–126.

26 Ibid., pp. 131–3.

27 Redford, Donald B., review in *The American Historical Review*, Vol. 87, No. 1, February, 1982, pp. 157–8.

28 Quirke, Stephen, review in *Discussions in Egyptology*, Oxford, Vol. 6, 1986, pp. 101–4.

29 Wilkinson, Toby A. H., *Royal Annals of Ancient Egypt: The Palermo Stone and Its Associated Fragments*, Kegan Paul International, 2000.

30 Ibid., p. 21.

31 O'Mara, *The Palermo Stone*, op. cit., p. 137, and Fig. 48 on p. 156.

32 Lacau, Pierre, and Lauer, Jean-Philippe, *Fouilles à Saqqarah: La Pyramide à Degrés*, Tome IV, *Inscriptions Gravées sur les Vases*, Premier Fasc.: Planches, Institut Français d'Archéologie Orientale, Cairo, 1959. The three photos of these inscriptions which entirely fill Pl. 4 are numbered 19–21.

33 Ibid., Tome V (1965), p. 49, where seven examples are given, and one inscription is shown in Fig. 73.

34 Brunton, Guy, and Caton-Thompson, Gertrude, *The Badarian Civilisation and Predynastic Remains near Badari*, British School of Archaeology in Egypt, London, 1928, pp. 20–2.

35 *Ibid.*, pp. 38–42.

36 An example of a dissenting voice is Willem M. van Haarlem, 'Were the Archaic Kings Buried at Sakkara or Abydos?', in *Discussions in Egyptology*, Oxford, Vol. 17, 1990, pp. 73–4.

37 Caulfeild, A. St. G., *The Temple of the Kings at Abydos*, Egyptian Research Account Eighth Year 1902, London, 1903, with Archaeological Notes by W. M. F. Petrie.

38 Emery, Walter B., *Excavations at Saqqara*, op. cit.

39 Ibid., p. 1.

40 Allen, James P., 'Menes the Memphite', *Göttinger Miszellen: Beiträge zur Ägyptologischen Diskussion*, Göttingen, Germany, Vol. [Heft] 126, 1992, pp. 19–22.

41 As a curious aside, I might mention that Olivia and I often stayed in a 'White Walls', but it was not Memphis. It was a cottage in Fowey, Cornwall, which friends often loaned to us, and where we translated much of our Aesop book for Penguin Classics. You might call this our 'Memphite Period'. I couldn't resist mentioning this, as I have never in my life come across any other place called 'White Walls', and the fact that we became accustomed

to speaking often and casually of 'White Walls' is such a coincidence, if you believe in coincidences.

[42] Wilson, John A., 'Buto and Hierakonpolis in the Geography of Egypt', in *Journal of Near Eastern Studies*, Vol. XIV, No. 4, October, 1955, pp. 209–36.

[43] Baumgaertel, Elise, *The Cultures of Prehistoric Egypt*, 2 vols., Griffith Institute, Ashmolean Museum, Oxford, Vol. I, 1949 (I have a signed copy of this volume in my Egyptological library), and Vol. II, 1960. Palettes are discussed in Vol. II, pp. 81–105.

[44] Davis, Whitney, *Masking the Blow: The Scene of Representation in Late Prehistoric Art*, University of California Press, Berkeley, USA, 1992.

[45] Wilkinson, Toby A. H., *State Formation in Egypt: Chronology and Society*, British Archaeological reports Series 651, Cambridge Monographs in African Archaeology 40, Oxford, 1996, p. 94.

[46] Ranke, Hermann, 'Alter und Herkunft der Ägyptischen "Löwenjagd-Palette"' ('Age and Origin of the "Lion-Hunt Palette"', *Sitzungsberichte der Heidelberger Akademie der Wissenschaften: Philosophisch-Historische Klasse*, 1924/5 Vol., Fifth Treatise, Heidelberg, 1925, published as an offprint of twelve pages with three full-page plates. My copy of this is the original offprint, so I do not know the pagination in the full volume; it is possible that this was only issued separately, in which case it must be extremely difficult to find in any major library, as it is so small and fragile.

[47] Goedicke, Hans, 'The Pharaoh *Ny-Swth*', in *Zeitschrift für Ägyptische Sprache und Altertumskunde*, Leipzig, Vol. 81, Pt 1, 1956, pp. 18–24.

[48] Ibid., p. 18.

[49] Emery, *Archaic Egypt*, op. cit., pp. 91–2.

[50] Ibid., p. 97.

[51] Swelim, Nabil M. A., *Some Problems on the History of the Third Dynasty*, op. cit.

[52] Derry, D. [Donald] E., 'The Dynastic Race in Egypt', in *Journal of Egyptian Archaeology*, London, Vol. 42, 1956, pp. 80–5.

[53] Emery, Walter B., *Saqqara and the Dynastic Race*, University College London, 1952, 12 pages.

Chapter Seven

[1] Petrie, [Sir] W. M. Flinders, *The Pyramids and Temple of Gizeh*, op. cit., Chapter XIV, 'The Granite Temple and Other Remains', pp. 128–37.

[2] Ricke, Herbert, *Der Harmachistempel*, op. cit.

[3] Hölscher, Uvo, *Das Grabdenkmal*, op. cit.

4   Ibid., p. 1.
5   Hassan, Selim, *The Great Sphinx and Its Secrets: Historical Studies in the Light of Recent Excavations*, Vol. VIII of Hassan's series *Excavations at Giza, 1936–1937*, Government Press, Cairo, 1953. This rare book is not the same as Hassan's earlier and very brief book *The Sphinx: Its History in the Light of Recent Excavations*, Government Press, Cairo, 1949, which is widely available and is so severely abridged that it is not sufficient for scholarly and archaeological purposes. Many people are not even aware that Hassan published the longer book, and many libraries possess no copy. I am extremely fortunate that I have been able to obtain one privately from my friend Simon Cox, as I have never seen one for sale on the open market.
6   Hölscher, *Das Grabdenkmal*, op. cit., p. 1.
7   Ibid., pp. 9–10.
8   Ibid., pp. 2–11.
9   Ibid., Ch. VI, 'Individual Finds: A. Statue Fragments of the Old Kingdom', pp. 89–104. Seventy-one objects are illustrated and described in detail. Borchardt was very thorough.
10 Ibid.
11 Petrie, op. cit., pp. 129–30.
12 Ibid., Pl. VI at the back of the book.
13 By a misprint, Petrie's text says the N.W. corner, which is wrong.
14 Petrie, [Which book?] op. cit., p. 130.
15 Ibid., p. 131.
16 Ibid., pp. 132–3.
17 Ibid., p. 133.
18 Hölscher, op. cit., p. 80.
19 Ibid., Chapter VI, 'Individual Finds. B: The Remaining Finds', pp. 105–15.
20 Hornung, Erik, Rolf Krauss and David A. Warburton, eds., *Ancient Egyptian Chronology*, with contribution by Jochen Kahl 'Dynasties 0–2' on pp. 94–15, Brill, Leiden, 2006.
21 Reisner, George A., *Mycerinus*, op. cit., p. 102.
22 Emery, Walter B., *Archaic Egypt*, op. cit., 1984, p. 97.
23 Rice, Michael, *Egypt's Making*, 2nd edn, Routledge, London, 2003, pp. 146–7.
24 Verbrugghe, Gerald P., and John M. Wickersham, *Berossos and Manetho*, op. cit. p. 188.
25 O'Mara, Patrick F., *The Palermo Stone and the Archaic Kings of Egypt*, Paulette Publishing Co., La Canada, California, USA, 1979, p. 166.
26 Hölscher, *Das Grabdenkmal*, op. cit., pp. 80–1.
27 Reisner, *Mycerinus*, op. cit., p. 102.

[28] Ibid., p. 179.

[29] Ibid., p. 102.

[30] Hölscher, *Das Grabdenkmal*, op. cit., pp. 10–11.

[31] Ibid., p. 11.

[32] Temple, Robert, *The Crystal Sun: Rediscovering a Lost Technology of the Ancient World*, Century, London, 2000, pp. 375–6.

[33] Ibid., Pl. 30, with caption on pp. 216–17.

[34] Ibid., p. 421 and Pl. 60, with caption on p. 406.

[35] Cotsworth, Moses, *The Rational Almanac*, York, England, 1902, p. 176.

[36] Hölscher, *Das Grabdenkmal*, op. cit., p. 37.

[37] *Ibid.*, pp. 18–20.

[38] Graindorge-Héreil, Catherine, *Le Dieu Sokar à Thebes au Nouvel Empire* [The God Sokar at Thebes during the New Kingdom], Harrassowitz, Weisbaden, 1994 pp. 34–9.

[39] Hölscher, *Das Grabdenkmal*, op. cit., p. 40.

[40] Maragioglio, V., and C. Rinaldi, *L'Architettura delle Piramidi Mefite*, Parte V, Testo [The Architecture of the Pyramids of Memphis, Pt V, Text], including an English translation by A. E. Howell, Rapallo, 1966, pp. 76–88 and 128–30.

[41] Ibid., Parte V, Tavole [Pt V, Plates], Pl. 14, 15 and 16.

[42] Ibid., Pl.16.

[43] Ibid., 'Testo', p. 76.

[44] Ibid., p. 128 (Observation 36).

[45] Ibid., pp. 128–30 (Observation 38).

[46] Petrie, [Sir] W. M. Flinders, *The Pyramids*, op. cit., pp. 130–1.

[47] Ricke, *Der Harmachistempel*, op. cit., p. 8.

[48] Ibid., p. 29.

[49] Ibid., p. 25.

[50] Maragioglio and Rinaldi, *L'Architettura*, op. cit., 'Text', p. 136. There is a typographical error on this page of their book, which I will take this opportunity of correcting for them. In l. 34 of the English text, the word 'north' should be deleted and replaced with the word 'south', so that it reads: Here the door is near the south corner of the west wall . . .' There are also errors on folding Pl. 14 which accompanies this volume, and contains the plan of the Sphinx Temple; the 'outer magazine' in the northwest corner is wrongly labeled PN, whereas it should be labeled RN. (Also missing from the plan are the labels SW and PW, which are the western equivalents to SE and PE in the east of the temple. And, as I have mentioned in my main text, the North Trench adjoining the temple extends much further to the west than is shown in the plan: this may be substantiated by my photos, Pl. 21 and others on the website. As for the Valley Temple plan which also appears

on this plate, none of the concealed features which I have explored, photographed and described is even hinted at.)

51 Ibid., pp. 138–40.
52 Ibid., p. 136.
53 Hassan, Selim, *The Great Sphinx*, op. cit., p. 25. Maragioglio and Rinaldi ('Text', p. 134) give the wrong reference for this, erroneously citing p. 28.
54 Maragioglio and Rinaldi, *L'Architettura*, op. cit., p. 134.
55 Ricke, *Der Harmachistempel*, op. cit., p. 16.
56 Ibid., pp. 18–19.
57 Ibid., p. 9.
58 Maragioglio and Rinaldi, *L'Architettura*, op. cit., 'Text', p. 134.
59 Hassan, Selim, *The Great Sphinx*, op. cit., p. 26.
60 Ibid., p. 26, Note 1.
61 Grinsell, Leslie, *Egyptian Pyramids*, John Bellows, Gloucester, England, 1947, p. 109.
62 Maragioglio and Rinaldi, L'Architettura, op. cit., 'Text', p. 138.
63 Ibid.
64 Ricke, *Der* Harmachistempel, op. cit., p. 12.
65 Arnold, Dieter, *The Encyclopaedia of Ancient Egyptian Architecture*, I. B. Tauris, London, 2003, p. 60.

Chapter Eight

1 Petrie, [Sir] W. M. Flinders, 'The Metals in Egypt', *Ancient Egypt*, London, Vol. 2, Pt 1, 1915, p. 17.
2 Petrie, [Sir] W. M. Flinders, reviewing *The Antiquity of Iron* by G. F. Zimmer in *Ancient Egypt*, London, Vol. 2, Pt 4, 1915, p. 190.
3 Petrie, 'The Metals in Egypt', op. cit., p. 17.
4 Petrie, 'The Metals in Egypt'. op. cit., pp. 21–2, where he says: '. . . that the iron was not meteoritic is proved by its malleability . . .' For some recent excavated examples of non-meteoritic iron objects, see Gale, Noel, and Stos-Galse, Zofia, 'The "Fingerprinting" of Metals by Lead Isotopes and Ancient Iron Production at Timna', in *Discussions in Egyptology*, Vol. 1, 1985, pp. 7–13. The authors state for instance: 'Analyses of the [twelve] iron objects from Timna by Professor Bachmann and at Oxford show, by the absence of nickel, that they are made of smelted, not meteoritic iron.' (These were found in the Hathor Temple at Timna and dated from the Nineteenth and Twentieth Dynasties.)
5 Paul Bovier-Lapierre, 'Note sur le Traitement Métalurgique du fer aux environs d'Assouan', *Annales du Service*, Tome XVII, 1917.

6   Watkins, Rev. M. G., *Gleanings from the Natural History of the Ancients*, London, 1885, p. 231.

7   Strabo, *The Geography of*, translated by H. L. Jones, Loeb Classical Library, Harvard University press, USA, 1988, 8 vols, Vol. II, pp. 156–7 (Bk III, Ch. 5, 11).

8   Strabo, *The Geography of*, translated by H. C. Hamilton, George Bell, Bohn's Libraries, London, 1887, 3 vols, Vol. I, p. 262 (Bk III, Ch. 5, 11).

9   de Montalbán y de Mazas, César Luis, *Las Mazmorras de Tetuán su limpieza y Exploración*, Comp. Ibero-Americana, 1929.

10 Whishaw, Ellan M., *Atlantis in Andalucía*, Rider, London, no date, but 1929, Fig. 33, opposite p. 164. See discussion of this photo on p. 198.

11 Thom, Alexander, *Megalithic Sites in Britain*, Oxford University Press, 1967, reprinted with corrections in 1971 and 1972, 1974, 1976 and 1979; Thom, Alexander, *Megalithic Lunar Observatories*, Oxford University Press, 1971, reprinted with corrections in 1973 and 1978; Thom, Alexander, and Thom, Archibald S., *Megalithic Remains in Britain and Britanny*, Clarendon Press, Oxford, 1978. Examples of articles written by the two Thoms for the *Journal for the History of Astronomy*, ed. M. A. Hoskin, Science History Publications, Chalfont St Giles, Buckinghamshire, England, are: 'The Astronomical Significance of the Large Carnac Menhirs', Vol. 2, Pt 3, No. 5, 1971, pp. 147–60; 'The Carnac Alignments', Vol. 3, Pt 1, 1972, pp. 11–26; 'The Uses of the Alignments at Le Menec Carnac', Vol. 3, Pt 3, No. 8, 1972, pp. 151–64. Reference to the Pythagorean triangle of 12, 35, 37 on which megalithic ellipses were constructed may be found in *Megalithic Sites in Britain*, pp. 27 and 77–8.

12 Geoffrey of Monmouth, *The British History of*, translated from the Latin by A. Thompson and J. A. Giles, James Bohn, London, 1842, p. 158 (Bk 8, Ch. 11).

13 *Hesiod, the Homeric Hymns and Homerica*, translated by H. G. Evelyn-White, Loeb Classical Library, Harvard University Press, 1982, pp. 94–5.

14 *Hésiode*, traduit par Paul Mazon, Paris, 1960, pp. 39–40.

15 Diodorus Siculus, *Diodorus of Sicily (The History)*, translated by C. H. Oldfather, Loeb Classical library, Harvard University Press, USA, 12 vols., Vol. II, pp. 278–9 (Bk III, 60, 1).

16 Diodorus Siculus, *The Historical Library of Diodorus the Sicilian*, translated by G. Booth, London, 1700, p. 115 (Book III, Chapter 4, 135, which is a different reference numbering system than that later used by the Loeb series). I am fortunate to own a copy of this rare book, which is not easily found. I generally try to collect all existing translations of key classical works, in order to compare them. It is often the earliest which are the most fascinating.

17 Thom and Thom, *Megalithic Remains*, op. cit., p. 181.

18 Aeschylus, translated by H. W. Smyth, Loeb Classical Library, Harvard University Press, 1922, 2 vols., Vol. I, pp. 246–7.

19 Aeschylus, *The Tragedies of*, translated by Theodore Alois Buckley, George Bell, Bohn's Classical Library, London, 1899, p. 12.

20 *Aristotle in Twenty-Three Volumes*, Loeb Library, Harvard University Press, USA, Vol. XII, 1983, includes *Movement of Animals*, translated by E. S. Forster, pp. 448–9.

21 Smith, J. A., and Ross, W. D., eds, *The Works of Aristotle Translated into English*, Vol. 5, Clarendon Press, Oxford, 1912; *De Motu Animalium* (*On the Movement of Animals*), translated by A. S. L. Farquharson (these editions have no pagination and the references are found by textual references alone).

22 Strabo, *The Geography of*, trans. Jones, op. cit., Vol. II, pp. 134–7 (Bk 3, 5,5); Strabo, *The Geography of*, trans. Hamilton and Falconer, op. cit., Vol. I, p. 255.

23 Ibid., pp. 136–9; p. 256: 'the assertion that neither the little islands, nor yet the mountains, bear much resemblance to pillars, strictly so called, [set up] either as the termination of the habitable earth, or of the expedition of Hercules, has at all events some reason in it; it being an ancient usage to set up such boundary marks.'

24 Tacitus, *The Agricola and the Germania*, translated by H. Mattingly and S. A. Handford, Penguin, Harmondsworth, Middlesex, England, 1971, p. 130.

25 *The Works of Tacitus: The Oxford Translation, Revised with Notes*, trans. Anonymous, George Bell & Sons, London, but bound as Bohn's Classical Library [Bohn acquired Bell], London, 2 vols, 1896–8; Vol. II, *Germania*, Chapter 34, pp. 324–5.

26 In the *Wörterbuch*, *negeg* may be found on page 350 of Vol. 2 (Adolf Erman and Hermann Grapow, *Wörterbuch der Aegyptischen Sprache*, Leipzig, 1928.) Fortunately, I have my copies of these volumes, and I see that an alternative meaning is 'the cry of a falcon', which would be the cry of the resurrected Horus, the risen sun, as he appears in the sky.

27 Eissa, Ahmed, 'Zur Etymologie des modernen Namens vom grossen Amuntempel in Theben: "Karnak"' [On the Etymology of the Modern Name of the Great Temple of Amun at Thebes: 'Karnak'], in *Göttinger Miszellen*, Göttingen, Germany, Volume 144, 1995, pp. 31–41. I have omitted numerous mythological details, such as the 'Great Cackler', the 'Sacred Goose of Amun', etc.

28 *Hesiod, the Homeric Hymns and Homerica*, translated by H. G. Evelyn-White, op. cit., p. 89. Also one may see *Hesiod and Theognis*, translated by Dorothea Wender, Penguin, Harmondsworth, Middlesex, England, 1973, p. 28.

29 Lucan, *The Civil War (Pharsalia)*, translated by J. D. Duff, Loeb Classical Library, Harvard University Press, USA, 1928, p. 218 (Bk 4, l. 589).

30 Geoffrey of Monmouth, *The Historia Regum Britanniae of*, ed. by Acton Griscom and translated from the Welsh manuscript by Robert Ellis Jones, Longmans Green, London, 1929, p. 251 (folio 47 recto of the MS).

31 Petrie, [Sir] W. M. Flinders, review of *Der Name und das Tier des Gottes Set* [The Name of the God Set and the Set-Animal], in *Ancient Egypt*, London, Vol. One, Pt 3, 1914, p. 133.

32 *Wörterbuch*, Vol. 5, p. 231 ('*Widersacher*').

33 *Wörterbuch*, Vol. 1, pp. 97–8.

34 Clement of Alexandria, *The Writings of*, trans. By Rev. William Wilson, Vols. IV–V of Roberts, Rev. Alexander, and Donaldson, James, eds, *Ante-Nicene Christian Library*, Edinburgh, 1867, Vol. IV, p. 401.

35 Diodorus Siculus, Loeb Library, op. cit., pp. 156–7 and footnote 3 on p. 157.

36 Tacitus, *The Life of Agricola*, in *The Works of Tacitus*, The Oxford translation revised [Anonymous], 2 vols, George Bell and Bohn's Library, London, 1898, Vol. II, p. 353 (Ch. 11).

37 Tacitus, *The Agricola and the Germania*, trans. Mattingly and Handford, op. cit., p. 61.

38 See entry for Silures in Wikipedia.

39 Nennius, *History of the Britons*, in *Six Old English Chronicles*, ed. By J. A. Giles, Henry Bohn, London, 1848, p. 389 (Book III, chapter 13).

40 Griscom, Acton, *The Historia Regum Britanniae of Geoffrey of Monmouth*, together with a literal translation of the Welsh Manuscript No. LXI of Jesus College, Oxford, by Robert Ellis Jones, Longmans Green, London, 1929, pp. 240-1.

41 *Geoffrey of Monmouth, The British History of*, translated from the Latin by A. Thompson, new edition revised and corrected by J. A. Giles, James Bohn, London, 1842, pp. 16–7 (Bk I, Chs 11 and 12).

42 Ibid., p. 22 (Bk I, Ch. 16).

43 Strabo, *The Geography of*, Hamilton and Falconer trans., op. cit., Vol. I, p. 255 (Bk III, Ch.5, 5); Loeb trans., op. cit., Vol. II, pp. 134–5.

44 Lethbridge, T. C., *The Painted Men*, Andrew Melrose, London, 1956, pp. 186–7. (This book is largely devoted to the Picts, who were 'the painted men'.)

45 Peet, T. Eric, *Rough Stone Monuments*, Harper, London and New York, 1912.

46 Ibid., pp. 146–53.

47 Cowper, H. S. [Henry Swainson Cowper], *The Hill of the Graces: A Record of Investigation among the Trilithons and Megalithic Sites of Tripoli*, Methuen, London, 1897.

48 Ibid., p. 170.

49 Ibid., pp. 169–71.

50 Goodchild, R.G., 'Roman Tripolitania: Reconnaissance in the Desert Frontier Zone', *The Geographical Journal*, London, Vol. 115, No. 4/6 (April–June 1950), pp. 161–71.

51 Newberry, Percy E., 'The Wooden and Ivory Labels of the First Dynasty', in *Proceedings of the Society of Biblical Archaeology*, December, 1912, p. 288. (My copy of this article is an original offprint, so I do not have the volume number, not having taken it from a bound volume. The article as a whole is pp. 279–89, with three pages of plates, numbered XXXI–XXXIII.)

52 Newberry, Percy E., '*Ta-Tehenu* – "Olive Land"', in *Ancient Egypt*, Vol. Two, Pt 3, 1915, pp. 97–102 with plate (Fig. 4) facing p. 97.

53 Bates, Oric, *The Eastern Libyans*, Macmillan, London, 1914, pp. 159–60.

54 Reyna, Simeon Gimenez, *Die Dolmen von Antequera*, Antequera, 1978.

55 Leisner, Georg, and Leisner, Vera, *Die Megalithgräber der Iberischen Halbinsel* (*The Megalithic Graves of the Iberian Peninsula*), Berlin, 1943 onwards, several volumes including plates volumes.

56 Bates, Oric, *The Eastern* Libyans, op. cit.

57 Ibid., pp. 39–41.

58 Ibid.. p. 160.

59 Petrie, [Sir] W. M. Flinders, 'The Alphabet in the XIIth Dynasty', in *Ancient Egypt*, 1921–2, Pt 1, pp. 2–3.

60 Petrie, [Sir] W. M. Flinders, archaeological report for the year, in *Ancient Egypt*, 1921–2, Pt 1, p. 33.

61 Bruijning, F. F., 'The Tree of the Herakleopolite Nome', in *Ancient Egypt*, 1921–2, Pt 2, p. 1.

62 Petrie, [Sir] W. M. Flinders, 'The Palace Titles', in *Ancient Egypt*, 1924, pp. 114–5.

63 Petrie, [Sir] W. M. Flinders, ''The Peoples of Egypt', in *Ancient Egypt*, 1931, p. 78.

64 Petrie, [Sir] W. M. Flinders, review in *Ancient Egypt*, 1931, p. 113.

65 Petrie, [Sir] W. M. Flinders, review in *Ancient Egypt*, 1935, Pt 2, p. 119.

66 Nibbi, Alessandra, 'Some "Libyans" in the Thera Frescoes?' in *Discussions in Egyptology*, Oxford, Vol. 31, 1995, p. 89.

67 Breasted, James Henry, *The History of Egypt*, London, 1906, pp. 6–7, 31–2.

COLOUR PLATE SECTION CAPTIONS

PLATE 1

The subway beneath the Chephren Causeway which leads to the Osiris Shaft, seen from the south, with the Great Pyramid in the background. The remains of a clumsily-built later superstructure may be seen protruding from the top of the Causeway, directly above the initial shaft which descends to Level One, the other entry to which is on the left as you enter the subway from this direction. The superstructure and the portion of the shaft which has been cut down through the Causeway would have facilitated the re-use of this early shaft and the lowering of the five smaller sarcophagi which are now missing, having been removed since 1944 by persons unknown.
(Photo by Robert Temple)

PLATE 2

The deep shaft from Level One to Level Two of the Osiris Shaft. Two ladders have been affixed to the shaft wall, side by side. The shaft is approximately a hundred feet deep, and it was here that we were left hanging in space when the lights suddenly went out.
(Photo by Robert Temple)

PLATE 3

Sarcophagus Two in Level Two of the Osiris Shaft, in a northern niche at the western end of the chamber. This is one of the most extraordinary objects in Egypt, made of a stone which apparently is not used for any other object known to Egyptology, dacite. The lid has been shoved to one side, and the sarcophagus is empty and without inscriptions. Our dating of this sarcophagus shows that it is of extreme antiquity, with a dating span ranging from Pre-Dynastic times to shortly after the time of Chephren himself, under whose Causeway it is to be found. According to these dating results, this sarcophagus could be as early as 850 years before the time of Chephren.
(Photo by Robert Temple)

PLATE 4

A general view of the Tomb of Osiris. To the left is the portion of the water canal which runs along the west wall, and encircles the island except for the entry path which leads from the south. In 1940, the four pillars at each corner of the island were still intact, but they have all now been smashed, leaving only stumps at the top and bottom of each. Since it is unlikely that this was done in a search for treasure, intentional damage to this Osirian centre is suspected. Rubble from the destroyed pillars still litters the central island.
(Photo by Robert Temple)

PLATE 5

I am sitting on a step at the top of the huge descending shaft at Abu Ruash, which is oriented perfectly to the meridian (geographical north-south line). In my opinion the shaft was used as an astronomical observation shaft, for studying meridian transits of stars. (The shaft would probably have had a roof of perishable materials, long vanished.) The shaft was carved out of the solid bedrock on top of a hill overlooking Giza, the highest point in that part of Egypt, and an excellent choice for an astronomical observatory. Meridian transits were crucial for time-keeping and the maintaining of a precise calendar. The shaft is not believed to be later than fourth Dynasty in date, but its 'twin' at Zawiyet el-Aryan was not later than Third Dynasty in date, since two occurrences of the name of the Third Dynasty pharaoh Neferka (or Nebka) were found there by archaeologists. Attempts to suggest that the two giant shafts and the huge open 'chambers' they lead to were meant to be covered by pyramids which were never built are wholly unsubstantiated and unconvincing. No existing pyramids contain such gigantic shafts and 'chambers'. These shafts and 'cham-

bers' were used for astronomical purposes, I am certain, though they may well have doubled for ceremonial occasions as well.
(Photo by Olivia Temple)

PLATE 6

Olivia clambers up the Abu Ruash shaft. At that point of the shaft, the surviving stonework suggests that there was an obstacle erected, most of which has been removed. It seems as if it might have been a stone base for a wooden superstructure, which could perhaps have been intended for narrowing the view. If the shaft were for astronomical observation purposes, a narrowing of the shaft at some point for better observation of the meridian (in the dead centre of the shaft) would have been expected.
(Photo by Robert Temple)

PLATE 7

The Abu Ruash Shaft seen from above, looking down and facing directly north. In the lower centre of the floor of the shaft, the sockets definitely suggest fixtures of some kind (presumably wooden), perhaps for refining the meridian observations by narrowing and widening the view as appropriate. The feet and lower legs of Olivia are seen at top right, which gives scale.
(Photo by Robert Temple)

PLATE 8

The Egyptologist Jean-Philippe Lauer, standing at the edge of the vast descending shaft of Zawiyet el-Aryan, which leads down to an uncovered chamber. In the far distance may be seen the two main pyramids at Giza. This shaft apparently dates to the Third Dynasty. Although it is often spoken of as an 'unfinished pyramid' and attributed to the Fourth Dynasty, there is no evidence for either contention. It was probably used for either astronomical observations or ritual ceremonial occasions, or both. Because it is in a closed military zone, it has not been studied by archaeologists for more than half a century. This photo is Figure 1 from Lauer's article 'Reclassement des Rois des IIIe et IVe Dynasties Égyptiennes par l'Archéologie Monumentale' ('Rearranging of the Kings of the Third and Fourth Egyptian Dynasties on the Basis of the Archaeology of the Monuments'), *Comptes Rendus 1962, Académie des Inscriptions & Belles-Lettres*, Paris, 1963, pp. 290-309, with a response by Pierre Montet on pages 309-10. Lauer points out in his article that although the shaft at Zawiyet el-Aryan resembles that at Abu Ruash, it is in fact much bigger, and contains an abundance of enormous blocks of granite.

PLATE 9

Looking northwards along the rising open shaft, which is oriented precisely to the geographical north, at Zawiyet el-Aryan. From G. [Sir Gaston] Maspero, *Histoire Générale de l'Art: Égyte*, Librairie Hachette, Paris, 1912, Figure 78 on page 47.

PLATE 10

The Step Pyramid at Saqqara, built for King Zoser, the first king of the Third Dynasty (reigned 2707 BC - 2670 BC according to conventional dating), by his architect and vizier, Imhotep.
(Photo by Robert Temple)

PLATE 11

This marvellous statue of the Pharaoh Mycerinus (Menkaure) was excavated at his Valley Temple at Giza, at the eastern end of the Causeway extending from the Pyramid of Mycerinus. At left is the goddess Hathor, and at right is the 'god of Thebes'. In this portrait, Mycerinus wears the White Crown of Upper Egypt (the South), where Thebes was the southern Capital. The statue is in the Egyptian Museum at Cairo.
(Photo by Robert Temple)

PLATE 12

(a) The granite blocks in the left two-thirds of this photo are casing stones on the east side of the Pyramid of Mycerinus. This closeup photo shows very clearly how the limestone blocks at right, which were part of the Funerary Temple of Mycerinus, were rudely jammed up against the pyramid at a later date, without any attempt at sophistication or even any finishing-off.
(Photo by Robert Temple)

(b) At right, we see granite casing stones of the Pyramid of Mycerinus. At left, we see the limestone blocks of the Funerary Temple of Mycerinus rudely and crudely jammed up against the pyramid. The unsophisticated nature of this construction is truly astonishing. This proves conclusively that the funerary temple was a later edifice which was constructed with far less care and precision. Doubtless, if the funerary temples of the pyramids of Cheops and Chephren were sufficiently preserved, we would have seen a similar sight in each case to this. I am not aware that anyone has ever called attention to this detail, or published a photo showing it, although it is readily available for any curious tourist to inspect.
(Photo by Robert Temple)

PLATE 13

This photo appeared in *McClures Magazine* (USA) for January 1902, to accompany an article by Cleveland Moffett entitled 'In and Around the Great Pyramid'. Fortunately, I have for years collected *McClures Magazines*! It is the best photo I have ever seen of the top 'relieving chamber' directly above the King's Chamber inside the Great Pyramid. This photo shows that the chamber was completely covered in Victorian graffiti, including the name 'Campbell's Chamber' at the base of the photo which was painted on the instructions of Howard Vyse. The vast profusion of graffiti in this supposedly remote chamber in Victorian times shows just how unreliable the chamber's 'ancient graffiti' really are as evidence of anything, and how likely it is that they were forged, as elucidated in the main text on the basis of Vyse's own journal entries.
(Photo by Cleveland Moffett)

PLATE 14

Looking up the Grand Gallery of the Great Pyramid. The ladder at the top has been erected to enable access to Davison's Chamber, the bottom 'relieving chamber' over the King's Chamber, which is reached by way of a narrow passage from the top of this gallery. No one knows the purpose of the strange ramps with holes which run along the ramp at each side of the Grand Gallery. The wooden rails and steps are modern installations to facilitate tourist access.
(Photo by Robert Temple)

PLATE 15

The Sphinx (left), Valley Temple (bottom right), and Sphinx Temple (upper right), from the air. The Chephren Causeway may be seen extending beside the Sphinx and leading into the Valley Temple. This is an uncredited aerial photo reproduced by Herbert Ricke as half of his frontispiece in his book *Der Harmachistempel des Chefren in Giseh* (*The Harmachis Temple of Chephren at Giza*), Wiesbaden, 1972. This photo is an old one, as there is no car park at far right, and there is no modern road going up towards the pyramids along the top of the photo, as there would be today. The photo must therefore date from sometime between 1936 and 1960 at the latest. The most probable date is late 1940s. The Sphinx has not had its 'modern restoration', and the ravaged and heavily eroded rear is particularly evident when seen from above. One strange feature which is not normally evident, but which can be seen in this particular photo, is that the Sphinx is not oriented at right angles to the western wall of the Sphinx Temple in front of it, but instead his face is looking directly at the North Trench just beyond it, over which the Romans built their grand descending staircase when the Sphinx Temple was buried in sand and forgotten. A very strange conclusion to be drawn from this photo is that Ricke's plans of the Sphinx and Sphinx Temple (see Figure X as an example) are inaccurate and are not surveyed properly, since in them he has the Sphinx directly facing the western wall of the temple, which this photo proves conclusively is not the case. The fact that Ricke reproduced this very photo in his own book and did not notice that it discredited his plans appearing in the same book shows that he must have been asleep at the wheel, and that his eyes were turned off.

PLATE 16

The strange channel or conduit cut into the bedrock and running beneath the wall of the Sphinx Temple. It is plugged with a basal granite slab, which has a central groove tightly filled with a succession of small granite blocks 24 cm wide. Beneath them runs a tiny 'channel' which slopes inwards into the temple and cannot be a drain. It is estimated that the granite slab weighs as much as 100 tons. It runs under the north wall of the temple and enters a natural cliff face. This is in my opinion a classic example of one of several cable grooves, heavily weighted down on top, to guide the cables which lowered immensely heavy stone sarcophagi down into subterranean tombs. I believe that at the far end of this cable groove, where the stone ceases, a shaft leads to an intact tomb which cannot be later than the time of King Chephren.

(Photo by Robert Temple)

PLATE 17

A close-up of the tiny 9 cm-high cable groove sloping inwards which runs underneath the granite blocks set into the basal granite slab of the Sphinx Temple northern channel. It opens to a maximum of 13 cm in width. Apart from the fact that this groove descends inwards rather than outwards, it is too small to carry any significant amount of fluid of any kind, so cannot have been the 'waste water drain' both excavators assumed it to be. Prominent signs of wear on the granite to either side of the groove seem to indicate that something rubbed them very hard in a sideways direction, back and forth with great force, and this must have been the cable.

(Photo by Robert Temple)

PLATE 18

The Sphinx as seen from the floor of the north-east corner of the Sphinx Temple. In the foreground at right may be seen the depression cut out of the bedrock for the insertion of the granite cable channel. Immediately to the left of it, in the centre of the photograph, is the hole also cut out of the bedrock to enable a person to crouch beside the entry hold of the cable groove.

(Photo by Robert Temple)

PLATE 19

Behind me is the north wall of the Sphinx Temple, and seen immediately over my head is a gigantic block of limestone in the centre of the wall. It in turn holds down the small limestone plug stone directly below the centre of it, seen to the right of my head. It is this small plug-stone, obviously inserted last, which lies on top of the granite cable channel. I am crouching in the area cut out of the bedrock floor which allows a person to be at the level of the cable groove. The hacking of such a huge rough hole from the bedrock of the temple floor can have only one purpose, namely access to the end of the cable conduit by two people guiding the double-cable along the conduit during the lowering process for the sarcophagus at the other end of the cables.

(Photo by Olivia Temple)

PLATE 20

This photo shows the channel cut out of the limestone bedrock entering the northern cliff face, which constitutes the north wall of the North Trench. I have shoved the tourist rubbish

(which blows in the wind and is everywhere on the Giza plateau) up beneath the cliff, in order to clear as much of the channel as possible for the photograph. At the point where the sand changes colour from pale to dark, the inlaid granite conduit ends. From that point on (beneath the dark portion), there is no stone at all beneath the sand, and it seems that the sand has there filled a vertical shaft. I dug my hands down into the sand as far as I could, and I jabbed with the pointed chisel which I had with me, and could detect nothing but sand. This therefore seems to be the place into which the cable descended from the cable groove. I have taken great care to clear with my hands one of the granite blocks laid down over the cable groove; barely discernible to either side of it, but more on the right side, may be seen the actual granite conduit, still mostly covered by sand, as I had no way to clear it properly to make it better visible.
(Photo by Robert Temple)

PLATE 21

The channel as it emerges from under the north wall of the Sphinx Temple into the North Trench. The large limestone block resting above the channel protrudes from the wall, and beneath it a small limestone block has been roughly wedged into the channel to block it. The rectangular stone which shows quite clearly in the channel is one of the succession of granite blocks which an archaeologist at some time appears to have levered out of the basal incision in the granite slab conduit beneath it, and then when replacing it could not get it to go all the way down again. This may have been done by Selim Hassan or Herbert Ricke, the excavators. Raising this small block would reveal nothing but another piece of granite underneath, so the investigator would have been deterred from proceeding further.
(Photo by Robert Temple)

PLATE 22

The North Trench from its western end, showing the prominent channel cut out of the bedrock crossing it from beneath the north wall of the temple (at right) and entering the cliff face at left.
(Photo by Robert Temple)

PLATE 23

This is the southern cable channel, cut out of the bedrock of the floor of the Sphinx Temple but plugged with limestone blocks rather than with granite. It passes beneath a wall here, and contains rubble which neither Hassan nor Ricke bothered to remove, because they assumed that this was just a waste water drain and hence of no interest. Of course, this channel should be cleared and studied properly, because it probably leads to another access shaft to the subterranean tombs and structures beneath the temple.
(Photo by Robert Temple)

PLATE 24

(a) An Old Kingdom basalt pulley, excavated by Selim Hassan, and which would have been used in connection with lowering the heavy stone sarcophagi into the tombs at Giza. (This is Plate XVII A in Selim Hassan, *The Great Pyramid of Khufu and Its Mortuary Chapel*, Cairo, 1960.)

(b) A side view of the basalt pulley of Old Kingdom date excavated at Giza by Selim Hassan, and which is seen in Plate 23a. This is Plate XVII B in the Hassan book. The three grooves at the top of this pulley allow for three parallel cables to be used for heavy objects, and to steady their ascent or descent.

(c) This is the 'Chephren channel', another one of the granite cable channels, which was excavated beneath the plaster floor of the Funerary Temple of Chephren by Uvo Hölscher in 1909, directly in front of the Pyramid of Chephren. It is highly likely that this cable channel was used for the cable which was used to lower the sarcophagus of Pharaoh Chephren into his tomb, which I believe must lie beneath this spot. A photo of the granite plug sealing the top of the channel at the end may be seen in Plate 50. This photo is a view facing south, showing the channel passing from the court of the temple underneath the middle of the southern wall of the court. (This is Figure 47 on page 57 of Uvo Hölscher, *Das Grabdenkmal des Königs Chephren* (*The Funerary Monument of King Chephren*), Leipzig, 1912.)

(d) This is the outer, southern end of the granite cable channel which was concealed by the plaster floor of the Funerary Temple of Chephren and passed beneath the southern wall of the court of the temple. Here, as with the channel in the Sphinx Temple, we see the same feature of a snugly-fitting granite plug on top of the channel to keep the cable from flying up, and to keep it steady while lowering the sarcophagus. (This is Figure 48 on page 57 of Uvo Hölscher, *Das Grabdenkmal des Königs Chephren* (*The Funerary Monument of King Chephren*), Leipzig, 1912.)

PLATE 25

This is Plate 34–B in George A. Reisner's *Mycerinus*, Harvard University Press, USA, 1931. (The photo is taken looking West.) The cable conduit may be seen in the foreground at left, terminating in a large rectangular pit carved out of a solid block of limestone, which has been transported to this spot and embedded in the gravel floor. (It takes the place of the similar 'crouching-pit' hacked out of the bedrock in equivalent position at the Sphinx Temple.) The conduit passes under the central stone pathway and terminates beneath a limestone wall, though that cannot be seen in this photo. Some of the stone blocks set down into the channel are still in place, as may be seen, so that this conduit closely resembles the north conduit in the Sphinx Temple in having a groove in stone, covered with tightly-fitting smaller stones on top.

PLATE 26

The portion of the limestone burial chamber of Khasekhemui which was visible at the time of our visit. The chamber is still largely filled with sand, but it is not at all deep, extending downwards for a mere six courses of limestone blocks. Here, the top course and part of the second course are exposed, which was sufficient for our dating samples to be taken. The photo is taken from the south, looking towards the north.
(Photo by Robert Temple)

PLATE 27

A closeup photo of the top course of limestone masonry on the east side of the burial chamber of Khasekhemui, with part of the second course visible. The limestone blocks are rough and unfinished , rudely hacked and clumsily joined. Behind them the dark mudbrick may be seen. It is hard to believe that incompetent masonry such as this preceded by only twenty or thirty years the construction of the huge Step Pyramid at Saqqara (see Plate 10).

PLATE 28

The Tomb of Khasekhemui at Abydos, first excavated by Sir William Flinders Petrie in 1900, and here exposed by the re-excavation in 2001 by Gunter Dreyer. The tomb structure is entirely of mudbrick and wood with the exception of the small rectangular patch in the foreground, which is the limestone burial chamber dated by us. This photo is taken from the south, looking north.
(Photo by Robert Temple)

PLATE 29

This is a statue of Imhotep, the Vizier and Chief Architect of Egypt under King Zoser (Djoser), first king of the Third Dynasty. Imhotep designed and built the Step Pyramid at Saqqara. This statue is of Ptolemaic date, and is Object N4541 on display at the Louvre.
(Photo by Olivia Temple)

PLATE 30

A small limestone portrait statue of King Khasekhemui, last king of the Second Dynasty, preserved in the Ashmolean Museum, at Oxford. He was originally called King Khasekhem ('The Appearance of the Power'), but later changed his name to Khasekhemui ('The Appearance of the Two Powers') after he unified the northern and southern regions of Egypt. In this statue he only wears the white crown of Upper Egypt, his land of origin, before his conquest of all or part of the north. He is also wearing the garment of the Sed Festival, which was a kingship renewal ritual. He is said to have been a physical giant, more than eight feet tall.

(Photo by Robert Temple)

PLATE 31

'The Fort' at Hieraconpolis.
(Photo by Robert Temple)

PLATE 32

The passage leading up to the entrance to 'the Fort' at Hieraconpolis. The wall on the right is part of 'the Fort', showing a well preserved portion of mudbrick recessed panelling typical of large royal structures of this period of Egyptian history.
(Photo by Robert Temple)

PLATE 33

The Step Pyramid of Enezib at Saqqara, as it looked in 1937 after excavation by Walter Emery. The pyramid was 75 feet long at the base and 43 feet high originally, with a slope of 49 degrees to its sides. The pyramid was built as a tomb by King Enezib, fifth king of the First Dynasty. The pyramid was 'decapitated' by the succeeding pharaoh, King Semerkhet, who covered it with a conventional rectangular mastaba tomb, which completely disguised it until Emery dug deeper and found this structure concealed underneath. The size may be appreciated by the man standing on top. This is Plate 77 from Walter B. Emery, 'A Preliminary report on the Architecture of the Tomb of Nebetka', *Annales du Service*, Cairo, Vol. 38, 1938. (At first Emery thought the tomb was that of Nebetka or Nebitka, a royal official under Enezib, but he was later forced to revise his opinion.) A fuller report on this tomb was published eleven years later in Walter B. Emery, *Great Tombs of the First Dynasty*, Volume I, Cairo, 1949, where this photo appears again as Plate 35-A, but is reproduced much less well, and the tomb was then numbered and re-named 'Tomb 3038'. Emery announced that it was King Enezib's tomb in 1961, in his book *Archaic Egypt*.

PLATE 34

The 'Petrie Fragment', or 'London Fragment', or 'Petrie/London Fragment of the Cairo Stone', which Sir Flinders Petrie bought from a 'petty dealer' in antiquities at Cairo 'while I was [digging] at Memphis'. Enquiries undertaken unofficially by Petrie from dealers revealed a story claiming 'that it was found in Upper Egypt, had been brought down and sold to a Cairo dealer: from whom it had been passed to a Memphite dealer, and so finally to myself.' It is now preserved at the Petrie Museum at University College London. This photo was reproduced in the periodical *Ancient Egypt*, Volume 8, 1916, p. 119. Patrick O'Mara's analysis suggests that this fragment, like all the 'Cairo fragments' but one (the only one which was obtained by excavation, and which alas has almost no text), are fakes made by antiquities forgers for sale by dealers. Their acceptance as genuine, despite the strong evidence of their being fakes, has distorted the accepted chronologies and historical accounts and interpretations of Egypt prior to Fifth Dynasty (currently dated circa 2500 BC).

PLATE 35

Dr. Patrick O'Mara, who demonstrated that the 'Cairo Stone' fragments were fakes made by antiquities forgers in 1910. He was thus able to 'purge' Archaic chronology in Egypt of false elements invented by the forgers.
(Photo courtesy of his daughter, Mrs. Kathleen Kottler, of California)

PLATE 36

A cubit rod or rule of the New Kingdom, preserved in the Louvre. Every scribe was required to have one. The main reason why the Cairo fragments must be fakes is that, unlike the Palermo Stone, the inscriptions were not laid out according to such a cubit rule.
(Photo by Robert Temple)

PLATE 37

(a) This is one of the most mysterious of the many stone bowls and vases of the Archaic Period in Egypt. It was excavated by Walter Emery at Saqqara in the tomb of a First Dynasty royal official named Sabu, a tomb which is known simply as 'Tomb 3111'. The central hole is bizarre, to say the least, and this item has caused a lot of controversy, some people joking that it reminds them of a modern turbine blade. It is important to remember that this is supposed to be made out of a single piece of carved stone. It is 61 cm wide and 10 cm high. This is one of the 'lipped bowls' which call into question the very idea that these could possibly have been carved from solid stone. Some 'lipped bowls' have four lips, such as one perfect specimen of diorite which I saw exhibited at the Grand Palais in Paris a few years ago, and this one has three lips. These lips are folded over as if they had been made of soft clay. Joseph Davidovits and I believe that these objects made from very hard stone (not the soft alabaster ones) were not really carved from solid stone at all but were fabricated from weathered stone fragments mixed in a geopolyermic binder as a kind of concrete or mortar, shaped when soft, and then allowed to go hard. That would explain how it was possible to make such 'lipped bowls'. The tomb of Sabu dates from the reigns of the kings Udimu (also called Den and 'Horus who strikes') and Enezib (also called Anedjib and 'safe is his heart'), as shown by jar sealings of their reigns found in the tomb.
(Plate 40-A in Walter B. Emery, *Great Tombs of the First Dynasty*, Volume I, Cairo, 1949.)

(b) Side view of the First Dynasty 'schist bowl' with the three folded lips.(Plate 40-B in Walter B. Emery, *Great Tombs of the First Dynasty*, Volume I, Cairo, 1949.)

PLATE 38

King Narmer, mace in hand and wearing the crown of the south, in the symbolic act of smiting his northern enemies from the Delta. The falcon Horus, symbol of royal authority, grips a braided rope which is round the neck of a 'Delta Libyan', who is further identi-fied by the papyrus plants behind him. (Papyrus only grows in still water and never grew along the flowing Nile, but only north of Memphis in the Delta swamps.) Narmer's name in archaic hieroglyphics is in the centre at top, in a 'serekh', or rectangular box ornamented with the 'palace façade' wall motif.
(Photo by Robert Temple)

PLATE 39

The central motif of the reverse side of the Narmer Palette. The two strange beasts, called by archaeologists 'serpopards' for lack of a better name, and presumably based upon the giraffe, are here held by ropes round their necks, as they form this heraldic device of entwined necks with heads facing one another. It appears to be a zoomorphic attempt to simulate the hieroglyph *shen*, which means 'infinity', surmounted by the two heads gazing at one another, which symbolize the north and the south regarding each other forever as a united and intertwined entity, henceforward to be what we call Egypt.
(Photo by Robert Temple)

PLATE 40
Ioannis Liritzis (right) and myself at Giza, with the Pyramid of Chephren in the background.
(Photo by Olivia Temple)

PLATE 41
An aerial photo of the Sphinx taken sometime after 1937, probably by a military plane during the Second World War. The Great Pyramid is at top of the photo. Directly in front of the Sphinx is the ruined Sphinx Temple, and to its left the much more substantial Valley Temple, behind which the long Chephren Causeway extends up towards the Pyramid of Chephren, which cannot be seen in this photo. (The small rectangular ruin at an angle just above the Sphinx Temple, between it and the road in the photo, is the Temple of Amenhotep IV, of the New Kingdom, which was built when the Sphinx Temple was completely covered in sand and its existence forgotten.) This photo provides clear evidence that Selim Hassan's clearance of 1936-7 extended to the front of the Sphinx Temple as well, where traces of quays are visible. These have been covered over again by sand for so long (probably since the 1950s) that no one remembers they were ever cleared, and this photo is the only evidence of it that I have ever seen.
(Collection of Robert Temple)

PLATE 42
Ioannis (right) and myself inside one of the upper magazines of the Valley Temple, attempting to find a suitable dating sample. I am wearing my hat not because of some strange eccentricity, but to try to keep all the spiders out of my hair; the magazines were all criss-crossed with thick spider webs when we entered them, so that we had to rip our way through them. The far wall and ceiling are of red granite, but the walls are of travertine ('Egyptian alabaster'). There are six magazines altogether laid out in two stories one on top of another: three form a top row, and three form a bottom row. They are highly resonant to sound, like pipes. They are only open at one end. No one knows their purpose. Archaeologists presume they may have been used for storage, hence their name of 'magazines', which is an old-fashioned word meaning a storage chamber. (I suppose the modern use of the word magazine to describe a periodical is because it is stuffed full of things.) We discovered from our Geiger counter that the Valley Temple magazines are so intensely radioactive that the priests serving in the temple every day would be bound to get leukaemia or some other cancer within twenty years. My theory is that such magazines, as well as the many granite sarcophagi (which are even more radioactive) would have irradiated and killed bacteria, and aided in the preservation of mummified corpses. Perhaps these magazines were one filled with mummies, prior to burial. They may have been stored here during their seventy-day 'curing' process.
(Photo by Olivia Temple)

PLATE 43
An Osiris Eye as painted on the wall of the Temple of Seti I at Abydos (*Photo by Robert Temple*). Superimposed is the geometrical analysis of the design, showing how the key points such as the centre of the pupil, the top centre edge of the iris, and the centre right edge of the iris, as well as the left end of the eyebrow, are all joined by lines making triangular and rectangular patterns defined by a total of five 'golden angles' of 26° 33' 54", which was the sacred angle used in all Egyptian sacred art and architecture throughout the ages. The 'golden angle' is derived from 'the Golden Section' by means of a 'golden triangle'. (See lengthy description in my previous book with Olivia Temple, *The Sphinx Mystery*, 2009.) The superimposed design is by Robert Temple, improved, corrected and drawn for the computer by my graphics collaborator Jonathan Greet.

PLATE 44

Looking down on the middle corridor of the western end of the Pillared Hall of the Valley Temple, giving the proportions of the granite columns and architraves by comparison with the figures standing on the alabaster floor.
(Photo by Robert Temple)

PLATE 45

Trying to obtain a viable sample from the travertine wall of the staircase inside the Valley Temple. Unfortunately, we discovered later that Ioannis's technique of optical thermoluminescence does not work with travertine ('Egyptian alabaster') because the stone is translucent and not opaque. Therefore, we cannot date anything made of that stone.
(Photo by Olivia Temple)

PLATE 46

Olivia and a woman antiquities inspector looking out onto the roof of the Valley Temple from the granite-framed doorway at the top of the stairway. The only way today to leave the doorway and gain access to the roof is to creep along the ledge at bottom left of the photo, which is above the Ascending Passage, so that a fall would be injurious onto the stone far below. I had some difficulty persuading anyone to follow me, but finally Ioannis and the male antiquities inspector risked it. I believe the only people who had been on the roof for many, many years were the electricians, who had obviously used their own ladders for access from the outside of the temple.
(Photo by Robert Temple)

PLATE 47

The roof of the Valley Temple, filmed from the top of the stairway, and looking towards the southwest corner of the temple. The strange limestone 'box', probably containing a chamber, is in the top centre of the photo. Ioannis is kneeling down, flanked by two inspectors, taking the limestone sample which he has dated to the New Kingdom period, thereby proving that this roof was accessible at that time although the rest of the temple was probably buried, It can be seen that the stones which Ioannis is sampling here are paler than the main wall, and appear to be later additions of some kind, which is indeed what they are (of New Kingdom date) The spot where Ioannis is crouching is directly over the western end of the magazines.
(Photo by Olivia Temple)

PLATE 48

The view of the roof of the Valley Temple looking north, from the southern wall. In the far distance is the road which leads to the Great Pyramid, with people walking along it. Then there is the massively thick north limestone wall of the temple, and the door in the upper centre of the photo, surrounded by red granite blocks, is the opening of the stairway onto the roof. Olivia sits there in the shade while her mad husband leaps from pillar to pillar like some demented gazelle, something I could not persuade anyone to join me in doing. The row of red granite blocks slanting upwards is the Ascending Passage, which leads through the west wall (extreme left) and out onto the Causeway. In the foreground are the many red granite architraves of the T-shaped Pillared Hall, which are largely intact, resting on their pillars. The hall has sixteen such granite pillars.
(Photo by Robert Temple)

PLATE 49

Inside the Blind Room of the Valley Temple, looking out towards the passage which leads to the magazines. The bottom of this hole, from which a stone has been removed to permit entry, is at normal chest height when standing in the passage, and you have to climb up to get in. Originally, this Blind Room would have been invisible from the passage, because a

granite block would have filled this space. It was probably removed in the 19th century by Mariette or Petrie. Beneath the floor of this Blind Room, to the right of the photo, is the mysterious space from which an acid solution leaked through a special drain over a long period in the Old Kingdom, as shown in Plate 25. There must be a space beneath the entire Blind Room, and it is probably a substantial chamber. No one but Petrie ever even referred to the existence of this large and impressive Blind Room. It was never even mentioned in Hölscher's excavation report of the temple. At the rear (behind the camera), this Blind Room connects with passages which run east-west within the south wall of the temple, both of which passages are blocked (the granite plug blocking the eastern one may be seen in Plate 50), and also opens into a huge vertical shaft. All of these features may be seen in the many additional photos on this book's website www.egyptiandawn.info.
(Photo by Robert Temple)

PLATE 50

a) Here I am standing at the bottom of the Blind Room of the Valley Temple at Giza, taking a photo up the vertical shaft leading down into it through the south wall of the temple.
(Photo by Olivia Temple)

(b) Inside the Blind Room of the Valley Temple may be found this opening containing a large stone plug, one of the many mysteries of the chamber. It blocks a passage leading eastwards within the south wall.
(Photo by Robert Temple)

PLATE 51

(a) Looking down the first NE vertical shaft inside the north wall of the Valley Temple.
(Photo by Robert Temple)

(b) Looking down the second NE vertical shaft inside the north wall of the Valley Temple. An electrician's cable used for the *son et lumière* lights affixed to the roof has been fed down it, proving that the electricians know more about this building than any archaeologist does. A horizontal passage appears to lead off from the left, but I had no way to suspend myself down the shaft to inspect it, nor do I believe any electrician has ever done it, as they just throw the cables down and catch them at the bottom (accessing the bottom from the horizontal internal passage at ground level, see Plates X and X). At bottom left we can clearly see a stone shelf protruding into the shaft. I am certain that in the Old Kingdom period, these vertical shafts had wooden stairways affixed inside, as there are evidences of slots, shelves, and indentations in the stonework, to indicate that such wooden fixtures were accommodated and used constantly to facilitate the movement by the priests throughout the complex network of passages, chambers, and shafts, which honeycombs the temple. The shelf which we see here was, I believe, a platform to anchor the stairway at this high level and act as a landing for passing into the uppermost horizontal passageway. I believe there were probably three successive stories of horizontal passageways riddling the walls of the temple, linking the shafts, and leading to chambers. This internal network has never been explored and was completely ignored by the German excavators at the beginning of the 20th century. No study of the temple has been done since that time, until my report in this book.
(Photo by Robert Temple)

PLATE 52

Looking upwards from the base of the second vertical shaft, North Shaft Two, in the northeast corner of the north wall of the Valley Temple. The base of this shaft is linked to the base of another shaft by a horizontal passage inside the wall at ground level, along which I crawled, as it has windblown sand in it. Although the shaft has had an electric cable thrown

down from the roof by the workmen, for conveying the electricity for the *son et lumière* light fixtures, none of the antiquities inspectors had the slightest awareness of the existence of any of the vertical shafts which I discovered, as they clearly never ask the electricians about where they run their cables. It is obvious that this shaft, like the others, was not created by stone-robbers but is an original and integral feature of the construction of the temple. I am convinced that each vertical shaft originally contained an interior wooden stairway for access to the roof, and to the side-passages and various chambers within the walls.
(Photo by Robert Temple)

PLATE 53

I took this photo from deep inside the limestone north wall of the Valley Temple, looking north and outwards, at ground level. The figure crawling towards me is the intrepid Olivia. This is a low north-south passage leading to an internal chamber which connects with an east-west passage which joins the bases of the two vertical shafts (Number One and Number Two) in the north wall at its eastern end. As can be seen, a great deal of windblown sand impeded our progress. None of these shafts, chambers, and passages has ever been examined by an archaeologist. They all need to be cleared and properly plotted onto a plan of the temple.
(Photo by Robert Temple)

PLATE 54

The Sphinx Temple as seen from the top of the Valley Temple. The massive central courtyard dominates the scene, with remnants of limestone pillars. The floor is of levelled bedrock. Some archaeologists have speculated that this temple once had a pavement of 'Egyptian alabaster', which was stripped away in antiquity (which would have had to be prior to circa 2000 BC, as the temple was then covered with sand continuously until 1936), but this is pure speculation, and there is no evidence for it whatever. It is most unlikely that this temple ever had a stone floor of any kind, and that whatever flooring was used from time to time was perishable, but not wooden (no traces of wood were found during the excavations of this structure by Hassan or Ricke). I have suggested in *The Sphinx Mystery* that during the three months of the Inundation period at the time of the Old Kingdom, the Egyptians may have allowed the floor of this temple to become naturally flooded with Nile water. See Plate X, of the northwest magazine of the temple, which I suggest was used to store a ceremonial boat used on these occasions in connection with rituals of some kind which were performed on the water of this temple, which never had a roof.
(Photo by Robert Temple)

PLATE 55

A portrait of al Uted and his friends. Al Uted is the only menhir still standing within the Mezorah Ring, the others having fallen. One fallen menhir's base may be seen just to the right of al Uted, as it has fallen outwards and away from the direction of this view. To the left of al Uted, three of the stones have been broken off. At right in this photo, three large stones remain standing, one of which is leaning significantly, and two other stones have partially subsided. In all, there are eleven stones or remains of stones of the Ring visible in this photo. In the far distance, a corrugated iron roof of a local dwelling may be glimpsed. In the middle distance, stones comprising another formation may be seen in a row in the grass, mostly broken very low down. There are outer groups of stones at Mezorah which have not been properly plotted or studied, and many stones which are wholly or partially buried. Some are also incorporated within dwellings.
(Photo by Robert Temple)

PLATE 56

Looking at the standing menhir al Uted and many, largely fallen and broken, stones of the Mezorah Ring of which it is a part. An unbroken mini-menhir may be seen not far beyond

it in the Ring, which is still standing. The way in which many of the stones of the Ring have been overturned and broken off is seen clearly here. No less than 24 stones of the Ring may be seen here, most of them fallen, broken, or moved. The edge of the inner tumulus is seen at right. In the far right distance may be seen a portion of a local dwelling, with two windows showing.
(Photo by Robert Temple)

PLATE 57
Six of the Mezorah stones are seen here, the third from the right having been broken off so that only its stump remains. This is one tiny portion of the Mezorah Ring.
(Photo by Robert Temple)

PLATE 58
This is the wonderful and wild landscape of Morocco as seen from the site of the Mezorah Ring. Some of the trees surrounding the area of this site are large wild quince trees, far taller than garden quince trees normally grow.
(Photo by Robert Temple)

PLATE 59
(a) A quince growing in my garden in England. The Greek word for a quince, as recorded by the Roman naturalist Pliny, translates as 'golden apple'.
(Photo by Olivia Temple)

(b) Bound captive Libyan chieftains in their traditional garb, with their customary beards, as depicted in a New Kingdom Egyptian relief of the time of Pharaoh Rameses III. These captives were seized in Rameses III's war against the Libyans of the North. From *Geschichte Ägyptens (History of the Egyptians)*, by Georg Steindorff, Leipzig, 1931, plate opposite page 384.

PLATE 60
The megalithic group ('*senam*') of trilithons at Messa in Libya, a photo taken by Herbert Weld-Blundell and published as Figure 49, on page 169, of H. S. Cowper, *The Hill of Graces: A Record of Investigation among the Trilithons and Megalithic Sites of Tripoli*, London, 1897. Messa is at a place called Zawieh Beida, forty miles from Greanah in Libya, in the Cyrenaica region. It is clear that originally stones were laid continuously along the tops of the upright stones to form a continuous line of trilithons, closely resembling the use trilithon constructions at Stonehenge in England. It is suggested that North African and British megalithic peoples were in frequent sea contact over a prolonged period. The similarity of the name Messa in Libya with the name Mezorah in Morocco may not be coincidental. Also, the contemporary name of Egypt amongst Egyptians is spelled in English letters as *Misr* or *Mesr*, pronounced approximately like 'Mezrr', and although the name is recognised as having ancient origins, they are a bit vague, with no one being absolutely certain about the details or what the true ancient meaning of the name really was. However, modern Egyptians are most insistent upon using this name for their country, which they never call 'Egypt' except to foreigners. (The photographer, Herbert Joseph Weld-Blundell, lived 1852-1935, and shortened his name to Herbert Weld in 1924.)

PLATE 61
Senam Semana (Terr'gurt). Figure 21, page 91, from H. S. Cowper, *The Hill of the Graces: A Record of Investigation among the Trilithons and Megalithic Sites of Tripoli*, London, 1897.

PLATE 62
Senam el-Khab (M'Salata).). Figure 33, page 141, from H. S. Cowper, *The Hill of the Graces: A Record of Investigation among the Trilithons and Megalithic Sites of Tripoli*, London, 1897.

PLATE 63

Libyan trilithon known as Senam Bu-Saiedeh surrounded by fallen stones. Figure 54 on page 190 from H. S. Cowper, *The Hill of Graces: A Record of Investigation among the Trilithons and Megalithic Sites of Tripoli*, London, 1897.

PLATE 64

(a) Libyan trilithon known as the Senam at Kom Nasr. Figure 38 on page 147 from H. S. Cowper, *The Hill of Graces: A Record of Investigation among the Trilithons and Megalithic Sites of Tripoli*, London, 1897.

(b) Frontispiece to H. S. Cowper, *The Hill of Graces: A Record of Investigation among the Trilithons and Megalithic Sites of Tripoli*, London, 1897. This shows the Libyan trilithon known as Senam el-Gharabah.

INDEX

(page numbers in italic face denote
illustrations)

Abu Ruash 90–7, *91*, *92*, *93*, *95*, 309, 445
Abydos 9, 73–4, 77–8, 99–100, 108–9,
    194, 255
  Khasekhemui's tomb at, *see*
      Khasekhemui
  Osireion at 65, 67, 71, 72, 77, 99, 254
  Osiris Island at 65, 66, 72, 78
  religious ritual at 71–2, 72–4
  tombs (versus cenotaphs) at 254–7
Abydos king list 215–16, *215*, *216*, 217,
    224–5, 233–4, 254
Adams, Barbara 209
*Additional Unlabeled Lunar Dates from the
    Old Kingdom in Egypt* (O'Mara) 236
Agnew, Henry Crichton 29
Akhenaten, King 219, 233
Akhet-hotep 306
Alexander the Great 234
Algeria 401, 408, 412, 418, 425
Allen, James P. 257–9, 260
Alpha Draconis 21
Amenophis II 341
Amun 264, 395, 425
Ancient Egypt 229
Ancient Egypt Stone Vessels (Aston) 61
Ancient Egyptian Minerals and Industries
    (Lucas, Harris) 61
Ancient Records of Egypt (Breasted) 125
Anedjib, *see* Enezib
Annales du Service 147, *149*, 214
Antaios 386, 387, 388, 396–9

Antequera 419, 432
Apophis, King 363
Arbuthnot, Sir Robert 134
Archaic Egypt (Emery) 106, 199, 214, 216–
    17, 271–2, 301
Aristotle 392
Armenia 381–2, 395
Arnold, Dieter 130, 360
arsenic 371
Ashmolean Museum 203, 270
Aston, Barbara 61
Aswan 54, 55, 58, 62, 112, 125, 166, 179,
    318, 372
Athothis, King 242
Atlantis 13, 14, 15, 46, 47, 370, 373, 375
Atlantis in Andalucía (Whishaw) 378
Atlas 13, *369*, 387–8, 389–91, *390*, 392–3,
    396, 399

Bach, Johann Sebastian 40
Badarian Civilisation The (Brunton,
    Caton-Thompson) 251–2
Band, Erster 185
Barsanti, Alessandro 69
Barth, Dr Henry 417
Barthoux, Jules 61–2, 66
Basques 376, 402
Bates, Oric 189, 416, 420, 421–2, 429
Baumgaertel, Elise 262–3, 264
Bauval, Robert 57
Bedjau, King 233
Belzoni, Giovanni Battista 457–8, *459*
Berlin Museum 292, 462
Betchau, King 201

Bikheris (Biuf/Biufre), King 90
  in 'mini' king list *87*, 88, 89–90
Bikui-nub (Cheops) 129
Biometrika 276
Birch, Samuel 137–8, 143, 146
Biuf-Biufre, *see* Bikheris, King
Bonani, Georges 147
Borchardt, Ludwig 229–31, 238, 287, 291,
  292–3, 431, 453, 462
bowls, vases, *see* pottery
Brandi, Annibale 48, 50, 288, 437
Breasted's Chronology 83–4, 99, 149, 431
Breasted, James Henry 83–4, 125–6, 203,
  231, 431–2
Brettel, Mr 134
Brewer, Humphries 144–5
Britain 374–5, 376, 379–80, 395, 396, 397,
  400, 402, 403–4, 404–5
British Museum 50, 134, 137, 264, 372–3
bronze 370–1, 374
Brooke, Sir Arthur de Capell 382
Browne, Gordon 383–4
Brunton, Guy 251–2
Brutus 403–4
Budge, Wallis 201, 264
Building in Egypt (Arnold) 130
*Bulletin de l'Institut Français d'Archéologie
  Orientale* 223
Burton, James 47–8, 50, 51–2, 138, 442–3
Buto 260, 433

Cadiz 374, 375, 393, 394, 404
Cairo 12, 20, 43, 268, 451
  German Institute in 82, 194, 211
  Museum 175, 209, 228, 231, 238, 288,
    290, 414, 459, 460
Cairo Stone 10, 203, 228–32, 235–6, 237–
  45, 273
Calder, C. S. T. 381
carbon dating 1, 111, 146–50, 198, 210–11
Carey, Henry 183
Carnac 381, 395–6; *see also* Karnak
Carthage 370
Caton-Thompson, Gertrude 251–2
Caulfeild, A. St G. 254
Caviglia, Captain Giambattista 7–8, 47–9,
  50–2, 120, 287–8, 439–42, 459
Cayce, Edgar 46–7
cenotaphs 97, 100, 207, 253–7, 260
Charles I of England 259
Cheops (Khufu), King 4, 6, 43, 63, 73, 83,
  90, 101, 102–4, 129, 152, 268, 366,
  367–8, 420, 454
  death of 86
  fixation of, on Great Pyramid 102, 118
  Funerary Temple of, *see* Cheops's
    Funerary Temple
  graffiti of name of 103–4, 118–19, 122–
    3, 124–46 *passim*, *139*, *141*
  Horus name of 129
  Khnumu-Khufu alternative name of
    124–6, 129, 144
  in 'mini' king list *87*, 87
  Petrie on 124
  Pyramid, *see* Great Pyramid
  tomb of 59, 98, 153, 170, 180, 182–6
Cheops's Funerary Temple *181*, *182*, 182–
  3, 186
  conduits/channels/grooves beneath 184
Chephren (Khafre/Raqaf), King 4, 6, 8,
  43, 68–9, 73, 84, 90, 101, 103–4,
  152, 166, 175, 233, 268, 282, 292,
  295, 299, 300, 302, 364–5, 366–8,
  454
  Funerary Temple of, *see* Chephren's
    Funerary Temple
  in 'mini' king list *87*, 89
  statues of 175, 288, 290–1, *295*, 302,
    312, 314, 316, 318, 343, 352–3, 355,
    357–8, 359, 364, 365, 460, 461
  tomb of 59, 98, 153, 170, 180, 182–4,
    188
Chephren Causeway 4, 43, 51–5 *passim*,
  68–9, 76, 165, 174, 175, *181*, 186,
  279, *280*, 281, 287, 288, 291, 305–6,
  307, 312, 315, 323, 354, 441
Chephren Pyramid 26–9 *passim*, *23*, 34,
  35, 36, 38–9, 40, 43, 51, 54, 76, 84,
  165, 186, 188, 279, *280*, 281, 283,
  303, 306, 315, 320, 322, 354, 419,
  451, 453–4, 457–8
  Belzoni's Chamber in 142
  blocks used in 110, 419
  date range of, from samples 149
  king predated by 6, 117, 149–50
  Shadow Square and, *see* Shadow
    Square
  solstice shadow from 29, 306
  see also Giza Plateau; pyramids of Giza
Chephren's Funerary Temple *51*, 165,
  185, 281, 291, 315, 334, 354, 356,
  358, 456–7, 462

conduits/channels/grooves beneath 186–9

Chester Beatty Papyrus Number One 29

Chipiez, Charles 128

Chronology of the Palermo and Turin Canons, The (O'Mara) 236

Classical Review 264

Cleopatra, Queen 234

cobras 8

Coffin Texts 152

Comma of Pythagoras 40–1, 307

Complete Pyramids (Lehner) 125

Constantine, Emperor 35

copper 370–1, 374

Corineus 397, 399

Cornwall 371, 397, 401–2

cosmic order 22, 40, 306, 308, 309

Cotsworth, Moses B. 19, 20, 24, 308–9

Cowper, H. S. 407, 409, 410–11

Crystal Sun, The (Temple) 19, 29, 30, 40, 98, 175, 179, 237, 247, 306, 307, 308, 309, 314, 338, 340, 372, 387

cubits, explained 236–7

Cultures of Prehistoric Egypt, The (Baumgaertel) 262–3

Cyprus 370–1, 401

dacite 61–3, 66, 69, 313

Daily Telegraph 52–3

Daressy, Georges 69, 238, 434

Darius I, King 46, 363

Das Grabdenkmal des Königs Chephren (Hölscher) 52, 185, 283, 295

Dashur 267

   pyramids at 100, 111, 119, 423

   Red Pyramid at 111

'Dated Texts of the Old Kingdom' (Spalinger) 85, 127

David, Rosalie 71–2, 73

Davidovits, Joseph 248–9

Davis, Whitney 263

Davison, Nathaniel 122–3, 131

Dawn of Astronomy, The (Lockyer) 215

Debono, Fernand 87, 88

DeMille, Cecil B. 104

Den, King 207, 208, 220

Denderah, Temple of 74

Derry, D. E. 11, 274, 276–7, 278

Devine, James. M. 147

Die Annalen (Borchardt) 229

Discussions in Egyptology 12, 429–30

Djebel Moussa 393

Djedefre (Radjedef), King 84–6, 90–1, 103, 233, 420

   in 'mini' king list *87*, 88, 89–90

Djer (Zer), King *241*, 242

Djeser-nub, King 232

Djet, King 220

Djoser/Djeser, *see* Zoser

Dreyer, Dr Gunter 105–6, 108, 194, 195, 196, 197, 202

Droiton, Etienne 87, 88, 89, 90

dynamite 126, 130, 133, 138, 331

Dynastic Race 273–4, 275–8

'Dynastic Race in Egypt, The' (Derry) 11, 276

Dynasties:

   1st 11, 69–70, 82, 86, 99–100, 103, 109, 113, 117, 118, 206, 207, 208, 213–27, 230, 232, 239, 241, 242, 246, 253–7 *passim*, 259, 260, 265, 272, 371, 413, 415, 420

   2nd 8–9, 36, 69, 82, 86, 89, 107, 109, 118, 170, 171, 197, 199, 200, 201–2, 203, 208, 212, 217, 227, 228, 232, 233, 246, 253, 272, 299, 301, 302, 303–4

   3rd 9, 12, 81, 82, 92, 94, 95, 97, 105, 107, 109, 129, 201, 205, 207, 210, 212, 216, 227, 227, 246, 253, 272–3, 299, 368, 371, 420

   4th 6, 8, 58, 68, 69, 79, 82, 83, 84, *87*, 88, 90, 95, 97, 103, 104, 113, 117, 118, 129, 132, 145, 151, 166, 167, 170, 171, 193, 209, 225, 227, 232, 245, 265, 272, 276, 277, 282, 301, 304, 344, 352, 368, 420, 451–2

   5th 10, 66, 67, 68, 97, 110, 170, 202, 209, 227, 232, 233, 238, 276, 352, 353, 365, 415

   6th 66, 67, 82, 97, 110, 118, 169, 170, 175, 209, 227, 277, 288, 303, 314, 353, 371

   12th 73, 84, 88, 232

   19th 215, 233, 363

   22nd 15, 423

   25th 235, 421

   26th (Saitic Period) 46, 53–4, 59, 63, 68, 75, 79, 113, 144, 301, 363

   early, confusion concerning 9

Hyksos 235

Manetho's division into 234–5
overlapping 83
Eastern Libyans, The (Bates) 420, 429
Edgar, J. and M. 372
Egypt Before the Pharaohs (Hoffman) 107, 200
Egypt:
  1st Intermediate Period of 15, 66, 67, 71, 169, 227, 259, 288
  2nd Intermediate Period of 67
  3rd Intermediate Period of 198
  African influences in 275
  Amratian culture of 424–5
  Archaic Period of 15, 83, 106, 109, 198, 216, 217, 227, 242
  Badarian culture of 250–3, 263, 423, 424
  cattle counts in 86
  chronology issues of, examined 227–8
  Civil Year in 246
  Delta 12, 13–14, 203, 363, 264–5, 376, 399, 421, 428, 431–2, *433*, *434*
  Middle Kingdom of 15, 60, 67, 68, 73, 78, 79, 84, 271
  Muslim Brotherhood of 65
  Nasser takes over 65
  New Kingdom 71, 88, 163, 169, 198, 199, 200, 224, 254, 257–8, 259–60, 281, 282, 310, 322, 343, 363
  Old Kingdom 4, 15, 46, 63, 66, 67, 70, 71, 81, 99, 148, 155, 162, 171, 187, 198, 216, 225, 227, 228, 259, 271, 282, 288, 295, 302–3, 310, 314, 336, 338, 343, 371–2, 422
  Persian invasion of 8, 363
  plague, social collapse and chaos in 15
  pottery from, *see main entry*
  predynastic 11, 69, 113, 150, 216, 225, 260, 261, 268, 276–7, 424, 433; *see also* Libyans
  religio-geometrical mania in 30
  simultaneous civilisations in 4, 9, 211
  unification of 11, 15, 113, 117, 226, 255, 263, 270
  see also dynasties; *individual pyramids, temples etc.*
Egypt's Making (Rice) 200, 301
Egyptian Dawn website (www.egyptiandawn.info) 5, 8, 22, 30, 42, 55, 60, 62, 64, 77, 92, 112, 152, 153, 159, 173, 180, 184, 185, 186, 208, 209, 246, 261, 285, 288, 296, 297, 298, 306, 307, 312, 313, 315, 318, 325, 327, 329, 331, 332, 333–9 *passim*, 347, 348, 355, 359, 362, 363, 372, 388, 417, 419, 431, 450
Egyptian Heritage: Based on the Edgar Cayce Readings (Lehner) 46
Egyptian Muslim Brotherhood 65
Egyptian Pyramids, The (Lepre) 126
Egyptian Supreme Council of Antiquities 5, 44, 114, 152, 172, 294
Eissa, Ahmed 395
el Ardi, Abd 48–9
Emery, Walter 99–100, 106, 107, 117, 199, 204–7, 213–18, 248, 249, 255, 256–7, 271–2, 276, 277–8, 301
Encyclopaedia of Ancient Egyptian Architecture (Arnold) 361
Enezib (Anedjib), King 213–14, 215, 217–27, 256
Enezib Pyramid 32, 213–23, *214*, 225–6, 304
Engelbach, R. 209
English Civil War 259
Ennead 29
Excavations at Giza (Hassan) 53
Excavations at Saqqara (Emery) 256
Eye of Ra 31, 32, 33–6, *34*, 41

faked evidence 4, 10, 203
  Vyse's 6–7, 104, 123, 130, 131, 132–46
  see also Cairo Stone
Fawcett, C. D. 276
Fayyum 62
Firth, Cecil 189
Fischer, Henry 250, 271
Fox Television Network 45
Frankfort, Henri 254
Freemasons 65
Freud, Sigmund 96

Gaballah, G. A. 115
Gauthier, Henri 238, 271
Gauthier, Joseph Étienne 271
Gebel Dukhan 62
Gebel Ferani 62
Gebel Um-Sidri 62
Genius of China, The (Temple) 18, 405
Geoffrey of Monmouth 14–15, 380, 397, 403–4, 411

Geographical Journal 411
Giza Drawing Board 233
Giza Plateau:
  Campbell's Tomb 48, 53, 131, 132, 133
  Comma as generator of complex
    features of, *see* Comma of
    Pythagoras
  earlier sealed royal tombs at 151; *see*
    also intact royal tombs
  Golden Plan 17, 22, 101
  large caves beneath 7
  maps of 16–17
  Osiris Shaft at, *see main entry*
  Perfect Square of, *see main entry*
  Plan 16–17, 19, 22, 25
  planned as unified design concept 16
  pyramids on, *see individual pyramids*;
    pyramids of Giza
  sealed royal tombs at, *see* intact royal
    tombs
  Shadow Square, *see main entry*
  sloping 17
  Sphinx at, *see main entry*
  Sphinx Temple at, *see main entry*
  triple-plan of 22
  Valley Temple of, *see* Valley Temple
  Winter Solstice Shadow Centre 29
  see also individual pyramids
Gizeh and Rifeh (Petrie) 69
Gleanings from the Natural History of the
  Ancients (Watkins) 374
Gnostics 35
Godley, A. D. 183
Godron, G. 205
Goedicke, Hans 271
Gogmagog 397, 399, 404
Goitein, Prof. D. D. 383
golden angle/slope 29, 179, 306, 307, 308,
  340
Goodchild, R. G. 411–13, 415, 416
Göttinger Miszellen 236, 429–30
Graindorge-Héreil, Catherine 321
grave robbers, *see* robbers
Great Flood 382
Great (Cheops) Pyramid 17–21 *passim*,
  23–30 *passim*, 35–40 *passim*, 41, 43,
  48, 94, 186, 287–8, 308, 341, 370,
  372, 455
  apothegm on 30
  Ascending Passage of 29, 306
  base area of 5, 24–5

boat pits beside 85, 86, 102
Brandi on Caviglia's work in 437–41
Breasted's Chronology and 83, 149
Campbell's Chamber in 127, 132, 137,
  140, 142, 143
Cheops's fixation on 102
Cheops predated by 6, 103, 117, 149–
  50
cross-correlation in design of 101
date range of, from samples 149
Davison's Chamber in 120, 123, *123*,
  440
Descending Passage of 21, 29, 94, 306,
  438, 439, 440
diagonal of 27–8
dynamite used in 126, 130–1, 133
faked evidence in, *see* Vyse
geometrical projection of plan of 27
graffiti linking Cheops to 103–4, 118–
  19, 122–3, 124–46 *passim*, *139*, *141*
Grand Gallery of 123, 124, *128*, 440
Grotto in 8, 131, 439, 442
height of, measuring 24
King's Chamber in 6, 118, *120*, *121*,
  122, *123*, 124, 125, *128*, 130
Lady Arbuthnot's Chamber in 122,
  132, 134, 137, 140, 142
'lost' passage beneath 8
meridian line bisecting 76
Nelson's Chamber in 122, 132, 133,
  140, 142
Queen's Chamber in 142
'recycled' by Cheops? 103
relieving chambers in 118, 119, *120*,
  121, 122–3, *123*, 124, 125, 126–7,
  128, 130–1, 132–3, 137, 138–42,
  141
section view of *21*
Shadow Square and, *see* Shadow
  Square
solstice shadow on 29, 306, 308
Subterranean Chamber of 8, 94, 131,
  287, 314, 439–40, 442–3
'well shaft' in 66, 131, 372, 439, 440,
  441, 442
Wellington's Chamber in 138, 140, 142
world's largest stone structure 104
  see also Giza Plateau; pyramids of Giza
Great Pyramid of Khufu and Its Mortuary
  Chapel, The (Hassan) 181, 182
Great Pyramid Passages (Edgar, Edgar) 372

Great Sphinx and Its Secrets, The (Hassan) 162–3, 285–6
Great Tombs of the First Dynasty (Emery) 214, 216, 249
Greco, Stefano 7, 48
Green Frederick 261
Greet, Jonathan 16–17, 24, 30, 32, 34, 38
Grinsell, Leslie 356, 357
Group of Nine 29

Haas, Herbert 147
Hall of Records 47, 152
Hamilton, William 133
Harmachis 159, 163–4, 165, 280, 281–2, 341, 349, 456
Harris, J. R. 61
Hassan, Selim 44, 46, 52–5, 58–9, 68, 70, 75, 78, 103, 157, 171, 181, 182, 189, 285–6, 287, 344–5, 346, 349, 355–6, 357
    conduit account of 162–3
    Osiris Shaft account of 53–4, 64
Hatshepsut, Queen 233
Hawara Quarry 172
Hawass, Dr Zahi 44–7, 48, 56, 57, 58, 63, 64, 65, 77, 105, 114–15, 116–17, 367
    in TV documentary 119
Hecataeus of Abdera 119
Hecataeus of Miletus 119
Hein, Heinrich 123
Helck, Wolfgang 86
Heliopolis 245, 451, 457
Helwan 207
Hemaka 100
Herakleopolis 268, 423, 424
Hercules 387, 388, 389, 394, 396–9
    Pillars of 14, 375, 393–5, 396, 403
Herodotus 98, 118, 151, 183, 374, 432, 438, 456
Hesperides 13, 388–9, 391, 396–7
Hetepheres (daughter of Cheops) 420
Hetepheres (mother of Cheops) 102
Hierakonpolis (Nekhen) 203, 208–9, 260, 261, 414
Hierakonpolis (Quibell) 203
Hill, J. R. 132, 133, 143, 145
Himmler, Heinrich 419
Histoire de l'Art dans l'Antiquité (Perrot, Chipiez) 128
History of Egypt, A (Breasted) 203, 431–2

History of Phoenicia, A (Rawlinson) 376
Hoffman, Michael 107, 200
Hölscher, Uvo 52, 176, 177, 179, 185, 186–7, 189, 272, 282–3, 284–5, 287, 288–92, 293, 295, 298–9, 301, 302–3, 305, 310–11, 313, 315–18, 321–2, 326, 337, 362, 431
Homer 371
Hor-Aha, King 99, 103, 256, 260, 262, 263, 268
Hordjedef, King 90
    in 'mini' king list 87, 88, 89–90
Hornung, Erik 200, 300, 301
Horus 200
    Eye of 40, 41
    names 129, 199
    sons of 80
    Temple of 74, 261
Horus Medjedu 129
Hotepsekhemui, King 170, 303
Huni, King 111, 242, 270–1
Hunter's Palette 264–5

Ikhernofret Stela 73
Iliad 371
Illustrated London News 53
Imhotep 105, 107, 110, 196, 219, 220, 222, 223, 225, 227, 246–7, 250
industrial diamonds 247–8, 338
intact royal tombs 4, 7, 42, 59, 80, 150–93 *passim*
    earlier 151
    precise sites of 183–4
    see also Cheops: tomb of; Chephren: tomb of
International Congress of Egyptologists 263
Introduction to the Study of the Egyptian Hieroglyphics (Birch) 137
Ireland 380, 403, 405
iron 371–2
Isis 73, 352

jar sealings 197, 202, 217, 265
Jaritz, Dr Horst 163, 285
Jesus 'of Nazareth' 12, 35, 44, 65, 97
Jews and Arabs (Goitein) 383
Journal of Egyptian Archaeology 11, 207, 276

Kahl, Jochen 300
Kaiser, Werner 200

Karnak 74, 264, 395–6; *see also* Carnac
Khafre/Raqaf, *see* Chephren, King
Khaiu 268, 269
Khasekhem (Hudjefa), King 199–205, 210
Khasekhemui (Bebti), King 105–6, 109,
    110, 194, 197–212, 222, 228, 232,
    267
   tomb of, *see* Tomb of Khasekhemui
Kheneres, King 200
Khnum 248
Khufu, *see* Cheops
Killare 380
king lists 10, 36, 82, 111, 199, 200, 203,
    223–5, 227, 232–4, 246, 253, 259
   'mini' *87*, 88–90
   competing 83
   specific, *see* Abydos king list; Cairo
    Stone; Giza Drawing Board;
    Palermo Stone; Redford, Donald;
    Pharaonic King Lists; Saqqara king
    list; Wadi Hammamat
Kolber, Suzy 45, 46, 47
Kottler, Kathleen 236
Krauss, Rolf 300, 301
Kronick, William 122

La Dieu Sokar (Graindorge-Héreil) 321
La Pyramide à Degrés 246
Lacau, Pierre 246, 250
Lauer, Jean-Philippe 95, 181, 220, 221–3,
    246–7, 250, 273
Leahy, Anthony 430–1
Lebanon 12
Lee, Michael 266, 268
Lehner, Mark 46, 122, 125, 126, 146–7
Leipzig University Museum 292
Leisner, Georg 419, 424, 427
Leisner, Vera 419, 424, 427
Lepre, J. P. 126, 127
Leprohon, Ronald 129
Lethbridge, T. C. 404–5
Libya (Ta Tahenu) 14, 245, 401, 402, 407,
    408–9, 410, 412, 413–17, 418, 425,
    431
Libya and Egypt (Leahy) 430
Libyans 12–15, 203, 212, 220, 263, 264,
    265, 373, 376, 399, 400, 420, 422–5,
    425, 427, 429, 430–2
Life and Work at the Great Pyramid
    (Piazzi-Smyth) 120
Liritzis, Prof. Ioannis 1–3, 6, 56, 60, 62,

81, 111–12, 113, 114, 116, 117, 150,
    152, 154, 194, 211, 228, 297, 315,
    331, 337, 364
Lixus *377*, 378, 386, 387, 388
Lockyer, Sir Norman 215
Louvre 246, 290, 459
Luxor (Thebes) 55, 224, 359, 395, 396

MacIver, David 416
Mahu 232
Maillet, Benoit de 438, 440, 453, 453
Malta 425
Mamun, Caliph 457
Mandelbrot, Benoit 33
Manetho 199, 200, 203, 234–5, 253, 257,
    272, 299, 301, 302, 414
Manneville, E. de 425
Maragioglio, M. 107, 322–4, 338, 345–6,
    347–8, 349, 350, 356–8
Mariette, Auguste 282, 286–7, *287*, 288,
    289, 290, 291, 293, 294, 300, 326,
    331, 333, 353, 362, 451, 459–61
Masking the Blow (Davis) 263
Maspero, Gaston 209, 238, 453
mastabas 54, 55, 70, 76, 81, 100, 104, 129,
    219–22, 223, 291, 306, 371
Mathuisieulx, H. Méhier de 416, 417, 431
Mavor, James Watt Jr 379, 384, 385–7, 417
Megalithic Remains in Britain and Brittany
    (Thom) 381, 390
megaliths 4, 13, 370, 376, 377, 379–84,
    387, 390, 391, 395–6, 401–2, 405–
    11, *408*, *409*, *412*, 415–20, *418*,
    421–2, 432
   builders of 14, 370, 371, 373, 375–6,
    387, 390, 393, 399, 400, 404–5, 410,
    419, 421, 424
   see also Antequera; Carnac; Messa;
    Mezorah; Stonehenge; Zoraz Kar
Meidum 14, 268
   pyramid at 100, 111, 119, 423
Mekhet 268, 269
Memphis 15, 20, 72, 109, 125, 174, 229,
    245, 257–8, 259, 307, 451, 457
Mendelssohn, Kurt 107
'Menes', King 11, 113, 225, 242, 262, 263,
    414, 415
   name of 257–60
Menkaure, *see* Mycerinus, King
Meresankh 242
Merlin 380, 411

Mer-Neith 15, 220, 420
Merneith, Queen, tomb of *220*
Mersyankh III, Queen 73
Mesopotamia 106
Messa 409–10, 415
Meyer, Eduard 238
Mezorah 376, 378–9, 380, 382–93, 396,
    397, 398–9, 410, 417, 420
Monroe, Marilyn 88
Montalbán, César Luis de 378, 420
Montet, Pierre 95
Morocco 13, 375, 378, 380, 387, 388, 391,
    396, 420
mummies 42, 58, 60, 253, 297, 319, 334,
    335
  bacteria in 60, 297
Muslim fanatics 64–5
Mycerinus (Menkaure), King 6, 86, 101,
    112–13, 129, 190, 454
  crew-name graffiti of 129
  forged coffin of 104
  Funerary Temple of 112, 189
  Valley Temple of, *see* Valley Temple of
      Mycerinus
Mycerinus (Reisner) 190, 191, 300–1
Mycerinus Pyramid 23, 28, 38, 39, 86,
    103, 111–13, 116–17, 144, 148, 228,
    283, 441, 454
  casing stones of 111–12, 116
  date range of, from samples 149
  dating sample from 111–12, 116, 117
  geometrical projection 27
  king predated by 6, 113, 117, 149–50
  Shadow Square and, *see* Shadow
      Square
  see also Giza Plateau; pyramids of Giza
'Mysteries of the Great Pyramids' 122
'Mysteries of the Pyramids . . . Live, The'
    119, 121

Naqada 256, 276, 423–4
Narmer, King 256, 256, 258, 260–3
    passim, *262*, 264, 265, 268, 270, 414
Narmer Palette 261–3, *262*, 264
Nasser, Gamal Abdel 65
National Geographic 119
Natural History Museum 7, 173
Nazlett el-Sammann 152, 279, 311
Nebetka 214, 216
Neb-Kaw-Her 306
Nebra (Reneb), King 170, 303

nebti names 199
Neferka, King 92, 94, 129
  inscriptions of name of *95*, *273*
'negative pyramids', *see* 'pyramids-in-reverse'
Neheb 268, 269
Neith 15, 220, 265, 268, 414, 424
Neith-Hotep 15, 256, 265, 420
Nekhbet 205
Nekhen, *see* Hierakonpolis 260
Nennius 403
Nephthys 352
Netjerykhet, *see* Zoser
'New Portions of the Annals' (Petrie) 229
Newberry, Percy 413–15
Nh-Shufu 124
Nibbi, Alessandra 12, 13, 427–30
Nile inundations 50, 55, 74, 273, 265, 283,
    318, 343, 347, 359, 360, 444
Ninetjer, King 232, 267, 301
Noah 382

occultism 65
O'Connor, David 208–9
olives 245, 407, 409, 411–14, 415–17
O'Mara, Dr Patrick F. 202–3, 235–44,
    246, 302, 430
'Opening the Lost Tombs: Live from
    Egypt' 45–6
*Operations Carried on at the Pyramids of
    Gizeh in 1837* (Vyse, R. H.) 48–9
Oppel, Karl 425
optical thermoluminescence 1–3, 6, 198,
    211
optically stimulated luminescence 2
Osiris 43–4, 65, 67, 72–3, 307, 319, 321,
    353
  drowning of 72, 73
  mystery play depicting 73
  Temple of 71, 352
  tomb of, *see* Tomb of Osiris
  see also Abydos; Sokar
Osiris Shaft 4, 5–6, 43–80 *passim*, *51*, 117,
    122, 150, 288, 306, 372, 441
  in Assan's account 53–4
  Caviglia discovers 47, 50
  dacite in 61–3, 66, 69, 313
  dating considerations of 44–5, 46, 57–
    8, 59, 63, 69, 75, 79, 228
  disputed depth of 46
  elementary part of total design 68
  in Fox TV programme 45–7

holes in Level 3 walls of 77
international curiosity attracted by 44
iron veins in rock of 66
Level 1 of 46, 51, 58
Level 2 of 45, 46, 49, 50, 51, 52, 57,
    58, 59, 60, 64, 67–8, 70, 75, 79, 122
Level 3 of 49, 50, 51, 52, 57, 59–60,
    63, 64, 66, 67, 68, 70, 75, 77
only map showing location of 76
pottery in 46
radioactivity in 60, 297
reuse of, for Saitic burials 75
sarcophagi in 44, 48, 53–4, 55, 57, 58–
    9, 60–4, 66–7, 69, 70–6 *passim*, 79,
    122, 313
Sarcophagus 1 in 60, 63
Sarcophagus 2 in 60, 61, 62, 66, 67, 68,
    69, 79
Sarcophagus 3 in 63, 66–7, 74, 75, 78,
    98–9
significance of location of 76
vandalism in 55, 64–5
Our Inheritance in the Great Pyramid
    (Piazzi-Smyth) 21

Palermo Stone 10, 82, 202, 228–9, 231–2,
    235, 236–46, 265–70, *266*, *268*, 269,
    414, 432
measurements 444–9
*Palermo Stone and the Archaic Kings of
    Egypt, The* (O'Mara) 236
Parker, Richard 84
Peet, T. Eric 405–7, 408
Perfect Square 21, 24, 30–4, *31*, 35, *37*,
    38–9, 40, 41–2
    Eye of Ra created within, demonstrated
        33–6, *34*
Peribsen, King 200, 205, 233
Perring, John S., 50, 95, 131, 132, 133,
    134, 137, 458–9, 463
Perrot, Georges 128
Petrie, Sir Flinders 29, 69, 123, 124–5,
    129, 194, 197, 201, 203, 207, 238,
    262, 273–4, 276, 281, 287, 293–4,
    296, 298, 305, 326, 332, 334–5, 337,
    338, 371, 372, 397, 422–4, 424–5,
    425, 427, 451, 453, 462, 463
    on Cairo Stone 229–31
Petrie Museum 228, 229, 238, 244, 251
Pharaonic King Lists (Redford) 233, 235,
    246

Philae 84
Phoenicians 370, 373, 374, 375, 377, 402,
    404, 422
Piankoff, Alexandre 168
Piazzi-Smyth, Charles 21, 85, 120, 121,
    287, 305, 308–9, 451, 462
Pillars of Hercules 14
Pliny 279, 289, 388, 438
Plutarch 73, 386–7
Porter & Moss epigraphical survey 125
Poseidon 387
pottery 70, 210, 246–53, *249*
    26th Dynasty 46
    Badarian 250–3
    dating 1–2, 198
Povich, Maury 45, 46
Protestantism 35
Ptah 245, 307–8, 320
Ptolemies 74, 89 234, 235, 438
pulleys 58
Pyramid Texts 152, 170, 344, 360, 395
pyramids of Giza:
    appropriated by kings 103
    architectural development of 81
    Breasted's Chronology and 83, 99, 149
    carbon dating of 1, 111, 146–50
    casing stones of *85*
    cast limestone used in 249
    dating difficulties concerning 6, 11, 69,
        81–150
    early burial use of 69, 70
    geographical alignments of 63
    Middle Subsidiary 102
    North Subsidiary 102
    real builders of 7
    size and weight of blocks in 110
    South Subsidiary 102
    Stonehenge connection with 14, 15
    Subsidiaries 102
    'three queens' pyramids 102
    tomb theory concerning 82, 86, 97–100
    unified design concept 16, 101
    see also individual pyramids
'pyramids-in-reverse' 94–7
Pyramids and Temples of Gizeh, The
    (Petrie) 123–4, 332

Quibell, James 203, 209, 261
Quirke, Stephen 244

Ra (Re) 34, 35, 87, 168

Eye of 31, 32, 33–6, *34*, 41
  name of 36
radioactivity 60, 297
Radjedef, *see* Djedefre, King
Radwan, Mansour 157
Rambova, N. 168
Rameses II, King 224, 234, 254, 460
Raneb, King 36, 89, 170, 303
Ranke, Hermann 264–5
Raven, Mr 134, 143, 145
Rawlinson, George 377
Redford, Donald 224–5, 233, 235, 243,
  244, 246
Reed, Eleonore 284–5
Reformation 35
Reisner, George 102, 129–30, 144, 189–
  92, 276–7, 283, 299, 300–1, 303,
  452
Religious Ritual at Abydos (David) 71–2
Reyna, Simeon 419
Rice, Michael 200, 301
Ricke, Herbert 154, 156, 157, 159–60,
  161–2, 163–6, 168–9, 171, 187, 189,
  280, 281–2, 285, 286, 341–2, 346,
  349, 350, 358, 451
Riddle of the Pyramids, The (Mendelssohn)
  107
Rinaldi, C. 107, 322–4, 338, 346, 347–8,
  349, 350, 356–8
robbers 4, 21, 60, 70, 71, 77, 102, 198, 253
Rock of Gibraltar 393
ropes 59
Rosetta Stone 127
Rosicrucians 65
Rossellini, Ippolito 132, 138
Rostau 152, 321
Rough Stone Monuments (Peet) 405–6, 408
Royal Annals of Ancient Egypt (Wilkinson)
  244
Royal Tombs of the Earliest Dynasties, The
  (Petrie) 195

Saad, Zaki 207
Saguir, Mohammed 115
Sahu, King 249, 303
Sahure, King 414, 415
St Paul 12
Sais 220, 265, 414, 421, 424, 432, 433
Saitic Period, *see* Dynasties: 26th
Salt, Henry 443
Saqqara 82, 99–100, 101, 108–9, 255, 274

1st Dynasty pyramid at 117, 213–23,
  214, 225–6
  cenotaphs (versus tombs) at 254–7
  predynastic cemeteries at 276
  Step Pyramid at 9, 31, 81, 97, 105,
    106–8, 109–10, 147, 196, 206, 208,
    218, 219, 220–3 *221*, *222*, *223*, 225,
    218, 246–7, 250, 304
Saqqara and the Dynastic Race (Emery)
  276
Saqqara king list 215, 217, 224, 225, 217,
  302
Scorpion, King 261, 270, 302
Scotland 376, 403
Scott, Michael 383–4
Secret Chamber (Bauval) 57
Secret of the Great Pyramid, The (Hein)
  123
Secrets of the Great Pyramids (Tompkins)
  127
Seka 268, 269
Semerkhet, King 213, 214, 215, 217–21
  passim, 223, 224, 225, 227–8, 256,
  304
Send (Sened/Sendji), King 8–9, 36, 82,
  170, 272, *299*, 299–302, 304
Senusret III 257
Sertoirus, Quintus 386–7
Sesostris III, King 73
Set 73, 200, 397
Sethe, Kurt 238, 397
Seti I, King 71, 74, 234, 254–5, 256, 259
  Temple of *see* Temple of Seti
Shadow Square 17–32 *passim*, *23*, *31*, 40,
  41
  establishing centre of 27
  Perfect Square derived from *37*
Sharif, Omar 122
Shepseskaf, King 190, 452, 454, 456
Sheri 301
Sheshet 209
Shu-Shufu 124
Siculus, Diodorus 387, 389, 390, 401, 422,
  438, 457, 438, 457
Sieglin, Ernst von 185, 282, 291, 293
Sinai 12
Sirius 16, 83
Sirius Mystery, The (Temple) 16
Sitchin, Zechariah 146
Skinner-Simpson, Nigel 45
Smith, Elliot 276–7

Sneferu, King 111, 117, 171, 232, 242, 245, 265, *267*, 270, 304, 366
Sokar (later Osiris) 151, 319–1, 352, 353, 366, 425
  priests of *319*
  see also Osiris
Some Indirect Sothic and Lunar Dates from the Middle Kingdom in Egypt (O'Mara) 236
Some Lunar Dates from the Old Kingdom in Egypt (O'Mara) 236
Some Problems on the History of the Third Dynasty (Swelim) 107–8
'Sothic Dating of the Twelfth and Eighteenth Dynasties, The' (Parker) 84
Spain (Iberia) 275, 375, 383, 402, 403, 406–7, 418–20, 424, 427
Spalinger, Anthony 85–6, 127, 129
Sphinx 16, 28, 35, 39, 101, 280, 340–1, 343–5, 350, 49, 440, 455, 459, 460
  Harmachis name of, *see main entry*
  Temple, *see main entry*
  see also Giza Plateau
Sphinx Mystery, The (Temple) 17, 22, 29, 31, 38, 64, 73, 98, 101, 152, 287–8, 306, 308, 313, 314, 316, 333, 339, 341, 343, 345, 346, 348, 351, 354, 360, 364, 368, 380, 441
  website of (www.sphinxmystery.info) 22, 38, 64, 308, 341, 344
Sphinx Pit/Moat 286, 341, 343–4, 359, 364
Sphinx Temple 7, 8, 28, 152, 153–74, *157*, *159*, 187–9 *passim*, 191, 279–82, *280*, 285–6, 287, 304, *307*, 311, 318, 321, 327, 329, 340–68, 451
  'alabaster' beneath 172–3
  cavern complex beneath 171–2, 175, 368
  Central Court of 159, 187, 350, 352, 355
  conduits/channels/grooves beneath 154–71, 174, 192–3
  dating results for 363–4, 365–6, 367
  limestone cavern beneath 173
  North Trench beneath 156–60 *passim*, *159*, 162–3, 164, 322, 323, 348, 356
  pillars in 352, 355–7, 358, 360–1
  as 'Setepet' 345, 353–4, 359
  stalactite beneath 173–4

Stadelmann, Rainer 85–6
State Formation in Egypt (Wilkinson) 264
Steindorff, Georg 185, 291, 300, 301, 452, 453
Stonehenge 14–15, 376, 381, 387, 407, 409–10, 411
'Stonehenge in Africa' *see* Mezorah
Strabo 374–5, 393–4, 395, 404, 438, 457
Strudwick, Nigel 129
Sumerians 264
sun god 29
Swelim, Nabil 107–8, 272–3
Swiss Institute, Cairo 163, 285

Tacitus 394, 402
Taylor, John 25
Temple, Olivia 13, 56–7, 58, 114, 152, 154, 194, 209, 250, 329, 331, 335, 343, 359–60, 376, 388
'Temple of the Royal Ancestors' 215, 254
Temple of Seti I 65, 71, 99, 215, 216, 234, 254–5, 259, 342, 360
Teti, King:
  pyramid of 82
  several of 10–1, 82, 118, 232, 233
Texts from the Pyramid Age (Strudwick, Leprohon) 129
Thebes (Luxor) 55, 224, 359, 395, 396
thermoluminescence 1, 2, 198
Thesh 268, 269
This 218
Thom, Prof. Alexander 379–80, 381, 390
Thom, Dr Archibald 380, 381, 390
Thoth 74, 290–1, 313, 398
  Priestess of 73
Thutmosis IV, King 459, 460
tin 370–1, 373, 374, 401
Tiu 268, 269
Tjuloy 224, 225
Tomb of Khasekhemui 194–5, 197, 198, 208, 226, 254, 366
  carbon dating of 198, 210–11
Tomb of Osiris 5, 43–80 *passim*
  extraordinary importance of 79
  replica of 44, 46, 48, 57, 65, 71
Tomb of Ramesses VI (Piankoff, Rambova) 168
tomb robbers, *see* robbers
Tunisia 401, 416
Turin Papyrus 86, 200, 233, 302
Tutankhamun, King 98, 170, 233

Uadjet Eye 307
Uadji, King 100
Uazanez 268, 269
Udimu, King 100
'unfinished pyramid' 91
University College, London 229, 238, 240
unuti priests 20, 96, 310
Userkaf, King 232

Valley Temple 8, 36, 52, 69, 82, 152–3, 170–1, 174–80, *179*, *180*, 279–8, *280*, 282–5, 286–340 *passim*, *289*, *295*, *312*, *317*, 342, 343, 345, 346, 348, 350, 351, 352, 353, 354, 358, 359, 361–7
  'alabaster' in 174–5
  Ascending Passage of 174, 175, 179, 289, 293, 306–7, *307*, 312, 313, 314, 315, *317*, 320, 340
  Blind Room in 332–7, 339
  cavern complex beneath 175
  conduits/channels/grooves beneath 175–80, *176*, *177*, *180*
  dating results for 362–3, 364–7
  Hölscher's report on, Introduction to 450–6
  keeper of time 309–10, 312, 351
  limestone cavern beneath 173
  magazines in 289, 294, 296–7, *317*, 332, 337, 347, 366
  Osirian rites at 72
  Pillared Hall in *177*, *180*, *295*, 297, *307*, 311, 312, 313, 316, *317*, 320, 352
  quay in front of 318, 321
  radioactivity in 297
  shafts in 324–5, 236–30, 331
  unknown aspects of 324–40
Valley Temple of Mycerinus *190*, *191*, 303, 452
  conduits/channels/grooves beneath 189–93
vases, bowls, *see* pottery
Verbrugghe, Gerald P. 199–200

Veröffentlichungen der Ernst von Sieglin-Expedition (Band) 185
vesica piscis 34, 35
Vyse, Col. Richard Howard 48–50, 51, 52, 55, 76, 91, 92, 93, 97, 122, 124, 130–46 *passim*, 458–9
  coffin lid faked by 144
  dynamite used by 126, 130–1, 133, 138
  graffiti 'evidence' faked by 6–7, 104, 123, 130, 131, 132–46

Wadi Hammamat 87, 88, 232
Wadi Mouelih 62
Wadi Ranga 62
Wales 402
Warburton, David 300
Watkins, M. G. 374
Weeks, Dr Kent 107
Weigall, Arthur 205–6
Weld-Blundell, Herbert 409, 410
Wenke, Robert J. 147
Westcar Papyrus 313
Whishaw Ellen M. 378
Wickersham, John M. 199–200
Wilkin, Anthony 416
Wilkinson, Sir Gardner 132, 137, 138
Wilkinson, Toby 244–5, 265, 290, 460
William I of England 258–9
Wilson, John 260
Wölfli, Willy 147
Wood, Wendy 207–8

Zawiyet el-Aryan 92, 93–7, 272, 273, 309, 445
Zer, King 99
Zer, King, *see* Djer
Zimmer, G. F. 371
Zoraz Kar 381–2, 395
Zoser (Djoser/Djeser/Netjerykhet), King 32, 97, 101, 105–6, 107–8, 109, 197–8, 201, 202, 203, 212, 219–20, 222, 225, 226, 246, 304
  step pyramid of, *see* Saqqara: Step Pyramid at
Zyhlarx, E. 425–6